Defining and Acquiring Interests in Property

ASPEN SELECT SERIES

Defining and Acquiring Interests in Property
Second Edition

Bridget M. Fuselier
Professor of Law
Baylor University School of Law

Wolters Kluwer

Printed in the United States of America.

1 2 3 4 5 6 7 8 9 0

ISBN 978-1-5438-0899-5

Library of Congress Cataloging-in-Publication Data

Names: Fuselier, Bridget M., author.
Title: Defining and acquiring interests in property / Bridget M. Fuselier, Professor of Law, Baylor University School of Law.
Description: Second edition. | New York : Wolters Kluwer, [2019] | Series: Aspen select Series | Includes index.
Identifiers: LCCN 2019010290 | ISBN 9781543808995
Subjects: LCSH: Property--United States. | Acquisition of property--United States. | Homestead law--Texas. | Property--Texas. | LCGFT: Casebooks (Law)
Classification: LCC KF560 .F87 2019 | DDC 346.7304--dc23
LC record available at https://lccn.loc.gov/2019010290

SUSTAINABLE
FORESTRY
INITIATIVE

Certified Chain of Custody
Promoting Sustainable Forestry

www.sfiprogram.org
SFI-01347

About Wolters Kluwer Legal & Regulatory U.S.

Wolters Kluwer Legal & Regulatory U.S. delivers expert content and solutions in the areas of law, corporate compliance, health compliance, reimbursement, and legal education. Its practical solutions help customers successfully navigate the demands of a changing environment to drive their daily activities, enhance decision quality and inspire confident outcomes.

Serving customers worldwide, its legal and regulatory portfolio includes products under the Aspen Publishers, CCH Incorporated, Kluwer Law International, ftwilliam.com and MediRegs names. They are regarded as exceptional and trusted resources for general legal and practice-specific knowledge, compliance and risk management, dynamic workflow solutions, and expert commentary.

To Paul, Elise, and Evan.
Thank you for your love, encouragement, and support.
None of this would be possible without you.

Summary of Contents

Table of Contents

Acknowledgments

Thank you to Baylor Law student Amy Jowers Waller who provided invaluable assistance in preparing this second edition.

The following material has been reprinted with permission:

Restatement of the Law First, Property copyright © 1944 by The American Law Institute. All rights reserved. Reproduced with permission.

Restatement of the Law Third, Property (Servitudes) copyright © 2000 by The American Law Institute. All rights reserved. Reproduced with permission.

Chapter 1
Defining the Bundle of Sticks

A. Introduction to Property

Of all the first-year courses, property is often the one most dreaded by law students. However, for many it turns out to be the most enjoyable and exciting learning experience. To have that result, students must come to this material with an open mind and quickly understand some things are very different from what they appear. During this course the goal will be to achieve the following objectives:

(1) Understand a new definition of property; think of "property" in a different light;
(2) Learn the various forms of property interests that the law creates;
(3) Understand what impact these property interests have on others;
(4) Understand what impact other laws and interests of society have on the property interests; and
(5) Learn some of the means of acquiring these property interests.

Before getting any further in the reading, let's start thinking about how to define property. The thoughts that students have at this point are usually dramatically different from the ideas that form during the reading on this topic.

Start by answering the following True/False questions:
1. **"Property" refers only to land.**
2. **"Property" refers only to land and improvements affixed thereon.**
3. **"Property" is the relationship of people and things.**
4. **Intangible items are property.**
5. **Only tangible items are property.**
6. **The right to vote is property.**
7. **A job held by a government employee is property.**
8. **Some property is non-transferrable.**

B. Defining Property

What is property? Some scholars say that is an unanswerable question, but it does not have to be. There are a variety of definitions of the word *property*;

however, the following definitions are the ones that can be most helpful to a new property student.

Property: (1) That which is peculiar or proper to any person; that which belongs exclusively to one.

(2) An aggregate of rights that are guaranteed and protected by the government. More specifically, ownership; the unrestricted and exclusive right to a thing; the right to dispose of a thing in every legal way, to possess it, to use it, and to exclude everyone else from interfering with it.

What these definitions tell us is that most new law students need to adjust their way of thinking about "property." Property does not refer to some "thing" but rather to a bundle of rights, often referred to as a bundle of sticks. The nature of the sticks in the bundle defines what type of interest a person has in the thing and what type of relationship exists. This should lead to the understanding that the law of property is not about things, but rather is about the relationship of people to things.

C. Types of Property

The law is essentially divided into laws that apply to people and laws that apply to property. Therefore, there are more different types of property than most people realize. The primary focus of this first-year property course will be on real property. But as we begin the study of property, it is important to consider the different types of property that exist.

1. Personal Property

Personal property, also referred to as personalty, is, in a broad and general sense, everything that is the subject of ownership not coming under the denomination of real estate. It may refer to animate as well as inanimate property, money, notes, bonds, stocks, and causes of action generally, as well as intangible property like the right to vote, the interest in a government job, or ideas and inventions.

We know that after the abolition of slavery you cannot own a person, because people are not property. However, can you own your own organs, cells, blood, tissue, or reproductive material?

Henrietta Lacks & John Moore: Property Rights in Human Cells[1]

In 1950, Henrietta went to Johns Hopkins for indigent medical treatment. After examination, Dr. Jones determined Henrietta had cervical cancer that was growing at an alarming rate. Dr. Jones' boss, Dr. TeLinde was involved with medical research to support a theory he had developed about cervical cancer. He believed if he could prove his theory to be correct, he could save the lives of millions of women.

When Henrietta returned to Johns Hopkins for surgery and treatment, she signed a form to allow the staff "to perform any operative procedures and under any anesthetic . . . that they may deem necessary in the proper surgical care and treatment of" Henrietta. Dr. TeLinde often used patients in the public ward for research without their knowledge believing it was his right to do so because the patients were receiving free medical care.

The surgeon on duty performed the surgical procedure necessary to treat Henrietta's cervical cancer. However, he also shaved two dime-sized pieces of tissue from Henrietta's cervix—one from the tumor and one from the nearby healthy cervical tissue. The samples were taken to the lab.

Henrietta and her family were not informed of what took place, nor were they informed that even after Henrietta's death her cells lived on in medical labs around the world as research was, and still is, conducted on her cells.

In 1970, after 20 years of significant and profitable medical research was conducted using Henrietta's cells, her identity was finally released in connection with the cells. In 1973, without explaining what was being done, researchers at Johns Hopkins accessed Henrietta's family's medical records, contacted her spouse and children and obtained blood samples from them. The doctors admitted there was no effort to obtain informed consent because they were not patients, only research subjects.

Henrietta's daughter, Deborah, thinking she was being treated for the same cancer that had killed her mother, gave multiple blood samples to the researchers.

These cells are known in the scientific community as HeLa (for Henrietta Lacks). They are sold at a price of $256 per vial and are distributed throughout the world. Some companies make products from these cells that sell from $100 to $10,000 per vial.

---

[1] See Skloot, Rebecca. The Immortal Life of Henrietta Lacks, Broadway Books (2011). This book by Rebecca Skloot is a fascinating history of this important figure in medical history. The contributions made unknowingly by Henrietta Lacks and her family have allowed significant discoveries and medical treatments.

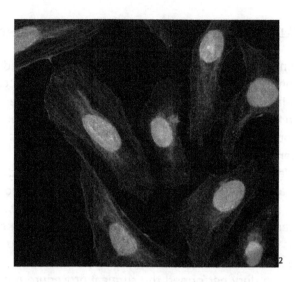

Henrietta's cells were used to develop the polio vaccine and uncover the secrets of cancer, viruses, and effects of the atom bomb. They have led to important advances like in vitro fertilization, cloning, and gene mapping. They have been part of research in space. And they have been bought and sold by the billions. In 1984, research using HeLa cells discovered a new strain of sexually transmitted virus called HPB-18.

In 1976, the same year Henrietta's family found out about the buying and selling of the cells, John Moore was working as a surveyor on the Alaska pipeline. He was having problems with bleeding gums, bruises covering his body, and his belly swelling. At the age of 31, Moore was diagnosed with hairy-cell leukemia, a rare and deadly cancer that filled the spleen with malignant blood cells.

Moore's local doctor referred him to Dr. Golde, a UCLA cancer researcher. Dr. Golde told him his only option was to have his spleen removed. Moore signed a consent form allowing the hospital to "dispose of any severed tissue or member by cremation."

The spleen was removed and Moore continued flying from Seattle to Los Angeles for the next seven years for Dr. Golde to take bone marrow, blood, and semen samples. In 1983, he was asked to sign a consent form that stated: "I (do, do not) voluntarily grant to the University of California all rights I, or my heirs, may have in any cell line or any other potential product which might be developed from the blood and/or bone marrow obtained by me."

Moore first circled "do" but on his next visit when given the same form, he circled "do not." Golde mailed him a form instructing Moore to circle "do." Moore

---

[2] Photo is that of HeLa cells stained with antibody to actin (green), vimentin (red), and DNA (blue).jpg. Uploaded by Gerry Shaw. Created 8/3/12. This photo can be located at https://commons.wikimedia.org/wiki/File:HeLa_cells_stained_with_antibody_to _actin_%28green%29_,_vimentin_%28red%29_and_DNA_%28blue%29.jpg.

refused. Another letter came from Golde telling Moore "to stop being a pain" and "sign the form."

Moore sent the form and letter to a lawyer.

Moore's cells carried a rare virus that was related to HIV, during a time when researchers were hoping to create a vaccine to stop the AIDS epidemic. Drug companies paid enormous sums to work with these cells. Had Moore known before Golde obtained a patent on the "Mo Line," Mr. Moore could have approached the drug companies and sold them himself.

John Moore v. The Regents of the University of California, et al.
Supreme Court of California, 1990
51 Cal. 3d 120

[Moore, the plaintiff in this case, began treatment for hairy-cell leukemia at the UCLA Medical Center. According to Moore, based upon recommendations from one of the defendants that he needed to return to UCLA for his health and well-being, he made several trips from his home in Seattle, Washington, to UCLA between 1976 and 1983. In fact, the defendants were conducting research on Moore's cells, and they developed a cell line from Moore's T-lymphocytes. Apparently, Moore's T-lymphocytes were interesting to the defendants because they overproduced certain proteins, making it easier to locate genetic information related to the human immune system. The defendants sought and received a patent for the cell line, which patent listed two of the defendants as inventors. Moore estimated that the defendants might potentially reap more than a billion dollars from marketing the products developed from his cell line, referred to as the "Mo-Line." Moore's complaint included 13 causes of action, including a claim for conversion. "Conversion" is an unauthorized exercise of ownership over the personal property belonging to another, to the exclusion of, or inconsistent with, the rights of the claimed true owner. This excerpt addresses Moore's conversion claim. Most footnotes have been omitted.]

Conversion
Moore also attempts to characterize the invasion of his rights as a conversion—a tort that protects against interference with possessory and ownership interests in personal property. He theorizes that he continued to own his cells following their removal from his body, at least for the purpose of directing their use, and that he never consented to their use in potentially lucrative medical research. Thus, to complete Moore's argument, defendants' unauthorized use of his cells constitutes a conversion. As a result of the alleged

conversion, Moore claims a proprietary interest in each of the products that any of the defendants might ever create from his cells or the patented cell line.

No court, however, has ever in a reported decision imposed conversion liability for the use of human cells in medical research. While that fact does not end our inquiry, it raises a flag of caution. In effect, what Moore is asking us to do is to impose a tort duty on scientists to investigate the consensual pedigree of each human cell sample used in research. To impose such a duty, which would affect medical research of importance to all of society, implicates policy concerns far removed from the traditional, two-party ownership disputes in which the law of conversion arose. Invoking a tort theory originally used to determine whether the loser or the finder of a horse had the better title, Moore claims ownership of the results of socially important medical research, including the genetic code for chemicals that regulate the functions of every human being's immune system.

We have recognized that, when the proposed application of a very general theory of liability in a new context raises important policy concerns, it is especially important to face those concerns and address them openly. Moreover, we should be hesitant to "impose [new tort duties] when to do so would involve complex policy decisions."

Accordingly, we first consider whether the tort of conversion clearly gives Moore a cause of action under existing law. We do not believe it does. Because of the novelty of Moore's claim to own the biological materials at issue, to apply the theory of conversion in this context would frankly have to be recognized as an extension of the theory. Therefore, we consider next whether it is advisable to extend the tort to this context.

Moore's Claim Under Existing Law

"To establish a conversion, plaintiff must establish an actual interference with his ownership or right of possession. . . . Where plaintiff neither has title to the property alleged to have been converted, nor possession thereof, he cannot maintain an action for conversion." (Del E. Webb Corp. v. Structural Materials Co. (1981) 123 Cal. App. 3d 593, 610–611, 176 Cal. Rptr. 824. *See also* General Motors A. Corp. v. Dallas (1926) 198 Cal. 365, 370, 245 P. 184.)

Since Moore clearly did not expect to retain possession of his cells following their removal, to sue for their conversion he must have retained an ownership interest in them. But there are several reasons to doubt that he did retain any such interest. First, no reported judicial decision supports Moore's claim, either directly or by close analogy. Second, California statutory law drastically limits any continuing interest of a patient in excised cells. Third, the subject matters of the Regents' patent—the patented cell line and the products derived from it—cannot be Moore's property.

Neither the Court of Appeal's opinion, the parties' briefs, nor our research discloses a case holding that a person retains a sufficient interest in excised cells to support a cause of action for conversion. We do not find this surprising, since the laws governing such things as human tissues, transplantable organs, blood, fetuses, pituitary glands, corneal tissue, and dead bodies deal with human biological materials as objects sui generis, regulating their disposition to achieve policy goals rather than abandoning them to the general law of personal property. It is these specialized statutes, not the law of conversion, to which courts ordinarily should and do look for guidance on the disposition of human biological materials.

Lacking direct authority for importing the law of conversion into this context, Moore relies, as did the Court of Appeal, primarily on decisions addressing privacy rights. One line of cases involves unwanted publicity. (Lugosi v. Universal Pictures (1979) 25 Cal. 3d 813, 160 Cal. Rptr. 323, 603 P.2d 425; Motschenbacher v. R.J. Reynolds Tobacco Company (9th Cir. 1974) 498 F.2d 821 [interpreting Cal. law].) These opinions hold that every person has a proprietary interest in his own likeness and that unauthorized, business use of a likeness is redressible as a tort. But in neither opinion did the authoring court expressly base its holding on property law.

Another privacy case offered by analogy to support Moore's claim establishes only that patients have a right to refuse medical treatment. (Bouvia v. Superior Court (1986) 179 Cal. App. 3d 1127, 225 Cal. Rptr. 297.) In this context the court in *Bouvia* wrote that " '[e]very human being of adult years and sound mind has a right to determine what shall be done with his own body. . . .' " (Id., at p. 1139, 225 Cal. Rptr. 297, quoting from Schloendorff v. Society of New York Hospital, *supra*, 211 N.Y. 125, 105 N.E. at p. 93.) Relying on this language to support the proposition that a patient has a continuing right to control the use of excised cells, the Court of Appeal in this case concluded that "[a] patient must have the ultimate power to control what becomes of his or her tissues. To hold otherwise would open the door to a massive invasion of human privacy and dignity in the name of medical progress." Yet one may earnestly wish to protect privacy and dignity without accepting the extremely problematic conclusion that interference with those interests amounts to a conversion of personal property.

The next consideration that makes Moore's claim of ownership problematic is California statutory law, which drastically limits a patient's control over excised cells. [The court cites Health and Safety Code § 7054.4, which prescribes how human tissue, body parts, etc. are to be disposed of.] By restricting how excised cells may be used and requiring their eventual destruction, the statute eliminates so many of the rights ordinarily attached to property that one cannot simply assume that what is left amounts to "property" or "ownership" for purposes of conversion law.

Finally, the subject matter of the Regents' patent—the patented cell line and the products derived from it—cannot be Moore's property. This is because the patented cell line is both factually and legally distinct from the cells taken from Moore's body. Federal law permits the patenting of organisms that represent the product of "human ingenuity," but not naturally occurring organisms. (Diamond v. Chakrabarty (1980) 447 U.S. 303, 309–310, 100 S. Ct. 2204, 2208, 65 L. Ed.2d 144.)

Should Conversion Liability Be Extended?

As we have discussed, Moore's novel claim to own the biological materials at issue in this case is problematic, at best. Accordingly, his attempt to apply the theory of conversion within this context must frankly be recognized as a request to extend that theory. While we do not purport to hold that excised cells can never be property for any purpose whatsoever, the novelty of Moore's claim demands express consideration of the policies to be served by extending liability (*cf.* Nally v. Grace Community Church, *supra*, 47 Cal. 3d at pp. 291–300, 253 Cal. Rptr. 97, 763 P.2d 948; Foley v. Interactive Data Corp., *supra*, 47 Cal. 3d at pp. 694-700, 254 Cal. Rptr. 211, 765 P.2d 373; Brown v. Superior Court, *supra*, 44 Cal. 3d at pp. 1061–1066, 245 Cal. Rptr. 412, 751 P.2d 470) rather than blind deference to a complaint alleging as a legal conclusion the existence of a cause of action.

There are three reasons why it is inappropriate to impose liability for conversion based upon the allegations of Moore's complaint. First, a fair balancing of the relevant policy considerations counsels against extending the tort. Second, problems in this area are better suited to legislative resolution. Third, the tort of conversion is not necessary to protect patients' rights. For these reasons, we conclude that the use of excised human cells in medical research does not amount to a conversion.

Of the relevant policy considerations, two are of overriding importance. The first is protection of a competent patient's right to make autonomous medical decisions. That right, as already discussed, is grounded in well-recognized and long-standing principles of fiduciary duty and informed consent. (*See, e.g.,* Cobbs v. Grant, *supra*, 8 Cal. 3d at pp. 242–246, 104 Cal. Rptr. 505, 502 P.2d 1; Bowman v. McPheeters, *supra*, 77 Cal. App. 2d at p. 800, 176 P.2d 745.) This policy weighs in favor of providing a remedy to patients when physicians act with undisclosed motives that may affect their professional judgment. The second important policy consideration is that we not threaten with disabling civil liability innocent parties who are engaged in socially useful activities, such as researchers who have no reason to believe that their use of a particular cell sample is, or may be, against a donor's wishes.

To reach an appropriate balance of these policy considerations is extremely important. In its report to Congress, the Office of Technology Assessment emphasized that "[u]ncertainty about how courts will resolve disputes between specimen sources and specimen users could be detrimental to both academic researchers and the infant biotechnology industry, particularly when the rights are asserted long after the specimen was obtained." The assertion of rights by sources would affect not only the researcher who obtained the original specimen, but perhaps other researchers as well.

Finally, there is no pressing need to impose a judicially created rule of strict liability since enforcement of physicians' disclosure obligations will protect patients against the very type of harm with which Moore was threatened. So long as a physician discloses research and economic interests that may affect his judgment, the patient is protected from conflicts of interest. Aware of any conflicts, the patient can make an informed decision to consent to treatment, or to withhold consent and look elsewhere for medical assistance. As already discussed, enforcement of physicians' disclosure obligations protects patients directly, without hindering the socially useful activities of innocent researchers.

For these reasons, we hold that the allegations of Moore's third amended complaint state a cause of action for breach of fiduciary duty or lack of informed consent, but not conversion.

ARABIAN, Justice, concurring.

I join in the views cogently expounded by the majority. I write separately to give voice to a concern that I believe informs much of that opinion but finds little or no expression therein. I speak of the moral issue.

Plaintiff has asked us to recognize and enforce a right to sell one's own body tissue for profit. He entreats us to regard the human vessel—the single most venerated and protected subject in any civilized society—as equal with the basest commercial commodity. He urges us to commingle the sacred with the profane. He asks much.

BROUSSARD, Justice, concurring and dissenting.

When it turns to the conversion cause of action, . . . , the majority opinion fails to maintain its focus on the specific allegations before us. Concerned that the imposition of liability for conversion will impede medical research by innocent scientists who use the resources of existing cell repositories—a factual setting not presented here—the majority opinion rests its holding, that a conversion action cannot be maintained, largely on the proposition that a patient generally possesses no right in a body part that has already been removed from his body. Here, however, plaintiff has alleged that defendants interfered with his legal rights before his body part was removed. Although a patient may not retain any legal interest in a body part after its removal when he has properly consented to its removal and use for scientific purposes, it is clear under California law that before a body part is removed it is the patient, rather than his doctor or hospital, who possesses the right to determine the use to which the body part will be put after removal. If, as alleged in this case, plaintiff's doctor improperly interfered with plaintiff's right to control the use of a body part by wrongfully withholding material information from him before its removal, under traditional common law principles plaintiff may maintain a conversion action to recover the economic value of the right to control the use of his body part. Accordingly, I dissent from the majority opinion insofar as it rejects plaintiff's conversion cause of action.

MOSK, Justice, dissenting.

I dissent.

The majority's first reason [for finding Moore's allegations insufficient to claim conversion] is that "no reported judicial decision supports Moore's claim, either directly or by close analogy." [Citation omitted.] Neither, however, is there any reported decision rejecting such a claim. The issue is as new as its source—the recent explosive growth in the commercialization of biotechnology.

Being broad, the concept of property is also abstract: rather than referring directly to a material object such as a parcel of land or the tractor that cultivates it, the concept of property is often said to refer to a "bundle of rights" that may be exercised with respect to that object—principally the rights to possess the property, to use the property, to exclude others from the property, and to dispose of the property by sale or by gift. "Ownership is not a single concrete entity but a bundle of rights and privileges as well as of obligations." (Union Oil Co. v. State Bd. of Equal. (1963) 60 Cal. 2d 441, 447, 34 Cal. Rptr. 872, 386 P.2d 496.) But the same bundle of rights does not attach to all forms of property. For a variety of policy reasons, the law limits or even forbids the exercise of certain rights over certain forms of property. For example, both law and contract may limit the right of an owner of real property to use his parcel as he sees fit. Owners of various forms of personal property may likewise be subject to restrictions on the time, place, and manner of their use. Limitations on the disposition of real property, while less common, may also be imposed. Finally, some types of personal property may be sold but not given away, while others may be given away but not sold, and still others may neither be given away nor sold.

In each of the foregoing instances, the limitation or prohibition diminishes the bundle of rights that would otherwise attach to the property, yet what remains is still deemed in law to be a protectable property interest. "Since property or title is a complex bundle of rights, duties, powers and immunities, the pruning away of some or a great many of these elements does not entirely destroy the title. . . ." (People v. Walker (1939) 33 Cal. App. 2d 18, 20, 90 P.2d 854 [even the possessor of contraband has certain property rights in it against anyone other than the state].) The same rule applies to Moore's interest in his own body tissue. . . .

NOTES & QUESTIONS:

1. In thinking about Henrietta and Moore,
    a. What interests are at issue?

b. What reasons would support classifying human cells as property?
c. If classified as property, how would that help Henrietta, Moore, and others like them?
d. What reasons support an argument against cells being property?
e. How would you resolve this conflict? Why?
f. If property, can we place a value on these cells? How?

2. Could the court have recognized that Moore had a property interest in his cells even after they were removed from his body but that the property interest is limited in that he could not sell his cells for profit just as he cannot sell his organs? What if he wanted to donate them to some other research facility?

3. There have been very few instances where a court has had to decide the disposition of reproductive material at death and it has been in the context of sperm. Two reported California cases have addressed the issue of how to treat cryopreserved sperm at death.

In Hecht v. Superior Court,[3] Bill Kane died with a will that left his cryopreserved sperm to his girlfriend Debra Hecht. His surviving adult children challenged the bequest in the will. Although the court seemed reluctant to discuss the sperm in terms of "property," the court determined the decedent's interest in his cryogenically preserved sperm was "property" that could be within the jurisdiction of the probate court. The court cited to the American Fertility Society's ethical statement that "it is understood that the gametes and concepti are the property of the donors. The donors therefore have the right to decide at their sole discretion the disposition of these items, provided such dispositions are within medical and ethical guidelines."[4] The court concluded that the sperm was a unique "property." The court could not have properly ordered the sperm destroyed by applying the provisions of the will.

Additionally, in the case of In re Estate of Kievernagel[5] the decedent died with cryopreserved sperm and instructions that the sperm were to be destroyed upon his death. Although his surviving spouse requested the sperm, the court agreed with the Hecht court finding the gametic material to be a unique type of property and thus not governed by the general laws relating to gifts of personal property or the transfer of personal property upon death. At the time of his death, he still had an

---

[3] 20 Cal. Rptr. 2d 275 (Cal. App. 1993).
[4] Id. at 282.
[5] 83 Cal. Rptr. 3d 311 (Cal. App. 2008).

ownership interest that gave him decision-making authority as to the use of his gametic material for reproduction.

If the sperm bank had transferred Kane's sperm to someone else either during his life or after his death, would Kane or his girlfriend have been able to pursue a claim of conversion? Why or why not would that situation be any different from that in *Moore*?

2. Real Property

Real property is land and generally whatever is erected or growing upon or affixed to land. The laws governing real property are more complex than personal property due to the importance that land has always played in society. During feudal times, land ownership allowed a man to have status in society and avoid being a landless serf. During the colonization of America, land ownership again gave a person status in society and allowed for the development of the family farm. Additionally, for quite some time in our country's history, only landowners had the right to vote. Land is an essential part of our current economy and market system. The turmoil in the real estate market in the United States had far reaching effects across the globe. The focus of the first-year property course primarily focuses on real property due to the complex system of laws to address the unique characteristics of land.

D. Methods of Acquiring Property

Regardless of the nature of property, there are many ways of acquiring property. While the focus of Property I is on the different interests that exist, it will aid in the understanding of property to briefly consider acquisition. There are ways that property is possessed and acquired for the first time, like capture, creation, and discovery. There are also means that property is acquired subsequently like find, purchase, gift, and adverse possession. The focus of Property II is the acquisition of rights in property focusing on subsequent acquisition—purchase, gift, and adverse possession. For now, we will turn our attention to capture and find.

1. The Rule of Capture

Pierson v. Post
Supreme Court of New York, 1805
3 Cal. R. 175

This cause comes before us on a return to a certiorari directed to one of the justices of Queens County.

The question submitted by the counsel in this cause for our determination is, whether Lodowick Post, by the pursuit with his hounds in the manner alleged in his declaration, acquired such a right to, or property in, the fox as will sustain an action against Pierson for killing and taking him away? → WILD *[handwritten]*

[handwritten margin note: ISSUE]

It is admitted that a fox is an animal *ferae naturae*, and that property in such animals is acquired by occupancy only. These admissions narrow the discussion to the simple question of what acts amount to occupancy, applied to acquiring right to wild animals.

If we have recourse to the ancient writers upon general principles of law, the judgment below is obviously erroneous. Justinian's Institutes (lib. 2, tit. 1, sec. 13), and Fleta (lib. 3, ch. 2, p. 175), adopt the principle, that pursuit alone vests no property or right in the huntsman; and that even pursuit, accompanied with wounding, is equally ineffectual for that purpose, unless the animal be actually taken. The same principle is recognized by Breton (lib. 2, ch. 1, p. 8).

[handwritten margin note: JUSTINIAN/ BRETON   PURSUIT ≠ PROPERTY]

Puffendorf (lib. 4, ch. 6, sec. 2 and 10) defines occupancy of beasts *ferae naturae*, to be the actual corporeal possession of them, and Bynkershock is cited as coinciding in this definition. It is indeed with hesitation that Puffendorf affirms that a wild beast mortally wounded or greatly maimed, cannot be fairly intercepted by another, whilst the pursuit of the person inflicting the wound continues. The foregoing authorities are decisive to show that mere pursuit gave Post no legal right to the fox, but that he became the property of Pierson, who intercepted and killed him.

[handwritten margin note: PUFF   PURSUIT + WOUND = PROPERTY]

It, therefore, only remains to inquire whether there are any contrary principles or authorities, to be found in other books, which ought to induce a different decision. Most of the cases which have occurred in England, relating to property in wild animals, have either been discussed and decided upon the principles of their positive statute regulations, or have arisen between the huntsman and the owner of the land upon which beasts *ferae naturae* have been apprehended; the former claiming them by title of occupancy, and the latter ratione soli. Little satisfactory aid can, therefore, be derived from the English reporters.

Barbeyrac, in his notes on Puffendorf, does not accede to the definition of occupancy by the latter, but, on the contrary, affirms that actual bodily seizure is not, in all cases, necessary to constitute possession of wild animals. He does not, however, describe the acts which, according to his ideas, will amount to an appropriation of such animals to private use, so as to exclude the claims of all other persons, by title of occupancy, to the same animals; and he is far from averring that pursuit alone is sufficient for that purpose. To a certain extent, and as far as Barbeyrac appears to me to go, his objections to Puffendorf's definition of occupancy are reasonable and correct. That is to say, that actual bodily seizure is not indispensable to acquire right to, or possession of, wild beasts; but that, on the contrary, the mortal wounding of such beasts, by one not abandoning his pursuit, may, with the utmost propriety, be deemed possession of him; since thereby the pursuer manifests an unequivocal intention of appropriating the animal to his individual use, has deprived him of his natural liberty, and brought him within his certain control. So, also, encompassing and securing such animals with nets and toils, or otherwise intercepting them in such a manner as to deprive them of their natural liberty, and render escape impossible, may justly be deemed to give possession of them to those persons who, by their industry and labor, have used such means of apprehending them. Barbeyrac seems to have adopted and had in view in his notes, the more accurate opinion of Grotius, with respect to occupancy. . . . The case now under consideration is one of mere pursuit, and presents no circumstances or acts which can bring it within the definition of occupancy by Puffendorf, or Grotius, or the ideas of Barbeyrac upon that subject.

The case cited from 11 Mod. 74, 130, I think clearly distinguishable from the present; inasmuch as there the action was for maliciously hindering and disturbing the plaintiff in the exercise and enjoyment of a private franchise; and in the report of the same case (3 Salk. 9), Holt, Ch. J., states, that the ducks were in the plaintiff's decoy pond, and so in his possession, from which it is obvious the court laid much stress in their opinion upon the plaintiff's possession of the ducks, *ratione soli*.

We are the more readily inclined to confine possession or occupancy of beasts *ferae naturae*, within the limits prescribed by the learned authors above cited, for the sake of certainty, and preserving peace and order in society. If the first seeing, starting or pursuing such animals, without having so wounded, circumvented or ensnared them, so as to deprive them of their natural liberty, and subject them to the control of their pursuer, should afford the basis of actions against others for intercepting and killing them, it would prove a fertile source of quarrels and litigation.

However uncourteous or unkind the conduct of Pierson towards Post, in this instance, may have been, yet this act was productive of no injury or damage for which a legal remedy can be applied. We are of opinion the judgment below was erroneous, and ought to be reversed.

LIVINGSTON, J, dissenting:

My opinion differs from that of the court. Of six exceptions, taken to the proceedings below, all are abandoned except the third, which reduces the controversy to a single question.

Whether a person who, with his own hounds, starts and hunts a fox on waste and uninhabited ground, and is on the point of seizing his prey, acquires such an interest in the animal as to have a right of action against another, who in view of the huntsman and his dogs in full pursuit, and with knowledge of the chase, shall kill and carry him away.

This is a knotty point, and should have been submitted to the arbitration of sportsmen, without poring over Justinian, Fleta, Bracton, Puffendorf, Locke, Barbeyrac, or Blackstone, all of whom have been cited: they would have had no difficulty in coming to a prompt and correct conclusion. In a court thus constituted, the skin and carcass of poor Reynard would have been properly disposed of, and a precedent set, interfering with no usage or custom which the experience of ages has sanctioned, and which must be so well known to every votary of Diana. But the parties have referred the question to our judgment, and we must dispose of it as well as we can, from the partial lights we possess, leaving to a higher tribunal the correction of any mistake which we may be so unfortunate as to make. By the pleadings it is admitted that a fox is a "wild and noxious beast." Both parties have regarded him, as the law of nations does a pirate, *"hostem humani generis,"* and although *"de mortuis nil nisi bonum"* be a

---

[6] Illustration by Hunter Ratcliff, Baylor Law J.D., *cum laude*, 2017.

maxim of our profession, the memory of the deceased has not been spared. His depredations on farmers and on barnyards, have not been forgotten; and to put him to death wherever found, is allowed to be meritorious, and of public benefit. Hence it follows, that our decision should have in view the greatest possible encouragement to the destruction of an animal, so cunning and ruthless in his career. But who would keep a pack of hounds; or what gentleman, at the sound of the horn, and at peep of day, would mount his steed, and for hours together, *"sub jove frigido,"* or a vertical sun, pursue the windings of this wily quadruped, if, just as night came on, and his stratagems and strength were nearly exhausted, a saucy intruder, who had not shared in the honors or labors of the chase, were permitted to come in at the death, and bear away in triumph the object of pursuit? Whatever Justinian may have thought of the matter, it must be recollected that his code was compiled many hundred years ago, and it would be very hard indeed, at the distance of so many centuries, not to have a right to establish a rule for ourselves. In his day, we read of no order of men who made it a business, in the language of the declaration in this cause, "with hounds and dogs to find, start, pursue, hunt, and chase," these animals, and that, too, without any other motive than the preservation of Roman poultry; if this diversion had been then in fashion, the lawyers who composed his institutes, would have taken care not to pass it by, without suitable encouragement. If anything, therefore, in the digests or pandects shall appear to militate against the defendant in error, who, on this occasion, was the fox hunter, we have only to say *tempora mutantur;* and if men themselves change with the times, why should not laws also undergo an alteration?

It may be expected, however, by the learned counsel, that more particular notice be taken of their authorities. I have examined them all, and feel great difficulty in determining, whether to acquire dominion over a thing, before in common, it be sufficient that we barely see it, or know where it is, or wish for it, or make a declaration of our will respecting it; or whether, in the case of wild beasts, setting a trap, or lying in wait, or starting, or pursuing, be enough; or if an actual wounding, or killing, or bodily tact and occupation be necessary. Writers on general law, who have favored us with their speculations on these points, differ on them all; but, great as is the diversity of sentiment among them, some conclusion must be adopted on the question immediately before us. After mature deliberation, I embrace that of Barbeyrac as the most rational and least liable to objection. If at liberty, we might imitate the courtesy of a certain emperor, who, to avoid giving offense to the advocates of any of these different doctrines, adopted a middle course, and by ingenious distinctions, rendered it difficult to say (as often happens after a fierce and angry contest) to whom the palm of victory belonged. He ordained, that if a beast be followed with large dogs and hounds, he shall belong to the hunter, not to the chance occupant; and in like manner, if he be killed or wounded with a lance or sword; but if chased with beagles only, then he passed to the captor, not to the first pursuer. If slain with a dart, a sling, or a bow, he fell to the hunter, if still in chase, and not to him who might afterwards find and seize him.

Now, as we are without any municipal regulations of our own, and the pursuit here, for aught that appears on the case, being with dogs and hounds of imperial stature, we are at liberty to adopt one of the provisions just cited, which comports also with the learned conclusion of Barbeyrac, that property in animals *ferae naturae* may be acquired without bodily touch or manucaption, provided the pursuer be within reach, or have a reasonable prospect (which certainly existed here) of taking what he has thus discovered an intention of converting to his own use.

When we reflect also that the interest of our husbandmen, the most useful of men in any community, will be advanced by the destruction of a beast so pernicious and incorrigible, we cannot greatly err in saying that a pursuit like the present, through waste and unoccupied lands, and which must inevitably and speedily have terminated in corporeal possession, or bodily seisin, confers such a right to the object of it, as to make any one a wrong-doer who shall interfere and shoulder the spoil. The justice's judgment ought, therefore, in my opinion, to be affirmed.

Judgment of reversal.

NOTES:

1. There is an interesting story that goes along with Pierson v. Post. Allegedly, Post was part of the nouveau riche and liked to make quite a show when fox hunting. Pierson was old money and a gentleman who wanted nothing to do with the likes of Post. This difference made the men dislike each other. Pierson evidently had had enough that day, and although he knew full well that Post was in pursuit of the fox, Pierson acted very ungentlemanly and got the fox for himself!

2. The majority rule of capture is still in force today. A contemporary example is the ocean fishery. Many ocean fisheries are governed by the rule and as a result, countries like Russia and Japan have developed boats that allow them to catch fish very effectively.

   Rule of capture also comes into play in the context of oil and gas. While the law of oil and gas is its own body of law, the context is viewed as similar to that of the wild animal roaming freely because oil and gas reserves can migrate under the land. Therefore, courts dealing with oil and gas issues have had to look to the rule of capture to address ownership issues and disputes. This rule has also impacted another natural resource that is migratory—water.

We will also look at the rule of capture and whether it has a role in the context of a more recent case involving a baseball.

2. Rule of Finders

In the context of acquiring property by "find" we think of the old saying "finders keepers, losers weepers." It is in this context we discuss the idea of possession of property. With the rule of capture, the person in possession of the property is the first one to possess it and acquire ownership of it. However, with the rule of finders, the person in possession is a subsequent possessor. The possessor did not acquire a right in the property by purchasing it. A property right was not given to him as through a legal gift. In this instance someone who is not the "true owner" takes possession of some property and does develop a legal relationship with the property.

Armory v. Delamirie
93 Eng. Rep. 664, 1722

Finder of a jewel may maintain trover.

The plaintiff being a chimney sweeper's boy found a jewel and carried it to the defendant's shop (who was a goldsmith) to know what it was, and delivered it into the hands of the apprentice, who under pretence of weighing it, took out the stones, and calling to the master to let him know it came to three halfpence, the master offered the boy the money, who refused to take it, and insisted to have the thing again; whereupon the apprentice delivered him back the socket without the stones. And now in trover against the master these points were ruled:

1. That the finder of a jewel, though he does not by such finding acquire an absolute property or ownership, yet he has such a property as will enable him to keep it against all but the rightful owner, and consequently may maintain trover.

2. That the action well lay against the master, who gives a credit to his apprentice, and is answerable for his neglect.

3. As to the value of the jewel several of the trade were examined to prove what a jewel of the finest water that would fit the socket would be worth; and the Chief Justice (Pratt) directed the jury, that unless the defendant did produce the jewel, and shew it not to be of the finest water, they should presume the strongest case against him, and make the value of the best jewels the measure of their damages: which they accordingly did.

NOTES & QUESTIONS:

1. The rule of finders is that the finder prevails against all *except* for (1) the actual owner; and (2) any prior possessor. Additionally, the law of finders is categorized based on different types of found property—was it abandoned, lost, or mislaid by the original true owner? In the *Armory* case, was the jewel abandoned, lost, or mislaid by the true owner?

2. Abandoned property is property that the owner intentionally and voluntarily relinquishes all right, title, and interest in. The owner no longer desires to be the owner and casts off the cloak of property ownership. This allows the next person to come along and take possession to become the new true owner of the property through the rule of finders. In the *Armory* case, what if the facts were that the homeowner threw the jewel away in the trash? If the homeowner came back and demanded the jewel from the chimney sweep, would the homeowner be entitled to its return?

3. Lost property is property that the owner unintentionally and involuntarily parts with through neglect or inadvertence and then does not know where it is. In the *Armory* case, what if the homeowner had lost the jewel when it fell out of his pants pocket? If the homeowner came back and demanded the jewel from the chimney sweep, would the homeowner be entitled to its return?

4. Mislaid property is property that the owner voluntarily puts in a particular place, intending to retain ownership, but then fails to reclaim it or forgets where it is. In the *Armory* case, what if the homeowner had moved the jewel from a dresser drawer in the bedroom to a drawer in the kitchen, intending to come back and get it, but forgot the new location? If the homeowner came back and demanded the jewel from the chimney sweep, would the homeowner be entitled to its return?

5. Why would the law be interested in protecting a finder from a subsequent possessor? The key idea behind this rule is that it promotes the public order. It puts in place a system that honors the traditional rule of "first in time, first in right." But, is that really the result that the rule achieves?

E. Defining the Bundle of Sticks

There are many different rights associated with property. However, even though a person possesses property and enjoys certain rights, those rights may also be limited due to public policy considerations and balancing of interests involved.

→ = Right To Use

While there are many rights that can be included in the bundle, the essential rights that help to define the interest are (1) right to include, (2) right to exclude, (3) right to transfer, and (4) right to possess. The right to include encompasses the right to dictate who can use and enjoy the thing. The right to exclude involves the ability to prohibit others from using and enjoying the thing. The right to transfer gives the ability to transfer *inter vivos* (during life) or upon death. The right to transfer may not be a part of the bundle or it may be somewhat limited. The right to possession involves exerting dominion and control over the thing.

In defining the relationship of the person and thing, the combination of sticks and size of the sticks will vary. Each bundle of sticks for property does not have to be the same and will not be the same.

Jacque v. Steenberg Homes, Inc.
Supreme Court of Wisconsin, 1997
563 N.W.2d 154

WILLIAM A. BABLITCH, Justice.

Steenberg Homes had a mobile home to deliver. Unfortunately for Harvey and Lois Jacque (the Jacques), the easiest route of delivery was across their land. Despite adamant protests by the Jacques, Steenberg plowed a path through the Jacques' snow-covered field and via that path, delivered the mobile home. Consequently, the Jacques sued Steenberg Homes for intentional trespass. Although the jury awarded the Jacques $1 in nominal damages and $100,000 in punitive damages, the circuit court set aside the jury's award of $100,000. The court of appeals affirmed, reluctantly concluding that it could not reinstate the punitive damages because it was bound by precedent establishing that an award of nominal damages will not sustain a punitive damage award. We conclude that when nominal damages are awarded for an intentional trespass to land, punitive damages may, in the discretion of the jury, be awarded.

The relevant facts follow. Plaintiffs, Lois and Harvey Jacques, are an elderly couple, now retired from farming, who own roughly 170 acres near Wilke's Lake in the town of Schleswig. The defendant, Steenberg Homes, Inc. (Steenberg), is in the business of selling mobile homes. In the fall of 1993, a neighbor of the Jacques purchased a mobile home from Steenberg. Delivery of the mobile home was included in the sales price.

Steenberg determined that the easiest route to deliver the mobile home was across the Jacques' land. Steenberg preferred transporting the home across the Jacques' land because the only alternative was a private road which was covered in up to seven feet of snow and contained a sharp curve which would require sets of "rollers" to be used when maneuvering the home around the curve. Steenberg asked the Jacques on several separate occasions whether it could move the home across the Jacques' farm field. The Jacques refused. The Jacques were sensitive about allowing others on their land because [of earlier problems with neighbors].

On the morning of delivery, Mr. Jacque observed the mobile home parked on the corner of the town road adjacent to his property. He decided to find out where the movers planned to take the home. The movers, who were Steenberg employees, showed Mr. Jacque the path they planned to take with the mobile home to reach the neighbor's lot. The path cut across the Jacques' land. Mr. Jacque informed the movers that it was the Jacques' land they were planning to cross and that Steenberg did not have permission to cross their land. He told them that Steenberg had been refused permission to cross the Jacques' land.

One of Steenberg's employees called the assistant manager, who then came out to the Jacques' home. In the meantime, the Jacques called and asked some of their neighbors and the town chairman to come over immediately. Once everyone was present, the Jacques showed the assistant manager an aerial map and plat book of the township to prove their ownership of the land, and reiterated their demand that the home not be moved across their land.

[Steenberg's] assistant manager asked Mr. Jacque how much money it would take to get permission [to cross Mr. Jacque's land]. Mr. Jacque responded that it was not a question of money; the Jacques just did not want Steenberg to cross their land. Mr. Jacque testified that he told Steenberg to "[F]ollow the road, that is what the road is for."

At trial, one of Steenberg's employees testified that, upon coming out of the Jacques' home, the assistant manager stated: "I don't give a — what [Mr. Jacque] said, just get the home in there any way you can." The other Steenberg employee confirmed this testimony and further testified that the assistant manager told him to park the company truck in such a way that no one could get down the town road to see the route the employees were taking with the home. The assistant manager denied giving these instructions, and Steenberg argued that the road was blocked for safety reasons.

The employees, after beginning down the private road, ultimately used a "bobcat" to cut a path through the Jacques' snow-covered field and hauled the home across the Jacques' land to the neighbor's lot. One employee testified that upon returning to the office and informing the assistant manager that they had gone across the field, the assistant manager reacted by giggling and laughing. The other employee confirmed this testimony. The assistant manager disputed this testimony.

When a neighbor informed the Jacques that Steenberg had, in fact, moved the mobile home across the Jacques' land, Mr. Jacque called the Manitowoc County Sheriff's Department. After interviewing the parties and observing the scene, an officer from the sheriff's department issued a $30 citation to Steenberg's assistant manager.

The Jacques commenced an intentional tort action in Manitowoc County Circuit Court, Judge Allan J. Deehr presiding, seeking compensatory and punitive damages from Steenberg.

We turn first to the individual landowner's interest in protecting his or her land from trespass. The United States Supreme Court has recognized that the private landowner's right to exclude others from his or her land is "one of the most essential sticks in the bundle of rights that are commonly characterized as property." Kaiser Aetna v. United States, 444 U.S. 164, 176, 100 S. Ct. 383, 391, 62 L. Ed. 2d 332 (1979)). This court has long recognized "[e]very person['s] constitutional right to the exclusive enjoyment of his own property for any purpose which does not invade the rights of another person." Diana Shooting Club v. Lamoreux, 114 Wis. 44, 59, 89 N.W. 880 (1902). Thus, both this court and the Supreme Court recognize the individual's legal right to exclude others from private property.

Yet a right is hollow if the legal system provides insufficient means to protect it.

Harvey and Lois Jacque have the right to tell Steenberg Homes and any other trespasser, "No, you cannot cross our land." But that right has no practical meaning unless protected by the State, [and a nominal dollar award] does not constitute state protection.

A series of intentional trespasses, as the Jacques had the misfortune to discover in an unrelated action, can threaten the individual's very ownership of the land.[7]

In sum, the individual has a strong interest in excluding trespassers from his or her land.

Society has an interest in punishing and deterring intentional trespassers beyond that of protecting the interests of the individual landowner. Society has an interest in preserving the integrity of the legal system. Private landowners should feel confident that wrongdoers who trespass upon their land will be appropriately punished. When landowners have confidence in the legal system, they are less likely to resort to "self-help" remedies.

In conclusion, we hold that when nominal damages are awarded for an intentional trespass to land, punitive damages may, in the discretion of the jury, be awarded. Our decision today shall apply to Steenberg Homes. Finally, we hold

---

[7]The conduct of an intentional trespasser, if repeated, might ripen into prescription or adverse possession and, as a consequence, the individual landowner can lose his or her property rights to the trespasser. See Wis. Stat. § 893.28.

that the $100,000 punitive damages awarded by the jury is not excessive. Accordingly we reverse and remand to the circuit court for reinstatement of the punitive damage award.

Reversed and remanded with directions.

NOTE:

Avoiding self-help is a common theme throughout the law of property. In *McWilliams,* the court recognized the importance of " 'prevent [ing] the practice of dueling, [by permitting] juries [ ] to *punish* insult by exemplary damages.' " *McWilliams,* 3 Wis. at 428. Although dueling is rarely a modern form of self-help, one can easily imagine a frustrated landowner taking the law into his or her own hands when faced with a brazen trespasser, like Steenberg, who refuses to heed no trespass warnings.[8]

State of New Jersey v. Peter K. Shack and Frank Tejeras
Supreme Court of New Jersey, 1971
58 N.J. 297

WEINTRAUB, C.J.

Defendants entered upon private property to aid migrant farmworkers employed and housed there. Having refused to depart upon the demand of the owner, defendants were [convicted of trespassing].

Before us, no one seeks to sustain these convictions. The complaints were prosecuted in the Municipal Court and in the County Court by counsel engaged by the complaining landowner, Tedesco. However Tedesco did not respond to this appeal, and the county prosecutor, while defending abstractly the constitutionality of the trespass statute, expressly disclaimed any position as to whether the statute reached the activity of these defendants.

Complainant, Tedesco, a farmer, employs migrant workers for his seasonal needs. As part of their compensation, these workers are housed at a camp on his property.

Defendant Tejeras is a field worker for the Farm Workers Division of the Southwest Citizens Organization for Poverty Elimination, known by the acronym SCOPE, a nonprofit corporation funded by the Office of Economic Opportunity pursuant to an act of Congress, 42 U.S.C.A. §§ 2861-2864. The role of SCOPE includes providing for the 'health services of the migrant farm worker.'

Defendant Shack is a staff attorney with the Farm Workers Division of Camden Regional Legal Services, Inc., known as 'CRLS,' also a nonprofit corporation funded by the Office of Economic Opportunity pursuant to an act of

---

[8] Jacque v. Steenberg Homes, Inc., 563 N.W.2d 154, 160-161 (Wis. 1997).

Congress, 42 U.S.C.A. § 2809(a)(3). The mission of CRLS includes legal advice and representation for these workers.

Differences had developed between Tedesco and these defendants prior to the events which led to the trespass charges now before us. Hence when defendant Tejeras wanted to go upon Tedesco's farm to find a migrant worker who needed medical aid for the removal of 28 sutures, he called upon defendant Shack for his help with respect to the legalities involved. Shack, too, had a mission to perform on Tedesco's farm; he wanted to discuss a legal problem with another migrant worker there employed and housed. Defendants arranged to go to the farm together. Shack carried literature to inform the migrant farmworkers of the assistance available to them under federal statutes, but no mention seems to have been made of that literature when Shack was later confronted by Tedesco.

Defendants entered upon Tedesco's property and as they neared the camp site where the farmworkers were housed, they were confronted by Tedesco who inquired of their purpose. Tejeras and Shack stated their missions. In response, Tedesco offered to find the injured worker, and as to the worker who needed legal advice, Tedesco also offered to locate the man but insisted that the consultation would have to take place in Tedesco's office and in his presence. Defendants declined, saying they had the right to see the men in the privacy of their living quarters and without Tedesco's supervision. Tedesco thereupon summoned a State Trooper who, however, refused to remove defendants except upon Tedesco's written complaint. Tedesco then executed the formal complaints charging violations of the trespass statute.

The constitutionality of the trespass statute, as applied here, is challenged on several scores.

These constitutional claims are not established by any definitive holding. We think it unnecessary to explore their validity. The reason is that we are satisfied that under our State law the ownership of real property does not include the right to bar access to governmental services available to migrant workers and hence there was no trespass within the meaning of the penal statute. The policy considerations which underlie that conclusion may be much the same as those which would be weighed with respect to one or more of the constitutional challenges, but a decision in non-constitutional terms is more satisfactory, because the interests of migrant workers are more expansively served in that way than they would be if they had no more freedom than these constitutional concepts could be found to mandate if indeed they apply at all.

Property rights serve human values. They are recognized to that end, and are limited by it. Title to real property cannot include dominion over the destiny of persons the owner permits to come upon the premises. Their well-being must remain the paramount concern of a system of law. Indeed the needs of the occupants may be so imperative and their strength so weak, that the law will deny the occupants the power to contract away what is deemed essential to their health, welfare, or dignity.

Here we are concerned with a highly disadvantaged segment of our society. We are told that every year farmworkers and their families numbering more than one million leave their home areas to fill the seasonal demand for farm labor in the United States. The migrant farmworkers come to New Jersey in substantial numbers.

The migrant farmworkers are a community within but apart from the local scene. They are rootless and isolated. Although the need for their labors is evident, they are unorganized and without economic or political power. It is their plight alone that summoned government to their aid. In response, Congress provided under Title III-B of the Economic Opportunity Act of 1964 (42 U.S.C.A. § 2701 et seq.) for "assistance for migrant and other seasonally employed farmworkers and their families." Section 2861 states "the purpose of this part is to assist migrant and seasonal farmworkers and their families to improve their living conditions and develop skills necessary for a productive and self-sufficient life in an increasingly complex and technological society."

These ends would not be gained if the intended beneficiaries could be insulated from efforts to reach them. It is in this framework that we must decide whether the camp operator's rights in his lands may stand between the migrant workers and those who would aid them. The key to that aid is communication. Since the migrant workers are outside the mainstream of the communities in which they are housed and are unaware of their rights and opportunities and of the services available to them, they can be reached only by positive efforts tailored to that end.

A man's right in his real property of course is not absolute. It was a maxim of the common law that one should so use his property as not to injure the rights of others. Although hardly a precise solvent of actual controversies, the maxim does express the inevitable proposition that rights are relative and there must be an accommodation when they meet. Hence it has long been true that necessity, private or public, may justify entry upon the lands of another.

The subject is not static. As pointed out in 5 Powell, Real Property (Rohan 1970) § 745, pp. 493-494, while society will protect the owner in his permissible interests in land, yet ". . . (s)uch an owner must expect to find the absoluteness of his property rights curtailed by the organs of society, for the promotion of the best interests of others for whom these organs also operate as protective agencies. The current balance between individualism and dominance of the social interest depends not only upon political and social ideologies, but also upon the physical and social facts of the time and place under discussion."

Thus approaching the case, we find it unthinkable that the farmer-employer can assert a right to isolate the migrant worker in any respect significant for the worker's well-being. The farmer, of course, is entitled to pursue his farming activities without interference, and this defendants readily concede. But we see no legitimate need for a right in the farmer to deny the worker the opportunity for aid available from federal, State, or local services, or from recognized charitable groups seeking to assist him. Hence representatives of these agencies and organizations may enter upon the premises to seek out the worker at his living quarters. So, too, the migrant worker must be allowed to receive visitors there of his own choice, so long as there is no behavior hurtful to others, and members of the press may not be denied reasonable access to workers who do not object to seeing them.

It is not our purpose to open the employer's premises to the general public if in fact the employer himself has not done so. We do not say, for example, that solicitors or peddlers of all kinds may enter on their own; we may assume or the present that the employer may regulate their entry or bar them, at least if the employer's purpose is not to gain a commercial advantage for himself or if the regulation does not deprive the migrant worker of practical access to things he needs.

And we are mindful of the employer's interest in his own and in his employees' security. Hence he may reasonably require a visitor to identify himself, and also to state his general purpose if the migrant worker has not already informed him that the visitor is expected. But the employer may not deny the worker his privacy or interfere with his opportunity to live with dignity and to enjoy associations customary among our citizens. These rights are too fundamental to be denied on the basis of an interest in real property and too fragile to be left to the unequal bargaining strength of the parties. See Henningsen v. Bloomfield Motors, Inc., 32 N.J. 358, 403-404, 161 A.2d 69 (1960); Ellsworth Dobbs, Inc. v. Johnson, 50 N.J. 528, 555, 236 A.2d 843 (1967).

It follows that defendants here invaded no possessory right of the farmer-employer. Their conduct was therefore beyond the reach of the trespass statute. The judgments are accordingly reversed and the matters remanded to the County Court with directions to enter judgments of acquittal.

For reversal and remand.

Alex Popov v. Patrick Hayashi
Superior Court, San Francisco County, California, 2002
2002 WL 31833731

In 1927, Babe Ruth hit sixty home runs. That record stood for thirty-four years until Roger Maris broke it in 1961 with sixty-one home runs. Mark McGwire hit seventy in 1998. On October 7, 2001, at PacBell Park in San Francisco, Barry Bonds hit number seventy three. That accomplishment set a record which, in all probability, will remain unbroken for years into the future.

The event was widely anticipated and received a great deal of attention.

The ball that found itself at the receiving end of Mr. Bond's bat garnered some of that attention. Baseball fans in general, and especially people at the game, understood the importance of the ball. It was worth a great deal of money and whoever caught it would bask, for a brief period of time, in the reflected fame of Mr. Bonds.

With that in mind, many people who attended the game came prepared for the possibility that a record setting ball would be hit in their direction. Among this group were plaintiff Alex Popov and defendant Patrick Hayashi. They were unacquainted at the time. Both men brought baseball gloves, which they anticipated using if the ball came within their reach.

They, along with a number of others, positioned themselves in the arcade section of the ballpark. This is a standing room only area located near right field. It is in this general area that Barry Bonds hits the greatest number of home runs. The area was crowded with people on October 7, 2001, and access was restricted to those who held tickets for that section.

Barry Bonds came to bat in the first inning. With nobody on base and a full count, Bonds swung at a slow knuckleball. He connected. The ball sailed over the right-field fence and into the arcade.

Josh Keppel, a cameraman who was positioned in the arcade, captured the event on videotape. Keppel filmed much of what occurred from the time Bonds hit the ball until the commotion in the arcade had subsided. He was standing very near the spot where the ball landed and he recorded a significant amount of information critical to the disposition of this case.

In addition to the Keppel tape, seventeen percipient witnesses testified as to what they saw after the ball came into the stands. The testimony of these witnesses varied on many important points. Some of the witnesses had a good vantage point and some did not. Some appeared disinterested in the outcome of the litigation and others had a clear bias. Some remembered the events well and others did not. Some were encumbered by prior inconsistent statements which diminished their credibility.

The factual findings in this case are the result of an analysis of the testimony of all the witnesses as well as a detailed review of the Keppel tape. Those findings are as follows:

When the seventy-third home run ball went into the arcade, it landed in the upper portion of the webbing of a softball glove worn by Alex Popov. While the glove stopped the trajectory of the ball, it is not at all clear that the ball was secure. Popov had to reach for the ball and in doing so, may have lost his balance.

Even as the ball was going into his glove, a crowd of people began to engulf Mr. Popov. He was tackled and thrown to the ground while still in the process of attempting to complete the catch. Some people intentionally descended on him for the purpose of taking the ball away, while others were involuntarily forced to the ground by the momentum of the crowd.

Eventually, Mr. Popov was buried face down on the ground under several layers of people. At one point he had trouble breathing. Mr. Popov was grabbed, hit and kicked. People reached underneath him in the area of his glove. Neither the tape nor the testimony is sufficient to establish which individual members of the crowd were responsible for the assaults on Mr. Popov.

The videotape clearly establishes that this was an out of control mob, engaged in violent, illegal behavior. Although some witnesses testified in a manner inconsistent with this finding, their testimony is specifically rejected as being false on a material point.

Mr. Popov intended at all times to establish and maintain possession of the ball. At some point the ball left his glove and ended up on the ground. It is impossible to establish the exact point in time that this occurred or what caused it to occur.

Mr. Hayashi was standing near Mr. Popov when the ball came into the stands. He, like Mr. Popov, was involuntarily forced to the ground. He committed no wrongful act. While on the ground he saw the loose ball. He picked it up, rose to his feet and put it in his pocket.

Although the crowd was still on top of Mr. Popov, security guards had begun the process of physically pulling people off. Some people resisted those efforts. One person argued with an official and another had to be pulled off by his hair.

Mr. Hayashi kept the ball hidden. He asked Mr. Keppel to point the camera at him. At first, Mr. Keppel did not comply and Mr. Hayashi continued to hide the ball. Finally after someone else in the crowd asked Mr. Keppel to point the camera at Mr. Hayashi, Mr. Keppel complied. It was only at that point that Mr. Hayashi held the ball in the air for others to see. Someone made a motion for the ball and Mr. Hayashi put it back in his glove. It is clear that Mr. Hayashi was concerned that someone would take the ball away from him and that he was unwilling to show it until he was on videotape. Although he testified to the contrary, that portion of his testimony is unconvincing.

Mr. Popov eventually got up from the ground. He made several statements while he was on the ground and shortly after he got up which are consistent with his claim that he had achieved some level of control over the ball and that he intended to keep it. Those statements can be heard on the audio portion of the tape. When he saw that Mr. Hayashi had the ball he expressed relief and grabbed for it. Mr. Hayashi pulled the ball away. Security guards then took Mr. Hayashi to a secure area of the stadium.

It is important to point out what the evidence did not and could not show. Neither the camera nor the percipient witnesses were able to establish whether Mr. Popov retained control of the ball as he descended into the crowd. Mr. Popov's testimony on this question is inconsistent on several important points, ambiguous on others and, on the whole, unconvincing. We do not know when or how Mr. Popov lost the ball.

Perhaps the most critical factual finding of all is one that cannot be made. We will never know if Mr. Popov would have been able to retain control of the ball had the crowd not interfered with his efforts to do so. Resolution of that question is the work of a psychic, not a judge.

Plaintiff has pled causes of actions for conversion, trespass to chattel, injunctive relief and constructive trust.

Conversion is the wrongful exercise of dominion over the personal property of another. There must be actual interference with the plaintiff's dominion. Wrongful withholding of property can constitute actual interference even where the defendant lawfully acquired the property. If a person entitled to possession of personal property demands its return, the unjustified refusal to give the property back is conversion.

The act constituting conversion must be intentionally done. There is no requirement, however, that the defendant know that the property belongs to another or that the defendant intends to dispossess the true owner of its use and enjoyment. Wrongful purpose is not a component of conversion.

The injured party may elect to seek either specific recovery of the property or monetary damages.

Trespass to chattel, in contrast, exists where personal property has been damaged or where the defendant has interfered with the plaintiff's use of the property. Actual dispossession is not an element of the tort of trespass to chattel.

In the case at bar, Mr. Popov is not claiming that Mr. Hayashi damaged the ball or that he interfered with Mr. Popov's use and enjoyment of the ball. He claims instead that Mr. Hayashi intentionally took it from him and refused to give it back. There is no trespass to chattel. If there was a wrong at all, it is conversion.

Conversion does not exist, however, unless the baseball rightfully belongs to Mr. Popov. One who has neither title nor possession, nor any right to possession, cannot sue for conversion. The deciding question in this case then, is whether Mr. Popov achieved possession or the right to possession as he attempted to catch and hold on to the ball.

The parties have agreed to a starting point for the legal analysis. Prior to the time the ball was hit, it was possessed and owned by Major League Baseball. At the time it was hit it became intentionally abandoned property. The first person who came in possession of the ball became its new owner.

The parties fundamentally disagree about the definition of possession. In order to assist the court in resolving this disagreement, four distinguished law professors participated in a forum to discuss the legal definition of possession. The professors also disagreed.

The disagreement is understandable. Although the term possession appears repeatedly throughout the law, its definition varies depending on the context in which it is used. Various courts have condemned the term as vague and meaningless.

This level of criticism is probably unwarranted.

While there is a degree of ambiguity built into the term possession, that ambiguity exists for a purpose. Courts are often called upon to resolve conflicting claims of possession in the context of commercial disputes. A stable economic environment requires rules of conduct which are understandable and consistent with the fundamental customs and practices of the industry they regulate. Without that, rules will be difficult to enforce and economic instability will result. Because each industry has different customs and practices, a single definition of possession cannot be applied to different industries without creating havoc.

This does not mean that there are no central principles governing the law of possession. It is possible to identify certain fundamental concepts that are common to every definition of possession.

Professor Roger Bernhardt has recognized that "[p]ossession requires both physical control over the item and an intent to control it or exclude others from it. But these generalizations function more as guidelines than as direct determinants of possession issues. Possession is a blurred question of law and fact."

Professor Brown argues that "[t]he orthodox view of possession regards it as a union of the two elements of the physical relation of the possessor to the thing, and of intent. This physical relation is the actual power over the thing in question, the ability to hold and make use of it. But a mere physical relation of the possessor to the thing in question is not enough. There must also be manifested an intent to control it."

The task of this court is to use these principles as a starting point to craft a definition of possession that applies to the unique circumstances of this case.

We start with the observation that possession is a process which culminates in an event. The event is the moment in time that possession is achieved. The process includes the acts and thoughts of the would be possessor which lead up to the moment of possession.

The focus of the analysis in this case is not on the thoughts or intent of the actor. Mr. Popov has clearly evidenced an intent to possess the baseball and has communicated that intent to the world. The question is whether he did enough to reduce the ball to his exclusive dominion and control. Were his acts sufficient to create a legally cognizable interest in the ball?

Mr. Hayashi argues that possession does not occur until the fan has complete control of the ball. Professor Brian Gray, suggests the following definition[:] "A person who catches a baseball that enters the stands is its owner. A ball is caught if the person has achieved complete control of the ball at the point in time that the momentum of the ball and the momentum of the fan while attempting to catch the ball ceases. A baseball, which is dislodged by incidental contact with an inanimate object or another person, before momentum has ceased, is not possessed. Incidental contact with another person is contact that is not intended by the other person. The first person to pick up a loose ball and secure it becomes its possessor." (Gray's Rule)

Mr. Popov argues that this definition requires that a person seeking to establish possession must show unequivocal dominion and control, a standard rejected by several leading cases. (Citations omitted). Instead, he offers the perspectives of Professor Bernhardt and Professor Paul Finkelman who suggest that possession occurs when an individual intends to take control of a ball and manifests that intent by stopping the forward momentum of the ball whether or not complete control is achieved.

Professors Finkelman and Bernhardt have correctly pointed out that some cases recognize possession even before absolute dominion and control is achieved. Those cases require the actor to be actively and ably engaged in efforts to establish complete control. Moreover, such efforts must be significant and they must be reasonably calculated to result in unequivocal dominion and control at some point in the near future.

This rule is applied in cases involving the hunting or fishing of wild animals or the salvage of sunken vessels. The hunting and fishing cases recognize that a mortally wounded animal may run for a distance before falling. The hunter acquires possession upon the act of wounding the animal not the eventual capture. Similarly, whalers acquire possession by landing a harpoon, not by subduing the animal.

In the salvage cases, an individual may take possession of a wreck by exerting as much control "as its nature and situation permit."

Inadequate efforts, however, will not support a claim of possession. Thus, a "sailor cannot assert a claim merely by boarding a vessel and publishing a notice, unless such acts are coupled with a then present intention of conducting salvage operations, and he immediately thereafter proceeds with activity in the form of constructive steps to aid the distressed party."

These rules are contextual in nature. They are crafted in response to the unique nature of the conduct they seek to regulate. Moreover, they are influenced by the custom and practice of each industry. The reason that absolute dominion and control is not required to establish possession in the cases cited by Mr. Popov is that such a rule would be unworkable and unreasonable. The "nature and situation" of the property at issue does not immediately lend itself to unequivocal dominion and control. It is impossible to wrap ones arms around a whale, a fleeing fox or a sunken ship.

The opposite is true of a baseball hit into the stands of a stadium. Not only is it physically possible for a person to acquire unequivocal dominion and control of an abandoned baseball, but fans generally expect a claimant to have accomplished as much. The custom and practice of the stands creates a reasonable expectation that a person will achieve full control of a ball before claiming possession. There is no reason for the legal rule to be inconsistent with that expectation. Therefore Gray's Rule is adopted as the definition of possession in this case.

The central tenant of Gray's Rule is that the actor must retain control of the ball after incidental contact with people and things. Mr. Popov has not established by a preponderance of the evidence that he would have retained control of the ball after all momentum ceased and after any incidental contact with people or objects. Consequently, he did not achieve full possession.

That finding, however, does not resolve the case. The reason we do not know whether Mr. Popov would have retained control of the ball is not because of incidental contact. It is because he was attacked. His efforts to establish possession were interrupted by the collective assault of a band of wrongdoers.

A decision which ignored that fact would endorse the actions of the crowd by not repudiating them. Judicial rulings, particularly in cases that receive media attention, affect the way people conduct themselves. This case demands vindication of an important principle. We are a nation governed by law, not by brute force.

As a matter of fundamental fairness, Mr. Popov should have had the opportunity to try to complete his catch unimpeded by unlawful activity. To hold otherwise would be to allow the result in this case to be dictated by violence. That will not happen.

For these reasons, the analysis cannot stop with the valid observation that Mr. Popov has not proved full possession.

The legal question presented at this point is whether an action for conversion can proceed where the plaintiff has failed to establish possession or title. It can. An action for conversion may be brought where the plaintiff has title, possession or the right to possession.

Here Mr. Popov seeks, in effect, a declaratory judgment that he has either possession or the right to possession. In addition he seeks the remedies of injunctive relief and a constructive trust. These are all actions in equity. A court sitting in equity has the authority to fashion rules and remedies designed to achieve fundamental fairness.

Consistent with this principle, the court adopts the following rule. Where an actor undertakes significant but incomplete steps to achieve possession of a piece of abandoned personal property and the effort is interrupted by the unlawful acts of others, the actor has a legally cognizable pre-possessory interest in the property. That pre-possessory interest constitutes a qualified right to possession which can support a cause of action for conversion.

Possession can be likened to a journey down a path. Mr. Popov began his journey unimpeded. He was fast approaching a fork in the road. A turn in one direction would lead to possession of the ball he would complete the catch. A turn in the other direction would result in a failure to achieve possession he would drop the ball. Our problem is that before Mr. Popov got to the point where the road forked, he was set upon by a gang of bandits, who dislodged the ball from his grasp.

Recognition of a legally protected pre-possessory interest, vests Mr. Popov with a qualified right to possession and enables him to advance a legitimate claim to the baseball based on a conversion theory. Moreover it addresses the harm done by the unlawful actions of the crowd.

It does not, however, address the interests of Mr. Hayashi. The court is required to balance the interests of all parties.

Mr. Hayashi was not a wrongdoer. He was a victim of the same bandits that attacked Mr. Popov. The difference is that he was able to extract himself from their assault and move to the side of the road. It was there that he discovered the loose ball. When he picked up and put it in his pocket he attained unequivocal dominion and control.

If Mr. Popov had achieved complete possession before Mr. Hayashi got the ball, those actions would not have divested Mr. Popov of any rights, nor would they have created any rights to which Mr. Hayashi could lay claim. Mr. Popov, however, was able to establish only a qualified pre-possessory interest in the ball. That interest does not establish a full right to possession that is protected from a subsequent legitimate claim.

On the other hand, while Mr. Hayashi appears on the surface to have done everything necessary to claim full possession of the ball, the ball itself is encumbered by the qualified pre-possessory interest of Mr. Popov. At the time Mr. Hayashi came into possession of the ball, it had, in effect, a cloud on its title.

An award of the ball to Mr. Popov would be unfair to Mr. Hayashi. It would be premised on the assumption that Mr. Popov would have caught the ball. That assumption is not supported by the facts. An award of the ball to Mr. Hayashi would unfairly penalize Mr. Popov. It would be based on the assumption that Mr. Popov would have dropped the ball. That conclusion is also unsupported by the facts.

Both men have a superior claim to the ball as against all the world. Each man has a claim of equal dignity as to the other. We are, therefore, left with something of a dilemma.

Thankfully, there is a middle ground.

The concept of equitable division was fully explored in a law review article authored by Professor R.H. Helmholz in the December 1983 edition of the Fordham Law Review. Professor Helmholz addressed the problems associated with rules governing finders of lost and mislaid property. For a variety of reasons not directly relevant to the issues raised in this case, Helmholz suggested employing the equitable remedy of division to resolve competing claims between finders of lost or mislaid property and the owners of land on which the property was found.

There is no reason, however, that the same remedy cannot be applied in a case such as this, where issues of property, tort and equity intersect.

The principle at work here is that where more than one party has a valid claim to a single piece of property, the court will recognize an undivided interest in the property in proportion to the strength of the claim.

The court noted that possession requires both physical control and the intent to reduce the property to one's possession. Control and intent must be concurrent.

Here, the issue is not intent, or concurrence. Both men intended to possess the ball at the time they were in physical contact with it. The issue, instead, is the legal quality of the claim. With respect to that, neither can present a superior argument as against the other.

Mr. Hayashi's claim is compromised by Mr. Popov's pre-possessory interest. Mr. Popov cannot demonstrate full control. Their legal claims are of equal quality and they are equally entitled to the ball.

The court therefore declares that both plaintiff and defendant have an equal and undivided interest in the ball. Plaintiff's cause of action for conversion is sustained only as to his equal and undivided interest. In order to effectuate this ruling, the ball must be sold and the proceeds divided equally between the parties.

The parties are ordered to meet and confer forthwith before Judge Richard Kramer to come to an agreement as to how to implement this decision. If no decision is made by December 30, 2002, the parties are directed to appear before this court on that date at 9:00 a.m.

The court retains jurisdiction to issue orders consistent with this decision. The ball is to remain in the custody of the court until further order.

NOTES & QUESTIONS:

1. What definition would you formulate for "possession" in the context of a baseball in the stands?

2. Would you require a different definition of possession for a football that ends up in the stands? A basketball? A golf ball that lands at the foot of a spectator?

3. Would possession of land require a different definition? Why or why not?

4. If we use Gray's Rule, as adopted in Popov v. Hayashi, what should be the outcome in the following situation?

At the last home game at Yankee Stadium, a homerun ball is hit into the stands. The ball lands in the netting over the crowd and a fan grabs the ball. As the fan attempts to pull the ball through the net, he is instructed by a security guard to stop so the net is not damaged. The security guard instructs the fan to let the ball go and the security guard will return it to him.

The fan lets the ball go and as it rolls down the net, another fan grabs the ball. Security tells him to let go. The second fan lets go, security retrieves the ball and returns it to fan #1.

Which fan is the owner of the ball? Why?

5. Apply the rules in *Popov* to the following situation:

Jennifer, a 12-year-old girl, attends her first major league baseball game where player Ryan Howard hit a home run that made him reach 200 career home runs faster than any other player in history. The girl got the ball in the stands and was then approached by a Phillies employee telling her if she gave him the ball she could meet Ryan Howard after the game and he would autograph it. She handed over the ball and was given cotton candy and a soda.

At the end of the game, she was given a different ball, being told that the player Ryan Howard was going to keep the home run ball.

When she contacts you to be her attorney, who do you tell her has the legal right to the ball? Explain.

Chapter 2
Possessory Interests in Land: Freehold Estates

There are a variety of relationships that can be formed with land. Most people think of land ownership in the sense that it's mine and I can do whatever I want with it while I'm alive and leave it to whomever I want when I die. That is one form of land ownership, which will be labeled the Fee Simple Absolute. However, there are many more.

The material involving the freehold estates, as they are known, is something relatively unknown to the lay person. A freehold estate is an exclusive right to enjoy the possession and use of a parcel of land for an indefinite period. The freehold is compared to a leasehold estate, which is a right in land for a fixed, definite period.[1]

The freehold estate system is the foundation on which much of property law is built. This historical and traditional body of law is essential to understanding fundamental concepts of property law. The fact that one piece of paper could be conveying multiple interests in one parcel of land at the same time is often a surprising revelation.

It is time to take a journey back in time.

A. History of the Estate System

Imagine the year is 1066 and the Norman Conquest is completed. William the Conqueror was crowned the King of England on Christmas Day 1066. He was the illegitimate son of Duke Robert the Devil. At the end of a bloody and chaotic period in history, William completed the establishment of feudalism in England, compiling detailed records of land and property. In 1085, William ordered extensive surveying of the shires of England.[2]

By 1086, the Domesday Book with extensive property records was complete.[3] This first draft of the book contained records for 13,418 settlements

---

[1] http://www.businessdictionary.com/definition/freehold-estate.html.
[2] http://www.britroyals.com/kings.asp?id=william1.
[3] *Id.*

in the English counties that bordered Scotland at the time.[4] The whole point of the survey and compiling these records was to determine how much land belonged to England and the amount of taxes William could raise.[5] The history of the feudal system will often reveal that the motivation behind a rule or practice was taxes!

Due to the grand and comprehensive scale on which the Domesday survey took place, people compared it to the Last Judgement, or "Doomsday," described in the Bible.[6] The Domesday Book, which remains on display in the National Archives in London, provides extensive records of landholders; their tenants; the amount of land they owned; how many people occupied the land; the amounts of woodland, meadow, animals, fish, and ploughs on the land; and other resources and any buildings present.[7]

Feudalism, as established by William the Conqueror, is a social system of rights and duties based on land tenure and personal relationships.[8] This means that the produce of an appropriate number of peasants or serfs must underwrite the expenses of the fighting man when there is a warrior caste society.[9] In order to have an orderly system, there is a relationship between lord and vassal where the lord gives the vassal an income-yielding fief. The vassal does homage to the lord, formalizing the relationship.[10] The largest fiefs were conveyed from the monarchs to noblemen or barons, who then subcontracted parts of these fiefs to vassals of their own. Both the benefits and obligations were shared in this system to ensure that there were sufficient soldiers in the field. The king's vassals were sure of bringing their promised contingent of armed men into the field, and a pyramid of loyalty was created.

Additionally, the actual conveyance of an interest in real property was not accomplished through a written document. At the time, the use of writing was rare. After the Norman invasion, writing was used more often, and eventually over a period of hundreds of years, the delivery of a charter or deed came to replace the ceremony.[11] The livery of seisin ceremony was designed to symbolically convey the title to the land. The parties went to the land to be conveyed and were joined by many witnesses. The *feoffer* (*grantor* in today's terms) would hand over dirt, sticks, and leaves that represented the land being conveyed. The feoffer would speak words indicating the conveyance of the title

---

[4] http://www.domesdaybook.co.uk/.

[5] *Id.*

[6] *Id.*

[7] *Id.*

[8] http://history-world.org/feudalism.htm.

[9] http://www.historyworld.net/wrldhis/PlainTextHistories.asp?historyid=ac35.

[10] *Id.* Homage and fealty were the most significant features of feudal society. Each military tenant pledged utter support to his lord in a solemn ceremony.

[11] http://legal-dictionary.thefreedictionary.com/Livery+of+seisin.

to the land. It is also reported that the youngest members of the village were present at the ceremony and struck or even beaten so that they would remember the ceremony.[12] As the youngest, they would be alive the longest to attest to the fact that the land had indeed been conveyed.

The Real Property Act of 1845 (8 & 9 Vict. ch. 106 [Eng.]) allowed deeds to be used freely as granting devices and the livery of seisin ceremony was no longer necessary. However, it was not until 1925 that English law finally abolished the ceremony as a valid means to transfer property ownership.[13]

This is the context in which all of the classifications and rules were made. Because the ownership of land is what gave power to the kings and lords, the system of land ownership had very different goals than our market-based economy today. There developed over several hundred years a complex system that had at its core the goal to continue to have land return to the king. This resulted in a variety of estates in land that either *will* come to an end or *might* come to an end and only one that will never come to an end.

It is important to keep this history in place while learning the classifications and characteristics of the present and future interests. These interests were created in a different era when the goals were completely different from what we have today. However, there is a well-defined system with rules in place that provide a degree of certainty that is necessary when dealing with interests in land. Sometimes the distinctions may seem illogical and even artificial, and indeed they may be. Interests evolved over time to work through changing desires of landowners that sometimes clashed with the feudal lords who desperately wanted to retain power. Sometimes the land owners were trying to find a way to lessen taxes while the crown wanted to retain the revenue stream, which is a theme that remains common today. Mastering this material is going to require understanding of these concepts, not just memorization of them. So, let's delve into the estate system.

B. Introduction to the Estate System

Imagine a client walks through the door and wants your assistance with disposing of some assets that include real property. The client tells you, I own three tracts of land. I want one to go to my oldest daughter Ann, but I want to keep living there for now until I die. I want one parcel to go to my son Brian, but only if he settles down and gets married. I want the third parcel to go to my other daughter Cindy, but only if she graduates from law school. If Brian doesn't settle down and Cindy doesn't graduate from law school, then I want all of the land to

---

[12] Leslie Kiefer Amann, Property Law: A Survey of Transfer and Ownership Law for Trustees, https://www.naepc.org/journal/issue04k.pdf.

[13] http://legal-dictionary.thefreedictionary.com/Livery+of+seisin.

go to Ann. And, I don't want them to have to worry about a will, so you need to make sure all of this happens without a will. How can you make this happen? You must know what can be created and how. This is where the estate system comes in.

An estate is an interest in land that (1) is or may become possessory; and (2) is ownership measured in terms of duration.[14] The estate system is studied in two components—present possessory estates and future interests. When dealing with the estate system, it is important to think of the ownership and possession of property in terms of a time line. Property interests can be divided temporally as well as physically. With the estate system, we are dealing with ways that real property is being divided temporally. The person who owns and possesses a piece of real property today may not be the same person who owns and possesses it tomorrow. That change of ownership and possession can occur for a variety of reasons that will be discussed throughout the course.

The initial focus will be to understand what a possessory estate in land is and how such an estate is created. We will then move to the concept of future interests and understand how a person can own an interest in real property while not in possession and actually may never come into possession. However, it is still ownership of a valid real property interest.

Keep in mind during the reading and class discussions that the laws of property with respect to the estate system are grounded in the land's feudal history. Some classifications and distinctions are completely artificial and seemingly impractical. However, due to the lengthy history and evolution of interests in land, these are the rules of law that you must understand and master.

As discussed in the introductory material for the course, possession plays a central role in defining property interests. What is a possessory interest in land? Even when discussing possession in the context of personal property, the definition was slightly different depending on the thing involved—wild animal, baseball, items of personal property. Now in dealing with land, possession must once again be defined. And, there is present possession and future possession. How do the present possessory estates differ from the future interests? How do these possessory estates differ from nonpossessory property interests that will be covered later? Consider those questions throughout the material.

The Restatement (First) of Property provides the following definition and illustrations for a possessory interest in land:

> A possessory interest in land exists in a person who has a physical relation to the land of a kind which gives a certain degree of physical control over the land, and an intent so to exercise such

---

[14] *See* Restatement (First) of Property § 9 (1936).

control as to exclude other members of society in general from
any present occupation of the land.

Illustrations:
1. *A* owns land in fee simple absolute. *A* transfers the land to *B* for ten years.
    B takes possession. *A* has a nonpossessory and B has a possessory interest
    in the land. (Note: *B* will have a term of years nonfreehold estate as the
    present possessory estate and *A* will retain a reversion in fee simple
    absolute, which is a future interest.)

2. *A* owns land in fee simple absolute. *B* obtains a judgment against *A*, takes
    out execution, and levies upon the land. *A* has a possessory and *B* has a
    nonpossessory interest in the land. (Note: *A* still has the present
    possessory estate of a fee simple absolute. In this case there is no future
    interest created but merely a nonpossessory lien.)

3. *A* owns land in fee simple absolute.
    I.   *B* is entitled to cut all trees now growing on the land. *A* has a
         possessory and *B* a nonpossessory interest (profit) in the land.
         (Note: *A* still has the present possessory fee simple absolute. *B*
         has a profit, which is a nonpossessory interest that is not an
         estate in land but a servitude.)

    II. *B* is the owner in fee simple absolute of an adjacent piece of land
         to which is appurtenant an easement of way over the land owned
         by *A*. *A* has a possessory interest and *B* a nonpossessory interest
         (easement) in the land owned by *A*.[15]
         (Note: *A* again still holds the present possessory fee simple
         absolute. The interest created in *B* is a nonpossessory easement,
         which is a servitude and not an estate in land.)

---

[15] Restatement (First) of Property § 7 (1936). Although the Restatement Illustrations
use "*A*" as the identification of the original grantor of the property in the conveyances,
most often you will see "*O*" as the identification of the original grantor or owner of the
property.

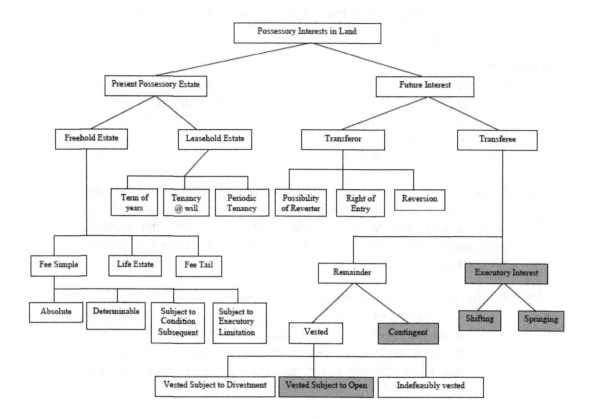

This diagram provides a depiction of the various present and future interests that will be covered in this course. This can help in studying how these interests relate to one another.

1. The Conveyance: Present and Future Interests in Land

At its core, the estate system is composed of present interests in real property or land. These are studied first for a couple of reasons. First, the present possessory estates are easier to define and understand. Second, the classification of future interests rests in part on first correctly identifying the present possessory estate it will follow. Thus, we turn to the introduction of present interests.

a. Present Interests

A present interest is an interest in land, or in a thing other than land, which includes a right to the immediate beneficial enjoyment of the affected thing.[16]

Basically, what this boils down to is the party who holds the right to actual possession right now has the present possessory estate.[17] There are different categories of possessory estates for both the freehold estates (this part of the material) and nonfreehold estates (which will be coming in the next chapter on landlord and tenant relationships). Although there are different ways to group these estates we will cover them in this manner: Fee Simple Absolute, Life Estates, Fee Tail, and Defeasible Estates.

> **(1) Fee Simple Absolute (FSA):** "The fee simple absolute is the largest, most complete estate a person can hold."[18] In theory, *O* could hold the property forever.[19] There is no future interest.[20] There is no inherent restriction or condition on his use of the land.[21] He has the right to alienate the property, meaning he can transfer it to anyone he wants.[22] Although the fee simple absolute is only one part of the fee simple estates, it warrants a category in and of itself due to the nature of the estate.

> **(2) Finite Estates: Life Estate and Fee Tail:**[23] The life estate and fee tail are two types of finite estates. Whereas the FSA *will* last forever, and the defeasible estates *may* last forever, provided the condition does not occur, a finite estate *must* end.[24]

> The *Life Estate* lasts for the duration of the grantee's life.[25] The life estate is usually a life estate (absolute) but may also be defeasible.

> Defeasible life estates are extremely rare.

---

[16] *Id.* § 153(3).

[17] *See* Peter T. Wendel, A Possessory Estates and Future Interests Primer 1 (2d ed. 2005).

[18] *Id.* at 7.

[19] *Id.* at 6.

[20] *Id.*

[21] *Id.*

[22] *Id.*

[23] There are also nonfreehold estates that are finite estates. We will discuss the different leasehold estates in the landlord tenant law section.

[24] Wendel, *supra* note 17, at 36.

[25] *Id.* at 37.

The *Fee Tail* is essentially a series of life estates in a family blood line.[26]

(3) Defeasible Estates: There are both defeasible fee estates and defeasible life estates. Defeasible fee estates are those that look like FSAs at first, but there is a condition or limitation placed on the estate that could cause the estate to terminate.[27] There are three types of defeasible fee estates: (1) the fee simple determinable (FSD); (2) the fee simple subject to a condition subsequent (FSSCS); and (3) the fee simple subject to an executory limitation/interest (FSSEI).

The defeasible life estate, while extremely rare, may be created. A defeasible life estate is one that may end by the death of the life tenant *or sooner* if a stated condition occurs before the death of the life tenant. There are also three types of defeasible life estates: (1) life estate determinable, (2) life estate subject to a condition subsequent, and (3) life estate subject to an executory interest.

b. Future Interests

The second component of the system is future interests. The future interests are more complicated and, as stated earlier, depend on a proper determination of the present possessory estate.

"A 'future interest' is defined as a property interest in which the privilege of possession or of other enjoyment is future and not present."[28] Or more simply, it is the "present right to possess the property in the future."[29] The party who holds the right to take actual possession of the property in the future has the future interest.[30] Each possessory estate *other than a fee simple absolute* must be coupled with a future interest.[31]

The various future interests will be categorized as those future interests in the transferor and in the transferee. Due to the nature of each future interest, we will match them with certain present possessory estates. *Mastering these*

---

[26] *Id.* at 39.

[27] "[W]here an estate is devised in language sufficient to create a fee simple absolute, and a subsequent provision is made in the will for a gift over on the happening of a future event or contingency, the subsequent provision will have the effect of modifying the estate already devised, to make it a defeasible fee." Cragin v. Frost Nat'l Bank, 164 S.W.2d 24, 28 (Tex. Civ. App.–San Antonio 1941, writ ref'd w.o.m.).

[28] Aloysius A. Leopord, Texas Practice Series, Land Titles and Title Examination § 13.2 (3d ed. 2006).

[29] Wendel, *supra* note 17, at 24.

[30] *Id.* at 1.

[31] *Id.* at 24.

pairings will assist you greatly in future coverage in other courses that involve the estate system.

Because the law of property favors the free alienability of land, at the end of our coverage of the estate system, we will briefly introduce the concept of Rules Promoting Alienability including the Destructability of Contingent Remainders, the Rule in Shelley's Case, the Doctrine of Worthier Title, and the illusive Rule Against Perpetuities and their impact on the future interests that are created.

2. Construction of the Grant

In learning to classify these present and future interests, much attention to detail is required. The focus is on the language used in conveyances to determine what is being created by the grantor. Consider what words were used historically and are used in modern times to create certain possessory estates and future interests. There are different rules that will aid in the interpretation of conveyances where the language seems to be ambiguous.

At the time the conveyance takes effect, there is the potential that multiple interests in property have been created by a single instrument of conveyance. It is important to distinguish between the two instruments of conveyance that can be used—the deed and the will. A deed is a written instrument that transfers title to the land in an *inter vivos* transaction. A will is a written instrument that transfers title to the land through a testamentary transfer. This boils down to meaning that deeds are used for conveyances by the owner during life and wills are used to convey at death. Thus the effective date of the documents is different. A deed becomes effective upon proper execution, delivery, and acceptance. Those terms will be studied in greater detail later in the course. At this point, the facts will indicate that there is a valid deed or a valid execution, delivery, and acceptance. With that, it is understood that the deed has effectively conveyed whatever interest or interests are created therein.

Because a will is used to convey property at death, the effective date is later in time. The will can be properly drafted, signed by the testator, and witnessed, but nothing has happened to the ownership of the property yet. A will does not take effect until the testator dies and the will is admitted to probate. So, if *A* drafts a will today in 2015 and does not die until 2025, nothing has changed with respect to the ownership of the property during those ten years unless *A* engages in some *inter vivos* conveyance. The will did nothing at the time. *A* continued to own the property and could do with it whatever he wanted. *A* could revise the will multiple times or even give away everything he owns before he dies. The beneficiaries named in the will have no legal basis to complain because they did not yet own anything.

In these documents, whether deeds or wills, there can be present and future interests; there can be multiple people with present interests; there can be multiple people with future interests; there may be possessory and nonpossessory interests created. A detailed analysis of the specific language, with the aid of a time line, will allow for the correct identification of all interests created by the conveyance. This is one area where practice, practice, practice is required. There are worksheets in this chapter that provide the opportunity for some of that needed practice.

In order to really understand all the pieces that must be utilized in navigating the estate system today, it is essential to go back in time to examine the rules and taxonomy that have existed for hundreds of years.

C. Present Possessory Estates

The study of present possessory estates begins with the fee simple absolute, which is known as the benchmark estate. After understanding the characteristics of the fee simple absolute (commonly referred to as fee simple) it is clear that this is the type of ownership most people think of as being associated with land ownership. In most cases this will be the form of ownership, but there are many times when it is not.

1. The Fee Simple Absolute: An Estate with No End

Fee Simple Estates (Including the Fee Simple Absolute)
An estate in fee simple is an estate which:
   (a) has a duration
       i.   potentially infinite; or
      ii.   terminable upon an event which is certain to occur but is not certain to occur within a fixed or computable period of time or within the duration of any specified life or lives; or
     iii.   terminable upon an event which is certain to occur, provided such estate is one left in the conveyor, subject to defeat upon the occurrence of the stated event in favor of a person other than the conveyor; and
   (b) if a limited in favor of a natural person, would be inheritable by his collateral as well as by his lineal heirs.[32]

---

[32] Restatement (First) of Property § 14 (1936).

a. Characteristics of the Fee Simple Absolute

The fee simple estates are a category of estates in land that include the specific estate of the fee simple absolute. While all estates within the fee simple category are on the same level of the estate hierarchy, the fee simple absolute is the greatest estate possible. As defined by the restatement, the fee simple absolute is "an estate in fee simple that is not subject to a special limitation (defined in § 23) or a condition subsequent (defined in § 24) or an executory limitation (defined in § 25)."[33]

The fee simple absolute estate (FSA) is the largest possible estate that can be created and, as previously stated, is the estate or ownership of property that most people think of. There are no limitations of any kind put on the ownership of property in FSA. The fee simple absolute property can be sold, gifted, devised, and inherited. This type of ownership of property includes both legal and equitable title to the land and includes everything from the top of the ground to the center of the earth.[34]

Generally, where an estate in land is granted and not limited by express words or by fair construction, a fee simple estate is favored. This is drastically different from the feudal origins that created the system of land ownership between the lords and the vassals. The common law rule in feudal times dictated that in order to make a fee simple absolute estate it had to be clearly created with particular words "and his heirs" or "and her heirs." Without those precise words, only a life estate would be conveyed. However, that common law rule is not followed in Texas or any other state today.[35]

Tex. Prop. Code[36]
§ 5.001. Fee Simple
    (a) An estate in land that is conveyed or devised is a fee simple unless the estate is limited by express words or unless a lesser estate is conveyed or devised by construction or operation of law. Words previously necessary at common law to transfer a fee simple estate are not necessary.

---

[33] *Id.* § 15.

[34] *See generally* County School Trustees of Upshur County v. Free, 154 S.W.2d 5 (Tex. 1947); Cragin v. Frost Nat'l Bank, 164 S.W.2d 24 (Tex. Civ. App.–San Antonio 1942, writ ref'd w.o.m.).

[35] *See generally* Pythian Home for Orphans at Weatherford v. Barrow, 346 S.W.2d 426 (Tex. Civ. App.–Amarillo 1961, writ ref'd n.r.e.).

[36] Acts 1983, 68th Leg., p. 3480, ch. 576, § 1, eff. Jan. 1, 1984. The fee simple absolute is commonly referred to as the fee simple in practice. When the court means to refer to a defeasible fee estate then it is referred to with the full name of fee simple determinable, fee simple subject to condition subsequent, or fee simple subject to executory limitation.

(b) This section applies only to a conveyance occurring on or after February 5, 1840.

This section of the property code supersedes the historic common law approach requiring the inclusion of specific language. Other states have comparable statutes to no longer require specific language for fee simple estates.

However, even if a person attempts to convey fee simple absolute, he can never convey more than he owns, no matter the language of the conveyance. The following Texas Property Code provision gives the statutory language that follows the common law concept that a person cannot convey more than he owns.

§ 5.003. Partial Conveyance[37]

(a) An alienation of real property that purports to transfer a greater right or estate in the property than the person making the alienation may lawfully transfer alienates only the right or estate that the person may convey.

Once the common law presumption of a life estate was reversed by statute, the fee simple estates became the favored estates and are devisable and inheritable. Remember, the fee simple absolute will last forever. Even the defeasible fee estates might last forever. This means that at the end of the owner's lifetime, the title to the real property will pass either through a will or through the laws of intestate succession. There is a body of vocabulary that must be learned in order to effectively discuss what can occur. The following are some of those essential terms.

Heir:[38] At common law, the person appointed by law to succeed to the estate in case of intestacy. One who inherits property, whether real or personal. One who would receive his estate under statute of descent and distribution.

Heirs is a larger category that includes within it ancestors, issue, and collateral.

Under the Texas Estates Code, "heir" means a person who is entitled under the statutes of descent and distribution to a part of the estate of a decedent who dies intestate. The term includes the decedent's surviving spouse.[39]

---

[37] Section (b) is omitted.

[38] *Black's Law Dictionary*, p. 724 (6th ed. 1990).

[39] Tex. Estates Code § 22.015 (added by Acts 2009, 81st Leg., ch. 680, § 1, eff. Jan. 1, 2014).

No one is heir of the living; a living person has no heirs (yet!). If there is a conveyance "to the heirs of *A*" (a living person), we do not know who will take until *A* dies and *A*'s heirs are ascertained. We would basically take a snapshot at the funeral and figure out who is alive at that time and would qualify as an heir. While a class of people, heirs are all determined at one time.

> **Issue:** This is a subcategory of the inviduals who make up the larger category of heirs. Issue include lineal descendants and offspring. This group includes children, grandchildren, great-grandchildren coming from the decedent.

> **Ancestors:** This is another subcategory of individuals who make up the larger category of heirs. Issue include those going back in time before the decedent, such as parents, grandparetns, great-grandparents, and so forth.

> **Collaterals:** The last category of indivudials included within the group of heirs. These blood relatives are not in line directly before or following the decident. These are other blood relatives who would include aunts and uncles, siblings, cousins. They are not in the direct bloodline.

> **Escheat:**[40] A reversion of property to the state in consequence of a want of any individual competent to inherit. Escheat at feudal law was the right of the lord of a fee to re-enter upon the same when it became vacant by the extinction of the blood of the tenant. The word "escheat" in this country merelyindicates the preferable right of the state to an estate left vacant, and without there being any one in existence able to make claim thereto.

NOTES, QUESTIONS & PROBLEMS:

1. Closely evaluate the language in the following conveyances. What is conveyed to *A* in each example (1) if in 1600 and (2) if today with application of the Texas Property Code.

   a. *O* to *A* and his heirs.
   b. *O* to *A* in FSA.
   c. *O* to *A*.
   d. *O* to *A* forever.
   e. Oliver grants and conveys to Alice.
   f. Oliver grants, sells, and conveys to Alice and her heirs.

---

[40] *Black's Law Dictionary* 545 (6th ed. 1990).

     g. Oliver devises and bequeaths to Alice and her heirs.

     h. In any of these conveyances would *B*, *A*'s only heir, have an interest in the land?

2. What happens if Oliver owns Blackacre in fee simple absolute and dies intestate and without issue? Who would own Blackacre? If Oliver dies intestate and without heirs, who would own Blackacre?

3. Oliver, the owner of Blackacre, is a widower and has three children, Ann, Bob, and Charles. Bob is married to Emily and they have two children, Fiona and Gail. Bob dies in 2012 and is survived by his wife and children. He had a will leaving all of his property to his wife. Oliver dies intestate in 2015 still owning Blackacre. Upon Oliver's death, who are Oliver's heirs? Who are his issue? Collateral? Will Bob's wife Emily be entitled to a share of Blackacre?

b. Examining the Language of the Conveyance

Clarity is key when dealing with conveyances of interests in land, especially in modern times with the presumption that the grantor has conveyed the greatest estate possible. However, drafters are not always clear. And sometimes lay persons even engage in their own drafting, which can make matters even more complicated. Given the fact that there is often a lack of clarity, courts must use a system of rules of construction to try to determine what is conveyed by the words on the page. The following cases provide some examples of how difficult the task may be. Pay close attention to the language used in each case. Consider how the court is reaching the conclusion in each case and reflect on whether you would come to the same conclusion.

<u>**Texas Electric Ry. Co. et al. v. Neale et al.**</u>
Supreme Court of Texas, 1952
252 S.W.2d 451

SMEDLEY, Justice.

Respondents William F. Neale and E. C. Street sued petitioners Texas Electric Railway Company and others for the title and possession of a tract or strip of land containing 6.60 acres, which was acquired by the Southern Traction Company by conveyance in 1912 and was used by that company and its successor, respondent Texas Electric Railway Company, as part of the right of way of an electric interurban railway operated by the two companies until December 31, 1948, when operation was discontinued and abandoned.

The trial court's judgment for respondents was affirmed by the Court of Civil Appeals, which held that the deed to the Southern Traction Company conveyed only an easement and not the estate in fee to the land described. 244 S.W.2d 329.

The decision of the case turns on the construction of the deed, which is as follows, except that we have numbered the paragraphs of the deed for convenient reference, and have omitted the signatures and the certificate of acknowledgment:

"(1) Know All Men By These Presents: That We Geo. S. McGhee, Mrs. Dora Behrens and Abe Gross, for and in consideration of One Dollar to me in hand paid and the benefits which will accrue to my other property by reason of the construction of the Interurban Railway hereinafter mentioned, do by these presents grant, sell and convey unto Chas. H. Allyn, W. D. Lacy, J. K. Parr, S. M. Dunlap, J. Baldridge, J. Houston Miller and W. R. McDaniel, Trustees of the Southern Traction Company, their successors and assigns, the following described piece or parcel of land, to wit:

. . .

(3) It being the intention of this deed to convey a strip of land 100 feet wide for 550 feet, and 80 feet wide for the balance of the way through the property of J J Dean in the Tomas de la Vega Eleven League Grant.

(4) It is further understood herein that the above strip of land is conveyed upon the further condition and consideration that said Southern Traction Company will, as soon as it begins operation, establish a stop on the right of way hereinabove conveyed about the center thereof for the purpose of letting passengers on and off its cars which stop shall be as near a street crossing as possible and said Co., shall forever keep up and maintain said stop when so established, and said company further agrees to allow to be opened and dedicated as streets across said right of way such streets as may be opened by grantors herein, it being understood that the property through which this right of way is given is to be opened up as an addition to the city of Waco,

(5) To have and to hold the same unto the said Trustees, their successors and assigns, forever free of all encumbrances, including telephone, telegraph and transmission lines.

(6) However, this deed is made as a right-of-way deed for an Interurban Railway from Dallas to Waco, Texas, and in case said railway shall not be constructed over said land then this conveyance shall be of no effect. Witness our hands this 4th day of Sept. A. D. 1912."

The one, or the principal, question to be determined is: Did the deed convey to the grantee merely an easement, that is, the right to use the land for a right of way, or did it convey the title in fee? This question has been before the courts of this state many times. There are two lines of authorities, the one represented by Right of Way Oil Co. v. Gladys City Oil, etc., Co., 106 Tex. 94, 157 S.W. 737, 51 L.R.A., N.S., 268, and the other by Calcasieu Lumber Co. v. Harris, 77 Tex. 18, 13

S.W. 453, and Brightwell v. International-Great Northern R. Co., 121 Tex. 338, 49 S.W.2d 437, 84 A.L.R. 265. Generally stated, the rules announced by these decisions are: First, that, as in the *Right of Way Oil Company* case, (106 Tex. 94, 157 S.W. 739) a deed which by the terms of the granting clause grants, sells and conveys to the grantee a "right of way" in or over a tract of land conveys only an easement; and second, that, as in the *Calcasieu Lumber Company* case and in the *Brightwell* case, a deed which in the granting clause grants, sells and conveys a tract or strip of land conveys the title in fee, even though in a subsequent clause or paragraph of the deed the land conveyed is referred to as a right of way.

Looking to the granting clause of the deed, paragraph No. 1, we find that it grants, sells and conveys to the grantee "the following described piece or parcel of land." 244 S.W.2d 331. The quoted words are followed in the deed by a description of the 6.06 acres by metes and bounds and then by the recital, paragraph 3, that it is the intention of the deed "to convey a strip of land 100 feet wide for 550 feet, and 80 feet wide for the balance of the way through the property of J. J. Dean" in a named survey. The habendum clause, paragraph No. 5, is "To have and to hold the same unto the said Trustees, (of the Southern Traction Company) their successors and assigns, forever free of all encumbrances, including telephone, telegraph and transmission lines." These parts of the deed evidence the intention on the part of the grantor to convey the title to the tract or strip of land, and the Court of Civil Appeals agrees that they do. That Court, however, found in paragraphs numbered 4 and 6 expressions which in its opinion disclose an intention "that the instrument as a whole should evidence a conveyance of right-of-way as distinguished from land". And it then expressed the conclusion that if the language employed in paragraphs numbered 4 and 6 did not clearly express that intention, they made the meaning of the instrument uncertain and ambiguous as to the nature of the estate conveyed so that extrinsic evidence was admissible and could be considered as an aid in ascertaining the true intention of the parties. Respondents, relying on the recitals in the fourth and sixth paragraphs of the deed, as did the Court of Civil Appeals, insist that the deed conveys only an easement. They especially stress the statement in the sixth paragraph that "this deed is made as a right-of-way deed" and construe that statement to mean or to say that "a right of way is conveyed," that is, an easement merely, and they give that statement controlling effect over the granting clause; which conveys a piece or parcel of land. In this way respondents would bring the case under the rule of Right of Way Oil Co. v. Gladys City Oil, etc., Co., 106 Tex. 94, 157 S.W. 737, 51 L.R.A., N.S., 268.

It is our opinion, after careful consideration of the deed and the decisions, that the case is ruled by Calcasieu Lumber Co. v. Harris, 77 Tex. 18, 13 S.W. 453, and Brightwell v. International-Great Northern R. Co., 121 Tex. 338, 49 S.W.2d 437, 84 A.L.R. 265, rather than by the *Right of Way Oil Company* case. In the case last mentioned the granting clause of the deed granted and conveyed "the right of way, two hundred feet in width, over and upon the above-described tract of land", whereas the granting clause in the deed here under construction grants, sells and conveys to the grantee "the following described piece or parcel of land." It does not purport to convey merely a right of way or merely an easement. There do appear in the deed words which show the purpose for which the grant is made, but those words do not undertake to reduce or debase what has been granted from a fee title to a mere easement.

FEE TITLE

The fourth paragraph provides that the grantee will as soon as it begins operation "establish a stop on the right of way hereinabove conveyed" at a designated place, and will forever maintain the stop, and that the grantee will allow streets to be opened and dedicated "across said right of way." These provisions show that the property is to be used as a right of way. The grantee is obligated to "establish a stop on the right of way hereinabove conveyed." The words "right of way" here used clearly refer to the piece or parcel of land that is conveyed for a right of way. The stop is to be established on the tract or parcel of land. It could not be established on an intangible right, that is, an easement. The same is true of the obligation to allow streets to be opened "across said right of way." "The term 'right of way' has a two-fold signification. It sometimes is used to describe a right belonging to a party, a right of passage over any tract; and it is also used to describe that strip of land which railroad companies take upon which to construct their road-bed." Joy v. City of St. Louis, 138 U.S. 1, 11 S. Ct. 243, 256, 34 L. Ed. 843, 857; *see also* New Mexico v. United States Trust Co., 172 U.S. 171, 19 S. Ct. 128, 43 L. Ed. 407, 411; Johnson v. Valdosta, M. & W. R. Co., 169 Ga. 559, 150 S. E. 845, 847. In our opinion the words "establish a stop on the right of way hereinabove conveyed" mean nothing more than that a stop shall be established on the strip or parcel of land that has been conveyed by the deed for right of way purposes. They do not undertake to define or limit the estate or title that has been granted.

EASEMENT

Confusion @ Right of Way Meaning

The deed construed in Calcasieu Lumber Co. v. Harris, 77 Tex. 18, 13 S.W. 453, 454, shows that the strip of land conveyed was intended to be used as a railroad right of way. The granting clause recites that "I James Manor . . . do grant, bargain, sell and release to the Houston and Texas Central Railroad Company, a strip of two hundred feet of land over the tracts of land particularly described as follows," etc. The habendum clause is in the usual form and refers to "the said premises." The deed contains after the habendum clause the grant to the said company of a full release from all claims for damages that may be sustained by their work "in the construction and for the right-of-way of said Railroad, over any of the said lands." Notwithstanding this reference in the deed to the land conveyed as "right-of-way" the court in its opinion stated that the deed "conveyed to the railway company the estate in fee to this strip of land."

Right-of-Way ≠ Easement

The deed construed in Brightwell v. International-Great Northern R. Co., 121 Tex. 338, 49 S.W.2d 437, 439, 84 A.L.R. 265, is, as is observed in the opinion in that case, "the same in every substantial detail" as that involved in the *Calcasieu Lumber Company* case. It grants "a strip of (200) Two Hundred feet in width of land over the tracts of land . . . and has the same habendum as that contained in the deed construed in the *Calcasieu Lumber Company* case. After the habendum clause the deed grants "to said Company such earth, material, timber and rock as may be found on my lands herein mentioned, and granted herein as right-of-way which may be required for the construction of said Railroad." There is also in the deed the same release of claims for damages that may be sustained by work in the construction and for the "right-of-way." The words "and granted herein as right-or-way" were relied upon by *Brightwell* as evidencing an intention on the part of the grantor to convey a mere easement and not the fee. The court rejected that contention and held that the words quoted were not used for the purpose of limiting the title granted, but to confine to the land granted, the two hundred foot strip, the right given to take earth, material and rock. Thus the words "right of way" were regarded by the court as descriptive of the strip of land granted and not as defining the right or title conveyed. We have in the *Brightwell* case the distinct decision that the use in the deed of the words "granted herein as right-of-way" did not limit the estate granted. On the authority of that decision the words "right of way hereinabove conveyed" in the fourth paragraph of the deed here involved and the words "this deed is made as a right-of-way deed" in the sixth paragraph do not have the effect of reducing to an easement the fee title conveyed by the granting clause.

The court's opinion in the *Brightwell* case contains the statement that the decision made in the *Calcasieu Lumber Company* case "has become a rule of property under which titles and securities of immense value have been acquired in this state, and it should not now be disturbed or changed." The same is true of the decision in the *Brightwell* case.

There are on the other hand a number of decisions by the courts of this state following Right of Way Oil Co. v. Gladys City Oil, Gas & Mfg. Co., 106 Tex. 94, 157 S.W. 737, 51 L.R.A., N.S., 268, in holding that when the deed grants and conveys not a tract or strip of land but a right of way over or upon land, an easement only is acquired. Among them are the following cases cited in the opinion of the Court of Civil Appeals and by respondents: Houston & T. C. R. Co. v. Central Texas Securities Corp., 68 S.W.2d 585; Gulf Coast Water Co. v. Hamman Exploration Co., 160 S.W.2d 92; Boles v. Red, 227 S.W.2d 310. In each of those cases the right or interest conveyed was described in the granting clause as "right of way".

The fourth paragraph of the deed here involved was inserted for the purpose of obligating the grantee to establish and maintain a stop on the right or way; and the sixth paragraph, beginning with the word "however," has for its purpose the imposition of a condition precedent upon the title conveyed which, without the sixth paragraph, would be an unconditional fee title. The record shows that the condition was performed by the construction of the interurban railway, which was operated continuously for many years.

Appropriate use was made of the words "right of way" in the fourth and sixth paragraphs of the deed, for, as has been said, the words sometimes describe the strip of land over which a railway is constructed and sometimes describe a right of passage or easement. And since the words as there used clearly have reference to the land and not to an intangible right, they are not contradictory of the granting clause. In the use of the words "right of way" in the two paragraphs the purpose for which the land is conveyed, the use intended to be made of it, is indicated. This fact, however, does not change the effect of the conveyance, for the declaration in a deed of the purpose for which land is conveyed or the use to be made of it does not impose a condition upon the title granted; nor does it operate to limit the grant to a mere easement. Stanberry v. Wallace, Tex. Comm. App., 45 S.W.2d 198; Texas & Pacific Ry. Co. v. Martin, 123 Tex. 383, 71 S.W.2d 867; Hughes v. Gladewater County, etc., School District, 124 Tex. 190, 76 S.W.2d 471; City of Stamford v. King, Tex. Civ. App., 144 S.W.2d 923, *application for writ of error refused*; Green v. Kunkel, Tex. Civ. App., 183 S.W.2d 585.

[*Conclusion*]

In view of our conclusion that the deed conveying the land in controversy to petitioners' predecessor in title by its terms plainly and clearly discloses the intention to grant and convey title to the land and not merely an easement over it, we do not consider extrinsic evidence to ascertain the intention. Anderson & Kerr Drilling Co. v. Bruhlmeyer, 134 Tex. 574, 583, 136 S.W.2d 800, 127 A.L.R. 1217; Universal C.I.T. Credit Corp. v. Daniel, 150 Tex. —, 243 S.W.2d 154, 157.

[*Neale backup plan: defeas. fee estate*]

Respondents present by counter point the contention that by reason of the obligation in the fourth paragraph of the deed that the grantee establish and forever maintain a stop on the right of way the estate granted by the deed terminated when the operation of the railway was abandoned. The provision is that "the above strip of land is conveyed upon the further condition and consideration that said Southern Traction Company will, as soon as it begins operation, establish a stop on the right of way hereinabove conveyed . . . and said Co., shall forever keep up and maintain said stop when so established." (244 S.W.2d 331). It is argued that by reason of this provision the deed conveyed either an estate on condition subsequent or a determinable fee. In our opinion the obligation imposed by the fourth paragraph to establish and maintain the stop is a covenant. The deed does not expressly provide that title shall revert to the grantor in case of nonperformance on the part of the grantee; nor does it provide that title shall terminate when the stop is no longer maintained. Conditions and limitations that work forfeiture or termination of title are not favored, and in case of doubtful language the promise or obligation of the grantee will be construed to be a covenant. . . .

Miller, et al. v. The Atchison, Topeka and Santa Fe Railway Co.
United States District Court for the Eastern District of Missouri,
Northern Division, 1971
325 F. Supp. 604

WANGELIN, District Judge.

This matter is before the Court on defendant's motion for summary judgment with supporting affidavits and suggestions in support of the motion. Plaintiffs filed suggestions in opposition to the motion and the parties were heard on the matter.

This action was commenced in the Circuit Court of Scotland County, Missouri, and thereafter removed to this Court on the basis of diversity of citizenship and amount in controversy.

For purposes of the questions presented in this motion, there is no dispute as to the facts. Plaintiffs claim to be the heirs of W.G. and Barbara Miller. Defendant is the Atchison, Topeka & Santa Fe Railway Company, the successor to the Chicago, Santa Fe & California Railway Company of Iowa. Plaintiffs are claiming they own a fee simple absolute interest in a portion of land located in Scotland County, Missouri, over which run the main-line tracks of the defendant railroad. Santa Fe has denied the plaintiffs have any interest in the land in question.

By general warranty deed, dated May 20, 1887, W.G. Miller and Barbara Miller, his wife, conveyed certain land to the defendant's predecessor. The deed contains the following language:

> "Should said above named Rail-way or its assigns fail to erect and maintain a depot and bridge on said above described premises then this Deed to be void.
>
> And should said above named Railway or its assigns fail to erect and maintain said depot at a point designated by stake No. 2300 and being about 1100 feet from the South West corner of Section 9, Twp. 64, Range 10, along said R.R. survey, or between that stake and a stake numbered 2298 as heretofore agreed upon between said parties to this deed then this deed to be void."

Pursuant to the deed, defendant's predecessor erected a depot and a bridge in 1888. The bridge has been and is being maintained by the railroad. The depot was maintained from 1888 until 1963 when the depot was closed pursuant to order of the Missouri Public Service Commission. The depot was later removed.

Under plaintiffs' original pleading, the contentions of the parties on defendant's motion for summary judgment are directed to the issue of the claimed reversion of the title to the land in dispute to the plaintiffs under the provisions of the deed. It is the plaintiffs' position that since the railroad no longer maintains a depot, under the terms of the deed, title to the land is vested in them. It is the position of the defendant that title remains in the defendant since defendant maintained the depot for seventy five years and still maintains the bridge.

However, during the argument on the motion, plaintiffs sought leave to amend the complaint to include the allegation that the plaintiffs are the adjoining landowners. Plaintiffs argued the theory that under the holdings in Brown v. Weare, 348 Mo. 135, 152 S.W.2d 649 (1941) and Quinn v. St. Louis-San Francisco Railway Co., 439 S.W.2d 533 (Mo. En Banc 1969), the railroad acquired only an easement to the land in 1887, and that defendant, having abandoned the depot in 1963, the use reverted to the adjoining landowners.

The Court finds the *Brown* case and the *Quinn* case inapposite. The facts are clearly distinguishable. The language of the deed in the present case is not similar to the deeds in the *Brown* and *Quinn* cases. But more importantly, the present case lacks the total abandonment present in *Brown* and *Quinn*. As the following discussion indicates, the sole issue to be determined on this motion is whether title to the land in question reverted to the heirs of W.G. and Barbara Miller in 1963 when the defendant ceased to maintain a depot.

At the outset, the Court notes that conditions subsequent and reverters are not favorites of the law. In Duncan v. Academy of Sisters of the Sacred Heart, 350 S.W.2d 814 (Mo. 1961), the Missouri Supreme Court discussed the requirements for a determinable fee, at p. 816:

> "The grant in such a case is not upon a condition subsequent, and no re-entry is necessary; but by the terms of the grant the estate is to continue until the happening of some event. And upon the happening of said event, the estate will cease and determine by its own limitation. The proper words for the creation of such an estate are, 'until,' 'during,' 'so long as,' and the like. . . . "

The deed in the present case uses no such words. In fact, the habendum clause of the deed contains the word "forever," and not the words "until," "so long as," "while" or "during."

The Court in the *Duncan* case pointed out that the distinctive characteristic of a conveyance of an estate upon condition subsequent is the existence of a provision for an entry upon breach of the condition. There is no provision for re-entry in the deed in the present case.

It is the opinion of this Court that the deed in the present case did not convey a determinable fee or an estate upon condition subsequent. In any event, it is the further opinion of this Court that the railroad has complied with the provisions of the deed.

Upon the facts of this case, title in fee simple absolute is vested in the railroad. The defendant's motion for summary judgment will be granted.

Rhobbin L. Cooley a/k/a Rhobbin Laverne Jebbia v. Marilyn L. Williams
Court of Appeals of Texas, Houston (1st Dist.), 2000
31 S.W.3d 810

COHEN, Justice.

Rhobbin Cooley (a/k/a Rhobbin Jebbia) appeals an order admitting the holographic will of her grandmother, Lillian McKee ("decedent"), to probate as a muniment of title and construing that will as conveying no interest to Cooley. We reverse and render.

Background
Decedent left the following holographic will:

> If I die all my possions [sic] go to my husband Paul Odis McKee and when he dies everything goes to Rhobbin LaVern Jabbia [sic]. Written by Lillian E. McKee (wife).

She was survived by her husband and two daughters, Margaret Elkund (Cooley's mother) and Marilyn Williams, both of whom are still alive. Decedent's husband died intestate fewer than two weeks after decedent's death. Cooley filed an application to probate decedent's will and to be appointed independent administrator. Williams contested it. After a hearing, the trial judge admitted the will to probate as a muniment of title, construed it to convey decedent's estate in fee simple absolute to decedent's husband with no "remainder" interest to Cooley, and ordered the estate's assets delivered to the administrator of decedent's husband's estate. Cooley appeals.

Discussion
In her sole issue, Cooley contends the trial judge erred in construing the will to convey a fee simple absolute interest to her grandfather. Instead, Cooley claims the will gave her grandfather a life estate, albeit with full power to dispose of the property during his lifetime, and a contingent remainder interest in herself. While we agree the judge erred, we disagree with Cooley's characterization of the devise.

1. Construction Rules

We look for the testator's intent as revealed in the language of the whole will. Welch v. Straach, 531 S.W.2d 319, 321 (Tex. 1975); *see also* Kelley v. Marlin, 714 S.W.2d 303, 305 (Tex. 1986) (testator's intent single most important factor). We harmonize all provisions if at all possible to give effect to that intent. *Welch,* 531 S.W.2d at 322. We presume decedent placed nothing superfluous or meaningless in her will and that she intended every word to play a part. Marlin v. Kelly, 678 S.W.2d 582, 587 (Tex. App.—Houston [14th Dist.] 1984), *aff'd,* 714 S.W.2d 303 (Tex. 1986). "Generally, the greatest estate will be conferred on a devisee that the terms of the devise permit; and when an estate is given in one part of a will, in clear and decisive terms, it cannot be cut down or taken away by any subsequent words that are not equally clear and decisive'. . . an estate clearly given in one part of a will cannot be disturbed by a subsequent clause which is ambiguous to uncertain in its meaning." Benson v. Greenville Nat'l Exch. Bank, 253 S.W.2d 918, 919 (Tex. Civ. App.—Texarkana 1952, writ ref'd n.r.e.); *see also* Gilliam v. Mahon, 231 S.W. 712, 713 (Tex. App. 1921). *Unless a lesser estate is created by express words or operation of law, we read a devise to be in fee simple absolute. Benson,* 253 S.W.2d at 922; *see also* Tex. Prop. Code Ann. § 5.001(a) (Vernon 1984) (for real property).

2. Applicable Estates

A "fee simple absolute" is an estate over which the owner has unlimited power of disposition in perpetuity without condition or limitation. Walker v. Foss, 930 S.W.2d 701, 706 (Tex. App.—San Antonio 1996, no writ).

An "executory limitation" is an event which, if it occurs, automatically divests one of devised property. Deviney v. Nations Bank, 993 S.W.2d 443, 448 (Tex. App.—Waco 1999, pet. denied). A fee simple estate subject to an executory limitation is called a "determinable fee simple estate."[41] *Id.* This is a fee simple interest in every respect, except that it passes to another if the contingency happens. Barker v. Rosenthal, 875 S.W.2d 779, 781 (Tex. App.—Houston [1st Dist.] 1994, no writ). The recipient upon the contingency's happening has an "executory interest." *Deviney,* 993 S.W.2d at 448-49.

A life estate is created by words showing intent to give the right to possess, use, and enjoy the property during life. *See* Eversole v. Williams, 943 S.W.2d 141, 143 (Tex. App.—Houston [1st Dist.] 1997, no writ). Additionally, the life tenant may expressly be given unlimited power to dispose of the property during his lifetime; if such power is exercised, it defeats the remainderman's interest in the disposed-of property. *See* Edds v. Mitchell, 143 Tex. 307, 184 S.W.2d 823, 825 (1945). However, the life tenant may not devise any of that property that remains

---

[41] A "determinable" fee simple estate is also known as a "base," "defeasible," "qualified," or "conditional" fee simple estate. *See* Smith v. Bynum, 558 S.W.2d 99, 101 (Tex. Civ. App.—Tyler 1977, writ ref'd n.r.e.).

at her death. Montgomery v. Browder, 930 S.W.2d 772, 777 (Tex. App.—Amarillo, writ denied). No particular language is required to make a life estate. *Welch*, 531 S.W.2d at 321.

3. Application

We hold the will created a determinable fee simple in decedent's husband with an executory interest in Cooley. The first half of the sentence gave decedent's husband a fee simple estate. See Killough v. Shafer, 358 S.W.2d 748, 749 (Tex. Civ. App.—Fort Worth 1962, writ ref'd n.r.e.) (holding "I wish all of my property to go to my wife Thelma . . ." created "absolute devise"). The second half of the sentence, however, also clearly gave "everything" after the husband's death to Cooley. To read the two halves together—without nullifying the second half and while preserving the greatest estate possible in the first devisee—is to construe decedent's husband's devise as a determinable fee simple. *See* Smith v. Bynum, 558 S.W.2d 99, 101 (Tex. Civ.A pp.—Tyler 1977, writ ref'd n.r.e.) (holding following language gave daughter determinable fee simple interest, not life estate: ". . . in case of the death of [the daughter] . . . without leaving bodily heirs, . . . the property herein above devised [in fee simple to that child] shall pass to and be vested in [the son]."). This is the same as, "If I die all my possessions go to my husband Paul Odis McKee and when he dies everything remaining goes to Rhobbin LaVern Jabbia," which is typical language for a determinable fee. *See Killough*, 358 S.W.2d at 749 (in this case on which Williams relies, court held determinable fee simple interest created by following language: "I wish all of my property to go to my wife . . . It is also my intention after [we] are both dead if there is any estate left that my part of such estate be apportioned to [other family]."). Accordingly, Cooley held an executory interest in decedent's estate: the contingency was her grandfather's dying with some of decedent's property. *See Harrell*, 215 S.W.2d at 878. He did. Therefore, she takes. This reading harmonizes both parts of the sentence; comports with decedent's evident intent, as indicated by naming two sequential devisees with fee simple language applicable to both (and without any language typical of a life estate); and gives the first devisee the greater estate (determinable fee simple, rather than life estate).

Our holding grants Cooley the relief she desires. Nevertheless, we note our respectful disagreement with Norris v. Methodist Home, on which Cooley relies, which held that a similarly worded will gave only a life estate with remainder interest. 464 S.W.2d 677, 678 (Tex. Civ. App.—Waco 1971, writ ref'd n.r.e.) ("It is my will and desire that . . . my property . . . shall become the property of my Husband . . . It is also my will and desire that all above mentioned property, at my Husband's death shall go to [a charity]."). The *Norris* court relied on three cases that used much clearer language indicating a life estate than was used in either *Norris* or the present case. Such clearer language is normally used to create a life estate. We disagree with Williams that the only alternative here is a fee simple absolute to the first devisee. The devise here and in *Norris* should be read to give a determinable fee simple followed by an executory interest. *See Smith*, 558 S.W.2d at 101. There is no other way to read the first devise, which evidences a fee simple interest but does not elsewhere contain life estate language . . . and still give meaning to the last clause of the will. Williams's construction of the will would render meaningless the words "and when he dies, everything goes to Rhobbin l aVern Jabbia."

Accordingly, we sustain the sole issue, reverse the order, and render an order construing decedent's will to give her husband a determinable fee simple interest and Cooley an executory interest that came into effect upon the husband's death.

QUESTIONS:

1. What was Lillian trying to accomplish with her will?

2. Should it matter to the court that this will was drafted by a layperson and not a lawyer who would know the precise language to use?

3. What did the court add to Lillian's actual language to reach the interpretation in this case?

4. When reading White v. Brown, Singleton v. Donalson, and Knopf v. Gray below, consider whether Lillian McKee, Jessie Lide, and Ruth Donalson were all trying to accomplish the same goals.

2. The Finite Estates: Estates That Must End

The fee simple absolute is the benchmark estate that will never end. The polar opposite is the category of finite estates, which include the life estate, fee tail, and leasehold estates. Because of this different aspect there will be many differences in the finite estates and the fee simple absolute.

a. Life Estates

An estate for life is an estate that is not an estate of inheritance, and

(a) is an estate that is specifically described as to duration in terms of the life or lives of one or more human beings, and is not terminable at any fixed or computable period of time; or

(b) though not so specifically described as is required under the rule stated in Clause (a), is an estate that cannot last longer than the life or lives of one or more human beings, and is not terminable at any fixed or computable period of time or at the will of the transferor.

Illustration:

1. Each of the following limitations when contained in an otherwise effective conveyance creates an estate for life:

   I.   To *A* for his own life.

   II.   To *A* for the joint lives of *B* and *C*.

   III. To *A* for lives of *A*, *B*, and *C* and the longest liver of them.[42]

As previously stated, at common law, the life estate was the default estate. If there were no express words of limitation, it was a life estate. Even if the conveyance said "*O to A in Fee Simple Absolute*," *A* would still hold a life estate at common law because at common law you had to use the words "and his heirs" to create the fee simple absolute estate.[43] The modern trend presumes, and Texas does so by statute, that the grantor intended to convey all that he has in the absence of express words of limitation indicating some intent to limit the estate being passed.[44] Under modern rules, the fee simple absolute is the default estate and in order to create a life estate there must be some words of limitation to evidence intent to measure the duration of the estate by someone's life. While there are no specific required words to use, "for life" are the classic words of limitation indicating a life estate.

By the very nature of a life estate, it terminates upon the death of the life tenant so that upon the life tenant's death there is no property interest—no estate to devise or be inherited.[45] However, a life estate may be sold or gifted during the life tenant's life. If such a conveyance occurs, a life estate *pur autre vie* is created. The life estate *pur autre vie* is a life estate held by one person and measured by the life of another.[46] It can be created when one life tenant transfers his or her interest to another person or it can be created in the original conveyance if the grantor indicates that the estate shall continue for *X*'s life and *X* is not the life tenant receiving the estate. If a life estate *pur autre vie* is created,

---

[42] Restatement (First) of Property § 18 (1936).
[43] Wendel, *supra* note 17, at 37-38.
[44] Tex. Prop. Code Ann. § 5.001 (Vernon 2003).
[45] Wendel, *supra* note 17, at 43.
[46] *Id.* at 37-38.

the life tenant holding the estate could possibly have an estate that could be devised or inherited.

If party A, holding a life estate, transfers his life estate to party B, because one cannot transfer more than one owns, the grantee/transferee B would hold a life estate measured by the original life tenant's life (A's life — or a life estate *pur autre vie*). While A is still alive, B's life estate *pur autre vie* is transferable, inheritable, and devisable, but upon A's death the life estate *pur autre vie* immediately expires—even if B is still alive.[47] If B dies, but A is still alive, B's life estate *pur autre vie* would go into B's probate estate, where B could devise it if he has a valid will; otherwise it would pass through intestacy.[48]

Life estates may be created by specific conveyances and they may also be created by operation of law. The Homestead life estate (or right of occupancy) that is covered at the end of this course is one example of a statute creating a life estate in a certain situation regardless of what the prior estate or ownership of the property may be. Other instances where a life estate is created by statute include the statutes of descent and distribution (Texas Estates Code § 201.001-.002) and in a judicial property division in divorce proceedings (Texas Family Code).[49] But keep in mind that regardless of how the life estate is created—by a conveyance or by operation of law—the rules governing the life estates are the same.

After a detailed discussion of how to create a life estate, we will cover the various rules that guide the actions to be taken by life tenants and the rights of the corresponding future interest holders. Keep in mind that even though the future interest holder is not entitled to possession until the end of the life tenant's present possessory estate, the future interest holder does indeed own a property interest and therefore has certain rights and the life tenant has certain obligations and responsibilities to that future interest holder. Finally, we will discuss why life estates are used as estate planning tools for clients and how particular language may be used to provide certain rights to life tenants that are not afforded simply by creating the life estate. I refer to these types of life estates as "super life estates."[50]

Life Estate Examples

Each of the following conveyances has been held to create a life estate in the grantee.

---

[47] *Id.*

[48] *Id.*

[49] Tex. Estates Code Ann. § 201.001-.002 (Vernon 2013); Tex. Family Code Ann. Ch. 7 (Vernon's 2003).

[50] This is not a legal term (like the life estate *pur autre vie*) but a term that I use to help explain what is involved in these types of life estates specifically created in conveyances, usually wills or trust documents.

1. *O* grants and transfers Blackacre to Jordan for so long as Jordan shall live; thereafter to Mallory.

2. Zena conveys to Alpha until she dies.

3. Orlando gives to Blake, and at Blake's death to Blake's children.

4. I, Ola, hereby devise to my husband, Ed, all my real property when I die; and when he dies, all my real property to my daughter, Diane.

5. Oscar grants to Elmo Blackacre for as long as Ernie lives.
   (This is actually an example of the life estate *pur autre vie*.)

How does this language compare to the language reviewed by the court in Cooley v. Williams? Also compare these life estate examples with the language in the following case.

White v. Brown
Supreme Court of Tennessee, 1977
559 S.W.2d 938

BROCK, J.

This is a suit for the construction of a will. The Chancellor held that the will passed a life estate, but not the remainder, in certain realty, leaving the remainder to pass by inheritance to the testatrix's heirs at law. The Court of Appeals affirmed.

Mrs. Jessie Lide died on February 15, 1973, leaving a holographic will which, in its entirety, reads as follows:

> April 19, 1972
>
> I, Jessie Lide, being in sound mind declare this to be my last will and testament. I appoint my niece Sandra White Perry to be the executrix of my estate. I wish Evelyn White to have my home to live in and <u>not</u> to be <u>sold</u>.
>
> I also leave my personal property to Sandra White Perry. My house is not to be sold.
>
> Jessie Lide
> (Underscoring by testatrix)

Mrs. Lide was a widow and had no children. Although she had nine brothers and sisters, only two sisters residing in Ohio survived her. These two sisters quitclaimed any interest they might have in the residence to Mrs. White. The nieces and nephews of the testatrix, her heirs at law, are defendants in this action.

Mrs. White, her husband, who was the testatrix's brother, and her daughter, Sandra White Perry, lived with Mrs. Lide as a family for some twenty-five years. After Sandra married in 1969 and Mrs. White's husband died in 1971, Evelyn White continued to live with Mrs. Lide until Mrs. Lide's death in 1973 at age 88.

Mrs. White, joined by her daughter as executrix, filed this action to obtain construction of the will, alleging that she is vested with a fee simple title to the home. The defendants contend that the will conveyed only a life estate to Mrs. White, leaving the remainder to go to them under our laws of intestate succession. The Chancellor held that the will unambiguously conveyed only a life interest in the home to Mrs. White and refused to consider extrinsic evidence concerning Mrs. Lide's relationship with her surviving relatives. Due to the debilitated condition of the property and in accordance with the desire of all parties, the Chancellor ordered the property sold with the proceeds distributed in designated shares among the beneficiaries.

Our cases have repeatedly acknowledged that the intention of the testator is to be ascertained from the language of the entire instrument when read in the light of surrounding circumstances. But, the practical difficulty in this case, as in so many other cases involving wills drafted by lay persons, is that the words chosen by the testatrix are not specific enough to clearly state her intent. Thus, in our opinion, it is not clear whether Mrs. Lide intended to convey a life estate in the home to Mrs. White, leaving the remainder interest to descend by operation of law, or a fee interest with a restraint on alienation. Moreover, the will might even be read as conveying a fee interest subject to a condition subsequent (Mrs. White's failure to live in the home).

In such ambiguous cases it is obvious that rules of construction, always yielding to the cardinal rule of the testator's intent, must be employed as auxiliary aids in the courts' endeavor to ascertain the testator's intent.

In 1851 our General Assembly enacted two such statutes of construction, thereby creating a statutory presumption against partial intestacy.

Chapter 33 of the Public Acts of 1851 (now codified as T.C.A. §§ 64-101 and 64-501) reversed the common law presumption that a life estate was intended unless the intent to pass a fee simple was clearly expressed in the instrument. T.C.A. § 64-501 provides:

> Every grant or devise of real estate, or any interest therein,
> shall pass all the estate or interest of the grantor or devisor,
> unless the intent to pass a less estate or interest shall appear by

express terms, or be necessarily implied in the terms of the instrument."

Chapter 180, Section 2 of the Public Acts of 1851 (now codified as T.C.A. § 32-301) was specifically directed to the operation of a devise. In relevant part, T.C.A. § 32-301 provides:

> "A will . . . shall convey all the real estate belonging to [the testator] or in which he had any interest at his decease, unless a contrary intention appear by its words and context."

Thus, under our law, unless the "words and context" of Mrs. Lide's will clearly evidence her intention to convey only a life estate to Mrs. White, the will should be construed as passing the home to Mrs. White in fee. "'If the expression in the will is doubtful, the doubt is resolved against the limitation and in favor of the absolute estate.'"

Several of our cases demonstrate the effect of these statutory presumptions against intestacy by construing language which might seem to convey an estate for life, without provision for a gift over after the termination of such life estate, as passing a fee simple instead. In Green v. Young, 163 Tenn. 16, 40 S.W.2d 793 (1931), the testatrix's disposition of all of her property to her husband "to be used by him for his support and comfort during his life" was held to pass a fee estate. Similarly, in Williams v. Williams, 167 Tenn. 26, 65 S.W.2d 561 (1933), the testator's devise of real property to his children "for and during their natural lives" without provision for a gift over was held to convey a fee. And, in Webb v. Webb, 53 Tenn. App. 609, 385 S.W.2d 295 (1964), a devise of personal property to the testator's wife "for her maintenance, support and comfort, for the full period of her natural life" with complete powers of alienation but without provision for the remainder passed absolute title to the widow.

Thus, if the sole question for our determination were whether the will's conveyance of the home to Mrs. White "to live in" gave her a life interest or a fee in the home, a conclusion favoring the absolute estate would be clearly required. The question, however, is complicated somewhat by the caveat contained in the will that the home is "not to be sold"—a restriction conflicting with the free alienation of property, one of the most significant incidents of fee ownership. We must determine, therefore, whether Mrs. Lide's will, when taken as a whole, clearly evidences her intent to convey only a life estate in her home to Mrs. White.

Under ordinary circumstances a person makes a will to dispose of his or her entire estate. If, therefore, a will is susceptible of two constructions, by one of which the testator disposes of the whole of his estate and by the other of which he disposes of only a part of his estate, dying intestate as to the remainder, this Court has always preferred that construction which disposes of the whole of the testator's estate if that construction is reasonable and consistent with the general scope and provisions of the will. A construction which results in partial intestacy will not be adopted unless such intention clearly appears. It has been said that the courts will prefer any reasonable construction or any construction which does not do violence to a testator's language, to a construction which results in partial intestacy.

The intent to create a fee simple or other absolute interest and, at the same time to impose a restraint upon its alienation can be clearly expressed. If the testator specifically declares that he devises land to A "in fee simple" or to A "and his heirs" but that A shall not have the power to alienate the land, there is but one tenable construction, viz., the testator's intent is to impose a restraint upon a fee simple. To construe such language to create a life estate would conflict with the express specification of a fee simple as well as with the presumption of intent to make a complete testamentary disposition of all of a testator's property. By extension, as noted by Professor Casner in his treatise on the law of real property:

> "Since it is now generally presumed that a conveyor intends to transfer his whole interest in the property, it may be reasonable to adopt the same construction, [conveyance of a fee simple] even in the absence of words of inheritance, if there is no language that can be construed to create a remainder." 6 American Law of Property § 26.58 (A. J. Casner ed. 1952).

In our opinion, testatrix's apparent testamentary restraint on the alienation of the home devised to Mrs. White does not evidence such a clear intent to pass only a life estate as is sufficient to overcome the law's strong presumption that a fee simple interest was conveyed.

Accordingly, we conclude that Mrs. Lide's will passed a fee simple absolute in the home to Mrs. White. Her attempted restraint on alienation must be declared void as inconsistent with the incidents and nature of the estate devised and contrary to public policy.

The decrees of the Court of Appeals and the trial court are reversed and the cause is remanded to the chancery court for such further proceedings as may be necessary, consistent with this opinion. Costs are taxed against appellees.

HARBISON, Justice, dissenting.

With deference to the views of the majority, and recognizing the principles of law contained in the majority opinion, I am unable to agree that the language of the will of Mrs. Lide did or was intended to convey a fee simple interest in her residence to her sister-in-law, Mrs. Evelyn White.

The testatrix expressed the wish that Mrs. White was "to have my home to live in and not to be sold". The emphasis is that of the testatrix, and her desire that Mrs. White was not to have an unlimited estate in the property was reiterated in the last sentence of the will, to wit: "My house is not to be sold."

The testatrix appointed her niece, Mrs. Perry, executrix and made an outright bequest to her of all personal property.

The will does not seem to me to be particularly ambiguous, and like the Chancellor and the Court of Appeals, I am of the opinion that the testatrix gave Mrs. White a life estate only, and that upon the death of Mrs. White the remainder will pass to the heirs at law of the testatrix.

The cases cited by petitioners in support of their contention that a fee simple was conveyed are not persuasive, in my opinion. Possibly the strongest case cited by the appellants is Green v. Young, 163 Tenn. 16, 40 S.W.2d 793 (1931), in which the testatrix bequeathed all of her real and personal property to her husband "to be used by him for his support and comfort during his life." The will expressly stated that it included all of the property, real and personal, which the testatrix owned at the time of her death. There was no limitation whatever upon the power of the husband to use, consume, or dispose of the property, and the Court concluded that a fee simple was intended.

In the case of Williams v. Williams, 167 Tenn. 26, 65 S.W.2d 561 (1933), a father devised property to his children "for and during their natural lives" but the will contained other provisions not mentioned in the majority opinion which seem to me to distinguish the case. Unlike the provisions of the present will, other clauses in the Williams will contained provisions that these same children were to have "all the residue of my estate personal or mixed of which I shall die possessed or seized, or to which I shall be entitled at the time of my decease, to have and to hold the same to them and their executors and administrators and assigns forever."

Further, following some specific gifts to grandchildren, there was another bequest of the remainder of the testator's money to these same three children. The language used by the testator in that case was held to convey the fee simple interest in real estate to the children, but its provisions hardly seem analogous to the language employed by the testatrix in the instant case.

In the case of Webb v. Webb, 53 Tenn. App. 609, 385 S.W.2d 295 (1964), the testator gave his wife all the residue of his property with a clear, unqualified and unrestricted power of use, sale or disposition. Thereafter he attempted to limit her interest to a life estate, with a gift over to his heirs of any unconsumed property. Again, under settled rules of construction and interpretation, the wife was found to have a fee simple estate, but, unlike the present case, there was no limitation whatever upon the power of use or disposition of the property by the beneficiary.

In the present case the testatrix knew how to make an outright gift, if desired. She left all of her personal property to her niece without restraint or limitation.

As to her sister-in-law, however, she merely wished the latter have her house "to live in," and expressly withheld from her any power of sale.

The majority opinion holds that the testatrix violated a rule of law by attempting to restrict the power of the donee to dispose of the real estate. Only by thus striking a portion of the will, and holding it inoperative, is the conclusion reached that an unlimited estate resulted.

In my opinion, this interpretation conflicts more greatly with the apparent intention of the testatrix than did the conclusion of the courts below, limiting the gift to Mrs. White to a life estate. I have serious doubt that the testatrix intended to create any illegal restraint on alienation or to violate any other rules of law. It seems to me that she rather emphatically intended to provide that her sister-in-law was not to be able to sell the house during the lifetime of the latter—a result which is both legal and consistent with the creation of a life estate.

In my opinion the judgment of the courts below was correct and I would affirm.

Knopf v. Gray
Supreme Court of Texas, 2018
61 Tex. 621

PER CURIAM

This case involves the construction of a will bequest of a tract of land. The primary issue presented is whether the testator intended to devise a fee-simple interest or a life-estate interest to her son. Both the trial court and the court of appeals held that the will unambiguously devised a fee-simple interest, entitling the son to summary judgment. We disagree and reverse the court of appeals' judgment.

Vada Wallace Allen's will disposed of her entire estate, including the land at issue in this case—approximately 316 acres of land in Robertson County. The provision through which she devised that land states:

> NOW BOBBY I leave the rest to you, everything, certificates of deposit, land, cattle and machinery, Understand the land is not to be sold but passed on down to your children, ANNETTE KNOPF, ALLISON KILWAY, AND STANLEY GRAY. TAKE CARE OF IT AND TRY TO BE HAPPY.

[handwritten margin note: Provision]

The provision thus begins with a residuary bequest to her son, William Robert "Bobby" Gray. A residuary bequest is "a bequest of the remainder of the testator's estate after the payment of the debts, legacies, and specific bequests." *Residuary Bequests*, Black's Law Dictionary (10th ed. 2014). That residuary bequest is immediately followed by instructional language referencing the "land" included in the residuary and Bobby's children.

Bobby and his wife, Karen, conveyed the land at issue in fee simple to Polasek Farms, LLC, via multiple warranty deeds. Knopf sued Bobby, Karen, and Polasek Farms (who collectively are the respondents here), seeking a declaratory judgment that Allen devised only a life estate to Bobby, thus precluding him from delivering a greater interest to Polasek Farms.

Polasek Farms and Knopf filed cross-motions for summary judgment. The trial court granted Polasek Farms' motion in two separate rulings and rendered final judgment for the respondents, finding that the contested provision contained an invalid disabling restraint, the will vested Bobby with a fee-simple interest in the property, and Knopf received no remainder interest. A divided court of appeals affirmed, agreeing with the trial court's findings and concluding that the will's language regarding passing the land on down to the children was merely an instruction to Bobby rather than a gift to the children. ___ S.W.3d ___, ___, 2017 WL 131863 (Tex. App.–Waco 2017) (mem. op.). The dissenting justice would have held that the provision's meaning was ambiguous and thus improper for resolution on summary judgment. *Id.* at ___ (Gray, C.J., dissenting).

When a will's meaning is ambiguous, its interpretation becomes a fact issue for which summary judgment is inappropriate. *See* White v. Moore, 760 S.W.2d 242, 243 (Tex. 1988) (citing Coker v. Coker, 650 S.W.2d 391, 394 (Tex. 1983)). A will is ambiguous when it is subject to more than one reasonable interpretation or its meaning is simply uncertain. *See El Paso Nat'l Bank*, 615 S.W.2d at 185. Whether a will is ambiguous is a question of law for the court. In re Estate of Slaughter, 305 S.W.3d 804, 808 (Tex. App.–Texarkana 2010, no pet.); *see* Kelley-Coppedge, Inc. v. Highlands Ins. Co., 980 S.W.2d 462, 464 (Tex. 1998) (holding same regarding contract construction).

The cardinal rule of will construction is to ascertain the testator's intent and to enforce that intent to the extent allowed by law. Sellers v. Powers, 426 S.W.2d 533, 536 (Tex. 1968); *see also* Bergin v. Bergin, 159 Tex. 83, 315 S.W.2d 943, 946 (1958). We look to the instrument's language, considering its provisions as a whole and attempting to harmonize them so as to give effect to the will's overall intent. Stephens v. Beard, 485 S.W.3d 914, 916 (Tex. 2016) (citations omitted); *Bergin*, 315 S.W.2d at 946–47. We interpret the words in a will as a layperson would use them absent evidence that the testator received legal assistance in drafting the will or was otherwise familiar with technical meanings. *Bergin*, 315 S.W.2d at 946.

Here, the parties dispute whether Allen intended to devise to Bobby a fee-simple interest in the land at issue or only a life estate. "An estate in land that is conveyed or devised is a fee simple unless the estate is limited by express words," Tex. Prop. Code § 5.001(a), but the law does not require any specific words or formalities to create a life estate, *see* Welch v. Straach, 531 S.W.2d 319, 321 (Tex. 1975). Therefore, the words used in the will must only evidence intent to create what lawyers know as a life estate. *See Bergin*, 315 S.W.2d at 947. A life estate is generally defined as an "estate held only for the duration of a specified person's life." *Life Estate*, Black's Law Dictionary (10th ed. 2014). Thus, a will creates a life estate "where the language of the instrument manifests an intention on the part of the grantor or testator to pass to a grantee or devisee a right to possess, use, or enjoy property during the period of the grantee's life." Fin. Freedom Senior Funding Corp. v. Horrocks, 294 S.W.3d 749, 755 (Tex. App.–Houston [14th Dist.] 2009, no pet.).

As noted, the contested provision in Allen's will states:

> NOW BOBBY I leave the rest to you, everything, certificates of deposit, land, cattle and machinery, Understand the land is not to be sold but passed on down to your children, ANNETTE KNOPF, ALLISON KILWAY, AND STANLEY GRAY. TAKE CARE OF IT AND TRY TO BE HAPPY.

Knopf argues that the instructional language in the second clause, read in conjunction with other language throughout the will, demonstrates Allen's intent to grant Bobby a life estate with the remainder interest going to her grandchildren. The respondents counter that the instructional language confirms Allen's intent to devise the land to Bobby in fee simple. In the alternative, they argue that the instructional language either constitutes an invalid disabling restraint, is nontestamentary, or is technically insufficient to create a life estate.

Arguments

Beginning with the contested provision itself, the parties focus largely on the meaning of the specific phrase "passed on down." However, this line of semantic argument misses the analytical forest for the trees. The provision's meaning depends on its overall intent, so narrow concentration on the possible meanings of three words is a diversion. We need only read the provision as a whole to see a layperson's clearly expressed intent to create what the law calls a life estate. Reading all three clauses together, Allen grants the land to Bobby subject to the limitations that he not sell it, that he take care of it, *and* that it be passed down to his children. This represents the essence of a life estate; a life tenant's interest in the property is limited by the general requirement that he preserve the remainder interest unless otherwise authorized in the will. *See, e.g.*, Richardson v. McCloskey, 276 S.W. 680, 685 (Tex. 1925) (stating that life tenants take the property's benefits with corresponding burdens of repair and upkeep); Moody v. Pitts, 708 S.W.2d 930, 936 (Tex. App.–Corpus Christi 1986, no writ) (recognizing the duty of life tenants not to destroy remainder interests except as authorized by the will); Maxwell v. Harrell, 183 S.W.2d 577, 580 (Tex. Civ. App.–Austin 1944, writ ref'd w.o.m.) (noting that a life tenant cannot alienate property to "defeat the estate of the remaindermen"). Allen's words in the contested provision unambiguously refer to elements of a life estate and designate her grandchildren, the petitioners, as the remaindermen. The language thus clearly demonstrates that the phrase "passed on down," as used here, encompasses a transfer upon Bobby's death.

Reading the provision in the context of the entire document only cements this conclusion. *See Stephens*, 485 S.W.3d at 916. Allen devised her entire estate to various family members, including approximately one dozen specific bequests to her grandchildren. She also selectively repeated the sentiment that certain property not be sold but be "passed on" or "given" or "handed down" to the devisees' children. Thus, the will as a whole indicates an intent to keep her property in her family and to bequeath certain property to multiple generations. Reading the contested provision to grant Bobby a life estate and to grant Knopf the remainder interest is fully consistent with the overall intent of the document.

The respondents attempt to rebut Knopf's interpretation by characterizing the words "the land is not to be sold" as an invalid disabling restraint on sale, as the trial court and court of appeals held. A disabling restraint is an attempt by the grantor, through the terms of a transfer, "to invalidate a [grantee's] later transfer of that [granted] interest, in whole or in part." RESTATEMENT (SECOND) OF PROPERTY § 3.1 (Am. Law Inst. 1983). The respondents would thus have us pluck a fragment out of context, construe it in isolation, strike it, and then return to the remaining text. This proposed approach inverts the analytical process and defies our rules of will construction. The nature of a granted interest (e.g., fee simple versus life estate) must be resolved *before* a court may determine whether a restraint on that interest is valid because the restraint's validity depends on the type of interest granted. *See Bergin*, 315 S.W.2d at 947. To the point, inherent in a life estate is a restraint on alienation of the remainder interest. *Id.* Accordingly, the phrase "the land is not to be sold" is an integral part of Allen's expression of intent to create a life estate. The respondents' suggested methodology would also violate our contextual approach to will construction and our rule against rewriting wills to arrive at a presumed intent. Shriner's Hosp. for Crippled Children v. Stahl, 610 S.W.2d 147, 151 (Tex. 1980) (noting that intent is derived from the words actually used and that courts cannot redraft wills to reflect presumed intent).

The respondents' remaining arguments also ultimately beg the question of the contested provision's intended meaning. For example, they contend that the instructional language following the residuary bequest is precatory, or nontestamentary, language with no legal effect. But whether language is precatory or testamentary is itself a question of intent. *See Bergin*, 315 S.W.2d at 947. Our determination that the provision clearly expresses Allen's intent to grant a life estate establishes that the instructional language *is* testamentary. Moreover, the fact that Allen selectively used these phrases evidences that she intended they have some effect.

Finally, the respondents also claim that any ambiguity in the contested provision favors them because a testator must clearly reduce a bequest from a fee simple to a life estate. *See id.* at 946. However, in light of our holding that the provision unambiguously conveyed a life estate, we need not address this argument.

Accordingly, without hearing oral argument, *see* Tex. R. App. P. 59.1, we grant Knopf's petition for review, reverse the court of appeals' judgment, and render judgment that the will granted Bobby Gray a life estate and the petitioners the remainder interest in the property at issue. The case is remanded to the trial court for further proceedings consistent with this opinion.

NOTES & QUESTIONS:

1. With the bundle of sticks for the fee simple absolute there is a right-to-transfer stick that cannot be restrained. The idea is that a restraint on alienability is fundamentally inconsistent with the bundle of sticks conveyed to the owner. However, with a life estate and other finite estates, the law takes a different approach. The finite estates are lesser estates and the bundle is not as large. Therefore, the law will allow restraints on the alienability of a finite estate. In White v. Brown, because the court ultimately concluded it was a fee simple absolute, the attempted restraint on the ability to sell the house was void and unenforceable. However, had the court determined the estate to be a life estate, the very same restraint would be valid.

2. Why would restraints on alienation be disfavored under the law when dealing with a fee estate? Remember, the modern approach is to promote free alienability of land so that it is marketable.

i. The Nature of the Relationship of the Life Tenant and Future Interest

When the classification is that of a life estate, there are then additional rules to consider. The present possessory estate will come to an end and the future interest owner, whether remainder or reversion, also owns an interest in the land that will result in possession at the end of the life estate. Do the future interest owners need to be concerned that what they ultimately possess will be drastically different from what existed at the time the interests were conveyed? The following cases provide examples of where this question commonly arises.

Davis v. Bond et al.
Commission of Appeals of Texas, Section B, 1942
158 S.W.2d 297
Error to Court of Civil Appeals of Sixth Supreme Judicial District

SMEDLEY, Commissioner.

Defendants in error, the surviving wife and children of J. B. Bond, deceased, filed this suit against plaintiff in error, Mrs. Elisa Bond Davis, and other defendants who made no contest, to recover the title to a lot in the town of Talco, in Titus County, upon which a producing oil well had been drilled, and to remove from their title clouds cast by recorded instruments, executed by Mrs. Davis and persons claiming under her, affecting the oil, gas and other minerals in the lot.

Defendants in error asserted title under a general warranty deed executed and acknowledged by plaintiff in error [Elisa Bond Davis], joined by her husband, on November 23, 1923, by which the lot was conveyed to J. B. Bond, plaintiff in error's son, for a recited consideration of $100 in cash and the further consideration that "the said Elisa Davis shall retain possession, use and control of said property hereby conveyed during the remainder of her lifetime and that said J. B. Bond shall have no control, use or possession of said property until after the death of said Elisa Davis." The important question in the case is whether there was a delivery of this deed.

[Ed. Note: Delivery of the deed, *i.e.*, relinquishing control of the deed or otherwise manifesting an intent that the conveyance be irrevocable, is necessary to have a valid conveyance by deed. The first three assignments of error addressed whether there was a valid delivery of the deed when Mrs. Elisa Bond Davis executed the deed and left it with a notary public with the instruction to deliver it to J. B. Bond upon her death. The court held that the legal effect under such facts is to invest the grantee presently with title to the land conveyed, but to postpone the right of possession until the grantor's death and that such delivery was valid where the grantee reserved no control over the instrument. According to the court, the deed took effect from the first delivery. The fourth assignment of error addressed what kind of interest a deed created under those circumstances, and the court confirmed that the deed served to reserve a life estate in the grantor, with the remainder to go to the grantees in the deed. Having decided that a life estate was created in Elisa Bond Davis, the court next considered her rights as a life tenant to oil and gas produced from the property and the rights of the holders of the remainder interest.]

The Court of Civil Appeals correctly approved that part of the trial court's judgment which awarded to defendants in error the proceeds received and to be received from the one-eighth royalty reserved in the oil and gas lease executed by plaintiff in error and J. B. Bond, with provision that the proceeds from the royalty should be held by the receiver and invested under the orders of the court and the income from the investment delivered to plaintiff in error during her life. Swayne v. Lone Acre Oil Co., 98 Tex. 597, 86 S.W. 740, 69 L.R.A. 986, 8 Ann. Cas. 1117.

Relying upon a statement in the opinion in the Swayne case that at common law conventional life estates, or those created by contract, were not impeachable for waste unless expressly made so by the conveyance, plaintiff in error takes the position that since (if there was an effective delivery of the deed) she is a conventional life tenant rather than a legal life tenant, as was the tenant in the Swayne case, she is entitled to the royalties during her lifetime. The old common law rule is correctly stated in the Swayne case, but, as pointed out in the opinion of the Court of Civil Appeals in this case, that rule was changed by statutes enacted several centuries before the common law was adopted as the rule of decision in this state, which statutes made conventional as well as legal life estates impeachable for waste, and the common law liability for waste as extended by the early statutes obtains in most of the states. 27 R.C. L. p. 1032, Sec. 21; 21 C.J. p. 948, Sec. 87; "Fee Simple Ownership of Oil and Gas in Texas" by A. W. Walker, Jr., 6 Texas Law Review, pp. 125, 142, 143; "Rights of a Life Tenant in Production and Use of "Oil and Gas" by Clarence A. Guittard, 4 Texas Bar Journal, pp. 265 and following. Summers says in substance, citing many authorities, that tenants for life or years, whether created by common law, by statute, by deed, devise or contract, are under a duty not to take oil or gas, as against the remainderman or reversioner. Summers' Law of Oil and Gas, Perm. Ed., Vol. 1, pp. 86-88, § 33. Tiffany announces the same rule as applicable generally to all tenants for life or years. Tiffany's Law of Real Property, 3d Ed., Vol. 2, pp. 634, 635, Sec. 633. See also Note 43 A.L.R. pp. 811-819.

In view of the foregoing authorities and the value of a uniform rule applicable both to life estates created by contract and to those created by operation of law, and because the taking of oil and gas is an injury to the inheritance, we conclude that the trial court did not err in awarding to defendants in error the proceeds from the royalty reserved and requiring their investment and the payment to plaintiff in error of the income therefrom during her lifetime.

It is important to observe that the land "had not been devoted to mining purposes" at the time of the creation of the tenancy. The oil and gas lease was executed and the well was drilled after the delivery to W. H. Crawford of the deed which conveyed the lot to J. B. Bond and reserved a life estate to plaintiff in error.

[margin note: LEASE + WELL CREATED AFTER CONVEYANCE]

The judgment of the Court of Civil Appeals is affirmed.

Opinion adopted by the Supreme Court.

QUESTION:

1. What should have been done to allow Elisa Bond Davis the right to the royalties?

Thompson v. Thompson et al.
Supreme Court of Texas, 1951
236 S.W.2d 779

GRIFFIN, Justice.

[Ed. Note: In Texas, the primary residence of a single adult or a family may be protected under the Texas Homestead laws provided that other conditions that you will learn later are satisfied. The rights in that primary residence or "homestead" are different from the rights one has in nonhomestead property in a variety of ways. Just one of the implications of having homestead property stems from the protection afforded to a surviving spouse. Under Texas law, if a married couple has a homestead and one spouse dies, the surviving spouse has, at a minimum, a life estate in the interest owned by the deceased spouse prior to his or her death, as a matter of law. For example, suppose that H owned a house on a property known as "Blackacre" prior to marrying W. This house would be his separate property, *i.e.*, not community property. Nonetheless, H and W move into Blackacre, and it is their homestead. If H dies, W as the surviving spouse has the right to continue possessing Blackacre until she either dies or abandons Blackacre as her homestead. This is a right that arises by law, and the surviving spouse is the only one who can opt not to take advantage of this homestead right. If H devised Blackacre to his daughter, D, or even his best friend F, neither would have a right to possess until after W's death or her abandonment of Blackacre. Note that this is precisely the way a life estate works: one person has the immediate right to possess (*i.e.*, the life tenant) while the remainderman will be delayed in his or her right to possess. In the example above, W has a life estate and F or D has a remainder by operation of the homestead laws.]

One R. W. (Robert W.) Thompson, who died October 19, 1948, married the petitioner, Edna Thompson, on October 18, 1916, and these parties lived together as husband and wife until the death of R. W. Thompson. At the time of his marriage he was a widower and had three children by his first marriage, and who are the respondents here (joined by the husbands of the daughters), and who were living in his household at the time of the second marriage. At the time of his marriage, R. W. Thompson owned an undivided one-half interest in the tract involved in this suit, and totaling approximately 334 acres. The son Roy Thompson, owned the other one-half of said land and lived on said land in a home of his own. Petitioner and R. W. Thompson, immediately upon their marriage, moved into a two-story frame house on the land owned by R. W. Thompson and continued to live in said house and occupy the land as a homestead at all times until the death of R. W. Thompson. Since his death petitioner has continued to occupy this house and land as her homestead down to date of the trial in the lower court. This land was the separate property of R. W. Thompson. R. W. Thompson owned only an undivided one-fourth of all the oil, gas and other minerals in and under his land.

On December 28, 1925, R. W. Thompson, joined by his wife, petitioner herein, executed an "unless" oil and gas and other mineral lease, vesting in the lessee the "exclusive right of mining and drilling for oil, gas, and other minerals, as well as such easements over and across the surface of said lands as were necessary for such mining and/or drilling operations, for a cash consideration, and the additional consideration of the obligation of such lessee to deliver to lessors as royalty one-eighth (1/8), in kind, of such oil as might be produced from said premises by said lessee. Said lands being the separate property of the said R. W. Thompson. . . ."

The Humble Oil & Refining Company became the owner of said lease and brought in a well under said lease shortly after its execution and this land has produced oil and gas continuously for more than 20 years prior to the death of R. W. Thompson, and at the time of his death there were 13 wells producing under said lease and R. W. Thompson had collected pay for the royalties reserved under said lease, and according to his ownership of the land.

We hold that R. W. Thompson and wife, Edna, did not abandon any part of their homestead by the execution of the lease in 1925, and that the widow has such an interest in the royalties payable under the lease as will support her claim to the use and enjoyment of such royalties.

As the surviving widow of R. W. Thompson, and having renounced any claim under his will, the petitioner herein is entitled to her statutory rights in the homestead being used by herself and her husband at the time of his death. Constitution of Texas, Art. XVI, Sec. 52, Vernon's Ann. St.; Vernon's Ann. Civ. St. Art. 3501.

It has been held by this Court that the homestead right of the survivor to continue to occupy the family homestead is in the nature of a life estate created by law. Sargeant v. Sargeant, 118 Tex. 343, 15 S.W.2d 589, 593; Rancho Oil Co. v. Powell, 142 Tex. 63, 173 S.W.2d 960, loc. cit. (9), 1st col., 965.

The rights of a life tenant in the production of oil from wells which were producing at the time the life tenancy came into being, are to have the use and enjoyment of that part of the production payable under the terms of the instrument permitting the production. The case of Swayne v. Lone Acre Oil Co., 98 Tex. 597, 86 S.W. 740, 69 L.R.A. 986, in an opinion by Judge Gaines discusses the rights of a life tenant in lands to receive the oil produced therefrom, and holds that oil is governed by the same rule that applies to other minerals. 86 S.W. loc. cit., bot. 2nd col., 742 to top of 1st col., 743.

In Petrus v. Cage Bros., Tex. Civ. App., 128 S.W.2d 537, 538, *writ refused*, suit was brought by the children of Ferdinand Petrus, deceased, against Cage Bros., the lessees and operators of a caliche pit upon the homestead of Ferdinand Petrus and his surviving widow, Laura, who continued to occupy said homestead upon the death of Ferdinand. The pit had been opened by Ferdinand prior to his death and was operated by him until his death. After he died the widow alone leased the pit to Cage Bros. and they were operating it at the time of the trial. Judgment for the defendants was affirmed by the Court of Civil Appeals at San Antonio. In its opinion the Court said: "The rule arrived at seems clearly to be that the right of survivors, such as Mrs. Petrus, is more than a mere right of possession and occupancy; it is an estate in land, in the nature of a life estate. She is a tenant for life in the homestead, the measure of her right in which is not the mere privilege of possession and enjoyment. The right encompasses 'every element of a life estate, and is therefore at least in the nature of a legal life estate, or, in other words, a life estate created by operation of law.' The authorities cited further hold that a life tenant by virtue of the operation of law (such as Mrs. Petrus) cannot use the property upon which she is such tenant for any purpose which would work an injury to the inheritance, 'save those (purposes) only to which it had been devoted at the time the life estate came into existence,' for, 'having once had the power of committing waste, he shall not be deprived of it by the act of God.' Swayne v. Lone Acre Oil Co., supra (98 Tex. 597, 86 S.W. 742). 'Applying the rules stated, Mrs. Petrus, upon the death of her spouse, took an estate for life, by operation of the law, in that part of the homestead which descended in fee, upon the death of the father, to their children, appellants herein, and by virtue of her said estate therein thus acquired, she had the right to continue to take caliche from the mine which had been opened prior to and was being operated at, the time her life estate came into existence, to-wit, at the death of her spouse, intestate.' "

White v. Blackman, Tex. Civ. App., 168 S.W.2d 531, 533, writ refused, want of merit, decided by the Texarkana Court of Civil Appeals is a case on all fours with the one at bar. The surviving widow brought suit against the heirs under the decedent's will to have a homestead set aside to her in two tracts of land, one of which was separate property of the decedent, and also to recover "all the oil and gas royalties and proceeds therefrom which had accrued subsequent to the death of J. M. Blackman and which would accrue so long as she continued to use and occupy said properties as her homestead." Decedent and his first wife had made an oil and gas lease on both tracts of land prior to the first wife's death. Under this lease there were 41 producing wells on the two tracts at the time of the death of J. M. Blackman. Judgment was for the plaintiff in the trial court and on appeal the Texarkana Court—much against its will and belief as to what the law should be—affirmed on authority of the refusal by the Supreme Court of a writ of error in the case of Petrus v. Cage Bros., *supra*, and "solely for such reason." This Court refused the application for writ of error "want of merit", thus approving the judgment awarding all of the royalties and proceeds therefrom to the widow, but not approving the reasoning advanced, nor all of the pronouncements of the Court of Civil Appeals as to the law. A reading of the opinion shows that it could not have been given a "straight refusal." *See also* Clayton v. Canida, Tex. Civ. App., 223 S.W.2d 264, 265, no writ history.

We hold that the petitioner is entitled to receive one-fourth of the royalties and the proceeds therefrom produced from those wells, which were opened at the time of the death of R. W. Thompson as long as she shall live and use the family homestead.

Joe Singleton, et al. v. George E. Donalson III
Court of Appeals of Texas, Beaumont, 2003
117 S.W.3d 516

[handwritten: Sum of Money Set aside for Named Beneficiary]

[handwritten right margin: Future Ownership → To revert back to owner after death of life tenant]

In 1976 Ruth Hooks Donalson executed a will devising a life estate in her separate property to her husband, George Donalson III, with a "reversionary interest" to other specified relatives. She died in 1977, and her will was probated the same year. A dispute arose between George and the holders of the "reversionary" interests over certain royalties and bonuses from the oil and gas produced from the estate property. Appellants argue that the royalties and bonuses are corpus of the estate, and that the will does not grant George the power to consume or dispose of the corpus. Appellants sued George for waste of the estate's assets, conversion, breach of fiduciary duty, fraud, and debt. The trial court granted George's motion for summary judgment. Appellants ask this Court to reverse the judgment.

Appellants' first issue attacks the assertion in George's summary judgment motion that the language in Ruth's will gives him the right to consume and dispose of the royalties and bonuses. A court's interpretation of a will is governed by the testator's intent, which is ascertained from the language found within the four corners of the will. *See* San Antonio Area Foundation v. Lang, 35 S.W.3d 636, 639 (Tex. 2000); McGill v. Johnson, 799 S.W.2d 673, 674 (Tex. 1990). If a will is unambiguous, a court may not go beyond the will's specific terms in search of the testator's intent. *Lang*, 35 S.W.3d at 639.

Ruth gave George a life estate, as set out in the following language of the will:

> My separate real property, hereinabove referred to in III A., including fee, surface, minerals, royalties, and mixed, and hereby intending to include all the rest, remainder and residue of my estate, not heretofore disposed of, I hereby give, devise and bequeath to my beloved husband, George E. Donalson, III., a Life Estate. My said husband is to enjoy the use and benefits of said properties, including the income derived from said properties, said income to become his separate property as paid. As stated,

my said husband is to enjoy the use and benefits of said properties and *to do with as he sees fit* for the rest of his life, with reversion of the corpus of said properties upon his death as follows:

A. To my beloved niece, Olga Prather Singleton, one fourth (1/4) of the reversionary interest from the life estate left to my husband. Should the said Olga Prather Singleton predecease George P. Donalson, III., then her one fourth (1/4) of said reversionary interest shall vest in the natural children of Olga Prather Singleton, living at the time of the death of George E. Donalson, III., share and share alike[.] (emphasis added).

In similar fashion, the will gives a one-fourth "reversionary interest" each to other nieces, and a one-eighth "reversionary interest" each to a grandniece and grandnephew.[51] In describing the life estate, the will expressly gives George the right to enjoy the "use and benefits" of that property, including the "income" therefrom. The will further provides that the income becomes George's separate property when paid to him. Significantly, George may "do with [the properties in the life estate] as he sees fit for the rest of his life."

As a general rule subject to exceptions, a life tenant may not dispose of the corpus of the estate, and oil and gas royalties and bonuses generally are considered corpus. *See Moore v. Vines*, 474 S.W.2d 437, 439 (Tex.1971); *Clyde v. Hamilton*, 414 S.W.2d 434, 438 (Tex. 1967). Exceptions exist. *Hudspeth v. Hudspeth*, 756 S.W.2d 29, 31 (Tex. App.–San Antonio 1988, writ denied). For example, under the open mine doctrine, which is applied only to leases executed by the testator and in effect at her death, royalties and bonuses belong to the life tenant. *Riley v. Riley*, 972 S.W.2d 149, 155 (Tex. App.—Texarkana 1998, no pet.) (citing *Clyde v. Hamilton*, 414 S.W.2d 434 (Tex. 1967)). Another exception arises when the testator expressly says otherwise in the will; controlling effect is given to the intent of the creator of the life estate. *See Hudspeth*, 756 S.W.2d at 31.

Where a will contains a provision that upon a certain contingency an estate given to one shall pass to another, the law favors the first taker. *Id.* at 33. Here, George is the first taker—he "takes" before the remainder interests. The testator's language should be construed so as to grant to the first taker the greatest estate which, by fair construction, the will is capable of passing. *Id.*

The summary judgment motion asserts that the will gave George a life estate with "additional powers of receiving all income from the mineral and royalty interests," as well as the power of disposition. A will creates a life estate where the language of the will manifests an intention on the testator's part to pass to the first taker a right to possess, use, or enjoy the property during his life. *Miller*

---

[51] The use of the term "reversionary," rather than "remainder," suggests life estate terms were not necessarily used precisely in the will.

v. Wilson, 888 S.W.2d 158, 161 (Tex. App.—El Paso 1994, writ denied). The testator may give a power of disposition with the life estate; this power is not necessarily inconsistent with the creation of a life estate. Edds v. Mitchell, 143 Tex. 307, 184 S.W.2d 823, 825 (Tex. 1945). Where a life tenant has unqualified power to dispose of property during his lifetime, the remainder beneficiaries have no justiciable interest in any property except that which has not been disposed of at the life tenant's death. In re Estate of Gibson, 893 S.W.2d 749, 751 (Tex. App.—Texarkana 1995, no writ). The power to dispose of the property in the life estate does not necessarily divest the remaindermen of all title or right to the proceeds derived from the sale of the property. Unless otherwise provided in the will, whatever is not disposed of when the life tenant dies will pass to the remaindermen. Edds, 184 S.W.2d at 825-26.

In determining whether Ruth's will gives George the power of consumption and disposition of royalties and bonuses, we are to give words their normal meaning in light of the testator's intent. See Barker v. Rosenthal, 875 S.W.2d 779, 781 (Tex. App.—Houston [1st Dist.] 1994, no writ). Under this will, George "is to enjoy" the described property's "use and benefits," including "income," and is to "do [with the property] as he sees fit for the rest of his life." Ruth specifically included "royalties" in describing the property she was giving to George. Although appellants argue the word "income," as used in oil and gas law, does not include royalties and bonuses, we must look to the meaning of the word in the context of this will. The term "benefits," which the will says includes "income," describes advantages flowing from the life estate property, such as income, rents, bonuses, revenues, and royalties. As used in the will, neither "benefits" nor "income" has a specialized or technical meaning. Further, the will imposes no limitation on George's use of the "benefits" during his lifetime, and the will contains no instructions to impound bonuses or royalties for the sole use of the remaindermen.

In Hudspeth, the San Antonio court of appeals considered the extent of the powers of a life tenant in the context of a will. Hudspeth, 756 S.W.2d at 29. The husband willed his wife "all rents, revenues and income of every kind and character derived from the real estate belonging to [him] at the time of [his] death during the span of [his wife's] natural life, or until her marriage." Id. at 30. The will provided that after payment of debts against properties in the estate, "the balance of said rental payments shall be the sole and separate property" of the wife "to apply as in her judgment may seem wise and proper." Id. The trial court construed the Hudspeth will to give the wife a life estate entitling her to receive and retain all income of every kind from the realty, including mineral lease bonuses and royalties.

The Hudspeth children contended they were entitled to the royalties and bonuses as a matter of law, because as a general rule royalties and bonuses are part of the corpus and a life tenant has no right to consume them. Id. at 31. The

San Antonio court indicated this general rule should be applied unless a contrary intent appeared in the instrument creating the life estate. *Id*. at 32. Construing the will's language, the court concluded the devise expressly directed that the wife (life tenant) could do what she deemed "wise and proper" with any and all income from the realty, and with no requirement to impound royalties and bonuses. Further, the court said the word "income" was not used in a strictly legal sense. The wife's conduct in consuming the bonuses and royalties was held to be in accord with the testator's intent.

Similarly, in this will the phrase "to enjoy the use and benefits of the property," and the language to "do with [the property] as he sees fit," indicate George may enjoy the use and benefit of the royalties and bonuses as he sees fit until his death. His power of disposition limits appellants' rights. *See* Montgomery v. Browder, 930 S.W.2d 772, 777 (Tex. App.—Amarillo 1996, writ denied). George's conduct in using the bonuses and royalties for his benefit is in accord with the testator's intent as expressed in her will. The trial court did not err in granting the summary judgment.

Given our disposition of issue one, we need not address issue two. The summary judgment is affirmed.

NOTES & QUESTIONS:

1. Due to the finite nature of the life estate, there are special rules to consider regarding the nature of the relationship between the life estate and the future interest or interests. One issue that is illustrated by the Davis v. Bond and Thompson v. Thompson cases above is the concept of waste. The life tenant must maintain the property and can possess and use the land in a manner consistent with its normal use.

   There are different forms of waste.

   Affirmative waste occurs when the life tenant makes use of the land in a way that harms its value. The typical situation involving affirmative waste is illustrated in the cases involving extraction of natural resources. The Open Mine Doctrine from the *Thompson* case is also important to consider as it might prevent a life tenant from being liable for damages for waste.

   Permissive waste occurs when inaction by the life tenant allows some harm to occur that will impact the value of the land. Permissive waste could occur when repairs need to be made and the life tenant's failure to make such repairs results in additional damage occurring.

Ameliorative waste occurs when the life tenant takes steps to substantially alter the property that results in an increased value. Although the value may increase, the future interest is entitled to receive the land and any improvements thereon in a certain condition. Just because the value may increase does not mean the change will be legally acceptable. Typically, the change will be permissible only if due to changed circumstances the land is no longer useful or useable in its current state.

As seen in the Singleton v. Donalson case, the life tenant can be granted additional powers which change the nature of the relationship. Why would Ruth Donalson have wanted to allow her husband George to do more than the normal life tenant?

2. All revenues, rents, and income derived from the land belong to the life tenant. This rule with respect to income from rental of the land is the same whether the land is rented out in whole or in part, or used by the life tenant in a business of his own.

3. Taxes on the property are also the responsibility of the life tenant. The payment of taxes is consistent with the fact that the life tenant has dominion and control over the land along with the use and enjoyment thereof.

4. The life tenant is not entitled to reimbursement for expenses incurred for ordinary repairs while using and occupying the property. The life tenant has a duty to maintain.

5. A life tenant does not have to make principle payments on a mortgage taken out by the life tenant and future interest holder. However, the life tenant is responsible for interest. Finally, the life tenant is not obligated to pay for insurance on the property.

6. At the time of creation, both the life estate and future interest or interests have a value. If a value is needed, the court is going to look at life expectancy tables as well as the present value of money to put a dollar figure on the value of the property interest of the life tenant vs. the property interest of the holder of the remainder or reversion in fee simple absolute. In practice, you'll hire an economist to do this for you!

b. The Fee Tail

At common law, an estate fee tail was an estate to an individual and his or her descendants, rather than his or her heirs generally. In order to create the fee tail, slightly different wording was used. Instead of the words "*O to A and his heirs,*" the conveyance would read "*O to A and the heirs of his body.*" Essentially, what was created was a life estate in *A* (the grantee) and a life estate to his or her children at death and then upon each child's death a life estate to that child's children and so on until there were no "children" to take the fee tail.[52]

The fee tail arises in old English literature like *Pride and Prejudice*[53] or in recent TV shows like the PBS hit *Downton Abbey*.[54] The fee tail is truly a feudal remnant that really no longer lives in harmony with the modern trend favoring alienability of land. The fee tail tied up land in bloodlines for hundreds of years. Because this was a series of life estates, often the life tenant had no incentive to make improvements or increase the value of the land. Additionally, due to the nature of the fee tail, the interest often could not be used as collateral because of the uncertainty of the duration of ownership.

Most states abolished the fee tail. However, in abolishing the fee tail, states have given different treatment to conveyances containing the language that would have created a fee tail estate. You must look to state statutes and constitutions to determine how the particular jurisdiction will handle the conveyance.[55]

Texas Const. Art. I, § 26 Perpetuities and monopolies; primogeniture or entailments

> Perpetuities and monopolies are contrary to the genius of a free government, and shall never be allowed, nor shall the law of primogeniture or entailments ever be in force in this State.

---

[52] Wendel, *supra* note 17, at 38. *See also* Restatement (First) of Property §§ 14-15 (1936).

[53] Austen, Jane. Pride and Prejudice (1813).

[54] One of the main plot lines for the first season of the show revolved around a fee tail male that was created to pass the property to the male heirs of the Earldom of Grantham. There were fee tails that could be restricted to only male heirs or only female heirs.

[55] Theoretically it is still possible to create a fee tail in Delaware, Maine, Massachusetts, and Rhode Island. However, the laws in those states allow the fee tail owner to easily avoid such an estate by entering into a two-step transaction referred to as a "straw" transaction. We will discuss straw transactions in more detail when we cover joint ownership or concurrent ownership of property.

The Texas Constitution abolished these estates in Texas.[56] A conveyance that would have created an estate in fee tail at common law is now construed as creating a fee simple estate.[57] While the common law interpretation of the conveyance actually created a future interest in the heirs of *A*'s body, this is no longer the case. The majority of states treat the fee tail in the same manner as Texas.

3. Defeasible Estates: Estates That Might End

a. Introduction to Defeasible Fee Estates

An estate in fee simple defeasible is an estate in fee simple that is subject to special limitation (defined in § 23), a condition subsequent (defined in § 24), an executory limitation (defined in § 25) or a combination of such restrictions.[58]

As introduced above, the fee simple estates and the finite estates may be absolute or defeasible. Although we did not speak specifically of the "life estate absolute" when discussing the life estate material, that was essentially our focus.[59] Our discussion involved a life estate that would end only by the death of the life tenant and not some additional condition or event, so in a sense, it is absolute.

The difference between an absolute estate and a defeasible estate has to with a restriction beyond the standard durational limitation that defines the estate. For example, the fee simple absolute has no durational limit. It will continue on forever if *O* could live forever. However, with the defeasible fee simple estate, some limitation or condition is placed on the fee simple absolute estate and transforms it into an estate that may end. If the conveyance begins with words that look like a fee simple estate but there is some limitation or

---

[56] Tex. Const. art. I, § 26.

[57] Reilly v. Huff, 335 S.W.2d 275, 280 (Tex. Civ. App.—San Antonio 1960, no writ) (construing repealed Tex. Rev. Civ. Statutes Art. 1291, predecessor to Tex. Prop. Code Ann. § 5.001) (Vernon 2006).

[58] Restatement (First) of Property § 16 (1936).

[59] However, lawyers do not refer to absolute life estates in that manner. They are simply referred to as life estates. The same may be said for the fee simple absolute. Most lawyers simply use the term *fee simple* when discussing the fee simple absolute, although that terminology is not precise. When the fee simple or life estate is defeasible, that particular designation must be included. For purposes of our class, you must use the full term *fee simple absolute* when referring to that particular estate and you will be expected to provide the complete name for any defeasible fee simple estate. With respect to the life estates, you may refer to the life estate "absolute" as merely a life estate (unless it is a life estate *pur autre vie*) but if the estate is some type of defeasible life estate, the complete name must also be given.

condition on the estate, it cannot be absolute but must be some type of defeasible fee simple estate.

The same holds true for the life estate. While the very nature of a life estate is that it must end when the life tenant dies, if a defeasible life estate is created the life estate will not last any longer than the life tenant's life but may terminate earlier upon the happening of some event or condition.

The use of defeasible estates is becoming less common in modern times and is extremely rare for a life estate. However, in the past the defeasible estate provided a means for the original owner of the property to restrict in some manner how the property would be used by the grantee[60] or how long the property would be held by the grantee depending on some event occurring or not occurring.[61] By allowing property owners to attach these types of restrictions on property being conveyed, these restrictions cause problems when the grantee wants to sell the property to someone else. Placing these restrictions on property causes a restraint on the alienability of the property.

Remember in Texas, as in most states, we favor the free alienability of property so that land can easily transfer from one owner to the next. Having some sort of restraint or limitation on the use of the property places a hurdle that is sometimes difficult to overcome. Restraints on alienability and the rules dealing with these issues are beyond the scope of this course. What we will focus on in this class is how to determine what particular present possessory defeasible estate has been created by the grant and what future interest exists. We will not cover the rules dictating whether or not these particular restrictions are actually valid.

b. Fee Simple Determinable vs. Fee Simple Subject to Condition Subsequent

(1) Fee Simple Determinable — Form of Limitation: An estate in fee simple determinable is created by any limitation that, in an otherwise effective conveyance of land,

  a. Creates an estate in fee simple; and
  b. Provides that the estate shall automatically expire upon the occurrence of a stated event.

---

[60] A conveyance might restrict the use of the land for a park or school or church. The conveyance might prohibit the sale of alcohol on the property. The cases we will cover will provide numerous examples of property owners controlling the use of the property in some manner within the terms of the grant.

[61] A conveyance might allow a woman to hold the property as long as she remains unmarried or unless she divorces. A conveyance might allow someone to hold the property as long as he does not smoke or drink alcohol.

Illustration:

1. *A*, owning Blackacre in fee simple absolute, transfers Blackacre "to *B* and his heirs so long as Town *C* remains unincorporated." *B* has an estate in fee simple determinable. *A* has a [future interest] despite the absence of specific words creating any interest in him. Town *C* is incorporated. *B*'s estate expires automatically and *A* becomes entitled forthwith to possession of Blackacre.[62]

A fee simple determinable (FSD) exists if a fee simple estate will terminate automatically and revert to the grantor on the occurrence of a stated event. A fee simple determinable may be created using "magic words" that indicate a durational limitation on the fee simple estate. The phrase "as long as" has been recognized as one of the "magic words" evidencing a fee simple determinable estate.[63] Other words that are recognized as "magic words" to create the fee simple determinable estate include "so long as," "until," "during," and "while." Again, the focus is on words that evidence some sort of duration of the estate.

The significance of this language is huge. If an FSD is created and the particular durational condition occurs, the present possessory estate automatically terminates and the future interest automatically becomes possessory without any action being taken on the part of the future interest holder.

Because of the presumption in Texas that a conveyance creates the largest possible estate (fee simple absolute), it is prudent practice to state an intent to create an FSD and to use the customarily recognized "magic words" to create such an estate.[64]

> **(2) Fee Simple Subject to a Condition Subsequent — Form of Limitation:** An estate in fee simple subject to a condition subsequent is created by any limitation that, in an otherwise effective conveyance of land,
>
> a. creates an estate in fee simple;
> b. provides that upon the occurrence of a stated event the conveyor or his successor in interest shall have the power to terminate the estate so created.

Illustration:

1. *A*, owning Blackacre in fee simple absolute, transfers Blackacre "to *B* and his heirs, but on condition that if liquor is sold upon the premises conveyed, *B*'s

---

[62] Restatement (First) of Property § 44 (1936).

[63] *See* Clark v. Perez, 679 S.W.2d 710, 712 (Tex. App.—San Antonio 1984, no writ).

[64] *See* Schwarz-Jordan, Inc. v. Delisle Construction Co., 569 S.W.2d 878, 881 (Tex. 1978).

estate shall be subject to *A*'s [future interest] for breach thereof." *B* sells liquor upon Blackacre. *A*, or his successor in interest, has the option of terminating the estate granted to B.[65]

The term "condition subsequent" denotes that part of the language of a conveyance, by virtue of which upon the occurrence of a stated event the conveyor, or his successor in interest, has the power to terminate the interest that has been created subject to the condition subsequent, but that will continue until this power is exercised.[66]

A fee simple subject to a condition subsequent (FSSCS) is a fee simple estate that may be cut short due to the occurrence of some condition. In determining whether a conveyance has created an FSSCS, the "magic words" used suggest a conditional termination of the estate rather than a durational one. The recognized "magic words" include "but if," "however if," "on condition that," and "provided that."

In order to further clarify the grantor's intent to create an FSSCS, it is prudent to include a clause expressly stating that *O* (the grantor) has the right to reenter and retake the property in the event the condition occurs. This aids in the distinction between the FSD and FSSCS and the creation of their respective future interests. Unlike the FSD, which terminates automatically upon the occurrence of the limitation, the FSSCS does not terminate automatically upon the occurrence of the condition but requires some affirmative steps to reenter and reclaim the property. In an FSSCS, the present possessory estate will continue even in the face of a violation of the condition unless and until the future interest holder takes some action.

Where the language is ambiguous as to whether the conveyance has created an FSD or FSSCS, the courts tend to favor an FSSCS because courts disfavor forfeiture of property.[67] The courts would rather make the future interest holder have to take some action to terminate the present possessory estate rather than allowing the automatic termination. However, if the conveyance is well crafted, an FSD may be created, enabling the automatic termination.

---

[65] Restatement (First) of Property § 45 (1936).

[66] *Id.* § 24.

[67] *See generally* Lawyers Trust Co. v. City of Houston, 359 S.W.2d 887 (Tex. 1962).

c. Fee Simple Subject to an Executory Interest (or Executory Limitation)

(1) Except as stated in Subsection (2), an estate in fee simple subject to an executory limitation exists when any limitation, in an otherwise effective conveyance of land,

 (a) Creates an estate in fee simple in a conveyee, or leaves an estate in fee simple in the conveyor or his successor in interest; and

 (b) Provides that the estate subject thererto, upon the occurrence of the stated event is to be divested, before the normal expiration thereof, in favor of another interest in a person other than the conveyor, or his successor in interest.

(2) Omitted.

Illustrations to Subsection (1):

1. *A*, owning Blackacre in fee simple absolute, transfers Blackacre "to *B* and his heirs but if *B* dies without issue surviving him at his death, then to *C* and his heirs." *A* creates in *B* an estate in fee simple subject to an executory limitation. [NOTE: This creates a shifting executory interest in *C*.]

2. *A*, owning Blackacre in fee simple absolute, transfers Blackacre "to *B* and his heirs from and after one year from the date of this instrument." *A* leaves in *A* an estate in fee simple subject to an executory limitation. [NOTE: This creates a springing executory interest in *B*.]

3. *A*, owning Blackacre in fee simple absolute, effectively devises Blackacre "to whichever of my brothers first arrives in the United States from Ireland." *A* dies survived by *B* as his sole heir. *A* leaves in *B*, as *A*'s successor in interest, an estate in fee simple subject to executory limitation. [NOTE: This is simply illustrating the point that once *A* has created the fee simple subject to executory limitation, it is an estate of inheritance but the successor can only receive what *A* had.][68]

The term "executory limitation" denotes that part of the language of a conveyance, by virtue of which

 (a) an estate in fee simple determinable, . . . or an estate in fee simple conditional, concurrently with its expiration, is to be succeeded forthwith

---

[68] Restatement (First) of Property § 46 (1936).

by another interest in a person other than the conveyor or his successor in interest.[69]

The fee simple subject to an executory interest or executory limitation (FSSEI) is another fee simple estate that may be cut short by some condition, event or duration. However, the only way that this particular defeasible fee estate may be created is if the future interest will be held by a third party—not the transferor/grantor and not the grantee A. The FSSEI looks a lot like an FSD or FSSCS, and is cut short by the same type of limitations, but the difference is that once the condition occurs to terminate the fee simple estate, the estate goes to a third party (transferee), not back to O (transferor).

If the future interest will be held by a third party, then there is no need to focus on any "magic words" because there are no requisite "magic words" to create this type of defeasible estate. Furthermore, the FSSEI is treated in the same manner as an FSD and the present possessory estate will automatically terminate upon the occurrence of the event, condition or duration. Texas retains all three of the defeasible estates although some states have not.[70]

Any estate may be made to be *defeasible*, meaning it will terminate, prior to its natural end point, upon the occurrence of some specified future event. For example, a life estate ends naturally at the death of the life tenant, whereas a defeasible life estate might end earlier than that (as in a conveyance that states, "*O* to *A* for life so long as the property is used only for residential purposes"). The most common defeasible freehold estates are the fees simple defeasible ("defeasible fees," as we will sometimes call them).

Every fee simple determinable is accompanied by a future interest. In the ordinary case the future interest is retained by the transferor, *O* in the above example, or his heirs, and called a *possibility of reverter*.[71] The possibility of reverter may be expressly retained or, as in the above example, arise by operation of law. It arises by operation of law because *O* has transferred less than his entire interest in Blackacre when he creates a determinable fee in the School Board.

d. Defeasible Fee Estate Examples

The following conveyances create fee simple determinable, fee simple subject to condition subsequent, and fee simple subject to executory limitation (or interest) estates.

---

[72]*Id.* § 25.

[70] Some states have chosen to statutorily abolish the distinction between the FSD and FSSCS, making all defeasible fee estates with a future interest in the transferor FSSCSs and all defeasible fee estates with a future interest in the transferee FSSELs.

[71] When a future interest following a determinable fee is created in a *transferee*, it is called an *executory interest. See* Gutierrez v. Rodriguez.

1. Alec grants Blackacre to Buzz and his heirs, but if the land is used for other than agricultural purposes, then Alec may reenter and resume his prior estate.

   Buzz has an FSSCS

2. Adam conveys to Zelda for so long as Zelda does not serve alcohol on the premises.

   Zelda has an FSD

3. Albert grants conveys Blackacre to Bill until Bill gets marries, then to Charlie and his heirs.

   Bill has an FSSEL

Consider the classification of the conveyance in the following case. What are the magic words? What can we determine to be in the intent of the grantor based on the language?

Mahrenholz v. County Board of School Trustees
Appellate Court of Illinois, 1981
417 N.E.2d 138

JONES, J., delivered the opinion of the court.

This case involves an action to quiet title to real property located in Lawrence County, Illinois. Its resolution depends on the judicial construction of language in a conveyance of that property. The case is before us on the pleadings, plaintiffs' third amended complaint having been dismissed by a final order. The pertinent facts are taken from the pleadings.

On March 18, 1941, W. E. and Jennie Hutton executed a warranty deed in which they conveyed certain land, to be known here as the Hutton School grounds, to the trustees of School District No. 1, the predecessors of the defendants in this action. The deed provided that "this land to be used for school purpose only; otherwise to revert to Grantors herein." [Ed. Note: The Huttons owned a 40-acre parcel of land. They executed this deed, conveying 1½ acres out of the 40-acre tract they owned, to be used for the school. The Huttons retained a future interest in that 1½-acre tract. The Huttons also retained ownership of the remaining 38½-acre tract.] W. E. Hutton died intestate on July 18, 1951, and Jennie Hutton died intestate on February 18, 1969. The Huttons left as their only legal heir their son Harry E. Hutton.

The property conveyed by the Huttons became the site of the Hutton School. Community Unit School District No. 20 succeeded to the grantee of the deed and held classes in the building constructed upon the land until May 30, 1973. After that date, children were transported to classes held at other facilities operated by the District. The District has used the property since then for storage purposes only.

Earl and Madeline Jacqmain executed a warranty deed on October 9, 1959, conveying to the plaintiffs over 390 acres of land in Lawrence County and which included the 40-acre tract from which the Hutton School grounds were taken. The deed from the Jacqmains to the plaintiffs excepted the 1 ½ acre tract that was the Hutton School grounds, but purported to convey the disputed future interest in the 1 ½ acre tract.

On May 7, 1977, Harry E. Hutton, son and sole heir of W. E. and Jennie Hutton, conveyed to the plaintiffs all of his interest in the Hutton School land. This document was filed in the recorder's office of Lawrence County on September 7, 1977. On September 6, 1977, Harry Hutton disclaimed his interest in the property in favor of the defendants. The disclaimer was in the form of a written document entitled "Disclaimer and Release." It contained the legal description of the Hutton School grounds and recited that Harry E. Hutton disclaimed and released any possibility of reverter or right of entry for condition broken, or other similar interest, in favor of the County Board of School Trustees for Lawrence County, Illinois, successor to the Trustees of School District No. 1 of Lawrence County, Illinois. The document further recited that it was made for the purpose of releasing and extinguishing any right Harry E. Hutton may have had in the "interest retained by W. E. Hutton and Jennie Hutton in that deed to the Trustees of School District No. 1, Lawrence County, Illinois dated March 18, 1941, and filed on the same date. The disclaimer was filed in the recorder's office of Lawrence County on October 4, 1977.

The plaintiffs filed a complaint in the circuit court of Lawrence County in which they sought to quiet title to the school property in themselves, by virtue of the interests acquired from the Jacqmains. On March 21, 1979, the trial court entered an order dismissing this complaint. In the order the court found that the

> "[W]arranty deed dated March 18, 1941, from W. E. Hutton and Jennie Hutton to the Trustees of School District No. 1, conveying land here concerned, created a fee simple subject to a condition subsequent followed by the right of entry for condition broken, rather than a determinable fee followed by a possibility of reverter."

Plaintiffs have perfected an appeal to this court.

The basic issue presented by this appeal is whether the trial court correctly concluded that the plaintiffs could not have acquired any interest in the school property from the Jacqmains or from Harry Hutton. Resolution of this issue must turn upon the legal interpretation of the language contained in the March 18, 1941, deed from W. E. and Jennie Hutton to the Trustees of School District No. 1: "this land to be used for school purpose only; otherwise to revert to Grantors herein." In addition to the legal effect of this language we must consider the alienability of the interest created and the effect of subsequent deeds.

The parties appear to be in agreement that the 1941 deed from the Huttons conveyed a defeasible fee simple estate to the grantee, and gave rise to a future interest in the grantors, and that it did not convey a fee simple absolute, subject to a covenant. The fact that provision was made for forfeiture of the estate conveyed should the land cease to be used for school purposes suggests that this view is correct.

The future interest remaining in this grantor or his estate can only be a possibility of reverter or a right of re-entry for condition broken. As neither interest may be transferred by will nor by inter vivos conveyance (Ill. Rev. Stat. 1979, ch. 30, par. 37b), and as the land was being used for school purposes in 1959 when the Jacqmains transferred their interest in the school property to the plaintiffs, the trial court correctly ruled that the plaintiffs could not have acquired any interest in that property from the Jacqmains by the deed of October 9, 1959.

Consequently this court must determine whether the plaintiffs could have acquired an interest in the Hutton School grounds from Harry Hutton. The resolution of this issue depends on the construction of the language of the 1941 deed of the Huttons to the school district. As urged by the defendants, and as the trial court found, that deed conveyed a fee simple subject to a condition subsequent, followed by a right of re-entry for condition broken. As argued by the plaintiffs, on the other hand, the deed conveyed a fee simple determinable followed by a possibility of reverter. In either case, the grantor and his heirs retain an interest in the property which may become possessory if the condition is broken. The type of interest held governs the mode of reinvestment with title if reinvestment is to occur. If the grantor had a possibility of reverter, he or his heirs become the owner of the property by operation of law as soon as the condition is broken. If he has a right of re-entry for condition broken, he or his heirs become the owner of the property only after they act to retake the property.

It is alleged, and we must accept, that classes were last held in the Hutton School in 1973. Harry Hutton, sole heir of the grantors, did not act to legally retake the premises but instead conveyed his interest in that land to the plaintiffs in 1977. If Harry Hutton had only a naked right of re-entry for condition broken, then he could not be the owner of that property until he had legally re-entered the land. Since he took no steps for a legal re-entry, he had only a right of re-entry in 1977, and that right cannot be conveyed inter vivos. On the other hand, if Harry

Hutton had a possibility of reverter in the property, then he owned the school property as soon as it ceased to be used for school purposes. Therefore, assuming (1) that cessation of classes constitutes "abandonment of school purposes" on the land, (2) that the conveyance from Harry Hutton to the plaintiffs was legally correct, and (3) that the conveyance was not pre-empted by Hutton's disclaimer in favor of the school district, the plaintiffs could have acquired an interest in the Hutton School grounds if Harry Hutton had inherited a possibility of reverter from his parents.

The difference between a fee simple determinable (or determinable fee) and a fee simple subject to a condition subsequent, is solely a matter of judicial interpretation of the words of a grant. As Blackstone explained, there is a fundamental theoretical difference between a conditional estate, such as a fee simple subject to a condition subsequent, and a limited estate, such as a fee simple determinable.

A fee simple determinable may be thought of as a limited grant, while a fee simple subject to a condition subsequent is an absolute grant to which a condition is appended. In other words, a grantor should give a fee simple determinable if he intends to give property for so long as it is needed for the purposes for which it is given and no longer, but he should employ a fee simple subject to a condition subsequent if he intends to compel compliance with a condition by penalty of a forfeiture.

Based on this, the Huttons would have created a fee simple determinable if they had allowed the school district to retain the property so long as or while it was used for school purposes, or until it ceased to be so used. Similarly, a fee simple subject to a condition subsequent would have arisen had the Huttons given the land upon condition that or provided that it be used for school purposes. In the 1941 deed, though the Huttons gave the land "to be used for school purpose only, otherwise to revert to Grantors herein," no words of temporal limitation, or terms of express condition, were used in the grant.

The plaintiffs argue that the word "only" should be construed as a limitation rather than a condition. The defendants respond that where ambiguous language is used in a deed, the courts of Illinois have expressed a constructional preference for a fee simple subject to a condition subsequent.

We believe that a close analysis of the wording of the original grant shows that the grantors intended to create a fee simple determinable followed by a possibility of reverter. Here, the use of the word "only" immediately following the grant "for school purpose" demonstrates that the Huttons wanted to give the land to the school district only as long as it was needed and no longer. The language "this land to be used for school purpose only" is an example of a grant which contains a limitation within the granting clause. It suggests a limited grant, rather than a full grant subject to a condition, and thus, both theoretically and linguistically, gives rise to a fee simple determinable.

The second relevant clause furnishes plaintiffs' position with additional support. It cannot be argued that the phrase "otherwise to revert to grantors herein" is inconsistent with a fee simple subject to a condition subsequent. Nor does the word "revert" automatically create a possibility of reverter. But, in combination with the preceding phrase, the provisions by which possession is returned to the grantors seem to trigger a mandatory return rather than a permissive return because it is not stated that the grantor "may" re-enter the land.

The terms used In the 1941 deed, although imprecise, were designed to allow the property to be used for a single purpose, namely, for "school purpose." The Huttons intended to have the land back if it were ever used otherwise. Upon a grant of exclusive use followed by an express provision for reverter when that use ceases, courts and commentators have agreed that a fee simple determinable, rather than a fee simple subject to a condition subsequent, is created.

Thus, authority from this State and others indicates that the grant in the Hutton deed did in fact create a fee simple determinable.

We hold, therefore, that the 1941 deed from W. E. and Jennie Hutton to the Trustees of School District No. 1 created a fee simple determinable in the trustees followed by a possibility of reverter in the Huttons and their heirs. Accordingly, the trial court erred in dismissing plaintiffs' third amended complaint which followed its holding that the plaintiffs could not have acquired any interest in the Hutton School property from Harry Hutton. We must therefore reverse and remand this cause to the trial court for further proceedings.

Reversed and remanded.

Batesburg-Leesville School District Number 3 v. Annie B. Tarrant, et al.
Court of Appeals of South Carolina, 1987
361 S.E.2d 343

GARDNER, J.

This case involves the construction of a deed to School District Number 18 of Saluda County. Respondent Batesburg-Leesville School District Number 3 (the school district), as successor to the original grantee of the deed in question, brought this declaratory judgment action to determine the ownership of the subject property.

The above-named respondents-appellants contend that they are co-tenant reversioners under the deed. The consideration expressed by the deed is "for and in consideration of the use by the hereinafter mentioned grantee of the tract of land herein conveyed for the uses and purposes mentioned by the trustees of School District Number 18 as trustees of School District Number 18 of Saluda County." The granting clause of the deed conveys the property to "School District

Number 18 of Saluda County, State of South Carolina, to be used for school purposes." The habendum clause is, "to have and to hold . . . the said premises before mentioned unto the said School District Number 18 of Saluda County, State of South Carolina, so long as it is used as a building site on which is erected a School Building." The special warranty of the deed and all renunciations of dower are limited by the same language or essentially the same language as the habendum clause.

The appealed order construed the deed as conveying to the school district a fee simple determinable estate which terminated when the school district ceased to use the property for school purposes and that thereupon the fee to the property reverted to the original grantors or their successors in title. The school district appeals. We affirm.

The school district first contends that the granting clause conveyed a fee simple absolute estate and that the grantors merely stated the purposes for the conveyance and did not restrict or place any condition on the fee simple absolute title conveyed. To support this thesis the school district relies on the familiar rule that once the fee is conveyed by the granting clause, it cannot be cut down by subsequent language in the deed. The school district argues that there is no case law in South Carolina which requires words of inheritance to be in the granting clause or habendum of a deed in order for it to convey fee simple absolute title to a school district. Additionally, the school district quotes Professor David H. Means' article entitled Words of Inheritance and Deeds of Land in South Carolina: A Title Examiner's Guide, 5 S.C.L.Q. 313, 326 (1952), in which it is stated, "Words of inheritance or succession are unnecessary in the conveyance by deed of a fee simple estate to the United States or to a State or subdivision thereof." Under this authority the school district asserts the granting clause of the land conveyed a fee simple estate.

For the reasons stated below, we hold that the above rule by Professor Means is not applicable to a situation where a clear intent to the contra is manifested by the deed when read as a whole.

In County of Abbeville v. Knox, 267 S.C. 38, 225 S.E. (2d) 863 (1976), the court referred to the case of Byars v. Cherokee County, 237 S.C. 548, 118 S.E. (2d) 324 (1961) and noted that the opinion in Byars did not contain a full record of the granting or habendum clauses of the deed. The court referenced the transcript of record of the Byars case and then held:

In Byars v. Cherokee County, supra, the grant was to Cherokee County without any words of inheritance or succession. The habendum clause contained the following language:

> "TO HAVE AND TO HOLD all and singular the said premises before mentioned unto the said Cherokee County—its— successors and Assigns forever.

"'Provided that in case the said lot of land shall cease to be used by the County of Cherokee for curing house purposes that the said Forrest Byars shall have the right to repurchase the said lot of land and have same reconveyed to him upon the payment of the said purchase price of $ 50.00, Cherokee County to have the right to remove therefrom at that time any improvements placed on the said land if desired.'"

This Court held in *Byars* that the provision in the habendum created a condition subsequent, and upon the happening of the event stated entitled the grantor to a reconveyance of the property.

We hold *Byars* to be determinative of the school district's argument that the granting clause of the deed conveyed a fee which could not be qualified by later provisions of the deed.

We further hold that the estate conveyed by the deed must be determined from the whole deed including the habendum clause. The cardinal rule of construction of a deed is to ascertain and effectuate the intention of the parties, unless that intention contravenes some well-settled rule of law or public policy. In ascertaining such intention the deed must be construed as a whole, and effect given to every part thereof, if such can be done consistently with the law. And also, the rule is well established in this state that where an indefinite estate is conveyed by the granting clause of a deed, resort may be had to the habendum clause for the purpose of ascertaining the intention of the grantors.

And we further hold that the deed, when read as a whole, is unambiguous.

The clear intent of the grantors was, we hold, to convey the property to the school district so long as the land be used for a school. The school district admittedly ceased to use the property for school purposes. The learned trial judge correctly ruled that the deed granted a fee simple determinable estate and when the land ceased to be used for school purposes, the fee reverted to the respondents-appellants. And we so hold.

For the reasons stated, the appealed order is affirmed.

Affirmed.

NOTES & QUESTIONS:

1. So what's the big deal? That is often the attitude of the law student being introduced to the magic words and subtle differences of the defeasible fee estates. While at first glance it may seem like surely in our modern world these little words could not possibly be important, further study will prove otherwise. A November 4, 2013, article in *Texas Lawyer* reported a lawsuit brought by a 79-year-old widow who claimed she had to go back to work after her husband's estate planning attorney did not

clearly effectuate her late husband's intent in his estate planning documents. The woman was suing the lawyer and his law firm, alleging negligence and negligent misrepresentation.[72]

2. When Baylor University acquired property from Dr. John Harrington's heirs, the University had to agree to terms that the building would not be torn down for at least 15 years. In 1974, the Harrington House became the first on-campus faculty dining facility and remained as the faculty dining facility until the fall of 2008 when the new dining facility opened. The Victorian style Harrington House still remains on the Baylor campus.[73]

3. Conditions on gifts of personal property also occur. In December 2008, Princeton University finally ended a long legal battle over a monetary gift that established an endowment to "educate graduate students for a career in government."[74]

4. *The Deseret Morning News* carried a story out of Provo, Utah, reporting that a school crisis was over.[75] What was the crisis? Title companies missed two handwritten deeds executed by Ed Loose in 1898 and 1910 that conveyed almost an acre of land in two parts. Both parcels were conveyed with the specific condition that the land always remain a playground for the elementary school or be returned to the family.

The school district closed the Maeser Elementary School in 2002 and it was purchased by a nonprofit housing authority to save the historic school building and redevelop the land. After millions of dollars in grant money had been invested in the project, the deeds were discovered by an heir of Ed Loose, his great-grandson Ed Peterson. Mr. Peterson believed his great-grandfather would have approved of the project so title insurance proceeds paid for memorials on the land for Charles Edwin Loose and Mary Jane Loose. Additional funds will go to a scholarship fund in the name of Edwin Peterson.

---

[72] Inadmissible: Estate Planning Suit Filed, Texas Lawyer, Nov. 4, 2013.

[73] This Old House: The History and Future of Harrington House, The Baylor Line, Summer 2008.

[74] Lewin, Tamar. Princeton Settles Money Battle over Gift, New York Times, www.nytimes.com (Dec. 11, 2008).

[75] Walch, Tad. Maeser School Crisis Over, Deseret Morning News, Sept. 25, 2007. Available at http://www.deseretnews.com/article/695212965/Maeser-School-crisis-over.html.

The executive director of the housing authority was shocked to learn of the condition. The officials at the title company stated that it was not uncommon to stop a title search before 100 years. According to the title company a possibility of reverter as the one contained in the Loose deeds is extremely rare. The vice-president of the title company stated, "I would have to say, in my 30 years in this business, this is the first time I've seen a right of reverter anywhere but in a law school exam. These type of things don't happen in today's world." Evidently, he was wrong about that.

5. Because of the harsh consequences of the differences in the magic words used, or the lack of clarity, some states have chosen to do away with the distinction between fee simple determinable and fee simple subject to condition subsequent. In those states, by statute the legislature has changed all defeasible fee estates with the future interest in the grantor to be a fee simple subject to condition subsequent, which prevents automatic forfeiture of title. In those states, the only automatic forfeiture of title occurs if a valid fee simple subject to executory interest is created with the future interest in another grantee. However, the vast majority of states have maintained the distinction between the fee simple determinable and fee simple subject to condition subsequent.[76]

While most states have not abolished the legal classifications, there is a preference for the fee simple subject to condition subsequent. If there is an ambiguity that can be resolved in favor of the fee simple subject to condition subsequent then it will be classified as such. The rationale is that there is a lesser chance of forfeiture of title because the present possessory estate will not end automatically.

6. The issue of substantial compliance with a condition was raised in the Miller v. ATSF case.[77] At the conclusion of the court's opinion, in dicta, the court stated that even if classified as a defeasible fee estate the actions of the railroad would constitute substantial compliance with the condition. So, how closely must the condition be followed? Should close be good enough? Courts have been struggling with this concept. Once the

---

[76] *See* Cal. Civ. Code § 885.020 (West 2007) and Ky. Rev. Stat. Ann. § 381.218 (2006) for examples of state statutes abolishing the fee simple determinable. The new Restatement also proposes eliminating the distinction between these two present estates, creating the "fee simple defeasible," which would be a present interest that terminates upon the happening of a condition or event that may or may not occur. Restatement (Third) of Property, Wills and Other Donative Transfers § 24.3 (Council Draft No. 6, 2008).

[77] 325 F. Supp. 604 (E.D. Mo. 1971).

legal classification is determined, often there is a fact question to follow regarding the meaning of the condition and whether it has been violated. While most courts will not say that close is good enough, often the appellate courts will construe the condition in such a way as to find compliance, again in an effort to avoid forfeiture of title.

7. Remember *Texas Electric Railway*, where the court was faced with Neale's final argument that if it was a fee simple conveyance it was a defeasible fee estate. If the court had classified the present possessory estate in that manner, he would have had a valid argument that the present estate terminated and as the holder of a future interest he was entitled to possession. The Texas Supreme Court managed to give effect to all of the language of the conveyance while still avoiding forfeiture of title. This was done by classifying the language as a covenant rather than a condition. The nonpossessory interest of covenants will be covered in depth in a later chapter. However, it is important to note at this time that violation of a covenant does not result in termination of the present possessory estate. Violation of a covenant can result in injunctive relief or damages for diminished market value of the land. Only conditions can cause the present possessory estate to actually terminate.

Think about *Mahrenholz*. How would the outcome have been different for the parties if the language could have been interpreted to be a covenant rather than a condition? What is different in the language in *Texas Electric, Mahrenholz, Miller,* and *Batesburg* to result in the different classifications?

Keeping all of this in mind, how would you classify the conveyance in the following case? Do you agree with the court's classification? Why or why not?

Porter Williamson et al. v. Dr. Allen Grizzard et al.
Supreme Court of Tennessee, 1965
215 Tenn. 544

Opinion by Justice WHITE.

The complainants, appellants here, in this case are the Trustees and the Manse Committee of the Cumberland Presbyterian Church at Goodlettsville. The appellees, defendants below, are two of the heirs at law of R. W. Grizzard and wife, Annie E. Grizzard, as well as some of the heirs at law of L. Hinton Grizzard and wife, Elizabeth Grizzard. The unknown heirs of both R. W. Grizzard and wife, and L. Hinton Grizzard and wife were made parties defendant to the suit.

This suit concerns a provision of a deed by which, many years ago, R. W. Grizzard and wife conveyed certain described property to the Cumberland Presbyterian Church at Goodlettsville. The provision reads as follows:

> "To have and told [and to hold] said lot with the improvements and everything pertaining thereto to the said church forever. Provided the following conditions are complied with, said lot of land with improvements thereon is to be used by said church as a parsonage and to be known as L. Linton [Hinton] and Elizabeth Grizzard Memorial Parsonage. Should said property cease to be needed as a parsonage for said Church, said property may be rented or leased and the proceeds realized therefrom may be applied to the support of a pastor or pulpit supply for said church. Should said property be used for any other purpose than above specified or should it cease to be used for the purposes above specified for a period of five consecutive years, then this conveyance to said church will be null and void and title to said property will become vested in the heirs at law of the said L. Hinton Grizzard, deceased, or their legal representatives."

The bill alleges that the property in question had been used for a church manse or parsonage for many years. The church parsonage had previously been located in a residential area, however, it is now surrounded by purely commercial property which makes it unsuited for the intended use, *i.e.*, a church manse.

Appellants seek to have the property sold free of the aforesaid provision with the express understanding that the proceeds of the sale be re-invested in another manse or parsonage for the Goodlettsville Cumberland Presbyterian Church to be known as the L. Hinton and Elizabeth Grizzard Memorial Parsonage, which new parsonage would be located in a more desirable residential district, the deed to such parsonage to contain the same provisions as to reversion as does the deed in question.

A demurrer was filed to the bill by the appellees (defendants), which was sustained by the chancellor on the following grounds:

(1) The court has no jurisdiction to divest the defendants of their rights in and to the property described in the bill and to create for them the same rights in other property without their consent.

(2) The deed contained in the bill creates the rights of the parties, and the interest of these defendants cannot be divested without their consent and approval.

(3) The bill seeks to enforce a penalty of forfeiture against the defendants by divesting them of their interest in the property, without their consent.

From the unfavorable ruling of the chancellor the complainants applied for and obtained a writ of error from the author of this opinion, under authority of T.C.A. sec. 27-601 et seq.

Errors to the action of the chancellor have been assigned which present the basic question for our determination, *i.e.*, whether, in light of the habendum provision of the deed, the law permits the sale of the described land with its restrictions and reversionary interests, and the subsequent reinvestment in a new tract of land which would be used for the same purposes and contain the same reversionary interests which the present deed contains.

It is the well accepted rule in this State that in attempting to determine the estate conveyed in a deed, we must examine the deed to determine the intention of the parties, or in this case the intention of the grantors.

We think it is clear that the intention of the grantors in this case was to give their property to the church so long as it was used for church purposes and, then, when not so used, the property was to revert to the grantors, or their heirs. The language of the deed is that

> "should said property be used for any other purpose than above specified then this conveyance to said church will be null and void and title to said property will become vested in the heirs at law of the said L. Hinton Grizzard, deceased, or their legal representatives."

Thus, it appears that the deed by which the described property was conveyed did not create an absolute title in fee simple. The provisions of the deed clearly show that the church's estate was and is limited, and might be termed a determinable fee or fee simple on condition subsequent, both of which estates are recognized by the property law of this State.

Of course, the result is the same in this case whether the estate created constituted a determinable fee or a fee simple on condition subsequent. If the deed created a determinable fee, it left in the heirs of the grantors a possibility of reverter. If it conveyed a fee simple on condition subsequent, it left in the grantors a right of re-entry. The only distinction between the two future interests is, in a determinable fee, upon the happening of the condition, the grantee's estate automatically terminates and the entire fee simple title reverts to the grantors or their heirs. If the estate created is a fee simple on a condition subsequent, some act of re-entry on the part of the grantors or their heirs is necessary upon the happening of the condition, to re-vest title in the grantors or their heirs.

It is the contention of the appellants that under their proposal the conditional aspects of the habendum clause of the deed would not be disregarded or ignored. The proposal is merely to substitute a new parcel of land which would have the same conditions and reversionary interests as the original deed. Thus, so the appellants reason, the grantors' charitable purpose could be fulfilled and at the same time the appellants would retain their reversionary interests in a tract of land of equal value.

Appellants cite as authority for their position the case of Banner Baptist Church v. Watson, *supra.* The deed involved in that case conveyed the land to the church to be used for church purposes with the proviso that if it should cease to be so used, the land would revert to the grantor's daughter. The Court held that the ousting of the church from the land by the State in the exercise of its sovereign power of eminent domain was not an abandonment of use for church purposes by the church. Therefore, the trustees of the church received the funds from the eminent domain proceedings as a substitute res.

Likewise, appellants rely on the Kentucky case of Lutes v. Louisville & N.R. Co., 158 Ky. 259, 164 S.W. 792 (1914), quoted with approval in the *Banner Baptist Church* case. That case held that where a railroad undertakes proceedings to condemn church property, the property donated for church purposes does not revert to the heirs of the grantor. Rather, the heirs' reversionary interest will be transferred to the property purchased from the proceeds of the donated property.

We are of the opinion that both of the above cases are distinguishable from the case at bar. We think the line of demarcation is that in both cases the sale of land was involuntary as condemnation proceedings either were eminent or had already been undertaken. There is no threat of condemnation in the case at bar, and any sale of land by the church would have to be termed voluntary. While the growth of the community may have affected the property, we think that the environmental change is not analogous to a condemnation or threatened condemnation situation.

Our interpretation of the grantors' intent is that they wished the church to use the land so long as it had a use for it, and then desired thereafter that their heirs receive the benefit therefrom. It appears from the bill that the described land may have served its usefulness to the church, and we conclude that the heirs should receive the land in accordance with the clear, intent and wish of the grantors, provided, of course, the church fails to use the land for the purposes specified in the deed.

We think the chancellor was eminently correct in relying on the case of Mountain City Missionary Baptist Church v. Wagner, *supra,* in sustaining the demurrer. In that case the grantor conveyed to the trustees of a church certain property to be used for church purposes, with a clause limiting the estate in much the same language as is found in the case at bar. The trustees of the church filed a bill to eliminate the condition of the deed so that the church might erect a new building and borrow money thereon. The Court held the estate created was a determinable fee, refused to overlook the conditional limitations of the deed, and stated:

> "When we thus read the deed, as a whole, we find that the unmistakable and clear intention of the grantor was to give this property to the church so long as it was used for church purposes and then when not so used the property was to revert to the grantor or his heirs." 193 Tenn. at 628, 249 S.W.2d at 876.
>
> "For the reasons heretofore stated we think that the deed in question created a valid determinable fee and that this cannot be considered a cloud on the title, and that we as a Court have no right to disturb this clause as created by the parties when the deed was made." 193 Tenn. at 630, 249 S.W.2d at 877.

We think the above case is controlling in this matter. Appellants, however, seek to distinguish this case contending that it is not their intention to destroy the possibility of reverter, but merely to sell the present land and re-invest in other property and to which the reversionary interests of appellees would be transferred.

Appellants' position is untenable. The practical effect of such a plan would be to severely limit the reversionary rights of the appellees. And also, the reversionary interest of the appellees was created in the particular tract of land described in the deed. A substitute parcel of land might be much less desirable to them in the event of an exercise of the reversionary rights, and it would be an obvious usurpation of the appellees' rights to permit the substitution.

Likewise, if the law allows the substitution, the church might, in subsequent years, sell and re-invest again, and again. In so doing, the probability of the appellees coming into their reversionary interests would be greatly reduced, if not done away with.

Such reasoning, in effect, would be to completely ignore the conditional aspect of the deed, and we are unwilling to do so. The intention of the grantors is clear and should not be deviated from. If the property ceases to be used for the purposes set forth in the deed, then the property reverts to the heirs of the grantors as expressly provided in the deed.

The chancellor is affirmed.

NOTES & QUESTIONS:

1. Keep in mind that these defeasible fee estates only come to an end if the specific condition is violated. Also, because this is a form of fee simple estate, the law of waste does not apply. The present possessory estate

may never end, so imposing the law of waste would tie up land from productive uses. One example of how these concepts come together is the case of Davis v. Skipper, 83 S.W.2d 318 (Tex. 1935). Land was given to a church as long as the building was used for church purposes. This language created a fee simple determinable estate. While church services were still being conducted on the property, oil and gas was discovered under the land. The church entered into an oil and gas lease and the successor to the original grantor who now held the possibility of reverter sought a judgment that title had reverted to them and also sought an injunction to stop the oil and gas production. The court held that title did not revert because the church building was still being used for a church and would not enjoin the oil and gas production because the present owner of a fee simple determinable has "all the incidents of a fee simple" and could extract oil from the land.

2. Remember that the fee simple determinable ends automatically if the condition occurs. However, the fee simple subject to condition subsequent does not end automatically. The holder of the right of entry must take steps to reenter and reclaim the land. This difference in the ending of the present possessory estate can have significant legal consequences.

First, there is some disagreement regarding transferability of the future interest involved. The modern view is to make all interests in land freely transferrable. The majority view today is that the possibility of reverter and right of entry are freely transferrable inter vivos or at death. However, some states continue to follow the rule in *Mahrenholz* that the interests are not transferrable *inter vivos* unless being released to the owner of the present possessory estate. A few states also distinguish between the two and allow free transferability of the possibility of reverter while only allowing the right of entry to be transferred through will or intestate succession. In Texas, as the *Lawyers Trust* case will illustrate, these interests are freely transferrable.

Second, due to the nature of the present possessory estate, the timing of adverse possession will be different. If a condition is violated with a fee simple determinable and the person remains in possession, the statute of limitations begins to run for purposes of adverse possession. However, with the fee simple subject to condition subsequent continuing on until the holder of the future interest takes steps, the time period for adverse possession does not begin to run immediately. The present possessory estate holder is still legally in possession of the land. This means the statute of limitations cannot begin until the holder of the right of entry takes steps to reenter. Does this mean that the future interest can be exercised at any time in the future? Consider that question as you read the next case.

Lawyers Trust Company v. City of Houston
Supreme Court of Texas, 1962
359 S.W.2d 887

SMITH, Justice.

This is a trespass to try title suit. On the 12th day of August, 1926, W. T. Carter Lumber & Building Company, executed an instrument wherein it was recited that the company had acquired title to certain lands in Harris County, Texas, and had plotted the several tracts so acquired into lots and blocks, to be known as "Garden Villas." The instrument, subject to certain reservations, dedicated unto the public certain described portions of such tracts for park and other purposes, all of which was delineated upon a map attached to and made a part of the dedicatory instrument. Among the rights reserved unto W. T. Carter Lumber & Building Company, its successors and assigns, was that expressed in reservation four (4), which reads[:]

> If, on or after the expiration of twenty-five (25) years from date hereof, any tract or tracts dedicated for parks, civic centers, schools or community places as shown on said plat, cease to be used for the purpose or purposes indicated thereon, the fee title to any such tract or tracts shall vest and be in W. T. Carter Lumber & Building Company.

Lawyers Trust Company, hereinafter designated as Lawyers Trust, successor in title to W. T. Carter Lumber & Building Company, filed this trespass to try title suit against the City of Houston, hereinafter referred to as the "City." Lawyers Trust based its suit upon the contention that the City, the representative of the public, had on and after August 12, 1951, the expiration date of the twenty-five (25) year term provided in the reservation, ceased to use the land described in its petition for park purposes, and, therefore, Lawyers Trust was the owner of the land and vested with all rights reserved by W. T. Carter Lumber & Building Company. The case was submitted to a jury upon special issue No. 1., which stated, "Do you find from a preponderance of the evidence that the land involved in this law suit had ceased to be used for park purposes on or after August 12, 1951?"

The jury in response thereto found that on and after August 12, 1951, the land involved had ceased to be used for park purposes. . . .

The trial court entered judgment against the City and awarded to Lawyers Trust the title to and possession of the tract of land sued for. The City appealed to the Court of Civil Appeals and that court reversed the judgment of the trial court and rendered judgment for the City.

The pertinent facts are these: On April 12, 1926, the date of dedication, the land was situated outside the city limits of Houston, Texas, and was owned by the dedicator, W. T. Carter Lumber & Building Company. The land involved here was designated on the map or plat as Park No. 1 and was used by the public for park purposes from the date of dedication through the year 1944. The city limits of Houston were extended in 1949 so as to include Park No. 1.

In 1947 the W. T. Carter Lumber & Building Company conveyed to the Carter Investment Company all of its rights to the property. Thereafter, in 1957, the Carter Investment Company conveyed to the Lawyers Trust Company its interest in the property.

Lawyers Trust Company contends that a conditional limitation was created by the deed of dedication and that consequently upon cessation of use of the property for park purposes on and after August 12, 1951, the estate created by the deed of dedication automatically terminated. Lawyers Trust makes the further contention that even though it may be held that the language of the deed of dedication was sufficient to create a condition subsequent, it had a right of re-entry from and after August 12, 1951, nevertheless, by virtue of the broken condition, and that it exercised such right of re-entry by the filing of this suit in trespass to try title in 1959.

The City contends that the language of the deed of dedication conclusively shows that a condition subsequent was created, but that a forfeiture resulting from the breach of the condition subsequent was waived, and that Lawyers Trust had forfeited its right to claim a forfeiture prior to the filing of this suit on February 18, 1959.

In view of the vigorous contention presented by Lawyers Trust that a conditional limitation was created by the language of the deed of dedication and that consequently cessation of use of the property for park purposes automatically terminated the estate, we deem it necessary to briefly state our reasons for holding to the contrary. The City contends that the deed of dedication imposed upon the estate a condition subsequent. We agree.

It is a cardinal rule in determining from the language of deeds whether a conditional limitation or a condition subsequent was intended by the parties that the instrument as a whole must be considered. Stevens v. Galveston H. & S. A. Ry. Co., 212 S.W. 639 (Tex. Comm. App. 1919). The pertinent provision of the deed before us begins with the word "if," a word of art which traditionally has been held to create a condition subsequent. American Law of Property, Section 4.7. By this we do not mean that by use of the word "if" a condition subsequent is created as a matter of law. We mention it merely as one portion of the deed which must be considered and given effect. It is a rather strong indication that the parties intended a condition subsequent. However, we do not treat its import as conclusive. When we turn to other language in the deed of dedication, we find that provision that the property 'shall vest and be in' the grantor in the event the property is not used for its designated purpose. The quoted language seems to provide that the estate will terminate automatically and that it will revest immediately upon the occurrence of the stated contingency. It seems to foreclose the necessity of a re-entry on the part of the grantor in order to terminate the estate. This unmistakably indicates a special limitation. But, here again, such indication is not conclusive. Similar language in other conveyances of this character has not been held to be prohibitive of the creation of a condition subsequent. Daggett v. City of Fort Worth, 177 S.W. 222 (Tex. Civ. App.—Amarillo 1915, no writ); Houston & T.C. R. Co. v. Ennis-Calvert Compress Co., 23 Tex. 441, 56 S.W. 367 (Tex. Civ. App. 1900, writ re'd); Stevens, et al. v. Galveston H. & S. A. Ry. Co., *supra*; Gulf C. & S. F. Ry. Co. v. Dunman, 74 Tex. 265, 11 S.W. 1094.

It is well settled that when there is doubt from the entire language of the instrument whether it fair construction imports a limitation or a condition subsequent the doubt must be resolved in favor of the latter as being in a sense less onerous upon the grantee in that, under such a construction, the estate does not terminate automatically with the occurrence of the stated contingency, but only after re-entry or its equivalent is made by the grantor. Stevens v. Galveston H. & S. A. Ry. Co., *supra*; Houston & T. C. R. Co. v. Ennis-Calvert Compress Co., *supra*.

The language in the deed before us presents an appropriate situation for the application of this principle. Part of the expressed provision would lead to the belief that a condition subsequent was created whereas another part indicates that a conditional limitation was intended by the parties. Therefore, in accordance with the above-mentioned constructional preference, we are led to the conclusion that a condition subsequent was created by the terms of the deed.

The Court of Civil Appeals has held that "the evidence is without dispute that the property had ceased to be used for park purposes since about 1944." The City does not contend that the property was used for park purposes at any time after 1944.

Although we do not agree with Lawyers Trust in its contention that the language of the deed of dedication created a conditional limitation and that the fee simple title automatically vested in W. T. Carter Lumber & Building Company, we do agree that as of August 12, 1951, the Carter Investment Company, the then owner of the title, had the right of re-entry by virtue of the broken condition, and that right was acquired by the Lawyers Trust Company by virtue of the deed to it as grantee executed in October, 1957 by the Carter Investment Company. This right of re-entry was properly exercised by Lawyers Trust by the filing of this suit in 1959. *See* Gulf C. & S. F. Ry. Co. v. Dunman, *supra*. Therefore, Lawyers Trust is entitled to recover the title to Park No. 1, the property involved in this suit, unless we conclude to sustain in City in either of its contentions of waiver and estoppel. We do not agree with either contention.

On the question of waiver, the City argues the delay of seven and one-half years before suit was filed effected a waiver of the right of re-entry. In effect, the City is saying that a grantor may lose his right to claim a forfeiture for breach of a condition subsequent merely because of lapse of time between the breach of a condition subsequent and the time of re-entry. Mere indulgence, acquiescence, or inaction is not ordinarily considered sufficient to constitute a waiver of a forfeiture for breach of a condition subsequent, 4 Thompson on Real Property, Section 2118, p. 665, and it has been held that a waiver or estoppel arises only when the grantor does some act inconsistent with his right of forfeiture, and where it would be unjust for him thereafter to insist upon a forfeiture. *See* Brown v. McKinney, 208 S.W. 565 (Tex. Civ. App. 1919, writ ref'd); City of Barnesville v. Stafford, 161 Ga. 588, 131 S.E. 487, 43 A.L.R. 1045. In Tiffany on Real Property, Third Edition, Vol. 1, Section 203, p. 338, it is said: " . . . But a mere silent acquiescence in the doing of an act involving a breach of the condition is not sufficient to show a waiver of its condition, so as to preclude the assertion of a right of forfeiture by reason of such act."

[margin note: SILENCE ≠ WAIVER]

A waiver of a breach of a condition subsequent may be presumed after a reasonable lapse of time has occurred without any assertion of right by the grantor under the condition. But, as said in 4 Thompson on Real Property, Section 2123, p. 668, it is incumbent upon the grantee to allege and prove such lapse of time. Waiver is a question of fact, and whether in any particular case there is a waiver is a matter of intention on the part of the grantor, to be ascertained from his acts and all the attendant circumstances of the case. Waiver of the right to claim a forfeiture has not been established as a matter of law.

It is true that delay in exercising the right of re-entry coupled with proof that the grantee was misled by such delay and as a result changed his position by making improvements on the property or investing money in it, then it can be said that the grantor has waived his right of re-entry and is estopped from asserting his claim of the right of forfeiture. *See* Benavides v. Hunt, 79 Tex. 383, 15 S.W. 396; Wisdom v. Michen, 154 S.W.2d (Tex. Civ. App.—Galveston 1941, writ re'd w.o.m.). There is no evidence of any act on the part of the grantor or its grantees, Carter Investment Company and Lawyers Trust, which could be calculated to mislead the City, nor is there any evidence that the City has changed its position on the strength of the failure to file suit prior to February, 1959.

[margin note: No MISLEADING No ESTOPPEL]

The judgment of the Court of Civil Appeals is reversed and that of the trial court is affirmed.

REVIEW PROBLEMS:

For these problems assume you are applying the law at modern times. *O* starts out owning a fee simple absolute. All of these conveyances occur in a deed that has been validly executed, delivered, and accepted.

1. *O* conveys Blackacre "to *A* and her heirs so long as it is used for school purposes only." What is *A*'s interest in Blackacre?

2. When *A* closes the school and opens a restaurant, what is *A*'s interest? *O*'s interest?

3. *O* conveys Blackacre "to *A* and her heirs, but if it is not used for school purposes, *O* has the right to re-enter and reclaim Blackacre." What is *A*'s interest in Blackacre?

4. When *A* closes the school and opens a restaurant, what is *A*'s interest? *O*'s interest?

5. *O* conveys Blackacre "to *A* and her heirs so long as it is used for school purposes, and if it is not used for school purposes *O* has the right to reenter and reclaim the land." What is *A*'s interest?

6. When *A* closes the school and opens a restaurant, what is *A*'s interest? *O*'s interest?

7. *O* conveys Blackacre "to *A* and her heirs while it is used for school purposes, then to *B*." What is *A*'s interest?

8. When *A* closes the school and opens a restaurant, what is *A*'s interest? *O*'s interest? *B*'s interest?

9. *O* conveys Blackacre "to *A* and her heirs to be used for school purposes." What is *A*'s interest?

10. When *A* closes the school and opens a restaurant, what is *A*'s interest? *O*s' interest? What remedies does *O* have against *A*?

D. Future Interests: The Rest of the Story

Present possessory estates are held by those who have an immediate right to possession at the time of the conveyance. Now that the coverage of present possessory estate is complete, the focus shifts. Because there are a multitude of present possessory estates that are not the complete fee simple absolute, there must be other types of interests to account for every moment in time when there will be a person who can be seized of the land. The focus now turns from the present possessory estates to the variety of future interests that accompany them. The future interests are more complicated and depend in part on a proper determination of the present possessory estate. The subject of future interests is a large and complex subject that cannot be completely covered in a first-year course. This material will cover the basic essentials of future interests to gain a general knowledge that will also serve as a foundation for trust law and estate planning.

1. Introduction to Future Interests

Think back to the bundle of sticks concept from the first days of the course. When conveyancing language is examined and a timeline of ownership is established, there are different bundles that every person on the timeline holds. The bundle of sticks for the future interest will not be exactly the same as those for present possessory estate. The sticks will be somewhat different when examining areas like possession and transferability. Once the biggest and best fee simple absolute bundle is divided up into smaller bundles, every single person holding a bundle must be identified to account for everything that was part of that fee simple absolute bundle. Each possessory estate *other than a fee simple absolute* must be coupled with a future interest. [78] The language of the conveyance must be read left to right with each interest being determined as it occurs. The first interest is the present possessory estate that has already been covered. Now the question to consider is what comes next?

In order to properly identify all of the interests involved and to make sure that the entirety of the ownership of the property is accounted for, time line diagrams are extremely helpful. Bundles must be defined until ultimately there is at least one holder of a future interest who could end up with fee simple absolute again one day. The labeling of the future interest consists of three parts: (1) who holds the future interest; (2) which future interest the person holds; and (3) what estate will be held if the interest becomes possessory. The future interest label holds the person's place on the timeline while we wait to see what will develop over time.

"A 'future interest' is defined as a property interest in which the privilege of possession or of other enjoyment is future and not present."[79] Or more simply, it is the "present right to possess the property in the future."[80] A future interest is

---

[78] Wendel , *supra* note 17, at 24.

[79] Leopord, *supra* note 28, § 13.2.

[80] Wendel , *supra* note 17, at 24.

an interest in land that is not, but may become, a present interest and is a segment of ownership measured in terms of duration.[81] The party who holds the right to take actual possession of the property in the future has the future interest.

If the present possessory estate is not the entire fee simple absolute, then the question must be posed, "who holds the future interest?" The material on future interests is divided into two categories—future interests in the transferor (grantor) and future interests in the transferee (grantee). Making this distinction aids in matching up future interests to the correct present possessory estate and also aids in future understanding of the Rule Against Perpetuities and other rules promoting alienability.

In covering the various future interests, they will be categorized as those future interests in the transferor and in the transferee. The future interest could be held by the grantor, as with a possibility of reverter or right of entry or a reversion, or it could be held by the grantee as with a remainder or an executory interest.[82] Due to the nature of each future interest, we will match them with certain present possessory estates. *Mastering these pairings will assist you greatly in future coverage in other courses that involve the estate system.*

Because the law of property favors the free alienability of land, at the end of our coverage of the estate system we will briefly introduce the concept of Rules Promoting Alienability including the illusive Rule Against Perpetuities and its application to these future interests that are created.

The future interests in transferors are:

(1) reversion,
(2) possibility of reverter, and
(3) right of entry (or power of termination).

The future interests in transferees are:

(1) remainders
    (a) indefeasibly vested remainder,
    (b) contingent remainder,
    (c) vested remainder subject to open, and
    (d) vested remainder subject to divestment

and

(2) executory interests
    (a) shifting executory interests, and
    (b) springing executory interests.

---

[81] Restatement (First) of Property § 153 (1936).
[82] Leopord, *supra* note 28, § 13.2.

Once the future interest piece of the puzzle snaps into place, it will be important to practice using the worksheets in this chapter. It is essential to master the present possessory estate plus future interest combinations and then be able to recognize them in written conveyances in order to determine what property rights exist and, as a result, what duties and obligations the various interest holders have.

2. Future Interests in Transferors: It was mine and now it's yours, but it could be mine again one day

The law first recognized the concept of the future interest in the transferor because that was consistent with the historic feudal goal of keeping the land coming back to the lord to keep land ownership concentrated. When the original presumed estate was a life estate, that meant the lord transferred a present possessory estate of lesser quantum than his fee simple absolute. When the lord was only transferring part of his bundle of sticks, he must have held back some of that bundle: the sticks that represented his ability to possess again in the future in fee simple absolute. The future interest in the transferor was essential for this form of land ownership. Even once the goal changed to free alienability of land, lesser estates may still be created if expressly done. This means that these future interests in the transferor remain essential to the estate system. Because this category of future interests is that of interests which remain with the original owner, they are favored under the law.

a. Reversion

A reversion arises when the transferor has conveyed an estate lesser than what he owns and the preceding estates in the grantees terminate other than by a condition subsequent or special limitation. Another way of saying this is that the reversion is the interest created in the transferor when the smaller estate conveyed is one that terminates naturally. A reversion may follow a life estate, a fee tail, or a leasehold estate, as those are all estates that terminate "naturally" because the present possessory estate holder is not divested of the estate. There is some natural end to the term of the present possessory estate due to the very nature of the estate, not because of some event or condition occurring. The main focus in this chapter will be on the reversion following the life estate, since the fee tail is abolished in Texas. The reversion also follows the leasehold estates, covered in the next chapter. The reversion simply sits back and waits patiently for the preceding estate to terminate and then becomes possessory.

The reversion is freely transferrable during life and upon death. This means that even if the transferor dies during the time of the present possessory estate, the reversion will be devised or inherited. The devisee or heir simply steps into the shoes of the transferor and holds the reversion. The nature of the future interest does not change. The transferor could only convey what he owned: the reversion.

The reversion is sometimes an interest that is certain to become possessory in the future, but sometimes it serves a function on the timeline which makes the reversion speculative in nature. If there is any possibility, no matter how unlikely, that the transferor may need to retake possession in the future, a reversion must remain.

Look at these two examples as a point of comparison.

Example #1: *O* to *A* for life.

Example #2: *O* to *A* for life, then to *B* if *B* survives *A*.

In **Example #1**, *O* started with a fee simple absolute and then conveyed a lesser present possessory estate to *A* in the form of a life estate. It is obvious that *A* will die and when that occurs the present possessory estate ends and the holder of the reversion, whether *O* or someone else, now takes possession. It is certain that this will happen. *O* has a reversion in fee simple absolute.

However, in **Example #2**, the situation is different. While *A* has still received a lesser present possessory estate in the form of a life estate, the transferor *O* had also created an interest in *B* that will become possessory at the end of *A*'s life estate, but only if *B* survives *A*. It is not certain that *B* will be able to take possession. There must be someone who can be seized of the land at all times which means the transferor *O* must still have part of the bundle of sticks. The transferor has a future interest that would follow *A*'s lesser estate that terminates naturally. This means that by definition *O* must have a reversion in fee simple absolute even though *B* has a future interest. *O*'s reversion in this example is speculative in nature and not certain like it was in Example #1. It is possible that when *A*'s life estate ends *B* will be alive and will take possession and *O*'s interest will disappear. However, it is also possible that *B* will die during *A*'s life estate and *O* will have to retake possession at the end of *A*'s life estate.

No matter the role the reversion plays, this future interest is not subject to the Rule Against Perpetuities. The Rule Against Perpetuities will void an interest that vests too remotely in time. The reversion may be speculative but it is considered vested or capable of becoming possessory again. The transferor who originally owned the entire bundle has retained some of the bundle and that will not be voided no matter how long it may take to become possessory again.

b. Possibility of Reverter

The possibility of reverter is another interest held by the transferor. However, the possibility of reverter follows the fee simple determinable estate. In this case, the estate of the grantee will not end naturally but will automatically end by the occurrence of some event set forth in the description of the estate in order for the transferor to retake possession of the estate. The automatic termination of the present possessory estate allows the estate to "revert" back to the transferor.

The possibility of reverter was introduced in the discussion of the *Mahrenholz* case in the section on defeasible fee estates. Under the modern approach, the possibility of reverter is freely transferrable. The possibility of reverter is similar to the reversion in that it will wait patiently for the previous estate to automatically end. The holder of this future interest does not have to do anything to be able to retake possession. This future interest in the transferor is always speculative. The fee simple determinable may never end. The condition or limitation placed on the present possessory estate may never occur. However, as one of the preferred future interests in the transferor, this future interest is also never subject to the Rule Against Perpetuities. While it is uncertain that it will ever become possessory, it is always capable of becoming possessory as soon as the prior estate ends.

Consider the difference between the following examples:

Example #1: *O* to *A* for life.

Example #2: *O* to *A* so long as the land is used for school purposes.

In both examples *O* has given a present possessory estate to *A* and has not given out the entire bundle of sticks. In **Example #1**, we know *A*'s life estate will end one day even if we do not know a date certain. In **Example #2**, we do not know that *A*'s fee simple determinable will end. The land could continue being used for school purposes forever. In that case *O* will never retake possession. This illustrates the distinction between the certainty of one and the speculative nature of the other. Something else to keep in mind, *O*'s interest in Example #2 cannot be classified as a reversion because it is not following a naturally ending present possessory estate and it does not follow a lesser estate. The defeasible fee estates are viewed to be on the same level of the estate hierarchy as the fee simple absolute because the defeasible fee estates may last forever. The life estate, however, is a finite estate that must end. *O*'s interest in Example #2 must be a possibility of reverter in fee simple absolute.

c. Right of Entry

The right of entry or power of termination is the third interest held by the transferor. This interest is what follows the fee simple subject to a condition subsequent. This is another situation where the estate of the grantee will not end naturally but will also not end automatically. The preceding present possessory estate will be cut short or interrupted by the occurrence of some event set forth in the description of the estate in order for the transferor to retake possession.

As indicated by the names given to this future interest, it indicates the fact that the future interest holder must take some action to regain possession of the estate once the event or condition has occurred. This feature distinguishes this future interest from both the reversion and the possibility of reverter. Because this future interest also follows a defeasible fee estate that may never end, it is similar to the possibility of reverter because it is speculative in nature. Under the modern trend this future interest is also freely transferrable. However, some states still treat this future interest differently since it is even more speculative than the others. This means that in some states the right of entry is still not transferrable inter vivos.

Consider the following examples to understand the differences in these future interests in the transferor.

All three of these future interests in the transferor have similarities and differences. It is because of the similarities that they are grouped together into one category and it is because of the differences that each one matches up with a distinct present possessory estate.

Example #1: *O* to *A* for life.

Example #2: *O* to *A* so long as the land is used for school purposes.

Example #3: *O* to *A*, but if the land is not used for school purposes, *O* retains the right to reenter and retake the land.

O's interest in both Examples 2 and 3 follow defeasible fee estates. By way of review, Example #3 is the fee simple subject to condition subsequent because it contains conditional magic words rather than the durational magic words seen in Example #2. This means that in Example #3, *O* has a right of entry in fee simple absolute. The interests in both Examples 2 and 3 are speculative in nature because the present possessory estates held by *A* may never end. The land could be used for school purposes forever. The right of entry is speculative, but *O* will have to take steps to retake possession of the land. *O* cannot sit back and wait patiently. Because of this, the interest is considered even more speculative in nature because in order to retake possession the condition must occur and *O* must take steps. However, even though this is incredibly speculative, it is not subject to the Rule Against Perpetuities. Again, *O* is seen as always capable of retaking the land in which he originally held the entire fee simple absolute bundle of sticks.

3. Future Interests in Transferees: It was mine and now it's yours, but it could be someone else's one day

The future interests in a transferee were created later in time and were treated less favorably under the law. There was some resistance to the idea of the original owner, *O*, being able to dictate for some time into the future who would own Blackacre. The law did not like uncertainty, so future interests in transferees that seem to be somewhat speculative are problematic and are still impacted today.

The future interests in the transferee break down into two categories: remainder and executory interest. Each type of interest has characteristics for the type as well as characteristics for the specific future interest. The remainder will have commonality with the reversion. The executory interest will have something in common with both the possibility of reverter and right of entry. The remainders and executory interests are generally freely transferrable. There may be some conditions placed on the future interest that would limit its transferability in some circumstances.

a. Remainder

A remainder is a future interest created in a transferee that is capable of becoming a possessory estate upon the natural termination of a prior estate created by the same instrument. If, at the time the future interest is created, it is not possible for it to become possessory upon the termination of the prior estate, the future interest is not a remainder.

Because the remainder interest follows the natural termination of an estate, it can only be created following a life estate, fee tail, or leasehold estate. Again, as with the reversion, we will focus on the remainder following the life estate.

Think back to these examples:

Example #1: *O* to *A* for life.

Example #2: *O* to *A* for life, then to *B* if *B* survives *A*.

Example #3: *O* to *A* for life, then to *B*.

In analyzing these conveyances before, the focus was on the reversion held by *O* in each example. **Example #1** illustrated the certain reversion in fee simple absolute in *O* and **Example #2** illustrated the need to have a reversion in fee simple absolute that is speculative in nature when there is a future interest in a transferee that is not certain to become possessory. The interest in *B* is not certain to become possessory so it will be classified as a contingent remainder in fee simple absolute. This introduces the distinctions between remainders and reversions. **Example #3** illustrates another type of remainder that is a different classification than that in Example #2. In Example #3 there is no uncertainty and *B* will have an indefeasibly vested remainder in fee simple absolute and there is no longer a need for any interest in *O*.

The common thread in all of these examples is that the future interests, whether reversion or remainder, all follow a naturally ending present possessory estate—the life estate. All of these future interests are simply waiting for the life estate to end. Both the reversion held by *O* in Example #1 and the remainder held by *B* in Example #3 are certain to become possessory at the end of *A*'s life estate. So, why have the different names? Remember, the names of the future interest serve a particular purpose. The future interest label explains the nature of the interest while it sits on the timeline waiting for possession to occur. A reversion by definition is an interest held by the transferor. This means that once *B*, a transferee, is identified as holding the future interest it cannot be labeled a reversion. There will be different types of remainders because their roles on the timeline are different. In Example #2, there is an interest in the transferor and an interest in a transferee. In this example both interests are speculative. This conveyance is written in such a way so that at the time of conveyance there are different options as to what will happen as facts develop over time.

If the conveyance reads "Oscar conveys Blackacre to Angela for life, then to Brad if Brad gives Angela a proper funeral," does Brad have a remainder? If not, why? Who would take possession after Angela's life estate?

In order to provide more flexibility in transferring interests in land, different types of remainders were created. Finally, one remainder was created as a legal problem solver. A definition and description of each of the remainders will provide a foundation to begin trying to recognize different patterns of language.

Remainders can be vested or contingent. There are four specific types: (1) contingent remainder; (2) indefeasibly vested remainder (vested remainder); (3) vested remainder subject to open (or partial divestment); and (4) vested remainder subject to divestment (or total divestment). Each will be examined separately.

i. Contingent Remainder

Contingent remainders are uncertain. A remainder is contingent if it is (1) subject to a condition precedent (other than the natural termination of the prior estate) **or** (2) created in an unascertainable person. The contingent remainder is like a closed door that will remain closed unless and until the condition precedent is met or the holder is identified.

So, think back to Example #2 above. *O to A for life, then to B if B survives A.* The interest in *B* has to be a remainder because it is held by a transferee and follows a naturally ending life estate. Although *B* is an ascertainable person, the words in italic are placing a condition precedent on *B*. *B* cannot take possession of Blackacre unless *B* is still alive at *A*'s death. *B*'s interest is speculative, uncertain, contingent. At the time of conveyance it cannot be determined with certainty who will possess Blackacre at every moment in time on the timeline.

Additionally, the interest will be contingent if there is an unascertainable person. What if instead the conveyance reads as follows?

O to A for life, then to A's widow.

At the time of the conveyance, *A* is married to *B*. Does that mean *B* holds an indefeasibly vested remainder and *O* no longer has an interest? No, not at all. *B* cannot hold an interest at this time. While *B* is currently *A*'s spouse, we do not know if *A* will have a widow until the time of death. *A* and *B* may divorce and *A* could be married to *C* at the time of death. Or, due to death or divorce, *A* may die single without a widow. This is a situation where there is an unascertainable person. This means that "*A*'s widow" has a contingent remainder in fee simple absolute and *O* still must have a reversion in fee simple absolute for in case there is no widow at the end of the life estate.

What happens if *O* wants to create a contingent remainder but does not want the land back if the condition is not satisfied but instead wants the land to go on to someone else? Before other future interests were recognized the only option was to create alternative contingent remainders.

> **Example:** *O to A for life, then to B if B survives A, but if B does not survive A, then to C.*

What does this language create? *A* still has a life estate and there are now two future interests in transferees. *B*'s remainder is subject to a condition precedent of survivorship. The condition precedent is included in the language of the clause creating the future interest in *B*. *B* must have a contingent remainder. However, *C* has an interest as well. *C*'s interest is also subject to a condition precedent. *C* will only be able to take possession if *B* does not survive *A*. This condition precedent is stated in the clause before the clause that creates the future interest in *C*. This means that *C* also has a contingent remainder. This practically means that *B* has a contingent remainder in fee simple absolute that may become possessory at the end of the life estate and *C* has a contingent remainder in fee simple absolute that may become possessory at the end of *A*'s life estate. The vesting of one means the destruction of the other. Only one or the other will happen. These are referred to as alternative contingent remainders.

Would there still be a reversion in *O*? The answer is yes for a couple of reasons. While it appears that there is no reason why the land would ever go back to *O*, there was the possibility that the life estate could terminate early before the end of *A*'s life. In feudal times the life estate could terminate for a variety of reasons, including the life tenant's failure to provide the required feudal incidents to *O*. Also, and still applicable at modern times, the life estate could potentially be terminated early due to waste. If the life estate ended early, the contingent remainders could not take possession because their interests were not yet vested, not capable of becoming possessory. And, under the common law rule of destructibility of contingent remainders, a contingent remainder was destroyed if at the termination of the preceding estate it was still possible for the contingency to occur, it was not yet vested. So, if *A*'s life estate is terminated before *A* dies, we cannot yet know whether *B* will survive *A* or not. Both interests in B and C would be destroyed and the land would return to *O* through a reversion in fee simple absolute that was retained.

The common law rule of destructibility of contingent remainders is abolished in the majority of states, Texas included, but may still be applicable in some states.[83] But, if the contingent remainders are not destroyed and they are not vested because *A*'s life estate terminates early due to waste, the land would still need to go back to *O* until the condition precedent can be satisfied. With the creation of some additional future interests, this situation can be avoided. We will come back to this example in the following material.

ii.   Vested Remainders

A remainder is vested if (1) it is given to an ascertained person *and* (2) it is not subject to a condition precedent other than the natural termination of the preceding estates. There are specific subsets of vested remainders.

---

[83] *See* Joseph William Singer, Introduction to Property 315 (2d ed. 2005); Hovenkamp & Kurtz, Principles of Property Law 178 (6th ed. 2005), citing to Blocker v. Blocker, 103 Fla. 285, 137 So. 249 (1931).

a. Indefeasibly Vested Remainders

This type of vested remainder is certain to become possessory in the future and cannot be divested. For this remainder there is an ascertainable person and there is no condition precedent.

Back to **Example #3** above: *O* to *A* for life, then to *B*.

In this conveyance, *B* is an ascertainable person and *B* does not have to satisfy any conditions. *B* has an indefeasibly vested remainder in fee simple absolute. As stated previously, even if *B* does not survive *A* in this example, *B*'s interest was devisable and inheritable and someone would be standing in *B*'s shoes to take at *A*'s death. This is the type of remainder that the law favored historically and still does. This remainder leaves no unanswered questions and promotes certainty.

b. Vested Remainder Subject to Open (or Subject to Partial Divestment)

This type of vested remainder is certain to become possessory in the future because there is no condition precedent and the identity of the interest holder is certain, but the size of the holder's share is uncertain. If more interest holders are identified then the share of each will diminish.

Example #3: *O* to *A* for life, then to *B*.

Example #4: *O* to *A* for life, then to *A*'s children.

This type of remainder is the one used for the class gift. Sometimes the owner wants to make a conveyance of an interest to a class of people like children, grandchildren, great-grandchildren, siblings, nieces, nephews, and others. This type of class gift is particularly useful in estate planning because when drafting a will *O* might not yet have any children or grandchildren yet wants to plan for such people to exist in the future. *O* could bequeath Blackacre to a class of people would receive an interest in the land and it would include every person who becomes a member of that class.

In **Example #4**, there is still a future interest in a transferee, but this time it is to a class of transferees. It will be important to know if at the time of conveyance anyone exists who is one of *A*'s children. Even though there is no condition precedent, if there is no ascertainable person then this would still have to be a contingent remainder in fee simple absolute. However, if *A* has at least one child at the time, there would be at least one member of the class who is ascertainable so that child would have a vested remainder subject to open.

This remainder requires some understanding of the class gift. It has already been stated that members can enter the class over time. How long can people enter the class? There is a concept of the class closing to help determine who would be eligible to take some interest in the property. There are two ways in which a class may close: (1) naturally or biologically; or (2) by convenience. Closing naturally or biologically occurs when no others members could be born into the class. For example, in the conveyance above Blackacre is conveyed to A for life, then to A's children. A, the life tenant, is the person who will determine the class. If a woman, A's children can only be born into the class during her life. If a man, A's children can be born into the class during his life plus nine months of gestation. This means that by the time A dies, all potential member of the class are identified. But, what if the conveyances changes to the following:

Example #5: *O to A for life, then to A's grandchildren.*

What is different about this example? Now A, the life tenant, does not determine who biologically enters the class. A's children determine whether or not grandchildren are born. What would happen if during A's lifetime grandchildren are born? Upon A's death, grandchildren P and Q are alive and are members of the class holding vested remainders subject to open. However, what if A's children, B and C, are still alive and could have more children who would be members of the class? This is an example of when the class would close by convenience. The class closes by convenience when there is at least one member of the class who can demand possession. Because P and Q have vested interests and the life estate has ended, they can demand possession. The class will close and even if B and C go on to have many more children who would otherwise be members of the class. They will not share in the property. They will be too late.

c. Vested Remainder Subject to Divestment (or Subject to Total Divestment): The Legal Problem-Solver

The vested remainder subject to divestment is often a source of confusion. Even looking to various scholarly materials there is a variety of definitions of this interest. You may find it stated that a vested remainder subject to divestment is a vested remainder that can be divested by the happening of a later event.[84] It is also is defined as "a remainder limited in favor of a born or ascertained person or in a class that is vested subject to open but is subject to the occurrence or nonoccurrence of a condition subsequent. Accordingly, the remainder may not

---

[84] Singer, *supra* note 86, at 314.

become possessory, or if it does, it may not remain possessory indefinitely."[85] John Gray explains that "whether a remainder is vested or contingent depends on the language employed. If the conditional element is incorporated into the description of, or into the gift to the remainderman, then the remainder is contingent; but if, after words giving a vested interest, a clause is added divesting it, the remainder is vested."[86]

With respect to this interest, the easiest way to understand it is to know that this is one of those instances where there is no logical reasoning that fits. Basically, the vested remainder subject to divestment was created as a way to place conditions just like those found with contingent remainders, but to avoid the pitfalls of the contingent remainder. There were many rules aimed at limiting the viability of the contingent remainder due to its uncertainty. There was also a problem that occurred once some rules were eliminated. This future interest was a legal way around all of that. By simply changing the pattern of the words, a different future interest was created. It is really that simple. Look for the pattern and the nature of the condition and you will reach the correct classification.

Going back to this earlier example:

> *O* to *A* for life, then to *B* if *B* survives *A*, but if *B* does not survive *A*, then to *C*.

This was an example of the alternative contingent remainder. Without any options like the vested remainder subject to divestment, coupled with the executory interest (covered next), *O* did not have any other options. With the vested remainder subject to divestment, *O* could instead create:

> *O* to *A* for life, then to *B*, but if *B* does not survive *A*, then to *C*.

That sounds the same, right? After the life estate *O* wants the land to go to *B* only if *B* is still alive, and if that is not the case it will pass to *C*. However, the order of the language is changed, the classification is different. There is still a condition that could keep *B* from ever taking possession of Blackacre. But, that condition is placed in a subsequent clause. In reading the sentence from left to right the language creates what looks like an indefeasibly vested remainder in *B* (*O* to *A* for life, then to *B*) and then goes on to place a condition (but if *B* does not survive *A*). This is the pattern of the vested remainder subject to divestment. Now, *C*'s interest cannot be a remainder. The remainder is an interest that will follow a naturally ending prior estate. *C* will take possession in this example only if *B* is divested. A remainder is not capable of divesting any interest. *C* will have an executory interest.

---

[85] Hovenkamp et al., *supra* note 86, at 176.

[86] John C. Gray, The Rule Against Perpetuities § 108 (4th ed. 1942).

A has a life estate, *B* has a vested remainder in fee simple subject to divestment, and *C* has a shifting executory interest in fee simple absolute. That is what the classification is at the time of conveyance. As facts develop over time, the interests may change. For example, what happens if *B* dies during *A's* life estate? *B's* interest is divested, there is nothing for anyone to inherit from *B* or to be devised from *B*. *C's* executory interest now changes to an indefeasibly vested remainder in fee simple absolute because at the end of *A's* naturally ending life estate *C* will be ready to take possession. What happens if the life estate ends and *B* is still alive. Now, *C's* executory interest disappears and *B* takes possession in fee simple absolute. The condition that had to be satisfied occurred and the land belongs to *B*.

Let's revisit the situation where the life estate ends early due to waste. *A* is still alive but we don't know yet if *B* is going to survive *A*. Does this mean there should be some reversion in *O* so that *O* can retake possession? No! By creating an interest in *B* that is *vested* subject to divestment, *B* is capable of taking possession at any time. That means that *B* would take possession, but of a fee simple subject to executory interest and *C* would still have a shifting executory interest in fee simple absolute. If *A* dies with *B* still alive, *B* will then hold the land forever and *C's* executory interest will essentially disappear. However, if *B* dies before *A*, *B's* estate will be divested by *C* and *C* will take in fee simple absolute. The vested characteristic allows for acceleration of possession and eliminates any need for *O* to retake possession of the land.

NOTES & QUESTIONS:

How does the law handle the situation where there is lack of clarity in whether an interest should be a contingent remainder or vested? The law prefers a vested remainder over a contingent one since that promotes certainty. So if there is any ambiguity, the court will go with a classification of vested rather than contingent remainder.

Additionally, remainders are favored over executory interests in part due to the feudal origins outlined below. This means that if there is ambiguity between a remainder and an executory interest, the court will attempt to first classify it as a remainder. Contingent remainders and executory interests are very similar in that neither is vested and they will not become possessory unless some condition is satisfied. The distinction is that the contingent remainder cannot divest a prior interest but an executory interest can.

b. Executory Interests

Not long after the contingent remainder was recognized by the courts, the executory interest arose to complicate matters further. The executory interest, made possible by the Statute of Uses (1536), developed to do what a remainder cannot do: divest or cut short the preceding interest. Before the Statute of Uses there could not be an interest in a transferee that could divest or cut short a freehold estate. However, they proved to be quite useful and after evolving in equity the Statute of Uses allowed this interest.

An executory interest is a future interest in a transferee that must, in order to become possessory:

1. divest or cut short some interest in another *transferee* (this is known as a shifting executory interest), or
2. divest the *transferor* in the future (this is known as a springing executory interest).[87]

An executory interest is a future interest in a transferee that can take effect only by divesting another interest. The difference between taking possession as soon as the prior estate ends and divesting the prior estate is the essential difference between a remainder and an executory interest. Because the executory interest can do something the remainder cannot, the executory interest is comparable to the utility player on a baseball team. This interest can field many positions on the timeline and has proved to be very useful in working with giving effect to the specific intent of the grantor or testator in conveyances.

Because of this distinction in how it can become possessory, the executory interest will follow the fee simple subject to an executory limitation (executory interest), the vested remainder subject to divestment, and can also exist with the vested remainder subject to open.[88]

i.   Shifting Executory Interest

The type of executory interest in which the interest is moving from one transferee to another is a shifting executory interest. It shifts from transferee #1 to transferee #2.

> **Example #1:** *O to A for life, then to B, but if B does not survive A, then to C.*

---

[87] We differentiate here between a shifting executory interest and a springing executory interest because we think it helps the student better understand what an executory interest is, but there is no legal difference in legal consequence between the two.

[88] Remember the class gift and the vested remainder subject to open. There could be a situation where there are members of the class who hold the vested remainder subject to open but there is a child in utero who could be born into the class. That unborn child technically has an executory interest that would partially divest the other members of the class.

C has a shifting executory interest because the property would shift from *B* (one transferee) to *C* (another transferee).

> **Example #2:** *O* to *A* as long as the land is used for agricultural purposes, otherwise to *B*.

B has a shifting executory interest following *A*'s fee simple subject to executory limitation. The property would shift from *A* (one transferee) to *B* (another transferee).

ii.   Springing Executory Interests

The executory interest that operates to divest or cut short the estate of the transferor is a springing executory interest. There are two situations where a springing executory interest can be created.

> **Example #1:** *O* to *A* if *A* graduates from law school.

This conveyance looks remarkably different from the previous examples in this chapter. What is *O* trying to accomplish here? *O* wants possession to transfer to *A* only if a certain condition is satisfied. This means that *O* is going to retain possession that may now be cut short if *A* satisfies this condition precedent. This is a future interest only conveyance. *O* has now transformed his FSA into a FSSEL. *A* has received a springing executory interest.

If and when *A*'s future interest becomes possessory, the estate will spring from the transferor directly to this transferee.

The executory interest may also come into play in the situation of a conveyance that includes a gap in time that must be accounted for. Let's turn to an example that was included earlier during the remainders to consider the nature of the contingent remainder.

> **Example #2:** Oscar conveys Blackacre to Angela for life, then to Brad if Brad gives Angela a proper funeral.

Remember we already identified that the interest created in Brad could not be a remainder because it would not be able to follow Angela's life estate. There was a condition that had to be satisfied first. This conveyance creates a "gap in time." Because we have to wait to see if the condition is satisfied, Oscar retained a reversion in a FSSEL. He might have possession again forever, but he might be cut short if Brad satisfies the condition precedent of giving Angela a proper funeral. So, there is a future interest in a transferee that follows a defeasible fee estate and is one that has to divest or cut short the transferor, Oscar. This means it has to be an executory interest and it must be a springing executory interest because the property would spring from Oscar (transferor) to Brad (transferee).

4. Rules Promoting Alienability

In the section on contingent remainders, we have already seen the destructibility of contingent remainders in action. This rule was regarding as promoting alienability of land by destroying uncertain interests, putting the land back in the hands of the original transferor so that the land could be conveyed to someone else rather than waiting to see if a condition would be satisfied. While that rule did promote alienability it has been destroyed in most jurisdictions due to the harsh nature of the rule and the fact that the outcome is often contrary to the transferor's intent.

There are other rules that were created for different reasons historically but in modern times tie into promoting alienability. Both the Rule in Shelley's Case and the Doctrine of Worthier Title were created originally to make sure that inheritance taxes could not be avoided. Today, some states still retain these rules because by destroying certain attempted conveyances they promote the alienability of land.

a. Rule in Shelley's Case

If one instrument creates a life estate in *A* and purports to create a remainder in persons described as *A*'s heirs and the life estate and remainder are both legal or equitable, the remainder becomes a remainder in fee simple in *A*.

Example: *O* to *A* for life, then to *A*'s heirs.

First, classify the interests at the time of conveyance. *A* has a life estate, *A*'s heirs have a contingent remainder in FSA, *O* has a reversion in FSA. Why would *O* do this? If both interests are created in the inter vivos conveyance, no inheritance occurs upon *A*'s death and those heirs take title free of any inheritance taxes. The crown was not going to allow this to happen so the Rule in Shelley's Case was a rule created to completely ignore *O*'s intent and would require reclassification.

So, if the rule applies, the remainder will now be an indefeasibly vested remainder in *A* in FSA. *O*'s reversion disappears. *A* now has a life estate and the vested remainder following the life estate. Due to the doctrine of merger, the present estate and vested future interest merge together and now create FSA in *A*. *A*'s heirs could still ultimately inherit the land from *A* upon *A*'s death, but they would have to pay inheritance taxes.

Most states today have abolished the Rule in Shelley's Case by statute.[89] In Texas, Texas Property Code § 5.042 abolished the Rule in Shelley's Case for conveyances taking effect after January 1, 1964. Therefore, in most states today we would not reclassify the interests and *O* is allowed to convey the life estate to *A* and a contingent remainder to the heirs of *A*.

b. Doctrine of Worthier Title

If there is conveyance of land by a grantor to a person and the same instrument purports to give a *remainder or executory interest* to the *grantor's heirs*, no future interest in the heirs is created; rather a reversion is retained by the grantor.

Example #1: *O* to *A* for life, then to *O*'s heirs.

First, classify the interests created in the conveyance. *A* has a life estate, *O*'s heirs have a contingent remainder in FSA and *O* holds a reversion in FSA. Why would *O* create such a conveyance? This was another attempt to avoid inheritance taxes. If *O* conveyed these interests inter vivos, upon *O*'s death there was nothing to pass, we would simply be able to identify the heirs who would take possession upon *A*'s death. The crown was also not going to allow this to happen so the Doctrine of Worthier Title was a rule created to completely ignore *O*'s intent and would require reclassification.

So, if the rule applied here, *A* would still have a life estate and now *O* would have a reversion in FSA. Now, if *O* wanted his heirs to take the land upon *A*'s death, *O* would have to devise his reversion or it would be inherited and thus subject to inheritance taxes.

Example #2: Oscar conveys Blackacre to Angela for life, then if Angela has a proper funeral, to the heirs of Oscar.

We start with classification, and this is the gap in time example again. Angela has a life estate, Oscar has a reversion in FSSEL, and the heirs of Oscar have springing executory interest in FSA. Now, instead of a remainder in the grantor's heirs we have an executory interest in the grantor's heirs. When applying the rule, *A* still would have a life estate and *O* would have the reversion in FSSEL as well as the executory interest. The FSSEL and the executory interest would merge together and Oscar would have a reversion in FSA. It would be as if the conveyance were Oscar to Angela for life.

---

[89] Thompson on Real Property, Thomas Edition § 30.22 (David A. Thomas ed. 1994); T.P. Gallianis, The Future of Future Interests, 60 Wash. & Lee L. Rev. 513, 534-542 (2003).

Much like the Rule in Shelley's Case, the Doctrine of Worthier Title has been abolished by statute in most states as well.[90] In Texas, Texas Property Code § 5.042 abolished the Rule in Shelley's Case for conveyances taking effect after January 1, 1964. Therefore, in most states today we would not reclassify the interests and *O* is allowed to convey a future interest to his heirs.

c. The Rule Against Perpetuities

The Rule Against Perpetuities was mainly created because the executory interests that were created did not fall within the Rule of Destructability of Contingent Remainders. Much of the concern of having uncertainty with remainders was addressed with the Rule. Executory interests would have been able to linger for too long a period without creating another rule. The Rule Against Perpetuities is a rule about time. It is another rule that defeats the intent of the grantor. The Rule operates to invalidate future interests that will vest too remotely in time. The Rule states:

> No interest is good unless it must vest, if at all, no later than 21 years after the death of some life in being at the creation of the interest.[91]

If your response to reading the rule is "what?," you are not alone. According to the California Supreme Court in a legal malpractice case against an attorney who incorrectly drafted a will, "it would not be proper to hold that defendant failed to use such skill, prudence, and diligence as lawyers of ordinary skill and capacity commonly exercise" when dealing with such a complicated rule.[92] The rule is really not as complicated as it initially appears. It is simply a tool that was crafted to ensure that interests would not linger too far into the future and thus tie up land with such uncertainty.

The Rule Against Perpetuities only applies to contingent remainders, executory interests (whether shifting or springing), and the vested remainder subject to open. Contingent remainders and executory interests make sense because those interests are subject to conditions precedent. The vested remainder subject to open is unusual because that interest is actually vested. The Rule applies, however, because of the idea of the class gift and the fact that people can become members of the class over time and someone could come into the class too remotely.

---

[90] William B. Stoebuck & Dale A. Whitman, The Law of Property § 3.15, at 110 (3d ed. 2000).

[91] John C. Gray, The Rule Against Perpetuities 191 (4th ed. 1942) (quoted in Thompson on Real Property, Thomas Edition § 28.01 (David A. Thomas ed. 1994).

[92] Lucas v. Hamm, 364 P.2d 685 (Cal. 1961).

For purposes of this course, we will not go into the application of the Rule. That will occur during Trusts and Estates because there have been statutory modifications to the Rule and they apply most commonly in the context of trusts. However, the following example can demonstrate the application of the Rule:

O to A as long as the land is used for agricultural purposes, then to B.

When classifying the interests, the language of the conveyance clearly creates a FSSEL in A with B holding a springing executory interest. Now that there is an executory interest, the Rule Against Perpetuities comes into consideration. The question would be, could everyone alive at the time of conveyance die and then 21 years pass before the land is no longer used for agricultural purposes? The answer is of course, yes. The land could be used for agricultural purposes for hundreds of years. This means the executory interest could possibly vest too remotely. This requires reclassification because B's interest is void. That leaves us with "O to A as long as the land is used for agricultural purposes." When we reclassify that leaves A with a fee simple determinable and O with a possibility of reverter in fee simple absolute. Because the Rule does not apply to future interests in the transferor, the condition is still valid and if violated it will revert back, not shift forward to another transferee. It does not matter that this is completely contrary to O's intent, the law is intent canceling.

E. Practice Problems

These problems are designed to help learn the estate system material as you go and also to review the concepts. Work through these examples over and over again to master the distinctions and patterns of language.

Assume that the original grantor has ownership of the property in fee simple absolute. Also, assume that the language used in the conveyance provides an adequate description of the property. Do not assume any other facts. If other facts are needed to fully identify all interests created in the property, indicate what facts are needed and why.

1. Dallas to Scott for life, then to Eliot and his heirs.

2. In his will, Oliver devises his fee simple estate Blackacre "to April and her heirs, if and when she becomes a lawyer." When Oliver dies, April is not yet a lawyer. Oliver's sole heir is Ben.

3. Danny to Ben and his heirs so long as he uses the land for educational purposes. FSD

4. Olivia to Amy for so long as Amy shall live; thereafter to Bethany.
   a. Now assume that Amy sells her interest to Charlie. How would the interests be classified?

5. Andrew to Ben for life, then to Charles and his heirs if he marries Heather, and if Charles does not marry Heather, to Danny and his heirs.

6. Oscar to Amy for life then to Beth and her heirs if Beth attends Amy's funeral.

7. Lauren to Heather for life, then to Chet if Chet graduates from law school.
   a. What is the classification if the destructibility of contingent remainders is applied and at the time of Heather's death Chet is alive and has not graduated from law school?
   b. What is the classification at modern time in Texas with the abolition of the rule of destructibility of contingent remainders?
   c. Would the classification in *A* or *B* be any different if the language read "Lauren to Heather for life, then to Chet if Chet graduates from law school before Heather's death."

8. Andrew to Erin for life, then to Gail for life, then to Heather's heirs and their heirs. Assume that Heather is still alive.

9. Lauren to Heather as long as she does not marry Charles, then to Margaret and her heirs.

10. Evan to Steven and the heirs of his body, then to Richard and his heirs.

11. Jana to Lindsay for 99 years. *LiFE ESTATE?*

12. Eliot to Scott and his heirs if he graduates from law school.

13. Andrew to Ben for life, then to Charles, but if Charles marries Heather, then to Danny and his heirs.
    a. Assume that Ben, Charles, Heather, and Danny are alive.
    b. Assume that Ben is dead and Charles, Heather, and Danny are still alive.

14. Olivia to Amy for life, then to Amy's children and their heirs.
    a. Assume Amy is alive and has no children.
    b. Assume Amy is alive and has one child, Beth.
    c. Assume Amy is alive and has a second child, Cameron.

     d.   Assume Amy dies and her children Beth and Cameron are alive.

     e.   Assume Amy dies without any children.

15. Margaret conveys Blackacre to Lindsay for life, then to Lindsay's surviving children.

16. Eliot to Dallas and his heirs as long as Dallas uses the land for dove hunting, then to Scott and his heirs.

17. David to Lauren and her heirs, but if Lauren starts smoking, then to Erin and her heirs.

18. In his will, Andrew gives his wife Jessica Blackacre and provides that on her death, "the property shall go to my children in fee simple absolute." On Andrew's death, he and Jessica have two children, Kristy and Lindsay. There are no children of Andrew in utero.

19. Daniel conveys Blackacre to Sarah for life, remainder to Jane's heirs.
     a.   Jane is alive at the time of the conveyance.
     b.   Jane is dead at the time of the conveyance.

20. Dallas conveys Blackacre to Evan for life then to Gail and her heirs, but if she dies before age 25, to Heather and her heirs.

21. Patrick conveys Blackacre to Ryan for life, remainder to Ryan's widow. At the time of the conveyance Ryan is alive and married to Margaret.

22. Andrew to Ben for life, then to Charles and his heirs. Ben transfers his interest to Danny.

23. Lisa grants and conveys Blackacre to Angela for life; one day after Angela's death to Michelle and her heirs.

24. Donna grants and conveys Blackacre to David to be used as a youth camp.

25. Susan conveys the land described herein to McLennan County for the purpose of constructing and maintaining thereon a county hospital in memorial to the gallant men of the Armed Forces of the United States of America from McLennan County, Texas.

26. Bob conveys Blackacre to Pat for two years; then to Sandra for life; then to the heirs of Art and their heirs.

27. Jenny conveys Blackacre to Kate for life, remainder to Lauren and his heirs if Lauren enters an LLM program by the age of 25, but if Lauren does not enter an LLM program by age 25, to Melissa and her heirs.

28. Lauren conveys Blackacre to Heather for life.
    a. Heather then immediately conveys her estate to Charles for 25 years. *(LEASEHOLD TO CHARLES) → REVERSION TO HEATHER IN LIFE ESTATE*
    b. If Heather dies 10 years later, who is entitled to possession of Blackacre and why? *→ LAUREN Bc HEATHER'S LIFE ESTATE TERMINATED*

29. Amy conveys Blackacre to Charles for life, and on his death to his children. At the time of the conveyance Charles is alive and has one son, Chet.

30. Danny to Ben and his heirs, but if he stops using the land for educational purposes Danny has the right to reenter and reclaim the land.

31. Lori conveys Blackacre to Colton for life, then to Ethan and his heirs, but if Ethan does not reach age 16, then to Dylan and his heirs.

32. Eliot grants and conveys Blackacre to Dallas to be used for dove hunting.

33. Jessica grants and conveys Blackacre to Sam on the condition that Sam does not move away from Seattle.

34. Scott conveys Blackacre to Thomas for life, then if Tony has finished law school by then, to Tony and his heirs; otherwise to Elise and her heirs.

35. Carrie conveys Blackacre to Erin for life, then to Gail and her heirs, but if Gail dies without issue surviving her, to Jenny and her heirs.

36. Rosalie grants to Jerry and his heirs the land described herein for "so long as any of my children who are alive at my death shall survive."

REVIEW PROBLEMS:

Assume that the original grantor has ownership of the property in fee simple absolute. Also, assume that the language used in the conveyance provides an adequate description of the property. Do not assume any other facts. If other facts are needed to fully identify all interests created in the property, indicate what facts are needed and why.

Also, indicate whether there are any interests that are subject to the Rule Against Perpetuities. You do not need to apply the Rule, simply identify the interests subjected to the Rule.

1. Oliver conveys Blackacre to Amy as long as the land is used for agricultural purposes.

2. Oliver conveys Blackacre to Amy if she completes a degree in agricultural science.

3. Oliver conveys Blackacre to Amy, but if she does not use the land for agricultural purposes, Oliver retains the right to re-enter and reclaim the land.

4. Oliver conveys Blackacre to Amy as long as the land is used for agricultural purposes, and if it is not used for agricultural purposes, to Ben and his heirs.

5. Oliver conveys Blackacre to Amy for life, then to Ben and his heirs.

6. Oliver conveys Blackacre to Amy for life, if Amy uses the land for Agricultural purposes, to Ben, otherwise to Cathy.

7. Oliver conveys Blackacre to Amy for life, then to Ben if Ben completes a degree in agricultural science, and if he does not complete a degree in agricultural science, to Cathy.

8. Oliver conveys Blackacre to Amy for life, then to Ben, but if Ben does not complete a degree in agricultural science, to Cathy.

9. Oliver conveys Blackacre to Amy for life, then to Ben, but if Ben does not use the land for agricultural purposes, to Cathy.

Chapter 3
Possessory Interests in Land: Nonfreehold Estates

A. Introduction to Landlord and Tenant Relationships

The material now transitions from the classification and rules of the freehold estates into the nonfreehold estates. Recall, a freehold estate is an exclusive right to enjoy the possession and use of a parcel of land for an indefinite period. Now we compare the freehold to the leasehold estate which is a right in land for a fixed, definite period or for as long as the landlord and tenant desire.

This area of property governing the landlord and tenant relationship is probably one of the most familiar areas to students while being unfamiliar at the same time. While just about everyone has rented an apartment, house, townhouse, condominium, or some type of property, most of the time the tenant is unfamiliar with the actual rules that apply to the landlord-tenant relationship and is at the mercy of the lease agreement used by the landlord. During our coverage of this material, we will focus primarily on the Texas Property Code and its application but will also discuss common law concepts that are still in use today and also how the common law was superseded by statute in many instances. The area of landlord-tenant law is filled with public policy considerations and balancing of interests.

While the leasehold estate is an estate in land that is considered a possessory interest in property, it is not full ownership of property—the tenant is not conveyed the whole bundle of sticks. However, one of the most fundamental bundles—possession—is the primary stick or right conveyed in this transaction. Technically, the leasehold estate is a legal interest that entitles the tenant to immediate possession of specified land, either for a fixed period of time or for as long as the landlord and tenant desire. There is no seisin passed in this conveyance so that the landlord retains an interest in the land after the leasehold estate terminates. In order to fully appreciate the laws at work today, in this area is it also important to consider the historic origins of these estates.

We start out again in feudal times. Landlord-tenant law originated with English common law principles established during the postfeudal era. Under this approach a lease was seen as a conveyance of a nonfreehold or a "leasehold" estate. The lands of the nobility and gentry were cultivated by landless serfs that had arrangements that differed very little from slavery. When the Black Plague decimated the supply of labor, the lords had to offer more attractive agreements to have labor to work their land. This evolved into a very rudimentary lease, where the former serf was allowed to use a particular tract of land for an agreed-upon term in exchange for a fixed rent. This gradually gave way to the landlord-tenant relationship.

The relationship really began more as a commercial lease rather than a residential lease, because the agreements during the medieval times were for farming land. The landlord was transformed into the "gentleman" whose social status precluded any manual labor and the landlord provided no services to the tenant, nor did the tenant expect any. Once the landlord transferred possession, his only remaining role was passive—receiving rent.

By 1500, this type arrangement was well solidified and molded to fit the farm lease situation. The lease was viewed as a conveyance of an estate in land and was governed by property law rather than contract law principles. However, what this meant was that under common law:

1. the tenant had the sole duty to repair and maintain the premises and any structure on the premises even if they were demolished by fire or other disaster;
2. the tenant was required to pay the rent even if the structures were destroyed;
3. the tenant was required to continue the tenancy and pay rent even if the landlord breached any lease obligations he had undertaken (the tenant's sole remedy was to sue for damages, not end the lease); and
4. the landlord had no duty to mitigate damages if the tenant abandoned the premises.

In the 1500s and 1600s, widespread residential leasing began in England as urbanization increased. Courts applied these standard landlord-tenant rules from the commercial farming leases. Traditionally, this area of the law was governed by principles that heavily favored the landlord. This landlord-favored relationship went on for centuries, until the conditions of residential leased property in urban areas in the United States had to be addressed.

In the 1970s, courts began to reexamine these traditional rules in light of modern conditions, particularly the plight of the urban residential tenant. May poor and unsophisticated residential tenants were at the mercy of the landlord for housing, and the conditions were deplorable. People were left with little choice but to live in unsafe and unsanitary conditions because they could afford little else. The tenant had no power to force the landlord to comply with the few laws that did exist for their protection. When these disputes started making their way to the courts across the country, a massive shift in the law toward enhanced protection for residential tenants resulted.

By contrast, commercial leases are still governed largely by traditional property rules, although there has been some modernization in this area as well. The commercial tenant is viewed as a sophisticated party with equal bargaining power to the landlord. The laws have not gone as far in this context to try to protect the tenant. We will find many instances in this area of the law where there are distinct differences at common law and by statute between the residential and commercial tenant.

As with other topics in a first-year Property course, this material cannot cover all of the intricacies and possibilities of the landlord and tenant relationship. The focus will primarily be on residential leases in some of the major areas of trouble in the landlord-tenant relationship, such as rights of possession, condition of the premises and repairs, subleases and assignments, and the always troublesome security deposit. Along the way there will be some comparisons to commercial leases where there are significant differences. But before getting into the specific rules, we start with classification of the leasehold estate.

1. Classification of the Leasehold Estate

There are three true leasehold estates or tenancies that can be created and a fourth category that is referred to as a tenancy but really isn't a true leasehold estate. They are the (1) Tenancy for Years (a/k/a Term of Years), (2) Periodic Tenancy, (3) Tenancy at Will, and (4) Tenancy at Sufferance.

a. Tenancy for Years (Term of Years)

A tenancy for years is one in which the tenancy has a specified beginning and ending date or can be computed by the information contained within the lease.[1] To create an estate for years or for any definite term, the lease must be certain or capable of being made certain as to the beginning, duration, and termination of the term. However, an estate may be created that will terminate subject to an earlier termination on the happening of a collateral event, such as the sale of the premises or like conditions. No notice of termination is necessary because the parties know from the outset when the tenancy will end.

This form of leasehold is particularly useful in the commercial context. It allows the parties to plan for the future with respect to renegotiation of lease terms, change in location of a business, or the landlord's desire to use the premises for a different purpose. The term of years could easily be used in the residential tenancies as well. However, typically, even if the leasehold begins with

---

[1] 49 Tex. Jur. 3d Landlord and Tenant § 10 (2007).

a term of years there is often a notice requirement added that will then operate to change the leasehold into a periodic tenancy.[2]

(1) Example Form: The form in this section illustrates a standard provision to express the term or basic effective period of a typical lease in which the parties intend to create a tenancy for a fixed term. The lease term usually is set out as the first article or section of a lease, immediately following the preamble and property description. The following examples demonstrate how the term of years can be created in the lease.

Term of Lease: This lease will begin on the 1st day of January, 2018 and will end on the 31st day of December, 2018.

Term of Lease: This lease will begin on the 1st day of January, 2018 lasting for a period of 5 years.

Term of Lease: This lease will begin on the 1st day of January, 2018 for a period of 6 months.

b. Periodic Tenancy

A lease without a definite ending date that calls for the periodic payment of rent usually is ill-advised but often employed in residential leases. It creates only a "periodic tenancy," with the parties having the power to terminate the tenancy on notice to the other party.[3] The parties can choose any period of time that will continue to automatically renew until either the landlord or tenant gives proper notice to terminate. The period could be days, weeks, months, years—really any leasehold that does not automatically end but continues to renew.

Unlike the term of years, the periodic tenancy can be created in several ways: (1) by express language in the lease; (2) by implication; or (3) by operation of law. The parties could specifically state that the tenancy will be from month to month or year to year, or whatever period they desire to specifically create. However, if there is no specific language to create the term of years, and no specific language to identify a periodic tenancy, the court must continue to look for an option. The court can try to determine if there is an implied periodic tenancy based on a regular rent payment period. If the parties did not specify month to month but

---

[2] The standard Texas Apartment Association lease begins with language that creates a term of years. Then by the language of the document there is a requirement to give notice to terminate and if proper notice is not given the leasehold then changes to a month-to-month periodic tenancy.

[3] Sellers v. Spiller, 64 S.W.2d 1049, 1051 (Tex. Civ. App.–Austin 1933, no writ); *see* Lynch v. Cock, 195 S.W.2d 773, 774 (Tex. Civ. App.–Texarkana 1946, ref. n.r.e.).

did specify a monthly rent payment, the classification would be a month-to-month periodic tenancy. A tenancy can be created by operation of law if (1) an attempted term of years or periodic tenancy fails to comply with the statute of frauds, or (2) a tenant holds over after the expiration of the original tenancy and the landlord accepts rent from the holdover tenant. In those instances the court will allow for the creation of a leasehold and will again look to the rent paid and accepted by the landlord. Whether a tenancy is from month to month or from year to year is a question of law to be determined by the court from the facts.[4]

A period tenancy will be created when a lease does not specify an ending date but requires the lessee to pay rent periodically until the lease is terminated by notice or breach. The effective date for termination by notice corresponds, as a general rule, to the rent-paying period but can be governed by statute. Notice given during a period is effective termination at the end of the next rent period.[5]

> Term of lease. The lease term will begin on January 1, 2018 and will continue thereafter as a month-to-month tenancy until terminated as provided elsewhere in this lease or by either party's giving the other at least 30 days' written notice of the intention to terminate the tenancy as of the end of the next rental period following the period in which the notice is given.

No matter how the periodic tenancy is created, it must end with proper notice being given by either the landlord or tenant. The requirement for proper notice to terminate the periodic tenancy is an area where there has been a great deal of change from the common law. At common law, the notice required for a periodic tenancy had to be the same as the length of the period up to a maximum of six months. This means that if L and T agreed to a month-to-month periodic tenancy, either party would have to give one-month's notice to properly terminate. If the period were three months, then three-months' notice would have to be given to properly terminate. If the period were six months, that would be the amount of notice required. However, once we move past a six-month period, the amount of notice stays at six months.

The other harsh reality was that the notice not only had to be the right time length, but it also had to be given timely so that the tenancy would terminate on a period ending date. If the period begins on the first of the month and runs through the last day of the month, the notice would need to be timed precisely to end on the period ending date, the last day of the month. This is a rule that would be more favorable to the landlord than the tenant. As a result, most states,

---

[4] 49 Tex. Jur. 3d Landlord and Tenant § 11 (2007).
[5] Texas Real Estate Guide § 40.22[4][a][ii]; *see also* Tex. Prop. Code Ann. § 91.001 (Vernon 2007).

if not all, have modified this by statute. Additionally, even if not changed by statute, a provision in a lease agreement can change the requirements for proper notice to terminate.

Tex. Prop. Code
§ 91.001. Notice for Terminating Certain Tenancies

(a) A monthly tenancy or a tenancy from month to month may be terminated by the tenant or the landlord giving notice of termination to the other.

(b) If a notice of termination is given under Subsection (a) and if the rent paying period is at least one month, the tenancy is terminates on whichever of the following days is the later:

(1) The day given in the notice for termination; or

(2) One month after the day on which the notice is given.

(c) Omitted.

(d) If a tenancy terminates on a day that does not correspond to the beginning or end of a rent-paying period, the tenant is liable for rent only up to the date of termination.

(e) Subsections (a), (b), (c) and (d) do not apply if:

(1) a landlord and tenant have agreed in an instrument signed by both parties on a different period of notice to terminate the tenancy or that no notice is required; or

(2) there is a breach of contract recognized by law.

PROBLEMS:

1. *L* and *T* enter into a lease agreement that states "*L* to *T*, beginning January 1, 2013, for two years." On December 31, 2014, *T* packs up and leaves, saying nothing to *L* and paying no additional rent. What result if *L* sues *T*?

2. *L* and *T* enter into a lease agreement that states "*L* to *T*, beginning January 1, 2013." On December 31, 2014, *T* packs up and leaves, saying nothing to *L* and paying no additional rent. What result if *L* sues *T*?

3. *L* and *T* enter into a lease agreement that states "*L* to *T*, beginning January 1, 2013, for a two-year period that will automatically renew until either *L* or *T* give proper notice to terminate." On December 31, 2014, *T* packs up and leaves, saying nothing to *L* and paying no additional rent. What result if *L* sues *T*?

4. *L* and *T* enter into a lease agreement that states "*L* to *T*, beginning January 1, 2013, with an annual rental of $12,000 per year, payable at $1,000 per month on the first of each month." On December 31, 2014, *T*

packs up and leaves, saying nothing to L and paying no additional rent. What result if *L* sues *T*?

5. *L* and *T* enter into a lease agreement that states "*L* to *T*, beginning January 1, 2013, to run from month-to-month with a rent of $12,000 per year, payable at $1,000 per month on the first of each month."

    a. On October 15, *T* sends written notice to *L* that she plans to vacate and terminate the lease on November 15. What result if *L* sues *T* in a common law jurisdiction? What result if *L* sues *T* in Texas?

    b. On October 15, *T* sends written notice to *L* that she plans to vacate and terminate the lease on October 31. What result if *L* sues *T* in a common law jurisdiction? What result if *L* sues *T* in Texas?

c. Tenancy at Will

One in lawful possession of premises by permission of the owner or landlord and for no fixed term but simply for as long as the landlord and tenant desire is a tenant at will. If a lease does not provide for a definite or certain lease term and does not provide a means of impliedly creating a periodic tenancy, the tenancy created by the lease will be deemed a "tenancy at will."[6] In such a tenancy, either party may terminate the leasehold estate at any time.[7] During its existence, however, a tenancy at will is a leasehold estate.[8]

A tenancy at will is typically not a desirable tenancy because it can be terminated at any time by a variety of ways. Either party can simply choose to end the tenancy. Additionally, the tenancy at will can terminate by: (1) the death of either party; (2) waste by the tenant; (3) assignment of the leasehold by the tenant; (4) transfer of title by landlord; or (5) lease by landlord to someone else.

If the lease provides that the tenancy can be terminated by one party, at modern times it is not necessarily at the will of the other. Complications in this statement are examined in the *Garner* and *Willis* cases below. Note, however, that a unilateral power to terminate a lease can be engrafted on a term of years or a periodic tenancy; for example, a lease by "*L* to *T* for 10 years or until *L* sooner terminates" creates a term of years determinable. If the parties truly desire to create a tenancy at will it should be expressly stated as clearly as possible.

---

[6] Philpot v. Fields, 633 S.W.2d 546, 547 (Tex. App.—Texarkana 1982, no writ).

[7] Urban v. Crawley, 206 S.W.2d 158, 160 (Tex. Civ. App.—Eastland 1947, writ ef. n.r.e.).

[8] Griffin v. Reynolds, 107 S.W.2d 634, 637 (Tex. Civ. App.—Texarkana 1937, writ dism'd).

Some modern statutes require a period of notice—say 30 days or time equal to the interval between rent payments—in order for one party or the other to terminate a tenancy at will, which seems to make it more like a periodic tenancy.[9] In Texas, there is no required notice to terminate the tenancy at will; however, in order to evict a tenant at will who will not leave, the property code will require a minimum of three-days' notice to vacate before an eviction suit may be brought against the tenant.

Garner v. Gerrish
Court of Appeals of New York, 1984
473 N.E.2d 223

Opinion by Judge WACHTLER.

The question on this appeal is whether a lease which grants the tenant the right to terminate the agreement at a date of his choice creates a determinable life tenancy on behalf of the tenant or merely establishes a tenancy at will. The courts below held that the lease created a tenancy at will permitting the current landlord to evict the tenant. We granted the tenant's motion for leave to appeal and now reverse the order appealed from.

In 1977 Robert Donovan owned a house located in Potsdam, New York. On April 14 of that year he leased the premises to the tenant Lou Gerrish. The lease was executed on a printed form and it appears that neither side was represented by counsel. The blanks on the form were filled in by Donovan who provided the names of the parties, described the property and fixed the rent at $ 100 a month. With respect to the duration of the tenancy the lease provides it shall continue "for and during the term of *quiet enjoyment* from the *first day* of *May, 1977* which term will end—*Lou Gerrish has the privilege of termination [sic] this agreement at a date of his own choice*" (emphasis added to indicate handwritten and typewritten additions to the printed form). The lease also contains a standard reference to the landlord's right to reentry if the rent is not timely paid, which is qualified by the handwritten statement: "Lou has thirty days grace for payment."

Gerrish moved into the house and continued to reside there, apparently without incident, until Donovan died in November of 1981. At that point David Garner, executor of Donovan's estate, served Gerrish with a notice to quit the premises. When Gerrish refused, Garner commenced this summary proceeding to have him evicted. Petitioner contended that the lease created a tenancy at will because it failed to state a definite term. In his answering affidavit, the tenant

---

[9] How, in such jurisdictions, does the tenancy at will differ from a periodic tenancy? *See* 1 American Law of Property §§ 3.28, 3.31 (1952 & Supp. 1977). Under a tenancy for no fixed period with rent reserved or paid periodically, a periodic tenancy—rather than a tenancy at will—arises in most jurisdictions by implication. *See id*. § 3.25.

alleged that he had always paid the rent specified in the lease. He also contended that the lease granted him a tenancy for life, unless he elects to surrender possession during his lifetime.

The County Court granted summary judgment to petitioner on the ground that the lease is "indefinite and uncertain as regards the length of time accorded respondent to occupy the premises. Although the writing specifies the date of commencement of the term, it fails to set forth the duration of continuance, and the date or event of termination." The court concluded that the original landlord leased the premises to the tenant "for a month-to-month term and that petitioner was entitled to terminate the lease upon the death of the lessor effective upon the expiration of the next succeeding monthly term of occupancy." In support of its decision the court quoted the following statement from our opinion in Western Transp. Co. v. Lansing, 49 N.Y. 499, 508: "A lease for so long as the lessee shall please, is said to be a lease at will of both lessor and lessee."

The Appellate Division affirmed for the same reasons in a brief memorandum.

On appeal to our court, the parties concede that the agreement creates a lease. The only question is whether it should be literally construed to grant to the tenant alone the right to terminate at will, or whether the landlord is accorded a similar right by operation of law.

At early common law according to Lord Coke, "when the lease is made to have and to hold at the will of the lessee, this must be also at the will of the lessor" (1 Co. Litt., § 55a). This rule was generally adopted in the United States during the 19th century and at one time was said to represent the majority view. However, it was not universally accepted and has been widely criticized, particularly in this century, as an antiquated notion which violates the terms of the agreement and frustrates the intent of the parties.

It has been noted that the rule has its origins in the doctrine of livery of seisin, which required physical transfer of a clod of earth, twig, key or other symbol on the premises in the presence of witnesses, to effect a conveyance of land interest. Although this ceremony was not required for leases, which were generally limited to a specified term of years, it was necessary to create a life tenancy which was viewed as a freehold interest. Thus, if a lease granting a tenant a life estate was not accompanied by livery of seisin, the intended conveyance would fail and a mere tenancy at will would result. The corollary to Lord Coke's comment is that the grant of a life estate would be enforceable if accompanied by livery of seisin and the other requisites for a conveyance. Because such a tenancy was terminable at the will of the grantee, there was in fact no general objection at common law to a tenancy at the will of the tenant. The express terms of a lease granting a life tenancy would fail, and a tenancy at will would result, only when livery of seisin, or any other requirement for a conveyance, had not been met.

Because livery of seisin, like the ancient requirement for a seal, has been abandoned, commentators generally urge that there is no longer any reason why a lease granting the tenant alone the right to terminate at will, should be converted into a tenancy at will terminable by either party. The Restatement adopts this view and provides the following illustration: "L leases a farm to T 'for as long as T desires to stay on the land.' The lease creates a determinable life estate in T, terminable at T's will or on his death." This rule has increasingly gained acceptance in courts which have closely examined the problem.

Seemingly perpetual leases are not favored by the law, and will not be enforced unless the lease clearly grants to the tenant or his successors the right to extend beyond the initial term by renewing indefinitely.

In the case now before us the lease does not provide for renewal, and its duration cannot be said to be perpetual or indefinite. It simply grants a personal right to the named lessee, Lou Gerrish, to terminate at a date of his choice, which is a fairly typical means of creating a life tenancy terminable at the will of the tenant. Thus the lease will terminate, at the latest, upon the death of the named lessee. The fact that it may be terminated at some earlier point, if the named tenant decides to quit the premises, does not render it indeterminate. Leases providing for termination upon the occurrence of a specified event prior to the completion of an otherwise fixed term, are routinely enforced even when the event is within the control of the lessee.

In sum, the lease expressly and unambiguously grants to the tenant the right to terminate, and does not reserve to the landlord a similar right. To hold that such a lease creates a tenancy terminable at the will of either party would violate the terms of the agreement and the express intent of the contracting parties.

Accordingly, the order of the Appellate Division should be reversed and the petition dismissed.

Order reversed, with costs, and petition dismissed.

Willis v. Thomas
Court of Civil Appeals of Texas, San Antonio, 1928
9 S.W.2d 423

SMITH, J.

R. M. Willis and T. V. Cobb operated the Star Drug Store in Corpus Christi in a building rented by them from Guggenheim & Cohn, the owners. Dr. J. R. Thomas was a practicing physician in Corpus Christi, but being impressed by a current real estate boom undertook to engage in the real estate brokerage business through a partnership he formed with one J. J. Prine. This partnership rented desk space in the Star Drug Store, from Willis and Cobb, under a lease which "shall begin not later than May 1, 1926, and shall terminate not later than December 31, 1927," a period of 20 months. The lessees agreed to pay rental in the lump sum of $1,500, payable monthly in advance at the rate of $75 per month. The lease contract contained these stipulations, among others usual to such agreements:

> "Said party of the second part (lessees) hereby agrees, binds and obligates themselves jointly and individually to pay unto party of the first part at their place of business, Corpus Christi, Tex., as rental for said space for said entire twenty (20) months the sum of fifteen hundred ($1,500.00) dollars payable as follows: Twenty (20) equal installments of seventy-five ($75.00) dollars each to be paid on the first day of each month for twenty (20) months, and if default be made in the payment of monthly installments as they accrue for a period of fifteen (15) days all of said installments not then due shall at the option of the parties of the first part and without notice to the parties of the second part become due and payable and the parties of the first part shall thereupon have the right to reenter into and upon said lease space and eject therefrom parties of the second part and take possession of said space without prejudice, however, to the right of parties of the first part to collect rental as aforesaid and as herein agreed, on said premises for the unexpired portion of said entire term of twenty (20) months.
>
> The parties of the first part (lessor) reserve the right to cancel this lease at any time they sell the Star Drug Store or, and the lease they have with Guggenheim & Cohn, and parties of the second part agree to the cancellation of this, their lease, in this case and agrees to vacate said space upon the payment to them of one hundred and fifty ($150.00) dollars by parties of the first part within fifteen (15) days after being notified of cancellation."

Dr. Thomas's partner, Prine, upon whom it seems Dr. Thomas depended to actively operate the new business, appears to have given up the project and left town at the end of the first two weeks, and the venture was suspended thenceforward. Dr. Thomas paid the first month's rent of $75, but made no further effort to operate the business or hold the rented space. On September 10, 1927, 3 months and 21 days before the expiration of the 20-month term fixed in the sublease to Dr. Thomas and his associate, Willis & Cobb surrendered their lease to the owners of the building. This was one of the contingencies under which it was stipulated that the sublease should terminate.

Willis, as the successor to Willis & Cobb, the landlord, brought this action against Dr. Thomas alone, seeking to recover of him the sum of $1,500, being the full amount of the agreed rental stipulated in the 20-month sublease. The trial court directed a verdict in favor of Thomas, denying any recovery to Willis, who has appealed.

The case seems to have gone off, primarily, upon the theory that the lease contract in question created a strict tenancy at will, terminable by the landlord at any time he might so elect, and therefore likewise terminable at the will of the tenant.

It is contended, by appellee, that although the term of the lease is definitely fixed in the contract to be for a period of 20 months, the certainty of the term so fixed is destroyed by the provision that the lease may be canceled by the landlord in the contingency that he sell his drug business and/or the lease under which he has sublet a part of his leased premises to appellee. It is contended that this proviso put it in the power of the landlord to terminate the lease at any time he pleased, by the device of selling his drug store or his lease, thus bringing the contract within the class which, being expressly terminable at the will of one of the parties, is impliedly terminable at the will of the other. It is remarkable that neither of the parties cites any case directly in point upon the facts, nor have we found any after a somewhat thorough search therefor.

T: He had at will term. rights

To create an estate for years, or for any definite term, the lease must be certain, or capable of being made certain, as to the beginning, duration, and termination of the term. A lease in general terms to run until the premises are sold, or similar conditions, is a tenancy at will only, constituting the lessee a tenant at the will of the lessor (Lea v. Hernandez, 10 Tex. 137), and such a lease is terminable at any time by either party, upon reasonable notice to the other. Taylor's Landlord and Tenant (9th Ed.) § 111; 16 R. C. L. 611; Hudson v. Wheeler, 34 Tex. 356; Robb v. St. Ry. Co., 82 Tex. 392, 18 S. W. 707; Emerson v. Emerson (Tex. Civ. App.) 35 S. W. 425; Buford v. Wasson, 49 Tex. Civ. App. 454, 109 S. W. 275, and cases cited in note to 34 L. R. A. (N. S.) 1069 et seq.

Applicable rules

But an estate may be created by a demise for a definite period, subject to an earlier termination contingent upon the happening of a collateral event, such as the sale of the premises, or like conditions. Taylor, § 76; 35 C. J. pp. 971, 1047; 16 R. C. L. p. 1108 et seq.

Such appears to be the character of the lease in controversy. It was for a definite period, fixed with certainty at 20 months. It is true it was terminable within a shorter period by the happening of the contingency of the sale of the landlord's drug business, and this contingency being within the control of appellant, it may be said, broadly, that the termination of the lease at any time lay within the power and pleasure of the landlord. But the latter could not exercise that power capriciously or by simulated transactions; the sale of the drug business must be negotiated and fully consummated in good faith in order to constitute the requisite contingency. This provision in the contract amounted to an option given the landlord to terminate the lease on the happening of that contingency, upon the payment of a bonus to the tenant as consideration for that

Landlord did not have full power to terminate at will

option. It is a form of contract recognizable and enforceable under the law, and very generally resorted to in the business world. 16 R. C. L. p. 1108, § 625 et seq. And the tenant cannot impair the landlord's right to collect the rent for the full term by abandonment of possession before the expiration of the term for which he has agreed to pay rent. 16 R. C. L. p. 969, § 481 et seq.; Goldman v. Broyles (Tex. Civ. App.) 141 S. W. 283.

We conclude, from the holdings of the authorities cited, that the contract was enforceable as against both parties for the period of 20 months, subject to earlier termination by the landlord under his option. By breaching the contract and abandoning the premises, and by refusing to make the payments as they accrued, appellant provoked the action of appellee in exercising his option to declare the rent due for the whole term as provided in the contract. But as the tenant should be favored in this character of contract, we think appellee should be credited with every amount he could have earned in the course the lease actually took. He would therefore be entitled to a credit of $75, actually paid by him, of $277.50 to cover the 3 months and 21 days deducted from the 20 months' term by reason of appellant's surrender of the original lease, and of $150 to which appellee would have been entitled as a bonus to be paid him by appellant in event of a cancellation of the lease prior to its normal expiration. These credits aggregate $502.50, leaving a balance of $997.50 due upon the contract amount. Reversed and rendered in favor of appellant.

2. Holding Over and the Tenant at Sufferance

A tenancy at sufferance is not a true tenancy but is one that arises under certain circumstances. A tenancy at sufferance typically arises in the case of a lessee holding over after the end of a lease without the permission of the lessor.[10] Unlike the implied periodic tenancy created by operation of law, a tenant in this case has not tendered rent that the landlord accepts. Here, the tenant remains on the property without the landlord's permission. A tenant at sufferance holds no estate in the real property.[11] This is basically the status of the tenant until the landlord elects how to handle the situation. The landlord has the ability to choose at that point of time. The landlord can choose to accept rent from the tenant and impose a new periodic tenancy or the landlord can choose to treat the tenant as a trespasser and sue to evict the tenant and collect damages.[12]

---

[10] Bockelmann v. Marynick, 788 S.W.2d 569, 571 (Tex. 1990).

[11] Griffin v. Reynolds, 107 S.W.2d 634, 637 (Tex. Civ. App.–Texarkana 1937, writ dism'd).

[12] Standard Container Corp. v. Dragon Realty, 683 S.W.2d 45, 48 (Tex. Civ. App.–Dallas 1984, writ ref. n.r.e.).

A written lease may or may not expressly cover the circumstance of the lessee's "holding over," that is, continuing to use and occupy the premises after the expiration of the primary term. When the lease includes a provision addressing the lessee's holding over, the provision will control over general rules applicable to a holdover tenancy.[13] In the usual case, the holdover provision gives the option to the lessor to accept continued possession as the lessee's agreement to be bound by the lease for another term or demand that the lessee vacate the premises.[14]

If the lease is silent about the effect of the lessee's holding over, and the facts are that the lessee continued in possession and paid rent accepted by the lessor, the courts will presume that the parties intended to renew the lease agreement on the same terms and conditions.[15]

3. The Lease

A lease is both an instrument of conveyance of an interest in real property **and** a contract. This means that the statute of frauds applies to the leasehold and certain requirements must be met. In a majority of states, Texas included, an oral lease may be valid if it is not for a term or period of more than one year.

The oral agreement must include the essential terms:

1. A physical property description of the leased property;
2. The term of the lease (or a way of impliedly establishing the term); and
3. The amount of the rent with time and manner of payment.

If the lease is longer than one year, then in addition to the above requirements, they must be in a writing or writings and be signed by the person to be charged with the promise or agreement or by someone lawfully authorized to sign for him.[16]

In Texas, the statute of frauds that applies to leases is found in the Texas Business and Commerce Code.

---

[13] Corpier v. Lawson, 356 S.W.2d 361, 362 (Tex. Civ. App.–Waco 1962, no writ).

[14] *Standard Container Corp.*, 683 S.W.2d 45, 48.

[15] Barragan v. Munoz, 525 S.W.2d 559, 561-562 (Tex. Civ. App.—El Paso 1975, no writ).

[16] *See* 49 Tex. Jur. Landlord and Tenant § 19.

Tex. Bus. & Com. Code
Effective: September 1, 2005

§ 26.01. Promise or Agreement Must Be in Writing[17]

   (a) A promise or agreement described in Subsection (b) of this section is not enforceable unless the promise or agreement, or a memorandum of it, is
   - (1) in writing; and
   - (2) signed by the person to be charged with the promise or agreement or by someone lawfully authorized to sign for him.
   (b) Subsection (a) of this section applies to:
   - (5) a lease of real estate for a term longer than one year;
   - (6) an agreement which is not to be performed within one year from the date of making the agreement;

Section 26.01(b)(5) provides the requirement that if the lease is for longer than one year it must be in writing. Subsection (b)(6) addresses the requirement of a writing if the lease cannot be completed with one year from the date of its making. This would be an applicable provision if the prospective landlord and tenant agree to a one-year term; however, when the agreement is reached verbally, the lease will not actually begin for two months. This means that even though the one-year lease would ordinarily not have to be in writing, because it cannot be performed within one year of the making of the agreement, it now must be in writing.

What happens if a prospective landlord and tenant negotiate essential lease provisions for a five-year lease through a series of email communications that contain an electronic signature block at the bottom of the message? Is there a valid lease that complies with the statute of frauds? Does the electronic "signature" fulfill the requirement? The answer requires a brief examination of the Uniform Electronic Transactions Act.

President Clinton signed the Electronic Signatures in Global and National Commerce Act (E-Sign) on June 30, 2000. Since then 47 states, D.C., Puerto Rico, and the Virgin Islands have adopted the Uniform Electronic Transactions Act (UETA). Only Illinois, New York, and Washington have not adopted UETA. Both acts validate the use of electronic records and signatures. Texas adopted its first version of the UETA in 2001. The most recent version of the UETA is found within the Business and Commerce Code.

Basically, the use of an electronic signature will turn on the question of intent of the parties. The provisions in Chapter 322 of the Texas Business and Commerce Code reflect the parties' ability to reach an agreement regarding the use of

---

[17] Subsections (b)(1)-(3) and (5)-(8) omitted.

electronic records and signatures for a transaction.[18] As defined in § 322.002, the agreement may be found in the parties' language or inferred from other circumstances and from rules, regulations, and procedures given the effect of agreements under laws otherwise applicable to a particular transaction. An "electronic signature" means an electronic sound, symbol, or process attached to or logically associated with a record and executed or adopted by a person with the intent to sign the record. Section 322.007 also provides that a record or signature may not be denied legal effect or enforceability solely because it is in electronic form. A contract may not be denied legal effect or enforceability solely because an electronic record was used in its formation. If a law requires a record to be in writing, an electronic record satisfies the law. If a law requires a signature, an electronic signature satisfies the law.

This means that when engaging in email communications regarding leases, the parties should be mindful of the fact that the communications could be used as a writing with electronic signatures to satisfy the statute of frauds.

B. Possession Issues

Because a leasehold estate is a possessory interest in land, there are many issues that arise in the landlord-tenant context. Is a tenant entitled to actual possession of the leasehold or merely a legal right to possess? What are the landlord's responsibilities if the tenant is disturbed in his possession during the lease term? How must the landlord deal with a tenant who defaults but remains in possession? What about if a tenant unlawfully abandons? These are all common questions that arise in this context. We will take each one by one and determine the rights and responsibilities of the parties.

1. Delivery of Possession

Law student enters into a lease agreement that is to run from August 1, 2015, through July 31, 2016. When law student arrives on August 1 to move into her apartment and get ready to start classes, landlord informs law student that the apartment is not ready for move-in due to a prior tenant holding over. Landlord does not have any other available options and tells law student, sorry, but you have to pay me rent because your lease has started. If law student wants to move in, she can figure out how to get the tenant evicted. What can the law student do? Does she have any recourse against landlord?

---

[18] Added by Acts 2007, 80th Leg., R.S., Ch. 885 (H.B. 2278), Sec. 2.01, eff. April 1, 2009.

Hannan v. Dusch
Supreme Court of Appeals of Virginia, 1930
153 S.E. 824

PRENTIS, C.J., delivered the opinion of the court.

The declaration filed by the plaintiff, Hannan, against the defendant, Dusch, alleges that Dusch had on August 31, 1927, leased to the plaintiff certain real estate in the city of Norfolk, Virginia, therein described, for fifteen years, the term to begin January 1, 1928, at a specified rental; that it thereupon became and was the duty of the defendant to see to it that the premises leased by the defendant to the plaintiff should be open for entry by him on January 1, 1928, the beginning of the term, and to put said petitioner in possession of the premises on that date; that the petitioner was willing and ready to enter upon and take possession of the leased property, and so informed the defendant; yet the defendant failed and refused to put the plaintiff in possession or to keep the property open for him at that time or on any subsequent date; and that the defendant suffered to remain on said property a certain tenant or tenants who occupied a portion or portions thereof, and refused to take legal or other action to oust said tenants or to compel their removal from the property so occupied. Plaintiff alleged damages which he had suffered by reason of this alleged breach of the contract and deed, and sought to recover such damages in the action. There is no express covenant as to the delivery of the premises nor for the quiet possession of the premises by the lessee.

The single question of law therefore presented in this case is whether a landlord, who without any express covenant as to delivery of possession leases property to a tenant, is required under the law to oust trespassers and wrongdoers so as to have it open for entry by the tenant at the beginning of the term—that is, whether without an express covenant there is nevertheless an implied covenant to deliver possession.

It seems to be perfectly well settled that there is an implied covenant in such cases on the part of the landlord to assure to the tenant the legal right of possession—that is, that at the beginning of the term there shall be no legal obstacle to the tenant's right of possession. This is not the question presented. Nor need we discuss in this case the rights of the parties in case a tenant rightfully in possession under the title of his landlord is thereafter disturbed by some wrongdoer. In such case the tenant must protect himself from trespassers, and there is no obligation on the landlord to assure his quiet enjoyment of his term as against wrongdoers or intruders.

Of course, the landlord assures to the tenant quiet possession as against all who rightfully claim through or under the landlord.

The discussion then is limited to the precise legal duty of the landlord in the absence of an express covenant, in case a former tenant, who wrongfully holds over, illegally refuses to surrender possession to the new tenant at the time fixed by the lease for the beginning of his term.

It is conceded by all that the two rules, one called the English rule, which implies a covenant requiring the lessor to put the lessee in possession, and that called the American rule, which recognizes the lessee's legal right to possession, but implies no such duty upon the lessor as against wrongdoers, are irreconcilable.

The English rule is that in the absence of stipulations to the contrary, there is in every lease an implied covenant on the part of the landlord that the premises shall be open to entry by the tenant at the time fixed by the lease for the beginning of his term.

It must be borne in mind, however, that the courts which hold that there is such an implied covenant do not extend the period beyond the day when the lessee's term begins. If after that day a stranger trespasses upon the property and wrongfully obtains or withholds possession of it from the lessee, his remedy is against the stranger and not against the lessor.

The lessee may also protect himself by having his lessor expressly covenant to put him in possession at a specified time, in which case, of course, the lessor is liable for breach of his covenant where a trespasser goes into possession, or wrongfully holds possession, and thereby wrongfully prevents the lessee from obtaining possession.

A case which supports the English rule is Herpolsheimer v. Christopher. In that case the court gave these as its reasons for following the English rule:

> "We deem it unnecessary to enter into an extended discussion, since the reasons pro and con are fully given in the opinions of the several courts cited. We think, however, that the English rule is most in consonance with good conscience, sound principle, and fair dealing. Can it be supposed that the plaintiff in this case would have entered into the lease if he had known at the time that he could not obtain possession on the 1st of March, but that he would be compelled to begin a lawsuit, await the law's delays, and follow the case through its devious turnings to an end before he could hope to obtain possession of the land he had leased? Most assuredly not. It is unreasonable to suppose that a man would knowingly contract for a lawsuit, or take the chance of one. Whether or not a tenant in possession intends to hold over or assert a right to future term may nearly always be known to the landlord, and is certainly much more apt to be within his knowledge than within that of the prospective tenant. Moreover, since in an action to recover possession against a tenant holding over, the lessee would be compelled largely to rely upon the lessor's testimony in regard to the facts of the claim

[handwritten margin note: English Rule Pro Tenant]

to hold over by the wrongdoer, it is more reasonable and proper to place the burden upon the person within whose knowledge the facts are most apt to lie. We are convinced, therefore, that the better reason lies with the courts following the English doctrine, and we therefore adopt it, and hold that, ordinarily, the lessor impliedly covenants with the lessee that the premises leased shall be open to entry by him at the time fixed in the lease as the beginning of the term."

Referring then to the American rule: Under that rule, in such cases, "the landlord is not bound to put the tenant into actual possession, but is bound only to put him in legal possession, so that no obstacle in the form of superior right of possession will be interposed to prevent the tenant from obtaining actual possession of the demised premises. If the landlord gives the tenant a right of possession he has done all that he is required to do by the terms of an ordinary lease, and the tenant assumes the burden of enforcing such right of possession as against all persons wrongfully in possession, whether they be trespassers or former tenants wrongfully holding over."

So that, under the American rule, where the new tenant fails to obtain possession of the premises only because a former tenant wrongfully holds over, his remedy is against such wrongdoer and not against the landlord—this because the landlord has not covenanted against the wrongful acts of another and should not be held responsible for such a tort unless he has expressly so contracted. This accords with the general rule as to other wrongdoers, whereas the English rule appears to create a specific exception against lessors.

There are some underlying fundamental considerations. Certainly, as a general rule, the lessee must protect himself against trespassers or other wrongdoers who disturb his possession. It is conceded by those who favor the English rule, that should the possession of the tenant be wrongfully disturbed the second day of the term, or after he has once taken possession, then there is no implied covenant on the part of his landlord to protect him from the torts of others. The English rule seems to have been applied only where the possession is disturbed on the first day, or perhaps more fairly expressed, where the tenant is prevented from taking possession on the first day of his term; but what is the substantial difference between invading the lessee's right of possession on the first or a later day? To apply the English rule you must imply a covenant on the part of the landlord to protect the tenant from the tort of another, though he has entered into no such covenant. This seems to be a unique exception, an exception which stands alone in implying a contract of insurance on the part of the lessor to save his tenant from all the consequences of the flagrant wrong of another person. Such an obligation is so unusual and the prevention of such a tort so impossible as to make it certain, we think, that it should always rest upon an express contract.

For the reasons which have been so well stated by those who have enforced the American rule, our judgment is that there is no error in the judgment complained of.

The law helps those who help themselves, generally aids the vigilant, but rarely the sleeping, and never the acquiescent.

Affirmed.

NOTES & QUESTIONS:

1. Under the American Rule, the tenant's remedies are against the person wrongfully in possession. The tenant may sue to recover possession and damages from the person wrongfully in possession. There is no action against the Landlord because the Landlord has not breached any duty or obligation to the tenant.

   In the situation with the law student being unable to enter the leased premises, she would have to determine who the holdover tenant is, sue the tenant, establish that she is entitled to possession, get a judgment against the holdover for damages she incurred, and then try to collect the judgment.

2. Is that what the average person would normally expect to be the answer? Why or why not? As compared to the English Rule:

   (1) The tenant may terminate the lease and sue for damages.

   (2) If a wrongdoer is in possession of only part of the premises, the tenant may take possession of the remainder with an appropriate abatement in rent and damages.

   (3) When possession is delayed, the tenant is not obligated to pay rent for the portion of the term during which he was kept out of possession and may collect appropriate damages.

   (4) The tenant may also go directly against the third party to recover possession or damages.

   Under the English Rule, the law student could choose which of these options would be better for her, which would include terminating the lease and just finding another place to live. The landlord would remain liable for any damages incurred as a result. Which rule do you prefer? Why?

3. Although the rule applied in *Hannan* is called the American Rule, it is actually the minority view in the United States today. Texas has followed

the English Rule since 1885 in the case of Hertzberg v. Beisenbach, 64 Tex. 262 (Tex. 1885) for residential properties and also applies the English rule to commercial tenancies.

4. Remember, nothing prevents this from being changed by agreement. Even if in an English Rule jurisdiction, the landlord could include language in the lease agreement that would essentially change the outcome to the application of the American Rule. Tenants must read leases carefully for language regarding actual possession of the premises in order to determine what the available rights and remedies will be.

2. Defaulting Tenant in Possession

Now, what happens if the tenant went into actual possession of the leasehold but is not complying with the terms of the lease. The landlord wants the tenant out. What can the landlord do to get the tenant to vacate the premises?

<u>Berg v. Wiley</u>
Supreme Court of Minnesota, 1978
264 N.W.2d 145

ROGOSHESKE, J.

Defendant landlord, Wiley Enterprises, Inc., and defendant Rodney A. Wiley (hereafter collectively referred to as Wiley) appeal from a judgment upon a jury verdict awarding plaintiff tenant, A Family Affair Restaurant, Inc., damages for wrongful eviction from its leased premises. The issues for review are whether the evidence was sufficient to support the jury's finding that the tenant did not abandon or surrender the premises and whether the trial court erred in finding Wiley's reentry forcible and wrongful as a matter of law. We hold that the jury's verdict is supported by sufficient evidence and that the trial court's determination of unlawful entry was correct as a matter of law, and affirm the judgment.

On November 11, 1970, Wiley, as lessor and tenant's predecessor in interest as lessee, executed a written lease agreement letting land and a building in Osseo, Minnesota, for use as a restaurant. The lease provided a 5-year term beginning December 1, 1970, and specified that the tenant agreed to bear all costs of repairs and remodeling, to "make no changes in the building structure" without prior written authorization from Wiley, and to "operate the restaurant in a lawful and prudent manner." Wiley also reserved the right "at [his] option [to] retake possession" of the premises "should the Lessee fail to meet the conditions of this Lease."[19] In early 1971, plaintiff Kathleen Berg took assignment of the lease from

---

[19] The provisions of the lease pertinent to this case provide:

the prior lessee, and on May 1, 1971, she opened "A Family Affair Restaurant" on the premises. In January 1973, Berg incorporated the restaurant and assigned her interest in the lease to "A Family Affair Restaurant, Inc." As sole shareholder of the corporation, she alone continued to act for the tenant.

The present dispute has arisen out of Wiley's objection to Berg's continued remodeling of the restaurant without procuring written permission and her consequent operation of the restaurant in a state of disrepair with alleged health code violations. Strained relations between the parties came to a head in June and July 1973. In a letter dated June 29, 1973, Wiley's attorney charged Berg with having breached lease items 5 and 6 by making changes in the building structure without written authorization and by operating an unclean kitchen in violation of health regulations. The letter demanded that a list of eight remodeling items be completed within 2 weeks from the date of the letter, by Friday, July 13, 1973, or Wiley would retake possession of the premises under lease item 7. Also, a June 13 inspection of the restaurant by the Minnesota Department of Health had produced an order that certain listed changes be completed within specified time limits in order to comply with the health code. The major items on the inspector's list, similar to those listed by Wiley's attorney, were to be completed by July 15, 1973.

During the 2-week deadline set by both Wiley and the health department, Berg continued to operate the restaurant without closing to complete the required items of remodeling. The evidence is in dispute as to whether she intended to permanently close the restaurant and vacate the premises at the end of the 2 weeks or simply close for about 1 month in order to remodel to comply with the health code. At the close of business on Friday, July 13, 1973, the last day of the 2-week period, Berg dismissed her employees, closed the restaurant, and placed a sign in the window saying "Closed for Remodeling." Earlier that day, Berg testified, Wiley came to the premises in her absence and attempted to change the locks. When she returned and asserted her right to continue in possession, he complied with her request to leave the locks unchanged. Berg also testified that at about 9:30 p.m. that evening, while she and four of her friends were in the restaurant, she observed Wiley hanging from the awning peering into

----

"Item # 5 The Lessee will make no changes to the building structure without first receiving written authorization from the Lessor. The Lessor will promptly reply in writing to each request and will cooperate with the Lessee on any reasonable request.

Item # 6 The Lessee agrees to operate the restaurant in a lawful and prudent manner during the lease period.

Item # 7 Should the Lessee fail to meet the conditions of this Lease the Lessor may at their option retake possession of said premises. In any such event such act will not relieve Lessee from liability for payment the rental herein provided or from the conditions or obligations of this lease."

the window. Shortly thereafter, she heard Wiley pounding on the back door demanding admittance. Berg called the county sheriff to come and preserve order. Wiley testified that he observed Berg and a group of her friends in the restaurant removing paneling from a wall. Allegedly fearing destruction of his property, Wiley called the city police, who, with the sheriff, mediated an agreement between the parties to preserve the status quo until each could consult with legal counsel on Monday, July 16, 1973.

Wiley testified that his then attorney advised him to take possession of the premises and lock the tenant out. Accompanied by a police officer and a locksmith, Wiley entered the premises in Berg's absence and without her knowledge on Monday, July 16, 1973, and changed the locks. Later in the day, Berg found herself locked out. The lease term was not due to expire until December 1, 1975. The premises were re-let to another tenant on or about August 1, 1973. Berg brought this damage action against Wiley and three other named defendants, including the new tenant, on July 27, 1973. A second amended complaint sought damages for lost profits, damage to chattels, intentional infliction of emotional distress, and other tort damages based upon claims in wrongful eviction, contract, and tort. Wiley answered with an affirmative defense of abandonment and surrender and counterclaimed for damage to the premises and indemnification on mechanics lien liability incurred because of Berg's remodeling. At the close of Berg's case, all defendants other than Rodney A. Wiley and Wiley Enterprises, Inc., were dismissed from the action. Only Berg's action for wrongful eviction and intentional infliction of emotional distress and Wiley's affirmative defense of abandonment and his counterclaim for damage to the premises were submitted by special verdict to the jury. With respect to the wrongful eviction claim, the trial court found as a matter of law that Wiley did in fact lock the tenant out, and that the lockout was wrongful.

The jury, by answers to the questions submitted, found no liability on Berg's claim for intentional infliction of emotional distress and no liability on Wiley's counterclaim for damages to the premises, but awarded Berg $31,000 for lost profits and $3,540 for loss of chattels resulting from the wrongful lockout. The jury also specifically found that Berg neither abandoned nor surrendered the premises.

On this appeal, Wiley seeks an outright reversal of the damages award for wrongful eviction, claiming insufficient evidence to support the jury's finding of no abandonment or surrender and claiming error in the trial court's finding of wrongful eviction as a matter of law.

The first issue before us concerns the sufficiency of evidence to support the jury's finding that Berg had not abandoned or surrendered the leasehold before being locked out by Wiley. Viewing the evidence to support the jury's special verdict in the light most favorable to Berg, as we must, we hold it amply supports the jury's finding of no abandonment or surrender of the premises. The jury could reasonably have concluded, based on Berg's testimony and supporting circumstantial evidence, that she intended to retain possession, closing temporarily to remodel. Thus, the lockout cannot be excused on ground that Berg abandoned or surrendered the leasehold.

The second and more difficult issue is whether Wiley's self-help repossession of the premises by locking out Berg was correctly held wrongful as a matter of law.

Minnesota has historically followed the common-law rule that a landlord may rightfully use self-help to retake leased premises from a tenant in possession without incurring liability for wrongful eviction provided two conditions are met: (1) The landlord is legally entitled to possession, such as where a tenant holds over after the lease term or where a tenant breaches a lease containing a reentry clause; and (2) the landlord's means of reentry are peaceable. Under the common-law rule, a tenant who is evicted by his landlord may recover damages for wrongful eviction where the landlord either had no right to possession or where the means used to remove the tenant were forcible, or both.

Wiley contends that Berg had breached the provisions of the lease, thereby entitling Wiley, under the terms of the lease, to retake possession, and that his repossession by changing the locks in Berg's absence was accomplished in a peaceful manner. In a memorandum accompanying the post-trial order, the trial court stated two grounds for finding the lockout wrongful as a matter of law: (1) It was not accomplished in a peaceable manner and therefore could not be justified under the common-law rule, and (2) any self-help reentry against a tenant in possession is wrongful under the growing modern doctrine that a landlord must always resort to the judicial process to enforce his statutory remedy against a tenant wrongfully in possession. Whether Berg had in fact breached the lease and whether Wiley was hence entitled to possession was not judicially determined. That issue became irrelevant upon the trial court's finding that Wiley's reentry was forcible as a matter of law because even if Berg had breached the lease, this could not excuse Wiley's nonpeaceable reentry. The finding that Wiley's reentry was forcible as a matter of law provided a sufficient ground for damages, and the issue of breach was not submitted to the jury.

In applying the common-law rule, we have not before had occasion to decide what means of self-help used to dispossess a tenant in his absence will constitute a nonpeaceable entry, giving a right to damages without regard to who holds the legal right to possession. Wiley argues that only actual or threatened violence used against a tenant should give rise to damages where the landlord had the right to possession. We cannot agree.

It has long been the policy of our law to discourage landlords from taking the law into their own hands, and our decisions and statutory law have looked with disfavor upon any use of self-help to dispossess a tenant in circumstances which are likely to result in breaches of the peace.

To facilitate a resort to judicial process, the legislature has provided a summary procedure whereby a landlord may recover possession of leased premises upon proper notice and showing in court in as little as 3 to 10 days. As we recognized in Mutual Trust Life Ins. Co. v. Berg, "the forcible entry and unlawful detainer statutes were intended to prevent parties from taking the law into their own hands when going into possession of lands and tenements."

In the present case, the tenant was in possession, claiming a right to continue in possession adverse to the landlord's claim of breach of the lease, and had neither abandoned nor surrendered the premises. Wiley, well aware that Berg was asserting her right to possession, retook possession in her absence by picking the locks and locking her out. The record shows a history of vigorous dispute and keen animosity between the parties. Upon this record, we can only conclude that the singular reason why actual violence did not erupt at the moment of Wiley's changing of the locks was Berg's absence and her subsequent self-restraint and resort to judicial process. Upon these facts, we cannot find Wiley's means of reentry peaceable under the common-law rule.

Our long-standing policy to discourage self-help which tends to cause a breach of the peace compels us to disapprove the means used to dispossess Berg. To approve this lockout, as urged by Wiley, merely because in Berg's absence no actual violence erupted while the locks were being changed, would be to encourage all future tenants, in order to protect their possession, to be vigilant and thereby set the stage for the very kind of public disturbance which it must be our policy to discourage.

We recognize that the growing modern trend departs completely from the common-law rule to hold that self-help is never available to dispossess a tenant who is in possession and has not abandoned or voluntarily surrendered the premises. This growing rule is founded on the recognition that the potential for violent breach of peace inheres in any situation where a landlord attempts by his own means to remove a tenant who is claiming possession adversely to the landlord. Courts adopting the rule reason that there is no cause to sanction such potentially disruptive self-help where adequate and speedy means are provided for removing a tenant peacefully through judicial process. At least 16 states[20] have adopted this modern rule, holding that judicial proceedings, including the summary procedures provided in those states' unlawful detainer statutes, are the exclusive remedy by which a landlord may remove a tenant claiming possession.

To make clear our departure from the common-law rule for the benefit of future landlords and tenants, we hold that, subsequent to our decision in this case, the only lawful means to dispossess a tenant who has not abandoned nor voluntarily surrendered but who claims possession adversely to a landlord's claim

---

[20] Annotation, 6 A.L.R.3d 177, 186, Supp. 13, shows this modern rule to have been adopted in California, Connecticut, Delaware, Florida, Georgia, Illinois, Indiana, Louisiana, Nebraska, North Carolina, Ohio, Tennessee, Texas, Utah, Vermont, and Washington.

of breach of a written lease is by resort to judicial process. Considered together, these statutory and judicial remedies provide a complete answer to the landlord. In our modern society, with the availability of prompt and sufficient legal remedies as described, there is no place and no need for self-help against a tenant in claimed lawful possession of leased premises.

Applying our holding to the facts of this case, we conclude, as did the trial court, that because Wiley failed to resort to judicial remedies against Berg's holding possession adversely to Wiley's claim of breach of the lease, his lockout of Berg was wrongful as a matter of law. The rule we adopt in this decision is fairly applied against Wiley, for it is clear that, applying the older common-law rule to the facts and circumstances peculiar to this case, we would be compelled to find the lockout nonpeaceable for the reasons previously stated. The jury found that the lockout caused Berg damage and, as between Berg and Wiley, equity dictates that Wiley, who himself performed the act causing the damage, must bear the loss.

Affirmed.

NOTES & QUESTIONS:

What should a landlord do when faced with the problem situation of having a defaulting tenant in possession of the premises? As we learned in Berg v. Wiley, even if a tenant has failed to meet her obligations, a landlord must lawfully remove the tenant. An eviction is a lawsuit filed by a landlord to remove persons and belongings from the landlord's property. In Texas, these are also referred to as "forcible entry and detainer" or "forcible detainer" suits. There are hundreds filed every day with Texas justice courts (also called justice of the peace or J.P. courts). The process that is available in J.P. courts provides a quick and inexpensive legal route for the landlord to remove a defaulting tenant in possession. There are safeguards in the process to eliminate situations that might lead to self-help by the landlord or a nonpeaceful response by the defaulting tenant.

The landlord is required to provide an initial notice to the tenant that he must leave by a certain date. In the standard form Texas Apartment Association lease, the landlord must only provide 24-hours' notice for the tenant to vacate before proceeding with an eviction action. This short time period is permitted by statute. Requirements for an initial notice will vary from state to state.

If the tenant does not leave voluntarily, the landlord will file suit and the tenant will be served with the lawsuit, being given the opportunity to answer and appear. The landlord often appears on his own behalf without assistance of counsel. Tenants often do not answer or appear; however, if a tenant does appear it is usually without assistance of counsel. The justice of the peace will hear both sides and make a determination of whether the landlord is entitled to regain possession. Even if a judgment is entered for the landlord with a writ of possession, the landlord still may not act on his own to remove the tenant. A law enforcement official, in Texas a constable, will assist with the actual physical removal of the tenant and her personal property.

Under the majority of proceedings, the tenants can typically be evicted in 30 days. However, depending on how long the landlord waits to act on the default and pursue legal action, this time period can be longer.

While the majority view, which Texas follows, is that the landlord cannot use self-help when dealing with a defaulting tenant in possession, the landlord has options to consider when the situation arises. The Texas Property Code even provides some specific guidance to the landlord that will allow the message to be sent to the tenant that the tenant needs to comply or vacate before eviction occurs.

---

[21] "No Self-Help!" Illustration by Hunter Ratcliff, Baylor Law J.D., *cum laude*, 2017.

Tex. Prop. Code Chapter 92: Residential Tenancies

§ 92.002 Application

This chapter applies only to the relationship between landlords and tenants of residential rental property.

§ 92.008 Interruption of Utilities

    (a) A landlord or a landlord's agent may not interrupt or cause the interruption of utility service paid for directly to the utility company by a tenant unless the interruption results from bona fide repairs, construction, or an emergency.

    (b) A landlord may not interrupt or cause the interruption of water, wastewater, gas, or electric service furnished to a tenant by the landlord as an incident of the tenancy or by other agreement unless the interruption results from bona fide repairs, construction, or an emergency.

    (c) to (e) Repealed by HB 882, § 3, 81st Leg., eff. Jan. 1, 2010.

    (f) If a landlord or a landlord's agent violates this section, the tenant may:

        (1) either recover possession of the premises or terminate the lease; and

        (2) recover from the landlord an amount equal to the sum of the tenant's actual damages, one month's rent or $500, whichever is greater, reasonable attorney's fees, and court costs, less any delinquent rents or other sums for which the tenant is liable to the landlord.

    (g) A provision of a lease that purports to waive a right or to exempt a party from a liability or duty under this section is void.

    (h) Subject to subsections (i), (j), (k), (m), and (o), a landlord who submeters electricity or allocates or prorates nonsubmetered master metered electricity may interrupt or cause the interruption of electric service for nonpayment by the tenant of an electric bill issued to the tenant if:

        (1) The landlord's right to interrupt electric service is provided by a written lease entered into by the tenant;

        (2) The tenant's electric bill is not paid on or before the 12th day after the date the electric bill is issued;

        (3) Advance written notice of the proposed interruption is delievered to the tenant by mail or hand delivery separately from any other written content [NOTE: There are particular requirements for the notice in form and substance.]

        (4) The landlord, at the same time the service is interrupted, hand delivers or places on the tenant's front door a written notice [NOTE: This written notice also has statutory requirements for form and substance.]

[NOTE: There are many additional provisions that govern the interruption of electricity for nonpayment of the electric bill. The landlord who is going to utilize this provision must be certain to follow all rules carefully.]

§ 92.0081 Removal of Property and Exclusion of Residential Tenant

(a) (omitted)

(b) A landlord may not intentionally prevent a tenant from entering the leased premises except by judicial process unless the exclusion results from:

(1) bona fide repairs, construction, or an emergency;

(2) removing the contents of premises abandoned by a tenant; or

(3) changing the door locks on the door to the tenant's individual unit of a tenant who is delinquent in paying at least part of the rent.

(c) If a landlord or a landlord's agent changes the door lock of a tenant who is delinquent in paying rent, the landlord or the landlord's agent must place a written notice on the tenant's front door stating:

(1) an on-site location where the tenant may go 24 hours a day to obtain the new key or a telephone number that is answered 24 hours a day that the tenant may call to have a key delivered within two hours after calling the number;

(2) the fact that the landlord must provide the new key to the tenant at any hour, regardless of whether or not the tenant pays any of the delinquent rent; and

(3) the amount of rent and other charges for which the tenant is delinquent.

(d) A landlord may not intentionally prevent a tenant from entering the leased premises under Subsection (b)(3) unless:

(1) the landlord's right to change the locks because of a tenant's failure to timely pay rent is placed in the lease;

(2) the tenant is delinquent in paying all or part of the rent; and

(3) the landlord has locally mailed not later than the fifth calendar day before the date on which the door locks are changed or hand-delivered to the tenant or posted on the inside of the main entry door of the tenant's dwelling not later than the third calendar day before the date on which the door locks are changed a written notice stating:

(A) the earliest date that the landlord proposes to change the door locks;

(B) the amount of rent the tenant must pay to prevent changing of the door locks;

(C) the name and street address of the individual to whom, or the location of the on-site management office at which, the delinquent rent may be discussed or paid during the landlord's normal business hours; and

(D) in underlined or bold print, the tenant's right to receive a key to the new lock at any hour, regardless of whether the tenant pays the delinquent rent.

(e) A landlord may not change the locks on the door of a tenant's dwelling under Subsection (b)(3) on a day, or on a day immediately before a day, on which the landlord or other designated individual is not available, or on which any on-site management office is not open, for the tenant to tender the delinquent rent.

(e-1) A landlord who changes the locks or otherwise prevents a tenant from entering the tenant's individual rental unit may not change the locks or otherwise prevent a tenant from entering a common area of residential rental property.

(f) A landlord who intentionally prevents a tenant from entering the tenant's dwelling under Subsection (b)(3) must provide the tenant with a key to the changed lock on the dwelling without regard to whether the tenant pays the delinquent rent.

(g) If a landlord arrives at the dwelling in a timely manner in response to a tenant's telephone call to the number contained in the notice as described by Subsection (c)(1) and the tenant is not present to receive the key to the changed lock, the landlord shall leave a notice on the front door of the dwelling stating the time the landlord arrived with the key and the street address to which the tenant may go to obtain the key during the landlord's normal office hours.

(h) If a landlord violates this section, the tenant may:

(1) either recover possession of the premises or terminate the lease; and

(2) recover from the landlord a civil penalty of one month's rent plus $1,000, actual damages, court costs, and reasonable attorney's fees in an action to recover property damages, actual expenses, or civil penalties , less any delinquent rent or other sums for which the tenant is liable to the landlord.

(i) If a landlord violates Subsection (f), the tenant may recover, in addition to the remedies provided by Subsection (h), an additional civil penalty of one month's rent.

(j) A provision of a lease that purports to waive a right or to exempt a party from a liability or duty under this section is void.

(k) A landlord may not change the locks on the door of a tenant's dwelling under Subsection (b)(3):

(1) when the tenant or any other legal occupant is in the dwelling; or

(2) more than once during a rental payment period.

(l) This section does not affect the ability of a landlord to pursue other available remedies, including the remedies provided in Chapter 24 [forcible entry and detainer suit].

3. The Tenant Who Has Abandoned Possession

A different situation from the tenant who defaults and remains in possession is the tenant who unlawfully abandons during the leasehold. The tenant entered into a five-year lease and leaves two years into the term. The landlord does not have to worry about eviction—or does he? As seen in Berg v. Wiley, sometimes the line between being a defaulting tenant in possession and an abandoning tenant can be a close call. If the landlord makes the wrong decision, it can be costly. Layer on this the concept of mitigation of damages and the landlord's position becomes even more difficult. Default, abandonment, and surrender are all closely related legal concepts and these concepts have very different legal implications for the landlord. Consider the facts and circumstances of *Berg* while reading the following case.

Sommer v. Kridel
Supreme Court of New Jersey, 1977
378 A.2d 767

PASHMAN, J.

We granted certification in these cases to consider whether a landlord seeking damages from a defaulting tenant is under a duty to mitigate damages by making reasonable efforts to re-let an apartment wrongfully vacated by the tenant. Separate parts of the Appellate Division held that, in accordance with their respective leases, the landlords in both cases could recover rents due under the leases regardless of whether they had attempted to re-let the vacated apartments. We now reverse and hold that a landlord does have an obligation to make a reasonable effort to mitigate damages in such a situation.

Sommer v. Kridel

This case was tried on stipulated facts. On March 10, 1972 the defendant, James Kridel, entered into a lease with the plaintiff, Abraham Sommer, owner of the "Pierre Apartments" in Hackensack, to rent apartment 6-L in that building.[22] The term of the lease was from May 1, 1972 until April 30, 1974, with a rent

---

[22] Among other provisions, the lease prohibited the tenant from assigning or transferring the lease without the consent of the landlord. If the tenant defaulted, the lease gave the landlord the option of reentering or reletting, but stipulated that failure to relet or to recover the full rental would not discharge the tenant's liability for rent.

concession for the first six weeks, so that the first month's rent was not due until June 15, 1972.

One week after signing the agreement, Kridel paid Sommer $690. Half of that sum was used to satisfy the first month's rent. The remainder was paid under the lease provision requiring a security deposit of $345. Although defendant had expected to begin occupancy around May 1, his plans were changed. He wrote to Sommer on May 19, 1972, explaining

> I was to be married on June 3, 1972. Unhappily the engagement was broken and the wedding plans cancelled. Both parents were to assume responsibility for the rent after our marriage. I was discharged from the U.S. Army in October 1971 and am now a student. I have no funds of my own, and am supported by my stepfather.
>
> In view of the above, I cannot take possession of the apartment and am surrendering all rights to it. Never having received a key, I cannot return same to you.
>
> I beg your understanding and compassion in releasing me from the lease, and will of course, in consideration thereof, forfeit the 2 month's rent already paid.
>
> Please notify me at your earliest convenience.

Plaintiff did not answer the letter.

Subsequently, a third party went to the apartment house and inquired about renting apartment 6-L. Although the parties agreed that she was ready, willing and able to rent the apartment, the person in charge told her that the apartment was not being shown since it was already rented to Kridel. In fact, the landlord did not re-enter the apartment or exhibit it to anyone until August 1, 1973. At that time it was rented to a new tenant for a term beginning on September 1, 1973. The new rental was for $345 per month with a six week concession similar to that granted Kridel.

Prior to re-letting the new premises, plaintiff sued Kridel in August 1972, demanding $7,590, the total amount due for the full two-year term of the lease. Following a mistrial, plaintiff filed an amended complaint asking for $5,865, the amount due between May 1, 1972 and September 1, 1973. The amended complaint included no reduction in the claim to reflect the six week concession provided for in the lease or the $690 payment made to plaintiff after signing the agreement. Defendant filed an amended answer to the complaint, alleging that plaintiff breached the contract, failed to mitigate damages and accepted defendant's surrender of the premises. He also counterclaimed to demand repayment of the $345 paid as a security deposit.

The trial judge ruled in favor of defendant. Despite his conclusion that the lease had been drawn to reflect "the 'settled law' of this state," he found that "justice and fair dealing" imposed upon the landlord the duty to attempt to re-let the premises and thereby mitigate damages. He also held that plaintiff's failure to make any response to defendant's unequivocal offer of surrender was tantamount to an acceptance, thereby terminating the tenancy and any obligation to pay rent. As a result, he dismissed both the complaint and the counterclaim. The Appellate Division reversed in a per curiam opinion, and we granted certification.

Riverview Realty Co. v. Perosio

This controversy arose in a similar manner. On December 27, 1972, Carlos Perosio entered into a written lease with plaintiff Riverview Realty Co. The agreement covered the rental of apartment 5-G in a building owned by the realty company at 2175 Hudson Terrace in Fort Lee. As in the companion case, the lease prohibited the tenant from subletting or assigning the apartment without the consent of the landlord. It was to run for a two-year term, from February 1, 1973 until January 31, 1975, and provided for a monthly rental of $450. The defendant took possession of the apartment and occupied it until February 1974. At that time he vacated the premises, after having paid the rent through January 31, 1974.

The landlord filed a complaint on October 31, 1974, demanding $4,500 in payment for the monthly rental from February 1, 1974 through October 31, 1974. Defendant answered the complaint by alleging that there had been a valid surrender of the premises and that plaintiff failed to mitigate damages. The trial court granted the landlord's motion for summary judgment against the defendant, fixing the damages at $4,050 plus $182.25 interest.

The Appellate Division affirmed the trial court, holding that it was bound by prior precedents. Nevertheless, it freely criticized the rule which it found itself obliged to follow:

> There appears to be no reason in equity or justice to perpetuate such an unrealistic and uneconomic rule of law which encourages an owner to let valuable rented space lie fallow because he is assured of full recovery from a defaulting tenant. Since courts in New Jersey and elsewhere have abandoned ancient real property concepts and applied ordinary contract principles in other conflicts between landlord and tenant there is no sound reason for a continuation of a special real property rule to the issue of mitigation.

We granted certification.

As the lower courts in both appeals found, the weight of authority in this State supports the rule that a landlord is under no duty to mitigate damages caused by a defaulting tenant. This rule has been followed in a majority of states and has been tentatively adopted in the American Law Institute's Restatement of Property.

Nevertheless, while there is still a split of authority over this question, the trend among recent cases appears to be in favor of a mitigation requirement.

The majority rule is based on principles of property law which equate a lease with a transfer of a property interest in the owner's estate. Under this rationale the lease conveys to a tenant an interest in the property which forecloses any control by the landlord; thus, it would be anomalous to require the landlord to concern himself with the tenant's abandonment of his own property.

For instance, in Muller v. Beck, [94 N.J.L. 311, 110 A. 831 (Sup. Ct. 1920),] where essentially the same issue was posed, the court clearly treated the lease as governed by property, as opposed to contract, precepts. The court there observed that the "tenant had an estate for years, but it was an estate qualified by this right of the landlord to prevent its transfer," and that "the tenant has an estate with which the landlord may not interfere." Similarly, in Heckel v. Griese [12 N.J. Misc. 211, 171 A. 148 (Sup. Ct. 1934)], the court noted the absolute nature of the tenant's interest in the property while the lease was in effect, stating that "when the tenant vacated, . . . no one, in the circumstances, had any right to interfere with the defendant's possession of the premises."

Yet the distinction between a lease for ordinary residential purposes and an ordinary contract can no longer be considered viable.

This Court has taken the lead in requiring that landlords provide housing services to tenants in accordance with implied duties which are hardly consistent with the property notions expressed in Muller v. Beck, supra, and Heckel v. Griese, supra.

Application of the contract rule requiring mitigation of damages to a residential lease may be justified as a matter of basic fairness. Professor McCormick first commented upon the inequity under the majority rule when he predicted in 1925 that eventually

> the logic, inescapable according to the standards of a 'jurisprudence of conceptions' which permits the landlord to stand idly by the vacant, abandoned premises and treat them as the property of the tenant and recover full rent, will yield to the more realistic notions of social advantage which in other fields of the law have forbidden a recovery for damages which the plaintiff by reasonable efforts could have avoided. [McCormick, "The Rights of the Landlord Upon Abandonment of the Premises by the Tenant," 23 Mich. L. Rev. 211, 221-22 (1925).]

Various courts have adopted this position.

The pre-existing rule cannot be predicated upon the possibility that a landlord may lose the opportunity to rent another empty apartment because he must first rent the apartment vacated by the defaulting tenant. Even where the breach occurs in a multi-dwelling building, each apartment may have unique qualities which make it attractive to certain individuals. Significantly, in Sommer v. Kridel, there was a specific request to rent the apartment vacated by the defendant; there is no reason to believe that absent this vacancy the landlord could have succeeded in renting a different apartment to this individual.

We therefore hold that antiquated real property concepts which served as the basis for the pre-existing rule, shall no longer be controlling where there is a claim for damages under a residential lease. Such claims must be governed by more modern notions of fairness and equity. A landlord has a duty to mitigate damages where he seeks to recover rents due from a defaulting tenant.

If the landlord has other vacant apartments besides the one which the tenant has abandoned, the landlord's duty to mitigate consists of making reasonable efforts to re-let the apartment. In such cases he must treat the apartment in question as if it was one of his vacant stock.

As part of his cause of action, the landlord shall be required to carry the burden of proving that he used reasonable diligence in attempting to re-let the premises. We note that there has been a divergence of opinion concerning the allocation of the burden of proof on this issue. While generally in contract actions the breaching party has the burden of proving that damages are capable of mitigation, here the landlord will be in a better position to demonstrate whether he exercised reasonable diligence in attempting to re-let the premises.

The Sommer v. Kridel case presents a classic example of the unfairness which occurs when a landlord has no responsibility to minimize damages. Sommer waited 15 months and allowed $4658.50 in damages to accrue before attempting to re-let the apartment. Despite the availability of a tenant who was ready, willing and able to rent the apartment, the landlord needlessly increased the damages by turning her away. While a tenant will not necessarily be excused from his obligations under a lease simply by finding another person who is willing to rent the vacated premises, here there has been no showing that the new tenant would not have been suitable. We therefore find that plaintiff could have avoided the damages which eventually accrued, and that the defendant was relieved of his duty to continue paying rent. Ordinarily we would require the tenant to bear the cost of any reasonable expenses incurred by a landlord in attempting to re-let the premises, but no such expenses were incurred in this case.

In Riverview Realty Co. v. Perosio, no factual determination was made regarding the landlord's efforts to mitigate damages, and defendant contends that plaintiff never answered his interrogatories. Consequently, the judgment is reversed and the case remanded for a new trial. Upon remand and after discovery has been completed, the trial court shall determine whether plaintiff attempted to mitigate damages with reasonable diligence, and if so, the extent of damages remaining and assessable to the tenant. As we have held above, the burden of proving that reasonable diligence was used to re-let the premises shall be upon the plaintiff.

In assessing whether the landlord has satisfactorily carried his burden, the trial court shall consider, among other factors, whether the landlord, either personally or through an agency, offered or showed the apartment to any prospective tenants, or advertised it in local newspapers. Additionally, the tenant may attempt to rebut such evidence by showing that he proffered suitable tenants who were rejected. However, there is no standard formula for measuring whether the landlord has utilized satisfactory efforts in attempting to mitigate damages, and each case must be judged upon its own facts.

The judgment in Sommer v. Kridel is reversed. In Riverview Realty Co. v. Perosio, the judgment is reversed and the case is remanded to the trial court for proceedings in accordance with this opinion.

NOTES & QUESTIONS:

1. What is abandonment? Abandonment occurs when the tenant vacates the leased premises without justification, lacks the intent to return, and defaults in the payment of rent. What can constitute a justification that would prevent the tenant from being considered an abandoning tenant? We will examine the covenant of quiet enjoyment and constructive eviction, which will provide a common law justification for a tenant. Additionally, we will look to the Texas Property Code warranty of habitability that also allows for a legal justification for departure due to certain repair issues.

    However, the Texas Property Code also includes specific statutes that serve as a legal justification for departure that will allow the tenant to avoid being in breach and being liable for additional rent under the lease. Texas Property Code § 92.016 addresses the right to vacate and avoid liability following family violence, and § 92.0161 addresses the right to vacate and avoid liability following certain sex offenses or stalking. Both of these provisions include statutory definitions and references to the specific conduct being addressed. These provisions provide relief to residential tenants under certain circumstances and both statutes specifically state that "a tenant may not waive a tenant's right to terminate a lease before the end of the lease term, vacate the dwelling, and avoid liability under this chapter."

Additionally, Texas Property Code § 92.017 provides a right to vacate and avoid liability following certain decisions related to military service. This statute allows servicemenbers the ability to terminate a lease early in the event of certain deployments or permanent change of duty station. There is a limited ability to waive this provision.[23]

2. Since the time of the Somer v. Kridel case in 1977, the majority view has switched to that of imposing a duty to mitigate damages on the landlord. While it is more pervasive in the residential setting, the majority of states also require mitigation in the commercial context as well. In residential properties, without a duty to mitigate, artificial housing shortages can occur. With commercial, a lack of a duty to mitigate could prevent land from being put to good economic use. The Texas Property Code reflects this majority view. The provision is found in Chapter 91, which applies to both residential and commercial tenancies.

§ 91.006 Landlord's Duty to Mitigate Damages
(a) A landlord has a duty to mitigate damages if a tenant abandons the leased premises in violation of the lease.
(b) A provision of a lease that purports to waive a right or to exempt a landlord from a liability or duty under this section is void.

Landlord/Tenant Hypothetical #1
Barney leased Blackacre to Ted for a term of five years. At the end of two years, when the lease still had three years to run, Ted offered to surrender the premises to Barney and requested that Barney accept such surrender of the leasehold. Barney refused to accept the surrender whereupon Ted tossed the keys to Blackacre to Barney and Barney caught them. Then Ted left, and has not been heard from again.

1. What should Barney do when considering § 91.006 of the Tex. Prop. Code? What additional facts would you want to know, if any. Why?

2. Assume that the lease between Barney and Ted called for rent at the rate of $300 per month, but at the time of Ted's offer of surrender, the fair rental value of Blackacre was $250 per month. What advice would you give to Barney and why? Would it matter that Marshall was willing to rent Blackacre at a rental rate of $175 per month. How so?

---

[23] Eff. Jan. 1, 2006; Amended by SB 83 § 1, 81st Leg., eff. Jan. 1, 2010. Acts 2005, 79th Leg., ch. 348, § 1, eff. Jan. 1, 2006.

3. Assume that the market value has increased since Ted's lease such that Marshall is willing to pay $400 per month. What advice would you give to Barney then, and why?

4. Is your advice any different if Barney does not only have this one house to rent but owns an apartment building that had four vacant units at the time Ted offered to surrender? Would it matter if Marshall specifically requested to rent Ted's vacant unit and Barney refused? Would it matter if Marshall specifically requested another vacant unit because he wanted one on the second floor and Ted's vacant unit was on the first floor? Would it matter if Marshall made no specific request and Barney intentionally placed him in one of the other vacancies?

4. Subleases and Assignments: The Right to Transfer a Leasehold

Because a lease is both a conveyance and a contract, there must be some examination of the right to transfer stick. Can the right to possess be transferred from one tenant to another? Depending on the jurisdiction, or the express language in a lease agreement, the tenant may need the landlord's permission to enter into an assignment or a sublease. In situations where that is the case, there is often a question of whether the landlord has the right to refuse a transfer of the leasehold. If so, on what grounds?

Once a leasehold is validly transferred, the focus then turns to what the potential liability is between the landlord and tenant for any promises in the original lease agreement. The landlord and tenant relationship is the area that first introduces the concept of the covenant that will be covered in a later chapter in the text. For now, this initial material will focus on the ability to transfer. Later material on the covenant will focus on the enforceability of certain promises when a transfer occurs.

Kendall v. Ernest Pestana, Inc.
Supreme Court of California, 1985
709 P.2d 837

BROUSSARD, J.

This case concerns the effect of a provision in a commercial lease that the lessee may not assign the lease or sublet the premises without the lessor's prior written consent. The question we address is whether, in the absence of a provision that such consent will not be unreasonably withheld, a lessor may unreasonably and arbitrarily withhold his or her consent to an assignment. This is a question of first impression in this court.

The allegations of the complaint may be summarized as follows. The lease at issue is for 14,400 square feet of hangar space at the San Jose Municipal Airport. The City of San Jose, as owner of the property, leased it to Irving and Janice Perlitch, who in turn assigned their interest to respondent Ernest Pestana, Inc. Prior to assigning their interest to respondent, the Perlitches entered into a 25-year sublease with one Robert Bixler commencing on January 1, 1970. The sublease covered an original five-year term plus four 5-year options to renew. The rental rate was to be increased every 10 years in the same proportion as rents increased on the master lease from the City of San Jose. The premises were to be used by Bixler for the purpose of conducting an airplane maintenance business.

Bixler conducted such a business under the name "Flight Services" until, in 1981, he agreed to sell the business to appellants Jack Kendall, Grady O'Hara and Vicki O'Hara. The proposed sale included the business and the equipment, inventory and improvements on the property, together with the existing lease. The proposed assignees had a stronger financial statement and greater net worth than the current lessee, Bixler, and they were willing to be bound by the terms of the lease.

The lease provided that written consent of the lessor was required before the lessee could assign his interest, and that failure to obtain such consent rendered the lease voidable at the option of the lessor. Accordingly, Bixler requested consent from the Perlitches' successor-in-interest, respondent Ernest Pestana, Inc. Respondent refused to consent to the assignment and maintained that it had an absolute right arbitrarily to refuse any such request. The complaint recites that respondent demanded "increased rent and other more onerous terms" as a condition of consenting to Bixler's transfer of interest.

The proposed assignees brought suit for declaratory and injunctive relief and damages seeking, inter alia, a declaration "that the refusal of Ernest Pestana, Inc. to consent to the assignment of the lease is unreasonable and is an unlawful restraint on the freedom of alienation. . . ." The trial court sustained a demurrer to the complaint without leave to amend and this appeal followed.

The law generally favors free alienability of property, and California follows the common law rule that a leasehold interest is freely alienable. Contractual restrictions on the alienability of leasehold interests are, however, permitted.

The common law's hostility toward restraints on alienation has caused such restraints on leasehold interests to be strictly construed against the lessor. Thus, in Chapman v. Great Western Gypsum Co., where the lease contained a covenant against assignment without the consent of the lessor, this court stated: "It hardly needs citation of authority to the principle that covenants limiting the free alienation of property such as covenants against assignment are barely tolerated and must be strictly construed."

Nevertheless, a majority of jurisdictions have long adhered to the rule that where a lease contains an approval clause (a clause stating that the lease cannot be assigned without the prior consent of the lessor), the lessor may arbitrarily refuse to approve a proposed assignee no matter how suitable the assignee appears to be and no matter how unreasonable the lessor's objection. The harsh consequences of this rule have often been avoided through application of the doctrines of waiver and estoppel, under which the lessor may be found to have waived (or be estopped from asserting) the right to refuse consent to assignment.

The traditional majority rule has come under steady attack in recent years. A growing minority of jurisdictions now hold that where a lease provides for assignment only with the prior consent of the lessor, such consent may be withheld only where the lessor has a commercially reasonable objection to the assignment, even in the absence of a provision in the lease stating that consent to assignment will not be unreasonably withheld.

For the reasons discussed below, we conclude that the minority rule is the preferable position. Although this is an issue of first impression in this court, several decisions of the Court of Appeal have reflected the changing trend in the law on this question.

The impetus for change in the majority rule has come from two directions, reflecting the dual nature of a lease as a conveyance of a leasehold interest and a contract. The policy against restraints on alienation pertains to leases in their nature as *conveyances*. Numerous courts and commentators have recognized that "[in] recent times the necessity of permitting reasonable alienation of commercial space has become paramount in our increasingly urban society."

Civil Code section 711 provides: "Conditions restraining alienation, when repugnant to the interest created, are void." It is well settled that this rule is not absolute in its application, but forbids only unreasonable restraints on alienation. Reasonableness is determined by comparing the justification for a particular restraint on alienation with the quantum of restraint actually imposed by it. "[The] greater the quantum of restraint that results from enforcement of a given clause, the greater must be the justification for that enforcement."

In Cohen v. Ratinoff, the court examined the reasonableness of the restraint created by an approval clause in a lease:

> Because the lessor has an interest in the character of the proposed commercial assignee, we cannot say that an assignment provision requiring the lessor's consent to an assignment is inherently repugnant to the leasehold interest created. We do conclude, however, that if such an assignment provision is implemented in such a manner that its underlying purpose is perverted by the arbitrary or unreasonable

withholding of consent, an unreasonable restraint on alienation is established." 147 Cal. App. 3d 321, 329 (1983).

The Restatement Second of Property adopts the minority rule on the validity of approval clauses in leases: "A restraint on alienation without the consent of the landlord of a tenant's interest in leased property is valid, *but the landlord's consent to an alienation by the tenant cannot be withheld unreasonably,* unless a freely negotiated provision in the lease gives the landlord an absolute right to withhold consent." (Rest. 2d Property, § 15.2(2) (1977), italics added.) A comment to the section explains:

> The landlord may have an understandable concern about certain personal qualities of a tenant, particularly his reputation for meeting his financial obligations. The preservation of the values that go into the personal selection of the tenant justifies upholding a provision in the lease that curtails the right of the tenant to put anyone else in his place by transferring his interest, but this justification does not go to the point of allowing the landlord arbitrarily and without reason to refuse to allow the tenant to transfer an interest in leased property. (*Id.*, com. a.)

Under the Restatement rule, the lessor's interest in the character of his or her tenant is protected by the lessor's right to object to a proposed assignee on reasonable commercial grounds. The lessor's interests are also protected by the fact that the original lessee remains liable to the lessor as a surety even if the lessor consents to the assignment and the assignee expressly assumes the obligations of the lease.

The second impetus for change in the majority rule comes from the nature of a lease as a contract. As the Court of Appeal observed in Cohen v. Ratinoff, supra, [since the majority rule was adopted], there has been an increased recognition of and emphasis on the duty of good faith and fair dealing inherent in every contract." 147 Cal. App. 3d at 329. Thus, "[in] every contract there is an implied covenant that neither party shall do anything which will have the effect of destroying or injuring the right of the other party to receive the fruits of the contract. . . ." Universal Sales Corp. v. Cal. etc. Mfg. Co. (1942). "[Where] a contract confers on one party a discretionary power affecting the rights of the other, a duty is imposed to exercise that discretion in good faith and in accordance with fair dealing." Cal. Lettuce Growers v. Union Sugar Co. (1955). Here the lessor retains the discretionary power to approve or disapprove an assignee proposed by the other party to the contract; this discretionary power should therefore be exercised in accordance with commercially reasonable standards.

Under the minority rule, the determination whether a lessor's refusal to consent was reasonable is a question of fact. Some of the factors that the trier of fact may properly consider in applying the standards of good faith and commercial reasonableness are: financial responsibility of the proposed assignee; suitability of the use for the particular property; legality of the proposed use; need for alteration of the premises; and nature of the occupancy, i.e., office, factory, clinic, etc.

Denying consent solely on the basis of personal taste, convenience or sensibility is not commercially reasonable. Nor is it reasonable to deny consent in order that the landlord may charge a higher rent than originally contracted for. This is because the lessor's desire for a better bargain than contracted for has nothing to do with the permissible purposes of the restraint on alienation—to protect the lessor's interest in the preservation of the property and the performance of the lease covenants. "'[The] clause is for the protection of the landlord *in its ownership and operation of the particular property*—not for its general economic protection.'" (Ringwood Associates v. Jack's of Route 23, Inc., *supra*, 379 A.2d at p. 512, quoting Krieger v. Helmsley-Spear, Inc. (1973) 62 N.J. 423, 302 A.2d 129, italics added.)

In conclusion, both the policy against restraints on alienation and the implied contractual duty of good faith and fair dealing militate in favor of adoption of the rule that where a commercial lease provides for assignment only with the prior consent of the lessor, such consent may be withheld only where the lessor has a commercially reasonable objection to the assignee or the proposed use. Under this rule, appellants have stated a cause of action against respondent Ernest Pestana, Inc.

The order sustaining the demurrer to the complaint, which we have deemed to incorporate a judgment of dismissal, is reversed.

NOTES & QUESTIONS:

1. In Texas, the property code requires the landlord's permission for the tenant to be able to assign or sublease. Under Texas Property Code § 91.005, even if the lease is silent, the landlord's permission is required by statute. The statute does not state, however, under what grounds the landlord can refuse an assignment or sublease.

2. The *Kendall* case raises the question of reasonableness in the commercial context and indicates that the growing majority view is that the landlord may refuse only for commercially reasonable justifications. Should the residential context be treated any differently? How would the landlord's duty to mitigate in the residential context match with the landlord's permission for assignments and subleases?

C. Duties, Rights, and Remedies (Especially Regarding the Condition of the Leased Premises)

Leases give rise to a rather obvious problem. Once a lease is entered into, the landlord has an incentive to neglect everyday repairs because the costs of neglect are borne primarily by tenants. Tenants, in turn, have an incentive to neglect maintenance, especially toward the end of the term, because the costs of neglect will soon shift to the landlord. How might the law deal with these difficulties? That question is the subject of this section. There has been a great deal of change over time. This is a prime area where there exists much interaction between common law concepts and statutes.

1. Landlord's Duties; Tenant's Rights and Remedies

In the beginning, there were no implied covenants regarding the condition of the premises. Property law took the stance of "let the lessee beware" and tenants took property "as is." Landlords were under no obligation to warrant the fitness of the property and the tenants had the duty to maintain the condition of the leased premises once the leasehold began. In the 1960s, the law started to change to what we have today.

What if we have the following situation:

A defective roof beam in *T*'s rented house collapses. What are *T*'s rights under these circumstances? Must *L* repair the roof? If *L* refuses to do so, can *T* terminate the lease and move out, remain in possession without paying rent, or use another remedy?

At common law, *T* would have no claim of any kind against *L*. Today, *L* would be obligated to repair the roof and if *L* failed to repair after due notice, *T* could terminate the lease or exercise other remedies. The reason for the dramatic change is the law's response to the problem of substandard housing. During the 19th century, large slum areas developed in the United States where housing conditions were both unhealthy and unsafe. The trend worsened in the 20th century. The landlord had no legal obligation to make repairs and the tenants often could not make the repairs. There were housing codes, but the fines for the violations were so minimal that the landlord just took his chances with getting fined. In 1965 in New York City, the average fine imposed for a housing code violation was 50 cents. In today's dollars that would be around $3.00. While there could also be jail time associated with violations, it was never imposed.

The 1960s brought concerns for the plight of the low-income residents trapped in slum housing; the courts and later legislatures began to reevaluate the traditional doctrines and make changes. This has had little impact on commercial leases; the rights and duties of commercial landlords are still largely governed by a "caveat lessee" standard.

Over the course of the past 40 years, the Texas Legislature has enacted a number of statutes addressing the responsibilities of the residential landlord, most of which are found in Chapter 92 of the Texas Property Code. Legislative bodies and courts in other states have similarly adopted doctrines different from those of the common law. The material in this section gives some idea of these developments, but does not cover them in detail or even list all of the possible variations.

Under the common law, and in Texas prior to the *Kamarath* decision, the landlord owed no duty to the residential tenant or others to furnish or maintain the premises in a safe or habitable condition. Shortly after the *Kamarath* case, the Texas Legislature superseded that case by enacting the statutory provisions that were the predecessors to the provisions of Chapter 92 regarding the residential landlord's duty to repair.[24] There are a great deal of protections afforded by the property code to the residential tenant and due to public policy concerns many of the protections cannot be waived at all and even if they are waivable, the waiver must be in writing.[25]

Regardless of the residential landlord's other statutory duties, the landlord has no statutory obligation to repair conditions caused by the intentional or negligent acts of the tenant. The Texas Supreme Court clarified that because the landlord has no liability for conditions caused by the tenant, the landlord can contractually require the tenant to repair those conditions, and the agreement is enforceable without regard to whether it complies with § 92.006. If, however, the landlord wishes to make the tenant responsible for repairing conditions for which the landlord would normally be liable (*i.e.*, conditions that materially affect the health and safety of the ordinary tenant), the agreement is not enforceable unless the landlord complies with § 92.006 of the Property Code.[26]

Unless the lease contains express language to the contrary, the landlord undertakes an implied covenant of quiet enjoyment by entering into the lease contract.[27] An eviction of the tenant by one having paramount title is one

---

[24] *See* Garza-Vale v. Kwiecien, 796 S.W.2d 500 (Tex. App. 1990). Another more recent case involving the landlord's duty to repair is Woods v. Taylor Housing Authority, No. 03-98-00249-CV, 1999 WL 298329 (Tex. App.—Austin May 13, 2002, no pet.) (not designated for publication).

[25] *See* Tex. Prop. Code Ann. § 92.006. (Vernon 2007).

[26] *See generally* Churchill Forge, Inc. v. Brown, 61 S.W.3d 368 (Tex. 2001).

[27] *See generally* L-M-S Inc. v. Blackwell, 233 S.W.2d 286 (Tex. 1950); Drummet v. Beal, 354 S.W.2d 701 (Tex. Civ. App.—Eastland 1962, err. ref'd, n.r.e.).

example of a breach of this covenant.[28] Furthermore, acts of the landlord that seriously affect the value or practicality of tenants' possession are sometimes regarded as breaches of the covenant of quiet enjoyment.[29]

We will compare from time to time Chapters 92 and 93 of the Texas Property Code. Chapter 93 applies to commercial landlord-tenant relationships. Chapter 93 does not offer as many modifications to the common law as does Chapter 92. You will come to understand and appreciate the difference in the commercial and residential tenancies due in large part to the nature of the parties involved as well as the purpose for the rental property.

2. Quiet Enjoyment and Constructive Eviction

Reste Realty Corp. v. Cooper
Supreme Court of New Jersey, 1969
251 A.2d 268

FRANCIS, J.

Plaintiff-lessor sued defendant-lessee to recover rent allegedly due under a written lease. The suit was based upon a charge that defendant had unlawfully abandoned the premises two and a quarter years before the termination date of the lease. The trial court, sitting without a jury, sustained tenant's defense of constructive eviction and entered judgment for defendant. The Appellate Division reversed, holding (1) the proof did not support a finding of any wrongful act or omission on the part of the lessor sufficient to constitute a constructive eviction, and (2) if such act or omission could be found, defendant waived it by failing to remove from the premises within a reasonable time thereafter. We granted defendant's petition for certification.

On May 13, 1958, defendant Joy M. Cooper, leased from plaintiff's predecessor in title a portion of the ground or basement floor of a commercial (office) building at 207 Union Street, Hackensack, N.J. The term was five years, but after about a year of occupancy the parties made a new five-year lease dated April 1959 covering the entire floor except the furnace room. The leased premises were to be used as "commercial offices" and "not for any other purpose without the prior written consent of the Landlord." More particularly, the lessee utilized the offices for meetings and training of sales personnel in connection with the business of a jewelry firm of which Mrs. Cooper was branch manager at the time. No merchandise was sold there.

---

[28] *See generally Drummet,* 354 S.W.2d 701.

[29] *See generally* Maple Terrace Apartment Co. v. Simpson, 22 S.W.2d 698 (Tex. Civ. App. 1929) (addressing failure to enforce pet restrictions against neighbors in apartment house).

A driveway ran along the north side of the building from front to rear. Its inside edge was at the exterior foundation wall of the ground floor. The driveway was not part of Mrs. Cooper's leasehold. Apparently it was provided for use of all tenants. Whenever it rained during the first year of defendant's occupancy, water ran off the driveway and into the offices and meeting rooms either through or under the exterior or foundation wall. At this time Arthur A. Donigian, a member of the bar of this State, had his office in the building. In addition, he was an officer and resident manager of the then corporate-owner. Whenever water came into the leased floor, defendant would notify him and he would take steps immediately to remove it. Obviously Donigian was fully aware of the recurrent flooding. He had some personal files in the furnace room which he undertook to protect by putting them on 2 x 4's in order to raise them above the floor surface. When negotiating with defendant for the substitute five-year lease for the larger space, Donigian promised to remedy the water problem by resurfacing the driveway. (It is important to note here that Donigian told Walter T. Wittman, an attorney, who had offices in the building and who later became executor of Donigan's estate, that the driveway needed "regrading and some kind of sealing of the area between the driveway which lay to the north of the premises and the wall." He also told Wittman that the grading was improper and was "letting the water into the basement rather than away from it.") The work was done as promised and although the record is not entirely clear, apparently the seepage was somewhat improved for a time. Subsequently it worsened, but Donigian responded immediately to each complaint and removed the water from the floor.

Donigian died on March 30, 1961, approximately two years after commencement of the second lease. Whenever it rained thereafter and water flooded into the leased floor, no one paid any attention to defendant's complaints, so she and her employees did their best to remove it. During this time sales personnel and trainees came to defendant's premises at frequent intervals for meetings and classes. Sometimes as many as 50 persons were in attendance in the morning and an equal number in the afternoon. The flooding greatly inconvenienced the conduct of these meetings. At times after heavy rainstorms there was as much as two inches of water in various places and "every cabinet, desk and chair had to be raised above the floor." On one occasion jewelry kits that had been sitting on the floor, as well as the contents of file cabinets, became "soaked." Mrs. Cooper testified that once when she was conducting a sales training class and it began to rain, water came into the room making it necessary to move all the chairs and "gear" into another room on the south side of the building. On some occasions the meetings had to be taken to other quarters for which rent had to be paid; on others the meetings were adjourned to a later date. Complaints to the lessor were ignored. What was described as the "crowning blow" occurred on December 20, 1961. A meeting of sales representatives from four states had been arranged. A rainstorm intervened and the resulting flooding placed five inches of water in the rooms. According to Mrs. Cooper it was impossible to hold the meeting in any place on the ground floor; they took it to a nearby inn. That evening she saw an attorney who advised her to send a notice of vacation. On December 21 she asked that the place be cleaned up. This was not done, and after notifying the lessor of her intention she left the premises on December 30, 1961.

Plaintiff acquired the building and an assignment of defendant's lease January 19, 1962. On November 9, 1964 it instituted this action to recover rent for the unexpired term of defendant's lease, i.e., until March 31, 1964.

At trial of the case defendant's proofs showed the facts outlined above. Plaintiff offered very little in the way of contradiction. It seemed to acknowledge that a water problem existed but as defense counsel told the court in his opening statement, he was "prepared to show that the water receded any number of times, and therefore the damage, if it was caused by an act that can be traced to the landlord, [the condition] was not a permanent interference" with the use and enjoyment of the premises. Plaintiff contended further that the water condition would not justify defendant's abandonment of the premises because in the lease she had stipulated that prior to execution thereof she had "examined the demised premises, and accept[ed] them in their [then] condition, and without any representations on the part of the landlord or its agents as to the present or future condition of the said premises"; moreover she had agreed "to keep the demised premises in good condition" and to "redecorate, paint and renovate the said premises as may be necessary to keep them in good repair and good appearance."

The trial judge found that the "testimony is just undisputed and overwhelming that after every rainstorm water flowed into the leased premises of the defendant" and nothing was done to remedy the condition despite repeated complaints to the lessor. He declared also that the condition was intolerable and so substantially deprived the lessee of the use of the premises as to constitute a constructive eviction and therefore legal justification for vacating them.

On this appeal the plaintiff-landlord claims that under the long-settled law, delivery of the leased premises to defendant-tenant was not accompanied by any implied warranty or covenant of fitness for use for commercial offices or for any other purpose. He asserts also that by express provision of both the first and second leases, the tenant acknowledged having examined the "demised premises," having agreed to accept them in their "present condition," and having agreed to keep them in good repair, which acknowledgment, as a matter of law, has the effect of excluding any such implied warranty or covenant.

It is true that as the law of leasing an estate for years developed historically, no implied warranty or covenant of habitability or fitness for the agreed use was imposed on the landlord. Because the interest of the lessee was considered personal property the doctrine of caveat emptor was applied, and in the absence of an express agreement otherwise, or misrepresentation by the lessor, the tenant took the premises "as is." Moreover, an awareness by legislatures of the inequality of bargaining power between landlord and tenant in many cases, and the need for tenant protection, has produced remedial tenement house and multiple dwelling statutes. It has come to be recognized that ordinarily the lessee does not have as much knowledge of the condition of the premises as the lessor. Building code requirements and violations are known or made known to the lessor, not the lessee. He is in a better position to know of latent defects, structural and otherwise, in a building which might go unnoticed by a lessee who rarely has sufficient knowledge or expertise to see or to discover them. A prospective lessee, such as a small businessman, cannot be expected to know if the plumbing or wiring systems are adequate or conform to local codes. Nor should he be expected to hire experts to advise him. Ordinarily all this information should be considered readily available to the lessor who in turn can inform the prospective lessee. These factors have produced persuasive arguments for reevaluation of the caveat emptor doctrine and, for imposition of an implied warranty that the premises are suitable for the leased purposes and conform to local codes and zoning laws. Proponents of more liberal treatment of tenants say, among other things, that if a lease is a demise of land and a sale of an interest in land in the commercial sense, more realistic consideration should be given to the contractual nature of the relationship. It will not be necessary to deal at any length with the suggested need for reevaluation and revision of the doctrines of caveat emptor and implied warranties in leases beyond consideration of matters projected into the case by the various contentions of the landlord.

Since the language of the two leases is the same, except that the second one describes the larger portion of the basement taken by the tenant, evaluation of the landlord's contentions will be facilitated by first considering the original lease and the factual setting attending its execution. Although the second or substitutionary lease is the controlling instrument, we take this approach in order to focus more clearly upon the effect of the change in the factual setting when the second lease was executed. This course brings us immediately to the landlord's reliance upon the provisions of the first lease (which also appear in the second) that the tenant inspected the "demised premises," accepted them in their "present condition" and agreed to keep them in good condition. The word "premises," construed most favorably to the tenant, means so much of the ground floor as was leased to Mrs. Cooper for commercial offices. The driveway or its surfacing or the exterior wall or foundation under it cannot be considered included as part of the "premises." In any event there is nothing to show that the inspection by Mrs. Cooper of the driveway or the ground floor exterior wall and foundation under it prior to the execution of the first lease would have given or did give her notice that they were so defective as to permit rainwater to flood into the leased portion of the interior. The condition should have been and probably was known to the lessor. If known, there was a duty to disclose it to the prospective tenant. Certainly as to Mrs. Cooper, it was a latent defect, and it would be a wholly inequitable application of caveat emptor to charge her with knowledge of it. The attempted reliance upon the agreement of the tenant in both leases to keep the "demised premises" in repair furnishes no support for the landlord's position. The driveway, exterior ground floor wall and foundation are not part of the demised premises. Latent defects in this context, i.e., those the existence and significance of which are not reasonably apparent to the ordinary prospective tenant, certainly were not assumed by Mrs. Cooper. In fact in our judgment present day demands of fair treatment for tenants with respect to latent defects remediable by the landlord, either within the demised premises or outside the demised premises, require imposition on him of an implied warranty against such defects. Such warranty might be described as a limited warranty of habitability. In any event we need not at this point deal with the scope of the warranty, nor with issues of public policy that might be involved in certain types of cases where express exclusion of such warranty is contained in the lease.

In Pines v. Perssion [14 Wis. 2d 590, 111 N.W.2d 409 (1961)], the Supreme Court of Wisconsin after noting that the frame of reference in which the old common law rule operated has undergone a change, declared:

> Legislation and administrative rules, such as the safe place statute, building codes and health regulations, all impose certain duties on a property owner with respect to the condition of his premises. Thus, the legislature has made a policy judgment—that it is socially (and politically) desirable to impose these duties on a property owner—which has rendered the old common law rule obsolete. To follow the old rule of no implied warranty of habitability of leases would, in our opinion, be inconsistent with the current legislative policy concerning housing standards. The need and social desirability of adequate housing for people in this era of rapid population increases is too important to be rebuffed by that obnoxious legal cliche, caveat emptor.

The letting of a one-family home to college students was involved in the case. Although the young men had gone through the house before renting it, the court pointed out they had no way of knowing that the plumbing, heating and wiring systems were defective. Under the circumstances an implied warranty of habitability was said to exist, and its breach by the landlord relieved the tenants of liability for rent, except for such rent as would be reasonable for the one month of their occupancy. Similarly we believe that at the inception of the original lease in the present case, an implied warranty against latent defects existed.

But the landlord says that whatever the factual and legal situation may have been when the original lease was made, the relationship underwent a change to its advantage when the second was executed. This contention is based upon the undisputed fact that in April 1959, after a year of occupancy, defendant, with knowledge that the premises were subject to recurrent flooding, accepted a new lease containing the same provisions as the first one. This acceptance, the argument runs, eliminates any possible reliance upon a covenant or warranty of fitness because the premises were truly taken then "as is." While it is true that a tenant's knowing acceptance of a defective leasehold would normally preclude reliance upon any implied warranties, the landlord's position here is not sustainable because it is asserted in disregard of certain vital facts—the agent's promise to remedy the condition and the existence of an express covenant of quiet enjoyment in the lease.

The evidence is clear that prior to execution of the substitutionary lease, the tenant complained to the owner's agent about the incursion of water whenever it rained. The agent conceded the problem existed and promised to remedy the condition. Relying upon the promise Mrs. Cooper accepted the new lease, and the landlord resurfaced the driveway. Unfortunately, either the work was not sufficiently extensive or it was not done properly because at some unstated time thereafter the water continued to come into the tenant's offices. The complaints about it resumed, and as noted above, until the building manager died he made prompt efforts to remove the water. In our opinion the tenant was entitled to rely upon the promise of its agent to provide a remedy. Thus it cannot be said as a matter of law that by taking the second lease she accepted the premises in their defective condition.

This brings us to the crucial question whether the landlord was guilty of a breach of a covenant which justified the tenant's removal from the premises on December 30, 1961. We are satisfied there was such a breach.

The great weight of authority throughout the country is to the effect that ordinarily a covenant of quiet enjoyment is implied in a lease. Where there is such a covenant, whether express or implied, and it is breached substantially by the landlord, the courts have applied the doctrine of constructive eviction as a remedy for the tenant. Under this rule any act or omission of the landlord or of anyone who acts under authority or legal right from the landlord, or of someone having superior title to that of the landlord, which renders the premises substantially unsuitable for the purpose for which they are leased, or which seriously interferes with the beneficial enjoyment of the premises, is a breach of the covenant of quiet enjoyment and constitutes a constructive eviction of the tenant.

Examples of constructive eviction having close analogy to the present case are easily found. Failure to supply heat as covenanted in the lease so that the apartment was "unlivable" on cold days amounted to constructive eviction.

Walker Realty Co., 1 N.J. Misc. 287 (Sup. Ct. 1923). So too, when the main waste pipe of an apartment building was permitted to become and remain clogged with sewage for a long period of time causing offensive odors and danger to health, the covenant of quiet enjoyment was breached and justified the tenant's abandonment of his premises.

As noted above, the trial court found sufficient interference with the use and enjoyment of the leased premises to justify the tenant's departure and to relieve her from the obligation to pay further rent. In our view the evidence was sufficient to warrant that conclusion, and the Appellate Division erred in reversing it. Plaintiff argued and the Appellate Division agreed that a constructive eviction cannot arise unless the condition interferes with the use in a permanent sense. It is true that the word "permanent" appears in many of the early cases. But it is equally obvious that permanent does not signify that water in a basement in a case like this one must be an everlasting and unending condition. If its recurrence follows regularly upon rainstorms and is sufficiently serious in extent to amount to a substantial interference with use and enjoyment of the premises for the purpose of the lease, the test for constructive eviction has been met. Additionally in our case, the defective condition of the driveway, exterior and foundation walls which permitted the recurrent flooding was obviously permanent in the sense that it would continue and probably worsen if not remedied. There was no obligation on the tenant to remedy it.

Plaintiff's final claim is that assuming the tenant was exposed to a constructive eviction, she waived it by remaining on the premises for an unreasonable period of time thereafter. The general rule is, of course, that a tenant's right to claim a constructive eviction will be lost if he does not vacate the premises within a reasonable time after the right comes into existence. What constitutes a reasonable time depends upon the circumstances of each case. In considering the problem courts must be sympathetic toward the tenant's plight. Vacation of the premises is a drastic course and must be taken at his peril. If he vacates, and it is held at a later time in a suit for rent for the unexpired term that the landlord's course of action did not reach the dimensions of constructive eviction, a substantial liability may be imposed upon him. That risk and the practical inconvenience and difficulties attendant upon finding and moving to suitable quarters counsel caution.

Here, plaintiff's cooperative building manager died about nine months before the removal. During that period the tenant complained, patiently waited, hoped for relief from the landlord, and tried to take care of the water problem that accompanied the recurring rainstorms. But when relief did not come and the "crowning blow" put five inches of water in the leased offices and meeting rooms on December 20, 1961, the tolerance ended and the vacation came ten days later after notice to the landlord. The trial court found as a fact that under the circumstances such vacation was within a reasonable time, and the delay was not sufficient to establish a waiver of the constructive eviction. We find adequate evidence to support the conclusion and are of the view that the Appellate Division should not have reversed it.

For the reasons expressed above, we hold the view that the trial court was correct in deciding that defendant had been constructively evicted from the premises in question, and therefore was not liable for the rent claimed. Accordingly, the judgment of the Appellate Division is reversed and that of the trial court is reinstated.

NOTES & QUESTIONS:

1. The covenant of quiet enjoyment and remedy of constructive eviction are often confused. Even the courts do not clearly explain the difference between the two concepts.

   The covenant of quiet enjoyment was originally a legal concept used in the context of a tenant being actually evicted or removed from the property either wrongfully by the landlord or by a third party with a superior interest to the tenant's. Remember the concept of possession discussed with obtaining actual possession. In the *Hannan* case, the court clarified that the issue did not involve a legal right to possession. In that context, everyone was in agreement that the landlord had a duty to provide a legal right to possession that was not impacted by some superior interest. However, with cases like *Reste Realty*, the courts used the concept of quiet enjoyment to apply in contexts where physical issues with the property could lead to a constructive eviction. However, there is a breach of the covenant of quiet enjoyment that lends itself to damages rather than utilizing the remedy of constructive eviction.

2. What if in the *Reste Realty* case, there was a constant leak from the ceiling every time it rained? There was no flooding, but a simple water leak. Would that amount to a constructive eviction? No. However, it would be a breach of the covenant of quiet enjoyment because the covenant is that in every lease the tenant impliedly has a promise on the part of the landlord that neither the landlord nor anyone with either a superior title or a title derivative of the landlord will wrongfully interfere with the tenant's use and enjoyment of the leased property.[30] If the landlord has a duty to maintain the premises and fails to do so, then that is wrongfully interfering with the tenant's use and enjoyment of the leased property.

---

[30] Hovenkamp & Kurtz, Principles of Property Law 269 (6th ed. 2005).

The facts of *Reste Realty* bring in the concept of a constructive eviction because the flooding in that case not only interfered with the tenant's use and enjoyment, it was a substantial interference that was permanent and the tenant vacated within a reasonable time.

Thus under the common law approach, either the breach is significant enough to justify termination of the lease by the tenant or the breach does not justify termination so the tenant must remain and sue for damages caused by the breach. These damages are often referred to as "difference money" because the tenant will be awarded the difference between the amount of rent under the lease less the fair rental value with the defect in place. This difference in amount paid versus value received will be the measure of damages. The tenant can also obtain a court order to make the landlord complete necessary repairs. However, this is a costly and time-consuming option for the tenant. And the option of constructive eviction is usually raised as an affirmative defense when the landlord sues the tenant for abandoning the premises and unpaid rent. Thus, either option can prove to be very costly for the tenant.

3. The remedy of constructive eviction with the common law covenant of quiet enjoyment is also difficult for the tenant to utilize. The tenant must give notice to the landlord. However, there is nothing specified as to the form of notice or the amount of time that the landlord must be allowed to make any needed repairs. This is of great concern to the tenant because if the tenant does not use this remedy properly then the tenant will be considered to have unlawfully abandoned and will be liable for the remaining rent due under the lease. Additionally, the tenant must vacate within a reasonable time or the constructive eviction claim will not be viable. How long is a reasonable time? It will depend on the particular facts and circumstances of the case.

These are just a couple of reasons why many states have enacted statutes governing the condition of the property and the landlord's obligations. The statutes generally provide more certainty to both landlords and tenants so that the law can be effectively utilized. Some pertinent provisions of the Texas Property Code are set forth below.

Tex. Prop. Code Chapter 92: Residential Tenancies

§ 92.006 Waiver or Expansion of Duties and Remedies
(a) A landlord's duty or a tenant's remedy concerning security deposits, security devices, the landlord's disclosure of ownership and management,

or utility cutoffs, as provided by Subchapter C, D, E, or G, respectively, may not be waived. A landlord's duty to install a smoke detector under Subchapter F may not be waived, nor may a tenant waive a remedy for the landlord's noninstallation or waive the tenant's limited right of installation and removal. The landlord's duty of inspection and repair of smoke alarms under Subchapter F may be waived only by written agreement.

(b) A landlord's duties and the tenant's remedies concerning security devices, the landlord's disclosure of ownership and management, or smoke detectors, as provided by Subchapter D, E, or F, respectively, may be enlarged only by specific written agreement.

(c) A landlord's duties and the tenant's remedies under Subchapter B, which covers conditions materially affecting the physical health or safety of the ordinary tenant, may not be waived except as provided in Subsections (d), (e), and (f) of this section.

(d) A landlord and a tenant may agree for the tenant to repair or remedy, at the landlord's expense, any condition covered by Subchapter B.

(e) A landlord and a tenant may agree for the tenant to repair or remedy, at the tenant's expense, any condition covered by Subchapter B if all of the following conditions are met:

(1) at the beginning of the lease term the landlord owns only one rental dwelling;

(2) at the beginning of the lease term the dwelling is free from any condition which would materially affect the physical health or safety of an ordinary tenant;

(3) at the beginning of the lease term the landlord has no reason to believe that any condition described in Subdivision (2) of this subsection is likely to occur or recur during the tenant's lease term or during a renewal or extension; and

(4) (A) the lease is in writing;

(B) the agreement for repairs by the tenant is either underlined or printed in boldface in the lease or in a separate written addendum;

(C) the agreement is specific and clear; and

(D) the agreement is made knowingly, voluntarily, and for consideration.

(f) A landlord and tenant may agree that, except for those conditions caused by the negligence of the landlord, the tenant has the duty to pay for repair of the following conditions that may occur during the lease term or a renewal or extension:

(1) damage from wastewater stoppages caused by foreign or improper objects in lines that exclusively serve the tenant's dwelling;

(2) damage to doors, windows, or screens; and

(3) damage from windows or doors left open.

This subsection shall not affect the landlord's duty under Subchapter B to repair or remedy, at the landlord's expense, wastewater stoppages or backups caused by deterioration, breakage, roots, ground conditions, faulty construction, or malfunctioning equipment. A landlord and tenant may agree to the provisions of this subsection only if the agreement meets the requirements of Subdivision (4) of Subsection (e) of this section.

(g) A tenant's right to vacate a dwelling and avoid liability under Section 92.016 or 92.017 may not be waived by a tenant or a landlord, except as provided by those sections.[31]

(h) A tenant's right to a jury trial in an action brought under this chapter may not be waived in a lease or other written agreement.[32]

Subchapter B: Repair or Closing of Leasehold

§ 92.051 Application

This subchapter applies to a lease executed, entered into, renewed, or extended on or after September 1, 1979.

§ 92.052 Landlord's Duty to Repair or Remedy

(a) A landlord shall make a diligent effort to repair or remedy a condition if:

(1) the tenant specifies the condition in a notice to the person to whom or to the place where rent is normally paid;

(2) the tenant is not delinquent in the payment of rent at the time notice is given; and

(3) the condition materially affects the physical health or safety of an ordinary tenant.

(b) Unless the condition was caused by normal wear and tear, the landlord does not have a duty during the lease term or a renewal or extension to repair or remedy a condition caused by:

(1) the tenant;

(2) a lawful occupant in the tenant's dwelling;

(3) a member of the tenant's family; or

(4) a guest or invitee of the tenant.

(c) This subchapter does not require the landlord:

---

[31] Section 92.016 allows tenants to terminate in situations of domestic violence provided the conditions set forth are satisfied; § 92.017 provides protection to persons in the military, allowing them to terminate under certain circumstances.

[32] The language of (h) was added by the legislature in the 2015 session. It applies to leases entered into as of January 1, 2016.

(1) to furnish utilities from a utility company if as a practical matter the utility lines of the company are not reasonably available; or

(2) to furnish security guards.

(d) The tenant's notice under Subsection (a) must be in writing only if the tenant's lease is in writing and requires written notice.

§ 92.056 Landlord Liability and Tenant Remedies; Notice and Time for Repair[33]

(a) A landlord's liability under this section is subject to Section 92.052(b) regarding conditions that are caused by a tenant and Section 92.054 regarding conditions that are insured casualties.

(b) A landlord is liable to a tenant as provided by this subchapter if:

(1) the tenant has given the landlord notice to repair or remedy a condition by giving that notice to the person to whom or to the place where the tenant's rent is normally paid;

(2) the condition materially affects the physical health or safety of an ordinary tenant;

(3) the tenant has given the landlord a subsequent written notice to repair or remedy the condition after a reasonable time to repair or remedy the condition following the notice given under Subdivision (1) or the tenant has given the notice under Subdivision (1) by sending that notice by certified mail, return receipt requested, by registered mail, or by another form of mail that allows tracking of delivery from the United States Postal Service or a private delivery service[34];

(4) the landlord has had a reasonable time to repair or remedy the condition after the landlord received the tenant's notice under subdivision (1) and, if applicable, the tenant's subsequent notice under Subdivision (3);

(5) the landlord has not made a diligent effort to repair or remedy the condition after the landlord received the tenant's notice under Subdivision (1) and, if applicable, the tenant's notice under Subdivision (3); and

(6) the tenant was not delinquent in the payment of rent at the time any notice required by this subsection was given.

(c) For purposes of Subsection (b)(4) or (5), a landlord is considered to have received the tenant's notice when the landlord or the landlord's agent or employee has actually received the notice or when the United States Postal Service has attempted to deliver the notice to the landlord.

---

[33] Updated Jan. 1, 2008.

[34] The language "or by another form of mail that allows tracking of delivery from the United States Postal Service or a private delivery service" was added during the 2013 legislative session. This applies to leases entered into on or after January 1, 2016.

(d) For purposes of Subsection (b)(3) or (4), in determining whether a period of time is a reasonable time to repair or remedy a condition, there is a rebuttable presumption that seven days is a reasonable time. To rebut that presumption, the date on which the landlord received the tenant's notice, the severity and nature of the condition, and the reasonable availability of materials and labor and of utilities from a utility company must be considered.

(e) Except as provided in Subsection (f), a tenant to whom a landlord is liable under Subsection (b) of this section may:

    (1) terminate the lease;

    (2) have the condition repaired or remedied according to Section 92.0561;

    (3) deduct from the tenant's rent, without necessity of judicial action, the cost of the repair or remedy according to Section 92.0561; and

    (4) obtain judicial remedies according to Section 92.0563.

(f) A tenant who elects to terminate the lease under Subsection (e) is:

    (1) entitled to a pro rata refund of rent from the date of termination or the date the tenant moves out, whichever is later;

    (2) entitled to deduct the tenant's security deposit from the tenant's rent without necessity of lawsuit or obtain a refund of the tenant's security deposit according to law; and

    (3) not entitled to the other repair and deduct remedies under Section 92.0561 or the judicial remedies under Subdivisions (1) and (2) of Subsection (a) of Section 92.0563.

(g) A lease must contain language in underlined or bold print that informs the tenant of the remedies available under this section and Section 92.0561.

§ 92.0561 Tenant's Repair and Deduct Remedies[35]

(a) If the landlord is liable to the tenant under 92.056(b), the tenant may have the condition repaired or remedied and may deduct the cost from a subsequent rent payment as provided in this section.

(b) The tenant's deduction for the cost of the repair or remedy may not exceed the amount of one month's rent under the lease or $500, whichever is greater. However, if the tenant's rent is subsidized in whole or in part by a governmental agency, the deduction limitation of one month's rent shall mean the fair market rent for the dwelling and not the rent that the tenant pays. The fair market rent shall be determined by the governmental agency subsidizing the rent, or in the absence of such a

---

[35] Updated July 1997.

determination, it shall be a reasonable amount of rent under the circumstances.

(c) Repairs and deductions under this section may be made as often as necessary so long as the total repairs and deductions in any one month do not exceed one month's rent or $500, whichever is greater.

(d) Repairs under this section may be made only if all of the following requirements are met:

(1) The landlord has a duty to repair or remedy the condition under Section 92.052, and the duty has not been waived in a written lease by the tenant under Subsection (e) or (f) of Section 92.006.

(2) The tenant has given notice to the landlord as required by Section 92.056(b)(1), and, if required, a subsequent notice under Section 92.056(b)(3), and at least one of those notices states that the tenant intends to repair or remedy the condition. The notice shall also contain a reasonable description of the intended repair or remedy.

(3) Any one of the following events has occurred:

(A) The landlord has failed to remedy the backup or overflow of raw sewage inside the tenant's dwelling or the flooding from broken pipes or natural drainage inside the dwelling.

(B) The landlord has expressly or impliedly agreed in the lease to furnish potable water to the tenant's dwelling and the water service to the dwelling has totally ceased.

(C) The landlord has expressly or impliedly agreed in the lease to furnish heating or cooling equipment; the equipment is producing inadequate heat or cooled air; and the landlord has been notified in writing by the appropriate local housing, building, or health official or other official having jurisdiction that the lack of heat or cooling materially affects the health or safety of an ordinary tenant.

(D) The landlord has been notified in writing by the appropriate local housing, building, or health official or other official having jurisdiction that the condition materially affects the health or safety of an ordinary tenant.

(e) If the requirements of Subsection (d) of this section are met, a tenant may:

(1) have the condition repaired or remedied immediately following the tenant's notice of intent to repair if the condition involves sewage or flooding as referred to in Paragraph (A) of Subdivision (3) of Subsection (d) of this section;

(2) have the condition repaired or remedied if the condition involves a cessation of potable water as referred to in Paragraph (A) of Subdivision (3) of Subsection (d) of this section and if the landlord has

       failed to repair or remedy the condition within three days following the tenant's delivery of notice of intent to repair;

    (3) have the condition repaired or remedied if the condition involves inadequate heat or cooled air as referred to in Paragraph (c) of Subdivision (3) of Subsection (d) of this section and if the landlord has failed to repair the condition within three days after delivery of the tenant's notice of intent to repair; or

    (4) have the condition repaired or remedied if the condition is not covered by Paragraph (A), (B), or (c) of Subdivision (3) of Subsection (d) of this section and involves a condition affecting the physical health or safety of the ordinary tenant as referred to in Paragraph (D) of Subdivision (3) of Subsection (d) of this section and if the landlord has failed to repair or remedy the condition within seven days after delivery of the tenant's notice of intent to repair.

(f) Omitted

(g) A landlord and a tenant may mutually agree for the tenant to repair or remedy, at the landlord's expense, any condition of the dwelling regardless of whether it materially affects the health or safety of an ordinary tenant. However, the landlord's duty to repair or remedy conditions covered by this subchapter may not be waived except as provided by Subsection (e) or (f) of Section 92.006.

(h) Omitted

(i) Omitted

(j) When deducting the cost of repairs from the rent payment, the tenant shall furnish the landlord, along with payment of the balance of the rent, a copy of the repair bill and the receipt for its payment. A repair bill and receipt may be the same document.

(k) Omitted

§ 92.0563 Tenant's Judicial Remedies[36]

The amended text in § 92.0563 below is effective for actions filed on or after Jan. 1, 2010. Actions filed before Jan. 1, 2010 are governed by the former law in effect at that time.

(a) A tenant's judicial remedies under Section 92.056 shall include:

    (1) an order directing the landlord to take reasonable action to repair or remedy the condition;

    (2) an order reducing the tenant's rent, from the date of the first repair notice, in proportion to the reduced rental value resulting from the condition until the condition is repaired or remedied;

---

[36] Amended by SB 1448, § 1, 81st Leg., eff. Jan. 1, 2010.

(3) a judgment against the landlord for a civil penalty of one month's rent plus $500;

(4) a judgment against the landlord for the amount of the tenant's actual damages; and

(5) court costs and attorney's fees, excluding any attorney's fees for a cause of action for damages relating to a personal injury.

(b) A landlord who knowingly violates Section 92.006 by contracting orally or in writing with a tenant to waive the landlord's duty to repair under this subchapter shall be liable to the tenant for actual damages, a civil penalty of one month's rent plus $2,000, and reasonable attorney's fees. For purposes of this subsection, there shall be a rebuttable presumption that the landlord acted without knowledge of the violation. The tenant shall have the burden of pleading and proving a knowing violation. If the lease is in writing and is not in violation of Section 92.006, the tenant's proof of a knowing violation must be clear and convincing. A mutual agreement for tenant repair under Subsection (g) of Section 92.0561 is not a violation of Section 92.006.

(c) The justice, county, and district courts have concurrent jurisdiction in an action under Subsection (a) of this section except that the justice court may not order repairs under Subdivision (1) of Subsection (a) of this section.

(d) If a suit is filed in a justice court requesting relief under Subsection (a), the justice court shall conduct a hearing on the request not earlier than the sixth day after the date of service of citation and not later than the 10th day after that date.

(e) A justice court may not award a judgment under this section, including an order of repair, that exceeds $10,000, excluding interest and costs of court.

(f) An appeal of a judgment of a justice court under this section takes precedence in county court and may be held at any time after the eighth day after the date the transcript is filed in the county court. An owner of real property who files a notice of appeal of a judgment of a justice court to the county court perfects the owner's appeal and stays the effect of the judgment without the necessity of posting an appeal bond.

4. One thing to keep in mind is the relationship between the covenant of quiet enjoyment at common law and this statutory warranty of habitability included in Chapter 92 of the Texas Property Code. The statutory warranty of habitability supersedes the common law on issues related to the physical health and safety of an ordinary tenant. Therefore, in a case like *Reste Realty* in Texas, the tenant would not claim the common law defense of constructive eviction. The tenant would have to

properly utilize the statute and assert the right to terminate the lease as one of the available remedies under the Texas Property Code. The next example will help you to work through the statute and its application.

Landlord/Tenant Hypothetical #2

In December, Elaine rented a house in the State of Texas from Newman on a one-year lease that will become a month-to-month after the first year. Elaine's rent is $600 per month. During the first two months of the lease, Elaine particularly enjoyed living in her house.

One day in January, when Elaine unplugged her toaster, she heard the crackling of electricity. Since that time, she has noticed a similar problem with certain other outlets in her rented house, and she has sometimes smelled something burning, although Elaine has never seen smoke or fire. Elaine has avoided those outlets for which she has observed a problem.

In February as a result of heavy spring showers, Elaine's roof started to leak. The water stained the ceiling and dripped onto her white sofa, causing stains to the sofa that cannot be removed.

When Elaine bumped into Newman at the post office in February, she told him of the problems, and although Newman promised to have the roof repaired and the electrical wiring inspected, nothing has been done with respect to either problem.

In addition, Elaine recently noted that the wooden railings on her staircase had dry rotted. Because she was afraid a guest may fall, she hired a neighbor to make a few minor repairs and deducted from her March rent the $150 the repairman charged. Elaine included a short note explaining her reason for paying only $450 instead of $600. She also asked if Newman had made any arrangements regarding the "other problems" about which they had spoken.

When Newman received Elaine's March rent and her note, he hit the roof. He called Elaine demanding that she immediately remit the $150 she had deducted and threatening to evict her if she didn't do so by 5 p.m. the next day.

Elaine's city has a housing code that regulates electrical wiring in houses, requiring in essence that the owner of the house repair immediately electrical wiring that poses a hazard at the risk of a fine or an order preventing habitation of the premises.

(1) What are Elaine's rights under Chapter 92 of the Texas Property Code? Please be precise in advising Elaine exactly what her rights are and any steps she must take before she can exercise her rights.

(2) What differences would there be, if any, if the leased premises were commercial property rather than residential property?

5. But, what if the issue is not a physical repair, but something else? Consider the following situations and evaluate whether the tenant could utilize the covenant of quiet enjoyment with the remedy of constructive eviction:

    a. Tenant's neighbor is manufacturing methamphetamine in his apartment. The toxic fumes are making tenant ill.

    b. Tenant's neighbor is a chain smoker and the cigarette smoke is seeping from the neighbor's unit into the unit of the nonsmoking tenant.

    c. Tenant's neighbor is loud and regularly has parties until 3 a.m. where he and his guests play loud music, pound on the walls, and generally prevent tenant from sleeping.

    d. Tenant's car has been broken into on several occasions by random third-party trespassers.

    e. Tenant is a gynecologist and performs abortions as part of his practice. His leased office space has been the target of demonstrations by antiabortion protestors who picket in the parking lot, sing and chant, approach patients, and enter into the lobby of the office to distribute literature and tell Tenant's patients that he "kills babies." Tenant complains for several months to the landlord but the landlord does nothing. The police will not take action against the protectors unless the landlord will also file a complaint. After several months of no action by the landlord, Tenant vacates.

3. Tenant's Duties; Landlord's Rights and Remedies

There has been much discussion thus far about what the landlord has to do, but what about the tenant? What is the tenant responsible for during the term of a leasehold estate? As discussed, we have moved from the tenant being responsible for almost everything to the landlord taking on a lot of the responsibilities. Although it is now implied, if not expressly stated in the lease agreement, the landlord has to provide a habitable property and is responsible for making repairs to the property to maintain that habitable condition. But there are limits to the landlord's responsibility for repairs and maintenance of the property.

a. Duty Not to Commit Waste

The leasehold is in the category of finite estates like the freehold life estate. This present possessory estate will come to an end and the landlord will retake possession due to the reversion he has retained. Thus, the law of waste that applied to life tenants also applies to tenants in the leasehold context.

Under the law of waste, the tenant still maintains a duty not to commit waste and this duty is breached if the tenant makes "such a change as to affect a vital and substantial portion of the premises; as would change its characteristics or appearance; the fundamental purpose of the erection; or the uses contemplated or a change of such nature as would affect the very realty itself, extraordinary in scope and effect, or unusual in expenditure."

For example, if the tenant leases land that is to be used as an apple orchard and proceeds to cut down all of the apple trees during the term of the lease, the tenant has committed waste and will be liable to the landlord for damages.

If a tenant leases property on which he will operate a service station and then does not comply with proper EPA regulations regarding disposal of oil, gasoline, solvents, etc. and damages the property due to the improper disposal, this will amount to waste and entitle the landlord to damages.

However, even if the tenant makes changes to the premises that do not amount to waste, the law of fixtures may be implicated. Fixtures are defined as any chattel permanently affixed to the premises by a tenant. The law of waste and fixtures are very closely related and a tenant must consider two questions: (1) Am I entitled to take the item with me at the end of the leasehold or has it become part of the realty? And (2) even if I can take the item with me, will its removal cause damage to the property that would either subject me to liability for repairs or damages for waste?

Suppose a tenant purchases a new chandelier and installs it in the dining room of her apartment. Five years later the tenancy ends. Can tenant take the chandelier with her? What if the tenant buys a washer and dryer and hooks them up in the laundry room in her apartment?

Washers and dryers are never considered fixtures and may always be removed. The question of the chandelier is a closer call. If the lease agreement addresses the concept of fixtures, the lease will govern. However, if the lease is silent, courts look to several factors to determine whether the item is still removable or has become part of the realty as a fixture.

The factors are:

(1) the degree of attachment to the property;
(2) the custom associated with the item;
(3) the degree of harm caused by removal of the item;
(4) whether the item is used in a trade or business;
(5) the intent of the party who installed the items.

Today, the intent of the installing tenant is really the most significant factor. The change with respect to the law of fixtures is one that actually started with the commercial context. Being procommerce, the law evolved to allow commercial tenants to remove trade fixtures before the tenancy expired. However, if the trade fixtures were not timely removed, they became the property of the landlord.

b. Duty to Pay Rent

The other significant duty of the tenant is the tenant's duty to pay rent. This obligation is governed by a term of the lease agreement that specifies the amount and manner of repayment. Residential leases normally provide for a specific rent while often commercial leases calculate rent based on some percentage of the tenant's revenues. Although the realm of rent agreements used to be off limits to laws, in recent decades some jurisdictions have enacted statutes that can limit how much a landlord can charge.

c. Recovery of Security Deposits

A lessee has a common law duty to use reasonable care to protect the leased premises from injury other than that caused by ordinary wear and tear.[37]

The duty is often expressed as the duty to prevent waste. The basic tort concepts apply so that the lessee will be liable to the lessor for the harm proximately caused to the property by the lessee's failure to exercise reasonable care.[38] The measure of damages for the breach is either the reasonable cost of repairs or the loss of market value of the property.[39]

Although the duty of the tenant to prevent waste will be implied under the common law even if not included in the lease, leases customarily include a provision embodying this common law duty. The usual lease requires the lessee to return the premises to the lessor in as good a condition and state of repair as when the lessee received possession. Such a provision does not expand the common law duty, nor does it impose the responsibility of an insurer on the lessee. The lessee is liable only for harm resulting from the lessee's intentional or negligent conduct.[40]

As a means of ensuring that the landlord can recover at least some of any damages that may be caused to the property, landlords require a security deposit.

---

[37] King's Court Racquetball v. Dawkins, 62 S.W.3d 229, 233 (Tex. App.—Amarillo 2001, no pet. hist.).

[38] *See* R.C. Bowen Estate v. Continental Trailways, 152 Tex. 260, 256 S.W.2d 71, 72 (1953); Texaco, Inc. v. Spires, 435 S.W.2d 550, 553 (Tex. Civ. App.—Eastland 1968, ref. n.r.e.).

[39] *See* Dunlap v. Mars Plumbing Supply Co., 504 S.W.2d 917, 919 (Tex. Civ. App.—San Antonio 1973, no writ).

[40] Orr v. Vandygriff, 251 S.W.2d 573, 574-576 (Tex. Civ. App.—Waco 1952, no writ).

In Texas, security deposits are governed by the property code.[41] Security deposits are often abused and are a hotbed of controversy in the landlord and tenant relationship.

The purpose behind the security deposit is to ensure that in the instance of a tenant's default or damage to the property that the landlord can recover at least some, if not all, of the amount owed by tenant. During the 1970s, it became clear that some landlords were wrongfully and routinely refusing to return security deposits to former tenants. Tenants didn't have a viable solution because the cost of litigation would far exceed the amount of money to be recovered. Due to this epidemic, over two thirds of the states enacted legislation to regulate security deposits.

Whether these reform measures have actually worked is a question that lingers. Most people have some sort of security deposit horror story usually involving some fact inquiry. Let's turn to the horror story in the *Pulley* case.

Ralph and Rubye Pulley v. Keith Milberger
Court of Appeals of Texas, Dallas, 2006
198 S.W.3d 418

Opinion by Justice LANG.

Ralph and Rubye Pulley appeal the trial court's take-nothing judgment against them in their lawsuit to recover their security deposit and in favor of their landlord, Keith Milberger, on his counterclaim for damages incurred in repairing the property. The Pulleys raise seven issues on appeal.

In issues two through four, the Pulleys argue the trial court erred when it rendered a take-nothing judgment against them and a judgment in favor of Milberger for damages because Milberger failed to plead: (1) the absence of bad faith to refund their security deposit or give them a written itemization of the charges for repairs; (2) the charges he offset against the security deposit were reasonable as required by the lease and section 92.109 of the Texas Property Code; and (3) he had a reasonable excuse for his failure to refund the security deposit or give them a written itemization of the charges for repairs.

In issues one and five through seven, the Pulleys argue the trial court erred when it rendered a take-nothing judgment against them and a judgment in favor of Milberger for damages because there was no evidence or, alternatively, insufficient evidence to: (1) establish Milberger gave them a written itemization of the charges for repairs as required by sections 92.104 and 92.109 of the Texas Property Code; (2) rebut the presumption that Milberger acted in bad faith when he failed to refund the security deposit or to give them a written itemization of

---

[41] Tex. Prop. Code Ann. §§ 92.101-109 (Vernon's 2007).

the charges for repairs; (3) establish the charges Milberger offset against the security deposit were reasonable as required by the lease and section 92.109 of the Texas Property Code; (4) establish Milberger had a reasonable excuse for his failure to refund the security deposit or to give them a written itemization of the charges for repairs; and (5) support the award of $2,000 in damages to Milberger, in excess of the security deposit.

We conclude Milberger was not required to plead as affirmative defenses the absence of bad faith, that the charges offset against the security deposit were reasonable, or that he had a reasonable excuse for failing to give the Pulleys an itemized list of the deductions. Also, we conclude there was sufficient evidence to support the trial court's take-nothing judgment against the Pulleys and judgment in favor of Milberger on his counterclaim awarding him $2,000 in damages. We decide all issues against the Pulleys. The trial court's judgment is affirmed.

Conclusion in Milberger favor

Factual and Procedural Background

Milberger is a petroleum engineer and the president of an oil and gas engineering firm, and his occupation requires him to travel extensively. Before 1997, Milberger leased his 2,400 square foot house located at 6643 Garlinghouse Lane, Dallas, Texas, to three different tenants. Milberger did not have any serious problems regarding the security deposits with his prior tenants.

On April 9, 1997, Milberger leased his house to Mr. Pulley, an attorney, and his wife. The lease agreement was on a form promulgated by the Greater Dallas Association of Realtors, Inc. Specific terms in the lease, relevant to this case, included: (1) a $3,700 security deposit; (2) Milberger may deduct from the security deposit reasonable charges for cleaning, deodorizing, damages, and repairs to the property or its contents beyond normal wear and tear as well as the cost of repairs for which the Pulleys are responsible; (3) the Pulleys were required to reimburse Milberger for any loss, property damage, or the cost of repairs or services to the property caused by the Pulleys' negligence or improper use of the property; and (4) Milberger was required to maintain the yard and the Pulleys were required to water the yard at reasonable and appropriate times.

Before the Pulleys began residing at the house, Milberger and his listing agent, Stacy Hamilton, walked through the house. Neither Milberger nor Hamilton observed any damage to the built-in china cabinet or the foundation. Also, four to five months before the Pulleys began residing at the house, Milberger had twenty-year, wear-dated Berber carpet installed. At the time the lease was signed, Milberger programmed the sprinkler system to water the yard pursuant to his discussions with the Pulleys and told Mr. Pulley that the system should remain turned on. During the time the Pulleys leased the house, Milberger paid for the maintenance and care of the yard.

The initial lease period was one year. After the first year, the Pulleys renewed their lease on a month-to-month basis. The Pulleys resided in the house for a total of six years. At one point during the Pulleys' tenancy, Mr. Pulley told Milberger he was having financial difficulties and asked Milberger to set aside half of the rent for four to six months. Milberger agreed and the Pulleys caught up on their rent payments four or five months afterward. The Pulleys were late in their rent payments thirteen times, but Milberger did not charge them any late fees as allowed by the lease. During the Pulleys' tenancy, Milberger did not increase the rent. On July 17, 2003, the Pulleys sent Milberger a letter notifying him that they would be vacating the house on August 18, 2003, and advising him that the sprinkler system was not working properly and needed repair.

Milberger asked Hamilton to re-lease the house when the Pulleys gave their notice. When Hamilton went to the house, she observed that the grass in the front yard was dead and the lawn was mainly soil. Milberger inspected the sprinkler system and found that it worked properly, but it had been turned off. Milberger had the front yard resodded and told the Pulleys the lawn had to be watered or the sod would die. The next morning, Milberger checked the sprinkler system and found that it had been turned off. Milberger turned the sprinkler system back on and wrapped a tie around it so it could not be turned off. However, when he checked the sprinkler system that evening, the tie wrap had been removed and, again, the sprinkler system had been turned off. Meanwhile, Hamilton tried to show the house to prospective lessees. However, there were problems with people being able to get in to see the house and, once inside, people would turn around and walk out because of the urine smell in the master bedroom. As a result, the house was taken off the market.

The Pulleys surrendered the premises on August 18, 2003, and, at the house, they left a handwritten note addressed to Milberger advising him of their forwarding address. Within two days of the Pulleys' surrender of the premises, Milberger inspected the house. A couple of days later, he inspected the house a second time with Hamilton. In addition to the issues with the lawn, they observed that the foundation was cracked, the built-in china cabinet had three scratches approximately 6 inches long and 1/4 inch deep, the garage floor had a deep oil stain approximately 3 feet wide and 7 feet long, the living room and master bedroom carpets were badly stained, the master bathroom wall was stained and the toilet was encrusted with stains, and the master bedroom and bathroom had the strong odor of urine. Milberger took photographs of the damage and obtained estimates on the cost of repairs.

[margin annotation: DAMAGES]

On August 22, 2003, Milberger sent the Pulleys a letter describing the damage to the house. Also, the letter stated, "As a result of the damages to the property that exceed what is considered reasonable wear and tear the resultant cost of repairs has exceed[ed] the [security] deposit." The Pulleys did not respond to his letter. As a result, Milberger telephoned the Pulleys once a week for three weeks, but no one took his calls and his messages were not returned. Then, on October 2, 2003, after thirty days had passed, the Pulleys sent Milberger a demand letter for the $3,700 security deposit and advised him that they had engaged an attorney who would begin the collection process if their security deposit was not returned by October 15, 2003. The next day, Milberger responded to the Pulleys' demand letter. In Milberger's response, he invited the Pulleys to meet with him to review the documented damages, photographs taken the day after they vacated the house, and the costs incurred to repair the damage.

Also, Milberger advised the Pulleys again that the damage was beyond normal wear and tear and the costs of the repairs exceeded the amount of their security deposit. The Pulleys did not respond to Milberger's invitation to review his documentation.

Milberger had the damage to the house repaired. When the carpet was pulled up, the smell was described as nauseating, the stains had permeated through to the back of the carpet and the padding, and the padding was crusty from urine residue. As a result, the carpet and padding had to be scraped up with a shovel and replaced. In the master bathroom, the drywall beside the toilet was cleaned with bleach, but the urine stains could not be removed so the drywall had to be replaced. Also, the toilet had to be removed because it was so heavily encrusted with urine stains. A month later, the bathroom had to be "redone" because the urine odor remained. The scratches on the counter top of the built-in china cabinet could not be repaired, so it was replaced. The oil on the garage floor was raked with a spatula and cleaned with acid. In addition, the foundation was repaired. It took approximately three months to repair the damage so the house could be shown to prospective lessees. Also, Milberger obtained the utility records for the house during the Pulleys' possession as well as similar houses in the neighborhood. After reviewing the utility records, he determined that the Pulleys had used thirty-five percent less water than similar houses in the neighborhood.

On June 9, 2004, approximately one year after the Pulleys notified Milberger they would be vacating the premises, the Pulleys sued Milberger to recover their security deposit. The Pulleys alleged that Milberger: (1) failed to return their security deposit within thirty days; (2) failed to account for the security deposit because, in bad faith, he did not furnish them with a written description and itemized list of the deductions; and, in the alternative, (3) improperly accounted for the security deposit because, in bad faith, he did not itemize the deductions and the sums were deducted for normal wear and tear. Milberger denied the allegations, asserted as an affirmative defense that he sent the Pulleys an itemized notice, and counterclaimed for $2,000 in damages above the amount of the security deposit. After a trial before the court, the trial court ordered that the Pulleys take nothing and awarded Milberger $2,000 for damages exceeding the Pulleys' security deposit, $160 in prejudgment interest, $4,000 in attorneys fees, and an additional $6,500 if he prevails on appeal, or $7,500 if a writ is granted.

The trial court entered the following findings of fact and conclusions of law:

The Pulleys' Claim Against Milberger

1. Pursuant to the written lease agreement in evidence, the parties had a landlord-tenant relationship.

2. The Pulleys, the tenants pursuant to the lease, gave notice of their forwarding address.

3. Keith Milberger, the landlord, did not act in bad faith when he failed to return the security deposit.

Keith Milberger's Claim Against the Pulleys

1. Milberger's damages exceed the security deposit by $2,000.

2. Through the trial of the case, Milberger's attorneys fees were $4,000; and for direct appeal, his attorneys fees would be $6,500; and if writ of error were granted, his attorneys fees would be $7,500.

The Pulleys requested additional findings of fact and conclusions of law and filed a motion for new trial, both of which the trial court denied.

Pleading Requirements

In issues two through four, the Pulleys argue the trial court erred when it rendered a take-nothing judgment against them and a judgment in favor of Milberger for damages because Milberger failed to plead: (1) the absence of bad faith to refund their security deposit or give them a written itemization of the charges for repairs; (2) the charges he offset against the security deposit were reasonable as required by the lease and section 92.109 of the Texas Property Code; and (3) he had a reasonable excuse for his failure to refund the security deposit or give them a written itemization of the charges for repairs. Milberger responds that he was not required to plead these issues as affirmative defenses and the Pulleys did not object to his failure to plead them as affirmative defenses at trial.

Section 92.109 provides a tenant with a cause of action against his landlord when the landlord fails to return a security deposit or to provide a written description of the damages and an itemized list of the deductions by the thirtieth day after the tenant surrenders the premises. See Tex. Prop. Code Ann. § 92.109 (Vernon 1995). When a tenant offers proof that the landlord's conduct was as set out in section 92.109, the landlord is presumed to have acted in bad faith. See id. § 92.109(d). Unless that presumption is rebutted, the landlord will be subject to the monetary sanctions imposed under section 92.109. See Tex. Prop. Code Ann. § 92.109(a), (b). In addition to rebutting the presumption of bad faith, in order to defend against the tenant's cause of action, the landlord has the burden to prove "the retention of any portion of the security deposit was reasonable." See Tex. Prop. Code Ann. § 92.109(c).

Pleading an affirmative defense permits the introduction of evidence, which does not tend to rebut the factual propositions asserted in the plaintiff's case, but seeks to establish an independent reason why the plaintiff should not recover. See Gorman v. Life Ins. Co. of N. Am., 811 S.W.2d 542, 546 (Tex. 1991). An affirmative defense is a matter asserted in avoidance of a party's argument or position, rather than a matter asserted in denial of that party's position. See

Gorman, 811 S.W.2d at 546; Compass Bank v. MFP Fin. Servs., Inc., 152 S.W.3d 844, 851 (Tex. App.–Dallas 2005, pet. denied).

A landlord's rebuttal of the statutory presumption of bad faith and proof of the reasonableness of his retention of the security deposit is asserted by his denial of the tenant's claims of bad faith retention of the security deposit. His denial is not asserted to establish an independent reason why the tenant should not recover. *See Gorman*, 811 S.W.2d at 546. Accordingly, we conclude Milberger was not required to plead as affirmative defenses the absence of bad faith, that the charges offset against the security deposit were reasonable, or that he had a reasonable excuse for failing to refund the security deposit or give the Pulleys an itemized list of the deductions.

Issues two through four are decided against the Pulleys.

Security Deposits—Landlord's Rights and Duties

Chapter 92, subchapter C of the Texas Property Code governs security deposits in residential leases. *See* Tex. Prop. Code Ann. §§ 92.101-92.109 (Vernon 1995 & Supp. 2005). A landlord's duty or a tenant's remedy concerning security deposits as provided in subchapter C may not be waived. *See* Tex. Prop. Code Ann. § 92.006(a) (Vernon Supp. 2005); Hardy v. 11702 Mem'l, Ltd., 176 S.W.3d 266, 275 (Tex. App.—Houston [1st Dist.] 2004, no pet.). A security deposit is defined as "any advance of money, other than an advance payment of rent, that is intended primarily to secure performance under a lease of a dwelling." Tex. Prop. Code Ann. § 92.102.

A landlord is required to refund a security deposit to the tenant on or before the thirtieth day after the date the tenant surrenders the premises. Tex. Prop. Code Ann. § 92.103(a). However, before returning a security deposit, the landlord may deduct from the security deposit damages and charges for which the tenant is legally liable under the lease or as a result of breaching the lease. Tex. Prop. Code Ann. § 92.104(a). The landlord may not retain any portion of the security deposit to cover normal wear and tear. Tex. Prop. Code Ann. § 92.104(b).

If the landlord retains all or part of the security deposit, the landlord shall give the tenant, within thirty days of the tenant's surrender of the premises: (1) the balance of the security deposit, if any; (2) a written description of the damages; and (3) an itemized list of all deductions. *See* Tex. Prop. Code Ann. § 92.104(c). However, the landlord is not obligated to return a tenant's security deposit or give the tenant a written description of the damages and an itemized list of the deductions until the tenant gives the landlord a written statement of the tenant's forwarding address for the purpose of returning the security deposit. *See* Tex. Prop. Code Ann. § 92.107(a).

Tenant's Claims

a. The Two Causes of Action

Chapter 92, subchapter C of the Texas Property Code establishes two causes of action that permit a tenant to seek recovery of his security deposit from his landlord. *See* Tex. Prop. Code Ann. § 92.109. Each of these causes of action provides the tenant with a different remedy. *See id.*

The first cause of action involves a landlord's bad faith retention of the security deposit and is established in section 92.109(a). *See id.* § 92.109(a). To prevail under this cause of action, the tenant must prove the landlord: (1) acted in bad faith; and (2) retained the security deposit in violation of chapter 92, subchapter C of the Texas Property Code. *See id.* When a landlord is found liable under section 92.109(a), the tenant may recover from the landlord: (1) an amount equal to the sum of $100; (2) three times the portion of the security deposit wrongfully withheld; and (3) the tenant's reasonable attorney's fees in a suit to recover the security deposit. *See id.*

The premise of the second cause of action is a landlord's bad faith failure to account for the security deposit. *See id.* § 92.109(b). To prevail under this cause of action, the tenant must prove the landlord: (1) acted in bad faith; and (2) failed to provide the tenant with: (a) a written description of the damages in violation of chapter 92, subchapter C of the Texas Property Code; and (b) an itemized list of the deductions in violation of chapter 92, subchapter C of the Texas Property Code. *See id.* A landlord who is found liable under section 92.109(b): (1) forfeits the right to withhold any portion of the security deposit; (2) forfeits the right to sue the tenant for damages to the premises; and (3) is liable for the tenant's reasonable attorney's fees in a suit to recover the security deposit. *See id.; see also* Ackerman v. Little, 679 S.W.2d 70, 73 (Tex. App.—Dallas 1984, no writ).

b. Presumption of Bad Faith

When a tenant sues a landlord to recover his security deposit under either of the two causes of action, section 92.109(a) or section 92.109(b), the tenant must prove the landlord acted in bad faith. *See* Tex. Prop. Code Ann. § 92.109(a), (b). Bad faith is presumed when a landlord fails to: (1) return the security deposit; or (2) provide a written description of the damages and an itemized list of all deductions within thirty days after the tenant surrenders the premises. *See* Tex. Prop. Code Ann. § 92.109(d). A landlord acts in bad faith when he retains the security deposit in dishonest disregard of the tenant's rights. *See* Reed v. Ford, 760 S.W.2d 26, 30 (Tex. App.—Dallas 1988, no writ); Alltex Constr., Inc. v. Alareksoussi, 685 S.W.2d 93, 94 (Tex. App.—Dallas 1984, writ ref'd n.r.e.). Bad faith implies an intention to deprive the tenant of a lawfully due refund. *See Reed*, 760 S.W.2d at 30; *Alltex Constr.*, 685 S.W.2d at 94; Wilson v. O'Connor, 555 S.W.2d 776, 780 (Tex. Civ. App.—Dallas 1977, writ dism'd); *Hardy*, 176 S.W.3d at 271; Leskinen v. Burford, 892 S.W.2d 135, 136 (Tex. App.—Houston [14th Dist.]

1994, no writ). Absent rebutting evidence, the presumption that the landlord acted in bad faith compels a finding of bad faith. *See Wilson*, 555 S.W.2d at 780; *Hardy*, 176 S.W.3d at 271.

To defeat the presumption of bad faith, the landlord must prove his good faith, *i.e.*, honesty in fact in the conduct or transaction concerned. *Wilson*, 555 S.W.2d at 780-81; *Hardy*, 176 S.W.3d at 271. Evidence that a landlord had reason to believe he was entitled to retain a security deposit to recover reasonable damages is sufficient to rebut the presumption of bad faith created by the Texas Property Code. *See Wilson*, 555 S.W.2d at 780; *Leskinen*, 892 S.W.2d at 136. Other evidence may include: (1) the landlord is an amateur lessor because the residence is his only rental property; (2) the landlord had no knowledge of the requirement to submit an itemized list of all deductions from the security deposit; (3) extensive damage was done to the residence; (4) the landlord attempted to do some of the repairs himself to save money; or (5) the landlord had a reasonable excuse for the delay, e.g., he was on vacation. *See Ackerman*, 679 S.W.2d at 74; *Wilson*, 555 S.W.2d at 781; *Leskinen*, 892 S.W.2d at 137-38.

c. Reasonable Retention of the Security Deposit

Even when a landlord defeats the presumption of bad faith in an action under section 92.109(a) as to the failure to return security deposits, the landlord has another hurdle. He must prove the retention of any portion of the security deposit was reasonable. *See* Tex. Prop. Code Ann. § 92.109(c) ("In an action brought by a tenant under this subchapter, the landlord has the burden of proving that the retention of any portion of the security deposit was reasonable."); *Ackerman*, 679 S.W.2d at 73; cf. *Wilson*, 555 S.W.2d at 779 (landlord has burden of proving reasonableness of deductions); *Jones*, 875 S.W.2d at 30. A landlord's retention of the security deposit may be reasonable if: (1) the tenant is legally liable under the lease or as a result of breaching the lease; (2) the damages did not exist before the tenant leased the premises; or (3) the damages or charges are equal to or in excess of the security deposit or the amount deducted from the security deposit. *See generally,* Jones v. Falcon, 875 S.W.2d 29, 31 (Tex. App.— Houston [14th Dist.] 1994, writ denied) (damage that existed before tenant moved in sufficient to raise fact issue regarding reasonableness of retention of security deposit); Thrift v. Johnson, 561 S.W.2d 864, 868-69 (Tex. Civ. App.— Houston [1st Dist.] 1977, no writ) (former statute construed to require landlord to prove tenant legally liable under lease or as result of breach, or charges equal to or in excess of security deposit or amount retained).

Damages

A landlord and tenant have the right to contract over whom will be responsible for conditions caused by the tenant, the tenant's occupant, or the tenant's guest. *See* Churchill Forge, Inc. v. Brown, 61 S.W.3d 368, 372 (Tex. 2001).

When there are no permanent damages to the premises, the landlord is entitled to the reasonable cost of repairs as the proper measure of damages if he waits until after the term of the lease has expired to seek damages. *See* Siegler v. Robinson, 600 S.W.2d 382, 386 (Tex. Civ. App.—Houston [1st Dist.] 1980, writ ref'd n.r.e.); *see also* King's Court Racquetball v. Dawkins, 62 S.W.3d 229, 235 (Tex. App.—Amarillo 2001, no pet.); Nielson v. Okies, 503 S.W.2d 614, 616 (Tex. Civ. App.—El Paso 1973, no writ). To establish the right to recover the costs of repair, it is not necessary for a landlord to use the words "reasonable" and "necessary" when introducing evidence of the cost of repairs. *See* Z.A.O., Inc. v. Yarbrough Drive Ctr. Joint Venture, 50 S.W.3d 531, 548 (Tex. App.—El Paso 2001, no pet.) (construing *Ebby Halliday Real Estate*, 916 S.W.2d 585, 589 (Tex. App.—Fort Worth 1996, writ denied)). Also, a landlord need not establish the amount of damages with mathematical precision. *See King's Court*, 62 S.W.3d at 236. Instead, a landlord needs only to present sufficient evidence to justify a finding that the costs were reasonable and the repairs were necessary by the trier of fact. *See Z.A.O.*, 50 S.W.3d at 548. A landlord needs only to bring forward the best evidence of the amount of damages that the situation admits and from which reasonable inferences can be made. *See King's Court*, 62 S.W.3d at 236.

Application of the Law to the Facts

We will address the Pulleys' issues by conducting our analysis in two parts so that similar legal issues are grouped together. The first part includes issues one, five, and seven, which address the Pulleys' claims for bad faith failure to return the security deposit and bad faith failure to account for the security deposit. The second part of our analysis includes issue six, which has two subissues that address the reasonableness of the retention of the security deposit and damages.

1. Bad Faith Failure to Return the Security Deposit and Bad Faith Failure to Account for the Security Deposit

The first group of issues, one, five, and seven, address two different causes of action that hinge on the ultimate issue of whether Milberger acted in bad faith under section 92.109(a) and (b) of the Texas Property Code. First, with respect to their claim for bad faith failure to return the security deposit, the Pulleys essentially contend that Milberger failed to rebut the presumption of bad faith and failed to establish a reasonable excuse for failing to refund the security deposit. Second, with respect to their claim for bad faith failure to account for the security deposit, the Pulleys essentially contend Milberger failed to rebut the presumption of bad faith, failed to establish a reasonable excuse for failing to itemize the deductions from the security deposit, and failed to establish he gave the Pulleys a written itemization of the deductions from the security deposit. In order to address the Pulleys' claim of bad faith failure to account, we will assume, without deciding, that Milberger failed to establish he gave the Pulleys a written itemization of the deductions from the security deposit.

Accordingly, in order to properly address the Pulley's sufficiency of the evidence argument, we condense issues one, five, and seven to challenges regarding: (1) the trial court's finding of fact that "[M]ilberger, the landlord, did not act in bad faith when he failed to return the security deposit;" and (2) because the trial court made no finding of fact as to the Pulleys' claim that Milberger failed to account for the security deposit, an implied finding of fact that Milberger did not act in bad faith when he failed to provide the Pulleys with an itemized list of the deductions. *See Carter*, 584 S.W.2d at 276 (presume all findings necessary to support judgment); *see generally, Hailey*, 176 S.W.3d at 383-84 (discussing implied findings for missing elements).

Milberger responds that he defeated the presumption of bad faith because: (1) his letters to the Pulleys were sufficient to comply with the statute because, in his first letter, he provided a written description of the damages within thirty days and, in his second letter, he offered to review the documented damages, his photographs, and the costs of repairs with the Pulleys; and (2) the Pulleys failed to respond to his letters and telephone calls.

The Pulleys argue Milberger failed to establish a reasonable excuse for both his failure to itemize the deductions from the security deposit and his failure to return the security deposit. However, a reasonable excuse is merely one means by which a landlord may rebut the presumption of bad faith. *See Ackerman*, 679 S.W.2d at 74; *Wilson*, 555 S.W.2d at 781; *Leskinen*, 892 S.W.2d at 137-38. A landlord may defeat the presumption of bad faith with evidence that he had reason to believe he was entitled to retain the security deposit to recover reasonable damages. *See Wilson*, 555 S.W.2d at 780; *Leskinen*, 892 S.W.2d at 136. Accordingly, we will review the evidence, if any, respecting "a reasonable excuse" in conjunction with other evidence to determine if the evidence is sufficient to rebut the presumption of bad faith.

At trial, there was evidence that Milberger was an amateur landlord. *See Ackerman*, 679 S.W.2d at 74 (evidence landlord was amateur landlord probative to show good faith); *Leskinen*, 892 S.W.2d at 137-38 (status as amateur lessor does not favor presumption of bad faith). He testified he is a petroleum engineer, the house is his only rental property, he had only three tenants before the Pulleys, and, prior to this dispute, he has not had problems regarding the security deposit. Also, there was evidence that, based on the terms of the lease and his discussions with Hamilton, Milberger believed he could retain the security deposit because of the damage to the house. *See Leskinen*, 892 S.W.2d at 136 (evidence landlord believed he was entitled to retain security deposit to recover reasonable charges or damages sufficient to rebut bad faith presumption). In addition, there was testimony that the damage to the house was extensive and photographs depicting that damage were admitted into evidence. Finally, even assuming

Milberger failed to give the Pulleys an itemized list of the deductions, which complies with the requirements of the statute, there was evidence that Milberger sent the Pulleys a written description of the damage and offered to show the Pulleys his documentation, photographs, and the costs of the repairs. However, the Pulleys did not respond.

Applying the prevailing standards of review, we conclude there was legally and factually sufficient evidence to support the trial court's finding of fact that "[M]ilberger, the landlord, did not act in bad faith when he failed to return the security deposit" and implied finding of fact that Milberger did not act in bad faith when he failed to provide the Pulleys with an itemized list of the deductions. Issues one, five, and seven are decided against the Pulleys.

2. Reasonableness of the Retention of the Security Deposit and Damages

Issue six includes two subissues, which comprises the second part of our analysis. First, we address the reasonableness of the retention of the security deposit. Second, we address the damages awarded to Milberger.

As it relates to the Pulleys' claims for bad faith failure to return the security deposit under section 92.109(a), which seeks, in part, to recover their security deposit, we will address the issue as a challenge to the trial court's implied finding of fact that Milberger's retention of the security deposit was reasonable under section 92.109(c). Also, as to Milberger's counterclaim for damages, we will address this issue as a challenge to the sufficiency of the evidence to support the trial court's: (1) finding of fact that "Milberger's damages exceed the security deposit by $2,000;" and (2) implied findings of fact that $2,000 was a reasonable cost for those repairs and the repairs were necessary. *See Carter*, 584 S.W.2d at 276 (presume all findings necessary to support judgment); *see generally, Hailey*, 176 S.W.3d at 383-84 (discussing implied findings for missing elements).

The Pulleys assert that proof of the reasonableness of the repair costs is the only proof that will satisfy Milberger's burden under section 92.109(c) to retain the security deposit and that Milberger may only deduct "reasonable charges" from the security deposit for "damages and repairs" pursuant to the lease. Further, they contend there was no proof that Milberger's charges were reasonable.

Although the Pulleys and Milberger both presented argument to us regarding the proof of "reasonable charges" or whether "the damages were reasonable," they did not focus first on the pivotal issue in section 92.109(c). That section states:

(c) In an action brought by a tenant under this subchapter, the landlord has the burden of proving that the retention of any portion of the security deposit was reasonable. *See* Tex. Prop. Code Ann. § 92.109(c).

When a landlord is sued under section 92.109(a), the landlord has the burden to prove that the retention of the security deposit was reasonable, not that the repair costs were reasonable. However, proof of the reasonableness of the repair costs may be necessary to satisfy the requirement of proving the reasonableness of the "retention." *See* Tex. Prop. Code Ann. § 92.104(a) (landlord may deduct from security deposit damages and charges for which the tenant is liable under the lease).

At trial, the lease was admitted into evidence showing the Pulleys were legally responsible for damage and repairs beyond normal wear and tear. The lease states, in part:

Deductions: Landlord may deduct reasonable charges from the security deposit for: (i) unpaid or accelerated rent; (ii) late charges; (iii) unpaid utilities; (iv) cleaning, deodorizing, damages, and repairs to the Property or its contents beyond normal wear and tear; (v) pet violation charges; (vi) cost of repairs for which Tenant is responsible; (vii) replacing unreturned keys, garage door openers or other security devices; (viii) the removal of unauthorized locks or fixtures installed by Tenant; (ix) pest control if required; (x) insufficient light bulbs; (xi) packing, removing, and storing abandoned property; (xii) costs of reletting, including brokerage fees; (xiii) attorney fees and costs of court incurred in any proceeding against Tenant; (xiv) any fee due for early removal of an unauthorized keybox; and (xv) other items provided by this Lease. If deductions exceed the security deposit, Tenant will pay the Landlord the excess within ten (10) days after Landlord makes written demand. The security deposit will be applied first to non-rent items, including late charges, returned check charges, repairs, brokerage fees, and periodic utilities, if any, then to any unpaid rent.

Although Milberger was required, under section 92.109, to prove that the retention of the security deposit was reasonable, the lease only permitted him to deduct reasonable charges from the security deposit. See also Tex. Prop. Code Ann. § 92.104(a). As a result, in order for Milberger's retention of the security deposit to be reasonable, the deductions must be for reasonable charges. Additionally, in order to collect damages in excess if the security deposit, the cost of the repairs must be reasonable charges. Accordingly, we review both the retention of the security deposit and the additional $2,000 in damages for sufficient evidence that the costs of the repairs were reasonable. At trial, there was evidence that the damage to the house did not exist before the Pulleys' occupancy. Milberger and Hamilton stated they did not observe any damage to the built-in china cabinet or the foundation before the Pulleys moved in. Also, Milberger stated the carpet was installed four to five months before the Pulleys occupied the house, the house was unleased when the carpet was installed, and it was brand new when the Pulleys took possession.

Milberger and Hamilton stated that the damage was beyond normal wear and tear. Milberger described the extent of the damage and his letter to the Pulleys detailing the damage to the premises was admitted into evidence. He stated that before he sent his first letter to the Pulleys describing the damage and stating that the cost of repairs exceeded the security deposit, he had professionals come to the house and provide him with estimates on the cost of repairs. Milberger described in detail the repairs made to the house and the extent to which the repairs required additional work, *e.g.*, the oil on the garage floor was so thick it had to be raked with a spatula and took two days to clean, the carpet was so crusty with urine it would break into little pieces and, as a result, it could not be pulled up in strips, but had to be scraped up with a shovel, and the urine stains on the master bathroom wall could not be cleaned with bleach so the drywall had to be replaced. Hamilton also testified regarding some of the damage to the house. She stated the house had to be removed from the market until the repairs were made because it was not in a marketable condition. In addition, there was photographic evidence of the damage to the premises.

Milberger testified regarding his total cost of the repairs in three different ways. However, the Pulleys did not present contrary evidence. First, Milberger described his total cost of repairs as $3,500 in excess of the $3,700 security deposit. Second, he stated his total cost of repairs was $6,000, not including the cost of the repairing the foundation. Third, he related that the total cost of repairs was $9,700. He specifically stated that the cost of repairing the foundation was $3,700 and the cost of painting and repairing the drywall in the master bathroom was $1,300. Also, Milberger stated he claimed only $2,000 in excess of the security deposit because he prorated the cost of repairs, *e.g.*, he calculated the Pulleys should pay $250 for the painting and replacement of the drywall in the master bathroom, instead of the full $1,300, because after six years they should not have to pay for painting the entire house, just the master bathroom where the wall was stained with urine. In addition, Milberger stated he did not include the cost of the sod in his request for damages. We conclude that, although Milberger's evidence did not employ the words "reasonable" and "necessary" when describing the cost of repairs, there is sufficient evidence for the fact-finder to reach that conclusion. *See Z.A.O.*, 50 S.W.3d at 548.

With respect to the Pulleys' lawsuit to recover their security deposit, we conclude there was legally and factually sufficient evidence to support the trial court's implied finding of fact that Milberger's retention of the security deposit was reasonable. As to Milberger's counterclaim for damages, we conclude there was legally and factually sufficient evidence to support the trial court's finding of fact that "Milberger's damages exceed the security deposit by $2,000" and implied findings of fact that $2,000 was a reasonable cost for those repairs and the repairs were necessary. *See Z.A.O.*, 50 S.W.3d at 548.

Issue six is decided against the Pulleys.

Conclusion

Milberger was not required to plead as affirmative defenses the absence of bad faith, that the charges offset against the security deposit were reasonable or that he had a reasonable excuse for failing to give them an itemized list of the deductions. Also, there was sufficient evidence to support the trial court's take nothing judgment against the Pulleys and judgment in favor of Milberger on his counterclaim and awarding him $2,000 in damages.

The trial court's judgment is affirmed.

NOTES & QUESTIONS:

The *Pulley* case provides an example of how security deposits operate in the residential context and the nature of the causes of action. All of the statutes are found in Chapter 92 of the Texas Property Code for handling of residential security deposits. However, there are similar statutes governing the commercial tenancy as well. Chapter 93 provides the commercial security deposit statutes and they have very few differences. The relevant sections are set forth below.

Tex. Prop. Code
§ 92.101 Application
This subchapter applies to all residential leases.

§ 92.102 Security Deposit[42]
A security deposit is any advance of money, other than a rental application deposit or an advance payment of rent that is intended primarily to secure performance under a lease of a dwelling that has been entered into by a landlord and a tenant.

§ 92.103 Obligation to Refund
   (a) Except as provided by Section 92.107, the landlord shall refund a security deposit to the tenant on or before the 30th day after the date the tenant surrenders the premises.
   (b) A requirement that a tenant give advance notice of surrender as a condition for refunding the security deposit is effective only if the requirement is underlined or is printed in conspicuous bold print in the lease.
   (c) The tenant's claim to the security deposit takes priority over the claim of any creditor of the landlord except a trustee in bankruptcy.

§ 92.104 Retention of Security Deposit; Accounting
   (a) Before returning a security deposit, the landlord may deduct from the deposit damages and charges for which the tenant is legally liable under the lease or as a result of breaching the lease.

---

[42] Updated Aug. 1999.

(b) The landlord may not retain any portion of a security deposit to cover normal wear and tear.

(c) If the landlord retains all or part of a security deposit under this section, the landlord shall give to the tenant the balance of the security deposit, if any, together with a written description and itemized list of all deductions. The landlord is not required to give the tenant a description and itemized list of deductions if:

    (1) the tenant owes rent when he surrenders possession of the premises; and

    (2) there is no controversy concerning the amount of rent owed.

§ 92.107 Tenant's Forwarding Address

(a) The landlord is not obligated to return a tenant's security deposit or give the tenant a written description of damages and charges until the tenant gives the landlord a written statement of the tenant's forwarding address for the purpose of refunding the security deposit.

(b) The tenant does not forfeit the right to a refund of the security deposit or the right to receive a description of damages and charges merely for failing to give a forwarding address to the landlord.

§ 92.109 Liability of Landlord

(a) A landlord who in bad faith retains a security deposit in violation of this subchapter is liable for an amount equal to the sum of $100, three times the portion of the deposit wrongfully withheld, and the tenant's reasonable attorney's fees in a suit to recover the deposit.

(b) A landlord who in bad faith does not provide a written description and itemized list of damages and charges in violation of this subchapter:

    (1) forfeits the right to withhold any portion of the security deposit or to bring suit against the tenant for damages to the premises; and

    (2) is liable for the tenant's reasonable attorney's fees in a suit to recover the deposit.

(c) In an action brought by a tenant under this subchapter, the landlord has the burden of proving that the retention of any portion of the security deposit was reasonable.

(d) A landlord who fails either to return a security deposit or to provide a written description and itemization of deductions on or before the 30th day after the date the tenant surrenders possession is presumed to have acted in bad faith.

§ 92.110 Lease Without Security Deposit; Notice Required[43]

(a) If a security deposit was not required by a residential lease and the tenenat is liable for damages and charges on surrender of the premises, the landlord shall notify the tenant in writing of the landlord's claim for damages and charges on or before the date the landlord reports the claim to a consumer reporting agency or third-party debt collector.

(b) A landlord is not required to provide the notice under subsection (a) if the tenant has not given the landlord the tenant's forwarding address as provided by Section 92.107.

(c) If a landlord does not provide the tenant the notice as required by this section, the landlord forfeits the right to collect damages and charges from the tenant. Forfeiture of the right to collect damages and charges from the tenant is the exclusive remedy for the failure to provide the proper notice to the tenant.

§ 93.001 Applicability of Chapter[44]

(a) This chapter applies only to the relationship between landlords and tenants of commercial rental property.

(b) For purposes of this chapter, "commercial rental property" means rental property that is not covered by Chapter 92.

§ 93.004 Security Deposit[45]

A security deposit is any advance of money, other than a rental application deposit or an advance payment of rent, that is intended primarily to secure performance under a lease of commercial rental property.

§ 93.005 Obligation to Refund Security Deposit[46]

(a) The landlord shall refund the security deposit to the tenant not later than the 60th day after the date the tenant surrenders the premises and provides notice to the landlord or the landlord's agent of the tenant's forwarding address under Section 93.009.

(b) The tenant's claim to the security deposit takes priority over the claim of any creditor of the landlord, including a trustee in bankruptcy.

---

[43] This provision was newly enacted in 2015. It is effective January 1, 2016.

[44] Added by Acts 1989, 71st Leg., ch. 687, § 2, eff. Sept. 1, 1989; Acts 1989, 71st Leg., ch. 689, § 2, eff. Sept. 1, 1989.

[45] Added by Acts 2001, 77th Leg., ch. 1460, § 1, eff. Sept. 1, 2001.

[46] Added by Acts 2001, 77th Leg., ch. 1460, § 1, eff. Sept. 1, 2001. Amended by Acts 2003, 78th Leg., ch. 1143, § 1, eff. Sept. 1, 2003.

§ 93.006 Retention of Security Deposit; Accounting[47]

(a) Before returning a security deposit, the landlord may deduct from the deposit damages and charges for which the tenant is legally liable under the lease or damages and charges that result from a breach of the lease.

(b) The landlord may not retain any portion of a security deposit to cover normal wear and tear. In this subsection, "normal wear and tear" means deterioration that results from the intended use of the commercial premises, including breakage or malfunction due to age or deteriorated condition, but the term does not include deterioration that results from negligence, carelessness, accident, or abuse of the premises, equipment, or chattels by the tenant or by a guest or invitee of the tenant.

(c) If the landlord retains all or part of a security deposit under this section, the landlord shall give to the tenant the balance of the security deposit, if any, together with a written description and itemized list of all deductions. The landlord is not required to give the tenant a description and itemized list of deductions if:

  (1) the tenant owes rent when the tenant surrenders possession of the premises; and

  (2) no controversy exists concerning the amount of rent owed.

§ 93.009 Tenant's Forwarding Address[48]

(a) The landlord is not obligated to return a tenant's security deposit or give the tenant a written description of damages and charges until the tenant gives the landlord a written statement of the tenant's forwarding address for the purpose of refunding the security deposit.

(b) The tenant does not forfeit the right to a refund of the security deposit or the right to receive a description of damages and charges for failing to give a forwarding address to the landlord.

§ 93.011 Liability of Landlord[49]

(a) A landlord who in bad faith retains a security deposit in violation of this chapter is liable for an amount equal to the sum of $100, three times the portion of the deposit wrongfully withheld, and the tenant's reasonable attorney's fees incurred in a suit to recover the deposit after the period prescribed for returning the deposit expires.

(b) A landlord who in bad faith does not provide a written description and itemized list of damages and charges in violation of this chapter:

---

[47] Added by Acts 2001, 77th Leg., ch. 1460, § 1, eff. Sept. 1, 2001.

[48] Added by Acts 2001, 77th Leg., ch. 1460, § 1, eff. Sept. 1, 2001.

[49] Added by Acts 2001, 77th Leg., ch. 1460, § 1, eff. Sept. 1, 2001. Amended by Acts 2003, 78th Leg., ch. 1143, § 2, eff. Sept. 1, 2003.

      (1) forfeits the right to withhold any portion of the security deposit or to bring suit against the tenant for damages to the premises; and

      (2) is liable for the tenant's reasonable attorney's fees in a suit to recover the deposit.

(c) In a suit brought by a tenant under this chapter, the landlord has the burden of proving that the retention of any portion of the security deposit was reasonable.

(d) A landlord who fails to return a security deposit or to provide a written description and itemized list of deductions on or before the 60th day after the date the tenant surrenders possession is presumed to have acted in bad faith.

Chapter 4
Nonpossessory Interests in Land: Servitudes

A. Introduction to Private Land Use Controls: The Law of Servitudes

As we depart from our coverage of the various forms of possessory interests in land, our focus now shifts to use. As defined earlier in the quarter, the terms *use* and *possession* are not synonymous. Possession incorporates a right of control, title, and ownership. Use is a very limited right to simply have access to something and not be a trespasser. Use does not transfer any title.

Consider the following situations as we compare possession and use:

1. Olivia buys a ticket to see a play at a theater.
2. Amy rents a room at a hotel for a night.
3. Migrant farm worker lives in barracks provided by Tedesco, the owner of the farm.
4. Bob holds the perpetual right of ingress and egress across Charlile's land to get to his neighboring property.
5. Kirby Lumber has the right to enter Old McDonald's property and remove timber.
6. David has the right to prevent his neighbor Emma from painting her house with blue and green stripes.

The first three scenarios are examples of licenses. A license is not even considered a property interest. It is permission to do something or be some somewhere based on contract principles. If removed from the theater, hotel, or farm, there is no property interest involving use or possession to argue to regain access to the premises. However, there could be a breach of contract action brought if wrongfully removed from the property. The concept of licenses will come up in the section on easements. A license is completely revocable and an easement will give a perpetual right to use the land of another. Sometimes a license can be transformed into an easement.

Scenarios four, five, and six do involve property rights. Bob having a perpetual right of ingress and egress across Charlie's land will be an easement. Bob is not given title to Charlie's land. Bob cannot exercise any dominion and control over Charlie's land. Bob may use Charlie's land for a specific purpose and nothing more. Kirby Lumber's right to remove timber from Old MacDonald's farm is a profit. This is a special form of easement that not only allows the right to enter another's land, but also the right to remove something of value, like timber.

The sixth scenario does not involve a right to use or possess but involves a right to dictate how another may use her land. This is the covenant. Covenants allow individuals to make promises with respect to how land will be used, impose architectural controls, and many others.

While there are many available public law doctrines that regulate the use of land and natural resources, there are private law devices as well. In the public law context we look to zoning, subdivision ordinances, and environmental and other regulatory provisions. These public law devices help to regulate and control the efficient use of land for its best economic purposes. The public regulations seek to ensure that the value of all land is protected while being put to its highest and best use. That is why in many cities you will notice that all industry is in one area, single family homes in another, multi-family dwellings and light commercial activity in another. The idea is that a systematic plan will benefit everyone.

It took many years for these public law regulations to develop and pass constitutional muster; in the meantime the use of land was changing. Large parcels of agrarian land began to be divided up into smaller parcels. Often a landowner was concerned about what might pop up on a parcel that he sold off to another. Would his farm now be right next to a smelly factory? Also, selling off parts of land could cause difficulty in simply getting to and from land, as there were limited available roads. Thus the change in our economy from agrarian and rural to more industrial and urban drove this system of laws that provides private land use regulation.

In the private law context we find easements, profits, and covenants running with the land. Our coverage begins with easements and profits as those are the first created under the common law. Covenants running with the land were a later development and have become much more expansive at modern times, especially in the context of the residential subdivision.

Private agreements are made between individuals to accomplish the same goals and objectives as the public land use regulations. These agreements typically impact two or more parcels of land, but sometimes may only involve one parcel. These agreements are allocating benefits and burdens to the land involved. Some land will be burdened with an obligation while other land is benefitted. For example, one parcel may be burdened by the obligation to use it only for residential and agricultural purposes to benefit the neighboring farm. Or one parcel may be burdened with the obligation to allow the neighboring landowner to drive across a private road in order to get to a public roadway. This will benefit the neighboring parcel that needs road access. These are the types of property interests we now consider. Because of the common idea of burdens in the law of easements, profits, and covenants all three are referred to under the category of "servitudes."

Section 1.1 of the Third Restatement of Property provides a definition of the various forms of servitudes:

(1) A servitude is a legal device that creates a right or an obligation that runs with the land or an interest in land.

    (a) Running with land means that the right or obligation passes automatically to successive owners or occupiers of land or the interest in land with which the right or obligation runs.

    (b) A right that runs with the land is called a "benefit" and the interest in land with which it runs may be called the "benefitted" or "dominant" estate.

    (c) An obligation that runs with land is called a "burden" and the interest in land with which it runs may be called the "burdened" or "servient" estate.

(2) The servitudes covered by this Restatement are easements, profits and covenants.[1]

As stated in the comments to Section 1.1, rights and obligations that run with the land are useful because they create land-use arrangements that remain intact despite changes in ownership of land, just as the public law options provide. Servitudes are widely used in land development because they can be individually tailored to meet the needs of particular projects. Servitudes are widely used for roads, utilities, pipelines, natural resource exploitation, and neighborhood development.

B. Introduction to Easements and Profits as Servitudes

The easement is one of the earliest forms of nonpossessory interests in land that allow use of the land of another. An easement is a nonpossessory interest in property classified as a servitude. Being granted an easement gives someone a legal right to use property in a particular way or for a particular purpose and prevents the holder of the easement from being a trespasser. The holder of the easement has no right to possession, but the easement is still an interest in land, not just a contract right. The easement burdens the land that is possessed by another, the person who owns the land. In the end it is simply stated as being given a right to use someone else's property.

A *profit a prendre*, or profit, is a special kind of easement. It gives the holder the right to use someone else's property and take things from it such as water,

---

[1] Sections (2)(a)-(c) and (3) are omitted.

timber, minerals, etc. It is also a nonpossessory interest in land. The law is the same for easements and profits, and as a result they will not be discussed separately.

There is a huge body of case law dealing with easements and the rules governing the creation, scope, modification, transfer, and termination of them. Our coverage will include the different types of easements that can be created and how they are created. We will then go on to cover the basic rules regarding scope, modification, transfer, and termination.

1. Historical Background and Terminology

Restatement (Third) of Property: Servitudes
§ 1.2 Easement and Profit Defined

(1) An easement creates a nonpossessory right to enter and use land in the possession of another and obligates the possessor not to interfere with the uses authorized by the easement.

(2) A profit a prendre is an easement that confers the right to enter and remove timber, minerals, oil, gas, game, or other substances from land in the possession of another. It is referred to as a "profit" in this Restatement.

(3) The burden of an easement or profit is always appurtenant.[2] The benefit may be either appurtenant or in gross.

(4) As used in this Restatement, the term "easement" includes an irrevocable license to enter and use land in the possession of another and excludes a negative easement. A negative easement is included in the term "restrictive covenant" defined in § 1.3.

Comments & Illustrations:
a. Historical note on classification of servitudes. Classification of servitudes into easements, profits, and covenants is relatively recent.

In the 19th century, categories were developed for easements and profits. English law recognized three types of easements: affirmative, negative, and spurious. Affirmative easements create rights to enter and use land in the possession of another; negative easements restrict the uses that can be made of property. In English law, the benefit of an easement could not be held in gross. When easements in gross were permitted, usually as the result of statute, they were called "spurious easements."

---

[2] Easement Appurtenant: An easement created to benefit another tract of land, the use of easement being incident to the ownership of that other tract. Black's Law Dictionary 586 (9th ed. 2009).

Profits a prendre are like affirmative easements in that they create rights to enter and use land in possession of another. However, they also create the right to remove something from the land. Rights to remove timber, minerals, and game, rights to cut wood, and rights to pasture cattle are profits.

b. Easements are affirmative easements. The term "easement" as used in this Restatement describes an "affirmative" easement, the right to make use of the land of another. A "negative" easement, the obligation not to use land in one's possession in specified ways, has become indistinguishable from a restrictive covenant, and is treated as such in this Restatement. See Comment e.

d. Easements and profits are not possessory interests in land. The extent of the use rights granted normally determines whether an interest is possessory or nonpossessory. The benefit of an easement or profit is considered a nonpossessory interest in land because it generally authorizes limited uses of the burdened property for a particular purpose. The holder of the easement or profit is entitled to make only the uses reasonably necessary for the specified purpose. The transferor of an easement or profit retains the right to make all uses of the land that do not unreasonably interfere with exercise of the rights granted by the servitude. For example, the transferor of an easement for an underground pipeline retains the right to enter and make any use of the area covered by the easement that is not specifically prohibited by the easement and that does not unreasonably interfere with use of the easement for pipeline purposes. The holder of the easement may only use the area for purposes reasonably related to the pipeline. By contrast, a transfer of possession generally transfers the right to make any use of the property that is not specifically prohibited. The transferor has no right to enter or use the land except as expressly reserved in the transfer. For example, the lessor who transfers a leasehold estate has no right to enter or use the leased premises except as expressly reserved in the lease, and the lessee may make any use that is not prohibited by the lease.

Easements and profits may authorize the exclusive use of portions of the servient estate, and may involve uses that make any actual use of the premises by the transferor unlikely, but they are still considered nonpossessory interests if the transferor is not excluded from the entire parcel and retains the right to make uses that would not interfere with the easement or profit. Unlike most possessory estates, easements and profits may be unilaterally terminated by abandonment, leaving the servient owner with a possessory estate unencumbered by the servitude. At the margin, it may be difficult to determine whether the parties intended to create a lease with extensive use restrictions or a servitude, or to create a fee simple, determinable on cessation of a particular use, or an easement or profit for the same use.

e. Profits are easements "plus." Profits are easements (rights to enter and use land in the possession of another) plus the right to remove something from the land. They are used most frequently for hunting and fishing rights and exploitation of natural resources through lumbering, mining, and other extractive activities. Generally, the rules governing creation, interpretation, transfer, and termination of easements and profits are the same in American law. The benefits of both may be created and held in gross. See § 2.6. The problems caused by dividing a benefit in gross are the same for both. See § 5.9. However, special rules may apply to profits used in the timber, oil and gas, and mining industries. To the extent that special rules apply, those profits are beyond the scope of this Restatement.

Recognizing that the same rules apply to easements and profits, the first Restatement of Property dropped the term "profit" in favor of the single term "easement." However, the term "profit" has remained in common use. Because it describes a distinctive subset of servitudes without causing confusion, the term "profit" is used in this Restatement.

f. Irrevocable licenses and executed parol licenses are easements. The difference between a license to enter and use land and an easement to make the same use is that the license is revocable at will by the owner of the burdened land. If the license becomes irrevocable, or revocable only on the occurrence of a condition, it is indistinguishable from an easement. An "executed parol license" is an easement that becomes effective despite failure to comply with the Statute of Frauds under the rule set forth in § 2.9, Exception to the Statute of Frauds. An irrevocable license is a license that becomes an easement by estoppel under the circumstances set forth in § 2.10, Servitudes Created by Estoppel.

g. Negative easements are restrictive covenants. In 19th century English law, there were substantial differences between negative easements and restrictive covenants. Negative easements were more limited in scope but more broadly enforceable. Negative easements could be created only to limit activity on the servient estate that would deny light, air, or support to the dominant estate, or that would prevent the flow of water in an artificial stream. Restrictive covenants, by contrast, could be created to limit any type of use of the burdened property. Negative easements, as legal interests, were enforceable against subsequent bona fide purchasers without notice; restrictive covenants, other than lease covenants, were equitable interests subject to the equitable bona fide purchaser defense. In English law, neither an easement nor a restrictive covenant could be created or held in gross.

The most common uses of negative easements in modern law have been to create conservation easements and easements for view. The perceived advantages of easements over restrictive covenants were that benefits in gross might be permitted with negative easements, but denied with restrictive covenants, and that the changed-conditions doctrine, which clearly applied to restrictive covenants, might not apply to negative easements. Sufficient doubt surrounded both these questions, however, that statutes authorizing and determining the attributes of conservation easements were enacted in the vast majority of states.

2. Creation of Easements

Easements are created in four basic ways:

1. by express agreement,
2. by estoppel,
3. by implication, or
4. by prescription.

Because an easement is an interest in property, it is subject to the statute of frauds and requires a writing. However, the express agreement is the only one created with a writing and the other three are really exceptions to the statute of frauds. They are equitable in nature while the express easement is a legal interest in property.

For the easement by estoppel, the easement is created through permissive use coupled with reliance or oral representations coupled with reliance. With the implied easements, there isn't even an agreement at all, the circumstances simply dictate that such an easement exists. And with the prescriptive easement, unauthorized and hostile use of someone else's property creates the easement.

Willard v. First Church of Christ, Scientist
Supreme Court of California, 1972
498 P.2d 987

PETERS, J.

In this case we are called upon to decide whether a grantor may, in deeding real property to one person, effectively reserve an interest in the property to another. We hold that in this case such a reservation vests the interest in the third party.

Plaintiffs Donald E. and Jennie C. Willard filed an action to quiet title to a lot in Pacifica against the First Church of Christ, Scientist (the church). After a trial, judgment was entered quieting the Willards' title. The church has appealed.

Genevieve McGuigan owned two abutting lots in Pacifica known as lots 19 and 20. There was a building on lot 19, and lot 20 was vacant. McGuigan was a member of the church, which was located across the street from her lots, and she permitted it to use lot 20 for parking during services. She sold lot 19 to one Petersen, who used the building as an office. He wanted to resell the lot, so he listed it with Willard, who is a realtor. Willard expressed an interest in purchasing both lots 19 and 20, and he and Petersen signed a deposit receipt for the sale of the two lots. Soon thereafter they entered into an escrow, into which Petersen delivered a deed for both lots in fee simple.

At the time he agreed to sell lot 20 to Willard, Petersen did not own it, so he approached McGuigan with an offer to purchase it. She was willing to sell the lot provided the church could continue to use it for parking. She therefore referred the matter to the church's attorney, who drew up a provision for the deed that stated the conveyance was "subject to an easement for automobile parking during church hours for the benefit of the church on the property at the southwest corner of the intersection of Hilton Way and Francisco Boulevard . . . such easement to run with the land only so long as the property for whose benefit the easement is given is used for church purposes. " Once this clause was inserted in the deed, McGuigan sold the property to Petersen, and he recorded the deed.

[handwritten margin note: EASEMENT]

[3] Google Earth V 6.2.2.6613. (January 12, 2009). Pacifica, California. 37° 37′ 57.43″N, 122° 29′ 24.03″W, Eye alt 891 feet, DigitalGlobe 2008. http://www.earth.google.com [January 12, 2009].

Willard paid the agreed purchase price into the escrow and received Petersen's deed 10 days later. He then recorded this deed, which did not mention an easement for parking by the church. While Petersen did mention to Willard that the church would want to use lot 20 for parking, it does not appear that he told him of the easement clause contained in the deed he received from McGuigan.

Willard became aware of the easement clause several months after purchasing the property. He then commenced this action to quiet title against the church. At the trial, which was without a jury, McGuigan testified that she had bought lot 20 to provide parking for the church, and would not have sold it unless she was assured the church could thereafter continue to use it for parking. The court found that McGuigan and Petersen intended to convey an easement to the church, but that the clause they employed was ineffective for that purpose because it was invalidated by the common law rule that one cannot "reserve" an interest in property to a stranger to the title.

The rule derives from the common law notions of reservations from a grant and was based on feudal considerations. A reservation allows a grantor's whole interest in the property to pass to the grantee, but revests a newly created interest in the grantor. While a reservation could theoretically vest an interest in a third party, the early common law courts vigorously rejected this possibility, apparently because they mistrusted and wished to limit conveyance by deed as a substitute for livery by seisin. Insofar as this mistrust was the foundation of the rule, it is clearly an inapposite feudal shackle today. Consequently, several commentators have attacked the rule as groundless and have called for its abolition.

California early adhered to this common law rule. In considering our continued adherence to it, we must realize that our courts no longer feel constricted by feudal forms of conveyancing. Rather, our primary objective in construing a conveyance is to try to give effect to the intent of the grantor. The common law rule conflicts with the modern approach to construing deeds because it can frustrate the grantor's intent. Moreover, it produces an inequitable result because the original grantee has presumably paid a reduced price for title to the encumbered property. In this case, for example, McGuigan testified that she had discounted the price she charged Petersen by about one-third because of the easement.

The highest courts of two states have already eliminated the rule altogether, rather than repealing it piecemeal by evasion. In Townsend v. Cable (Ky. 1964), the Court of Appeals of Kentucky abandoned the rule. It said: "We have no hesitancy in abandoning this archaic and technical rule. It is entirely inconsistent with the basic principle followed in the construction of deeds, which is to determine the intention of grantor as gathered from the four corners of the instrument." *Id*. at 808. Relying on *Townsend*, the Supreme Court of Oregon, in

Garza v. Grayson (1970), rejected the rule because it was "derived from a narrow and highly technical interpretation of the meaning of the terms 'reservation' and 'exception' when employed in a deed" (id. at p. 961), and did not sufficiently justify frustrating the grantor's intention. Since the rule may frustrate the grantor's intention in some cases even though it is riddled with exceptions, we follow the lead of Kentucky and Oregon and abandon it entirely.

Willard contends that the old rule should nevertheless be applied in this case to invalidate the church's easement because grantees and title insurers have relied upon it. He has not, however, presented any evidence to support this contention, and it is clear that the facts of this case do not demonstrate reliance on the old rule. There is no evidence that a policy of title insurance was issued, and therefore no showing of reliance by a title insurance company. Willard himself could not have relied upon the common law rule to assure him of an absolute fee because he did not even read the deed containing the reservation. This is not a case of an ancient deed where the reservation has not been asserted for many years. The church used lot 20 for parking throughout the period when Willard was purchasing the property and after he acquired title to it, and he may not claim that he was prejudiced by lack of use for an extended period of time.

The determination whether the old common law rule should be applied to grants made prior to our decision involves a balancing of equitable and policy considerations. We must balance the injustice which would result from refusing to give effect to the grantor's intent against the injustice, if any, which might result by failing to give effect to reliance on the old rule and the policy against disturbing settled titles. The record before us does not disclose any reliance upon the old common law rule, and there is no problem of an ancient title. Although in other cases the balancing of the competing interests may warrant application of the common law rule to presently existing deeds, in the instant case the balance falls in favor of the grantor's intent, and the old common law rule may not be applied to defeat her intent.

Willard also contends that the church has received no interest in this case because the clause stated only that the grant was 'subject to' the church's easement, and not that the easement was either excepted or reserved. In construing this provision, however, we must look to the clause as a whole which states that the easement 'is given.' Even if we assume that there is some ambiguity or conflict in the clause, the trial court found on substantial evidence that the parties to the deed intended to convey the easement to the church.

The judgment is reversed.

NOTES & QUESTIONS:

1. What type of easement did Genevieve create—appurtenant or in gross? If the church moved to another location several blocks away, could the

church still use the parking lot for automobile parking during church hours? Why or why not?

What would happen if the church sold the land to someone who opened a McDonald's on the land? Could the McDonald's customers use the parking lot? Why or why not?

2. Express easements are created in writing and require the same formalities as a valid deed. There must be a document that is valid on its face as well and having a valid execution, delivery, and acceptance. Express easements should be recorded in the public records so as to provide notice that the burden exists on the land involved.

3. A difficulty in the *Willard* case is distinguishing between the reservation of an easement and exception of an easement. The added complication comes from the involvement of a third party. The common law recognized that a grantor could reserve for himself an easement over land being conveyed. The problem was the reservation or exception for a "stranger to the deed."

Reserving an easement creates a new servitude that did not exist before as an independent interest but an exception grants some preexisting servitude on the land.

What is the difference between the two? The court in *Willard* concluded that the distinction and different treatment is really just an "unwarranted perpetuation of a useless historical distinction."

The terms *exception* and *reservation* are commonly used interchangeably by lawyers. Courts have not always adhered to a technical distinction. The key is to understand whether something is being created in the grantor or in someone else. There is a difference of opinion as to whether creating something for a third party should be allowed. In Texas, an interest cannot be reserved or excepted for a stranger to the deed. *See* Jackson v. McKenney, 602 S.W.2d 124, 126 (Tex. Civ. App.—Eastland 1980, writ ref'd n.r.e. 1981). The Restatement (Third) of Property, Servitudes § 2.6(2) (2000) states that an easement can be created in favor of a third party.

4. In order for Genevieve to be able to create the easement in favor of the church, what should have been done to avoid any problems with the common law rule?

a. Licenses and the Easement by Estoppel

Recall the license is permission to use the land of another that is completely revocable and is not even viewed as property. As stated at the beginning of this section on easements, the license is connected to the concept of easements because there are circumstances where a license can become an easement. This is describing the easement by estoppel. This is the first exception to the statute of frauds that we will consider. Not all states recognize this exception. Consider the following Restatement provision before reading the following cases.

Restatement (Third) of Property: Servitudes
§ 2.10 Creation by Estoppel

If injustice can be avoided only by establishment of a servitude, the owner or occupier of land is estoped to deny the existence of a servitude burdening the land when:

(1) the owner or occupier permitted another to use that land under circumstances in which it was reasonable to foresee that the user would substantially change position believing that the permission would not be revoked, and the user did substantially change position in reasonable reliance on that belief; or

(2) the owner or occupier represented that the land was burdened by a servitude under circumstances in which it was reasonable to foresee that the person to whom the representation was made would substantially change position on the basis of that representation, and the person did substantially change position in reasonable reliance on that representation.

<u>**Holbrook v. Taylor**</u>
Supreme Court of Kentucky, 1976
532 S.W.2d 763

STERNBERG, J.

This is an action to establish a right to the use of a roadway, which is 10 to 12 feet wide and about 250 feet long, over the unenclosed, hilly woodlands of another. The claimed right to the use of the roadway is twofold: by prescription and by estoppel. Both issues are heatedly contested. The evidence is in conflict as to the nature and type of use that had been made of the roadway. The lower court determined that a right to the use of the roadway by prescription had not been established, but that it had been established by estoppel. The landowners, feeling themselves aggrieved, appeal. We will consider the two issues separately.

In Grinestaff v. Grinestaff, Ky., 318 S.W.2d 881 (1958), we said that an easement may be created by express written grant, by implication, by prescription, or by estoppel. It has long been the law of this commonwealth that

> (an) easement, such as a right of way, is created when the owner of a tenement to which the right is claimed to be appurtenant, or those under whom he claims title, have openly, peaceably, continuously, and under a claim of right adverse to the owner of the soil, and with his knowledge and acquiescence, used a way over the lands of another for as much as 15 years.

Flener v. Lawrence, 187 Ky. 384, 220 S.W. 1041 (1920).

In 1942 appellants purchased the subject property. In 1944 they gave permission for a haul road to be cut for the purpose of moving coal from a newly opened mine. The roadway was so used until 1949, when the mine closed. During that time the appellants were paid a royalty for the use of the road. In 1957 appellants built a tenant house on their property and the roadway was used by them and their tenant. The tenant house burned in 1961 and was not replaced. In 1964 the appellees bought their three-acre building site, which adjoins appellants, and the following year built their residence thereon. At all times prior to 1965, the use of the haul road was by permission of appellants. There is no evidence of any probative value which would indicate that the use of the haul road during that period of time was either adverse, continuous, or uninterrupted. The trial court was fully justified, therefore, in finding that the right to the use of this easement was not established by prescription.

As to the issue on estoppel, we have long recognized that a right to the use of a roadway ever the lands of another may be established by estoppel. In Lashley Telephone Co. v. Durbin, 190 Ky. 792, 228 S.W. 423 (1921), we said:

> Though many courts hold that a licensee is conclusively presumed as a matter of law to know that a license is revocable at the pleasure of the licensor, and if he expend money in connection with his entry upon the land of the latter, he does so at his peril, yet it is the established rule in this state that where a license is not a bare, naked right of entry, but includes the right to erect structures and acquire an interest in the land in the nature of an easement by the construction of improvements thereon, the licensor may not revoke the license and restore his premises to their former condition after the licensee has exercised the privilege given by the license and erected the improvements at considerable expense.

In Gibbs v. Anderson, 288 Ky. 488, 156 S.W.2d 876 (1941), Gibbs claimed the right, by estoppel, to the use of a roadway over the lands of Anderson. The lower court denied the claim. We reversed. Anderson's immediate predecessor in title admitted that he had discussed the passway with Gibbs before it was constructed and had agreed that it might be built through his land. He stood by and saw Gibbs expend considerable money in this construction. We applied the rule announced

---

[4] Illustration by Hunter Ratcliff, Baylor Law J.D., *cum laude*, 2017.

in Lashley Telephone Co. v. Durbin, *supra*, and reversed with directions that a judgment be entered granting Gibbs the right to the use of the passway.

In McCoy v. Hoffman, Ky., 295 S.W.2d 560 (1956), the facts are that Hoffman had acquired the verbal consent of the landowner to build a passway over the lands of the owner to the state highway. Subsequently, the owner of the servient estate sold the property to McCoy, who at the time of the purchase was fully aware of the existence of the roadway and the use to which it was being put. McCoy challenged Hoffman's right to use the road. The lower court found that a right had been gained by prescription. In this court's consideration of the case, we affirmed, not on the theory of prescriptive right but on the basis that the owner of the servient estate was estopped. After announcing the rule for establishing a right by prescription, we went on to say:

> On the other hand, the right of revocation of the license is subject to the qualification that where the licensee has exercised the privilege given him and erected improvements or made substantial expenditures on the faith or strength of the license, it becomes irrevocable and continues for so long a time as the nature of the license calls for. In effect, under this condition the license becomes in reality a grant through estoppel.

In Akers v. Moore, Ky., 309 S.W.2d 758 (1958), this court again considered the right to the use of a passway by estoppel. Akers and others had used the Moore branch as a public way of ingress and egress from their property. They sued Moore and others who owned property along the branch seeking to have the court recognize their right to the use of the roadway and to order the removal of obstructions which had been placed in the roadway. The trial court found that Akers and others had acquired a prescriptive right to the use of the portion of the road lying on the left side of the creek bed, but had not acquired the right to the use of so much of the road as lay on the right side of the creek bed. Consequently, an appeal and a cross-appeal were filed. Considering the right to the use of the strip of land between the right side of the creek bed and the highway, this court found that the evidence portrayed it very rough and apparently never improved, that it ran alongside the house in which one of the protestors lived, and that by acquiescence or by express consent of at least one of the protestors the right side of the roadway was opened up so as to change the roadway from its close proximity to the Moore residence. The relocated portion of the highway had only been used as a passway for about six years before the suit was filed. The trial court found that this section of the road had not been established as a public way by estoppel. We reversed. In doing so, we stated:

We consider the fact that the appellees, Artie Moore, et al, had stood by and acquiesced in (if in fact they had not affirmatively consented) the change being made and permitted the appellants to spend money in fixing it up to make it passable and use it for six years without objecting. Of course, the element of time was not sufficient for the acquisition of the right of way by adverse possession. But the law recognizes that one may acquire a license to use a passway or roadway where, with the knowledge of the licensor, he has in the exercise of the privilege spent money in improving the way or for other purposes connected with its use on the faith or strength of the license. Under such conditions the license becomes irrevocable and continues for so long a time as its nature calls for. This, in effect, becomes a grant through estoppel. It would be unconscionable to permit the owners of this strip of land of trivial value to revoke the license by obstructing and preventing its use.

In the present case the roadway had been used since 1944 by permission of the owners of the servient estate. The evidence is conflicting as to whether the use of the road subsequent to 1965 was by permission or by claim of right. Appellees contend that it had been used by them and others without the permission of appellants; on the other hand, it is contended by appellants that the use of the roadway at all times was by their permission. The evidence discloses that during the period of preparation for the construction of appellees' home and during the time the house was being built, appellees were permitted to use the roadway as ingress and egress for workmen, for hauling machinery and material to the building site, for construction of the dwelling, and for making improvements generally to the premises. Further, the evidence reflects that after construction of the residence, which cost $25,000, was completed, appellees continued to regularly use the roadway as they had been doing. Appellant J. S. Holbrook testified that in order for appellees to get up to their house he gave them permission to use and repair the roadway. They widened it, put in a culvert, and graveled part of it with "red dog," also known as cinders, at a cost of approximately $100. There is no other location over which a roadway could reasonably be built to provide an outlet for appellees.

No dispute had arisen between the parties at any time over the use of the roadway until the fall of 1970. Appellant J. S. Holbrook contends that he wanted to secure a writing from the appellees in order to relieve him from any responsibility for any damage that might happen to anyone on the subject road. On the other hand, Mrs. Holbrook testified that the writing was desired to avoid any claim which may be made by appellees of a right to the use of the roadway. Appellees testified that the writing was an effort to force them to purchase a small strip of land over which the roadway traversed, for the sum of $500. The dispute was not resolved and appellants erected a steel cable across the roadway to prevent its use and also constructed "no trespassing" signs. Shortly thereafter, the suit was filed to require the removal of the obstruction and to declare the right of appellees to the use of the roadway without interference.

The use of the roadway by appellees to get to their home from the public highway, the use of the roadway to take in heavy equipment and material and supplies for construction of the residence, the general improvement of the premises, the maintenance of the roadway, and the construction by appellees of a $25,000 residence, all with the actual consent of appellants or at least with their tacit approval, clearly demonstrates the rule laid down in Lashley Telephone Co. v. Durbin, *supra*, that the license to use the subject roadway may not be revoked.

The evidence justifies the finding of the lower court that the right to the use of the roadway had been established by estoppel.

The judgment is affirmed.

NOTES & QUESTIONS:

1. In Carleton v. Dierks, a case considered by the Austin Court of Appeals in 1947, Texas recognized the easement by estoppel. For some 40 years, appellees used a roadway across appellant's property. In an oral agreement, the appellees agreed to relinquish the rights they had in that roadway, and to instead build a new road, which the appellees did at their own expense (over $500 on the road itself and $1,200 on improvements to their own land to change to the new road). The appellant later decided to place a gate across the road, and lock the gate, apparently because of fears of his animals being stolen. The court considered the issue of whether the appellants had granted merely a revocable license or whether an easement by estoppel had been created.

   The Austin Court of Appeals held that an easement was created based on the general rule that an owner of land may create an easement by a parol agreement or representation that has been so acted on by others as to create an estoppel in pais, *e.g.*, where there has been a parol agreement related to an easement and the other party has expended money that will be lost and valueless if the right is revoked. Equity will enjoin the owner of the first estate from preventing the use of it.

   The court rejected the idea that appellant could revoke the rights given upon the reimbursement to the appellees of the money they expended to make the road. Would that solution be more equitable? Why or why not?

2. Some states take the position that an easement by estoppel should not be recognized. In the case of Henry v. Dalton from the Supreme Court of Rhode Island, the court clearly rejected the concept. The primary rationale for rejecting the concept was that "a parol license to do an act on the land of the licensor, while it justifies anything done by the licensee before revocation, is nonetheless revocable at the option of the licensor, although the intention was to confer a continuing right and money had been expended by the licensee upon the faith of the license. This is plainly the rule of the statute [of frauds]. It is also, we believe, the rule required by public policy. It prevents the burdening of lands with restrictions founded upon oral agreements, easily misunderstood. It gives security and certainty to titles, which are most important to be preserved against defects and qualifications not founded upon solemn instruments."

b. Implied Easements by Prior Use

Another exception to the statute of frauds is the implied easement by prior use. The rationale behind allowing such an easement to be created is that although there is no writing and not even any oral representation, the recognition of this easement is giving effect to what the parties intended. If the particular elements of the implied easement by prior use are established, the circumstances are such that the parties intended for the easement to exist but simply forgot to reduce this understanding to writing. Consider that policy rationale while reading the following case.

Van Sandt v. Royster
Supreme Court of Kansas, 1938
83 P.2d 698

ALLEN, J.

The action was brought to enjoin defendants from using and maintaining an underground lateral sewer drain through and across plaintiff's land. The case was tried by the court, judgment was rendered in favor of defendants, and plaintiff appeals.

In the city of Chanute, Highland Avenue, running north and south, intersects Tenth Street running east and west. In the early part of 1904 Laura A. J. Bailey was the owner of a plot of ground lying east of Highland Avenue and south of Tenth Street. Running east from Highland Avenue and facing north on Tenth Street the lots are numbered respectively, 19, 20 and 4. In 1904 the residence of Mrs. Bailey was on lot 4 on the east part of her land.

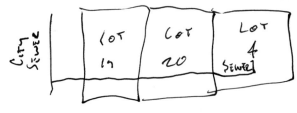

In the latter part of 1903 or the early part of 1904, the city of Chanute constructed a public sewer in Highland Avenue, west of lot 19. About the same time a private lateral drain was constructed from the Bailey residence on lot 4 running in a westerly direction through and across lots 20 and 19 to the public sewer.

On January 15, 1904, Laura A. J. Bailey conveyed lot 19 to John J. Jones, by general warranty deed with usual covenants against encumbrances, and containing no exceptions or reservations. Jones erected a dwelling on the north part of the lot. In 1920 Jones conveyed the north 156 feet of lot 19 to Carl D. Reynolds; in 1924 Reynolds conveyed to the plaintiff, who has owned and occupied the premises since that time.

In 1904 Laura A. J. Bailey conveyed lot 20 to one Murphy, who built a house thereon, and by mesne conveyances the title passed to the defendant, Louise H. Royster. The deed to Murphy was a general warranty deed without exceptions or reservations. The defendant Gray has succeeded to the title to lot 4 upon which the old Bailey home stood at the time Laura A. J. Bailey sold lots 19 and 20.

In March, 1936, plaintiff discovered his basement flooded with sewage and filth to a depth of six or eight inches, and upon investigation he found for the first time that there existed on and across his property a sewer drain extending in an easterly direction across the property of Royster to the property of Gray. The refusal of defendants to cease draining and discharging their sewage across plaintiff's land resulted in this lawsuit.

The drain pipe in the lateral sewer was several feet under the surface of the ground. There was nothing visible on the ground in the rear of the houses to indicate the existence of the drain or the connection of the drain with the houses.

As a conclusion of law the court found that "an appurtenant easement existed in the said lateral sewer as to all three of the properties involved in the controversy here." Plaintiff's prayer for relief was denied and it was decreed that plaintiff be restrained from interfering in any way with the lateral drain or sewer.

Plaintiff contends that the evidence fails to show that an easement was ever created in his land, and, assuming there was an easement created as alleged, that he took the premises free from the burden of the easement for the reason that he was a bona fide purchaser, without notice, actual or constructive.

Defendants contend: (1) That an easement was created by implied reservation on the severance of the servient from the dominant estate of the deed from Mrs. Bailey to Jones; (2) there is a valid easement by prescription.

In finding No. 11, the court found that the lateral sewer "was an appurtenance to the properties belonging to plaintiff and Louise Royster, and the same is necessary to the reasonable use and enjoyment of the said properties of the parties."

As an easement is an interest which a person has in land in the possession of another, it necessarily follows that an owner cannot have an easement in his own land. However, an owner may make use of one part of his land for the benefit of another part, and this is very frequently spoken of as a quasi easement.

> When one thus utilizes part of his land for the benefit of another part, it is frequently said that a quasi easement exists, the part of the land which is benefited being referred to as the 'quasi dominant tenement' and the part which is utilized for the benefit of the other part being referred to as the 'quasi servient tenement.' The so-called quasi easement is evidently not a legal relation in any sense, but the expression is a convenient one to describe the particular mode in which the owner utilizes one part of the land for the benefit of the other.
>
> If the owner of land, one part of which is subject to a quasi easement in favor of another part, conveys the quasi dominant tenement, an easement corresponding to such quasi easement is ordinarily regarded as thereby vested in the grantee of the land, provided, it is said, the quasi easement is of an apparent continuous and necessary character. [2 Tiffany, Real Property (2d Ed.) pp. 1272, 1273.]

Following the famous case of Pyer v. Carter, 1 Hurl. & N. 916, some of the English cases and many early American cases held that upon the transfer of the quasi-servient tenement there was an implied reservation of an easement in favor of the conveyor. Under the doctrine of Pyer v. Carter, no distinction was made between an implied reservation and an implied grant.

The case, however, was overthrown in England by Suffield v. Brown, 4 De G. J. & S. 185, and Wheeldon v. Burrows, 12 Ch. 31. In the former case the court said:

> It seems to me more reasonable and just to hold that if the grantor intends to reserve any right over the property granted, it is his duty to reserve it expressly in the grant, rather than to limit and cut down the operation of a plain grant (which is not pretended to be otherwise than in conformity with the contract between the parties), by the fiction of an implied reservation. If this plain rule be adhered to, men will know what they have to trust, and will place confidence in the language of their contracts and assurances. . . . But I cannot agree that the grantor can derogate from his own absolute grant so as to claim rights over the thing granted, even if they were at the time of the grant continuous and apparent easements enjoyed by an adjoining tenement which remains the property of him the grantor. [Pp. 190, 194.]

Many American courts of high standing assert that the rule regarding implied grants and implied reservations is reciprocal and that the rule applies with equal force and in like circumstances to both grants and reservations.

On the other hand, perhaps a majority of the cases hold that in order to establish an easement by implied reservation in favor of the grantor the easement must be one of strict necessity, even when there was an existing drain or sewer at the time of the severance.

Thus in Howley v. Chaffee et al., 88 Vt. 468, 474, 93 A. 120, L. R. A. 1915 D. 1010, the court said:

> With the character and extent of implied grants, we now have nothing to do. We are here only concerned with determining the circumstances which will give rise to an implied reservation. On this precise question the authorities are in conflict. Courts of high standing assert that the rule regarding implied grants and implied reservation of 'visible servitudes' is reciprocal, and that it applies with equal force and in like circumstances to both grants and reservations. But upon a careful consideration of the whole subject, studied in the light of the many cases in which it is discussed, we are convinced that there is a clear distinction between implied grants and implied reservations, and that this distinction is well founded in principle and well supported by authority. It is apparent that no question of public policy is here involved, as we have seen is the case where a way of necessity is involved. To say that a grantor reserves to himself something out of the property granted, wholly by implication, not only offends the rule that one shall not derogate from his own grant, but conflicts with the grantor's language in the conveyance, which, by the rule, is to be taken against him, and is wholly inconsistent with the theory on which our registry laws are based. If such an illogical result is to follow an absolute grant, it must be by virtue of some legal rule of compelling force. The correct rule is, we think, that where, as here, one grants a parcel of land by metes and bounds, by a deed containing full covenants of warranty and without any express reservation, there can be no reservation by implication, unless the easement claimed is one of strict necessity.

We are inclined to the view that the circumstance that the claimant of the easement is the grantor instead of the grantee, is but one of many factors to be considered in determining whether an easement will arise by implication. An easement created by implication arises as an inference of the intentions of the parties to a conveyance of land. The inference is drawn from the circumstances under which the conveyance was made rather than from the language of the conveyance. The easement may arise in favor of the conveyor or the conveyee. In the Restatement of Property, tentative draft No. 8, section 28, the factors determining the implication of an easement are stated:

REASONABLE

NECESSITY

> In determining whether the circumstances under which a conveyance of land is made imply an easement or a profit, the following factors are important: (a) whether the claimant is the conveyor or the conveyee, (b) the terms of the conveyance, (c) the consideration given for it, (d) whether the claim is made against a simultaneous conveyee, (e) the extent of necessity of the easement or the profit to the claimant, (f) whether reciprocal benefits result to the conveyor and the conveyee, (g) the manner in which the land was used prior to its conveyance, and (h) the extent to which the manner of prior use was or might have been known to the parties.

Comment j, under the same section, reads:

> The extent to which the manner of prior use was or might have been known to the parties. The effect of the prior use as a circumstance in implying, upon a severance of possession by conveyance, an easement or a profit results from an inference as to the intention of the parties. To draw such an inference, the prior use must have been known to the parties at the time of the conveyance, or, at least, have been within the possibility of their knowledge at the time. Each party to a conveyance is bound not merely to what he intended, but also to what he might reasonably have foreseen the other party to the conveyance expected. Parties to a conveyance may, therefore, be assumed to intend the continuance of uses known to them which are in a considerable degree necessary to the continued usefulness of the land. Also they will be assumed to know and to contemplate the continuance of reasonably necessary uses which have so altered the premises as to make them apparent upon reasonably prudent investigation. The degree of necessity required to imply an easement in favor of the conveyor is greater than that required in the case of the conveyee (see comment b). Yet, even in the case of the conveyor, the implication from necessity will be

aided by a previous use made apparent by the physical adaptation of the premises to it.

Illustrations:

9. A is the owner of two adjacent tracts of land, Blackacre and Whiteacre. Blackacre has on it a dwelling house. Whiteacre is unimproved. Drainage from the house to a public sewer is across Whiteacre. This fact is unknown to A, who purchased the two tracts with the house already built. By reasonable effort, A might discover the manner of drainage and the location of the drain. A sells Blackacre to B, who has been informed as to the manner of drainage and the location of the drain and assumes that A is aware of it. There is created by implication an easement of drainage in favor of B across Whiteacre.

10. Same facts as in illustration 9, except that both A and B are unaware of the manner of drainage and the location of the drain. However, each had reasonable opportunity to learn of such facts. A holding that there is created by implication an easement of drainage in favor of B across Whiteacre is proper.

At the time John J. Jones purchased lot 19 he was aware of the lateral sewer, and knew that it was installed for the benefit of the lots owned by Mrs. Bailey, the common owner. The easement was necessary to the comfortable enjoyment of the grantor's property. If land may be used without an easement, but cannot be used without disproportionate effort and expense, an easement may still be implied in favor of either the grantor or grantee on the basis of necessity alone. This is the situation as found by the trial court.

Neither can it be claimed that plaintiff purchased without notice. At the time plaintiff purchased the property he and his wife made a careful and thorough inspection of the property. They knew the house was equipped with modern plumbing and that the plumbing had to drain into a sewer. Under the facts as found by the court, we think the purchaser was charged with notice of the lateral sewer. It was an apparent easement as that term is used in the books.

The author of the annotation on Easements by Implication in 58 A. L. R. 832, states the rule as follows:

While there is some conflict of authority as to whether existing drains, pipes, and sewers may be properly characterized as apparent, within the rule as to apparent or visible easements, the majority of the cases which have considered the question have taken the view that appearance and visibility are not synonymous, and that the fact that the pipe, sewer, or drain may be hidden underground does not negative its character as an apparent condition; at least, where the appliances connected with and leading to it are obvious.

As we are clear that an easement by implication was created under the facts as found by the trial court, it is unnecessary to discuss the question of prescription. The judgment is affirmed.

NOTES & QUESTIONS:

1. The factors necessary for the implied easement by prior use are very specific and creation of an easement in this manner will be rare. However, that is the point. Easements are supposed to be in writing as they are interests in land. An easement will only be created without a writing in limited circumstances. The right set of facts must exist so that the conclusion must be that the parties intended this to be the result.

2. The court in *Van Sandt* addresses the question of how necessary the easement must be for the continued use and enjoyment of the now dominant estate. In *Van Sandt*, even though the easement would have been impliedly reserved by Mrs. Bailey, the court appeared to be requiring only reasonable necessity. The court stated that "the easement was necessary to the comfortable enjoyment of the grantor's property. If land may be used without an easement, but cannot be used without disproportionate effort and expense, an easement may still be implied in favor of either the grantor or grantee on the basis of necessity alone."

    Under the Restatement (Third) of Property, Servitudes § 2.12, there is no distinction between an implied easement by prior use that is reserved or granted. It simply provides that one of the elements is "continuance of the prior use was reasonably necessary to enjoyment of the parcel, estate, or interest previously benefited by the use." However, many states, Texas included, require a strict necessity when impliedly reserved by the grantor. *See* Houston Bellaire, Ltd. v. TCP LB Portfolio I, L.P., 981 S.W.2d 916 (Tex. Civ. App. 1998).

3. The circumstances of the *Van Sandt* case illustrate a prime situation where the implied easement by prior use will apply. There is another form of implied easement, which is the implied easement by necessity. The implied easement by necessity is a completely different easement and must not be confused with prior use. There are some common elements of the two so it is very important to keep them separate. While

the implied easement by prior use is recognized under the law because of circumstances that were occurring during the time of common ownership, the implied easement by necessity is created because of circumstances created at the time of severance.

4. For the implied easement by necessity, the necessity arises when the claimed dominant parcel is severed from the claimed servient parcel of land. The necessity didn't exist before and there was no prior use. The need for the easement is completely new at that time. The elements for the implied easement by necessity are: (1) unity of ownership of the now dominant and servient estates; (2) severance of one piece of property, creating a necessity for access at that time; and (3) a strong showing of necessity (strict necessity). A common element of both implied easements is the unity of ownership of what has become the new dominant and servient estates. What does this mean?

5. Unity of ownership may be satisfied in two ways. First, there could be separate parcels all owned by one person and a parcel is sold off (severed) from the others. This was the unity of ownership involved in *Van Sandt*. Mrs. Bailey originally owned all three parcels and then she sold off the lot that became servient to her other two parcels. Second, there could be one large tract that gets divided. That is the type of unity of ownership involved in the Crone v. Brumley case below.

   Sometimes the person wanting to establish the easement by necessity will have to go back for quite some time to find common ownership and will then have to establish going forward that the necessity has continued to be present since that time to avoid termination.

6. The policy reason for recognizing the implied easement by necessity is that parties probably did not intend to have a piece of land for which there is no access. Because of this reason for the easement's creation, there are some different nuances that must be understood. The implied easement by necessity is very fragile and limited in scope. The following cases will illustrate the challenges.

Crone v. Brumley
Court of Appeals of Texas, San Antonio, 2006
219 S.W.3d 65

Opinion by SARAH B. DUNCAN, Justice.

[handwritten: Issue: Necessity?]

The dispositive issue in this appeal is whether the evidence is legally sufficient to support the jury's findings that an easement south from the Brumleys' Ranch across Sandra Crone's Sycamore Ranch to Highway 2523 was "necessary" when the properties were severed in 1923 and at the time of trial. Because there is no evidence that a public road abutted the Sycamore Ranch on the south in 1923 and there is conclusive evidence of legal access to the Brumley Ranch from Highway 277/377 to the north, we hold the evidence is legally insufficient to support the jury's findings and therefore reverse the trial court's judgment and render a take-nothing judgment.

Factual and Procedural Background

[Ed. Note: Diagrams to help visualize the consecutive conveyances immediately follow the text.] This appeal involves what was once one large tract of ranch land owned by Abb Rose. On July 5, 1920, Abb severed his tract of land, keeping for himself the northern portion and conveying the southern portion to his son, Pat. In 1923, Pat conveyed the northern portion of his tract to E.S. DeLoach. It is undisputed that since the 1923 severance DeLoach's property has been "landlocked," surrounded on all sides by land owned by either Abb, Pat, or third-parties and without immediate access to a public road. However, the northwest corner of Abb's property bordered what is now Highway 277/377, a public road that runs from Sonora and Rocksprings in the north to Del Rio in the south. In 1924, Abb conveyed this corner of his land to H.I. North; and in 1931, Abb conveyed the land between the land he had conveyed to North and Pat's land to his son, Therrell. As of the date of the trial in this case, Pat's property was owned by his granddaughter Sandra Rose Crone; DeLoach's property was owned by Acton Brumley with a life estate in his mother Mary; the North property was owned by T.S. Hickman, Trustee; and Therrell Rose's property was divided between James and Anita Rollo and the Therrell Rose Pinon Ranch subdivision, all as shown on the [diagram that follows the case]:

[handwritten: No Access To Road]

No recorded document expressly grants an easement to what we will refer to as the DeLoach/Brumley Ranch north through what was once Abb's land to Highway 277/377 or south through what we will refer to as Crone's Sycamore Ranch to what was once Hamilton and Standart Lanes and are now Farm-to-Market Road 2523.

After they acquired the DeLoach/Brumley Ranch and until 2002, the Brumleys, as well as the hunters to whom they leased, accessed their ranch from the south on a private road over Crone's Sycamore Ranch by permission. However, after Crone noticed that water lines had been broken, household goods had been taken, a gate had been left open and livestock were missing, several head of livestock were found dead, and grasses had been torn up by the hunters' four-wheelers, Crone locked the gate on the road leading from her ranch to the DeLoach/Brumley Ranch, ultimately permitting only the Brumleys access to their property for maintenance purposes. In response, the Brumleys filed this lawsuit seeking to establish an easement by necessity south through Crone's Sycamore Ranch to Farm-to-Market Road 2523. The jury found "that when Pat Rose conveyed the property that is now the Brumley Ranch to E.S. DeLoach in 1923, the necessary and only reasonable access to the DeLoach property was south across what is now the Crone property to a public road" and "that since 1923 to the present, the necessary and only reasonable access to what is now the Brumley Ranch is south across what is now the Crone Ranch to what is now [Farm-to-Market Road] 2523." In accordance with these findings, the trial court signed a judgment awarding the Brumleys an easement by necessity south across Crone's property to Farm-to-Market Road 2523. Crone appeals, arguing the evidence is legally and factually insufficient to establish that an easement across her property was necessary either in 1923 or today.

Applicable Law and Standard of Review

When a grantee seeks an easement by necessity over land once owned by a common grantor but conveyed to third parties, he seeks a way of necessity by implied grant. *See, e.g.,* Bickler v. Bickler, 403 S.W.2d 354, 357 (Tex. 1966). "The elements needed to establish an implied easement by necessity are: (1) unity of ownership prior to separation; (2) access must be a necessity and not a mere convenience; and (3) the necessity must exist at the time of severance of the two estates." Koonce v. Brite Estate, 663 S.W.2d 451, 452 (Tex. 1984) (citing Duff v. Matthews, 158 Tex. 333, 311 S.W.2d 637 (1958)). "The way of necessity must be more than one of convenience for if the owner of the land can use another way, he cannot claim by implication to pass over that of another to get to his own." *Duff,* 311 S.W.2d at 640. However, an easement by necessity is not defeated by proof that the party seeking the easement has "a mere license to use a way across the land" of another. Bains v. Parker, 143 Tex. 57, 182 S.W.2d 397, 399 (1944). Rather, the party seeking to establish an easement by necessity must prove that he has no other legal access to his property. *See Bickler,* 403 S.W.2d at 357-59; *Duff,* 311 S.W.2d at 642-43; *Bains,* 182 S.W.2d at 399. Once an easement by necessity arises, it continues until "the necessity terminates." *Bains,* 182 S.W.2d at 399. The burden to prove all the facts necessary to establish an easement by necessity rests on the party seeking the easement. *Duff,* 311 S.W.2d at 640; *Bains,* 182 S.W.2d at 399 .

Crone argues that the "[s]ufficiency of the evidence is guided by the 'strict necessity' test." *See* Mitchell v. Castellaw, 151 Tex. 56, 246 S.W.2d 163, 168 (1952) (holding "[t]he question of strict necessity [or not] is one of mixed law and fact and accordingly one for the fact finder in the ordinary case."). The Brumleys, on the other hand, although initially setting out the requirements for an easement by necessity, proceed to conflate "necessity" and "reasonable" to argue that "the correct standard for the jury for an easement by necessity is 'reasonable necessity.'" However, absent a charge objection, we measure the sufficiency of the evidence against the jury charge actually given. *See* Romero v. KPH Consol., Inc., 166 S.W.3d 212, 221 (Tex. 2005).[5] The jury in this case was asked not whether an easement was "strictly necessary," as Crone argues, or whether it was a "reasonable necessity," as the Brumleys argue. Rather, the jury was asked whether an easement was "the necessary and only reasonable" means to access the DeLoach Ranch; and it was instructed that "[a] way of necessity . . . must be more than one of convenience." None of these terms were defined in the court's charge. But, in this context, "necessary" means "compulsory," "absolutely needed," or "required." WEBSTER'S NINTH NEW COLLEGIATE DICTIONARY 790 (Merriam-Webster, Inc. 1984). "Reasonable" means "not extreme or excessive," "moderate," "fair," or "inexpensive." *Id.* at 981. In common usage, "and" is "used as a function word to indicate connection or addition esp[ecially] of items within the same class or type" and "to join sentence elements of the same grammatical rank or function." *Id.* at 84.

"There is legally sufficient evidence of a matter when the proof and inferences from the proof furnish a reasonable basis for reasonable minds to reach differing conclusions as to the existence of the matter." Dew v. Crown Derrick Erectors, Inc., 49 Tex. Sup. Ct. J. 851, 2006 WL 1792216, at *10 (Tex. Jun. 30, 2006). Accordingly, the jury's findings that an easement south across Crone's Sycamore Ranch was and is "the necessary and only reasonable" access to the DeLoach/Brumley Ranch is supported by legally sufficient evidence only if "the proof and inferences from the proof furnish a reasonable basis to reach differing conclusions" both as to whether an easement is required and fair. We start, as we must, with whether an easement is "necessary" or "required." Cf. *Duff*, 311 S.W.2d at 640-43 (because Texas is committed to the doctrine of "strict" necessity, court uses strict necessity standard to measure the sufficiency of evidence even though jury was asked only whether easement was "necessary").

Necessity

As evidenced by the questions submitted to the jury, the Brumleys argued at trial that their right to an easement by necessity south across Crone's Sycamore Ranch arose out of Pat Rose's sale of the northern half of his land to DeLoach in 1923. Crone, on the other hand, argued that an easement by necessity north

---

[5] Although the record reflects Crone requested jury questions and instructions regarding the doctrine of strict necessity, it does not reflect the trial court ruled on her requests.

across what was Abb's land arose in 1920 when Abb sold the southern half of his land to Pat and continued through Pat's sale to DeLoach and DeLoach's sale to the Brumleys. We agree with Crone that the analysis must start with the severance of Abb's land in 1920.

As set forth above, a party seeking an easement by necessity must prove that he has no other legal access to his property. *See Duff*, 311 S.W.2d at 640. Legal access includes an easement by necessity. *See Bains*, 182 S.W.2d at 399. And once an easement by necessity arises, it continues until "the necessity terminates." *Id.* Accordingly, we must first determine whether Pat acquired an easement by necessity over Abb's lands to the north in 1920 and whether that way was still necessary when Pat transferred the northern half of his land to DeLoach in 1923.

Unity of title before Abb's transfer to Pat is undisputed. What is disputed is whether Pat had access from his land to a public road other than north through Abb's land to Highway 277/377. The Brumleys argue that he did—south to what was formerly Hamilton and Standart Lanes and is now Farm-to-Market Road 2523. In support of their argument, the Brumleys refer only to a 1936 Texas Highway Department map, a 1944 Corp. of Engineers map, and the testimony of Ray C. Hutto, who described Highway 2523 as a gravel, county-maintained road that "everybody used" traveling from Carta Valley to Del Rio in the 1920s when he was in school. However, maps dated 1936 and 1944 cannot establish the existence of a public road south of Pat's land in 1920 or 1923; nor do they furnish a basis for inferring that a public road existed some sixteen and twenty-four years before their publication. Nor does Hutto's testimony since he testified he was not born until 1920 and did not visit the ranches in this area until 1940. Indeed, the only competent evidence we have been able to find in the record on this issue is the testimony of Crone's expert William Blackburn, an attorney who specializes in real estate and who testified unequivocally that his review of the public records in the relevant counties revealed no evidence of a public roadway that abutted Pat's property to the south either in 1920 or in 1923.

From this evidence, we conclude, like Blackburn, that the 1920 severance created in Pat a way of necessity north over Abb's land to Highway 277/377; and this way of necessity was impliedly transferred to DeLoach in 1923 and later to the Brumleys upon their acquisition of the DeLoach/Brumley Ranch. *See, e.g.,* Rushin v. Humphrey, 778 S.W.2d 95, 97 (Tex. App.—Houston [1st Dist.] 1989, writ denied) ("As successors in interest to the admitted common source of title, the appellees are entitled to assert whatever easement rights were acquired at the time of the 1958 conveyance from Amy McKnight to Oscar Rushin."). Blackburn testified this is so even if there were no existing roads. But it is undisputed that there is a road out of the DeLoach/Brumley Ranch to the north across what was once Abb's property (and is now the Hickman and Rollo Ranches and Pinon Ranch subdivision) to Highway 277/377. Indeed, Crone's mother Frances, who lived with her husband Martin on their Sycamore Ranch in the early 1940s, testified that, unless DeLoach was paying a call on them and therefore using the road south across Sycamore Ranch by permission, he used the northern road out of the DeLoach/Brumley Ranch to Highway 277/377.

Acton Brumley also testified that, since Crone locked her gate, the hunters to whom he leases his lands have used this northern route out of the DeLoach/Brumley Ranch without interference. In Brumley's view, however, this northern route is not reasonable access because it is impassable without a four-wheel drive vehicle. However, " '[t]hose circumstances show that he has a way, which needs repair, and that until repaired it is impassable. But the impassability of the road gives to a party no right to an easement.'" *Duff*, 311 S.W.2d at 642-43 (quoting Carey v. Rae, 58 Cal. 159, 163 (1881)). Brumley's testimony thus establishes not that the road from the DeLoach/Brumley Ranch south across Crone's Sycamore Ranch to Highway 2523 is necessary but that it is more convenient than the northern road leading to Highway 277/377. *See Duff*, 311 S.W.2d at 642 ("It may be true that Matthews and other lot owners, as a matter of convenience, were not then using the upper road to reach their property and that the upper road had grown up in trees and underbrush and possibly washed out to the extent that it was no longer passable. These facts do not give Matthews a way of necessity. . . .").

Conclusion

Because there is no competent evidence that a public road abutted Pat Rose's land on the south in 1923 and there is conclusive evidence of a road out of the DeLoach/Brumley Ranch to the north in 1923 and today, we hold the evidence is legally insufficient to support the jury's findings that an easement south across Crone's Sycamore Ranch to Highway 2523 was "necessary" in 1923 and at the time of trial. We therefore reverse the trial court's judgment and render a take-nothing judgment.

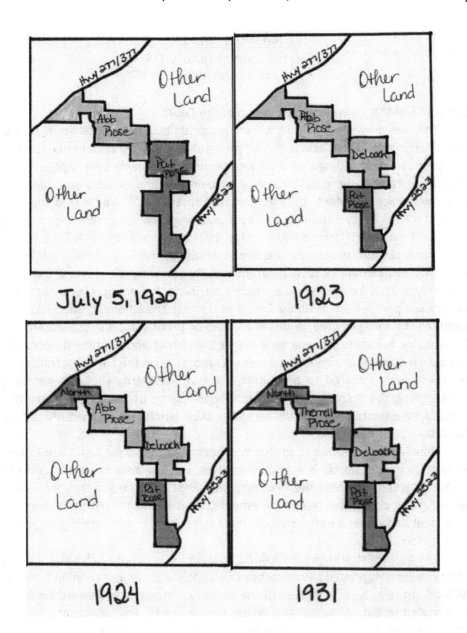

Hamrick v. Ward
Supreme Court of Texas, 2014
446 S.W.3d 377

Justice GUZMAN delivered the opinion of the Court.

This case presents the Court with an opportunity to provide clarity in an area of property law that has lacked clarity for some time: implied easements. For over 125 years, we have distinguished between implied easements by way of necessity (which we refer to here as "necessity easements") and implied easements by prior use (which we refer to here as "prior use easements"). We created and have utilized the necessity easement for cases involving roadway access to previously unified, landlocked parcels. Roadways by nature are typically substantial encumbrances on property, and we accordingly require strict, continuing necessity to maintain necessity easements. By contrast, we created and have primarily utilized the prior use easement doctrine for lesser improvements to the landlocked parcel, such as utility lines that traverse the adjoining tract. We have required, to some degree, a lesser burden of proof for prior use easements (reasonable necessity at severance rather than strict and continued necessity) because they generally impose a lesser encumbrance on the adjoining tract (*e.g.,* a power line compared to a roadway). Today, we clarify that the necessity easement is the legal doctrine applicable to claims of landowners asserting implied easements for roadway access to their landlocked, previously unified parcel.

Here, a party claims a road that was necessary for access to its landlocked, previously unified parcel is a prior use easement. The trial court and court of appeals agreed. We hold the necessity easement doctrine governs this claim. Because we clarify the law of easements, we reverse the court of appeals' judgment and remand to the trial court for the party to elect whether to pursue such a claim.

The trial court granted the Wards' motion for summary judgment, finding they conclusively proved the existence of a prior use easement running from the Wards' property across the rear of the Hamricks' property to Richardson Road. The trial court did not specifically designate a width for the easement. The trial court denied the Hamricks' motion for summary judgment, which raised affirmative defenses.

The Hamricks appealed, arguing the Wards failed to prove both beneficial use of the easement prior to severance and continuing necessity of the easement. The court of appeals found the summary judgment evidence conclusively established beneficial use of the road prior to severance as well as the necessity of the road, affirming the trial court. The court unanimously held that the Wards were required to prove necessity at the time of severance, not a continuing necessity as the Hamricks proposed.

II. Discussion

The parties raise three distinct issues; however, our disposition of the first issue precludes us from reaching the remaining two.

A. Implied Easement

The Hamricks argue the court of appeals erred by concluding the Wards were only required to demonstrate the necessity of the easement at the time of severance. The Wards counter that we have never before required continued necessity for prior use easements. As explained below, we determine the applicable doctrine for roadway access to previously unified, landlocked parcels is the necessity easement.

Under Texas law, implied easements fall within two broad categories: necessity easements and prior use easements. *See* Koonce v. J.E. Brite Estate, 663 S.W.2d 451, 452 (Tex.1984) (necessity easement); Bickler v. Bickler, 403 S.W.2d 354, 357 (Tex.1966) (prior use easement). But the unqualified use of the general term "implied easement" has sown considerable confusion because both a necessity easement and a prior use easement are implied and both arise from the severance of a previously unified parcel of land. Seber v. Union Pac. R. Co., 350 S.W.3d 640, 648 (Tex. App.-Houston [14th Dist.] 2011, no pet.). Further contributing to this confusion, courts have used a variety of terms to describe both necessity easements and prior use easements. Despite imprecise semantics, we have maintained separate and distinct doctrines for these two implied easements for well over a century. Today, we clarify that a party claiming a roadway easement to a landlocked, previously unified parcel must pursue a necessity easement theory.

1. Necessity Easement

"Anyone who grants a thing to someone is understood to grant that without which the thing cannot . . . exist." James W. Simonton, *Ways by Necessity,* 25 Colum. L. Rev. 571, 572 (1925). With similar emphasis on this ancient maxim, we recognized in 1867 that a necessity easement results when a grantor, in conveying or retaining a parcel of land, fails to expressly provide for a means of accessing the land. Alley v. Carleton, 29 Tex. 74, 78 (1867). When confronted with such a scenario, courts will imply a roadway easement to facilitate continued productive use of the landlocked parcel, rather than rigidly restrict access. *Id.*

To successfully assert a necessity easement, the party claiming the easement must demonstrate: (1) unity of ownership of the alleged dominant and servient estates prior to severance; (2) the claimed access is a necessity and not a mere convenience; and (3) the necessity existed at the time the two estates were severed. *Koonce,* 663 S.W.2d at 452. As this analysis makes clear, a party seeking a necessity easement must prove both a historical necessity (that the way was necessary at the time of severance) and a continuing, present necessity for the way in question. *Id.* Once an easement by necessity arises, it continues until "the necessity terminates." *Bains,* 182 S.W.2d at 399 ("[A] way of necessity is a temporary right, which arises from the exigencies of the case and ceases when the necessity terminates."); *see also Alley,* 29 Tex. at 76 (providing "if the necessity for its use ceases, the right also ceases"). The temporary nature of a necessity easement is thus consistent with the underlying rationale; that is, providing a means of roadway access to land only so long as no other roadway access exists. *Alley,* 29 Tex. at 78 ("A way of necessity, however, must be more than one of convenience, for if the owner of the land can use another way, he cannot claim by implication to pass over that of another to get to his own.").

Accordingly, it is no surprise that the balance of our jurisprudence on necessity easements focuses on roadway access to landlocked, previously unified parcels. *See Koonce,* 663 S.W.2d at 452 (assessing a roadway easement by the standard of an easement by necessity); Duff v. Matthews, 158 Tex. 333, 311 S.W.2d 637, 641 (1958) (same); Othen v. Rosier, 148 Tex. 485, 226 S.W.2d 622, 626 (1950) (same); *Bains,* 182 S.W.2d at 399 (same); *Alley,* 29 Tex. at 78 (same).

2. Prior Use Easements

Two decades after we established the necessity easement doctrine for roadways in *Alley,* we found that framework to be ill suited for other improvements that nonetheless are properly construed as implied easements. In Howell v. Estes, we addressed use of a stairwell to access two buildings. 71 Tex. 690, 12 S.W. 62, 62 (1888). In *Howell,* a father had constructed adjoining two-story buildings that jointly used a stairwell in one building. *Id.* When he died, he left one building to his son and the other to his daughter. *Id.* In the wake of a familial dispute, the sibling who owned the building with the stairwell denied use of it to the other sibling. *Id.*

Our preexisting doctrine for necessity easements could not adequately address such a situation. The party seeking the easement likely could not claim strict necessity, as he was still able to access his land and the bottom floor of his building. *Id.* But recognizing that the law should afford a remedy, we established an alternate doctrine for assessing whether to recognize implied easements for improvements across previously unified adjoining property as follows:

> [I]f an improvement constructed over, under, or upon one parcel of land for the convenient use and enjoyment of another contiguous parcel by the owner of both be open and usable and permanent in its character . . . the use of such improvement will pass as an easement, although it may not be absolutely necessary to the enjoyment of the estate conveyed. *Id.* at 63. Unlike necessity easements, which are implied out of the desire to avoid the proliferation of landlocked—and therefore, unproductive—parcels of land, the rationale underlying the implication of an easement based on prior use is not sheer

necessity. Rather, as this Court has expressly recognized, "[t]he basis of the doctrine [of prior use easements] is that the law reads into the instrument that which the circumstances show both grantor and grantee must have intended, had they given the obvious facts of the transaction proper consideration." Mitchell v. Castellaw, 151 Tex. 56, 246 S.W.2d 163, 167 (1952). There is a presumption that parties contracting for property do so "with a view to the condition of the property as it actually was at the time of the transaction," and therefore, absent evidence to the contrary, such conditions which openly and visibly existed at the time are presumed to be included in the sale. Miles v. Bodenheim, 193 S.W. 693, 696–97 (Tex. Civ. App.—Texarkana 1917, writ ref'd).

This Court has explained the requirements for establishing a prior use easement as "fairly standardized," such that the party claiming a prior use easement must prove: (1) unity of ownership of the alleged dominant and servient estates prior to severance; (2) the use of the claimed easement was open and apparent at the time of severance; (3) the use was continuous, so the parties must have intended that its use pass by grant; and (4) the use must be necessary to the use of the dominant estate. Drye v. Eagle Rock Ranch, 364 S.W.2d 196, 207–08 (Tex.1962). Because the actual intent of the parties at the time of severance is often elusive, these factors effectively serve as a proxy for the contracting parties' intent.

It is worth noting that we have elevated the proof of necessity for a subset of prior use easement cases. A prior use easement may arise either by reservation (where the grantor of the previously unified parcel retains the landlocked parcel) or by grant (where the grantor conveys the landlocked parcel). We have expressly held that to establish a prior use easement implied by reservation, a party must demonstrate strict necessity with respect to the easement claimed. Mitchell, 246 S.W.2d at 168. But, with respect to a prior use easement implied by grant, some ambiguity remains as to whether a party must demonstrate strict necessity or reasonable necessity for a party to succeed. See Drye, 364 S.W.2d at 208–09. Because we hold below that the Wards must pursue an implied easement by way of necessity theory, we need not reach this question.

The factual circumstances in which we have discussed the prior use easement illuminate its purpose. We have used the prior use easement doctrine to assess situations such as use of a stairwell in an adjacent building, grazing cattle, and recreational use of adjoining property. In addition to access, we have also discussed the application of the prior use easement doctrine to "a part[ition] wall," "a drain or aqueduct," "a water [gas] or sewer line into the granted estate," "a drain from the land," "light and air," "lateral support," and "water." Drye, 364 S.W.2d at 207–08. In light of the history and the purpose behind these two types of implied easements, we clarify when parties should pursue each type of easement.

3. Roadway Easements to Landlocked, Previously Unified Parcels Must Be Tried as Implied Easements by Way of Necessity

The Hamricks claim that we should inject continued necessity as a requirement for prior use easements. The Wards claim that, despite the confusion between necessity easements and prior use easements, we have never required continued necessity for prior use easements. We view the pertinent question not as whether continuing necessity is required of prior use easements but rather as whether the Wards' use of the roadway is appropriate to assess under the prior use easement doctrine.

We clarify that courts adjudicating implied easements for roadway access for previously unified, landlocked parcels must assess such cases under the necessity easement doctrine. Admittedly, the express elements required for prior use easements do not restrict themselves to certain easement purposes. *Drye,* 364 S.W.2d at 207–08. As a result, we have previously encountered a party asserting a prior use easement for a roadway to access his previously unified, landlocked parcel. *See Bickler,* 403 S.W.2d at 357. But we developed the two types of implied easements for discrete circumstances. The less forgiving proof requirements for necessity easements (strict and continuing necessity) simply serve as acknowledgment that roadways typically are more significant intrusions on servient estates. By contrast, improvements at issue in prior use easements (*e.g.,* water lines, sewer lines, power lines) tend to involve more modest impositions on servient estates. Accordingly, for such improvements, we have not mandated continued strict necessity but instead carefully examine the circumstances existing at the time of the severance to assess whether the parties intended for continued use of the improvement. Our clarification today in no way should impact the continued ability of such improvements to qualify as prior use easements.

Applying this distinction to the Wards' claimed easement does not entail prolonged analysis. Their claimed easement concerns a roadway to access a previously unified, landlocked parcel. This is precisely the factual scenario for which we created the necessity easement doctrine well over a century ago, and here, the Wards must pursue a necessity easement rather than a prior use easement.

NOTES & QUESTIONS:

1. There is some disagreement over the degree of necessity required for the implied easement by necessity. Most courts require strict necessity and it may be rather strict. The Wisconsin Supreme Court refused to recognize an easement by necessity when the landlocked parcel had access to a public road because the owner could travel by foot down a steep cliff to a public road. Schwab v. Timmons, 589 N.W.2d 1 (Wis. 1999).

Some courts, however, have taken more of a reasonable necessity approach. An Illinois appellate court recognized the easement when there was access to the land but it was too difficult, inadequate, or costly. *See* Weaver v. Cummins, 751 N.E.2d 628 (Ill. App. 2001). In some instances an implied easement by necessity will not be recognized if there is access to the land by navigable water.

2. Some courts have defined the necessity existing when the parcel is entirely surrounded and has no easement or other legal right of access to cross adjoining land to reach a public road. It must be more than mere convenience.

   In Reyes v. Saenz, the San Antonio Court of Appeals reversed a summary judgment establishing an easement because there was some evidence of alternate routes existing that raised a fact question. The case had to be remanded to make a factual determination whether another legal means of access existed. The court did state that it must be more than a license because that is not a property interest and is completely revocable. 54 S.W.3d 431 (Tex. App.—San Antonio, 2001).

   Another case from the San Antonio Court of Appeals considered the availability of an implied easement by necessity when building a bridge to cross a creek to reach the land from a public road would cost more than the fair market value of the land. The court concluded that under those circumstances there was a sufficient necessity to warrant creating an easement over adjoining land. Daniel v. Fox, 917 S.W.2d 106 (Tex. App.—San Antonio 1996, writ denied).

   Also, the Texas Supreme Court has held that the offer of an easement or a current license does not negate strict necessity. Bains v. Parker, 182 S.W.2d 397 (Tex. 1944).

3. The necessity must arise at the time of severance in order to create the easement. If at the time of severance the land has road access and then that later changes, an implied easement by necessity is not created.

   For example, George owned two parcels of land and sold the acreage that fronted Highway 183 to Rick and retained the acreage that connected to FM 1725. George's parcel is not landlocked when the severance occurs. However, due to maintenance issues and costs, FM 1725 is closed and George's lot then becomes landlocked. George is not entitled to an implied easement by necessity over Rick's land.

4. Another key component to the easement by necessity is the possibility that the easement will terminate if the necessity ends. Even if the necessity later arises again, the easement is not revived.

So, take the example of George and Rick again. At the time George sells the acreage to Rick that fronted Highway 183, there is no public road that allows access directly to George's retained acreage. At the time of severance an implied easement by necessity is created over Rick's land. However, a few years later FM 1725 is established and George then has direct road access. His land is no longer landlocked; the necessity ends and the easement terminates. Even if George's road access is later destroyed and his land is landlocked once more, his earlier implied easement by necessity does not revive.

This highlights the fact that the implied easement by prior use is a better alternative for the landowner because if the necessity that created that easement ends, the easement does not. *But*, with this implied easement by necessity, if the strict necessity ends the easement ends. However, as held by the Texas Supreme Court in *Hamrick*, the implied easement by prior use is not available for easements needed for landlocked parcels.

5. In some western states, statutes allow a landlocked landowner to bring a condemnation action to force the creation of an easement in exchange for just compensation to the landowner. These statutes allow for this action no matter how or when the land became landlocked. Prior unity of ownership is not required. Really, these statutes are better for the servient landowner because, while the land will be burdened with the easement, there will be compensation. When an implied easement by necessity is recognized under the common law, the easement burdens the land with no compensation to the landowner.

c. Prescriptive Easements

The final means of creating an easement without an express writing is the prescriptive easement. These prescriptive easements are similar in concept to adverse possession that will be covered when our focus changes to acquiring interests in property. However, adverse possession involves obtaining title and ownership to land through possession (exercising dominion and control) while the prescriptive easement allows the trespasser the right to continue using another's land for a limited purpose. While adverse possession involves specific statutes, prescriptive easements do not. However, the elements and time periods for prescriptive easements are very similar to adverse possession except for the difference in use versus possession.

Toal v. Smith
Court of Appeals of Texas, Waco, 2001
54 S.W.3d 431

BOBBY L. CUMMINGS, Justice (Retired)

This is an appeal from a verdict finding the existence of a prescriptive easement and failing to find abandonment of that easement. The owner of the land on which the easement lies, Marion Toal, challenges the legal and factual sufficiency of the evidence to support the jury's findings. We will affirm the judgment.

Facts

Jim Smith built a home on a tract of land in Ellis County in 1901. From 1901 until 1981, Smith and his descendants (the Smiths) lived in this house and used a driveway [the easement] built on leased land to access the house. That land was leased from a railroad company under a "pasture lease" and includes land north of the Smith homestead. The Smiths used the easement until 1981, when the home was abandoned.

The lease with the railroad was for a term of 100 years, expected to expire in 2001. However, after the Smith homestead became unoccupied in 1981, Marion Toal approached the railroad and requested that it cancel the Smith lease. The railroad agreed, cancelled the Smith lease, and entered into a new lease with Toal. Toal leased the land until 1992, when he purchased it from the railroad. Paul Smith (Paul) visited the Smith property periodically during this time, but no one lived there. When Paul again visited the Smith homestead in 1995, Toal informed him that he now owned the entire tract of land in front of the Smith homestead, including the easement, and the Smiths had no right to use the land for access to the home. After some consideration, Paul offered to buy the land in front of the homestead, but Toal was unwilling to sell it. Paul brought suit on behalf of his parents, Earl and Bessie alleging easement by prescription, easement by estoppel, and misrepresentation.

The court entered a directed verdict on the issues of easement by estoppel and fraud and submitted the issue of easement by prescription to the jury. The jury found that the Smiths had acquired an easement by prescription and that the easement had never been abandoned. Paul was awarded an ingress-egress easement plus attorney's fees. Toal appeals, asserting that the evidence is legally and factually insufficient to support the jury's findings.

Easement by Prescription

To burden a party's land with an easement by prescription, the plaintiff must show that his use of the land was: (1) open and notorious; (2) adverse to the owner's claim of right; (3) exclusive; (4) uninterrupted; and (5) continuous for a period of ten years. Brooks v. Jones, 578 S.W.2d 669, 673 (Tex. 1979); Johnson v. Dale, 835 S.W.2d 216, 218 (Tex. App.—Waco 1992, no writ); Wiegand v. Riojas, 547 S.W.2d 287, 289 (Tex. Civ. App.—Austin 1977, no writ). Burdening another's property with a prescriptive easement is not well-regarded in the law. Wiegand, 547 S.W.2d at 289.

Toal challenges the sufficiency of the evidence to support each of the required elements for easement by prescription. Toal only acknowledges the use of the land after 1981, when he acquired the lease from the railroad. His only reference to the time prior to 1981 is found in a footnote to his brief. He states:

> Based on his assertion that the Smiths had a "Pasture Lease" with the railroad, [Paul] Smith has consistently asserted that their use of the driveway was inconsistent with and adverse to the railroad, despite the landlord-tenant relationship. No Smith lease was ever produced. Moreover, the implications and effects of that position on all of the leased agriculture land in Texas is mind boggling.

Paul contends that the use of the leased land from 1901 and continuing until 1995, or any ten year time period between, met the requirements of use to obtain a prescriptive easement. He asserts that the Smith family acquired the easement long before Toal bought the property from the railroad. Thus, we are faced with two periods of time during which this prescriptive easement could have been acquired, 1901-1981 and 1981-1995. We first consider whether a prescriptive easement was acquired during the period when the Smiths leased the land from the railroad, 1901 until 1981.

Prescriptive Easement on Leased Land: 1901-1981

Initially, we consider whether a prescriptive easement may be acquired on leased land. Toal asserts that it cannot be and relies on Sassman v. Collins and Boles v. Red to support this assertion. Sassman v. Collins, 53 Tex. Civ. App. 71, 115 S.W. 337, 339 (1908, writ ref'd); Boles v. Red, 227 S.W.2d 310, 316 (Tex. Civ. App.—Eastland 1950, writ ref'd).

We agree that this is the general proposition, but disagree that Sassman controls here. The court states that where the tenant had control over the servient estate, the period of tenancy must be excluded in computing the prescriptive period. Id. Sassman implies no limitation on the lease in question. Likewise, in Boles there was no discussion of a limited lease. Here, the Smiths arguably did not have control over the land on which the easement was built because the lease limited their use of the land to using it as pasture.

More recently, the Supreme Court has stated that a tenant may acquire an easement by prescription once "the tenancy has been repudiated, and notice of such repudiation has been brought home to the titleholder." Tex-Wis Co. v. Johnson, 534 S.W.2d 895, 899 (Tex. 1976). Notice of repudiation does not have to be actual, but may be made by inference by using the land "inconsistent with the original use of the property. . . ." *Id.* at 901.

Accordingly, by using land in a manner inconsistent with the purpose for which the land is leased, a leasee may acquire a prescriptive easement, provided all of the elements for establishing the easement are met.

The Smith lease was not produced at trial, however Paul testified that it was a "pasture lease," identical to that acquired by Toal in 1981. That lease was admitted into evidence. It is entitled "Pasturage Lease" and limits the authorized use of the land to "pasturage purposes." Paul stated that Toal testified in a deposition that his lease was the same as the Smith lease and, thus, the language regarding using the land for "pasturage purposes" was identical. There was no objection.

Paul testified that his family openly used the easement from 1901-1981 without interruption and never used the land as pasture. The Smiths also used the easement to the exclusion of anyone else. He personally used the easement approximately 30 times a year when he was a child, and then "several times a year" after that until 1975. The easement could be seen in plain view, and is visible in the aerial photographs introduced at trial. Thus, there is a necessary inference of repudiation of the lease and notice of that repudiation to the railroad. *Dalo*, 636 S.W.2d at 588. He further stated that the railroad never used the easement. Considering only the evidence and inferences which support the finding in the light most favorable to the finding and disregarding evidence and inferences to the contrary, we find probative evidence to support it. *Browning-Ferris, Inc.*, 865 S.W.2d at 928. Thus, issues one and two are overruled. There is no evidence controverting Smith's testimony regarding the use of the land prior to 1981. Therefore, we do not find the jury's verdict to be so contrary to the overwhelming weight of the evidence as to be clearly wrong and unjust. *Cain*, 709 S.W.2d at 176. Issue three is overruled. Because we have determined that the evidence is sufficient to support a finding that the Smiths acquired an easement by prescription during the time between 1901 and 1981, we do not consider whether the events post 1981 were sufficient to support a finding that they acquired the easement during that time.

Abandonment of the Easement

In his last issue, Toal asserts that, because the Smiths essentially abandoned their homestead in 1981 and rarely visited the property after that, they lost their right to access the land. Additionally, Toal asserts, his "consistent use and modification of the land, and undisputed ownership of the land further supports [abandonment]." His complaint is one of insufficient evidence. We note that Toal fails to cite any authority on abandonment, but merely states that the argument in the prior issues along with the record "fairly address and support his final point of error."

The intent to abandon an easement "must be established by clear and satisfactory evidence." Milligan v. Niebuhr, 990 S.W.2d 823, 826 (Tex. App.—Austin 1999, no pet.) (citing Dallas County v. Miller, 140 Tex. 242, 166 S.W.2d 922, 924 (1942)). Abandonment of an easement will not result from non-use alone; instead, the "circumstances must disclose some definite act showing an intention to abandon and terminate the right possessed by the easement owner." *Id.*

Because mere non-use is insufficient to show abandonment of an easement, and because Toal has not identified any evidence showing that the Smiths intended to abandon the easement, we cannot say the verdict is so contrary to the overwhelming weight of the evidence as to be clearly wrong and unjust. *Cain*, 709 S.W.2d at 176.

Issue four is overruled.

Conclusion

Having overruled each issue presented, we affirm the judgment.

NOTES & QUESTIONS:

1. The element that most often comes into question is whether the use was adverse and hostile. If the use is permitted by the landowner, then none of the time will count toward the required time period for a prescriptive easement. In *Toal*, that was the first argument raised using the fact that the parties claiming a prescriptive easement had a lease on the land. However, if the use was outside the scope of what was permitted in the lease, then it was nonpermissive.

2. Sometimes a court will conclude that use is permissive if it is nonexclusive. Exclusivity is one of the elements for prescriptive easements but not all jurisdictions define exclusivity in the same manner. Some states, like Illinois, state that exclusivity does not require a showing that only the claimant made use of the land but that the claimant's use of the land does not depend upon similar rights in others. Page v. Bloom, 584 N.E.2d 813, 815 (Ill. App. 1991). In most states a prescriptive easement can be obtained even though the land is also used by the servient landowner. That is because this is just the right to use, not the right to possess. The

person acquiring the easement is not trying to exercise dominion and control.

In Texas, in order to acquire a prescriptive easement there must be exclusivity in use that does not include shared use with the servient landowner. Thus, it is more difficult to acquire a prescriptive easement in Texas than in most other states. Public prescriptive easements can be obtained. However, the use by the general public must be of such a nature and degree that it would put the landowner on notice that an adverse right is being claimed by the general public. It is claimed that in Rockefeller Center in New York City, a private street is located between the GE Building and the skating rink. Each year the street is closed to all traffic for one day to interrupt the use by the public and prevent a public prescriptive easement from being obtained.

Easement Problem #1

In 2000, Thurston Howell owned Lots I and II; Gilligan owned Lot III; Maryann owned Lot IV, including the road on that lot; and Ginger owned Lot V. There was a gravel road across Lot I as shown, and Howell used it to reach Lot II from Public Road 101. (See the diagram on the next page.) In 2005, Howell conveyed Lot II to Gilligan. The deed made no mention of an easement. Gilligan thereafter often used the gravel road to reach Lot II from PR 101. In 2007, Gilligan conveyed Lot II to the Skipper and this deed made no mention of an easement. In 2010, Howell told the Skipper that he could not cross Lot I on the gravel road anymore.

1. What are the Skipper's rights?

2. What if Howell did not refuse access to the Skipper until 2015?

3. Is the analysis any different if this is set in Texas?

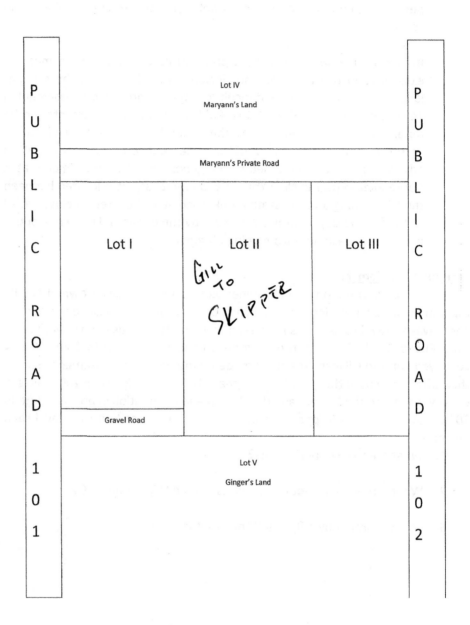

3. Scope and Modification of Easements

Once easements are created, regardless of the manner of creation, they are perpetual in nature. The interrelationship of the dominant and servient estates can cause tension over time. This section will focus on common issues with respect to this ongoing relationship. One common source of dispute is the location of the easement and the ability to relocate it.

Cozby et al. v. Armstrong et ux.
Court of Civil Appeals of Texas, Fort Worth, 1947
205 S.W.2d 403

HALL, Justice.

[Ed. Note: This case involves a 250-acre plot of land that was bisected by railroad tracks. In 1933, the land was subdivided into what eventually amounted to three lots, and after the subdivision, two of the lots had access across the railroad tracks only via an easement over the western-most lot because the only crossing over the tracks was on the western-most subdivided lot. The easement was expressly granted by Church Willburn and Reuben Willburn to the Armstrongs in 1939.]

Rueben Willburn, the owner of the western-most plot, agreed to sell to Goostree who was acting as the agent of Mrs. Cozby and her husband. In connection with that sale, Goostree (on behalf of Cozby), Church Wilburn, and Reuben Willburn entered into an agreement to relocate the easement if and when the Armstrongs, owners of one of the other lots, either abandoned the easement or agreed to relocate it. The agreement contained the following terms:

> Now Therefore, as an inducement unto said Goostree to so purchase said 62 ½ acre tract, it is covenanted and agreed between the parties hereto, that it such time as the said Armstrong and wife, their heirs or assigns, shall abandon the use of said roadway, or at such time as they shall agree to the change herein provided, it is covenanted and agreed between all parties hereto that the said Church O. Willburn and wife, their heirs and assigns, as the owners of said 37 ½ acre tract will, at his or their own proper cost and expense, construct and gravel a roadway from said 150 acre tract over and across said 37 ½ acre tract to a point near the intersection of the South line of the T. & P. Railway Company right-of-way with the E. line of said 62 ½ acre tract; and that the said Goostree, or other owner of the said 62 ½ acre tract, shall, at his or their own proper cost and expense, construct and gravel a road thence Southwesterly with the South line of said Railway right-of-way to the present crossing over said railway tracks, and thereby provide free and easy access from said 150-acre tract and said 37 ½ acre tract, and that thereafter the presently existing easement for roadway over said 37 ½ acre tract and said 62 ½ acre tract, appurtenant to the said 150-acre tracts, shall be limited to the roadway to be so constructed.

Arms Not
Parties

The Armstrongs, however, were not parties to the agreement to relocate the easement. At such time as the easement was relocated, according to the agreement, the then existing easement would be plowed under. The relocation was planned so that the road on the western-most plot would not run so close to the front door of the house on that plot.

In 1944, the parties to the agreement to relocate the road made the necessary changes notwithstanding that the Armstrong's had neither abandoned the easement nor agreed to a change. The old easement was plowed up and Mrs. Cozby the owner of the western-most lot, blocked both ends.

This case has been before this court before on a temporary injunction and a detailed statement of the contention of the parties is outlined in the opinion in 191 S.W.2d 786. However, the plaintiffs' pleadings have been changed some in accordance with the holding in said opinion but the principal contentions of the parties have not, and said opinion is referred to for a more detailed analysis.

It is undisputed that the only railroad crossing is located on the Cozby tract which is on the West side of the original Willburn 250 acre and that the major portion of the land owned by appellee Armstrong and wife is located on the East side of said original Willburn tract so that the only access appellees Armstrong have to the highway is obtained by the use of said railroad crossing on the Cozby land. It is admitted by Mrs. Cozby that the only road which the Armstrongs could use and were using, at the time she and her husband purchased the land, ran by her front door and then turned north toward the railroad crossing and the Benbrook highway.

In accordance with the last part of the agreement between Goostree, Reuben Willburn and Church Willburn, Reuben B. Willburn established and built a road along his west line to the railroad right-of-way and graveled the same. Appellant Cozby established and graveled a road connecting with the graveled road, built by Mr. Wilburn, along the railroad right-of-way across her land to the railroad crossing, thereby diverting the road from in front of her house down the fence row between her and Reuben Willburn and along the railroad right-of-way. This was done in 1944. In 1945 she plowed up the old road going in front of her house, put a yard fence over a portion of it and blocked the entrance at both ends, thereby establishing the new road in the place of the old one.

At this point was when this law suit was filed, and at the end of the trial upon its merits, the court entered a judgment for appellees, reestablishing the old road and enjoining defendant Cozby and other land owners from interfering with the rebuilding of the old road and allowing only three gates to be across said road.

Three of the issues submitted by the trial court and the jury's answers are as follows:

Special Issue No. 1:

"Question: Do you find from the preponderance of the evidence that by the use of the old road from the Armstrong property to and across the Texas and

Pacific railroad right-of-way, and taking into consideration what the parties said and did during such period of use, that the plaintiffs Armstrong and the defendants, Reuben Willburn and Church O. Willburn, intended thereby to fix the said old road as the final and permanent location for the way across the said land to the crossing on the Texas and Pacific right-of-way? Answer 'yes' or 'no.'

"Answer: Yes.

"Special Issue No. 2:

"Question: Do you find from the preponderance of the evidence that the use of the old road by the plaintiffs across the premises of Grace Cozby deprived her of the reasonable and practical use of her residence and land lying south of the railroad? Answer 'yes' or 'no.'

"Answer: Yes.

"Special Issue No. 3:

"Question: Do you find from the preponderance of the evidence that the new road is as suitable, convenient, and economical for the plaintiffs as the old road? Answer 'yes' or 'no.'

"Answer: Yes."

The executed easements of 1939 did not pass title to nor designate a particular right-of-way by metes and bounds.

There was no house on appellee's land until he built his residence in 1940. Up until then the testimony shows that he did not know positively where he himself wanted the road. Appellees did not have actual knowledge of ownership of any of the land until many years after the partition deeds of 1933 were executed. E. C. D. Willburn, who partitioned the land among his children, used this old road as a pasture road, leading from his home, which is the present home of appellant Cozby, over into the east side of his pasture, now the land owned by appellant. Gravel haulers had also used it when he, Willburn, sold gravel from pits on what is now known as appellees' land.

The testimony shows that it was a plain and visible pasture road and well known to the parties. It ran in a curve in front of appellant Cozby's house, and then northward across the railroad track and then on the Benbrook Highway. This old road was used under a right of easement for the first time in 1939, and under these stated facts, appellees contend that since the jury found that the grantors of the easement intended to fix the road as the permanent location of the easement, title to such road as above described became vested in the Armstrongs and could not thereafter be changed except by said Armstrongs' agreement.

Be that it may, parties in the Goostree agreement of 1944, supra, recognized this old road as the permanent easement. The language in the first part of said instrument sets out the fact that the easements of 1939 were acquired; that the mentioned roadway is well defined on the ground over and across said tracts; that the same has been used for some time; and that it was agreed by the parties that at such time said Armstrong and wife, their heirs or assigns, shall abandon the use of said roadway, or at such time as they shall agree to the change herein provided, then such change may be made. In the same instrument the servient owners designated the new way.

If the case had been tried upon this theory, and by such language in the agreement, appellant could not make such contemplated change in said right-of-way until appellee Armstrong should abandon said road, or should agree to the change, then in that event the question arises whether or not the trial court erred in not submitting appellant's theory of the case to the jury, which was raised by the conflicting testimony, to the effect that by use of the new road by Armstrong, did said Armstrong accept the new road as the location across the Cozby and Willburn tracts, and/or did such use by the Armstrongs establish abandonment of the old road, and/or did T. M. Armstrong tell Mrs. Cozby that he was not going to use the old road any more. These requested issues and other similar ones were refused by the court.

The facts further show that the new change in the road increased the length of travel from between 195 feet to 320 feet. The new road was graveled by Mrs. Cozby and Willburn. There were three gates to open over the old route, and only one over the new one.

The extent of the old road cut off begins on or near the east line of the Cozby tract and runs 165 feet west through her front yard near her front door and then north a short distance to the railroad tract, which cuts off a small tract of land lying east and north of her house.

By the closing of this portion of said old road, she testified that it assisted her in the use of her property in the form of orchards, gardens, and removing the dust and lights from her home caused by automobiles going around said curve immediately in front of her residence.

The jury found that the use of the old road by appellee deprived appellant, Mrs. Cozby, of the reasonable and practical use of her residence and land lying south of the railroad; and that the new road is just as suitable, convenient and economical road for appellees to travel and use as the old one.

Most of the text books are in harmony with the general rule that the location of an easement may not be changed by the easement owner or the servient tenement without the consent of both parties, even though the way so located becomes detrimental to the use and convenience of the servient estate. 28 C.J.S., Easements, § 84.

However, Texas Jurisprudence points out, in volume 15, page 804, that "the owner of an easement does not acquire the right unnecessarily to continue it as originally used, if such use would in effect destroy the right of the owner of the fee to the enjoyment of his property."

28 Corpus Juris Secundum, Easements, § 80, recites that: "Where a conveyance of a right of way does not definitely fix its location, the grantee is

entitled to a convenient, reasonable, and accessible way within the limits of the grant. What constitutes a way of this character depends upon the condition of the place and the purposes for which it was intended, and the acts of those having the right of user. However, the location must be reasonable as respects the rights of the grantor as well as the grantee."

And in 28 C.J.S., Easements, § 80, the text reads as follows: "Unless a contrary intention appears from the terms of the grant, when a right of way is granted over certain land without fixing its location, but there is a way already located at the time of the grant, this will be held to be the location of the way granted, and the grantee cannot be compelled to accept a substitute therefor. Under the circumstances it will be presumed that the parties had in mind the way already located."

In 9 R.C.L., page 791, § 48, the rule is laid down as: "if an easement in land is granted in general terms, without giving definite location and description to it, the grantee does not thereby acquire a right to use the servient estate without limitation as to the place or mode in which the easement is to be enjoyed. The right to locate belongs to the owner of the servient tenement, but he must exercise it in a reasonable manner, having due regard to the rights and interests of the owner of the dominant estate." *See also* 110 A.L.R., page 176.

And in 9 R. C. L. § 49, of the same text, we find the following language: "When an easement granted in indefinite terms has been once selected and located, its location cannot be changed by either the owner of the land or the owner of the easement without the consent of the other party, for it would be an incitement to litigation to treat such an easement as a shifting one, and would greatly depreciate the land on which it is charged and discourage its improvement."

In 15 Texas Jurisprudence, page 769, we find the definition of an easement to be as follows: "An easement is a liberty, privilege, or advantage in land without profit, existing distinct from the ownership of the soil."

In 130 A.L.R., page 768, it is pointed out, among other things, that the use of an easement is limited to those which are reasonably necessary and convenient and as little burdensome to the servient estate as possible for the use contemplated.

In the instant case, the servient owners, including appellant, through the Goostree agreement, and while recognizing the old road as the right-of-way, stipulated and designated in said instrument the proposed change as therein outlined, the fulfillment of which being the basis for the controversy in this case.

The right-of-way easement having been established by the servient owners, the next pertinent question is did the servient owners have a right to relocate this small portion of the recognized right-of-way, without the consent of the dominant owner under the facts in this case wherein it was found by the jury:

1. That the new way is as suitable and economical for grantee to travel as the old way.
2. Especially (if it is found by the jury), that by the continued use of such portion of the old road so abolished by the servient owners, deprived appellant of the reasonable and practical use of her residence and of her land.

Most of the law pertaining to change of location has to do with the making of a complete new right-of-way, including the change of the termini, and/or the closing of a road without establishing a new way, which cannot be done by one owner without the consent of the other one. In this case, we find that the termini remain the same, and even though the new way made a drastic change in a small portion of the road and that such change was made for the benefit and convenience of one of the servient owners; wherein it deviated the road from in front of her house by running the same down a fence line and connecting with the old road at the railroad crossing, thus enabling the appellant Cozby to eliminate the dust and the lights of automobiles from entering her house and in a small way allowing her a greater privilege in the use of her land cutoff by the old road. Yet the jury found such change did not discommode the appellees in any way.

All states recognize the general rule that it is the duty of the dominant owner to build and maintain the easement right-of-way. Appellee testified that he had not spent one penny on his easement way. Appellant Cozby testified that she and Reuben Willburn hauled many yards of gravel and graveled the new portion of said road. At least this gesture on the part of appellant Cozby does not show bad faith.

Under the court's judgment and under the testimony there would be three gates to open if the old road is reopened, while traveling the new way there would be only one gate, the same being the one leading out of appellees' land. In their brief however, the appellees submitted the following argument: "If the Armstrongs are required to use the new road, there is nothing to keep Mrs. Cozby or Puryear, who now owns the 37 ½ acre tract, from erecting a gate across the new way between the Cozby and Puryear lands. The parties in interest in the Spring of 1940 recognized that the owners of the servient estates were entitled to a gate between their property lines. Is there anything to prevent them from erecting a gate on their property line across the new way?" While we do not find it necessary to answer this question, yet we find the rule laid down, in the case of Chaney v. Martin, 205 Ark. 962, 171 S.W.2d 961, is plausible.

We therefore find that the jury decided the two ultimate issues in favor of appellant, and further find that such change in the road was not so drastic as to impair the rights and title of the appurtenant easement of appellee. Kelsay v. Lone Star Gas Co., Tex. Civ. App., 296 S.W 954, writ dismissed; Terry et al. v.

Boston et al., 246 Ky. 222, 54 S.W.2d 909; Gabbard v. Campbell et al., 296 Ky. 216, 176 S.W.2d 411.

The judgment of the trial court is reversed and rendered for appellant.

Goodwin v. Johnson
Court of Appeals of South Carolina, 2003
591 S.E.2d 34

ANDERSON, J.:

Troy K. Goodwin and Fonda E. Goodwin (the Goodwins) appeal the master-in-equity's order relocating their easement by necessity. We affirm.

Facts/Procedural Background

The Goodwins originally brought this cause of action against Martha and Ernie Johnson (the Johnsons) on December 18, 1996, in an effort to establish an easement across the Johnsons' property. The disputed property consisted of a road that ran from a public highway through the Johnsons' property to the Goodwins' property. The Goodwins argued they were entitled to the easement under several theories. After hearing from the parties, the master granted the Goodwins an easement by necessity and an easement by prescription. The master found the location of the easement or road was as set forth in a plat recorded in the Recorder of Deeds Office in Berkeley County.

The Johnsons appealed the master's finding to the Court of Appeals. An opinion was issued on June 19, 2001. *See* Goodwin v. Johnson, Op. No.2001-UP-323 (S.C. Ct. App. filed June 19, 2001). This Court affirmed the master's decision by finding there was evidence in the record to support his determination that an easement by necessity existed. *Id.* We declined to address further grounds.

Following our decision, the Johnsons moved to clarify the master's order and the Goodwins asked permission to execute on the judgment. The Johnsons desired to relocate the easement from its current location to another part of their property due to its proximity to their home and dangers it created for their children and pets. The Goodwins claimed that relocating the easement would make it both unsafe and unusable, as it would no longer link with a passable portion of their property.

In an order dated June 18, 2002, the master granted the Johnsons' request and ordered the construction of a new road along the side of the Johnsons' property.

Issue

Does a court of equity possess the plenary power to relocate an existing easement by necessity?

Law/Analysis

The Goodwins contend the master did not have the authority to move an existing easement, or alternatively, even if he did have the authority, the master erred in doing so under the facts of this particular case. We disagree.

The issue asseverated in this case is novel. Irrefutably, the question presented is of particular importance to trial courts.

The traditional rule concerning easements is that "the location of an easement once selected or fixed cannot be changed by either the landowner or the easement owner without the other's consent, which can be express or implied." 25 Am. Jur. 2d Easements and Licenses § 79 (1996) (footnotes omitted). Thus, "[a]fter a way has been located, it cannot be changed by either party without the consent of the other, even if the way so located becomes detrimental to the use and convenience of the servient estate." *Id.; see also* Samuelson v. Alvarado, 847 S.W.2d 319, 323 (Tex. Ct. App.1993) ("Once established, the location of the easement cannot be changed by either the easement owner or the servient owner without the consent of both parties, even though the use of the easement where located becomes detrimental to the use of the servient estate."); 28A C.J.S. Easements § 157 (1996) ("As a general rule, in the absence of statutes to the contrary, the location of an easement cannot be changed by either party without the other's consent, after it has been once established either by the express terms of the grant or by the acts of the parties, except under the authority of an express or implied grant or reservation to this effect.") (footnotes omitted); F.M. English, Annotation, Relocation of Easements, 80 A.L.R.2d 743 § 4 (1961) ("Language is frequently found in the cases to the general effect that an easement, once located, cannot be relocated without the consent of the parties thereto.").

Although South Carolina courts have yet to address this particular issue, the Goodwins cite several cases from other jurisdictions in support of the traditional rule regarding easements, including MacMeekin v. Low Income Hous. Inst., Inc., 111 Wash. App. 188, 45 P.3d 570 (2002), and Soderberg v. Weisel, 455 Pa.Super. 158, 687 A.2d 839 (1997). In *MacMeekin,* an action to quiet title to an easement, the Court of Appeals of Washington was confronted with the issue of whether a court had the power to relocate an existing easement by prescription without the permission of the owner of the dominant estate. After reviewing cases from other jurisdictions, the court decided: "Washington adheres to the traditional rule that easements, *however created,* are property rights, and as such are not subject to relocation absent the consent of both parties." *MacMeekin,* 45 P.3d at 579 (emphasis added).

Soderberg, while acknowledging the general rule, ultimately adopted a position inconsistent with that championed by the Goodwins. *See Soderberg,* 687 A.2d at 842. In that case, the owners of the servient parcel brought an action against the owners of the dominant parcel seeking to quiet title or, in the

[handwritten margin note: Rule @ MovinG]

alternative, to relocate an easement that was established by prescription. The easement in issue was a road in close proximity to the servient owner's home that posed dangers to their small children. *Id.* at 841. In contrast to *MacMeekin,* the Superior Court of Pennsylvania adopted the minority rule, holding "a court may compel relocation of an easement if that relocation would not substantially interfere with the easement holder's use and enjoyment of the right of way and it advances the interest of justice." *Id.* at 844.

Many of the cases adopting the traditional rule deal with express easements-not with easements created by necessity. We recognize that it *should be* more difficult to relocate an express easement, as it is akin to a contract and is bargained for by the parties. *MacMeekin,* cited by the Goodwins for the traditional approach, supports this position by acknowledging that most of the cases addressing the issue of whether a court can relocate an easement without the consent of both parties deal with express easements. *MacMeekin,* 45 P.3d at 575-76.

Before adopting the minority view, the *Soderberg* court explained:

> Prescriptive easements are . . . quite different from express grant easements. Express grant easements, once acquired, are much more difficult to alter. A prescriptive easement, however, differs markedly from an express grant easement, because the prescriptive easement is not fixed by agreement between the parties or their predecessors in interest.

Soderberg, 687 A.2d at 843 n. 3 (citation omitted). The court further expounded that "alterations of easements expressly granted will be interpreted under contract law principles; permission to alter must be intended by words or meaning of grant." *Id.* (citation omitted). The court found prescriptive easements, because they are not fixed by agreement among the parties, should be handled differently than express easements. *Id.* We agree with this reasoning and conclude the same is true with easements created by necessity.

The approach adopted by the *Soderberg* court is consonant with the position adopted by the drafters of the Restatement (Third) of Property: Servitudes § 4.8 (2000), which provides that, in certain situations, the owner of the servient estate can relocate an easement unilaterally. Section 4.8 of the Restatement reads in pertinent part:

> Except where the location and dimensions are determined by the instrument or circumstances surrounding creation of a servitude, they are determined as follows:

(3) Unless expressly denied by the terms of an easement, . . . the owner of the servient estate is entitled to make reasonable changes in the location or dimensions of an easement, at the servient owner's expense, to permit normal use or development of the servient estate, but only if the changes do not

(a) significantly lessen the utility of the easement,

(b) increase the burdens on the owner of the easement in its use and enjoyment, or

(c) frustrate the purpose for which the easement was created.

Id.

Authority exists specifically supporting the power of a court sitting in equity to relocate easements created by necessity. *See* William B. Johnson, Annotation, Locating Easement of Way Created by Necessity, 36 A.L.R.4th 769 § 2 (1985) (once an easement by necessity's location has been fixed, it cannot be changed except by agreement of the parties *or by a court for equitable reasons*). The Court of Appeals of Maryland addressed this issue in Hancock v. Henderson, 236 Md. 98, 202 A.2d 599 (1964). In that case, current owners of a dominant estate brought an action to prevent the servient owners from obstructing a claimed right-of-way. *Id.* at 600. The court found the dominant owners were entitled to an easement by necessity for the purpose of ingress and egress to and from their land. *Id.* at 603. Although a road was located on the servient estate in the past for this purpose, the road had fallen into disrepair and there was evidence it had not been used for many years. *Id.* The court articulated: "We do not think this slight activity so long ago was sufficient to establish with exactitude the location of an easement claimed now by a remote grantee of the dominant tract." *Id.* Because the current location of the road was located in such a way as to be considerably inconvenient to the servient owner and the uses of the respective properties had changed over the years, the court remanded the case to the trial court for an equitable determination of where the easement should be located. *Id.* Although on remand the parties had the option of working out a location on their own, the appellate court stated that in the absence of agreement, the trial court "should exercise jurisdiction in locating an adequate right of way over the servient tenement in a manner so as to permit ingress and egress of vehicular traffic, but also in a manner least burdensome to the servient tenement." *Id.*

In Michael v. Needham, 39 Md. App. 271, 384 A.2d 473 (1978), after determining that the dominant owner was entitled to an easement by necessity, the Court of Special Appeals of Maryland concluded that because the servient owner had expended a considerable amount of funds in making improvements to his property in the vicinity where the easement was claimed to lie, the case should be remanded to determine the best location for the easement. *Id.* at 479.

As in *Hancock,* the court held that, in the absence of agreement among the parties, "it will be the responsibility of the chancellor to take such testimony as might be required and to locate the right of way after due consideration of the equities of the matter." *Id.*

Significantly, the facts surrounding the current dispute are remarkably similar to those discussed in *Hancock.* Both concern easements created by necessity and relate to roads that were commonly used at one time but had since fallen into disrepair. *Hancock,* 202 A.2d at 603. In *Hancock,* the old road dissected the servient owner's property; whereas, in this case the old road comes within ten feet of the Johnsons' home. *Id.* Additionally, the Goodwins testified they have never used the old road to access their property. It is clear from the testimony presented at trial that the Goodwins were aware when they bought the property that there may be problems obtaining access. Finally, as in *Hancock,* the use to which the servient land was put has changed since the prior road was used as a way to access the property purchased by the Goodwins. In the past, the land was farmland. Currently, the land serves as the Johnson home.

The factors articulated by the drafters of the Restatement provide excellent guidance to courts of equity when faced with the task of relocating an easement created by necessity. A court using its equity powers may relocate an easement when the relocation will not "(a) significantly lessen the utility of the easement, (b) increase the burdens on the owner of the easement in its use and enjoyment, or (c) frustrate the purpose for which the easement was created." Restatement (Third) of Property: Servitudes § 4.8.

Indubitably, a relocation of the easement in question will not significantly lessen its utility. The Goodwins have never used the old road. Although Mrs. Goodwin testified they planned on building a house on the land, they have yet to do so and it remains undeveloped property. Relocation of the easement could not increase the burden on the Goodwins because they have never used any easement through the Johnsons' property. Finally, relocation of the easement will not frustrate the purpose for which the easement was created. The easement was created so the Goodwins would have a way into and out of their property. The master's order establishing the new road mandated that it be constructed to South Carolina Department of Transportation standards completely at the Johnsons' expense.

The Goodwins maintain they will be burdened by the master's location of the new road. They allege the new road will not link up with a passable portion of their property and the new road meets the public highway in such a way that it is unsafe when entering and exiting. Frankly, there is no evidence in the record to support these assertions. While it may be true that relocation of the road will prevent it from linking with the old road on the Goodwins' property, because the property at this point is nothing more than an undeveloped lot, we fail to see how this significantly burdens the Goodwins. Because the master mandated that the new road meet requirements imposed by the South Carolina Department of Transportation, and there is no evidence in the record to support the Goodwins' contention that the entrance of the new road will be unsafe, we agree with the master's decision.

Conclusion

We align South Carolina with those jurisdictions providing that courts of equity have the power to relocate existing easements created by necessity. We adopt the minority rule that a court of equity possesses the plenary power to relocate an easement by necessity when the evidence supports such a move.

Accordingly, the master-in-equity's decision is

Affirmed.

NOTES & QUESTIONS:

1. In addition to disputes about location, it is very common to have disputes about what is included in the scope of the easement. An easement allows the holder to make use of the land of another for a specific purpose. Can/does that purpose evolve over time? How do we determine whether the party is acting within the scope of the easement or if he has gone beyond that and become a trespasser?

Marcus Cable Associates, L.P. d/b/a Charter Communications, Inc. v. Krohn
Supreme Court of Texas, 2002
90 S.W.3d 697

Justice O'NEILL delivered the opinion of the Court.

In this case, we must decide whether an easement that permits its holder to use private property for the purpose of constructing and maintaining "an electric transmission or distribution line or system" allows the easement to be used for cable-television lines. We hold that it does not. Accordingly, we affirm the court of appeals' judgment reversing summary judgment in the cable company's favor.

I. Background

This case centers around the scope of a property interest granted over sixty years ago. In 1939, Alan and Myrna Krohn's predecessors in interest granted to the Hill County Electric Cooperative an easement that allows the cooperative to use their property for the purpose of constructing and maintaining "an electric transmission or distribution line or system." The easement further granted the right to remove trees and vegetation "to the extent necessary to keep them clear of said electric line or system."

In 1991, Hill County Electric entered into a "Joint Use Agreement" with a cable-television provider, which later assigned its rights under the agreement to Marcus Cable Associates, L.P. Under the agreement, Marcus Cable obtained permission from Hill County Electric to attach its cable lines to the cooperative's poles. The agreement permitted Marcus Cable to "furnish television antenna service" to area residents, and allowed the cable wires to be attached only "to the extent [the cooperative] may lawfully do so." The agreement further provided that the electric cooperative did not warrant or assure any "right-of-way privileges or easements," and that Marcus Cable "shall be responsible for obtaining its own easements and rights-of-way."

Seven years later, the Krohns sued Marcus Cable, alleging that the company did not have a valid easement and had placed its wires over their property without their knowledge or consent. The Krohns asserted a trespass claim, and alleged that Marcus Cable was negligent in failing to obtain their consent before installing the cable lines. The Krohns sought an injunction ordering the cable wires' removal, as well as actual and exemplary damages. In defense, Marcus Cable asserted a right to use Hill County Electric's poles under the cooperative's easement and under Texas statutory law.

Both parties filed motions for summary judgment. The Krohns moved for partial summary judgment, arguing that Marcus Cable's wires constituted a trespass. The Krohns requested the court to order the wires' removal and to set for trial the determination of damages. Marcus Cable filed a response and its own summary-judgment motion, arguing that the Hill County Electric easement gave it the legal right to place its wires on the Krohns' property.

The trial court granted summary judgment in Marcus Cable's favor. The court of appeals reversed and remanded, holding that the easement did not allow Marcus Cable's use. 43 S.W.3d at 579. We granted review to consider whether the cooperative's easement permits Marcus Cable to attach cable-television lines to Hill County Electric's utility poles without the Krohns' consent.

II. Common Law

A property owner's right to exclude others from his or her property is recognized as "'one of the most essential sticks in the bundle of rights that are commonly characterized as property.'" Dolan v. City of Tigard, 512 U.S. 374, 384, 114 S. Ct. 2309, 129 L.Ed.2d 304 (1994) (quoting Loretto v. Teleprompter Manhattan CATV Corp., 458 U.S. 419, 433, 102 S. Ct. 3164, 73 L. Ed. 2d 868 (1982) (quoting Kaiser Aetna v. United States, 444 U.S. 164, 176, 100 S. Ct. 383, 62 L. Ed. 2d 332 (1979))); see also II W. Blackstone, Blackstone's Commentaries 139 (Tucker ed. 1803). A landowner may choose to relinquish a portion of the right to exclude by granting an easement, but such a relinquishment is limited in nature. Cf. San Jacinto Sand Co. v. Southwestern Bell Tel. Co., 426 S.W.2d 338, 345 (Tex. Civ. App.—Houston [14th Dist.] 1968, writ ref'd n.r.e.); see generally II George W.

Thompson, Thompson On Property §§ 315-16, 319, at 6-7, 14-16, 32-34. Unlike a possessory interest in land, an easement is a nonpossessory interest that authorizes its holder to use the property for only particular purposes. *See* Restatement (Third) of Property (Servitudes) § 1.2 cmt. d.

Marcus Cable claims rights under Hill County Electric's express easement, that is, an easement conveyed by an express grant. *See* DeWitt County Elec. Coop., Inc. v. Parks, 1 S.W.3d 96, 103 (Tex. 1999). While the common law recognizes that certain easements may be assigned or apportioned to a third party, the third party's use cannot exceed the rights expressly conveyed to the original easement holder. *See* Cantu v. Cent. Power & Light Co., 38 S.W.2d 876, 877 (Tex. Civ. App.— San Antonio 1931, writ ref'd); Keokuk Junction Ry. Co. v. IES Indus., Inc., 618 N.W.2d 352, 356, 362 (Iowa 2000); Buhl v. U.S. Sprint Communications Co., 840 S.W.2d 904, 910 (Tenn. 1992); *cf.* Carrithers v. Terramar Beach Cmty. Improvement Assoc., 645 S.W.2d 772, 774 (Tex. 1983) ("[A]n easement may not create a right or interest in a grantee's favor which the grantor himself did not possess."). Marcus Cable's rights, therefore, turn on whether the cooperative's easement permits the Krohns' property to be used for the purpose of installing cable-television lines.

Marcus Cable raises three arguments to support its contention that the original easement encompasses cable-television use. First, it argues that easements must be interpreted to anticipate and encompass future technological developments that may not have existed when the easement was originally granted. Second, Marcus Cable contends that courts should give strong deference to the public policy behind expanding the provision of cable-television services. Third, Marcus Cable argues that its use is permitted because adding cable-television wires does not increase the burden on the servient estate. These arguments, however, ignore fundamental principles that govern interpreting easements conveyed by express grant. Those principles lead us to conclude that the original easement does not encompass Marcus Cable's use.

A. Express Easements

We apply basic principles of contract construction and interpretation when considering an express easement's terms. *DeWitt County,* 1 S.W.3d at 100; Armstrong v. Skelly Oil Co., 81 S.W.2d 735, 736 (Tex. Civ. App.—Amarillo 1935, writ ref'd). The contracting parties' intentions, as expressed in the grant, determine the scope of the conveyed interest. *See DeWitt County,* 1 S.W.3d at 103 (stating that "the scope of the easement holder's rights must be determined by the terms of the grant"); *see also* Houston Pipe Line Co. v. Dwyer, 374 S.W.2d 662, 664-65 (Tex. 1964) (holding that parties' intentions are determined by interpreting the real-property grant's language); Garrett v. Dils Co., 157 Tex. 92, 299 S.W.2d 904, 906 (1957) (same); City of Dallas v. Etheridge, 152 Tex. 9, 253 S.W.2d 640, 642 (1952) (same); Restatement (Third) of Property (Servitudes) §

4.1 (providing that an easement "should be interpreted to give effect to the intention of the parties ascertained from the language used in the instrument, or the circumstances surrounding the creation of the servitude, and to carry out the purpose for which it was created").

When the grant's terms are not specifically defined, they should be given their plain, ordinary, and generally accepted meaning. *DeWitt,* 1 S.W.3d at 101; *see also* Restatement (Third) of Property (Servitudes) § 4.1 cmt. d ("[Easement] language should be interpreted to accord with the meaning an ordinary purchaser would ascribe to it. . . ."); Restatement (Second) of Contracts § 202(3)(a) ("Unless a different intention is manifested, where language has a generally prevailing meaning, it is interpreted in accordance with that meaning."). An easement's express terms, interpreted according to their generally accepted meaning, therefore delineate the purposes for which the easement holder may use the property. *See DeWitt,* 1 S.W.3d at 100, 103; *see also* Coleman v. Forister, 514 S.W.2d 899, 903 (Tex. 1974); Vahlsing v. Harrell, 178 F.2d 622, 624 (5th Cir. 1949) (applying Texas law). Nothing passes by implication "except what is reasonably necessary" to fairly enjoy the rights expressly granted. *Coleman,* 514 S.W.2d at 903; Bland Lake Fishing & Hunting Club v. Fisher, 311 S.W.2d 710, 715-16 (Tex. Civ. App.—Beaumont 1958, no writ). Thus, if a particular purpose is not provided for in the grant, a use pursuing that purpose is not allowed. *See Coleman,* 514 S.W.2d at 903; Kearney & Son v. Fancher, 401 S.W.2d 897, 904-05 (Tex. Civ. App.—Fort Worth 1966, writ ref'd n.r.e.); *cf.* Bickler v. Bickler, 403 S.W.2d 354, 359 (Tex. 1966). If the rule were otherwise,

> then the typical power line or pipeline easement, granted for the purpose of constructing and maintaining a power line or pipeline across specified property, could be used for any other purpose, unless the grantor by specific language negated all other purposes.

Kearney & Son, 401 S.W.2d at 904-05 (citing Lange, 4 Texas Practice, Land Titles § 384, at 173); *see also* City of Pasadena v. California-Michigan Land & Water Co., 17 Cal. 2d 576, 110 P.2d 983, 985 (1941) ("It is not necessary for [the easement grantor] to make any reservation to protect his interests in the land, for what he does not convey, he still retains.").

The common law does allow some flexibility in determining an easement holder's rights. In particular, the manner, frequency, and intensity of an easement's use may change over time to accommodate technological development. Restatement (Third) of Property (Servitudes) § 4.10. But such changes must fall within the purposes for which the easement was created, as determined by the grant's terms. *See id.* § 1.2 cmt. d ("The holder of the easement . . . is entitled to make only the uses reasonably necessary for the specified purpose."); § 4.10 & cmt. a (noting that manner, frequency, and intensity of easement may change to take advantage of technological advances, but only for purposes for which easement was created); *see, e.g.,* Edgcomb v. Lower Valley Power & Light, Inc., 922 P.2d 850, 854-55, 858 (Wyo. 1996) (holding that, under easement granted for an electric or telephone line, the easement holder could increase the electricity-carrying capacity and replace the static-telephone line with fiber-optics line as a matter of "normal development of the respective rights and use"); City Pub. Serv. Bd. of San Antonio v. Karp, 585 S.W.2d 838, 841-42 (Tex. Civ. App.—San Antonio 1979, no writ) (holding that a "transformer easement" permitted its holder to replace a malfunctioning underground transformer with an aboveground one as "a matter of normal development"); Lower Colo. River Auth. v. Ashby, 530 S.W.2d 628, 629, 632-33 (Tex. Civ. App.—Austin 1975, writ ref'd n.r.e.) (holding that, under the electric-transmission easement at issue, the easement holder could replace wooden towers with new steel towers and could increase the electricity-carrying capacity); Restatement (Third) of Property (Servitudes) § 4.10 illus. 13 (stating that, under a 1940s telephone easement, easement holder could mount transmitters on its poles for cellular-telephone transmissions unless doing so would unreasonably interfere with enjoyment of the servient estate). Thus, contrary to Marcus Cable's argument, an express easement encompasses only those technological developments that further the particular purpose for which the easement was granted. *See* Restatement (Third) of Property (Servitudes) §§ 1.2 cmt. d., 4.2 cmt. a, 4.10 & cmt. a. Otherwise, easements would effectively become possessory, rather than nonpossessory, land interests. *See id.* § 1.2 cmt. d (distinguishing between an easement that permits its owner to use land for only specified purposes, and a possessory land interest that permits its owner to make any use of the property).

The emphasis our law places upon an easement's express terms serves important public policies by promoting certainty in land transactions. In order to evaluate the burdens placed upon real property, a potential purchaser must be able to safely rely upon granting language. *See* Restatement (Third) of Property (Servitudes) § 4.1 cmt. d. Similarly, those who grant easements should be assured that their conveyances will not be construed to undermine private-property rights—like the rights to "exclude others" or to "obtain a profit"—any more than what was intended in the grant. *See Loretto,* 458 U.S. at 436, 102 S. Ct. 3164.

Marcus Cable suggests that we should give greater weight to the public benefit that results from the wide distribution of cable-television services, arguing that technological advancement in Texas will be substantially impeded if the cooperative's easement is not read to encompass cable-television use.[6] But

---

[6] We note that the summary-judgment evidence indicates that Marcus Cable has readily available alternatives to attaching its cable lines to Hill County Electric's utility

even if that were so, we may not circumvent the contracting parties' intent by disregarding the easement's express terms and the specific purpose for which it was granted. *See* Restatement (Third) of Property (Servitudes) § 4.1 & cmt. d (indicating that a court may not adopt an easement interpretation based on public policy unless that interpretation is supported by the grant's terms). Adhering to basic easement principles, we must decide not what is most convenient to the public or profitable to Marcus Cable, but what purpose the contracting parties intended the easement to serve. *See* Dauenhauer v. Devine, 51 Tex. 480, 489-90 (1879). Hill County Electric could only permit Marcus Cable to use its easement "so long as that use is devoted exclusively to the purposes of the grant." *Cantu,* 38 S.W.2d at 877.

Finally, Marcus Cable contends that its use should be allowed because attaching cable-television wires to Hill County Electric's utility poles does not materially increase the burden to the servient estate. But again, if a use does not serve the easement's express purpose, it becomes an unauthorized presence on the land whether or not it results in any noticeable burden to the servient estate. *See* McDaniel Bros. v. Wilson, 70 S.W.2d 618, 621 (Tex. Civ. App.—Beaumont 1934, writ ref'd) ("[E]very unauthorized entry upon land of another is a trespass even if no damage is done or the injury is slight . . . ."); *see also* Rio Costilla Co-op. Livestock Ass'n v. W.S. Ranch Co., 81 N.M. 353, 467 P.2d 19, 25 (1970); Beckwith v. Rossi, 157 Me. 532, 175 A.2d 732, 735-36 (1961). Thus, the threshold inquiry is not whether the proposed use results in a material burden, but whether the grant's terms authorize the proposed use. With these principles in mind, we turn to the easement at issue in this case.

B. Hill County Electric's Easement

Both parties urge us to determine Marcus Cable's easement rights as a matter of law. When an easement is susceptible to only one reasonable, definite interpretation after applying established rules of contract construction, we are obligated to construe it as a matter of law even if the parties offer different interpretations of the easement's terms. *DeWitt,* 1 S.W.3d at 100. Because the easement here can be given a definite meaning, we interpret it as a matter of law.

The easement granted Hill County Electric the right to use the Krohns' property for the purpose of constructing and maintaining an "electric transmission or distribution line or system." The terms "electric transmission" and "electric distribution" are commonly and ordinarily associated with power companies conveying electricity to the public. *See, e.g.,* Texas Power & Light Co. v. Cole, 158 Tex. 495, 313 S.W.2d 524, 526-27, 530 (1958); Resendez v. Lyntegar Elec. Coop., Inc., 511 S.W.2d 350, 352-53 (Tex. Civ. App.—Amarillo 1974, no writ); Upshur-Rural Elec. Coop. Corp. v. State, 381 S.W.2d 418, 424 (Tex. Civ. App.—

---

poles. Furthermore, it is undisputed that cable-television providers may place their lines on public property in unincorporated areas. *See* Tex. Util. Code § 181.102.

Austin 1964, writ dism'd) (using terms electric transmission and/or distribution to describe equipment used by power companies to convey electricity); *see also* Restatement (Third) of Property (Servitudes) § 4.10 illus. 3 & 12 (using "electric-transmission lines" to designate lines operated by power companies); Tex. Util. Code § 39.157(a), (d)(3) (providing that Public Utility Commission shall regulate market-power abuses in the sale of electricity by utilities "providing electric transmission or distribution services"). Texas cases decided around the time the cooperative's easement was granted strongly suggest that this was the commonly understood meaning of those terms. *See, e.g.,* City of Bryan v. A & M Consol. Indep. Sch. Dist., 179 S.W.2d 987, 988 (Tex. Civ. App.—Waco 1944), *aff'd,* 143 Tex. 348, 184 S.W.2d 914 (1945); Texas-New Mexico Utils. Co. v. City of Teague, 174 S.W.2d 57, 59 (Tex. Civ. App.—Fort Worth 1943, writ ref'd w.o.m.); Arcola Sugar Mills Co. v. Houston Lighting & Power Co., 153 S.W.2d 628, 629-30 (Tex. Civ. App.—Galveston 1941, writ ref'd w.o.m.); McCulloch County Elec. Co-op., Inc. v. Hall, 131 S.W.2d 1019, 1020, 1022 (Tex. Civ. App.—Austin 1939, writ dism'd); Willacy County v. Central Power & Light Co., 73 S.W.2d 1060, 1061 (Tex. Civ. App.—San Antonio 1934, writ dism'd) (using term electric transmission to describe equipment used by power companies to convey electricity). Accordingly, we construe the easement's terms to allow use of the property for facilities to transmit electricity.

Marcus Cable does not argue that the generally prevailing meaning of the easement's grant encompasses cable-television services. Instead, it claims that, for reasons of public policy, we should construe the easement to embrace modern developments, without regard to the easement's language. In support of that position, Marcus Cable cites a number of decisions in other jurisdictions that have allowed the use of easements predating cable technology to allow installation of cable transmission lines.

The cases Marcus Cable cites, however, involve different granting language and do not support the proposition that we may disregard the parties' expressed intentions or expand the purposes for which an easement may be used. To the contrary, those cases involve easements containing much broader granting language than the easement before us. Most of them involved easements granted for communications media, such as telegraph and telephone, in addition to electric utility easements. In concluding that the easements were broad enough to encompass cable, the reviewing courts examined the purpose for which the easement was granted and essentially concluded that the questioned use was a more technologically advanced means of accomplishing the same communicative purpose.

For example, in *Salvaty v. Falcon Cable Television,* the 1926 easement permitted its holder to maintain both electric wires *and* telephone wires. 165 Cal. App. 3d 798, 212 Cal. Rptr. 31, 32, 35 (1985). The court held that cable-television lines were within the easement's scope, observing that cable television is "part of the natural evolution of *communications* technology." *Id.* at 34-35 (emphasis added); *accord* Witteman v. Jack Barry Cable TV, 228 Cal. Rptr. 584, 589 (Cal. Ct. App. 1986) (same). Similarly, the Fourth Circuit held that an easement allowing its holder to use the land for the purpose of maintaining pole lines for "electrical and telephone service" was sufficiently broad to encompass cable-television lines. C/R TV, Inc. v. Shannondale, Inc., 27 F.3d 104, 106, 109-10 (4th Cir. 1994) (applying West Virginia law). In reaching its conclusion, the court relied on the similar communicative aspects of both "telephone services" and cable-television services. *Id.* at 109-10. Other cases Marcus Cable cites also involved easements granted for communications-transmission purposes. *See, e.g.,* Cousins v. Alabama Power Co., 597 So. 2d 683, 686-87 (Ala. 1992) (involving easements—granted for the purpose of maintaining "electric transmission lines and all telegraph and telephone lines"—that the landowners conceded included the right to maintain fiber-optics telecommunications lines); Jolliff v. Hardin Cable Television Co., 26 Ohio St. 2d 103, 55 O.O.2d 203, 269 N.E.2d 588, 591 (1971) (concluding that cable-television wires were a burden "contemplated at the time of the grants [to the power company], as evidenced by the specific reference to telegraph and telephone wires" in the 1940 easement); Am. Tel. & Tel. Co. of Mass. v. McDonald, 273 Mass. 324, 173 N.E. 502, 502-03 (1930) (concluding that easement granted for the purpose of maintaining "lines of telephone and telegraph" could be apportioned by the easement holder to a telephone company seeking to install a telephone cable, and that "[n]othing granted to the [company] enables it to do anything which the original grantee could not have done"); Henley v. Continental Cablevision of St. Louis County, Inc., 692 S.W.2d 825, 827, 829 (Mo. Ct. App. 1985) (concluding that cable television fell within the 1922 easement grantors' expressed intention to provide "electric power and telephonic communications" to subdivision residents); Hoffman v. Capitol Cablevision Sys., Inc., 52 A.D.2d 313, 383 N.Y.S.2d 674, 676, 677 (N.Y. App. Div. 1976) (involving easements for the "distribution of electricity and messages," and concluding that cable-television wires were no greater burden "than that contemplated by the original easements").

We express no opinion about whether the cases Marcus Cable relies upon were correctly decided. But, unlike the cases Marcus Cable cites, Hill County Electric's easement does not convey the right to use the property for purposes of transmitting communications. While cable television may utilize electrical impulses to transmit communications, as Marcus Cable claims, [7] television

---

[7] Marcus Cable did not offer any evidence about the nature of cable-television transmissions; thus, the record is silent on this point. But we note that, in recent years, many telecommunications providers, including cable-television operators, have moved toward fiber-optics cables that use light lasers, rather than electrical impulses, to transmit communications over their lines to the public. *See, e.g.,* Mike Mills, Fine Lines of Telecommunications, *The Wash. Post*, Aug. 5, 1996, at F17.

transmission is not a more technologically advanced method of delivering electricity. Thus, the above-referenced cases do not support Marcus Cable's argument that the easement here encompasses the additional purpose of transmitting television content to the public.

Marcus Cable cites only two cases involving easements whose grants did not include telephone or telegraph services, and neither supports its position. In *Centel Cable Television, Inc. v. Cook,* the court interpreted easement language that permitted its holder to maintain "a line for the transmission and/or distribution of electric energy thereover, *for any and all purposes for which electric energy is now, or may hereafter be used.*" 58 Ohio St.3d 8, 567 N.E.2d 1010, 1014 (1991) (emphasis added). Observing that cable-television broadcasting "*utilize[s]* . . . 'electric energy,' " the court concluded that the grant language was broad enough to encompass cable television. *Id.* (emphasis added). And *Hise v. BARC Electric Cooperative,* 254 Va. 341, 492 S.E.2d 154, 158 (1997), involved a right-of-way easement by prescription that had been used for cable-television lines during the prescriptive period and that was later widened through eminent domain. It did not involve a privately-negotiated, express easement. *See, e.g., Nishanian v. Sirohi,* 243 Va. 337, 414 S.E.2d 604, 606 (1992) ("The use of an [express] easement must be restricted to the terms and purposes on which the grant was based." (citing *Robertson v. Bertha Mineral Co.,* 128 Va. 93, 104 S.E. 832, 834 (1920))). The easements in Marcus Cable's cited cases are simply not comparable to the more limited, express easement presented here.

Finally, Marcus Cable cites *San Antonio & Aransas Pass Railway v. Southwestern Telegraph & Telephone Co.,* 93 Tex. 313, 55 S.W. 117 (1900), for the proposition that an easement must be interpreted to embrace technological change. But that case does not support the idea that a court may ignore the contracting parties' intent as reflected in their written language. There, we were called upon to determine whether a statute granting condemnation power to "telegraph" companies applied equally to "telephone" companies. *Id.* Relying upon later statutory enactments that reflected the Legislature's intent to treat both the same, and recognizing that telegraph and telephone are two different means of accomplishing the same communicative purpose, we held that the statute at issue applied to telephone companies. *Id.* at 118-19.

The dissenting Justice would hold that the easement could properly be read to encompass cable because electricity is used in the transmission of cable television signals. Under such a reading, however, the easement could also be used for telegraph or telephone lines. Obviously, the Krohns' predecessors could have granted an easement for those purposes. But the easement's specific terms cannot be read so broadly.

In sum, the easement language here, properly construed, does not permit cable-television lines to be strung across the Krohns' land without their consent. However laudable the goal of extending cable service might be, we cannot disregard the easement's express terms to enlarge its purposes beyond those intended by the contracting parties. To the extent the trial court granted Marcus Cable summary judgment on this basis, it erred, and the court of appeals correctly reversed.

IV. Conclusion

We hold that Hill County Electric's easement does not convey the right to string cable-television wires over the Krohns' private property. Accordingly, we affirm the court of appeals' judgment reversing and remanding this case to the trial court for further proceedings.

NOTES & QUESTIONS:

What if the question that arises is not one of cable versus electric lines, but instead deals with what land can receive the benefit of the easement? In the case of Brown v. Voss, the easement holder is using the easement for ingress and egress. There is no question that is what was permitted by the easement. However, he is using it for ingress and egress to two parcels of land but the original easement was only for the benefit of one of those parcels. Is the easement holder exceeding the scope?

Easement Problem #2

In 1980, Marshall owned Blackacre in fee simple absolute, and he gave an easement to Barney who owned the adjacent farm of Greenacres. The instrument that granted the easement stated the following:

> an easement in the east 20 feet of Blackacre, from Farm
> Road 101 on the south to Green acres on the North, for the
> purposes of road access to Greenacres.

From 1980 until recently, Barney used the strip of land for access to Greenacres. During this time, Greenacres was used for agricultural and residential purposes. Approximately one month ago, Barney subdivided Greenacres into 50 lots, each containing 3 acres, and provided streets connecting the lots to the easement over Blackacre. Now Marshall consults with you. Marshall wants to stop Barney's grantees of the lots from using the strip across Blackacre. Further, Barney wants to pave the easement so it can carry the increased traffic. What do you tell Marshall on each of these questions and why?

What if instead, Barney split the land into two parcels and sold the land to Ted and Robin. Are they allowed to continue using the easement?

Instead of splitting the land into separate parcels,

    (a) Barney builds a 500-unit condo. Can all of the residents use the easement?

    (b) Barney builds a shopping center. Can all of the customers and delivery vehicles use the easement?

4. Termination of Easements

Because easements are perpetual in nature, at some point the servient landowner may want to establish that the easement has terminated and his land is no longer burdened. How can this be accomplished? There are a variety of means of terminating easements that are fairly straightforward. The one fact-intensive method is abandonment. The following case provides an example of a dispute over abandonment.

---

[8] Illustration by Hunter Ratcliff, Baylor Law J.D., *cum laude*, 2017.

Preseault v. United States
United States Court of Appeals, Federal Circuit, 1996
100 F.3d 1525

PLAGER, J.

In this Takings case, the United States denies liability under the Fifth Amendment of the Constitution for actions it took pursuant to the Federal legislation known as the Rails-to-Trails Act. The original parties to the case were the property owners, J. Paul and Patricia Preseault, 3 plaintiffs, and the United States (the "Government"), defendant. The State of Vermont (the "State"), claiming an interest in the properties involved, intervened and, under the joinder rules of the Court of Federal Claims, entered its appearance as a co-defendant. The Court of Federal Claims, on summary judgment after hearings and argument, concluded that the law was on the Government's side, and rendered judgment against the complaining property owners. The property owners appeal.

[W]e conclude that, for the reasons we shall explain, the trial court erred in giving judgment for the Government; that judgment is reversed. The case is remanded to the trial court for further proceedings to determine the just compensation to which the property owners are entitled.

A. Introduction and Summary

In brief, the issue in this case is whether the conversion, under the authority of the Rails-to-Trails Act and by order of the Interstate Commerce Commission, of a long unused railroad right-of-way to a public recreational hiking and biking trail constituted a taking of the property of the owners of the underlying fee simple estate. At this point we shall refer to the railroad's interest in the property by the term "right-of-way." That term is sufficient to indicate that the railroad had obtained a property interest allowing it to operate its equipment over the land involved.

In summary, we conclude that the trial court was correct in finding that the 1899 transfers to the railroad created easements for use for railroad purposes; the fee estates remained with the original property owners. (Part C.1.) We accept the Government's position that ultimately this is a matter to be decided under controlling federal law and Constitution, but we reject the Government's central thesis that general federal legislation providing for the governance of interstate railroads, enacted over the years of the Twentieth Century, somehow redefined state-created property rights and destroyed them without entitlement to compensation. (Part C.2.) The trial court erred in accepting that thesis.

As far as the Government's defenses based on the state's property law are concerned, we conclude that even if these easements were still in existence at the time the trail was created, there was no legal justification for the intrusion upon the Preseault's property. We find no support in Vermont law for the proposition, propounded by the defendants and accepted by the dissent, that the scope of an easement limited to railroad purposes should be read to include public recreational hiking and biking trails (Part D). But we find no clear error in the trial court's determination that in fact these easements had been abandoned years before the creation of [1531] the trail (Part E), and that determination is affirmed.

Finally, we conclude that the taking that resulted from the establishment of the recreational trail is properly laid at the doorstep of the Federal Government. Whether the State's role in the matter should have resulted in liability for the State, or whether the State could absolve itself by pointing to the Federal Government, as the State Court held, is immaterial. The Federal Government authorized and controlled the behavior of the State in this matter, and the consequences properly fall there. (Part E.)

B. Factual Background

The Preseaults own a fee simple interest in a tract of land near the shore of Lake Champlain in Burlington, Vermont, on which they have a home. This tract of land is made up of several previously separate properties, the identities of which date back to before the turn of the century. The dispute centers on three parcels within this tract, areas over which the original railroad right-of-way ran. The areas are designated by the trial court as Parcels A, B, and C. Two of those parcels, A and B, derive from the old Barker Estate property. The third parcel, C, is part of what was the larger Manwell property.

The Rutland-Canadian Railroad Company, a corporation organized under the laws of Vermont, acquired in 1899 the rights-of-way at issue on Parcels A, B, and C, over which it laid its rails and operated its railroad.

Meanwhile, ownership of the properties over which the rights-of-way ran passed through the hands of successors in interest, eventually arriving in the hands of the Preseaults. A map of the Preseault tract, showing the various parcels and the areas subject to the railroad's rights-of-way, is reproduced in Figure 4.4.

C. The Property Interests

In *Preseault II*, Justice Brennan writing for the Supreme Court noted the importance of determining the nature of the interests created by these turn-of-the-century transfers:

> The alternative chosen by Congress [the Rails-to-Trails program] is less costly than a program of direct federal trail acquisition because, under any view of takings law, only some rail-to-trail conversions will amount to takings. Some rights-of-way are held in fee simple. Others are held as easements that do

not even as a matter of state law revert upon interim use as nature trails. 494 U.S. 1, 16 (1990).

Clearly, if the Railroad obtained fee simple title to the land over which it was to operate, and that title inures, as it would, to its successors, the Preseaults today would have no right or interest in those parcels and could have no claim related to those parcels for a taking. If, on the other hand, the Railroad acquired only easements for use, easements imposed on the property owners' underlying fee simple estates, and if those easements were limited to uses that did not include public recreational hiking and biking trails ("nature trails" as Justice Brennan referred to them), or if the easements prior to their conversion to trails had been extinguished by operation of law leaving the property owner with unfettered fee simples, the argument of the Preseaults becomes viable.

The determinative issues in the case, then, are three: (1) who owned the strips of land involved, specifically did the Railroad by the 1899 transfers acquire only easements, or did it obtain fee simple estates; (2) if the Railroad acquired only easements, were the terms of the easements limited to use for railroad purposes, or did they include future use as public recreational trails; and (3) even if the grants of the Railroad's easements were broad enough to encompass recreational trails, had these easements terminated prior to the alleged taking so that the property owners at that time held fee simples unencumbered by the easements.

1. The Interests Created

The question of what estates in property were created by these turn-of-the-century transfers to the Railroad requires a close examination of the conveying instruments, read in light of the common law and statutes of Vermont then in effect.

With regard to the two parcels, A and B, derived from the Barker Estate, the trial judge examined, as have we, the document referred to as a "Commissioner's Award," dated September 2, 1899, as well as the relevant cases and statutes of Vermont. The Commissioner's Award, which is the only document that memorializes the event, is unlike a deed in that it does not contain the usual premises (the clause describing the parties to and purposes of the transaction) or habendum clause (defining the extent of the ownership interest conveyed). Usually in a deed the habendum clause would define the exact interest to be conveyed, whether a fee simple or a lesser interest, although the premises clause sometimes serves as well. Here, the Commissioner's Award simply confirms that "the Rutland-Canadian Railroad Company . . . for the purposes of its railroad has located, entered upon and occupied lands owned by [the Barkers] . . . described as follows [and here follows a metes and bounds description of the strip of

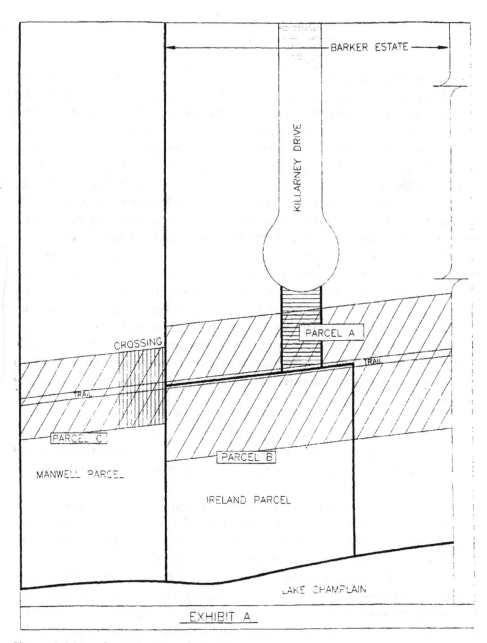

BARKER ESTATE

KILLARNEY DRIVE

PARCEL A

CROSSING

TRAIL

TRAIL

PARCEL C

PARCEL B

MANWELL PARCEL

IRELAND PARCEL

LAKE CHAMPLAIN

EXHIBIT A

Figure 4.4 Map from the Court's Opinion

land]." . . . The references to the purposes of the Railroad, and to the provisions of the Act incorporating it, are to 1898 Vermont Acts No. 160, entitled "An Act to Incorporate the Rutland-Canadian Railroad Company," approved November 4, 1898. That Act provided that certain named individuals constituted and created a body politic and corporate by the name of the "Rutland-Canadian Railroad

Company," for the purpose and with the right of constructing, maintaining and operating a railroad for public use in the conveyance of persons and property by the power of steam or otherwise . . . . Said Corporation shall have and enjoy the right of eminent domain . . . [and] may . . . take . . . such real and personal estate as is necessary or proper in the judgment of such corporation, for the construction, maintenance and accommodation of such railroad . . . as the purposes of the corporation may require . . . . 1898 Vt. Acts No. 160, § 1. The Act goes on to state that the corporation shall have all privileges and rights given by the general law to railroad companies for acquiring title and possession to property covered by its location.

In her opinion, the trial judge concluded that, in the context of the Vermont procedure for commissioners' awards for railroad rights-of-way, and in light of the Vermont case law, cited and discussed in the trial court's opinion, "the portion of the right-of-way consisting of the parcel of land condemned from the Barker Estate and taken by commissioner's award is indisputably an easement under the law of the State of Vermont." 24 Cl. Ct. at 827.

As a result of our independent examination of the question we conclude that there is little real dispute about this. That was the rule in the early Vermont cases, and continues to be the rule today. *See, e.g.,* Dessureau v. Maurice Memorials, Inc., 132 Vt. 350, 351, 318 A.2d 652 (1974) ("The taking, pursuant to statutory authority, gave the railroad only an easement, not a fee, and upon abandonment, the property reverts to the former owner.") (citing Troy & Boston R.R. v. Potter, 42 Vt. 265, 274 (1869)). . . . With few exceptions the Vermont cases are consistent in holding that, practically without regard to the documentation and manner of acquisition, when a railroad for its purposes acquires an estate in land for laying track and operating railroad equipment thereon, the estate acquired is no more than that needed for the purpose, and that typically means an easement, not a fee simple estate. The trial court fully and correctly analyzed the matter; it hardly needs further elaboration. We find no error in the trial court's analysis and conclusion, and it is affirmed.

Determining the provenance of the third parcel, C, derived from the Manwell tract, tests the above stated proposition even further. The operative instrument is a warranty deed, dated August 2, 1899, from Frederick and Mary Manwell to the Railroad. The deed contains the usual habendum clause found in a warranty deed, and purports to convey the described strip of land to the grantee railroad "to have and to hold the above granted and bargained premises . . . unto it the said grantee, its successors and assigns forever, to its and their own proper use, benefit and behoof forever." The deed further warrants that the grantors have "a good, indefeasible estate, in fee simple, and have good right to bargain and sell the same in manner and form as above written . . . ." In short, the deed appears to be the standard form used to convey a fee simple title from a grantor to a grantee.

But did it?

At trial, the Preseaults argued that, although the Manwell deed purports to grant a fee simple, the deed was given following survey and location of the right-of-way and therefore it should be construed as conveying only an easement in accordance with Vermont railroad law. The Government responded that, while it was true that survey and location of the railroad's right-of-way had occurred, no "formal" eminent domain proceedings had taken place, and therefore the deed should be taken at its face as a conveyance in fee simple. Each side cited Vermont cases to support its position. The trial court, after reviewing and discussing at length the cases and other relevant materials, concluded that "under well-settled Vermont law, the property interests in the parcel . . . conveyed following survey and location by warranty deed, amounted to [an] easement[] . . . ." 24 Cl. Ct. at 830.

Our independent review of the state of Vermont law on this issue leads us to conclude, despite some uncertainties in the matter, that the trial court is correct.

In Hill v. Western Vermont Railroad, 32 Vt. 68, the railroad had a contract with one Josiah Burton to purchase some land for railroad purposes. The bond, or contract, entered into before the railroad had surveyed their right-of-way called for Burton to convey such lands "as shall be required" for the company's road. Plaintiff, a creditor of the railroad, attempted to levy on a part of the land potentially subject to the contract. The railroad defended against the levy by arguing that the tract at issue was not needed by the railroad for its purposes, and thus Burton could not have been made to sell it to the railroad. Since, it was argued, the claimed land was not subject to contract enforcement, it was not subject to the levying creditor. The Vermont Supreme Court held for the railroad. The court observed that railroads acquire needed land either by order of a designated public body (through the exercise of eminent domain) or by consent of the landowner, although even in the latter case "the proceeding is, in some sense, compulsory." Id. at 75. Thus,

> in either mode of appropriating land for the purposes of the company, there is this implied limitation upon the power, that the company will take only so much land or estate therein as is necessary for their public purposes. It does not seem to us to make much difference in regard to either the quantity or the estate whether the price is fixed by the commissioners or by the parties.

Id. at 76. The court held that the estate which Burton was to convey would be "a mere easement for a particular use," and under the governing statute would not be subject to a levy. Id. at 77.

Parcel C
only Esmt

Thus it is that a railroad that proceeds to acquire a right-of-way for its road acquires only that estate, typically an easement, necessary for its limited purposes, and that the act of survey and location is the operative determinant, and not the particular form of transfer, if any. Here, the evidence is that the Railroad had obtained a survey and location of its right-of-way, after which the Manwell deed was executed confirming and memorializing the Railroad's action. On balance it would seem that, consistent with the view expressed in Hill, the proceeding retained its eminent domain flavor, and the railroad acquired only that which it needed, an easement for its roadway. Nothing the Government points to or that we can find in the later cases would seem to undermine that view of the case; the trial court's conclusion that the estate conveyed was an easement is affirmed.

Estate Conveyed = Easement

We thus conclude that fee simple title to all three parcels in dispute remained with their original owners, subject only to the burden of the easements in favor of the Railroad. Those titles passed through various hands, coming to rest eventually in the hands of the Preseaults, where they lay in 1986 when the public recreational trail was created by the Government's action.

F.S. Stays w/ Original Owners

D. The Scope of the Railroad's Easement

We turn then to the question of whether the easements granted to the Railroad, to which the Preseaults' title was subject, are sufficiently broad in their scope so that the use of the easements for a public recreational trail is not a violation of the Preseaults' rights as owners of the underlying fee estate. Both the Government and the State argue that under the doctrine of "shifting public use" the scope of the original easements, admittedly limited to railroad purposes, is properly construed today to include other public purposes as well, and that these other public purposes include a public recreational hiking and biking trail. Under that theory of the case, the establishment in 1986 of such a trail would be within the scope of the easements presumably now in the State's hands, and therefore the Preseaults would have no complaint. On the other hand, if the Government's use of the land for a recreational trail is not within the scope of the easements, then that use would constitute an unauthorized invasion of the land to which the Preseaults hold title. The argument on this issue assumes that the easements were still in existence in 1986, and for purposes of this part of the discussion we assume they were. . . .

In the absence of a Vermont case on point, we must seek the answer in traditional understandings of easement law, recognizing as we must that Vermont follows and applies common law property principles. The easements involved here are express easements, meaning that the scope of the easements are set out in express terms, either in the granting documents or as a matter of incorporation and legal construction of the terms of the relevant documents.

The extent of an easement created by a conveyance is fixed by the conveyance. . . . [W]hen precise language is employed to create an easement, such terminology governs the extent of usage. . . . The general rule does not preclude the scope of an easement being adjusted in the face of changing times to serve the original purpose, so long as the change is consistent with the terms of the original grant:

> It is often said that the parties are to be presumed to have contemplated such a scope for the created easement as would reasonably serve the purposes of the grant. . . . This presumption often allows an expansion of use of the easement, but does not permit a change in use not reasonably foreseeable at the time of establishment of the easement.

Richard R. Powell, 3 Powell on Real Property § 34.12[2] (Patrick J. Rohan ed., 1996).

Bernards v. Link, 199 Ore. 579, 248 P.2d 341 (Or. 1952), is a good example of the application of the test. The question was whether an easement for a logging railroad, granted to defendant's predecessor, would permit the substitution of a logging road for trucks, when the logging industry had moved to the use of such vehicles. The owners of the servient estate did not claim that the new use had subjected their property to any additional servitude, but that the new use constituted an abandonment of the original easement. The court reviewed the history of transportation in the logging industry, noting that the use of logging trucks and of logging roads had been an evolutionary development in the Northwest's logging industry: "improvements in trucks and the inexorable demand for lower cost of operation have made the logging road the successor to the logging railroad in divers places." 248 P.2d at 346. The court stated that

> the evidence renders it clear that the paramount purpose of the parties was to enable the grantee to bring to Carlton, over the right of way described in the deed, the logs which were being produced near Tillamook Gate. . . . We do not believe that the grantor intended to restrict the grantee to the specific type of equipment which was then in use.

Id. at 351-52. The court concluded that the use of logging trucks, after logging railroads became obsolete, was within the proper scope of the easement.

When the easements here were granted to the Preseaults' predecessors in title at the turn of the century, specifically for transportation of goods and persons via railroad, could it be said that the parties contemplated that a century later the easements would be used for recreational hiking and biking trails, or that it was necessary to so construe them in order to give the grantee railroad that for which it bargained? We think not. Although a public recreational trail could be described as a roadway for the transportation of persons, the nature of the usage is clearly different. In the one case, the grantee is a commercial enterprise using the easement in its business, the transport of goods and people for compensation. In the other, the easement belongs to the public, and is open for use for recreational purposes, which happens to involve people engaged in exercise or recreation on foot or on bicycles. It is difficult to imagine that either party to the original transfers had anything remotely in mind that would resemble a public recreational trail.

Furthermore, there are differences in the degree and nature of the burden imposed on the servient estate. It is one thing to have occasional railroad trains crossing one's land. Noisy though they may be, they are limited in location, in number, and in frequency of occurrence. Particularly is this so on a relatively remote spur. When used for public recreational purposes, however, in a region that is environmentally attractive, the burden imposed by the use of the easement is at the whim of many individuals, and, as the record attests, has been impossible to contain in numbers or to keep strictly within the parameters of the easement. [A]n easement created to serve a particular purpose ends when the underlying purpose no longer exists [and] when an easement for railway purposes is found, it is generally considered to end when it is no longer used for the stated purposes.

Most state courts that have been faced with the question of whether conversion to a nature trail falls within the scope of an original railroad easement have held that it does not.

Given that the easements in this case are limited by their terms and as a matter of law to railroad purposes, we are unable to join the dissent's effort to read into Vermont law a breadth of scope for the easements that is well outside the parameters of traditional common law understanding.

E. Abandonment

Even assuming for sake of argument that the Government and the State are correct and [we] permit reading the original conveyances in the manner for which they argue, there remains yet a further obstacle to the Government's successful defense. The Preseaults contend that under Vermont law the original easements were abandoned, and thus extinguished, in 1975. If that is so, the State could not, over ten years later in 1986, have re-established the easement even for the narrow purposes provided in the original conveyances without payment of the just compensation required by the Constitution. *See, e.g., Loretto*, 458 U.S. at 441. It follows that if the State could not in 1986 use the parcels for railroad purposes without that use constituting a taking, then it surely could not claim the right to use the property for other purposes free of Constitutional requirements. *See*

Preseault 1, 24 Cl. Ct. at 835 (concluding that a "shifting public use" doctrine could not apply because of discontinuity of use of the easement by State between 1975 and 1985).

We have established that the effect of the turn-of-the-century transfers regarding Parcels A, B, and C was to create in the transferee Railroad an easement carrying the right to exclusive possession of the surface of the strips of land described in the conveyances for the limited purposes of railroad use, and to leave in the original owners of the property their fee simple estate, subject to the easement. An easement is not a possessory estate of freehold, but merely gives the easement holder a right to make use of the land over which the easement lies for the purposes for which it was granted.

Typically the grant under which such rights-of-way are created does not specify a termination date. The usual way in which such an easement ends is by abandonment, which causes the easement to be extinguished by operation of law. See generally Restatement of Property § 504. Upon an act of abandonment, the then owner of the fee estate, the "burdened" estate, is relieved of the burden of the easement. In most jurisdictions, including Vermont, this happens automatically when abandonment of the easement occurs.

Vermont law recognizes the well-established proposition that easements, like other property interests, are not extinguished by simple non-use. As was said in Nelson v. Bacon, 113 Vt. 161, 32 A.2d 140, 146 (1943), "one who acquires title to an easement in this manner [by deed in that case] has the same right of property therein as an owner of the fee and it is not necessary that he should make use of his right in order to maintain his title." Thus in cases involving a passageway through an adjoining building (Nelson), or a shared driveway (Sabins v. McAllister, 116 Vt. 302, 76 A.2d 106 (1950), overruled in part on other grounds by Lague v. Royea, 152 Vt. 499, 568 A.2d 357 (1989)), the claimed easement was not extinguished merely because the owner had not made use of it regularly.

Something more is needed. The Vermont Supreme Court in *Nelson* summarized the rule in this way: "In order to establish an abandonment there must be in addition to nonuser, acts by the owner of the dominant tenement conclusively and unequivocally manifesting *either* a present intent to relinquish the easement or a purpose inconsistent with its future existence." *Nelson*, 32 A.2d at 146 (emphasis added); *see also Lague*, 152 Vt. at 503, 568 A.2d at 359; Barrett v. Kunz, 158 Vt. 15, 604 A.2d 1278 (1992). The record here establishes that these easements, along with the other assets of the railroad, came into the hands of the State of Vermont in the 1960s. The State then leased them to an entity called the Vermont Railway, which operated trains over them. In 1970, the Vermont Railway ceased active transport operations on the line, which included the right-of-way over the parcels at issue, and used the line only to store railroad cars. In 1975 the Railroad removed all of the railroad equipment, including switches and tracks, from the portion of the right-of-way running over the three parcels of land now owned by the Preseaults. *See* 24 Cl. Ct. at 822. In light of these facts, the trial court concluded that under Vermont law this amounted to an abandonment of the easements, and adjudged that the easements were extinguished as a matter of law in 1975.

Under Vermont law, "the question whether there has been an abandonment . . . is one of fact," *Lague*, 152 Vt. at 503, 568 A.2d at 359 (citation omitted), and "the fact that the question relates to a right of way taken by a railroad company does not make it one of law," Stevens v. MacRae, 97 Vt. 76, 122 A. 892 (1923).

The question to be decided here is what was the intent or purpose of the Railroad in 1975, when, for all practical purposes, it ended railroad operations on this easement. It is enough, under the circumstances of this case and given the fullness of the factual record before the trial judge, as well as her carefully considered analysis, that we here accord her traditional deference for factual determinations, and test her judgment against the usual standard of clear error. To do less would embroil this court in determining factual matters more intensively than customary for appellate courts, a position for which appellate courts are ill-equipped.

The Government and the State argue that there are facts inconsistent with that determination, but we are not persuaded that any of them significantly undercut the trial court's conclusion. For example, when the Vermont Railway removed its tracks in 1975, it did not remove the two bridges or any of the culverts on the line, all of which remained "substantially intact." That is not surprising. The Railroad was under no obligation to restore the former easement to its original condition. Tearing out existing structures would simply add to its costs, whereas the rails that were taken up could be used for repairs of defective rails elsewhere on the line. It is further argued that, since the rail line continues to operate to a point approximately one and one-third miles south of the Preseaults' property, it is possible to restore the line to full operation. The fact that restoration of the northern portion of the line would be technically feasible tells us little. The question is not what is technically possible to do in the future, but what was done in the past.

Almost immediately after the tracks were removed, members of the public began crossing over the easement. Perhaps illustrating the difficulty in getting government paperwork to catch up with reality, or perhaps indicating that revenue collectors do not give up easily, the State of Vermont and Vermont Railway, as they had done before the removal of the tracks, continued to collect fees under various license and crossing agreements from persons wishing to establish fixed crossings. In January 1976, the Preseaults executed a crossing agreement with the Vermont Railway which gave the Preseaults permission to cross the right-of-way. In March 1976, the Preseaults entered into a license agreement with the State and the Vermont Railway to locate a driveway and underground utility service across the railroad right-of-way. As late as 1991, 985 Associates (through Paul Preseault) paid a $10 license fee to "Vermont Railroad" (sic), presumably pursuant to one of the 1976 agreements. The Preseaults paid "under protest." Much of this activity suggests that, initially at least, the adjacent property owners decided it was cheaper to pay a nominal license fee to the State than to litigate the question of whether the State had the right to extract the fee.In view of all the contrary evidence [1548] of physical abandonment, we find this behavior by the State's revenue collectors unconvincing as persuasive evidence of a purpose or intent not to abandon the use of the right-of-way for actual railroad purposes.

One uncontrovertible piece of evidence in favor of abandonment is that, in the years following the shutting down of the line in 1970 and the 1975 removal of the tracks, no move has been made by the State or by the Railroad to reinstitute service over the line, or to undertake replacement of the removed tracks and other infrastructure necessary to return the line to service. The declarations in the 1985 lease between the State of Vermont, Vermont Railway, and the City of Burlington, which refer to the possible resumption of railroad operations at some undefined time in the future are of course self-serving and not indicative of the facts and circumstances in 1975. Other events occurring after 1975 are also of little probative value.

The trial judge in this case, after extensive recitation of the undisputed facts, and after reviewing cases such as Proctor, concluded that as a fact the Railroad had effected in 1975 an abandonment of the easement running over parcels A, B, and C. Even without giving the trial judge the deference due her, our review of the facts and circumstances leading up to the events of 1975 persuades us that the trial judge is correct. When we accord the trial judge due deference with regard to this factual determination, there is hardly a basis for finding clearly erroneous her conclusion that an abandonment of the easements occurred. . . .

We affirm the determination of the trial court that abandonment of the easements took place in 1975. That determination provides an alternative ground for concluding that a governmental taking occurred.

F. The Taking

The Preseaults had acquired Parcel C, the Manwell Parcel, in 1966. At that time it was still subject to the railroad's easement. In 1975, following the abandonment by the railroad of the easement across Parcel C, the Preseaults owned Parcel C in fee simple free of the encumbering easement. The Preseaults acquired Parcels A and B in 1980. At that time the easement had been extinguished for five years; the parcels they purchased were in fee simple, again free of the encumbrance.

Ten years later, in June 1985, the State of Vermont Agency of Transportation, joined by the Vermont Railway, as lessors, and the City of Burlington as lessee, entered into a lease by which the lessors purported to lease the former right-of-way over Parcels A, B, and C to the City of Burlington for use as a bicycle and pedestrian path.

In due course an eight foot wide paved strip was established on the former right-of-way over Parcels A, B, and C. The path is some 60 feet from the Preseaults' front door. On each side of the Preseaults' driveway, where it crosses the easement, two concrete posts and one metal post were installed to block automobile traffic. The city also erected two stop signs on the path and built a water main under and along the path. The Preseaults have been unable to build on the land under the easement or to construct a driveway connecting their land through Parcels A and B to the nearest public street.

The path is used regularly by members of the public for walking, skating, and bicycle riding. On warm weekends up to two hundred people an hour go through the Preseaults' property. People using the path often trespass on the Preseaults' front yard. On one occasion Mr. Preseault was nearly run over by a cyclist as he walked across the path.

[I]f the Preseaults have interests under state property law that have traditionally been recognized and protected from governmental expropriation, and if, over their objection, the Government chooses to occupy or otherwise acquire those interests, the Fifth Amendment compels compensation. The record establishes two bases on which the Preseaults are entitled to recover.

One, if the easements were in existence in 1986 when, pursuant to ICC Order, the City of Burlington established the public recreational trail, its establishment could not be justified under the terms and within the scope of the existing easements for railroad purposes. The taking of possession of the lands owned by the Preseaults for use as a public trail was in effect a taking of a new easement for that new use, for which the landowners are entitled to compensation. As discussed previously, some courts consider that the establishment of a use outside the scope of an existing easement has the effect of causing an abandonment, and thus termination, of the existing easement. *See, e.g.,* Lawson v. State, 107 Wash. 2d 444, 730 P.2d 1308 (Wash. 1986). Either way, the result is the same—a new easement for the new use, constituting a physical taking of the right of exclusive possession that belonged to the Preseaults.

Two, as an alternative basis, in 1986 when the ICC issued its Order authorizing the City to establish a public recreational biking and pedestrian trail on Parcels A, B, and C, there was as a matter of state law no railroad easement in existence on those parcels, nor had there been for more than ten years. The easement had been abandoned in 1975, and the properties were held by the Preseaults in fee simple, unencumbered by any former property rights of the Railroad. When the City, pursuant to federal authorization, took possession of Parcels A, B, and C and opened them to public use, that was a physical taking of the right of exclusive possession that belonged to the Preseaults as an incident of their ownership of the land.

When the Federal Government puts into play a series of events which result in a taking of private property, the fact that the Government acts through a state agent does not absolve it from the responsibility, and the consequences, of its actions.

Summary and Conclusion

We do not hold that every exercise of authority by the Government under the Rails-to-Trails Act necessarily will result in a compensable taking. Obviously if the railroad owns the right-of-way in fee simple, there is no owner of a separate underlying property interest to claim the rights of the servient estate holder. And even if an easement rather than fee title is the nature of the property interest held by the railroad at the time of the conversion to a public trail, if the terms of the easement when first granted are broad enough under then-existing state law to encompass trail use, the servient estate holder would not be in a position to complain about the use of the easement for a permitted purpose.

Whether, at the time a railroad applies to abandon its use of an easement limited to railroad purposes, a taking occurs under an ICC order to "railbank" the easement for possible future railroad use, and allowing in the interim for use of the easement for trail purposes, is a question not now before us. We offer no opinion at this time on that question. We conclude that the occupation of the Preseaults' property by the City of Burlington under the authority of the Federal Government constituted a taking of their property for which the Constitution requires that just compensation be paid. Neither the Government nor the State of Vermont have demonstrated a valid reason why the Preseaults are not entitled to what the Constitution mandates. The judgment of the Court of Federal Claims, holding the Government not liable, is reversed. The matter is remanded to that court for further proceedings consistent with this opinion.

Reversed and remanded.

C. Introduction to Covenants Running with the Land as Another Form of Servitude

The initial focus of this course was on possession and how it defines a property interest. The last material we covered, easements, moved us into the nonpossessory interest realm. We saw how someone could be granted the right to use the property of another without having possession and without having fee ownership. The easement was the first form of servitude created because it involved use of another's property. Now we move even further away from possession and use with the concept of the covenant running with the land (or covenant). The covenant developed later in time as a nonpossessory interest in land that does not even involve the right to use land. It does, however, give one landowner the ability to dictate how another landowner can make use of land.

This material ties in several different concepts. In the chapter on leaseholds, the topic of assignments and subleases arose in looking at the right to transfer sticks in the leasehold bundle. In that chapter, the focus was on the relationship of the parties after an assignment or sublease and the ability of a landlord to restrict the tenant's right to transfer. In this chapter, the law of covenants will explain how some promises and rights will continue on to successor tenants and landlords not based on contractual principles but on property law principles. This chapter also relates to the easement material as this is another form of servitude. As the covenant originally developed in the freehold context it was referred to as a negative easement. As that application did not work well, the covenant was formed. Additionally, this chapter will explore the creation of covenants as they relate to property that is subject to a freehold form of ownership. It will also consider what is required for enforcement and how the covenants may ultimately be terminated.

In order to understand how covenants work today, we must understand their origins, creation, and required elements for enforcement.

1. Historical Background of Covenants

a. Development and Application with the Leasehold

The original application of the property law of covenants arose in the leasehold context. Only one parcel of land was involved, but two different estates in land existed. The landlord held the reversion in fee simple while the tenant held some form of present possessory tenancy—term of years, periodic tenancy, or the tenancy at will. The original lease agreement between the landlord and tenant is a contract that contains promises made by the landlord and tenant. If the original landlord and tenant have a dispute, there is potential liability based on the contractual relationship and also based on property law principles related to the leasehold. But we also explored the sublease and assignment where a new party comes into possession of the premises without entering into a lease agreement with the original landlord. There is no contractual relationship between them, so in order to have promises burdening the new tenant, the property law of covenant applies. Additionally, if the original landlord sells the leased premises, the original tenant or an assignee does not enter into a new lease agreement. However, the tenant will want to enforce the original landlord's promises of making repairs and keeping the premises in a habitable condition. That is where the property law of covenants comes in again.

In its basic application, the law of covenants will allow a party who did not personally agree to the promise at issue to be held responsible for it. Does that seem fair? In some instances it would not be. That is why the law of covenants has many required elements depending on the parties to the dispute and the relief sought. Additionally, the nature of the promise will be closely examined to make sure that the right types of obligations will "run with the land" to a successor landlord or tenant. The following case provides an illustration of the distinction between assignments and subleases, which ties back to Chapter 3. It also helps us to examine the law of covenants in its original context of landlord and tenant.

Ernst v. Conditt
Court of Appeals of Tennessee, 1964
390 S.W.2d 703

CHATTIN, J.

Complainants, B. Walter Ernst and wife, Emily Ernst, leased a certain tract of land in Davidson County, Tennessee, to Frank D. Rogers on June 18, 1960, for a term of one year and seven days, commencing on June 23, 1960.

Rogers went into possession of the property and constructed an asphalt race track and enclosed the premises with a fence. He also constructed other improvements thereon such as floodlights for use in the operation of a Go-Cart track.

We quote those paragraphs of the lease pertinent to the question for consideration in this controversy:

> 3. Lessee covenants to pay as rent for said leased premises the sum of $4,200 per annum, payable at the rate of $350 per month or 15% of all gross receipts, whether from sales or services occurring on the leased premises, whichever is the larger amount. The gross receipts shall be computed on a quarterly basis and if any amount in addition to the $350 per month is due, such payment shall be made immediately after the quarterly computation. All payments shall be payable to the office of Lessors' agent, Guaranty Mortgage Company, at 316 Union Street, Nashville, Tennessee, on the first day of each month in advance. Lessee shall have the first right of refusal in the event Lessors desire to lease said premises for a period of time commencing immediately after the termination date hereof.
>
> 5. Lessee shall have no right to assign or sublet the leased premises without prior written approval of Lessors. In the event

[handwritten margin note: RELEVANT PARTS OF LEASE]

of any assignment or sublease, Lessee is still liable to perform the covenants of this lease, including the covenant to pay rent, and nothing herein shall be construed as releasing Lessee from his liabilities and obligations hereunder.

9. Lessee agrees that upon termination of this contract, or any extensions or renewals thereof, that all improvements above the ground will be moved at Lessee's expense and the property cleared. This shall not be construed as removing or digging up any surface paving; but if any pits or holes are dug, they shall be leveled at Lessors' request.

Rogers operated the business for a short time. In July, 1960, he entered into negotiations with the defendant, A. K. Conditt, for the sale of the business to him. During these negotiations, the question of the term of the lease arose. Defendant desired a two-year lease of the property. He and Rogers went to the home of complainants and negotiated an extension of the term of the lease which resulted in the following amendment to the lease, and the sublease or assignment of the lease as amended to Conditt by Rogers:

By mutual consent of the parties, the lease executed the 18th day of June 1960, between B. Walter Ernst and wife, Emily H. Ernst, as Lessors, and Frank G. Rogers as Lessee, is amended as follows:

1. Paragraph 2 of said lease is amended so as to provide that the term will end July 31, 1962 and not June 30, 1961.

2. The minimum rent of $350 per month called for in paragraph 3 of said lease shall be payable by the month and the percentage rental called for by said lease shall be payable on the first day of the month following the month for which the percentage is computed. In computing gross receipts, no deduction or credit shall be given the Lessee for the payment of sales taxes or any other assessments by governmental agencies.

3. Lessee agrees that on or prior to April 1, 1961, the portion of the property covered by this lease, consisting of about one acre, which is not presently devoted to business purposes will be used for business purposes and the percentage rent called for by paragraph 3 of the original lease will be paid on the gross receipts derived therefrom. In the event of the failure of the Lessee to devote the balance of said property to a business purpose on or before April 1, 1961, then this lease shall terminate as to such portion of the property.

4. Lessee agrees to save the Lessor harmless for any damage to the property of the Lessor, whether included in this lease or not, which results from the use of the leased property by the Lessee or its customers or invitees. Lessee will erect or cause to be erected four (4) 'No Parking' signs on the adjoining property of the Lessor not leased by it.

5. Lessor hereby consents to the subletting of the premises to A. K. Conditt, but upon the express condition and understanding that the original Lessee, Frank D. Rogers, will remain personally liable for the faithful performance of all the terms and conditions of the original lease and of this amendment to the original lease.

Except as modified by this amendment, all terms and conditions of the original lease dated the 18th day of June, 1960, by and between the parties shall remain in full force and effect.

In witness whereof the parties have executed this amendment to lease on this the 4 day of August, 1960.

B. Walter Ernst
Emily H. Ernest
Lessors
Frank D. Rogers
Lessee

For value received and in consideration of the promise to faithfully perform all conditions of the within lease as amended, I hereby sublet the premises to A. K. Conditt upon the understanding that I will individually remain liable for the performance of the lease.

Frank D. Rogers
Frank D. Rogers

The foregoing subletting of the premises is accepted, this the 4 day of Aug, 1960.

A. K. Conditt
A. K. Conditt

Conditt operated the Go-Cart track from August until November, 1960. He paid the rent for the months of August, September and October, 1960, directly to complainants. In December, 1960, complainants contacted defendant with reference to the November rent and at that time defendant stated he had been advised he was not liable to them for rent. However, defendant paid the basic monthly rental of $350.00 to complainants in June, 1961. This was the final payment received by complainants during the term of the lease as amended. The record is not clear whether defendant continued to operate the business after the last payment of rent or abandoned it. Defendant, however, remained in possession of the property until the expiration of the leasehold.

On July 10, 1962, complainants, through their Attorneys, notified Conditt by letter the lease would expire as of midnight July 31, 1962; and they were demanding a settlement of the past due rent and unless the improvements on the property were removed by him as provided in paragraph 9 of the original lease; then, in that event, they would have same removed at his expense. Defendant did not reply to this demand.

On August 1, 1962, complainants filed their bill in this cause seeking a recovery of $2,404.58 which they alleged was the balance due on the basic rent of $350.00 per month for the first year of the lease and the sum of $4,200.00, the basic rent for the second year, and the further sum necessary for the removal of the improvements constructed on the property.

The theory of the bill is that the agreement between Rogers, the original lessee, and the defendant, Conditt, is an assignment of the lease; and, therefore, defendant is directly and primarily liable to complainants.

The defendant by his answer insists the agreement between Rogers and himself is a sublease and therefore Rogers is directly and primarily liable to complainants.

The Chancellor found the instrument to be an assignment. A decree was entered sustaining the bill and entering judgment for complainants in the sum of $6,904.58 against defendant.

Defendant has appealed to this Court and has assigned errors insisting the Chancellor erred in failing to hold the instrument to be a sublease rather than an assignment.

To support his theory the instrument is a sublease, the defendant insists the amendment to the lease entered into between Rogers and complainants was for the express purpose of extending the term of the lease and obtaining the consent of the lessors to a "subletting" of the premises to defendant. That by the use of the words "sublet" and "subletting" no other construction can be placed on the amendment and the agreement of Rogers and the acceptance of defendant attached thereto.

Further since complainants agreed to the subletting of the premises to defendant "upon the express condition and understanding that the original lessee, Frank D. Rogers, will remain personally liable for the faithful performance of all the terms and conditions of the original lease and this amendment to the original lease," no construction can be placed upon this language other than it was the intention of complainants to hold Rogers primarily liable for the performance of the original lease and the amendment thereto. And, therefore,

Rogers, for his own protection, would have the implied right to re-enter and perform the lease in the event of a default on the part of the defendant. This being true, Rogers retained a reversionary interest in the property sufficient to satisfy the legal distinction between a sublease and an assignment of a lease.

It is then urged the following rules of construction of written instruments support the above argument:

> Where words or terms having a definite legal meaning and effect are knowingly used in a written instrument the parties thereto will be presumed to have intended such words or terms to have their proper legal meaning and effect, in the absence of any contrary intention appearing in the instrument. [12 Am. Jur., Contracts, Section 238.]
>
> Technical terms or words of art will be given their technical meaning unless the context, or local usage shows a contrary intention. [3 Williston on Contracts, Section 68, Sub. S. 2.]

As stated in complainants' brief, the liability of defendant to complainants depends upon whether the transfer of the leasehold interest in the premises from Rogers is an assignment of the lease or a sublease. If the transfer is a sublease, no privity of contract [or privity of estate] exists between complainants and defendant; and, therefore, defendant could not be liable to complainants on the covenant to pay rent and the expense of the removal of the improvements. But, if the transfer is an assignment of the lease, [privity of estate] does exist between complainants and defendant; and defendant would be liable directly and primarily for the amount of the judgment. [While there would still be no privity of contract, only one of the relationships is necessary to establish liability.]

The general rule as to the distinction between an assignment of a lease and a sublease is an assignment conveys the whole term, leaving no interest nor reversionary interest in the grantor or assignor. Whereas, a sublease may be generally defined as a transaction whereby a tenant grants an interest in the leased premises less than his own, or reserves to himself a reversionary interest in the term.

The common law distinction between an assignment of a lease and a sublease is succinctly stated in the case of Jaber v. Miller, 239 S.W.2d 760: "If the instrument purports to transfer the lessee's estate for the entire remainder of his term it is an assignment, regardless of its form or of the parties' intention. Conversely, if the instrument purports to transfer the lessee's estate for less than the entire term—even for a day less—it is a sublease, regardless of its form or of the parties' intention."

The modern rule which has been adopted in this State for construing written instruments is stated in the case of City of Nashville v. Lawrence, 284 S.W. 882:

"The cardinal rule to be followed in this state, in construing deeds and other written instruments, is to ascertain the intention of the parties."

It is our opinion under either the common law or modern rule of construction the agreement between Rogers and defendant is an assignment of the lease.

The fact that Rogers expressly agreed to remain liable to complainants for the performance of the lease did not create a reversion nor a right to re-enter in Rogers either express or implied. The obligations and liabilities of a lessee to a lessor, under the express covenants of a lease, are not in anywise affected by an assignment or a subletting to a third party, in the absence of an express or implied agreement or some action on his part which amounts to a waiver or estops him from insisting upon compliance with the covenants. This is true even though the assignment or sublease is made with the consent of the lessor. By an assignment of a lease the privity of estate between the lessor and lessee is terminated, but the privity of contract between them still remains and is unaffected. Neither the privity of estate or contract between the lessor and lessee are affected by a sublease.

Thus, the express agreement of Rogers to remain personally liable for the performance of the covenants of the lease created no greater obligation on his part or interest in the leasehold, other than as set forth in the original lease.

The argument that since the agreement between Rogers and defendant contains the words, "sublet" and "subletting" is conclusive the instrument is to be construed as a sublease is, we think, unsound.

> A consent to sublet has been held to include the consent to assign or mortgage the lease; and a consent to assign has been held to authorize a subletting. [51 C.J.S. Landlord and Tenant § 36, page 552.]

Prior to the consummation of the sale of the Go-Cart business to defendant, he insisted upon the execution of the amendment to the lease extending the term of the original lease. For value received and on the promise of the defendant to perform all of the conditions of the lease as amended, Rogers parted with his entire interest in the property. Defendant went into possession of the property and paid the rent to complainants. He remained in possession of the property for the entire term. By virtue of the sale of the business, defendant became the owner of the improvements with the right to their removal at the expiration of the lease.

Rogers reserved no part or interest in the lease; nor did he reserve a right of re-entry in event of a breach of any of the conditions or covenants of the lease on the part of defendant.

It is our opinion the defendant under the terms of the agreement with Rogers, had a right to the possession of the property for the entire term of the lease as amended, including the right to remove the improvements after the expiration of the lease. Rogers merely agreed to become personally liable for the rent and the expense of the removal of the improvements upon the default of defendant. He neither expressly, nor by implication, reserved the right to re-enter for a condition broken by defendant.

Thus, we are of the opinion the use of the words, "sublet" and "subletting" is not conclusive of the construction to be placed on the instrument in this case; it plainly appearing from the context of the instrument and the facts and circumstances surrounding the execution of it the parties thereto intended an assignment rather than a sublease.

It results the assignments are overruled and the decree of the Chancellor is affirmed with costs.

NOTES & PROBLEMS:

1. Why would Rogers have signed the lease amendment with Ernst that specifically stated that he would continue to remain liable under the lease? Whether he signed such an agreement or not, that is a correct statement of his liability. When the landlord and tenant enter into a lease agreement they have a relationship based on a contract, or privity of contract. That relationship continues until the agreement ends or the landlord agrees to release the tenant from the obligation, which the landlord will almost never do. This means that regardless of an assignment or sublease situation the original tenant will always remain liable to the landlord unless the landlord specifically agrees to terminate the contractual relationship.

2. Although Ernst could have sued Rogers, he wanted to go directly after Conditt as that was the party who was in possession and should be responsible for the obligations. However, in looking at the series of documents in this case, no document was ever directly entered into between Ernst and Conditt. Additionally, Conditt did not expressly agree to take the assignment subject to the terms of the original lease. Had Conditt made such a promise, under the contract doctrine of the third-party beneficiary Ernst could make the argument that such a promise was really for his benefit, not Rogers, and thus there would be a privity of contract.

   Without such a relationship the difference between an assignment and a sublease is critical because we must look to estate principles to find where privity of estate exists. Privity of estate is one of the elements essential to the covenant analysis when a real covenant is being enforced. In this case Mr. and Mrs. Ernst were seeking monetary damages from the breach of the covenant—past due rent and the cost of removing the improvements from the property. The correct privity relationship had to exist to be able to impose liability.

In an assignment, the original tenant is transferring all of his interest to the new tenant. In this case, Conditt was stepping into Rogers's shoes on the timeline. He would now hold the present possessory estate that would come to an end and allow Ernst to retake possession under his reversion.

In a sublease, the situation is very different. In a sublease, Rogers would have been taking his present possessory term of years and dividing it up into a shorter present possessory estate carved out for Conditt, and Rogers would actually have a reversion in his original term of years. That means that the initial timeline would not be disturbed and the estate-based relationship would remain between Ernest and Rogers. Therefore, in a sublease the landlord and sublessee do not have privity of estate or privity of contract unless the third-party beneficiary doctrine comes into play.

The principles developed hundreds of years ago still remain today. They were imported into the freehold system, and we will now turn to the historical development in that context.

b. Development and Application with the Freehold

The covenant has been stretched well beyond its origins to the common interest communities that have developed in the past 40 or 50 years. Think of all the orderly residential subdivisions that exist today. They exist, in part, due to the creation of the covenant. However, its origin was much simpler than and more limited than what is involved today in a residential subdivision or master-planned community.

In addition to being classified as a nonpossessory property interest, covenants are also private law devices that allow for limitations and controls to be placed on the use of land. For example, the covenant may prevent land from being used for something other than residential purposes; may dictate the architectural requirements of a structure built on the property; they may even control the number of pets you have on the property or how long your Christmas lights can be displayed.

The concept of the covenant is similar to the public law concept of zoning. With zoning laws, a governmental body dictates how land in a certain area may be used—residential, business, mixed use—and even further delineates use within those categories. The most commonly disputed area of zoning law is the regulation of the "sexually oriented business" or SOB. Zoning laws exist in many places and provide a baseline of use regulation. However, the private restrictive covenant can come in and even further define regulations on use as long as they are not discriminatory or in violation of public policy.

Zoning laws and covenants can work together. For example, an area may be zoned as residential, but then a certain area subject to covenants dictates that those residences must be single-family residences only, they must be a certain square footage, they must be constructed of all brick or stone, and the garages may not face the front of the house. Covenants can also do the job of zoning laws where no such laws exist. For example, the city of Houston, Texas, prides itself on having no zoning laws. All of the regulation of land use in the city is done privately through covenants.

So, where did all of this begin? We return again to the late 1500s and early 1600s when industrialization and urbanization were on the rise. Old McDonald had his 2,000-acre farm and he no longer had the need for all of the acreage. He decided to sell off 1,000 acres. However, Old McDonald is going to continue living on and farming the acreage he retains. He is concerned that with all of the new industry happening he might end up next to some smelly factory or really loud industry. He wants to make sure that does not happen. He could get a written agreement with the person he sells the land to originally, but what if the land is later sold again? When Old McDonald eventually sells or devises his other 1,000 acres he would like to provide assurances to his successors that they also will not be bothered by some loud or smelly factory. He does not want the land back if condition on use were violated, so a defeasible fee estate is not a desirable option. What can he do?

This is where covenants developed in the freehold estate system. However, unlike the leasehold estates, there are two parcels of land with separate estates. There was nothing in place to allow for the type of restrictions that Old McDonald wanted to place on the land. The only nonpossessory interest that existed was that of easements. However, easements are different. Recall, in the context of easements one person was being given the right to use the land of another. Old McDonald does not want to grant the right to use his land, he wants to convey the land in fee simple but restrict its use. Also, the easements involve affirmative promises—you can drive across my land, you can have your sewer line, you can walk across the path. The promise Old McDonald wants to extract is a negative one—you cannot build a factory, you cannot do anything with the land other than use it for agricultural or residential purposes.

The courts developed the concept of the negative easement. The negative easement did not work well. The English courts recognized four types of negative easements, which included the right to stop your neighbor from: (1) blocking your windows; (2) interfering with a defined channel of air flow to your land; (3) removing support of your building by excavating or removing a supporting wall; and (4) interfering with the natural flow of water. These negative easements made sense at the time. There was no electricity and no public utilities like we have today. People depended on natural light and air to be able to live. They needed a natural flow of water.[9]

While these negative easements were somewhat helpful they did not solve Old McDonald's problem. They were also troublesome because of the differences in the nature of the promises. With easements that involve affirmative promises, a subsequent landowner could discover even absent a written document that there was a burden on the land in the form of an easement. However, with a negative promise (to refrain from doing something) it would be difficult, if not impossible to discover such a negative obligation without a written document. And with the law of easements, there are several ways to establish an easement without a written document. A specific problem in this context was the prescriptive easement. It would be possible for a landowner to claim that since something had not been done on the land for 20 years it could not ever be done. There were other concerns and objections raised that ultimately led to the end of the expansion of negative easements.

The negative easement did transfer to the United States only with the four recognized in England and appears to also be a nonexpanding legal concept. However, there have been a few additional negative easements added in the U.S. legal system. Some western states have recognized an easement of unobstructed view. There have also been solar easements recognized. A more common form of negative easement created by statute is the conservation easement.[10] With the development of the law of covenants there really is no need to continue to expand the negative easement.

---

[9] The prohibition against damaging your neighbor's lateral and subjacent support still exists today and strict liability arises if it occurs.

[10] Conservation easements are growing in popularity across the United States. Conservation easements are created by statute and are really a hybrid of the characteristics of both the easement and the covenant.

2. Analyzing Covenants Running with the Land

a. Elements Generally Applicable to the Analysis

Covenants start as contractual promises made between parties. These promises may be affirmative promises to do something, but most likely are negative promises to refrain from doing something. The negative promise was most easily accepted by the courts and the affirmative promise was looked at with a little more scrutiny by the courts. Affirmative covenants are still examined more closely by courts; however, affirmative covenants of the right nature are enforceable today.

Because a covenant is an interest in real property, the covenants must be in writing. Unlike the easement, there are not a variety of methods to create a covenant without a written document. There is only one limited exception to the requirement of a promise in writing and it will only work in the context of the subdivision. This will be developed more in the coming material. The written promise may be in a lease agreement, a deed, a signed agreement among the parties involved, or in a subdivision plat.

The intent element is subjective, but as with all subjective concepts, we look for objective evidence of subjective intent. In this context, the court looks at the language of the agreement for evidence of intent. Language indicating that the promise is "for the benefit of A, his successors, and assigns" would indicate intent for the benefit to run with the land. Additionally, language stating that the promise is "intended to burden the grantee, his successor and assigns" would be language of intent for the burden to run with the land. However, if there is no evidence for or against intent, this element will be implied if all other needed elements are satisfied.

"Touch and concern" is the one element that looks at the substance of the promise. This is the way the law prevents personal promises from becoming part of the land and burdening subsequent owners. The touch-and-concern element has been defined in different ways over time. Originally, the touch-and-concern element looked for promises that impacted the physical use of the land. Does the promise exercise direct influence on the occupation, use, or enjoyment of the burdened premises that results in a benefit to other real property? Remember Old McDonald's desire to prevent the smelly factor from being next to his land. The original touch-and-concern element allowed promises such as residential use only, agricultural use only, or only single-family residences. This impacted the land ownership and the actual use of the land itself.

However, over time the touch-and-concern element began to change and stretch somewhat. A more modern definition of touch and concern has evolved to be: Does the promise enhance the value of the dominant estate and does the burden detract from the value of the servient estate? Is there a legal obligation imposed on the servient estate that enhances the value of the dominant estate? Keep in mind this change of definition as we explore the cases below. This change in definition has allowed the role of the covenant to expand and has helped created the residential subdivision.

The next element—notice—is involved only when considering the burden of a real covenant or equitable servitude. The concept of notice is introduced here in its most basic form. This concept will be visited in depth later in the course when addressing recording statutes. The basic premise with this element is that the party who takes the servient estate either knows or had some opportunity to find out about the promise burdening the land. The relevant period in time to determine notice is the time when the landowner took title to the land. This is not a common law element for real covenants. The notice concept arose with the recording statutes that exist in all 50 states. For the equitable servitude, in Tulk v. Moxhay, the next case in the text, the court of equity required notice as an element of an equitable servitude burden.

The final elements are horizontal and vertical privity. These elements focus on two different relationships and different points in time. Horizontal privity is only a part of the analysis of a real covenant burden. Horizontal privity focuses on the original promisor and promisee. No matter how many successors removed, the analysis of horizontal privity goes back to the beginning. The majority inquiry for horizontal privity is that horizontal privity exists if the promisee and promisor have some shared interest in the land in addition to the promise itself.[11]

The final element is vertical privity. Vertical privity focuses on the relationship of the original promisor or promisee and his successor. There are two standards for vertical privity. If looking to see if the burden of a real covenant will run, there must be full vertical privity between the original promisor and the successor promisor. This means that the successor must have succeeded to the entire estate of the original promisor. For the benefit of a real covenant to run, the successor promisee must have only succeeded to part of the original promisee's estate. Therefore, if the original promisee had a fee simple and the successor promisee has a life estate, that is sufficient for partial vertical privity. However, if the original promisor had a fee simple and the successor promisee only has a life estate, there is not full vertical privity for the burden to run.

As a starting point in the analysis, it is important to consider the parties involved in the dispute and what role they played in the formulation of the promises. When looking at the original promisor (person taking on the obligation,

---

[11] The English rule for horizontal privity is that horizontal privity only exists in a landlord and tenant relationship because there is a close relationship of two estates in one parcel of land. This means that still in England today, a real covenant cannot be enforced in a situation that involves two freehold estates. But, horizontal privity is not required for an equitable servitude so that type of enforcement does exist in the freehold estate context.

burden) and promisee (the person receiving the benefit of the promise), there is no need to look to the property law of covenants. Property law steps in once land has been conveyed and either one or both of the original parties are no longer involved.

There are different combinations that can establish the framework of a dispute. There could be:

(1) original promisor v. original promisee = contract law
(2) original promisor v. successor promisee = does the benefit run
(3) successor promisor v. original promisee = does the burden run
(4) successor promisor v. successor promisee = does the benefit run and does the burden run

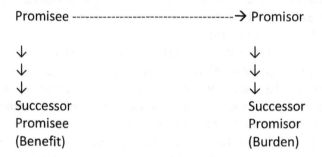

Promisee -----------------------------------→ Promisor

↓   ↓
↓   ↓
↓   ↓
Successor   Successor
Promisee   Promisor
(Benefit)   (Burden)

While any form of dispute can occur, the dispute between successors to the promisor and promisee are the most common. The promises are in place and many years later parties have a dispute. Then the law must determine if it is appropriate to burden someone with a promise he did not make for the benefit of someone who did not secure the promise. That is the idea of the burden and benefit running with the land. The promise must be of such a nature and made in such a manner so that the law can determine that the promise has become a part of the land itself.

b. Real Covenants vs. Equitable Servitudes

The other consideration in properly analyzing the burden and benefit is determining what the party wants as a remedy when bringing the action. Unlike the freehold and leasehold estates, where the focus was on particular words to distinguish between different classifications, with the covenant the distinguishing factor is the relief sought. Thinking back to Texas Electric Railway v. Neale, the court initially had to determine the classification of the interest based on the language in the deed. The court's conclusion was that the deed conveyed a fee simple absolute and the additional language about using the land as a railroad right-of-way was possibly a covenant. It would have been a contractual promise between the original grantor and grantee in the deed, but in the case the court was dealing with successors to the railroad as well as heirs of the original grantors. The court did not go any further with the discussion of the language as a covenant because that was not raised in the case. If Neale then wanted to bring a claim based on breach of covenant because the railroad was no longer using the land as a railroad right-of-way, then the next determination would be what Neale wanted as a remedy. The distinction between real covenant and equitable servitude would not come from language in the deed but from Neale's desired relief.

If the plaintiff is seeking recovery of damages for the diminished fair market value of his land due to the covenant violation then the covenant must be able to be enforced as a real covenant or covenant-at-law. If the plaintiff is seeking injunctive relief to require the burdened party to comply, then the covenant must be able to be enforced as an equitable servitude. In going through the analysis for the benefit and burden of a real covenant, there will be more elements involved and it will be more difficult. The view is that if someone is going to have to pay monetary damages for violating a promise he did not make, there must be specific circumstances under property law to allow that to happen. However, if the desired relief is an injunction, the analysis of a benefit or burden of an equitable servitude is easier with fewer elements. This makes sense because the benefit is a plus not a minus. However, to be entitled to monetary relief there must be more specific circumstances than just to receive the equitable benefit of an injunction.

The elements required for each analysis are as set forth in the chart below.

Real Covenant Burden	Real Covenant Benefit	Equitable Servitude Burden	Equitable Servitude Benefit
Written Promise	Written Promise	Written Promise	Written Promise
Intent	Intent	Intent	Intent
Touch & Concern	Touch & Concern	Touch & Concern	Touch & Concern
Notice		Notice	
Horizontal Privity			
Full Vertical Privity	Partial Vertical Privity		

*Notice: No privity requirements for the equitable servitude.

c. Applying the Analysis of the Real Covenant and Equitable Servitude

Tulk v. Moxhay
Court of Chancery, England, 1848
2 Phillips 774, 41 Eng. Rep. 1143

In the year 1808 the Plaintiff, being then the owner in fee of the vacant piece of ground in Leicester Square, as well as of several of the houses forming the Square, sold the piece of ground by the description of "Leicester Square garden or pleasure ground, with the equestrian statue then standing in the centre thereof, and the iron railing and stone work round the same," to one Elms in fee: and the deed of conveyance contained a covenant by Elms, for himself, his heirs, and assigns, with the Plaintiff, his heirs, executors, and administrators,

Covenant

that Elms, his heirs, and assigns should, and would from time to time, and at all times thereafter at his and their own costs and charges, keep and maintain the said piece of ground and square garden, and the iron railing round the same in its then form, and in sufficient and proper repair as a square garden and pleasure ground, in an open state, uncovered with any buildings, in neat and ornamental order; and that it should be lawful for the inhabitants of Leicester Square, tenants of the Plaintiff, on payment of a reasonable rent for the same, to have keys at their own expense and the privilege of admission therewith at any time or times into the said square garden and pleasure ground.

The piece of land so conveyed passed by divers mesne conveyances into the hands of the Defendant, whose purchase deed contained no similar covenant with his vendor: but he admitted that he had purchased with notice of the covenant in the deed of 1808.

The Defendant having manifested an intention to alter the character of the square garden, and asserted a right, if he thought fit, to build upon it, the Plaintiff, who still remained owner of several houses in the square, filed this bill for an injunction; and an injunction was granted by the Master of the Rolls to restrain the Defendant from converting or using the piece of ground and square garden, and the iron railing round the same, to or for any other purpose than as a square garden and pleasure ground in an open state, and uncovered with buildings.

On a motion, now made, to discharge that order, Mr. R. Palmer, for the Defendant, contended that the covenant did not run with the land, so as to be binding at law upon a purchaser from the covenantor, and he relied on the dictum of Lord Brougham C. in Keppell v. Bayley, to the effect that notice of such a covenant did not give a Court of Equity jurisdiction to enforce it by injunction against such purchaser, inasmuch as "the knowledge by an assignee of an estate, that his assignor had assumed to bind others than the law authorized him to affect by his contract had attempted to create a burden upon property which was inconsistent with the nature of that property, and unknown to the principles of the law could not bind such assignee by affecting his conscience." In applying that doctrine to the present case, he drew a distinction between a formal covenant as this was, and a contract existing in mere agreement, and requiring some further act to carry it into effect; contending that executory contracts of the latter description were alone such as were binding in equity upon purchasers with notice; for that where the contract between the parties was executed in the form of a covenant, their mutual rights and liabilities were determined by the legal operation of that instrument, and that if a Court of Equity were to give a more extended operation to such covenant, it would be giving the party that for which he had never contracted.

Rule

[12]

THE LORD CHANCELLOR [Cottenham]

That this Court has jurisdiction to enforce a contract between the owner of land and his neighbour purchasing a part of it, that the latter shall either use or abstain from using the land purchased in a particular way, is what I never knew disputed. Here there is no question about the contract: the owner of certain houses in the square sells the land adjoining, with a covenant from the purchaser not to use it for any other purpose than as a square garden. And it is now

---

[12]   Redeveloped   Leicester   Square   in   London,   UK. https://en.wikipedia.org/wiki/Leicester_Square#/media/File:Redeveloped_Leicester_Sq uare.jpg. Uploaded by Romazur, July 11, 2012.

contended, not that the vendee could violate that contract, but that he might sell the piece of land, and that the purchaser from him may violate it without this Court having any power to interfere. If that were so, it would be impossible for an owner of land to sell part of it without incurring the risk of rendering what he retains worthless. It is said that, the covenant being one which does not run with the land, this Court cannot enforce it; but the question is, not whether the covenant runs with the land, but whether a party shall be permitted to use the land in a manner inconsistent with the contract entered into by his vendor, and with notice of which he purchased. Of course, the price would be affected by the covenant, and nothing could be more inequitable than that the original purchaser should be able to sell the property the next day for a greater price, in consideration of the assignee being allowed to escape from the liability which he had himself undertaken.

That the question does not depend upon whether the covenant runs with the land is evident from this, that if there was a mere agreement and no covenant, this Court would enforce it against a party purchasing with notice of it; for if an equity is attached to the property by the owner, no one purchasing with notice of that equity can stand in a different situation from the party from whom he purchased.

With respect to the observations of Lord Brougham in Keppell v. Bailey, he never could have meant to lay down that this Court would not enforce an equity attached to land by the owner, unless under such circumstances as would maintain an action at law. If that be the result of his observations, I can only say that I cannot coincide with it.

I think the cases cited before the Vice-Chancellor and this decision of the Master of the Rolls perfectly right, and, therefore, that this motion must be refused, with costs.

NOTES & QUESTIONS:

1. Tulk v. Moxay was the birth of the equitable servitude. The promise could not be enforced as a real covenant and thus the only choice was to try for some equitable relief. What was the element that prevented enforcement of a real covenant burden?

2. Now consider which elements are involved in the following case. *Neponsit* is another groundbreaking case. Identify the elements at issue and consider why the court's decision here had such an important impact on the use of covenants today.

Neponsit Property Owners' Association, Inc. v. Emigrant Industrial Savings Bank

Court of Appeals of New York, 1938

15 N.E.2d 793

LEHMAN, J.

The plaintiff, as assignee of Neponsit Realty Company, has brought this action to foreclose a lien upon land which the defendant owns. The lien, it is alleged, arises from a covenant, condition or charge contained in a deed of conveyance of the land from Neponsit Realty Company to a predecessor in title of the defendant. The defendant purchased the land at a judicial sale. The referee's deed to the defendant and every deed in the defendant's chain of title since the conveyance of the land by Neponsit Realty Company purports to convey the property subject to the covenant, condition or charge contained in the original deed.

It appears that in January, 1911, Neponsit Realty Company, as owner of a tract of land in Queens county, caused to be filed in the office of the clerk of the county a map of the land. The tract was developed for a strictly residential community, and Neponsit Realty Company conveyed lots in the tract to purchasers, describing such lots by reference to the filed map and to roads and streets shown thereon. In 1917, Neponsit Realty Company conveyed the land now owned by the defendant to Robert Oldner Deyer and his wife by deed which contained the covenant upon which the plaintiff's cause of action is based.

That covenant provides:

> "And the party of the second part for the party of the second part and the heirs, successors and assigns of the party of the second part further covenants that the property conveyed by this deed shall be subject to an annual charge in such an amount as will be fixed by the party of the first part, its successors and assigns, not, however exceeding in any year the sum of four ($4.00) Dollars per lot 20 x 100 feet. The assigns of the party of the first part may include a Property Owners' Association which may hereafter be organized for the purposes referred to in this paragraph, and in case such association is organized the sums in this paragraph provided for shall be payable to such association. The party of the second part for the party of the second part and the heirs, successors and assigns of the party of the second part covenants that they will pay this charge to the party of the first part, its successors and assigns on the first day of May in each and every year, and further covenants that said charge shall on said date in each year become a lien on the land and shall

continue to be such lien until fully paid. Such charge shall be payable to the party of the first part or its successors or assigns, and shall be devoted to the maintenance of the roads, paths, parks, beach, sewers and such other public purposes as shall from time to time be determined by the party of the first part, its successors or assigns. And the party of the second part by the acceptance of this deed hereby expressly vests in the party of the first part, its successors and assigns, the right and power to bring all actions against the owner of the premises hereby conveyed or any part thereof for the collection of such charge and to enforce the aforesaid lien therefor.

These covenants shall run with the land and shall be construed as real covenants running with the land until January 31st, 1940, when they shall cease and determine.

Every subsequent deed of conveyance of the property in the defendant's chain of title, including the deed from the referee to the defendant, contained, as we have said, a provision that they were made subject to covenants and restrictions of former deeds of record.

There can be no doubt that Neponsit Realty Company intended that the covenant should run with the land and should be enforceable by a property owners association against every owner of property in the residential tract which the realty company was then developing. The language of the covenant admits of no other construction.

Regardless of the intention of the parties, a covenant will run with the land and will be enforceable against a subsequent purchaser of the land at the suit of one who claims the benefit of the covenant, only if the covenant complies with certain legal requirements. These requirements rest upon ancient rules and precedents. The age-old essentials of a real covenant, aside from the form of the covenant, may be summarily formulated as follows: (1) it must appear that grantor and grantee intended that the covenant should run with the land; (2) it must appear that the covenant is one "touching" or "concerning" the land with which it runs; (3) it must appear that there is "privity of estate" between the promisee or party claiming the benefit of the covenant and the right to enforce it, and the promisor or party who rests under the burden of the covenant. Although the deeds of Neponsit Realty Company conveying lots in the tract it developed "contained a provision to the effect that the covenants ran with the land, such provision in the absence of the other legal requirements is insufficient to accomplish such a purpose." (Morgan Lake Co. v. N. Y., N. H. & H. R. R. Co., 262 N. Y. 234, 238.) In his opinion in that case, Judge Crane posed but found it unnecessary to decide many of the questions which the court must consider in this case.

The covenant in this case is intended to create a charge or obligation to pay a fixed sum of money to be "devoted to the maintenance of the roads, paths, parks, beach, sewers and such other public purposes as shall from time to time be determined by the party of the first part [the grantor], its successors or assigns." It is an affirmative covenant to pay money for use in connection with, but not upon, the land which it is said is subject to the burden of the covenant. Does such a covenant "touch" or "concern" the land? These terms are not part of a statutory definition, a limitation placed by the State upon the power of the courts to enforce covenants intended to run with the land by the parties who entered into the covenants. Rather they are words used by courts in England in old cases to describe a limitation which the courts themselves created or to formulate a test which the courts have devised and which the courts voluntarily apply. In truth the test so formulated is too vague to be of much assistance and judges and academic scholars alike have struggled, not with entire success, to formulate a test at once more satisfactory and more accurate. "It has been found impossible to state any absolute tests to determine what covenants touch and concern land and what do not. The question is one for the court to determine in the exercise of its best judgment upon the facts of each case." (Clark, op. cit. p. 76.)

Even though that be true, a determination by a court in one case upon particular facts will often serve to point the way to correct decision in other cases upon analogous facts. Such guideposts may not be disregarded. It has been often said that a covenant to pay a sum of money is a personal affirmative covenant which usually does not concern or touch the land. Such statements are based upon English decisions which hold in effect that only covenants, which compel the covenanter to submit to some *restriction on the use* of his property, touch or concern the land, and that the burden of a covenant which requires the covenanter to do an affirmative act, even on his own land, for the benefit of the owner of a "dominant" estate, does not run with his land. (Miller v. Clary, 210 N. Y. 127.). So this court has recently said:

> Subject to a few exceptions not important at this time, there
> is now in this State a settled rule of law that a covenant to do an
> affirmative act, as distinguished from a covenant merely negative
> in effect, does not run with the land so as to charge the burden
> of performance on a subsequent grantee. This is so though the
> burden of such a covenant is laid upon the very parcel which is
> the subject-matter of the conveyance." (Guaranty Trust Co. v. N.
> Y. & Queens County Ry. Co.).

Both in that case and in the case of Miller v. Clary the court pointed out that there were some exceptions or limitations in the application of the general rule. Some promises to pay money have been enforced, as covenants running with the land, against subsequent holders of the land who took with notice of the covenant. It may be difficult to classify these exceptions or to formulate a test of whether a particular covenant to pay money or to perform some other act falls within the general rule that ordinarily an affirmative covenant is a personal and not a real covenant, or falls outside the limitations placed upon the general rule. At least it must "touch" or "concern" the land in a substantial degree. It has been suggested that a covenant which runs with the land must affect the legal relations—the advantages and the burdens—of the parties to the covenant, as owners of particular parcels of land and not merely as members of the community in general, such as taxpayers or owners of other land. That method of approach has the merit of realism. The test is based on the effect of the covenant rather than on technical distinctions. Does the covenant impose, on the one hand, a burden upon an interest in land, which on the other hand increases the value of a different interest in the same or related land?

Even though we accept that approach and test, it still remains true that whether a particular covenant is sufficiently connected with the use of land to run with the land, must be in many cases a question of degree. A promise to pay for something to be done in connection with the promisor's land does not differ essentially from a promise by the promisor to do the thing himself, and both promises constitute, in a substantial sense, a restriction upon the owner's right to use the land, and a burden upon the legal interest of the owner. On the other hand, a covenant to perform or pay for the performance of an affirmative act disconnected with the use of the land cannot ordinarily touch or concern the land in any substantial degree. Thus, unless we exalt technical form over substance, the distinction between covenants which run with land and covenants which are personal, must depend upon the effect of the covenant on the legal rights which otherwise would flow from ownership of land and which are connected with the land. The problem then is: Does the covenant in purpose and effect *substantially* alter these rights?

Looking at the problem presented in this case from the same point of view and stressing the intent and substantial effect of the covenant rather than its form, it seems clear that the covenant may properly be said to touch and concern the land of the defendant and its burden should run with the land. True, it calls for payment of a sum of money to be expended for "public purposes" upon land other than the land conveyed by Neponsit Realty Company to plaintiff's predecessor in title. By that conveyance the grantee, however, obtained not only title to particular lots, but an easement or right of common enjoyment with other property owners in roads, beaches, public parks or spaces and improvements in the same tract. For full enjoyment in common by the defendant and other property owners of these easements or rights, the roads and public places must be maintained. In order that the burden of maintaining public improvements should rest upon the land benefited by the improvements, the grantor exacted from the grantee of the land with its appurtenant easement or right of enjoyment a covenant that the burden of paying the cost should be inseparably attached to the land which enjoys the benefit. It is plain that any distinction or definition which would exclude such a covenant from the classification of covenants which "touch" or "concern" the land would be based on form and not on substance.

Another difficulty remains. Though between the grantor and the grantee there was privity of estate, the covenant provides that its benefit shall run to the assigns of the grantor who "may include a Property Owners' Association which may hereafter be organized for the purposes referred to in this paragraph." The plaintiff has been organized to receive the sums payable by the property owners and to expend them for the benefit of such owners. Various definitions have been formulated of "privity of estate" in connection with covenants that run with the land, but none of such definitions seems to cover the relationship between the plaintiff and the defendant in this case. The plaintiff has not succeeded to the ownership of any property of the grantor. It does not appear that it ever had title to the streets or public places upon which charges which are payable to it must be expended. It does not appear that it owns any other property in the residential tract to which any easement or right of enjoyment in such property is appurtenant. It is created solely to act as the assignee of the benefit of the covenant, and it has no interest of its own in the enforcement of the covenant.

The arguments that under such circumstances the plaintiff has no right of action to enforce a covenant running with the land are all based upon a distinction between the corporate property owners association and the property owners for whose benefit the association has been formed. If that distinction may be ignored, then the basis of the arguments is destroyed. How far privity of estate in technical form is necessary to enforce in equity a restrictive covenant upon the use of land, presents an interesting question. Enforcement of such covenants rests upon equitable principles (Tulk v. Moxhay, 2 Phillips, 774; Trustees of Columbia College v. Lynch, 70 N.Y. 440), and at times, at least, the violation "of the restrictive covenant may be restrained at the suit of one who owns property, or for whose benefit the restriction was established, irrespective of whether there were privity either of estate or of contract between the parties, or whether an action at law were maintainable." (Cheseboro v. Moers, 233 N.Y. 75, 80.). The covenant in this case does not fall exactly within any classification of "restrictive" covenants, which have been enforced in this State, and no right to enforce even a restrictive covenant has been sustained in this State where the plaintiff did not own property which would benefit by such enforcement so that some of the elements of an equitable servitude are present. In some jurisdictions it has been held that no action may be maintained without such elements. We do not attempt to decide now how far the rule of Trustees of Columbia College v. Lynch (*supra*) will be carried, or to formulate a definite rule as to when, or even whether, covenants in a deed will be enforced, upon equitable principles, against subsequent purchasers with notice, at the suit of a party without privity of contract or estate. There is no need to resort to such a rule if the courts may look behind the corporate form of the plaintiff.

The corporate plaintiff has been formed as a convenient instrument by which the property owners may advance their common interests. We do not ignore the corporate form when we recognize that the Neponsit Property Owners Association, Inc., is acting as the agent or representative of the Neponsit property owners. As we have said in another case: when Neponsit Property Owners Association, Inc., "was formed, the property owners were expected to, and have looked to that organization as the medium through which enjoyment of their common right might be preserved equally for all." (Matter of City of New York [Public Beach], 269 N.Y. 64, 75.) Under the conditions thus presented we said: "it may be difficult, or even impossible, to classify into recognized categories the nature of the interest of the membership corporation and its members in the land. The corporate entity cannot be disregarded, nor can the separate interests of the members of the corporation" (p. 73). Only blind adherence to an ancient formula devised to meet entirely different conditions could constrain the court to hold that a corporation formed as a medium for the enjoyment of common rights of property owners owns no property which would benefit by enforcement of common rights and has no cause of action in equity to enforce the covenant upon which such common rights depend. Every reason which in other circumstances may justify the ancient formula may be urged in support of the conclusion that the formula should not be applied in this case. In substance, if not in form, the covenant is a restrictive covenant which touches and concerns the defendant's land, and in substance, if not in form, there is privity of estate between the plaintiff and the defendant.

The order should be affirmed, with costs, and the certified questions answered in the affirmative.

NOTES & QUESTIONS:

1. Did you identify the elements at issue? While the court discusses the enforceability by the association in terms of privity, vertical privity is not typically required for equitable servitudes. The issue was really getting to the heart of a distinction between covenants and easements. As explained in the material on easements earlier in this chapter, there can be easements in gross that do not benefit any other land. There cannot be a benefit in gross for a covenant. Covenants must always be for the benefit of land.

   In *Neponsit*, the association did not own any land to be benefited, so this is really comparable to the requiring of standing in any lawsuit. The plaintiff must have standing to sue—have a direct interest in the outcome of the dispute. With covenants, the plaintiff needs to be bringing the action for the benefit of land. The court went through a tortured privity analysis to explain how the association was just acting on behalf of landowners who were entitled to the benefit.

Many states have taken the same approach as Texas, and have enacted statutes allowing an association to enforce covenants. See the Texas Property Code provision below.

§ 202.004 Enforcement of a Restrictive Covenant

(a) An exercise of discretionary authority by a property owners' association or other representative designated by an owner of real property concerning a restrictive covenant is presumed reasonable unless the court determines by a preponderance of the evidence that the exercise of discretionary authority was arbitrary, capricious, or discriminatory.

(b) A property owners' association or other representative designated by an owner of real property may initiate, defend, or intervene in litigation or an administrative proceeding affecting the enforcement of a restrictive covenant or the protection, preservation, or operation of the property covered by the dedicatory instrument.

2. What other element did you identify? Compare the court's discussion of the touch and concern inquiry in *Neponsit* to the following Texas case.

Samuel Lynn Homsey v. University Gardens Racquet Club
Court of Appeals of Texas, El Paso, 1987
730 S.W.2d 763

This is a restrictive covenant case. Appeal is from a money judgment for dues and assessments based on recorded covenants and restrictions on the land in the addition where Appellant bought his home. The case was tried to the court without a jury. There were no findings of fact and conclusions of law. We affirm.

The covenant in question required the owner of a lot in the University Garden's addition to pay dues and assessments to the University Gardens Racquet Club. Homsey denied any actual notice of the requirement in that his deed made no reference to it. His title policy obtained at closing did make reference to the restrictions. Homsey and his family never used the club. There is no question that Homsey had constructive notice of the restrictions which were of record.

Appellant urges in three points that the trial court erred in holding the covenant to be valid and enforceable. The contention is that such restrictive covenant is not reasonable, is not pursuant to a general scheme to benefit the land, and is not for the exclusive use and benefit of the landowners.

We believe there is ample evidence in the record to establish that the covenant was reasonable and pursuant to a general scheme to benefit the land. Absent findings of fact and conclusions of law, we assume the trial judge found every issuable fact proposition to sustain the judgment if such fact proposition is raised by the pleadings and supported by the evidence. The judgment of the trial court must be affirmed if it can be on any reasonable theory supported by the evidence and authorized by law. Burnett v. Motyka, 610 S.W.2d 735 (Tex. 1980). We will, however, discuss Appellant's benefit to the land and exclusivity arguments.

Of the four requirements for a restrictive covenant to run with the land set forth in Billington v. Riffe, 492 S.W.2d 343, at 346 (Tex. Civ. App.—Amarillo 1973, no writ), Appellant principally emphasizes the absence of the essential that the covenant must touch or concern the land. Appellant's primary argument is that when the Class C membership was created subsequent to the original dedication, the club was open to the public and the exclusivity was destroyed. Originally, there were Class A and Class B members. Class A members were fee owners in the addition with voting rights and an obligation to pay dues and assessments. Class B members were developers with lifetime membership without dues and assessments. Thereafter, a Class C membership was created. Class C members did not have to live in the subdivision, but were subject to the approval of the board of directors, had to pay an initiation fee of $500.00 as well as dues and assessments, and had no voting rights.

A chief consideration of a covenant "touching and concerning the land" is whether it is so related to the land as to enhance its value and confer benefit upon it. Prochemco, Inc. v. Clajon Gas Co., 555 S.W.2d 189 (Tex. Civ. App.—El Paso 1977, writ ref'd n.r.e.). The benefit conferred on landowners here is immunity from payment of the $500.00 initiation fee, their automatic acceptance into the club by virtue of their purchase and without approval of the board, and their status as voting members. The power to vote gives the landowner a voice in changing the corporation and, hypothetically, to totally eliminate the complained of payment of the fees and assessments. Class C members, concerning whom Appellant focuses his attention in espousing nonexclusivity, have no such power.

There appear to be no cases in Texas that make a distinction between a club exclusively for the use of landowners and one open to the public. In Frey v. DeCordova Bend Estates Owners Association, 632 S.W.2d 877 (Tex. App.—Fort Worth 1982), aff'd, 647 S.W.2d 246 (Tex. 1983), cited by Appellant, the court upheld deed restrictions providing for various assessments and dues required of members of a homeowners' association. The members of the association owned land within the subdivision. In Selected Lands Corporation v. Speich, 702 S.W.2d 197 (Tex. App.—Houston [1st Dist.] 1985, writ ref'd n.r.e.), it appears that the club was for the exclusive benefit of landowners; however, the exclusivity of the club is not addressed. In Bessemer v. Gernsten, 381 So. 2d 1344 (Fla. 1980), cited by Appellant, the court recognized the concept that a developer, in carrying out a uniform plan of development in a subdivision, may arrange for services or maintenance of common facilities and may bind a purchaser to pay for them. The club in Bessemer was exclusive; however, the court makes no reference to that as a determining factor. It appears to us that the nonexclusivity of the club is not a material factor since the question is whether landowners are benefited, not if others are also benefited. The judgment is affirmed.

QUESTIONS:

1. What is the problem with enforcing an affirmative promise to pay money that provides a personal benefit?

2. Can you think of any situation where such a promise should be enforced? Why or why not?

3. What is difference, if any, in the promise made in the *Homsey* case (the *Neponsit* case)?

Amason et al. v. Woodman et al.
Supreme Court of Texas, 1973
498 S.W.2d 142

POPE, Justice.

Plaintiff, Walter J. Woodman, instituted this suit as a class action to enforce a restrictive covenant which prohibits mobile homes in a subdivision known as Grande Casa Ranchitos No. 2 in Ellis County. The trial court granted plaintiffs' prayer for injunction that defendants W. D. Amason and wife and Wayne O. Glick and wife permanently move their mobile home from their eight-acre lot. The court of civil appeals affirmed the judgment of the trial court. 484 S.W.2d 594. The only question presented is whether, as held by the court of civil appeals, the defendants had the burden to prove that they did not possess actual knowledge of certain unrecorded contracts of sale which were executed prior to a release of defendants' lot from the restrictive covenants by the original subdivision owners. We hold that the burden of proof was on the plaintiffs. We reverse the judgments of the courts below.

On February 28, 1968, Tom and Jane Sewell, Ben Atwell and A. M. Byram owned 371.2 acres of land in Ellis County. On that date they recorded a set of restrictive covenants on the land, one of which prohibited the use of house trailers on the land. Between May 11 and June 23, 1968, the owners sold three lots by contracts for deed to the Sitzs, McFadins and Selfs. [Ed. Note: The contract for deed is a special type of seller financing agreement where the deed—legal title—to the property is not delivered until the last payment is made to the seller. The seller is basically acting as a lender and is not transferring title until paid in full. Once the valid contract for deed is entered into, the buyer has equitable title to the land. Therefore, the title is actually split at that time and there exists legal title holders and equitable title holders.] None of those contracts was recorded.

One June 28,1968, all of the original owners of the subdivision executed and recorded a release of the restrictions insofar as they affected the eight-acre lot which is here in question. Those persons holding under the unrecorded contracts for deed did not join in the release. Tom and Jane Sewell then purchased the released lot on November 25, 1968, and they recorded their deed. The Sewells sold their lot to Wayne Glick on September 23, 1969, and in December, 1971, he moved a mobile home onto the lot. The Glicks' daughter, Mrs. Amason and her husband, were living in the mobile home at the time of trial. Plaintiff Woodman obtained his deed to a seven-acre lot in the subdivision on May 6, 1971.

Plaintiffs' proof consisted of the recorded restrictive covenants which reached the original 371 acres of land, the subsequent deed from the original owners to Woodman of a seven-acre lot within the subdivision, the several unrecorded contracts for a deed, and the fact that the defendants had moved a mobile home onto their eight-acre lot which was within the original 371-acre subdivision. The defendants then proved the release of the original restrictive covenants as to their eight-acre lot and their deed which was executed after the release was recorded. They proved that they purchased their lot for $8,902.09 and assumed a lien in the sum of $13,597.91. They denied any knowledge of the unrecorded contracts and asserted their belief that their lot was released from the restrictions. After the defense rested, plaintiffs offered in evidence, for impeachment purposes only, part of an affidavit which was recorded on December 2, 1968, in the Ellis County Clerk's office. The only part of the recorded affidavit which plaintiffs introduced is the one sentence: The only tracts sold under contracts of sale were as described by an unrecorded survey plat as Tract 1 of 4.718 acres sold to Henry Truman McFadin and wife, Mary Jane McFadin; Tracts No. 6 and 7 of 7.500 acres sold to Albert Gerry Sitz and wife, Ruby Nell Sitz; Tract No. 10 of 2.500 acres sold to Sammie Ray Dowell; Tract No. 29 of 3.178 acres sold to Danny L. Self and Wife, Gloria J. Self; and Tract No. 30 of 4.317 acres sold to Billy R. Jones, and wife, Barbara Jones.

The plaintiffs rely upon the rule that a release of restrictive covenants is not effective unless all persons who own property in the restricted subdivision join in the release. Smith v. Williams, 422 S.W.2d 168 (Tex. 1967); Farmer v. Thompson, 289 S.W.2d 351 (Tex. Civ. App. 1956, writ ref'd n.r.e.). They assert that the release was ineffective, because there were three persons who held equitable title to lots in the subdivision who failed to join in the release upon which the defendants relied. The defendants say that they purchased their eight-acre lot for value and they took without notice of the non-joinder of the equitable owners. *See* Clark, Real Covenants and other Interests which "Run with Land" (1947).

Contrary to the holding of the court of civil appeals, the plaintiffs had the burden to prove that the defendants purchased their lot with actual or constructive notice that the owners of equitable title failed to join in the release. The general rule in Texas, in other areas of the law, is that the one who relies upon an equitable title to land as against a subsequent owner of the legal title assumes the burden of showing that the latter is not an innocent purchaser for value without notice. Teagarden v. R. B. Godley Lumber Co., 105 Tex. 616, 154 S.W 973 (1913); Gillian v. Day, 179 S.W.2d 575 (Tex. Civ. App. 1944, writ ref'd); Ratcliffe v. Mahres, 122 S.W.2d 718, 723 (Tex. Civ. App.1938, writ ref'd); Lange, 4 Texas Practice, Land Titles § 465 (1961). This court in Curfee v. Walker, 112 Tex. 40, 244 S.W 497 (1922), stated that the correct rule governing restrictive covenants is stated in Hooper v. Lottman, 171 S.W 270 (Tex. Civ. App. 1914, no writ), wherein the court wrote in part: So the general rule may be safely stated to be that where there is a general plan or scheme adopted by the owner of a tract, for the development and improvement of the property by which it is divided into streets and lots, and which contemplates a restriction as to the uses to which lots may be put, or the character and location of improvements thereon . . . a purchaser and his assigns may enforce the covenant against any other purchaser, and his assigns, if he has bought with actual or constructive knowledge of the scheme, and the covenant was part of the subject-matter of his purchase.

The plaintiffs failed to prove that the defendants purchased their lot with either constructive or actual notice that there were some owners of equitable title to land within the subdivision who failed to join in the release of the restrictions. Plaintiffs relied upon the one sentence of the affidavit, but it was not proof either of constructive or actual notice to defendants. The sentence does not locate any lands by survey, subdivision or county. It does not disclose the author of the affidavit. There is no other proof that the defendants possessed actual notice of the contracts for deed. We conclude that the plaintiffs failed to discharge their burden to prove that the defendants were not good faith purchasers of their lot.

The judgments of the courts below are reversed, and judgment is here rendered dissolving the permanent injunction.

Covenant Hypothetical #1: It's a Festivus Miracle!

Art, the fee simple owner of two individual lots, constructed single-family residences on each lot. Art decided to sell Lot 2 and he retained Lot 1. In the deed conveying Lot 2, he included the following language:

> Grantee, on behalf of himself and his heirs and assigns, agrees to the following:
>
> 1. That he will pay an annual assessment, not to exceed $50 per year, which will be used for Festivus decorations for the light posts, trees, and other structures on Lots 1 and 2.
> 2. That he will pay a monthly assessment of $75 per month, which will be used for maintenance of a common party wall between the two lots.
> 3. That he will not build any fence other than a 6-ft. tall privacy fence, constructed of good quality wood.
> 4. That he will not sell or lease to anyone who is not a member of the Caucasian race.
>
> These promises are intended to run with the land and will continue to benefit Lot 1 and its successor owners and assigns.

Art sold Lot 2 to George and the deed was duly recorded in the public records of the county in which the land is located.

George subsequently sold his property in fee simple absolute to Kosmo. George's deed to Kosmo was expressly made subject to all existing covenants and conditions of record. Kramer subsequently sold Lot 2 to Newman, transferring fee simple absolute to him. Kosmo's deed made no reference to any covenants or restrictions on Lot 2.

Newman, whose ancestry traces back to Ebenezer Scrooge, deplores holiday celebrations. Moreover, he is a cheapskate. Therefore, when he received the bill for the annual assessment described above, he tore it up and threw it in the trash can. In addition, he has signed an agreement with Sears to install a 4-ft. tall chain link fence in his yard, and a Sears contractor has already erected the metal posts to which the chain link fence will attach.

Elaine owns a life tenancy in Lot 1, which she received as a gift from her former boss. He had purchased Lot 1 from Art and owns the reversion in fee simple absolute in Lot 1.

1. Elaine comes to your office and wants to seek enforcement of the promises. Can she enforce as a real covenant? Equitable servitude?

2. What if Art seeks to enforce the covenants in either manner?

3. If we change the facts so that in the transaction from Kosmo to Newman, Newman receives only a term of years rather than FSA, could anyone enforce the covenants against Newman as real covenant or equitable servitude?

4. What difference would this make, if any, if these lots were part of a 40-lot planned community subdivision known as "Blackacre Estates" and the Neighborhood Association wanted to enforce the covenants?

d. Implied Reciprocal Negative Easements a/k/a Implied Equitable Servitudes (the One Exception to the Statute of Frauds!)

The implied reciprocal negative easement is not an easement at all but is actually a covenant. This misnomer is confusing because as you have seen, easements are governed by completely different rules than covenants. The implied reciprocal negative easement is a servitude that is implicated in very limited circumstances and it not recognized by all courts. It has been recognized and upheld in Texas. A minority of jurisdictions refuse to imply equitable servitudes in this manner, usually on the basis that it would violate the statute of frauds.

The implied equitable servitude is basically used as an exception to the writing requirement of the statute of frauds. While the statute of frauds requires a promise to be in writing, this one may be implied from an express equitable servitude that is in writing. The instance where this doctrine applies is in the context of the common plan or scheme of a development. If the developer manifests some common plan or scheme to impose uniform restrictions on the property that he once commonly owned, most courts conclude that an equitable servitude will be implied.

Evans, et al. v. Pollock, et al.
Supreme Court of Texas, 1990
796 S.W.2d 465

Opinion by Justice RAY.

This is a restrictive covenant case involving the implied reciprocal negative easement doctrine. The trial court found that only the lakefront lots were impressed with restrictive covenants as part of the general plan of development, but the hilltop block was not. It implied the negative reciprocal easement on the developers' retained lakefront lots only, enjoining their use contrary to the restrictive covenants burdening the other lakefront lots. The court of appeals reversed and rendered, holding that a reciprocal negative easement can be imposed only when the general plan of development includes the entire subdivision tract and attaches to all the property retained by the common developer-owner. 793 S.W.2d 14 (Tex. App. 1989). We hold that there need only be a clearly-defined restricted district to which the restrictions apply as part of the plan of development, some lots of which are either retained by the owner-developer or sold to a purchaser with actual or constructive notice of the restrictions, for the doctrine to apply as to those lots. We reverse the judgment of the court of appeals and remand the cause to that court for consideration of factual sufficiency points.

The Implied Reciprocal Negative Easement Doctrine

Because it sets the legal context for the factual disputes, we first briefly discuss the legal theory of this controversy. The doctrine of implied reciprocal negative easements applies when an owner of real property subdivides it into lots and sells a substantial number of those lots with restrictive covenants designed to further the owner's general plan or scheme of development. The central issue is usually the existence of a general plan of development. The lots retained by the owner, or lots sold by the owner from the development without express restrictions to a grantee with notice of the restrictions in the other deeds, are burdened with what is variously called an implied reciprocal negative easement, or an implied equitable servitude, or negative implied restrictive covenant, that they may not be used in violation of the restrictive covenants burdening the lots sold with the express restrictions. A reasonably accurate general statement of the doctrine has been given as follows:

[W]here a common grantor develops a tract of land for sale in lots and pursues a course of conduct which indicates that he intends to inaugurate a general scheme or plan of development for the benefit of himself and the purchasers of the various lots, and by numerous conveyances inserts in the deeds substantially uniform restrictions, conditions and covenants against the use of the property, the grantees acquire by implication an equitable right, variously referred to as an implied reciprocal negative easement or an equitable servitude, to enforce similar restrictions against that part of the tract retained by the grantor or subsequently sold without the restrictions to a purchaser with actual or constructive notice of the restrictions and covenants. [Citations omitted.]

The implied reciprocal negative easement doctrine has long been recognized in many jurisdictions. Annot., 60 A.L.R. 1216 (1929); Annot., 144 A.L.R. 916 (1943). This court expressly approved the doctrine in Curlee v. Walker, 112 Tex. 40, 43-44, 244 S.W. 497, 498 (1922). Curlee was a standing case in which we expressly addressed whether the owner of a lot subject to a restrictive covenant had standing to assert the restrictive covenant in another landowner's deed; the case did not involve an implied reciprocal negative easement. Because the concept of a general plan of development is so frequently connected to the doctrine and standing questions, however, we wrote extensively on the implied reciprocal negative easement doctrine. The leading Texas case on implied reciprocal negative easements is Hooper v. Lottman, 171 S.W. 270 (Tex. Civ. App.—El Paso 1914, no writ), from which we quoted at length with approval in Curlee. We implicitly recognized the doctrine in MacDonald v. Painter, 441 S.W.2d 179 (Tex. 1969). Numerous intermediate appellate decisions have applied it, as we will examine below.

Facts

In September of 1947 Stanley and Sarah Agnes Hornsby (the Hornsbys), together with Charles and Bernice McCormick (McCormicks) platted a subdivision around Lake Travis from their commonly owned property in Travis County. They named the subdivision "Beby's Ranch Subdivision No. 1." The plat itself did not state any restrictions on land-use. The plat divided the property into seven blocks designated alphabetically "A" through "G". The plat did not further subdivide blocks C, D, E, and F, but blocks A, B, and G were divided into thirty-one lots. The subdivision is on a peninsula-like tract that extends into the lake, so that much of it has lake frontage. All of the platted lots are lakefront lots. Block G is located on the point of the peninsula. Block F is located on a hill and is surrounded by lakefront lots. Block F is also referred to as the "hilltop."

[The schematic diagram of the subdivision is at the end of this opinion.]

In October of 1947, before selling any lots other than two lots sold prior to the platting discussed below, the Hornsbys and McCormicks partitioned Beby's No. 1 between themselves. By partition deed the McCormicks received title to all of Blocks A, B, and C, and the Hornsbys got Blocks D, E, F, and G. Over the next several years, the Hornsbys and the McCormicks conveyed twenty-nine parcels of land from Beby's No. 1 to third parties or one another. Stanley Hornsby, a real estate attorney, and his law partner Louise Kirk, handled most of the legal work relating to the sale of lots, and the McCormicks made most of the sales. A real estate agent advertised some of the lakefront lots for sale in 1955, describing them as in "a restricted subdivision." Each deed from the Hornsbys and the McCormicks contained substantially the same restrictive covenants, including, among others, covenants: (1) prohibiting business or commercial use of the land conveyed; (2) restricting the land to residential use with only one dwelling per lot; and (3) providing that the restrictions could be changed by 3/4 of the property owners within the subdivision "voting according to front footage holdings on the 715 contour line" of the lake. In 1946 the McCormicks had conveyed two of the lakefront lots unburdened by any deed restrictions. When the original grantee conveyed the two lots to third parties in 1954, he had Hornsby draft the deeds. The deeds contained the restrictions that the property could not be used for any business or commercial purposes and that the restrictions could be altered by the "3/4 vote" along the 715 contour. Thus all lots conveyed ended up with substantially similar restrictions. All were lakefront lots, and voting rights under the restrictive covenants apparently were limited to lots with lake frontage.

The Hornsbys retained ownership of lots 4 through 8 in Block G and all of Block F. Both Hornsbys are now deceased, and the retained property passed to their devisees. The present dispute arose when the Hornsby devisees contracted to sell Thomas R. Pollock all of Block F and lots 4 and 5 in Block G for the purpose of building a marina, private club, and condominium development. Charles Evans and other owners whose deeds contained the restrictive covenants sued for equitable relief under the implied reciprocal negative easement doctrine. They sought declaration that the restrictive covenants enumerated above expressly imposed by deed upon their property were implied upon the Hornsby retained property. They further sought an injunction to prevent the Hornsby devisees from conveying the property without such deed restrictions.

Trial Court Findings and Holding

Trial was to the court. The testimony sharply conflicted as to Stanley Hornsby's oral representations of his intentions for the retained property. The evidence ranged from testimony that could reasonably be interpreted to mean that Hornsby intended all the subdivision property to be restricted, to testimony lending itself to the conclusion that Hornsby intended the retained property to be unrestricted in all respects. The trial court filed numerous findings of fact, including these:

17. The restrictions at issue were part of a general plan for development of the subdivision by the original subdividers, Stanley and Sarah Agnes Hornsby and Charles and Bernice McCormick.

18. This general plan of development involved protection/preservation of the strictly residential character of the subdivision, prohibition of business-commercial activities within the subdivision, and provision for change or modification of the restrictions by vote of the owners of parcels within the subdivision.

19. The general plan of development of the original subdividers (Stanley and Sarah Agnes Hornsby, Charles and Bernice McCormick) was that all lakefront property within the subdivision be burdened with the same restrictions.

20. Stanley Hornsby and his real estate broker represented to various purchasers that all lakefront parcels (i.e. all parcels except Block F) were restricted to residential use only and that business-commercial use thereof was prohibited.

22. Non-enforcement of the general plan of development as to the lakefront lots will decrease the value of the lots purchased and presently owned by Plaintiffs Arnold and Kay Sousares.

The trial court rendered judgment declaring that the restrictions at issue applied to the five lakefront lots owned by the Hornsby devisees and enjoining them from conveying any interest in the lots without including the restrictions in the conveyance.

Court of Appeals Action and Holding

All parties appealed the judgment. The Hornsby devisees and Pollock interests maintained that the restrictions should not have been implied on the retained property, and the Evanses and other property owners complained that the trial court should have also implied the restrictions against the hilltop and should have allowed them attorneys' fees. The court of appeals reversed and rendered judgment that plaintiffs take nothing, holding that none of the retained lots were restricted. The court of appeals reasoned that for the implied reciprocal negative easement doctrine to apply, the original grantors had to have intended that the entire subdivision be similarly restricted. Relying primarily on the language from Saccomanno v. Farb, 492 S.W.2d 709, 713 (Tex. Civ. App.—Waco 1973, writ ref'd n.r.e.), requiring proof "evidencing a scheme or intention that the entire tract should be similarly treated," the court wrote, "It is the scope of the plan which defeats application of the doctrine." 793 S.W.2d at 21.

No Requirement of "Inception" of Plan

Respondents urge that the court of appeals' holding should be construed to be that there was no evidence that the developer-grantors intended from the inception of the subdivision that there would be specific restrictions that applied to all property within the subdivision. Respondents cite Davis v. Huey, 620 S.W.2d 561, 567 (Tex. 1981), for the proposition that the general scheme or plan must exist when the subdivision is platted, or from the inception of the subdivision. We stated in Davis v. Huey, "Moreover, the meaning of Paragraph 8 and accordingly the nature of the notice thereby furnished to the Davises, is determined at the date of the inception of the general plan or scheme, i.e., in 1965, the date of filing of the restrictions in the Deed Records of Travis County." This statement should not be read out of the context of the case. Davis v. Huey involved express restrictive covenants recorded on the plat for an entire subdivision. There was an express setback requirement, and an architectural approval requirement ("Paragraph 8"). The developer had used the architectural approval requirement to impose an additional setback requirement (by denying approval) because other lot owners had actually built their houses further from the lot lines. The developer sought to enforce a setback uniformity beyond what existed when the Davises bought their lot, and admittedly beyond the types of architectural restrictions envisioned by the original plan of development. Davis v. Huey was a "notice" case. We wrote it was "essential that the party seeking to enforce the restrictions on the use of land establish that the purchaser had notice of the limitations on his title." 620 S.W.2d at 567. The requirement that the general plan exist from the inception of the subdivision applied only in the factual context of that notice case. In particular, we attach no significance to the fact that two lots were sold without restrictions before the owners formulated their general scheme or plan of development.

The Scope of a "Restricted District"

Provisions in restrictive covenants that the restrictions may be waived or modified by the consent of three-fourths of the lot owners constitute strong evidence that there is a general scheme or plan of development furthered by the restrictive covenants. Armstrong v. Leverone, 105 Conn. 464, 472, 136 A. 71, 74 (1927). The voting rights in the present case clearly attached only to lakefront lots. It was reasonable for the trial court to conclude that the restrictions were meant to apply only to the lakefront lots. The legal question is whether all the tracts in the development must be intended to be subject to the restrictions for the implied reciprocal negative easement doctrine to apply to any of the retained lots. We find it immaterial whether the question is phrased as whether the plan may be that some tracts are unrestricted while others are restricted, or whether the plan need only apply to certain similarly situated lots. We hold that the general plan or scheme may be that the restrictions only apply to certain well-defined similarly situated lots for the doctrine of implied reciprocal negative easements to apply as to such lots. Logical extensions of Texas decisions, as well as decisions from sister states, support our conclusion.

Texas cases support the conclusion that the restricted area need not be the whole subdivision. The facts in Curlee v. Walker were that after the creation of the Floral Heights Addition in the City of Wichita Falls, the developers set aside 18 blocks to be subject to restrictive covenants for ten years from date of purchase, that the land would be used for residential purposes only, that there would be one residence to two whole lots, and that the cost to construct the residence would be at least $3,000. This court in its opinion referred to the 18 blocks as the "restricted district" and referred to the plan as "[t]his general scheme or plan of creating a restricted residence district." 112 Tex. at 42, 244 S.W. at 497. Thus a general scheme or plan need not apply to the whole tract or subdivision. In Hooper v. Lottman, from which we quoted with approval, the restriction had been that no barns would be constructed within 60 feet of a specific street. The number of feet varied in each deed, so there was no absolute uniformity, but the "restricted district" to which the plan applied was obviously lots with frontage on that street. Similarly, in upholding the trial court's refusal to enforce restrictive covenants on other grounds, in Canyon v. Ferguson, 190 S.W.2d 831, 834 (Tex. Civ. App.—Fort Worth 1945, no writ), the appellate court wrote it was "not essential that there be a general scheme of restricting all of the lots in the additions. Valid restrictions could result from a scheme to restrict the lots in only one block, or those facing on only one street."

Likewise, in Crump v. Perryman, 193 S.W.2d 233, 235 (Tex. Civ. App.—Dallas 1946, no writ), the court wrote, "[W]e know of no rule of law requiring the particular improvement district to embrace an addition in its entirety," citing *Curlee*. Similar statements concerning the extent of the "restricted area" appear in Lehmann v. Wallace, 510 S.W.2d 675, 681 (Tex. Civ. App.—San Antonio 1974, writ ref'd n.r.e.), and Cambridge Shores Homeowners Ass'n v. Spring Valley Lodge Co., 422 S.W.2d 10, 14 (Tex. Civ. App.—Dallas 1967, no writ). Finally, in a case tried on the implied reciprocal negative easement theory, we expressly approved an opinion that found no error in the jury instruction requiring that the restrictions be "substantially uniform, and that they be imposed on substantially all the lots in the restricted area." Bethea v. Lockhart, 127 S.W.2d 1029, 1032 (Tex. Civ. App.—San Antonio 1939, writ ref'd).

The language from the Texas cases suggesting that the restricted district need not be the whole subdivision is in agreement with decisions from other states. In First Security National Bank & Trust Co. v. Peter, 456 S.W.2d 46 (Ky. Ct. App. 1970), the court found a restricted district comprising less than the whole subdivision including most lots that faced a particular street. Even more in point is the Kentucky case of Bellemeade Co. v. Priddle, 503 S.W.2d 734 (Ky. Ct. App. 1974). There the owners had platted and recorded sections I, II, III, IV and V of the Bellemeade subdivision. Sections I, II, III and IV had been marketed as restricted to one-family residential uses, but section V was a tract of approximately 12 acres adjacent to a major United States highway, different in character from the other sections. When the plat of section I went to record, there was a contract with the real estate firm marketing the subdivision which gave it the exclusive right to sell residential lots, but there was a separate provision giving those agents the exclusive right to sell, lease or develop section V as multi-family duplex housing, a shopping center and parking area. There was evidence of negotiations about section V with prospective buyers or developers for commercial enterprises both before and after the platting of the subdivision. After reviewing the marketing evidence, the court concluded there was no evidence that any lots in section V were offered for sale for residential purposes or evidence of confusion as to the developers' intent. The court held that the implied reciprocal negative easement doctrine applied as to retained lots in sections I through IV, but that section V was not part of the restricted area and could be sold for construction of a proposed Holiday Inn motel.

In Weber v. Les Petite Academies, Inc., 490 S.W.2d 278 (Mo. App. 1973), the original grantor had platted a subdivision composed of Lot A, Lot B, and a large number of numbered lots. All numbered lots sold were conveyed with deeds restricting them to residential purposes. It was conceded there was a common plan or scheme of development, but the owner contended Lots A and B were not part of the restricted area. On summary judgment evidence that the common grantor did not intend Lots A and B to be restricted to residential dwellings and that the character of Lots A and B was totally different from that of the rest of the lots in the subdivision in that Lots A and B were larger, abutted on a busy traffic artery, and were lettered on the plat rather than numbered, the appellate court held that summary judgment was improper because substantial factual questions were raised whether Lots A and B were part of the restricted area. Likewise, in Sharts v. Walters, 107 N.M. 414, 759 P.2d 201 (N.M. App. 1988), the owner had platted a Tract B consisting of a 15.044 acre tract. All lots in Tract A (except for two acres where there was a pre-existing restaurant) had been sold with residential restrictions. The appellate court upheld the trial court finding that Tract B was not burdened by implied reciprocal restrictions, holding that whether Tract B was part of the restricted area under the plan of development was a fact question of what was intended to be covered by the restrictions. The New Mexico court cited the Texas Lehmann v. Wallace case, which we discussed above. Finally, by way of further example, in Duvall v. Ford Leasing Development Corp., 220 Va. 36, 255 S.E.2d 470 (1979), the court held that when a larger tract is subdivided into sections and lots in stages, for purposes of the implied reciprocal Tract A consisting of a 60-acre tract and a negative easement doctrine, each separate recording created a separate and distinct subdivision with its own set of restrictions benefitting and burdening only the land in that particular subdivision. We have concluded that the weight of authority supports our conclusion that the restricted district need not be the whole subdivision nor include the whole retained tract.

We have reviewed the record and find there is some evidence to support all trial court findings that were attacked in the court of appeals. Because there were factual sufficiency points raised in the court of appeals upon which that court has not ruled, we remand this cause to the court of appeals for further consideration consistent with this opinion.

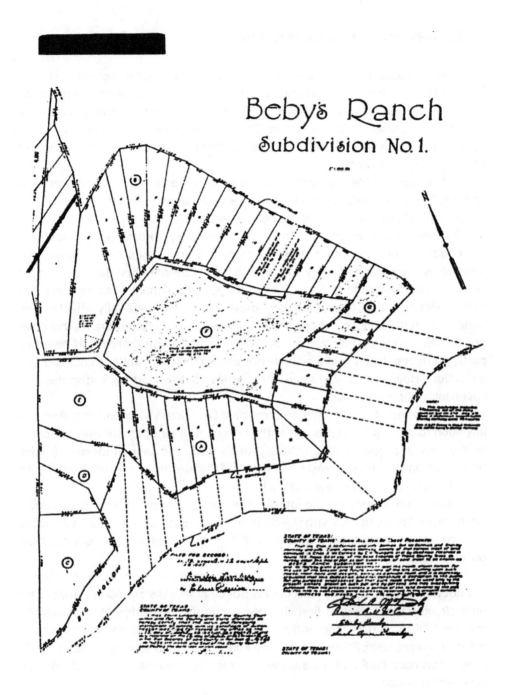

3. Termination of Covenants

Just as easements can be terminated by certain legal methods, so can covenants. Real covenants and equitable servitudes have some shared methods of termination—release, by the covenant's own terms, merger, eminent domain, recording acts, waiver, abandonment. The equitable servitude has one means of termination that is only available in equity and not at law and that is the concept of changed circumstances.

While most of the methods of terminating covenants are straightforward and easily understood, the concepts of waiver, abandonment, and changed circumstances are the ones that are often confused.

Waiver occurs when the covenant beneficiary (promisee or successor promisee) permits the covenant's violation. Waiver is used as an affirmative defense by the burdened party to argue that the covenant beneficiary suing for enforcement is not able to do so for this particular covenant because there has been a violation that the beneficiary knew about that materially affected the beneficiary but he chose not to pursue enforcement of the covenant. This does not technically mean the covenant is terminated, because there could be other parties with benefitted land who have not waived the covenant and could pursue an action. However, as between the parties to this particular dispute, the covenant is not enforceable.

Abandonment occurs when the covenant beneficiary's conduct manifests an intention to give up her rights under the covenant. Abandonment may be found in the way the covenant beneficiary deals with the benefited land (if the benefitted party acts with unclean hands and violates the covenant herself, the court is likely to find an abandonment).

Abandonment may also be found in the way the covenant beneficiary allows the burdened party to deal with the burdened land. Basically, if enough violations of a covenant occur then the court will find the covenant abandoned, thus terminated, as to all burdened land.

Changed circumstances is a means of terminating only equitable servitudes but not real covenants. What this means from a practical standpoint is that if the right circumstances exist to find changed circumstances sufficient to terminate the equitable servitude, the party seeking to enforce could not get injunctive relief to require compliance with the covenant, but could seek monetary relief if a real covenant could be established to receive monetary damages for the covenant violation.

a.   Changed Circumstances

Restatement (Third) of Property: Servitudes
§ 7.10 Modification and Termination of a Servitude Because of Changed Conditions

(1) When a change has taken place since the creation of a servitude that makes it impossible as a practical matter to accomplish the purpose for which the servitude was created, a court may modify the servitude to permit the purpose to be accomplished. If modification is not practicable, or would not be effective, a court may terminate the servitude. Compensation for resulting harm to the beneficiaries may be awarded as a condition of modifying or terminating the servitude.

(2) If the purpose of a servitude can be accomplished, but because of changed conditions the servient estate is no longer suitable for uses permitted by the servitude, a court may modify the servitude to permit other uses under conditions designed to preserve the benefits of the original servitude.

Comment:

a. Rationale. The potentially unlimited duration of servitudes creates substantial risks that, absent mechanisms for nonconsensual modification and termination, obsolete servitudes will interfere with desirable uses of land. . . . The rule stated in this section applies to easements as well as covenants and other types of servitudes. Rather than imposing a fixed time limit on servitude duration, it permits a party seeking relief from a servitude to seek court intervention at the point of need.

Because servitudes create property interests that are generally valuable, courts apply the changed-conditions doctrine with caution. Of the many changed-conditions cases that have produced appellate decisions, few result in modification or termination of a servitude. The test is stringent: relief is granted only if the purpose of the servitude can no longer be accomplished. When servitudes are terminated under this rule, it is ordinarily clear that the continuance of the servitude would serve no useful purpose and would create unnecessary harm to the owner of the servient estate.

The argument from public policy is that permitting the enforcement of servitudes after they have lost their utility reduces land values and turns the law into an instrument of extortion. Unless modification or termination is permitted, the servitude beneficiary can exact an unreasonably high price for release of an encumbrance that otherwise has no value and interferes with the ability of the servient owner to use his or her property.

In determining whether judicial intervention to modify or terminate a servitude is warranted, a court should consider whether there are serious obstacles to bargaining among the affected parties. Where transaction costs are likely to be high because large numbers of people are involved, or for other reasons, a court should be more ready to intervene than where transaction costs are likely to be low. If the servitudes provide a means for modification or termination by agreement of less than 100 percent of the servitude beneficiaries, a court should rarely intervene.

b. Relation to waiver, abandonment, and relative-hardship doctrines. Changed-conditions cases are often closely associated with waiver, but the two doctrines are distinct. Waiver arises when a servitude beneficiary has acquiesced in one or more breaches of a servitude obligation. When that same beneficiary later seeks to enforce the servitude with respect to a similar breach by a different person who is subject to a similar servitude obligation, or later seeks to enforce the same servitude against a new or different violation by the same person, waiver is raised as a defense to enforcement of the servitude against the later breach. If waiver is found, it affects the availability and selection of remedy under, but does not result in extinguishment of the servitude benefit unless the beneficiary has abandoned it. . . . Even though waiver precludes enforcement against some violations, the beneficiary retains the right to enforce it against violations that were not included in the scope of the waiver.

Extensive waiver of servitude violations may lead either to the conclusion that the servitude has been abandoned, and terminated, or to a situation in which further enforcement of the servitude will no longer serve the purpose for which it was created and the servitude may be modified or terminated because of changed conditions.

The changed-conditions doctrine is also closely related to abandonment. If a servitude has lost its utility, the beneficiary may well abandon it. However, changed conditions, unlike abandonment, does not require a finding that the beneficiary intended to relinquish the rights created by the servitude. The changed-conditions rule is used where, even though a servitude no longer serves its intended purpose, the beneficiary does not intend to abandon it.

c. Test and application. The test for finding changed conditions sufficient to warrant termination of reciprocal-subdivision servitudes is often said to be whether there has been such a radical change in conditions since creation of the servitudes that perpetuation of the servitude would be of no substantial benefit to the dominant estate. However, the test is not whether the servitude retains value, but whether it can continue to serve the purposes for which it was created. Increases in the cost of compliance to the servient estate are irrelevant except in the rare situations where the servient estate is no longer suitable for any use permitted by the servitude. The test is a stringent one, and few cases that have reached the appellate level have resulted in termination of servitudes.

Changes within an area covered by reciprocal servitudes generally are more significant than changes that take place outside the restricted area, *although changes outside may also provide grounds for termination*. If the changes include uses that violate the servitudes, the fact that they have taken place within the restricted area provides evidence that the servitudes have lost their value to the beneficiaries. If not, they would have challenged the violations. Changes outside the restricted area have no similar significance, however, because the servitude beneficiaries lack standing to challenge them. If the changes lead to a *situation where enforcement would produce no substantial benefit to the dominant estates*, however, *termination is warranted regardless of the location or source of the changes*.

Illustrations:
1. Green Acres is a small 10-lot subdivision subject to covenants restricting use to single-family dwellings. Lots 1 through 8 are condemned for construction of a state highway. The remaining two lots abut the new highway. The noise and traffic make the lots unsuitable for residential purposes. The owner of Lot 9 wants to convert it to commercial use; the owner of Lot 10 resists. Because the purpose of maintaining a single-family neighborhood can no longer be accomplished, the court would be justified in terminating the servitude on the basis of changed conditions. If the owner who resists will suffer damages as a result of the termination, termination may be conditioned on the payment of damages.

2. Same facts as Illustration 1, with the added fact that the property condemned included a commonly owned recreational facility maintained by the association of Green Acres lot owners. A covenant obligated the owners to pay assessments to the association for maintenance of the common property. Because the purpose of paying the assessments can no longer be accomplished, the covenant should be terminated.

3. Same facts as Illustration 1, except that Green Acres is a large subdivision of 500 lots and the lots taken lie along one edge of the subdivision. The lots abutting the new highway are no longer suitable for single-family residential use, but the balance of the subdivision remains intact. Because enforcement of the restrictions will protect the single-family residential character of the balance of the subdivision, a court would not be justified in terminating the restrictions as to the remaining lots. Modification of the restrictions on the buffer lots to permit multifamily use or limited commercial uses within single-family structures might be appropriate, under conditions designed to maximize their utility as a buffer and minimize the impact of the use changes on the interior lots.

THINK: So, what is needed for changed circumstances? Since this is an equitable principle, this is a very fact-intensive inquiry. Compare the following cases to understand the concept of changed circumstances. The court is looking for factors to indicate that there is no benefit remaining to the covenant's enforcement.

<u>Western Land Co. v. Truskolaski</u>
Supreme Court of Nevada, 1972
495 P.2d 624

BATJER, J.

The respondents, homeowners in the Southland Heights Subdivision in southwest Reno, Nevada, brought an action in the district court to enjoin the appellant from constructing a shopping center on a 3.5-acre parcel of land located within the subdivision at the northeast corner of Plumas and West Plumb Lane. In 1941 the appellant subdivided this 40-acre development, and at that time it subjected the lots to certain restrictive covenants which specifically restricted the entire 40 acres of the subdivision to single family dwellings and further prohibited any stores, butcher shops, grocery or mercantile business of any kind. The district court held these restrictive covenants to be enforceable, and enjoined the appellant from constructing a supermarket or using the 3.5 acres in any manner other than that permitted by the covenants. The appellant contends that the district court erred in enforcing these covenants because the subdivision had so radically changed in recent years as to nullify their purpose. We agree with the holding of the district court that the restrictive covenants remain of substantial value to the homeowners in the subdivision, and that the changes that have occurred since 1941 are not so great as to make it inequitable or oppressive to restrict the property to single-family residential use.

In 1941 the Southland Heights subdivision was outside of the Reno city limits. The property surrounding the subdivision was primarily used for residential and agricultural purposes, with very little commercial development of any type in the immediate area. At that time Plumb Lane extended only as far east as Arlington Avenue.

[13]

By the time the respondents sought equitable relief in an effort to enforce the restrictive covenants, the area had markedly changed. In 1941 the city of Reno had a population of slightly more than 20,000; that figure had jumped to approximately 95,100 by 1969. One of the significant changes, as the appellant aptly illustrates, is the increase in traffic in the surrounding area. Plumb Lane had been extended to Virginia Street, and in 1961 the city of Reno condemned 1.04 acres of land on the edge of the subdivision to allow for the widening of Plumb Lane into a four-lane arterial boulevard. A city planner, testifying for the appellant, stated that Plumb Lane was designed to be and now is the major east-west artery through the southern portion of the city. A person who owns property across Plumas from the subdivision testified that the corner of Plumb Lane and Plumas is "terribly noisy from 5:00 p.m. until midnight." One of the findings of the trial court was that traffic on Plumb Lane had greatly increased in recent years.

Another significant change that had occurred since 1941 was the increase in commercial development in the vicinity of the subdivision. On the east side of Lakeside Drive, across from the subdivision property, is a restaurant and the Lakeside Plaza Shopping Center. A supermarket, hardware store, drug store, flower shop, beauty shop and a dress shop are located in this shopping center. Still further east of the subdivision, on Virginia Street, is the Continental Lodge, and across Virginia Street is the Park Lane Shopping Center.

Even though traffic has increased and commercial development has occurred in the vicinity of the subdivision, the owners of land within Southland Heights testified to the desirability of the subdivision for residential purposes. The

---

[13] Google Earth V 6.2.2.6613. (June 25, 2008). Reno, Nevada. 39° 30' 20.81"N, 119° 48' 45.32"W, Eye alt 6194 feet. DigitalGlobe 2008. http://www.earth.google.com [June 25, 2008].

traffic density within the subdivision is low, resulting in a safe environment for the children who live and play in the area. Homes in Southland Heights are well cared for and attractively landscaped.

The trial court found that substantial changes in traffic patterns and commercial activity had occurred since 1941 in the vicinity of the subdivision. Although it was shown that commercial activity outside of the subdivision had increased considerably since 1941, the appellant failed to show that the area in question is now unsuitable for residential purposes.

Even though nearby avenues may become heavily traveled thoroughfares, restrictive covenants are still enforceable if the single-family residential character of the neighborhood has not been adversely affected, and the purpose of the restrictions has not been thwarted. Although commercialization has increased in the vicinity of the subdivision, such activity has not rendered the restrictive covenants unenforceable because they are still of real and substantial value to those homeowners living within the subdivision.

The appellant asks this court to reverse the judgment of the district court and declare as a matter of law that the objects and purposes for which the restrictive covenants were originally imposed have been thwarted, and that it is now inequitable to enforce such restrictions against the entity that originally created them. This we will not do. The record will not permit us to find as a matter of law that there has been such a change in the subdivision or for that matter in the area to relieve the appellant's property of the burden placed upon it by the covenants. There is sufficient evidence to sustain the findings of the trial court that the objects and purposes of the restrictions have not been thwarted, and that they remain of substantial value to the homeowners in the subdivision.

The case of Hirsch v. Hancock, 173 Cal. App. 2d 745, 343 P.2d 959 (1959) as well as the other authorities relied upon by the appellant are inapposite for in those cases the trial court found many changes within as well as outside the subdivision and concluded from the evidence that the properties were entirely unsuitable and undesirable for residential use and that they had no suitable economic use except for business or commercial purposes, and the appellate courts in reviewing those cases held that the evidence supported the findings and sustained the judgments of the trial courts.

On the other hand, in the case of West Alameda Heights H. Ass'n. v. Board of Co. Com'm., 169 Colo. 491, 458 P.2d 253 (1969), upon facts similar to those found in this case, the trial court decided that the changed conditions in the neighborhood were such as to render the restrictive covenants void and unenforceable. The appellate court reversed and held that the trial court misconceived and misapplied the rule as to change of conditions and said, "As long as the original purpose of the covenants can still be accomplished and substantial benefit will inure to the restricted area by their enforcement, the covenants stand even though the subject property has a greater value if used for other purposes."

There is substantial evidence in the record to support the trial court's findings of fact and conclusions of law that the covenants were of real and substantial value to the residents of the subdivision. Here the appellant has not carried its burden of showing that the subdivision is not now suitable for residential purposes because of changed conditions.

In another attempt to show that the restrictive covenants have outlived their usefulness, the appellant points to actions of the Reno city council. On August 1, 1968, the council adopted a Resolution of Intent to reclassify this 3.5-acre parcel from R-1 [residential] to C-1(b) [commercial]. The council never did change the zoning, but the appellant contends that since the council did indicate its willingness to rezone, it was of the opinion that the property was more suitable for commercial than residential use. This argument of the appellant is not persuasive. A zoning ordinance cannot override privately-placed restrictions, and a trial court cannot be compelled to invalidate restrictive covenants merely because of a zoning change.

Another of the appellant's arguments regarding changed conditions involves the value of the property for residential as compared to commercial purposes. A professional planning consultant, testifying for the appellant, stated that the land in question is no longer suitable for use as a single-family residential area. From this testimony the appellant concludes that the highest and best use for the land is non-residential. Even if this property is more valuable for commercial than residential purposes, this fact does not entitle the appellant to be relieved of the restrictions it created, since substantial benefit inures to the restricted area by their enforcement.

In addition to the alleged changed circumstances, the appellant contends that the restrictive covenants are no longer enforceable because they have been abandoned or waived due to violations by homeowners in the area. Paragraph 3 of the restrictive agreement provides that no residential structure shall be placed on a lot comprising less than 6,000 square feet. Both lot 24 and lot 25 of block E contain less than 6,000 square feet and each has a house located on it. This could hardly be deemed a violation of the restrictions imposed by the appellant inasmuch as it was the appellant that subdivided the land and caused these lots to be smaller than 6,000 feet. Paragraph 7 of the agreement provides that a committee shall approve any structure which is moved onto the subdivision, or if there is no committee, that the structure shall conform to and be in harmony with existing structures. The appellant did show that two houses were moved on to lots within the subdivision, but the appellant failed to show whether a committee existed and if so approved or disapproved, or whether the houses failed to conform or were out of harmony with the existing structures. Finally, in an effort to prove abandonment and waiver, the appellant showed that one house within the subdivision was used as a painting contractor's office for several years in the late 1940's, and that more recently the same house had been used as a nursery for a babysitting business. However, the same witnesses testified that at the time of the hearing this house was being used as a single-family residence.

Even if the alleged occurrences and irregularities could be construed to be violations of the restrictive covenants they were too distant and sporadic to constitute general consent by the property owners in the subdivision and they were not sufficient to constitute an abandonment or waiver. In order for community violations to constitute an abandonment, they must be so general as to frustrate the original purpose of the agreement.

Affirmed.

New Jerusalem Baptist Church, Inc. v. City of Houston
Court of Civil Appeals of Texas, Houston (14th Dist.), 1980
598 S.W.2d 666

Opinion by Judge PAUL PRESSLER.

This is an appeal from a permanent injunction, enjoining appellant from operating, conducting, or using two half lots in Shamrock Manor Subdivision, Houston, Texas, for church purposes or commercial activity in violation of the restrictions for such subdivision.

Appellant purchased the property in Shamrock Manor in 1974 with the intent of placing a church building thereon and conducting church services. Although its deed referred to the restrictions, appellant denied actual knowledge of them. They had existed since the development of the subdivision. Soon after the purchase, appellant cleared and leveled the property and placed a sign on it proclaiming it to be the future sight of The New Jerusalem Baptist Church. However, the testimony indicates that the sign became faded and partially overgrown with weeds, significantly reducing its legibility from the street on which the property fronted. The evidence further reflects that there were three or four ongoing non-conforming uses of property within the subdivision, including another church which was a very short distance from the property in question.

Arrangements were made in October 1978, for the construction of the building on a site far removed from the lots in question and its transfer in a nearly completed form to the property in Shamrock Manor. In February 1979, the civic club for the subdivision informed appellant that the restrictions limited the use of the property to single family residences. Appellant claims it had spent $41,000.00 by that time, primarily for the construction of the building. In spite of the warning, appellant proceeded with its plans and moved its virtually completed building onto the property in March 1979. Suit to enjoin violation of the restrictive covenant was brought April 2, 1979, and a temporary injunction was granted in May 1979. A permanent injunction was granted on July 26, 1979.

Appellant contends there was insufficient evidence to establish that the city's interest in enforcing the restrictive covenant outweighed the hardship to the church occasioned by its enforcement. We hold that there was sufficient evidence to support the conclusion reached by the trial court in weighing the equities. While Reverend Adams, a witness for appellant, testified that the church did not presently have the financial means to acquire a new site on which to relocate its building, there is no testimony that the lots in question could not be sold, yielding a substantial portion of the funds necessary for acquisition of an alternate site. Moreover, the evidence indicates that the building for which the majority of appellant's funds were expended is not permanently annexed to the property on which it presently rests in Shamrock Manor, and could be transported to another site with approximately the same ease and expense required in moving the building to its present site. As the value of appellant's investment in the building could thereby be preserved, the alleged harm suffered from the enforcement of the restrictive covenant is significantly mitigated. The other expenses associated with preparing the lots for the building either added to their value or were not significant.

On the other hand, there is evidence that several of the home owners in Shamrock Manor purchased their homes in reliance on the restrictive covenants. In recent years many of the owners in the subdivision have formed a civic club which has actively sought the enforcement of the restrictive covenant against owners of lots with non-conforming uses. In order for a court to refuse to enforce a restrictive covenant based on a balancing of the equities, a disproportion of "considerable magnitude" must be shown to exist between the harm suffered by the non-conforming user and the benefit received by those seeking enforcement. Cowling v. Colligan, 158 Tex. 458, 312 S.W.2d 943 (1958). There is insufficient evidence to indicate such a disproportion in the case before us.

Appellant contends that it was error to grant the permanent injunction as the great weight and preponderance of the evidence established that appellee had abandoned the restrictive covenant. In order to establish the affirmative defense of abandonment in a deed restriction case, the non-conforming user must prove that the violations then existing are so great as to lead the mind of the "average man" to reasonably conclude that the restriction in question has been abandoned. Among the factors to be considered by the "average man" are the number, nature, and severity of the then existing violations, any prior acts of enforcement of the restriction, and whether it is still possible to realize to a substantial degree the benefits intended through the covenant.

In the case before us, the evidence indicates that there are currently four non-conforming uses within the 169 lots of Shamrock Manor. There is some evidence of a salvage yard; however, there is conflicting evidence on whether a salvage business is being conducted therein. There is evidence of two beauty shops; however, both are allegedly incidental to the use of the property as residences (and as such should not be considered as evidence of a waiver of the covenant). Davis v. Hinton, 374 S.W.2d 723 (Tex. Civ. App.—Tyler 1964, writ ref'd n. r. e.). There is evidence of another church within the subdivision a short distance from appellant's lots. There was a great deal of evidence of prior non-conforming uses; however, these uses should not be considered in determining whether there is a present intent to abandon the restriction, as the applicability of the covenant is renewed once the violation of it ceases. Moreover, there is evidence of at least one recent enforcement of the covenant.

Based on the above, we hold there was sufficient evidence for the trial court to conclude that the "average man," when faced with these facts, would reasonably conclude that the restriction in question had not been abandoned nor its enforcement waived.

Affirmed.

b. Statute of Limitations for Covenants

Tex. Civ. Prac. & Rem. Code
§ 16.051

> Every action for which there is no express limitations period, except an action for the recovery of real property, must be brought not later than four years after the day the cause of action accrues.

The statute of limitations to enforce restrictive covenants is four years pursuant to Tex. Civ. Prac. & Rem. Code 16.051. A restrictive covenant enforcement action accrues upon breach of the covenant. The four-year statute begins to run from the first day of the breach. A party seeking the benefit of the discovery rule to avoid limitations has the burden of pleading and proving the discovery rule. For example, in Girsh v. St. John, 218 S.W.3d 921, 926 (Tex. App.—Beaumont 2007, no pet.), a neighbors' placement of a mobile home on their property in violation of a residential subdivision's restrictive covenant was not the type of injury that was unlikely to be discovered within the four-year limitations period for suits to enforce deed restrictions to allow the discovery rule to apply. In *Girsh*, the mobile home was present in the neighbors' backyard openly and there was no evidence of any efforts to camouflage or hide it. The question of when an injury should have been discovered so as to start the running of the limitations period is a question of fact.

It is important to note that if a violation of a covenant occurs long enough to pass the limitations period, the statute of limitations will be raised as an affirmative defense by the party against whom the covenant is being enforced, or the owner of the servient estate. The running of the statute of limitations will prevent enforcement of that particular covenant against that particular servient estate. However, this does not constitute an abandonment. The running of the statute of limitations for a covenant violation could play into a waiver argument. If enough violations occur that are outside of limitations to prevent enforcement, that could help establish an abandonment of the covenant as well.

It is also important to note that the limitations period runs for a particular violation. If there is a covenant violation that lasts long enough to prevent an action based on limitations, and the violation ceases, if a new violation of the same covenant then occurs, the limitations period begins running again for that new violation. Therefore, like the waiver affirmative defense, the statute of limitations defense is not technically a termination of a covenant.

Schoenhals, et al. v. Close
Court of Civil Appeals of Texas, Amarillo, 1970
451 S.W.2d 597

DENTON, Chief Justice.

This is an appeal from a temporary injunction enjoining the appellants from opening a beauty shop in violation of a restrictive covenant.

Plaintiff-appellants Mr. and Mrs. G. R. Close and defendants Schoenhals own adjoining lots in a residential section of Perryton, Texas. Each of the deeds to their respective lots derived from a common source and each contained a residential restriction and covenant which stated "that there shall never be erected upon said land hereinbefore described no improvements save and except improvements to be used for residential purposes. . . ."

In late 1959 appellant Schoenhals converted the inside of his garage into a beauty shop. In January of 1960 Schoenhals' daughter, appellant Gloria Griggs, opened the beauty shop for commercial operation. In October of 1960, the Closes purchased the house next to the Schoenhals' lot. At that time the beauty shop was in operation.

The beauty shop remained in commercial operation until some time in 1964. From 1964 until July 1969 appellant Gloria Griggs did some work in the beauty shop for some ten members of her church on a charitable basis. During this period when the commercial activity surrounding the beauty shop had ceased, plaintiff Close made over $30,000.00 in improvements to his property. In July, 1969, appellant Gloria Griggs made arrangements to resume commercial operations of the beauty shop. Three operators rented space, the drying chairs were replaced, and a business telephone was installed. When appellees learned of Gloria Griggs' intentions to resume the commercial operation of the beauty shop, they brought this suit. The trial court granted a temporary injunction and appellants have appealed to this court on two grounds. First, they contend that the four year statute of limitations applies in this case, Art. 5529, Vernon's Ann. Tex. Rev. Civ. St.; and that the appellees' cause of action is thus barred.

The four year statute of limitations does apply to violations of a restrictive covenant. Keene v. Reed, 340 S.W.2d 859 (Tex. Civ. App., writ ref'd); Arrington v. Cleveland, 242 S.W.2d 400 (Tex. Civ. App., writ ref'd). However, we have concluded the four year statute is not determinative in this case.

Gloria Griggs began to operate a beauty shop in 1960 in the appellant Schoenhals' garage in violation of the restrictive covenant. At that time the neighbors had a legal right to enforce the restrictive covenant and to prevent the operation of the beauty shop. In 1964, more than four years after the opening of the beauty shop, appellant Griggs ceased the commercial operation. At the time she ceased the commercial operation, the statute of limitation had run and she had, at that time, a right to continue the operation of the beauty shop. From 1964 appellant Gloria Griggs conducted a limited amount of charity work in the garage. If the restrictive covenant were in effect during that period, the charitable work would not have been in violation of the restrictive covenant, and the neighbors would not have had a cause of action. A small amount of non-profit work done inside one's home or garage would not violate a residential restrictive covenant. Allen v. Winner, 389 S.W.2d 599 (Tex. Civ. App., ref. n.r.e.).

When appellant Gloria Griggs resumed her commercial operation in July of 1969, the neighbors once again had a cause of action and statute of limitations began to run. The filing of this suit within the ten days after learning of appellants' plans would not raise a question of limitations with respect to the opening in July, 1969.

The question which must be decided in this case is whether a party who acquires a right through the statute of limitations to operate a commercial enterprise in contravention of a restrictive covenant may lose that right by abandonment?

Ordinarily, unless a restrictive covenant is removed either by the agreement of all the interested property owners or by a declaratory judgment, the restriction will not be removed. Simon v. Henrichson, 394 S.W.2d 249 (Tex. Civ. App., ref. n.r.e.). Even though the restriction has not been removed, it may become unenforceable with respect to the entire tract, either because 'of the acquiescence of the lot owners in such substantial violations within the restricted area as to amount to an abandonment of the covenant or a waiver of the right to enforce it,' or 'because there has been such a change of conditions in the restricted area or surrounding it that it is no longer possible to secure in a substantial degree the benefits sought to be realized through the covenant.' Cowling v. Colligan, 158 Tex. 458, 312 S.W.2d 943, 945.

Where there has been a single violation of a restrictive covenant in a neighborhood, the fact that one violation is protected by some valid defense does not have the effect of removing the restrictive covenant as it applies to the rest of the tract. Barham v. Reames, 366 S.W.2d 257 (Tex. Civ. App.).

A restriction may become unenforceable with respect to a particular lot in a tract under the defenses of the statute of limitations or waiver. Even though a party has violated a restrictive covenant and is able to continue to do so under one of the foregoing defenses, the restrictive covenant will continue to exist, 'even if the violation as it exists, continues.' Simon v. Henrichson, 394 S.W.2d 249, 252 (Tex. Civ. App., ref. n.r.e.). If the violation ceases, the covenant will once more become effective and will bar any future violations. Any other result would, in effect, seriously impair the usefulness and value of restrictive covenants, as any prospective purchaser of a home in a residential area could never be certain that a previous violation of a restrictive covenant in the neighborhood had not rendered that covenant ineffective.

In the case at hand, the beauty shop ceased its commercial activity some time in 1964. The converted garage did not appear to be a beauty shop from the outside and a casual observer in the neighborhood would have noticed nothing unusual about the garage during the period. When appellants ceased to violate the restrictive covenant, they waived the rights they may have acquired during the previous operation of the beauty shop. None of the neighbors would have been able to maintain a suit during this period as the appellants were not at that time violating the restrictive covenant.

When appellant Griggs reopened her beauty shop in July of 1969, she once again was in violation of the restrictive covenant. Appellees filed this suit within ten days after learning of appellants' plans. The concept of laches is based on the ground of unreasonable delay, and ten days is not an unreasonable delay.

Appellant contends that the four year statute of limitations is applicable and that appellees' cause of action is barred by that statute of limitations. Here there were two violations of the restrictive covenant and thus two causes of action. The first arose when appellant opened the beauty shop in 1960. The second cause of action arose in July, 1969, when appellant reopened her beauty shop in violation of the restrictive covenant. That cause of action was not barred by the statute of limitations at the time appellee filed this suit.

The judgment of the trial court is affirmed.

Covenant Hypothetical #2: The Attack of the Blue-Haired Ladies

There is a small residential neighborhood made up of four city streets, a total of 16 houses. The lots in this neighborhood are all burdened by the promises that the land shall be for residential purposes only, composed of single-family residences. In 1999, at the house at 1000 2nd Street, the owner begins running a babysitting business during the day where she watches two kids every Monday through Friday from 1999 to the present time. In 2001, the owner of the house at 2000 ABC Avenue begins working from home as a medical transcriptionist. She continues this work from home at the present time. From 2002 to 2004, the owner of the house at 3000 1st Street operates a catering business from her home. She converted her garage into a commercial grade kitchen, but since 2004 has only used it for her own entertaining at home.

In April 2007, Jan enclosed her garage to make a beauty shop so that she could work from home while caring for her ill mother. She created an entrance separate from her house and had additional concrete poured for ample parking in the front and along the side of the house. She has operated the beauty shop since 2007. Initially she was not very busy, but in the past year the traffic has greatly increased. She has many blue-haired old ladies coming and going in their rather large Cadillacs all during the day.

Jan's neighbor has known about the beauty shop since it started in 2007. At first it didn't really bother him because it did not really seem to impact the street or his house. However, the level of traffic and number of times his garbage has been spilled out all over the street after one of Jan's customers backed into his garbage cans has gotten to an irritating level.

Irritated Neighbor sues Jan in July 2010.

Jan comes to you seeking assistance in her defense against Neighbor's action to enforce the covenants as an equitable servitude or real covenant. What do you recommend?

Chapter 5
Concurrent Ownership

A. Introduction to Concurrent Interests

Concurrent ownership, or cotenancy, is a description of the relationship among property owners and not an estate in land. Everything that may be the subject of ownership may be owned in cotenancy—personal property, real property, mineral estates, etc. The terms *cotenancy* or *cotenants* refer to a general category and there are types of cotenancies to be classified based on how they are created. This is not another estate in land. This is an additional legal concept that layers on top of the form of estate in land that is already established. Recall the example where there was a conveyance *O* to *A* for life, then to *A*'s children. When *A* died she had two children *B* and *C*. *B* and *C* have a vested remainder subject to open during the life estate and then they both have fee simple absolute upon *A*'s death. However, we have two people both with a fee simple absolute bundle of sticks. How can that work? These rules regarding concurrent ownership answer that question.

As we follow through with the theme of possession, in this situation possession again is a key factor. The present right to possession of the property is an essential element of cotenancy; one who has no right to possession of property held in common is not a cotenant. Because of the possession element, a cotenancy cannot exist between a life tenant and the holder of the remainder interest or between multiple remainder interest holders. Life tenants owning undivided interests in the same life estate are cotenants because they both enjoy the present right to possess. There may be multiple remainder interest holders. They are not cotenants while they hold the future interest but once that future interest becomes the present possessory estate, those individuals are then cotenants.

One thing that is really important to remember throughout this material is that no matter real or personal property, the cotenants own fractional shares but do not own specific parts of the property. For example, if George and Susan own a horse as cotenants they each own a 50 percent share of ownership of the horse. That does not mean that we cut the horse in half and each person says "I own that piece of the horse!" While that may seem obvious when speaking of a horse, sometimes that concept gets lost when considering co-owners of land. If George and Susan own Blackacre, a 100-acre parcel of land, they each have a 50 percent share of ownership of the land. Neither can point to a specific 50 acres and say,

"That's mine!" And, they do not each own 50 acres of land. If they each have 50 percent of the value, depending on the makeup and topography of the land, presence of any natural resources, and road access, some acreage may be more valuable than others. If the cotenants choose to split up the land at some time in the future, George's 50 percent may be only 40 acres of land because it has better road access than the 60 acres Susan receives and thus his 40 acres actually represents 50 percent of the total value.

This chapter will first focus on establishing different forms of concurrent ownership in both land and personal property. Then it will develop the rules and responsibilities of the cotenants, regardless of the form of cotenancy relationship. Finally, the material will address the end of concurrent ownership through the escape hatch of partition.

1. Types of Cotenancies for Bank Accounts

Just as land can be owned by multiple people at the same time with interests divided into fractional shares, personal property can be the subject of concurrent ownership as well. In order to provide specific guidance with respect to concurrent ownership of money, the Texas Estates Code provides statutes governing different types of bank accounts. Some of these bank accounts do not actually include co-ownership of the funds in the accounts but rather provide for a nontestamentary disposition of cash in a bank account upon the owner's death. These accounts also provide for the manner in which the funds in the account can be the subject of concurrent ownership. Of course, as the Estates Code allows for joint tenancy with right of survivorship created by specific language and clear intent, comparable concepts appear in the Estates Code provisions governing bank accounts.

Texas Estates Code[1]

§ 113.001. General Definitions[2]
In this chapter:
(1) "Account" means a contract of deposit of funds between a depositor and a financial institution. The term includes a checking account, savings account, certificate of deposit, share account, or other similar arrangement.

---

[1] Enacted by Acts 2009, 81st Leg., ch. 680 (H.B. 2502), § 1, effective January 1, 2014; am. Acts 2011, 82nd Leg. ch. 1338 (S.B. 1198), § 2.07, effective January 1, 2014.

[2] Additional text from 2015 Tex. Sess. Law Serv. Ch. 255 (S.B. 1020), 84th Legislature, 2015 Reg. Session.

(2) "Beneficiary" means a person or trustee of an express trust evidenced by a writing who is named in a trust account as a person for whom a party to the account is named as trustee.

(3) "Payment" of sums on deposit includes a withdrawal, a payment on a check or other directive of a party, and a pledge of sums on deposit by a party and any set-off, or reduction of other disposition of all or part of an account under a pledge.

(4) "P.O.D. payee" means a person, trustee of an express trust evidenced by a writing, or charitable organization designated on a P.O.D. account as a person to whom the account is payable on request after the death of one or more persons.

(5) "Sums on deposit" means the balance payable on a multiple-party account including interest, dividends, and any deposit life insurance proceeds added to the account by reason of the death of a party.

(6) "Withdrawal" includes payment to a third person in accordance with a check or other directive of a party.

§ 113.002. Definition of Party

(a) In this chapter, "party" means a person who, by the terms of a multiple-party account, has a present right, subject to request, to payment from the account. Except as otherwise required by the context, the term includes a guardian, personal representative, or assignee, including an attaching creditor, of a party. The term also includes a person identified as a trustee of an account for another regardless of whether a beneficiary is named. The term does not include a named beneficiary unless the beneficiary has a present right of withdrawal.

(b) A P.O.D. payee, including a charitable organization, or beneficiary of a trust account is a party only after the account becomes payable to the P.O.D. payee or beneficiary by reason of the P.O.D. payee or beneficiary surviving the original payee or trustee.

§ 113.003. Definition of Net Contribution

(a) In this chapter, "net contribution" of a party to a joint account at any given time is the sum of all deposits made to that account by or for the party, less all withdrawals made by or for the party that have not been paid to or applied to the use of any other party, plus a pro rata share of any interest or dividends included in the current balance of the account. The term also includes any deposit life insurance proceeds added to the account by reason of the death of the party whose net contribution is in question.

(b) Omitted.

§ 113.004. Types of Accounts

In this chapter:

(1) "Convenience account" means an account that:

    (A) is established at a financial institution by one or more parties in the names of the parties and one or more convenience signers; and

    (B) has terms that provide that the sums on deposit are paid or delivered to the parties or to the convenience signers "for the convenience" of the parties.

(2) "Joint account" means an account payable on request to one or more of two or more parties, regardless of whether there is a right of survivorship.

(3) "Multiple-party account" means a joint account, a convenience account, a P.O.D. account, or a trust account. The term does not include an account established for the deposit of funds of a partnership, joint venture, or other association for business purposes, or an account controlled by one or more persons as the authorized agent or trustee for a corporation, unincorporated association, charitable or civic organization, or a regular fiduciary or trust account in which the relationship is established other than by deposit agreement.

(4) "P.O.D. account" means an account payable on request to:

    (A) one person during the person's lifetime and, on the person's death, to one or more P.O.D. payees; or

    (B) one or more persons during their lifetimes and, on the death of all of those persons, to one or more P.O.D. payees.

§ 113.102. Ownership of Joint Account During Parties' Lifetimes

During the lifetime of all parties to a joint account, the account belongs to the parties in proportion to the net contributions by each party to the sums on deposit unless there is clear and convincing evidence of a different intent.

§ 113.103. Ownership of P.O.D. Account During Original Payee's Lifetime

(a) During the lifetime of an original payee of a P.O.D. account, the account belongs to the original payee and does not belong to the P.O.D. payee or payees.

(b) If two or more parties are named as original payees of a P.O.D. account, during the parties' lifetimes rights between the parties are governed by Section 113.102.

§ 113.151. Establishment of Right of Survivorship in Joint Account; Ownership on Death of Party

(a) Sums remaining on deposit on the death of a party to a joint account belong to the surviving party or parties against the estate of the deceased party if the interest of the deceased party is made to survive to the surviving party or parties by a written agreement signed by the party who dies.

(b) Notwithstanding any other law, an agreement is sufficient under this section to confer an absolute right of survivorship on parties to a joint account if the agreement contains a statement substantially similar to the following: "On the death of one party to a joint account, all sums in the account on the date of the death vest in and belong to the surviving party as his or her separate property and estate."

(c) A survivorship agreement may not be inferred from the mere fact that the account is a joint account or that the account is designated as JT TEN, Joint Tenancy, or joint, or with other similar language.

(d) If there are two or more surviving parties to a joint account that is subject to a right of survivorship agreement:

(1) during the parties' lifetimes respective ownerships are in proportion to the parties' previous ownership interests under Sections 113.102, 113.103, and 113.104, as applicable, augmented by an equal share for each survivor of any interest a deceased party owned in the account immediately before that party's death; and

(2) the right of survivorship continues between the surviving parties if a written agreement signed by a party who dies provides for that continuation.

§ 113.152. Ownership of P.O.D. Account on Death of Party

(a) If the account is a P.O.D. account and there is a written agreement signed by the original payee or payees, on the death of the original payee or on the death of the survivor of two or more original payees, any sums remaining on deposit belong to:

(1) the P.O.D. payee or payees if surviving; or

(2) the survivor of the P.O.D. payees if one or more P.O.D. payees die before the original payee.

(b) If two or more P.O.D. payees survive, no right of survivorship exists between the surviving P.O.D. payees unless the terms of the account or deposit agreement expressly provide for survivorship between those payees.

§ 113.154. Ownership of Convenience Account on Death of Party

On the death of the last surviving party to a convenience account:

(1) a convenience signer has no right of survivorship in the account; and

(2) ownership of the account remains in the estate of the last surviving party.

§ 113.155. Effect of Death of Party on Certain Accounts Without Rights of Survivorship

The death of a party to a multiple-party account to which Sections 113.151, 113.152, and 113.153 do not apply has no effect on the beneficial ownership of the account, other than to transfer the rights of the deceased party as part of the deceased party's estate.

§ 113.158. Nontestamentary Nature of Certain Transfers

Transfers resulting from the application of Sections 113.151, 113.152, 113.153, and 113.155 are effective by reason of the account contracts involved and this chapter and are not to be considered testamentary transfers or subject to the testamentary provisions of this title.

2. Concurrent Ownership of Land and Other Property

When dealing with land and other personal property (outside of bank accounts), there are three types of cotenancies: (1) Tenancy in Common, (2) Joint Tenants with Right of Survivorship, and (3) Tenancy by the Entirety.

a. Forms of Concurrent Ownership

i. Tenancy in Common

Tenancy in Common is an undivided interest in property. Tenants in common hold by several distinct titles but have unity of possession. This means that all occupy the property in common or at least have the right to do so. At modern times the tenancy in common is the default form of concurrent ownership. Thus, there are many ways that a tenancy in common may be created.

A tenancy in common may be created:

(a) By any conveyance or devise to two or more unmarried people absent a clear intent to create a joint tenancy with right of survivorship;
(b) Through intestate succession;
(c) When a joint tenancy is severed;
(d) When a divorce severs a tenancy by the entirety; or
(e) When a conveyance attempts to create a joint tenancy or tenancy by the entirety and fails.

ii.   Joint Tenants with Right of Survivorship

The common law estate of joint tenancy was an estate held by two or more persons each having an equal right to share in enjoyment of the land during their lives. The distinguishing characteristic is the right of survivorship. At common law four unities were required to create this joint tenancy. No matter what the language may have said, the presence of the four unities was determinative of whether it would be a joint tenancy or tenancy in common. The modern approach today in the majority of states is to require the four unities plus specific language indicating an intent for survivorship. This follows the thinking today that we want to give effect to the grantor's intent. By requiring specific language parties can better give effect to intent.

The four unities are the unities of time, title, interest, and possession. Unity of time means all joint tenants received their interest at the same time. Unity of title means that all joint tenants received their interest in the same instrument of title or through the same adverse possession. Unity of interest requires all joint tenants to have the same size and type of interest. For example, *A* and *B* both have a 50 percent share and both own in fee simple absolute. Finally, there is the unity of possession. All joint tenants must be entitled to equal rights of possession.

In Texas, as long as the proper language is used as provided in the Texas Probate Code a joint tenancy with right of survivorship is created regardless of the unities. This actually allows for more flexibility in the creation of the joint tenancy.

Texas Estates Code[3]
§ 101.002 Effect of Joint Ownership of Property
If two or more persons hold an interest in property jointly and one joint owner dies before severance, the interest of the decedent in the joint estate:
   (1) Does not survive to the remaining joint owner or owners; and
   (2) Passes by will or intestacy from the decedent as if the decedent's interest had been severed.

§ 111.001 Right of Survivorship Agreements Authorized
   (a) Notwithstanding Section 101.002, two or more persons who hold an interest in property jointly may agree in writing that the interest of a joint owner who dies survives to the surviving joint owner or owners.
   (b) An agreement described by Subsection (a) may not be inferred from the mere fact that property is held in joint ownership.

---

[3] Added by Acts 2009, 81st Leg., ch. 680, § 1, eff. Jan. 1, 2014.

§ 111.002 Agreements Concerning Community Property

(a) Section 111.001 does not apply to an agreement between spouses regarding the spouses' community property.

(b) An agreement between spouses regarding a right of survivorship in community property is governed by Chapter 112.

iii. Tenancy by the Entirety

We will not focus our discussion on this tenancy because it has never been recognized in Texas; however, it does exist in some jurisdictions. A tenancy by the entirety is similar to the joint tenancy with right of survivorship but has a fifth unity—marriage. This cotenancy can exist only between a husband and wife when it is recognized. Texas is a community property state; therefore, the tenancy by the entirety has not been utilized.

NOTES & QUESTIONS:

1. Elaine executes a valid deed conveying interests in Blackacre, real property located in Texas (or a majority view state), as follows: "Elaine grants and conveys to Jerry, George, and Kramer each a 1/3 undivided interest in Blackacre." What is the state of the title for each? What if the original common law were applied to that conveyance?

2. In Texas or a majority view jurisdiction, Elaine by deed "grants and conveys undivided shares in Blackacre to George and Jerry . . ."
   a. jointly.
   b. as joint tenants.
   c. as joint tenants with right of survivorship.
   d. as joint tenants and the interests of either joint tenant who dies shall survive to the surviving joint owner or owners.
   e. as joint tenants and not as tenants in common.
   f. jointly with survivorship.

   Which of these conveyances validly create a joint tenancy with right of survivorship? Which create a tenancy in common?

3. Elaine executes a valid deed conveying interests in Blackacre, real property located in Texas (or a majority view jurisdiction), as follows:

   "Elaine grants and conveys to Jerry, George, and Kramer each a 1/3 undivided interest in Blackacre as Joint Tenants with Right of Survivorship."

What happens a year later when George dies and in his will leaves all of his real property to his friend Kenny?

4. Elaine executes a valid deed conveying interests in Blackacre, real property located in Texas (or a modern common law state), as follows:

> "Elaine grants and conveys to Jerry and George each a 1/3 undivided interest in Blackacre to have and to hold with Grantor as Joint Tenants with Rights of Survivorship."

What has Elaine created in each of them? What happens if one year later George dies and has a will leaving all of his real property to his friend Kenny?

If this were under original common law application, what would each have? What would happen if one year later George died with a will leaving all of his real property to his friend Kenny?

5. What if Elaine, Jerry, and George are joint tenants and George wants to convey his 1/3 share of ownership to his friend Kramer? Can he do that? If so, does it have any impact on Elaine or Jerry?

b. Severance of Joint Tenancies

Because the joint tenancy has the additional component of the right of survivorship, there are additional considerations for joint tenants. While creating a joint tenancy can be effective at allowing one person to ultimately own the entire property after all of the other cotenants have died, the joint tenancy is a fragile relationship. There are many things that can occur to defeat or sever the right of survivorship. This means that while other joint tenants hope to end up with the whole property, there are no guarantees with this relationship. We will look at several ways a joint tenancy could be impacted by the actions of only one joint tenant.

Keep in mind that if the joint tenancy is severed, it does not bring concurrent ownership to an end. It simply removes the right of survivorship from the affected interest. That share is now held as a tenant in common. The only concept that completely ends the cotenancy is that of partition, which we will cover last in this chapter.

Riddle v. Harmon
Court of Appeal of California, First District, 1980
162 Cal. Rptr. 530

POCHE, J.

We must decide whether Frances Riddle, now deceased, unilaterally terminated a joint tenancy by conveying her interest from herself as joint tenant to herself as tenant in common. The trial court determined, via summary judgment quieting title to her widower, that she did not. The facts follow.

Mr. and Mrs. Riddle purchased a parcel of real estate, taking title as joint tenants. Several months before her death, Mrs. Riddle retained an attorney to plan her estate. After reviewing pertinent documents, he advised her that the property was held in joint tenancy and that, upon her death, the property would pass to her husband. Distressed upon learning this, she requested that the joint tenancy be terminated so that she could dispose of her interest by will. As a result, the attorney prepared a grant deed whereby Mrs. Riddle granted to herself an undivided one-half interest in the subject property. The document also provided that "The purpose of this Grant Deed is to terminate those joint tenancies formerly existing between the Grantor, Frances P. Riddle, and Jack C. Riddle, her husband . . . ." He also prepared a will disposing of Mrs. Riddle's interest in the property. Both the grant deed and will were executed on December 8, 1975. Mrs. Riddle died 20 days later.

The court below refused to sanction her plan to sever the joint tenancy and quieted title to the property in her husband. The executrix of the will of Frances Riddle appeals from that judgment.

The basic concept of a joint tenancy is that it is one estate which is taken jointly. Under the common law, four unities were essential to the creation and existence of an estate in joint tenancy: interest, time, title and possession. If one of the unities was destroyed, a tenancy in common remained. Severance of the joint tenancy extinguishes the principal feature of that estate, the *Jus accrescendi* or right of survivorship.

An indisputable right of each joint tenant is the power to convey his or her separate estate by way of gift or otherwise without the knowledge or consent of the other joint tenant and to thereby terminate the joint tenancy. If a joint tenant conveys to a stranger and that person reconveys to the same tenant, then no revival of the joint tenancy occurs because the unities are destroyed. The former joint tenants become tenants in common.

At common law, one could not create a joint tenancy in himself and another by a direct conveyance. It was necessary for joint tenants to acquire their interests at the same time (unity of time) and by the same conveyancing instrument (unity of title). So, in order to create a valid joint tenancy where one of the proposed joint tenants already owned an interest in the property, it was first necessary to convey the property to a disinterested third person, a "strawman," who then conveyed the title to the ultimate grantees as joint tenants. This remains the prevailing practice in some jurisdictions. Other states, including California, have disregarded this application of the unities requirement "as one of the obsolete 'subtle and arbitrary distinctions and niceties of the feudal common law,' [and allow the creation of a valid joint tenancy without the use of a strawman]." (4A Powell on Real Property (1979) [para.] 616, p. 670, citation omitted.)

By amendment to its Civil Code, California became a pioneer in allowing the creation of a joint tenancy by direct transfer. Under authority of Civil Code section 683, a joint tenancy conveyance may be made from a "sole owner to himself and others," or from joint owners to themselves and others as specified in the code. The purpose of the amendment was to "avoid the necessity of making a conveyance through a dummy" in the statutorily enumerated situations. Accordingly, in California, it is no longer necessary to use a strawman to create a joint tenancy. This court is now asked to reexamine whether a strawman is required to terminate a joint tenancy.

Twelve years ago, in Clark v. Carter, the Court of Appeal considered the same question and found the strawman to be indispensable. 265 Cal. App. 2d 291, 295 (1968). As in the instant case, the joint tenants in Clark were husband and wife. The day before Mrs. Clark died, she executed two documents without her husband's knowledge or consent: (1) a quitclaim deed conveying her undivided half interest in certain real property from herself as joint tenant to herself as tenant in common, and (2) an assignment of her undivided half interest in a deed of trust from herself as joint tenant to herself as tenant in common. These documents were held insufficient to sever the joint tenancy.

After summarizing joint tenancy principles, the court reasoned that "[U]nder California law, a transfer of property presupposes participation by at least two parties, namely, a grantor and a grantee. Both are essential to the efficacy of a deed, and they cannot be the same person. A transfer of property requires that title be conveyed by one living person to another. Foreign authority also exists to the effect that a person cannot convey to himself alone, and if he does so, he still holds under the original title. Similarly, it was the common law rule that in every property conveyance there be a grantor, a grantee, and a thing granted. Moreover, the grantor could not make himself the grantee by conveying an estate to himself." (*Clark, supra,* at 295-296, citations omitted.)

That "two-to-transfer" notion stems from the English common law feoffment ceremony with livery of seisin. If the ceremony took place upon the land being conveyed, the grantor (feoffor) would hand a symbol of the land, such as a lump of earth or a twig, to the grantee (feoffee). In order to complete the investiture of seisin it was necessary that the feoffor completely relinquish possession of the land to the feoffee. It is apparent from the requirement of livery of seisin that one could not enfeoff oneself—that is, one could not be both grantor and grantee in a single transaction. Handing oneself a dirt clod is ungainly. Just as livery of seisin has become obsolete, so should ancient vestiges of that ceremony give way to modern conveyancing realities.

Thus, undaunted by the *Clark* case, resourceful attorneys have worked out an inventory of methods to evade the rule that one cannot be both grantor and grantee simultaneously.

The most familiar technique for unilateral termination is use of an intermediary "strawman" blessed in the case of Burke v. Stevens (1968). There, Mrs. Burke carried out a secret plan to terminate a joint tenancy that existed between her husband and herself in certain real property. The steps to accomplish this objective involved: (1) a letter written from Mrs. Burke to her attorney directing him to prepare a power of attorney naming him as her attorney in fact for the purpose of terminating the joint tenancy; (2) her execution and delivery of the power of attorney; (3) her attorney's execution and delivery of a quitclaim deed conveying Mrs. Burke's interest in the property to a third party, who was an office associate of the attorney in fact; (4) the third party's execution and delivery of a quitclaim deed reconveying that interest to Mrs. Burke on the following day. The Burke court sanctioned this method of terminating the joint tenancy, noting at one point: "While the actions of the wife, from the standpoint of a theoretically perfect marriage, are subject to ethical criticism, and her stealthy approach to the solution of the problems facing her is not to be acclaimed, the question before the court is not what should have been done ideally in a perfect marriage, but whether the decedent and her attorneys acted in a legally permissible manner."

Another creative method of terminating a joint tenancy appears in Reiss v. Reiss (1941). There a trust was used. For the purpose of destroying the incident of survivorship, Mrs. Reiss transferred bare legal title to her son, as trustee of a trust for her use and benefit. The son promised to reconvey the property to his mother or to whomever she selected at any time upon her demand. The court upheld this arrangement, stating, "We are of the opinion that the clearly expressed desire of Rosa Reiss to terminate the joint tenancy arrangement was effectively accomplished by the transfer of the legal title to her son for her expressed specific purpose of having the control and the right of disposition of her half of the property."

Moreover, this will not be the first time that a court has allowed a joint tenant to unilaterally sever a joint tenancy without the use of an intermediary. In Hendrickson v. Minneapolis Federal Sav. & L. Assn., decided one month after Clark, the Minnesota Supreme Court held that a tenancy in common resulted from one joint tenant's execution of a "Declaration of Election to Sever Survivorship of Joint Tenancy." No fictional transfer by conveyance and reconveyance through a strawman was required.

Our decision does not create new powers for a joint tenant. A universal right of each joint tenant is the power to effect a severance and destroy the right of survivorship by conveyance of his or her joint tenancy interest to another person. If an indestructible right of survivorship is desired—that is, one which may not be destroyed by one tenant—that may be accomplished by creating a joint life estate with a contingent remainder in fee to the survivor; a tenancy in common in simple fee with an executory interest in the survivor; or a fee simple to take effect in possession in the future.

We discard the archaic rule that one cannot enfeoff oneself which, if applied, would defeat the clear intention of the grantor. There is no question but that the decedent here could have accomplished her objective—termination of the joint tenancy—by one of a variety of circuitous processes. We reject the rationale of the *Clark* case because it rests on a common law notion whose reason for existence vanished about the time that grant deeds and title companies replaced colorful dirt clod ceremonies as the way to transfer title to real property. One joint tenant may unilaterally sever the joint tenancy without the use of an intermediary device.

The judgment is reversed.

Harms v. Sprague
Supreme Court of Illinois, 1984
473 N.E.2d 930

MORAN, J.

Plaintiff, William H. Harms, filed a complaint to quiet title and for declaratory judgment in the circuit court of Greene County. Plaintiff had taken title to certain real estate with his brother John R. Harms, as a joint tenant, with full right of survivorship. The plaintiff named, as a defendant, Charles D. Sprague, the executor of the estate of John Harms and the devisee of all the real and personal property of John Harms. Also named as defendants were Carl T. and Mary E. Simmons, alleged mortgagees of the property in question. Defendant Sprague filed a counterclaim against plaintiff, challenging plaintiff's claim of ownership of the entire tract of property and asking the court to recognize his (Sprague's) interest as a tenant in common, subject to a mortgage lien. At issue was the effect the granting of a mortgage by John Harms had on the joint tenancy. Also at issue was whether the mortgage survived the death of John Harms as a lien against the property.

The trial court held that the mortgage given by John Harms to defendants Carl and Mary Simmons severed the joint tenancy. Further, the court found that the mortgage survived the death of John Harms as a lien against the undivided one-half interest in the property which passed to Sprague by and through the will of the deceased. The appellate court reversed, finding that the mortgage given by one joint tenant of his interest in the property does not sever the joint tenancy. Accordingly, the appellate court held that plaintiff, as the surviving joint tenant, owned the property in its entirety, unencumbered by the mortgage lien.

Two issues are raised on appeal: (1) Is a joint tenancy severed when less than all of the joint tenants mortgage their interest in the property? and (2) Does such a mortgage survive the death of the mortgagor as a lien on the property?

A review of the stipulation of facts reveals the following. Plaintiff, William Harms, and his brother John Harms, took title to real estate located in Roodhouse, on June 26, 1973, as joint tenants. The warranty deed memorializing this transaction was recorded on June 29, 1973, in the office of the Greene County recorder of deeds.

Carl and Mary Simmons owned a lot and home in Roodhouse. Charles Sprague entered into an agreement with the Simmons whereby Sprague was to purchase their property for $25,000. Sprague tendered $18,000 in cash and signed a promissory note for the balance of $7,000. Because Sprague had no security for the $7,000, he asked his friend, John Harms, to co-sign the note and give a mortgage on his interest in the joint tenancy property. Harms agreed, and on June 12, 1981, John Harms and Charles Sprague, jointly and severally, executed a promissory note for $7,000 payable to Carl and Mary Simmons. The note states that the principal sum of $7,000 was to be paid from the proceeds of the sale of John Harms' interest in the joint tenancy property, but in any event no later than six months from the date the note was signed. The note reflects that five monthly interest payments had been made, with the last payment recorded November 6, 1981. In addition, John Harms executed a mortgage, in favor of the Simmonses, on his undivided one-half interest in the joint tenancy property, to secure payment of the note. William Harms was unaware of the mortgage given by his brother.

John Harms moved from his joint tenancy property to the Simmons property which had been purchased by Charles Sprague. On December 10, 1981, John Harms died. By the terms of John Harms' will, Charles Sprague was the devisee of his entire estate. The mortgage given by John Harms to the Simmonses was recorded on December 29, 1981.

Prior to the appellate court decision in the instant case no court of this State had directly addressed the principal question we are confronted with herein-the effect of a mortgage, executed by less than all of the joint tenants, on the joint tenancy.

Nevertheless, there are numerous cases which have considered the severance issue in relation to other circumstances surrounding a joint tenancy. All have necessarily focused on the four unities which are fundamental to both the creation and the perpetuation of the joint tenancy. These are the unities of interest, title, time, and possession. The voluntary or involuntary destruction of any of the unities by one of the joint tenants will sever the joint tenancy.

In a series of cases, this court has considered the effect that judgment liens upon the interest of one joint tenant have on the stability of the joint tenancy. In Peoples Trust & Savings Bank v. Haas, the court found that a judgment lien secured against one joint tenant did not serve to extinguish the joint tenancy. As such, the surviving joint tenant "succeeded to the title in fee to the whole of the land by operation of law." 328 Ill. 468, 471, 160 N.E. 85.

In yet another case involving the attachment of a judgment lien upon the interest of a joint tenant, Jackson v. Lacey (1951), 408 Ill. 530, 97 N.E.2d 839, the court held that the estate of joint tenancy had not been destroyed. The judgment creditor had levied on the interest of the joint tenant debtor. In addition, that interest was sold by the bailiff of the municipal court to the other joint tenant, who died intestate before the time of redemption expired. While the court recognized that a conveyance, even if involuntary, destroys the unity of title and severs the joint tenancy, it held that there would be no conveyance until the redemption period had expired without a redemption. As such, title was not as yet divested and the estate in joint tenancy was unaltered.

Clearly, this court adheres to the rule that a lien on a joint tenant's interest in property will not effectuate a severance of the joint tenancy, absent the conveyance by a deed following the expiration of a redemption period. It follows, therefore, that if Illinois perceives a mortgage as merely a lien on the mortgagor's interest in property rather than a conveyance of title from mortgagor to mortgagee, the execution of a mortgage by a joint tenant, on his interest in the property, would not destroy the unity of title and sever the joint tenancy.

Early cases in Illinois, however, followed the title theory of mortgages. In 1900, this court recognized the common law precept that a mortgage was a conveyance of a legal estate vesting title to the property in the mortgagee. Consistent with this title theory of mortgages, therefore, there are many cases which state, in dicta, that a joint tenancy is severed by one of the joint tenants mortgaging his interest to a stranger. Yet even the early case of Lightcap v. Bradley recognized that the title held by the mortgagee was for the limited purpose of protecting his interests. The court went on to say that "the mortgagor is the owner for every other purpose and against every other person. The title of the mortgagee is anomalous, and exists only between him and the mortgagor." Lightcap v. Bradley (1900), 186 Ill. 510, 522-23, 58 N.E. 221.

In *Kling*, the court was confronted with the question of when a separation of title, necessary to create an easement by implication, had occurred. The court found that title to the property was not separated with the execution of a trust deed but rather only upon execution and delivery of a master's deed. The court stated:

> In some jurisdictions the execution of a mortgage is a severance, in others, the execution of a mortgage is not a severance. In Illinois the giving of a mortgage is not a separation of title, for the holder of the mortgage takes only a lien thereunder. After foreclosure of a mortgage and until delivery of the master's deed under the foreclosure sale, purchaser acquires no title to the land either legal or equitable. Title to land sold under mortgage foreclosure remains in the mortgagor or his grantee until the expiration of the redemption period and conveyance by the master's deed.

3 Ill. 2d 455, 460, 121 N.E.2d 752.

We find, however, that implicit in *Kling* and our more recent cases which follow the lien theory of mortgages is the conclusion that a joint tenancy is not severed when one joint tenant executes a mortgage on his interest in the property, since the unity of title has been preserved. As the appellate court in the instant case correctly observed: "If giving a mortgage creates only a lien, then a mortgage should have the same effect on a joint tenancy as a lien created in other ways." (119 Ill. App. 3d 503, 507, 75 Ill. Dec. 155, 456 N.E.2d 976.)

A joint tenancy has been defined as "a present estate in all the joint tenants, each being seized of the whole." (Partridge v. Berliner (1927), 325 Ill. 253, 257, 156 N.E. 352.) An inherent feature of the estate of joint tenancy is the right of survivorship, which is the right of the last survivor to take the whole of the estate. Because we find that a mortgage given by one joint tenant of his interest in the property does not sever the joint tenancy, we hold that the plaintiff's right of survivorship became operative upon the death of his brother. As such plaintiff is now the sole owner of the estate, in its entirety.

Further, we find that the mortgage executed by John Harms does not survive as a lien on plaintiff's property. A surviving joint tenant succeeds to the share of the deceased joint tenant by virtue of the conveyance which created the joint tenancy, not as the successor of the deceased. The property right of the mortgaging joint tenant is extinguished at the moment of his death. While John Harms was alive, the mortgage existed as a lien on his interest in the joint tenancy. Upon his death, his interest ceased to exist and along with it the lien of the mortgage. Under the circumstances of this case, we would note that the mortgage given by John Harms to the Simmonses was only valid as between the original parties during the lifetime of John Harms since it was unrecorded. In addition, recording the mortgage subsequent to the death of John Harms was a nullity. As we stated above, John Harms' property rights in the joint tenancy were extinguished when he died. Thus, he no longer had a property interest upon which the mortgage lien could attach.

For the reasons stated herein, the judgment of the appellate court is affirmed.

Judgment affirmed.

NOTES & QUESTIONS:

1. The approach taken by the court in *Riddle* with respect to a unilateral severance of the joint tenancy is a modern approach but is not accepted by a majority of states. The reason for this is that it allows for a secret conveyance that could be fraudulent.

2. What would have happened if Mrs. Riddle drafted a deed to herself to sever the joint tenancy with her husband and she told no one and put the deed in a desk drawer or safety deposit box? If this deed affects a severance and she dies first, her husband is deprived of receiving her 50 percent share. He was always at risk of that happening so that outcome is not the real concern. However, what if Mrs. Riddle prepared the deed, put it in a desk drawer or safety deposit box and her husband died first? No one else knew of the deed so she tears it up and burns it in the fireplace, now claiming the 100 percent ownership in the property due to her right of survivorship. That is where there is concern over the secret conveyance.

   Some states have taken the approach that if a party wants to effect a unilateral severance, then the deed must be recorded in order to be valid. While the severance still may occur without the knowledge or participation of the other joint tenant or tenants, it eliminates the possibility of fraud.

3. Aside from the unilateral conveyance there are many ways a joint tenancy may be severed. If one joint tenant conveys his interest to a third party, that voluntary transfer does sever the right of survivorship. So, in in the earlier example, when George conveyed his 1/3 interest to Kramer, could he? What happened?

4. The *Harms* case illustrates different approaches taken to liens on real property. The majority view, Texas included, is that a mortgage is just a special type of lien. Liens are nonpossessory interests that do not impact the title unless foreclosed. So, if a joint tenant uses his fractional share as collateral for a debt, that does not destroy the right of survivorship in a majority of states.

What if a lien exists on the property and the lien is in default and the creditor is preparing to foreclose? At what point in the process do you think there would be a severance of the joint tenancy?

5. What would happen, if anything, to the joint tenancy if one cotenant wants to enter into a lease of the premises without the consent of the other cotenant(s)? Can he do that? Would it have any impact on the right of survivorship? Why or why not? *See* Schwartzbaugh v. Sampson below to help answer this question.

3. Relationships Among Cotenants

Each type of cotenancy is created differently and has distinct rules that apply. However, there are also general rules that will apply in all cotenant relationships. We will explore these common rules in our coverage of relationships among cotenants. There are rules that govern issues regarding possession and income; rents and profits; taxes, mortgages and other carrying costs; and rights of reimbursement or contribution for expenditures. Additionally, there are rules governing the termination of cotenant relationships through partition, which will be addressed in the next section on partition.

First, in considering the nature of a cotenant relationship, it is not one of a fiduciary. A fiduciary relationship exists when there is an obligation of special care to another. Cotenants do not have any special obligations, other than not to harm their cotenants' interests and each cotenant still cannot convey more than he owns. This means that both the tenant in common and joint tenant can always convey their fractional share of ownership and can make use of and possess the property. However, as seen in the prior sections, this can potentially impact the relationship.

Second, all cotenants have equal power to jointly manage the property. When parties cannot agree, the result is typically partition.

Third, in managing the property cotenants also are obligated to maintain it. There are differences among the states as to how repairs and maintenance costs should be addressed. Some states take the position that all cotenants have a duty to contribute to the necessary repairs of the property. However, many states disagree with this approach because sometimes it can be difficult to determine what is a "necessary" repair. Additionally, all states agree that a cotenant who voluntarily makes improvements to the property cannot seek contribution from the other cotenants. Sometimes it can be difficult to distinguish between a repair and an improvement. All states consider necessary repairs and improvements at the time of partition and factor that into the award of sales proceeds or distribution of the land.

Fourth, income from the renting of the property should be shared among the cotenants. A cotenant does not have a duty to pay rent for his own use and possession unless there is an agreement or ouster (majority view), but if income is made from renting the co-owned land to third parties then all are entitled to share.

Finally, all cotenants must share in necessary expenses for the property that are carrying charges. These are expenses that must be paid in order to keep the property. This would include taxes, assessments (including mandatory HOA dues), mortgage payments for mortgages entered into by all cotenants, and—in some states—property hazard insurance.

Spiller v. Mackereth
Supreme Court of Alabama, 1976
334 So. 2d 859

JONES, J.

This is an appeal from a suit based upon a complaint by John Robert Spiller seeking sale for division among tenants in common and a counterclaim by Hettie Mackereth and others seeking an accounting for Spiller's alleged "ouster" of his cotenants. By agreement of the parties, the trial Court entered a decree on the complaint ordering the sale of the property. A trial was then held *ore tenus* on the counterclaim.

At the conclusion of the trial, the Judge entered a finding that Spiller had ousted Mackereth. Based on these findings, the trial Judge awarded Mackereth $2,100 rental. Spiller appeals both the rental award. We reverse the rental award.

The pertinent facts are undisputed. In February, 1973, Spiller purchased an undivided one-half interest in a lot in downtown Tuscaloosa. Spiller's cotenants were Mackereth and the other appellees. At the time Spiller bought his interest, the lot was being rented by an automobile supply business called Auto-Rite. In May, 1973, Spiller offered to purchase Mackereth's interest in the property. Mackereth refused and made a counteroffer to purchase Spiller's interest which Spiller refused. Spiller then filed the complaint seeking sale for division on July 11, 1973.

In October, 1973, Auto-Rite vacated the building which it had been renting for $350 per month and Spiller begun to use the entire building as a warehouse. On November 15, 1973, Mackereth's attorney sent a letter to Spiller demanding that he either vacate one-half of the building or pay rent. Spiller did not respond to the letter, vacate the premises, or pay rent; therefore, Mackereth brought this counterclaim to collect the rental she claimed Spiller owed her.

On the question of Spiller's liability for rent, we start with the general rule that in absence of an agreement to pay rent or an ouster of a cotenant, a cotenant in possession is not liable to his cotenants for the value of his use and occupation of the property. Since there was no agreement to pay rent, there must be evidence which establishes an ouster before Spiller is required to pay rent to Mackereth. The difficulty in this determination lies in the definition of the word "ouster." Ouster is a conclusory word which is used loosely in cotenancy cases to describe two distinct fact situations. The two fact situations are (1) the beginning of the running of the statute of limitations for adverse possession and (2) the liability of an occupying cotenant for rent to other cotenants. Although the cases do not acknowledge a distinction between the two uses of "ouster," it is clear that the two fact situations require different elements of proof to support a conclusion of ouster.

The Alabama cases involving adverse possession require a finding that the possessing cotenant asserted complete ownership to the land to support a conclusion of ouster. The finding of assertion of ownership may be established in several ways. Some cases find an assertion of complete ownership from a composite of activities such as renting part of the land without accounting, hunting the land, cutting timber, assessing and paying taxes and generally treating the land as if it were owned in fee for the statutory period. Other cases find the assertion of complete ownership from more overt activities such as a sale of the property under a deed purporting to convey the entire fee. But whatever factual elements are present, the essence of the finding of an ouster in the adverse possession cases is a claim of absolute ownership and a denial of the cotenancy relationship by the occupying cotenant.

The normal fact situation which will render an occupying cotenant liable to out of possession cotenants is one in which the occupying cotenant refuses a demand of the other cotenants to be allowed into use and enjoyment of the land, regardless of a claim of absolute ownership.

The instant case involves a cotenant's liability for rent. We can affirm the trial Court if the record reveals some evidence that Mackereth actually sought to occupy the building but was prevented from moving in by Spiller. To prove ouster, Mackereth's attorney relies upon the letter of November 15, 1973, as a sufficient demand and refusal to establish Spiller's liability for rent. This letter, however, did not demand equal use and enjoyment of the premises; rather, it demanded only that Spiller either vacate half of the building or pay rent. The question of whether a demand to vacate or pay rent is sufficient to establish an occupying cotenant's liability for rent has not been addressed in Alabama; however, it has been addressed by courts in other jurisdictions. In jurisdictions which adhere to the majority and Alabama rule of nonliability for mere occupancy, several cases have held that the occupying cotenant is not liable for rent notwithstanding a demand to vacate or pay rent.

There is a minority view which establishes liability for rents on a continued occupancy after a demand to vacate or pay rent. We believe that the majority view on this question is consistent with Alabama's approach to the law of occupancy by cotenants. As one of the early Alabama cases on the subject explains:

> Tenants in common are seized *per my et per tout*. Each has an equal right to occupy; and unless the one in actual possession denies to the other the right to enter, or agrees to pay rent, nothing can be claimed for such occupation.

MAJORITY RULE

Thus, before an occupying cotenant can be liable for rent in Alabama, he must have denied his cotenants the right to enter. It is axiomatic that there can be no denial of the right to enter unless there is a demand or an attempt to enter. Simply requesting the occupying cotenant to vacate is not sufficient because the occupying cotenant holds title to the whole and may rightfully occupy the whole unless the other cotenants assert their possessory rights.

Besides the November 15 letter, Mackereth's only attempt to prove ouster is a showing that Spiller put locks on the building. However, there is no evidence that Spiller was attempting to do anything other than protect the merchandise he had stored in the building. Spiller testified that when Auto-Rite moved out they removed the locks from the building. Since Spiller began to store his merchandise in the building thereafter, he had to acquire new locks to secure it. There is no evidence that either Mackereth or any of the other cotenants ever requested keys to the locks or were ever prevented from entering the building because of the locks. There is no evidence that Spiller intended to exclude his cotenants by use of the locks. Again, we emphasize that as long as Spiller did not deny access to his cotenants, any activity of possession and occupancy of the building was consistent with his rights of ownership. Thus, the fact that Spiller placed locks on the building, without evidence that he intended to exclude the other cotenants, is insufficient to establish his liability to pay rent.

After reviewing all of the testimony and evidence presented at trial, we are unable to find any evidence which supports a legal conclusion of ouster. We are, therefore, compelled to reverse the trial Court's judgment awarding Mackereth $2,100 rental.

NOTES & QUESTIONS:

1. The rule that a cotenant does not owe rent absent agreement or ouster is the majority rule. Why would that be the case?

2. What should Mackereth have done to trigger Spiller's obligation to pay rent?

3. Keep in mind the rule regarding payments of rent while reading the next case.

Swartzbaugh v. Sampson
Court of Appeal of California, Fourth District, 1936
54 P.2d 73

MARKS, J.

This is an action to cancel two leases executed by John Josiah Swartzbaugh, as lessor, to Sam A. Sampson, as lessee, of two adjoining parcels of land in Orange county. A motion for nonsuit was granted at the close of plaintiff's case, and this appeal followed.

Defendant Swartzbaugh and plaintiff are husband and wife. They owned, as joint tenants with the right of survivorship, 60 acres of land in Orange county planted to bearing walnuts. In December, 1933, defendant Sampson started negotiations with plaintiff and her husband for the leasing of a small fraction of this land fronting on highway 101 for a site for a boxing pavilion. Plaintiff at all times objected to making the lease, and it is thoroughly established that Sampson knew she would not join in any lease to him.

The negotiations resulted in the execution of an option for a lease, dated January 5, 1934, signed by Swartzbaugh and Sampson. The lease, dated February 2, 1934, was executed by the same parties. A second lease of property adjoining the site of the boxing pavilion was signed by Swartzbaugh and Sampson. This was also dated February 2, 1934, but probably was signed after that date. Plaintiff's name does not appear in any of the three documents, and Sampson was advised that she would not sign any of them.

The walnut trees were removed from the leased premises. Sampson went into possession, erected his boxing pavilion, and placed other improvements on the property.

Plaintiff was injured in February, 1934, and was confined to her bed for some time. This action was started on June 20, 1934. Up to the time of the trial plaintiff had received no part of the rental of the leased property. Sampson was in possession of all of it under the leases to the exclusion of plaintiff.

There is but one question to be decided in this case which may be stated as follows: Can one joint tenant who has not joined in the leases executed by her cotenant and another maintain an action to cancel the leases where the lessee is in exclusive possession of the leased property? It seems necessary that we consider briefly the nature of the estate in joint tenancy and the rights of the joint tenants in it.

An estate in joint tenancy can be severed by destroying one or more of the necessary unities, either by operation of law, by death, by voluntary or certain involuntary acts of the joint tenants, or by certain acts or omissions of one joint tenant without the consent of the other. It seems to be the rule in England that a lease by one joint tenant for a term of years will effect a severance, at least during the term of the lease. We have found no case in the United States where this rule has been applied. From the reasoning used and conclusions reached in many of the American cases its adoption in this country seems doubtful.

One of the essential unities of a joint tenancy is that of possession. Each tenant owns an equal interest in all of the fee, and each has an equal right to possession of the whole. Possession by one is possession by all. Ordinarily, one joint tenant out of possession cannot recover exclusive possession of the joint property from his cotenant. He can only recover the right to be let into joint possession of the property with his cotenant. He cannot eject his cotenant in possession.

It is a general rule that the act of one joint tenant without express or implied authority from or the consent of his cotenant cannot bind or prejudicially affect the rights of the latter.

In the application of the foregoing rule, the courts have imposed a limitation upon it which, in effect, is a qualification of its broad language. This perhaps is due to the nature of the estate which is universally held to be joint in enjoyment and several upon severance. This limitation arises in cases where one joint tenant in possession leases all of the joint property without the consent of his cotenant, and places the lessee in possession. It seems to be based upon the theory that the joint tenant in possession is entitled to the possession of the entire property and by his lease merely gives to his lessee a right he (the lessor) had been enjoying, puts the lessee in the enjoyment of a right of possession which he (the lessor) already had, and by so doing does not prejudicially affect the rights of the cotenant out of possession; it being conceded that the joint tenant not joining in the lease is not bound by its terms and that he can recover from the tenant of his cotenant the reasonable value of the use and enjoyment of his share of the estate, if the tenant under the lease refuses him the right to enjoy his moiety of the estate.

In 2 Thompson on Real Property, p. 929, § 1715, it is said: "One joint tenant may make a lease of the joint property, but this will bind only his share of it." The same rule is thus stated in 1 Landlord and Tenant, Tiffany, 405: "One of two or more joint tenants cannot, by making a lease of the whole, vest in the lessee more than his own share, since that is all to which he has an exclusive right. Such a lease is, however, valid as to his share."

The foregoing authorities support the conclusion that a lease to all of the joint property by one joint tenant is not a nullity but is a valid and supportable contract in so far as the interest of the lessor in the joint property is concerned.

While the qualities of estates of joint tenancy and a tenancy in common differ, the rights of possession are quite similar. . . . This being so, decisions on similar questions to the one we are considering, where estates in common are concerned, have considerable weight.

In the case of Lee Chuck v. Quan Wo Chong & Co., 91 Cal. 593, 28 P. 45, the plaintiff, a tenant in common, brought an action to oust defendant who was holding under a lease from another tenant in common. The Supreme Court reversed the judgment in favor of plaintiff and said:

> The evidence does not support the judgment. It is expressly alleged in the complaint that "this plaintiff and one Chay Yune are successors in interest of said E. L. Goldstein, and to said building on the north-west corner of Dupont and Clay streets, and in and to said lease executed to Pee Han, and that they hold title to the same as tenants in common." The uncontradicted evidence shows that the defendants were in possession of the property, with the consent of said Chay Yune. All that the plaintiff was entitled to, therefore, was to be let into possession with the defendants,—to enjoy their moiety.
>
> "One tenant in common may, by either lease or license, confer upon another person the right to occupy and use the property of the co-tenancy as fully as such lessor or licensor himself might have used or occupied it if such lease or license had not been granted. If either co-tenant expel such licensee or lessee, he is guilty of a trespass. If the lessee has the exclusive possession of the premises, he is not liable to any one but his lessor for the rent, unless the other co-tenants attempt to enter, and he resists or forbids their entry, or unless being in possession with them, he ousts or excludes some or all of them." Freem. Co-Ten. § 253. There is no evidence tending to show that the defendants ever refused to allow the plaintiff to enjoy the use of the premises with them. The judgment does not confine the plaintiff's right of recovery to his own moiety, but provides that the plaintiff shall have and recover from defendants the restitution and possession of the premises described in the complaint.

As far as the evidence before us in this case is concerned, the foregoing authorities force the conclusion that the leases from Swartzbaugh to Sampson are not null and void but valid and existing contracts giving to Sampson the same right to the possession of the leased property that Swartzbaugh had. It follows they cannot be canceled by plaintiff in this action. Judgment affirmed.

NOTES & QUESTIONS:

1. An interesting note about the Swartzbaugh property. This land is now the home of the baseball field for the Los Angeles Angels at Anaheim. The trees were eventually removed and boxing arena destroyed to make way for the baseball stadium.

2. With Mrs. Swartzbaugh being stuck with the lease to Mr. Sampson, what could she do under the circumstances to protect her interests?

3. If Mr. Swartzbaugh died during the time of Mr. Sampson's lease, what happens to the lease?

4. If Mrs. Swartzbaugh is unhappy about the activity occurring on this land that she co-owns, should she seek partition? Consider that question as you read the material next on partition.

4. Right to Partition

Partition is different from a severance of a joint tenancy. When we discussed the concept of a severance, we were dealing with the destruction of the four unities required for a joint tenancy with right of survivorship. After the severance, a cotenancy relationship still exists but the nature of the tenancy has changed.

Partition is an "escape hatch" for cotenants. An action for partition ends the cotenant relationship completely and, instead of having a common interest in a single piece of property, the parties end up as neighbors, each owning separate pieces of land if the property is partitioned in kind or they each end up with money representing each share of the cotenant property if partitioned by sale.

Tex. Prop. Code
§ 23.001 Partition
A joint owner or claimant of real property or an interest in real property or a joint owner of personal property may compel a partition of the interest or the property among the joint owners or claimants under this chapter and the Texas Rules of Civil Procedure.

§ 23.004 Effect of Partition
(a) A person allotted a share of or an interest in real property in a partition action holds the property or interest in severalty under the conditions and covenants that applied to the property prior to the partition.
(b) A court decree confirming a report of commissioners in partition of real property gives a recipient of an interest in the property a title equivalent

to a conveyance of the interest by a warranty deed from the other parties in the action.

(c) Except as provided by this chapter, a partition of real property does not affect a right in the property.

Consider in this case the question of selling the property or physically dividing it up among the parties. Which is the better approach? Why?

Delfino v. Vealencis
Supreme Court of Connecticut, 1980
436 A.2d 27

HEALEY, J.

The central issue in this appeal is whether the Superior Court properly ordered the sale, pursuant to General Statutes § 52-500,[4] of property owned by the plaintiffs and the defendant as tenants in common.

The plaintiffs, Angelo and William Delfino, and the defendant, Helen C. Vealencis, own, as tenants in common, real property located in Bristol, Connecticut. The property consists of an approximately 20.5 acre parcel of land and the dwelling of the defendant thereon. The plaintiffs own an undivided 99/144 interest in the property, and the defendant owns a 45/144 interest. The defendant occupies the dwelling and a portion of the land, from which she operates a rubbish and garbage removal business.

Apparently, none of the parties is in actual possession of the remainder of the property. The plaintiffs, one of whom is a residential developer, propose to develop the property, upon partition, into forty-five residential building lots.

In 1978, the plaintiffs brought an action in the trial court seeking a partition of the property by sale with a division of the proceeds according to the parties' respective interests. The defendant moved for a judgment of in-kind partition and the appointment of a committee to conduct said partition. The trial court, after a

---

[4] General Statutes § 52-500 states: "Sale of Real or Personal Property Owned by Two or More. Any court of equitable jurisdiction may, upon the complaint of any person interested, order the sale of any estate, real or personal, owned by two or more persons, when, in the opinion of the court, a sale will better promote the interests of the owners. The provisions of this section shall extend to and include land owned by two or more persons, when the whole or a part of such land is vested in any person for life with remainder to his heirs, general or special, or, on failure of such heirs, to any other person, whether the same, or any part thereof, is held in trust or otherwise. A conveyance made in pursuance of a decree ordering a sale of such land shall vest the title in the purchaser thereof, and shall bind the person entitled to the life estate and his legal heirs and any other person having a remainder interest in the lands; but the court passing such decree shall make such order in relation to the investment of the avails of such sale as it deems necessary for the security of all persons having any interest in such land."

hearing, concluded that a partition in kind could not be had without "material injury" to the respective rights of the parties, and therefore ordered that the property be sold at auction by a committee and that the proceeds be paid into the court for distribution to the parties.

On appeal, the defendant claims essentially that the trial court's conclusion that the parties' interests would best be served by a partition by sale is not supported by the findings of subordinate facts, and that the court improperly considered certain factors in arriving at that conclusion.

It has long been the policy of this court, as well as other courts, to favor a partition in kind over a partition by sale. Due to the possible impracticality of actual division, this state, like others, expanded the right to partition to allow a partition by sale under certain circumstances. The early decisions of this court that considered the partition-by-sale statute emphasized that "[t]he statute giving the power of sale introduces . . . no new principles; it provides only for an emergency, when a division cannot be well made, in any other way. The court later expressed its reason for preferring partition in kind when it stated: "[A] sale of one's property without his consent is an extreme exercise of power warranted only in clear cases." Ford v. Kirk, 41 Conn. 9, 12 (1874). Although a court is no longer required to order a partition in kind even in cases of extreme difficulty or hardship it is clear that a partition by sale should be ordered only when two conditions are satisfied: (1) the physical attributes of the land are such that a partition in kind is impracticable or inequitable; and (2) the interests of the owners would better be promoted by a partition by sale. Since our law has for many years presumed that a partition in kind would be in the best interests of the owners, the burden is on the party requesting a partition by sale to demonstrate that such a sale would better promote the owners' interests.

The defendant claims in effect that the trial court's conclusion that the rights of the parties would best be promoted by a judicial sale is not supported by the findings of subordinate facts. We agree.

Under the test set out above, the court must first consider the practicability of physically partitioning the property in question. The trial court concluded that due to the situation and location of the parcel of land, the size and area of the property, the physical structure and appurtenances on the property, and other factors, a physical partition of the property would not be feasible. An examination of the subordinate findings of facts and the exhibits, however, demonstrates that the court erred in this respect.

It is undisputed that the property in question consists of one 20.5 acre parcel, basically rectangular in shape, and one dwelling, located at the extreme western end of the property. Two roads, Dino Road and Lucien Court, abut the property and another, Birch Street, provides access through use of a right-of-way. Unlike cases where there are numerous fractional owners of the property to be partitioned, and the practicability of a physical division is therefore drastically reduced in this case there are only two competing ownership interests: the plaintiffs' undivided 99/144 interest and the defendant's 45/144 interest. These facts, taken together, do not support the trial court's conclusion that a physical partition of the property would not be "feasible" in this case. Instead, the above facts demonstrate that the opposite is true: a partition in kind clearly would be practicable under the circumstances of this case.

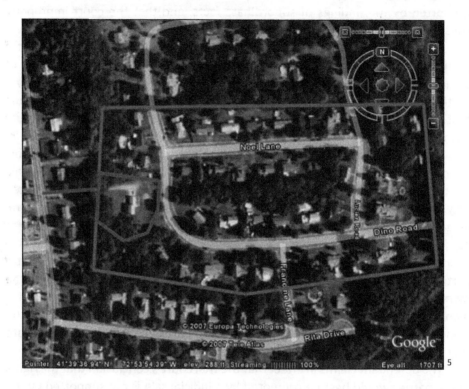

Although a partition in kind is physically practicable, it remains to be considered whether a partition in kind would also promote the best interests of the parties. In order to resolve this issue, the consequences of a partition in kind must be compared with those of a partition by sale.

The trial court concluded that a partition in kind could not be had without great prejudice to the parties since the continuation of the defendant's business would hinder or preclude the development of the plaintiffs' parcel for residential purposes, which the trial court concluded was the highest and best use of the property. The court's concern over the possible adverse economic effect upon the plaintiffs' interest in the event of a partition in kind was based essentially on four findings: (1) approval by the city planning commission for subdivision of the parcel would be difficult to obtain if the defendant continued her garbage hauling

---

[5] Google Earth V 6.2.2.6613. (January 19, 2009). 41° 39′ 36.94″N, 72° 53′ 54.39″W, Eye alt 1707 feet. DigitalGlobe 2007. http://www.earth.google.com [January 19, 2009].

business; (2) lots in a residential subdivision might not sell, or might sell at a lower price, if the defendant's business continued; (3) if the defendant were granted the one-acre parcel, on which her residence is situated and on which her business now operates, three of the lots proposed in the plaintiffs' plan to subdivide the property would have to be consolidated and would be lost; and (4) the proposed extension of one of the neighboring roads would have to be rerouted through one of the proposed building lots if a partition in kind were ordered. The trial court also found that the defendant's use of the portion of the property that she occupies is in violation of existing zoning regulations. The court presumably inferred from this finding that it is not likely that the defendant will be able to continue her rubbish hauling operations from this property in the future. The court also premised its forecast that the planning commission would reject the plaintiffs' subdivision plan for the remainder of the property on the finding that the defendant's use was invalid. These factors basically led the trial court to conclude that the interests of the parties would best be protected if the land were sold as a unified unit for residential subdivision development and the proceeds of such a sale were distributed to the parties.

Before we consider whether these reasons are sufficient as a matter of law to overcome the preference for partition in kind that has been expressed in the applicable statutes and our opinions, we address first the defendant's assignment of error directed to the finding of subordinate facts relating to one of these reasons. The defendant claims that the trial court erred in finding that the defendant's use of a portion of the property is in violation of the existing zoning regulations, and in refusing to find that such use is a valid nonconforming use. An examination of that portion of the parties' briefs directed to this issue discloses that, for some unexplained reason, the applicable zoning regulations and the date of their enactment were never introduced into evidence at the hearing below. Instead, the parties introduced only inconclusive and hearsay testimony to establish their respective positions on this issue. This deficiency in the evidence cuts both ways, however, and requires us to conclude that the particular paragraph of the defendant's draft finding cannot be added to the finding and that the court's finding in this regard must be stricken as unsupported by sufficient competent evidence. We are left, then, with an unassailed finding that the defendant's family has operated a "garbage business" on the premises since the 1920s and that the city of Bristol has granted the defendant the appropriate permits and licenses each year to operate her business. There is no indication that this practice will not continue in the future.

Our resolution of this issue makes it clear that any inference that the defendant would probably be unable to continue her rubbish hauling activity on the property in the future is unfounded. We also conclude that the court erred in concluding that the city's planning commission would probably not approve a subdivision plan relating to the remainder of the property. Any such forecast must be carefully scrutinized as it is difficult to project what a public body will decide in any given matter. In this case, there was no substantial evidence to support a conclusion that it was reasonably probable that the planning commission would not approve a subdivision plan for the remainder of the property. Moreover, there is no suggestion in the statute relating to subdivision approval that the undeveloped portion of the parcel in issue, which is located in a residential neighborhood, could not be the subject of an approved subdivision plan notwithstanding the nearby operation of the defendant's business. The court's finding indicates that only garbage trucks and dumpsters are stored on the property; that no garbage is brought there; and that the defendant's business operations involve "mostly containerized . . . dumpsters, a contemporary development in technology which has substantially reduced the odors previously associated with the rubbish and garbage hauling industry." These facts do not support the court's speculation that the city's planning commission would not approve a subdivision permit for the undeveloped portion of the parties' property.

The court's remaining observations relating to the effect of the defendant's business on the probable fair market value of the proposed residential lots, the possible loss of building lots to accommodate the defendant's business and the rerouting of a proposed subdivision road, which may have some validity, are not dispositive of the issue. It is the interests of all of the tenants in common that the court must consider and not merely the economic gain of one tenant, or a group of tenants. The trial court failed to give due consideration to the fact that one of the tenants in common has been in actual and exclusive possession of a portion of the property for a substantial period of time; that the tenant has made her home on the property; and that she derives her livelihood from the operation of a business on this portion of the property, as her family before her has for many years. A partition by sale would force the defendant to surrender her home and, perhaps, would jeopardize her livelihood. It is under just such circumstances, which include the demonstrated practicability of a physical division of the property, that the wisdom of the law's preference for partition in kind is evident.

As this court has many times stated, conclusions that violate "law, logic or reason or are inconsistent with the subordinate facts" cannot stand. Russo v. East Hartford, 179 Conn. 250, 255, 425 A.2d 1282 (1979). Since the property in this case may practicably be physically divided, and since the interests of all owners will better be promoted if a partition in kind is ordered, we conclude that the trial court erred in ordering a partition by sale, and that, under the facts as found, the defendant is entitled to a partition of the property in kind.

There is error, the judgment is set aside and the case is remanded for further proceedings not inconsistent with this opinion.

NOTES & QUESTIONS:

1. Because a court order to partition property by selling it and splitting the proceeds results in forcing individuals to sell their interest in real property, the courts are hesitant to do so. Originally, the only partition concept that was judicially recognized was partition in kind. However, as land ownership changed over time, it became impossible in some instances for the court to order physical partition. As a result, the remedy of having a court-ordered sale was recognized. With this history in mind, it makes sense that courts would first look to physical partition.

2. In the *Delfino* case, the court ultimately ordered a partition in kind. At the beginning we said that a person does not own a certain part of the land or a certain amount of acreage. Here the court awarded Helen the part of the land with her house and business. Did she essentially claim that land as her own by her actions? Why else would the court have awarded that land to her? In the partition, would Helen be required to share profits from her garbage business with the other cotenants? Did the court fairly divide up the acreage based on the value of the shares of ownership?

3. In the *Delfino* case, the court also entered a $16,000 owelty of partition judgment for damage that the garbage business might cause to the land in the future. What is the issue with this part of the judgment?

4. There is an additional partition concept known as equitable partition. An equitable partition is a remedy to protect some cotenants from one who has acted improperly. If a cotenant tries to sell his fractional share of ownership, that is within his rights. But, what if a cotenant tries to sell a particular number of acres to someone or the whole parcel, without the involvement of his other cotenants? What can the court do to give effect to the conveyance but also protect the interests of the other cotenants?

Chapter 6
Acquiring Property by Purchase: The Real Estate Transaction and Executory Period Issues

A. From Defining Interests in Property to Acquiring Them

During the first five chapters, the focus was on defining the different types of interests in land that a person can acquire and then also dealing with issues when more than one person owns the interest. These next chapters build upon that foundation in studying the acquisition of interests in property.

The real estate purchase is the model that most people are familiar with. However, there are a multitude of legal concepts involved in the basic purchase of a home. This material will cover all of the elements involved in the purchase, from the initial offers being made, to the executory period that exists once a contract has been negotiated, to the closing of the sale and transfer of legal title through a valid deed. The material will go on to address topics involving different types of deeds and the covenants of title that may be provided therein, the priority system, title searches and the problems that those searches can reveal, and then the remedies available for those problems.

After the sale of real property the legal doctrines of adverse possession and gifts will be a point of comparison. There are distinct legal elements that must be established for both transactions and they will be covered in detail.

Finally, in Texas, there are very significant homestead laws that provide special protections from creditors and also some protections that arise in the event of divorce and death. The final material in this course will focus on establishing the homestead and the legal consequences of such.

1. The Basics of the Real Estate Transaction

Every real estate transaction is different, but there are common elements that occur in every transaction. This will serve as a brief overview of what happens in the typical residential real estate transaction in Texas. Commercial transactions involve the same basic process; however, as seen in the leasehold material, residential and commercial transactions often have distinct legal treatment. The same is true in the purchase context. The primary focus of this material will be residential, but there may be some notes from time to time regarding a difference in the commercial transaction.

Some students come to law school already having engaged in one or more real estate transactions. For those students, this material may seem very simple. However, I encourage even the prior purchasers to look at this through a new lens. Not just from the position of a buyer or seller in a transaction but for the legal issues you were not even aware of when engaging in your prior transactions. On numerous occasions, students who have previously engaged in a real estate transaction often respond that they are relieved that nothing went wrong in their purchase or sale!

a. The Parties—The Buyer and Seller

The starting point of any transaction is a seller who is interested in selling real estate and a buyer who is in the market to buy. The parties in a residential transaction typically rely on a real estate professional to help with the transaction. The Texas Real Estate Commission licenses agents in the state of Texas. They have certain ethical and professional guidelines to follow. One guideline is that the agent cannot provide legal advice. So, you would think then that lawyers are involved in every transaction—they are not. In the standard residential transaction, a lawyer is rarely retained by either party.[1]

The seller who opts to use a real estate agent will sign a *listing agreement* with that agent, which will govern the relationship between them. The listing agreement will usually list the seller's asking price for the property and state the commission or other payment the seller will pay the agent if and when the property sells. The commission, typically a percentage of the sale price, is negotiable. Nonetheless, there tends to be a lot of consistency on the commission. In Texas, the usual commission is 6 percent of the actual sale price, but it is a negotiable item. Usually, the 6 percent commission is split between a buyer's agent and seller's agent and comes from the sales proceeds.

---

[1] If a title company is used for the closing, then the company will have a lawyer prepare all of the legal documents. Often in the residential process a lawyer gets involved only if something goes wrong.

The listing agreement will further describe what the agent, referred to as the seller's agent or the listing agent, will do for the seller. Typically, the listing agent promises to list the property in the local *multiple listing service*. A multiple listing service ("MLS") is a database of properties available for sale in a particular geographical area, including the listing price and other descriptive information about the property. Other agents who are members of the MLS can then search the database for properties that might be of interest to buyers they are representing. In other words, the MLS facilitates advertising the availability of properties for sale. Each multiple listing service establishes its own rules, including who is entitled to use it and its geographic area.

The seller's agent is rarely a lawyer, but will nonetheless often assist the seller in complying with any legal obligations the seller has. For example, Texas, as well as a number of other states, requires most sellers of residential real estate to disclose certain known defects with the property.[2] Unless the sale is not subject to the § 5.008 disclosure, the disclosure form must be completed and signed by the seller and provided to the buyer before the contract is signed. Failure to provide the buyer a copy of the disclosure form prior to his signing the contract essentially means that, notwithstanding his signature, the buyer is not bound by the contract until seven days after the buyer has in fact received the disclosure form. Of course, the form serves to alert the buyer to any problems with the property so that the buyer can decide whether to proceed with making an offer, and if so, at what price, or to keep looking for another property. As we move through the material, we will discuss the rights and obligations of the parties when there are undisclosed defects with property.

From the buyer's perspective, he has the option of retaining a *buyer's agent* who will help him locate properties that he might be interested in purchasing. Often, there is no charge to the buyer directly because the buyer's agent, as one of the agents that has helped sell the property, will share in the commission to be paid to the seller. Of course, because the commission is an expense of the seller that is usually taken out of the proceeds of the sale, it may impact the seller's selling price. Consequently, the buyer does pay the involved agents indirectly.

Other issues that may arise include what duties the real estate agents owe their clients. "Agency" suggests that there is a true agency relationship and the agent owes the client (legally referred to as the "principal") a fiduciary duty, that is, a high duty of trust and loyalty. That would suggest that one agent (or two agents in the same firm) could not represent both the buyer and the seller in the same transaction because of the conflict of interest. In other words, the seller wants to sell at the highest price possible, while the buyer wants to pay as little

---

[2] *See* Texas Property Code § 5.008.

as possible. In many states, including Texas, there are various arrangements allowed by law that modify the fiduciary relationship that might otherwise exist.[3]

b. The Real Estate Contract—The Executory Period Begins

Real estate transactions must be in in writing to comply with the statute of frauds, although there are exceptions. *See Hooks v. Bridgewater,* p. 401 of the text. Therefore, once the buyer has located a property that he might wish to buy, he and the seller can engage in informal negotiations or they may trade written offers and counteroffers. Eventually, their contract will need to be in writing and signed by each of them to be enforceable.

The contract is the first legal step in the real estate transaction. You should note that most real estate transactions occur in two steps: the contract followed by the closing.[4] There are different legal rules that apply depending on whether only the contract has been signed or the closing has occurred. When individuals say, for example, that they have "put a contract" on a property, they are referring to the first step.

At its most basic, the contract is the buyer's promise to purchase the property described in the contract at an agreed-upon price and the seller's promise to execute a deed transferring the property to the buyer. Because the contract must satisfy the statute of frauds, there are certain essential elements that must be included for the contract to be enforceable. These can vary among the jurisdictions, but at a minimum, the contract will need to include the seller's promise to convey, the buyer's agreement to purchase, a satisfactory land description, the price or a formula for determining the price, identification of the parties, and their signatures. If the agreement does not state a time for completing the transaction, a reasonable time will be inferred by the court if it becomes an issue.[5]

We will look specifically at what constitutes a valid property description for purposes of the contract, as well as other real estate documents that require a property description. In addition to the physical description of the property, the contract should include a description of the legal interest to be conveyed. As you should recall, there is a strong presumption of fee simple absolute. If the seller plans to convey, or only owns, less than fee simple absolute, the contract should

---

[3] *See* Patricia Wilson, Nonagent Brokers: Real Estate Agents Missing in Action, 52 Okla. L. Rev. 85 (1999).

[4] Conveyances of land that are gifts do not involve a contract. A contract would not be enforceable in any event because it would not have consideration.

[5] An interesting point to note is that in real estate transactions, time is not considered to be of the essence unless the contract specifically states such or it can be inferred from the circumstances.

reflect this. Otherwise, the seller will be in breach when he either cannot or will not convey the full fee simple estate.

Implied in every real estate contract is the seller's *marketable title covenant*, which, in short, is the seller's promise that he actually owns what he promised to sell in the contract, free of reasonable doubt. If the seller does not own what he promised to sell, the buyer will have certain rights based on the seller's breach of the covenant to convey marketable title to the property. Please note that this is not a promise of *economic* marketability, *i.e.*, that the property is worth some dollar amount, but rather a promise of *title* marketability, meaning the seller owns what he purports to sell.

Often, the contract contains many more provisions to protect the parties even though not required by the statute of frauds. The seller should require the buyer to pay *earnest money*.[6] *Earnest money* is paid by the buyer at the time of the contract that the buyer may lose if he breaches the contract. It provides security to the seller that if the buyer fails to complete the transaction, the seller has available money for all or part of the breach damages. If the transaction ultimately is completed, the earnest money is credited toward the purchase price.

The contract should provide the terms of the earnest money, including when the seller is entitled to retain the earnest money and when the buyer is entitled to return of the earnest money if the sale does not close, as well as who will hold the earnest money. In Texas, the title company often holds the earnest money in an account separate from its own accounts until it is known who is entitled to the earnest money. The amount of the earnest money is subject to negotiation, but in Texas, is often $500 to $1,000 for residential real estate transactions. It can be much higher, however, depending on the specific circumstances. As long as earnest money does not exceed 10 percent of the sales price, it is usually able to serve as liquidated damages if there is a breach.

The contract should also provide the buyer a right to inspect the property in order to discover any problems that may be costly to repair. Even if the seller is required to provide the § 5.008 disclosure form, the buyer would be foolish to rely on the disclosure form alone. Even a completely honest seller may be unaware of problems existing in the home. The buyer is wise to hire an experienced person to inspect the buildings, the electrical wiring, the roof, and other features of the property. In nonresidential transactions, in addition to inspecting the improvements and perhaps the land itself (soil tests, for example), the buyer may want to conduct environmental surveys or various other inspections to ensure that he will not be hindered by local or federal regulations in using the property as planned (*e.g.*, wetlands regulations).

---

[6] Because of the presence of earnest money in virtually every contract, you will often hear people refer to this as an "earnest money contract." They are speaking of this real estate contract that includes a provision for earnest money.

The contract should further provide what will happen if the buyer's inspections uncover problems. Will the seller be responsible for making needed repairs? If so, is there a limit on what the seller is obligated to pay to repair the property? At what point will either or both parties have the right to rescind the contract because of the problems? The well-drafted contract will specifically state the parties' rights and obligations. Due to the fact that the buyer will be having the property inspected *after* entering into the contract, the buyer should negotiate for an option period. The option period is a separate promise supported by separate consideration. This allows the buyer to purchase a brief time period within which the buyer could walk away from the transaction for any reason and the only money at risk is the money paid for the option. This is a provision that is completely negotiable. It is common, however, for a buyer to obtain a 10-day option for $150-200 or a 7-day option for $100. It is money well spent for peace of mind. In some instances an inspection may reveal a serious problem that even if it can be repaired the buyer may not want to take on.[7]

Another provision the buyer may want to include is an "out," that is, a way to rescind the contract, in the event he is unable to secure financing for the property. Most buyers will have to borrow money to purchase the property, and there is always the risk that a buyer may be denied credit. Realistically, if the buyer does not have the money, specific performance is not a practical remedy. Nonetheless, the buyer may lose his earnest money and be subject to other damages unless his contract provides him the right to terminate the contract because financing is unavailable. There is an addendum to the Texas form contract for residential sales that provides blanks for the parties to fill in the financing terms the buyer will seek and further provides that if he fails to obtain financing on those terms, the buyer has the right to terminate the contract with no penalty within a certain period of time. It does require an element of good faith on the part of the buyer to secure financing.

Finally, the parties should include a date by which to complete the deal. Certainly any lawyer involved in the deal should raise this matter with his client. The date can be a specific calendar date or it can be based on a formula. Either way, a closing date will help establish the parties' date for performance of their contract obligations.

We will examine many of the significant provisions of the form contract and you will also participate in an exercise where you will negotiate for the terms in a contract either as the buyer or seller in the transaction. Once you have negotiated your contract, we will use those contracts for discussion in class as our property's factual information changes and issues are raised with respect to what you actually contracted for.

---

[7] Common issues that arise that lead to termination are mold, termites, and foundation problems.

At this point when only the contract has been signed, the seller still owns the *legal title* to the property, meaning that title to the property is still held in the seller's name. The contract is the seller's promise to transfer the legal title to the buyer in the future. The law does recognize, however, that the buyer has an *equitable* interest in the property.[8] This is referred to as the doctrine of equitable conversion. This concept impacts many different issues in the executory period.

The buyer's equitable interest is a recognition that while the property is not held in the buyer's name, the seller holds the title subject to the buyer's right to obtain title, and the buyer may be considered the owner for other purposes, including losses that may occur to the property, such as destruction of improvements, prior to the second step of the transaction. The buyer's equitable title gives him certain rights, including the right to specific performance if the seller should balk at his promise to transfer title to the property. These are issues that we will study during this quarter. Now that there is a valid and enforceable contract, the parties are in the executory period.

c. The Executory Period—Where Everything Gets Done

The period between when the parties sign the contract and when the transaction is finally completed is referred to as the executory period, in recognition that one or both parties have performance obligations. As indicated above, the seller has legal title, and the buyer has equitable title.

The length of the executory period may be anywhere from a few weeks to many years, depending on the date set in the contract for completing the deal. In the typical real estate transaction, the executory period is only a few months at most for residential real estate, and perhaps as long as a year for commercial transactions. Again, however, it is a matter to be decided by the parties and included in the contract.

Typically, a lot of activity occurs during the few weeks or months of the executory period. The buyer must do his "due diligence" to discover any problems that may give him a right to rescind the contract or allow him to take other steps to protect his interests.

Assuming the buyer has the contractual right to perform certain inspections, those inspections will usually occur at this time.[9] In addition, the *title company*

---

[8] If this sounds similar to the way trusts work, where the trustee owns legal title to the trust property in his name while the beneficiaries own equitable title, you are on the right track. The concepts of title in the property once the contract has been signed and the concept of trusts are related ideas. The seller is sometimes said to hold the title to the property "in trust" for the buyer.

[9] The buyer can always seek the right to complete inspections before signing the contract. Again, almost everything is negotiable; the parties are not required to do what is typical.

will complete a *title search* of the *public records* to ensure that the seller owns what the seller promised to sell in the contract. The title company will be looking for any problems that may detract from what the seller actually owns, but it will be specifically looking for unpaid property taxes that could result in a *tax lien* on the property as well as other *liens* perfected against the property.

As we will discuss at various points in the course and particularly during the Priorities section, the owner of a lien has a right to have the property seized and sold to pay off some debt owed by the current owner or even a former owner of the property. As long as the former owner owned an interest in the property when the lien was created, that lien is enforceable even after the property is transferred to a new owner. That the owner-to-be did not create the debt or the lien will not prevent that individual from potentially losing title to the property because of the pre-existing lien. Therefore, the buyer will usually require that any liens on the property be cleared before or at the time the transaction is completed. It is fairly common that the property will have at least one lien—the *deed of trust lien* created when the current owner borrowed money to purchase the property and used the property as collateral for the loan. That lien will often be cleared at the time of the closing by using the proceeds from the sale to pay the remaining debt.

In addition to liens, the title company will also be looking for documents regarding easements, restrictive covenants, and other title defects that may mean that the current owner does not have good title to the property and thus cannot transfer good title to the buyer.[10] Covenants and easements are also other interests affecting the property that the title company is trying to locate. Remember, a purchaser is charged with constructive notice of anything filed of record in his chain or title. Therefore, the title company is searching for any of these types of interests in order to provide the buyer with actual knowledge to make an informed decision about the completion of the real estate transaction. If all appears well or mostly well with the title, the title company will issue a *title commitment*. The title commitment is the title company's promise to issue a *title insurance policy* insuring that the buyer has received good title as of the date the transaction is completed, subject to those title defects that are identified in the commitment and excluded from coverage.

Another activity that will occur during the executory period is the buyer's financing arrangements. If the buyer must borrow money to buy the property, which is typical, the buyer will need to finalize the loan. If the buyer applies to borrow from a bank or other institutional lender, the bank will determine whether the buyer is credit-worthy in general and how much the bank is willing to lend for the particular property the buyer has agreed to purchase, based on the bank's lending criteria. One of the bank's due diligence items will be

---

[10] We will visit the McLennan County Records Building to search the public records.

completing an appraisal to ensure that that particular property can support a loan of the size the buyer has requested. In addition, the bank will also want to ensure that the seller has fee simple to transfer to the buyer. The materials on real estate finance will contain more details about the bank's concerns about title and how that affects the bank's rights.

In addition, the bank or the buyer may order a survey of the land, particularly if the land is not in a developed subdivision.

If all goes well, the parties will eventually reach the second step of the process, namely the closing. As the name suggests, this is the culmination of everything that has happened thus far, and it will complete the real estate transaction. This is the event during which all the relevant documents will be signed by the different parties to the transaction, and legal title will finally transfer to the buyer; that is, the buyer will hold the property in his name and will be considered the owner. In Texas, the closing usually happens at the title company. Some of the typical closing documents include:

deed: This document transfers title of an interest in property to the named grantee. Deeds can be used to transfer a variety of property interests, including the different estates we discussed during the first quarter, easements (which we will discuss later in the course), mineral rights, etc. The deed is the seller's performance of his promise to convey, as stated in the contract. Only the seller signs the deed; the buyer does not sign it.

deed of trust: As mentioned several times already, most buyers will need to borrow money to buy the property, and most lenders will require that the property purchased be used as collateral to secure repayment of the loan. The deed of trust is the document that gives the purchased property (or any other property described therein) as collateral for the debt owed. In other words, the deed of trust is a specific kind of lien. We will discuss in further detail how the deed of trust actually works in practice. For now, you should know that the deed of trust gives the creditor the right to seize the property in the event of certain defaults on the promissory note and have it sold to pay off the debt. People often use the term *mortgage* to refer to the deed of trust.

Please note that deeds of trust are often used to purchase property, but deeds of trust can be given at any time on virtually any real property to secure new debts (*e.g.*, education loans) or debts that have already been created (*e.g.*, medical expenses). There will be some exceptions to this when the homestead material is introduced.

promissory note: The promissory note is the buyer/borrower's promise to repay the money borrowed, plus interest. It contains the terms of repayment, such as when payments are due, the term of the loan, and the interest rate. As with any contract, default can result in a lawsuit to obtain damages. The promissory note is governed by the Uniform Commercial Code and will be covered in somewhat more detail when we consider real estate finance, and even more detail in upper-quarter classes.

title policy: The title insurer will issue the policy that essentially promises that as of the date of closing (or the date otherwise stated in the policy), the seller's deed transferred good title to the buyer, subject to those exceptions and exclusions set out in the policy. If the buyer later discovers that as of the closing date he did not receive good title, the insurance company will pay on the policy, up to the buyer's purchase price. We will discuss title insurance issues briefly. For now, please become familiar with the idea that the policy covers defects with the title that existed at the date of the title policy. Defects in the buyer's title might not be discovered until long after closing, but if the problem existed at the time of the closing, albeit unknown to the title company, the buyer, or the seller, the title company is still liable on the policy. The title company is not liable for defects that occur after the closing.

Other events that will occur at the closing include the funding of the loan, assuming the buyer has borrowed from an institutional lender. The bank will have already approved the buyer, but will not release the loan proceeds until it has some assurance that the transaction is going to close and the documents are in order so that the bank is fully protected by the promissory note, the deed of trust, and the title insurance policy issued for the bank's protection.

The title company will be responsible for obtaining the signatures of the parties on a number of other documents. For consumer transactions that are financed by an institutional lender, the buyer will be asked to acknowledge receipt of the truth-in-lending statement, and to sign various other documents required by federal law for consumer transactions. Both the buyer and the seller may be asked to sign documents that contain various representations of facts that, if later found to be untrue, may result in fraud liability.

Finally, the title company will collect any money the buyer is responsible for having at closing and will disburse all funds to those who are entitled to receive them. An institutional lender will typically require that the buyer make a down payment on the purchase price, with the bank lending the difference between the buyer's down payment and the full purchase price. In addition, there will be other expenses the buyer is expected to pay in connection with the transaction, such as the cost of the appraisal, the buyer's share of taxes that have been prepaid by the seller, and various other expenses of which the buyer will have been advised shortly before the scheduled closing. The closer will collect the buyer's money.

The closer will also pay the real estate agents their commissions, make payment of any liens that must be cleared as a condition to the buyer accepting title, and pay off any other expenses for which the buyer or the seller is responsible for paying (including the premium for the title policy, which is usually the responsibility of the seller, but subject to negotiation). Any money left over after everything else has been paid goes to the seller.

Once the closing has occurred, the buyer is now the owner of legal title in the property. The seller no longer owns the interest conveyed in the deed. In addition, *merger* occurs. Once the deed is signed, all promises made related to the title of the property merge into the deed, and the deed is the legally operative document. What that means is that promises in the contract related to transfer of the title are no longer enforceable unless they are included in the deed or the contract specifically provided that the parties intended all or specific contract promises to survive execution of the deed.

There is a great deal of litigation on the issue of merger and which promises are related to the title and which are collateral promises, unrelated to the title, that are still enforceable although not included in the deed. The merger issue can be a difficult one to resolve. For example, is the seller's promise to repair physical problems with the property related to the title and thus unenforceable if not performed prior to closing or included in the deed? Or is that a collateral promise that the buyer can seek to enforce or for which damages are recoverable? Unfortunately, there is not a lot of consistency among jurisdictions as to what constitutes a collateral promise still enforceable after the deed, and what promises are no longer enforceable.

Attorneys involved in the transaction should always be attuned to the risk of not being specific if the parties know or expect that a promise contained in the contract cannot or will not be performed prior to closing. Fraud and mutual mistake are still relevant considerations, but for the most part, the deed is the only relevant document for determining the parties' rights and obligations.

The closing is an important event because the doctrine of *merger* has significant consequences. The closing is the dividing line between the rights the parties have under the contract, and the rights the parties have only pursuant to the deed. Please make sure you understand this idea because the rules are somewhat different depending on whether the parties are governed by the contract or the deed.

The final task to be completed is filing the various title documents (*e.g.*, the deed, deed of trust) in the public records of the property county. Filing the documents is the way the new owner gives notice of his interest in the property, and as we will discuss in the Priorities unit, recording is a necessary step to protect the new owner's interest. The deed will be recorded to protect the new owner and the deed of trust will be recorded to protect the lender. The title company usually files the documents.

d. Conclusion: Home Sweet Home

This is a very brief description of what happens in a real estate transaction. You should recognize that much of what is described above, particularly with respect to residential real estate transactions, occurs with only minimal involvement of attorneys. Real estate agents can fill in forms for most of the transaction, that—as well as the fact that agents tend to discourage their clients from involving attorneys—results in few buyers or sellers retaining an attorney. Consequently, unless the transaction is commercial in nature, lawyers may not be involved until there is a dispute.

The reliance on forms suggests that little is negotiable when, in fact, virtually *everything* is negotiable. One should recognize that while the forms are fairly complete, they may not work well for every transaction and should be modified to reflect clearly the parties' intent. Nonetheless, few will retain a lawyer, notwithstanding that many individuals engage in only two or three real estate transactions during a lifetime, and those transactions are often the largest single transactions in which they will engage. And so it goes.

Please plan to refer back to this overview throughout the remainder of the course.

B. Contract of Sale: Beginning the Executory Period

Because the contract involves the sale of real property, it must be in writing to be enforceable. The statute of frauds requires the most basic details of the transaction to be in writing to be enforceable. Because of the importance land has played and still plays in our society and also due to the desire for certainty with land titles, courts are reluctant to recognize exceptions to the statute of frauds in this context. First we will examine the requirements to satisfy the statute of frauds and then explore available exceptions.

1. The Statute of Frauds

The Texas statute of frauds is found in the Business and Commerce Code. The basic requirements to comply with the statute is that there is a writing (or writings) that identifies the parties, contains the promise of the seller to sell and the promise of the buyer to buy, a property description, the price or a means of determining the price, the closing date (or a reasonable time will be inferred), and the signatures of the parties.

Tex. Bus. & Com. Code § 26.01 Promise or Agreement Must Be in Writing[11]
   (a) A promise or agreement described in subsection (b) of this section is not enforceable unless the promise or agreement, or a memorandum of it, is
      (1) in writing; and
      (2) signed by the person to be charged with the promise or agreement or by someone lawfully authorized to sign for him.
   (b) Subsection (a) of this section applies to: (4) a contract for the sale of real estate.

Because the requirements are so simple, it is difficult to get an exception to allow for an oral promise to be enforceable. The following cases provide examples of the part performance and equitable estoppel. Consider the differences between the two exceptions. Which exception is easier to establish?

<u>**Hickey v. Green**</u>
Appeals Court of Massachusetts, 1982
442 N.E.2d 37, rev. denied,
445 N.E.2d 156 (1983)

CUTTER, J.

Mrs. Gladys Green owns a lot (Lot S) in the Manomet section of Plymouth. In July, 1980, she advertised it for sale. On July 11 and 12, Hickey and his wife discussed with Mrs. Green purchasing Lot S and "orally agreed to a sale" for $15,000. Mrs. Green on July 12 accepted a deposit check of $500, marked by Hickey on the back, "Deposit on Lot . . . Massasoit Ave. Manomet . . . Subject to Variance from Town of Plymouth." Mrs. Green's brother and agent "was under the impression that a zoning variance was needed and [had] advised . . . Hickey

---

[11] Subsections (b) (1)-(3) and (5)-(8) omitted.

to write" the quoted language on the deposit check. It turned out, however, by July 16 that no variance would be required. Hickey had left the payee line of the deposit check blank, because of uncertainty whether Mrs. Green or her brother was to receive the check and asked "Mrs. Green to fill in the appropriate name." Mrs. Green held the check, did not fill in the payee's name, and neither cashed nor endorsed it. Hickey "stated to Mrs. Green that his intention was to sell his home and build on Mrs. Green's lot."

"Relying upon the arrangements . . . with Mrs. Green," the Hickeys advertised their house on Sachem Road in newspapers on three days in July, 1980, and agreed with a purchaser for its sale and took from him a deposit check for $500 which they deposited in their own account. On July 24, Mrs. Green told Hickey that she "no longer intended to sell her property to him" but had decided to sell to another for $16,000. Hickey told Mrs. Green that he had already sold his house and offered her $16,000 for Lot S. Mrs. Green refused this offer.

The Hickeys filed this complaint seeking specific performance. Mrs. Green asserts that relief is barred by the Statute of Frauds contained in G.L. c. 259, § 1. The trial judge granted specific performance. Mrs. Green has appealed.

The present rule applicable in most jurisdictions in the United States is succinctly set forth in Restatement (Second) of Contracts, § 129 (1981). The section reads, "A contract for the transfer of an interest in land may be specifically enforced notwithstanding failure to comply with the Statute of Frauds if it is established that the party seeking enforcement, in reasonable reliance on the contract and on the continuing assent of the party against whom enforcement is sought, *has so changed his position that injustice can be avoided only by specific enforcement.*"[12] The earlier Massachusetts decisions laid down somewhat strict

---

[12] Comments a and b to § 129, read (in part): "a. . . . This section restates what is widely known as the 'part performance doctrine.' Part performance is not an accurate designation of such acts as taking possession and making improvements when the contract does not provide for such acts, but such acts regularly bring the doctrine into play. The doctrine is contrary to the words of the Statute of Frauds, but it was established by English courts of equity soon after the enactment of the Statute. Payment of purchase-money, without more, was once thought sufficient to justify specific enforcement, but a contrary view now prevails, since in such cases restitution is an adequate remedy. . . . Enforcement has . . . been justified on the ground that repudiation after 'part performance' amounts to a 'virtual fraud.' A more accurate statement is that courts with equitable powers are vested by tradition with what in substance is a dispensing power based on the promisee's reliance, *a discretion to be exercised with caution* in the light of all the circumstances . . . [emphasis supplied].

"b. . . . Two distinct elements enter into the application of the rule of this Section: first, the extent to which the evidentiary function of the statutory formalities is fulfilled by the conduct of the parties; second, the reliance of the promisee, providing a compelling substantive basis for relief in addition to the expectations created by the promise."

requirements for an estoppel precluding the assertion of the Statute of Frauds. Frequently there has been an actual change of possession and improvement of the transferred property, as well as full payment of the full purchase price, or one or more of these elements.

The present facts reveal a simple case of a proposed purchase of a residential vacant lot, where the vendor, Mrs. Green, knew that the Hickeys were planning to sell their former home (possibly to obtain funds to pay her) and build on Lot S. The Hickeys, relying on Mrs. Green's oral promise, moved rapidly to make their sale without obtaining any adequate memorandum of the terms of what appears to have been intended to be a quick cash sale of Lot S. So rapid was action by the Hickeys that, by July 21, less than ten days after giving their deposit to Mrs. Green, they had accepted a deposit check for the sale of their house, endorsed the check, and placed it in their bank account. Above their signatures endorsing the check was a memorandum probably sufficient to satisfy the Statute of Frauds. At the very least, the Hickeys had bound themselves in a manner in which, to avoid a transfer of their own house, they might have had to engage in expensive litigation. No attorney has been shown to have been used either in the transaction between Mrs. Green and the Hickeys or in that between the Hickeys and their purchaser.

There is no denial by Mrs. Green of the oral contract between her and the Hickeys. This, under § 129 of the Restatement, is of some significance. There can be no doubt (a) that Mrs. Green made the promise on which the Hickeys so promptly relied, and also (b) she, nearly as promptly, but not promptly enough, repudiated it because she had a better opportunity. The stipulated facts require the conclusion that in equity Mrs. Green's conduct cannot be condoned. This is not a case where either party is shown to have contemplated the negotiation of a purchase and sale agreement. If a written agreement had been expected, even by only one party, or would have been natural (because of the participation by lawyers or otherwise), a different situation might have existed. It is a permissible inference from the agreed facts that the rapid sale of the Hickeys' house was both appropriate and expected. These are not circumstances where negotiations fairly can be seen as inchoate.

We recognize also the cautionary language about granting specific performance in comment a to § 129 of the Restatement (see note 1, supra). No public interest behind G.L. c. 259, § 1, however, in the simple circumstances before us, will be violated if Mrs. Green fairly is held to her precise bargain by principles of equitable estoppel, subject to the considerations mentioned below.

Over two years have passed since July, 1980, and over a year since the trial judge's findings were filed on July 6, 1981. At that time, the principal agreed facts of record bearing upon the extent of the injury to the Hickeys (because of their reliance on Mrs. Green's promise to convey Lot S) were those based on the Hickeys' new obligation to convey their house to a purchaser. Performance of that agreement had been extended to May 1, 1981. If that agreement has been abrogated or modified since the trial, the case may take on a different posture. If enforcement of that agreement still will be sought, or if that agreement has been carried out, the conveyance of Lot S by Mrs. Green should be required now.

The case, in any event, must be remanded to the trial judge for the purpose of amending the judgment to require conveyance of Lot S by Mrs. Green only upon payment to her in cash within a stated period of the balance of the agreed price of $15,000. The trial judge, however, in her discretion and upon proper offers of proof by counsel, may reopen the record to receive, in addition to the presently stipulated facts, a stipulation or evidence concerning the present status of the Hickeys' apparent obligation to sell their house. If the circumstances have changed, it will be open to the trial judge to require of Mrs. Green, instead of specific performance, only full restitution to the Hickeys of all costs reasonably caused to them in respect of these transactions (including advertising costs, deposits, and their reasonable costs for this litigation) with interest. The case is remanded to the Superior Court Department for further action consistent with this opinion. The Hickeys are to have costs of this appeal.

So ordered.

NOTES & QUESTIONS:

Consider the two checks involved in the *Hickey* case. Could a check ever satisfy the statute of frauds? Consider what information is found on a check.

What information was on the check the Hickeys gave to Mrs. Green? What information was on the check the Hickeys received from their buyer? How does that impact the court's decision?

Which exception was used in the *Hickey* case? How would the dispute be decided if applying the law in the Texas cases found below

Hooks, et al. v. Bridgewater
Supreme Court of Texas, 1921
111 Tex. 122

Error to Court of Civil Appeals of First Supreme Judicial District.

PHILLIPS, C.J.

The plaintiff, Bob Bridgewater, brought the suit against the administrator of the estate of John W. Davis, deceased, and the heirs at law of Davis, to recover Davis' estate. The suit was in fact one to enforce a verbal agreement claimed to have been entered into by the plaintiff's father—at that time his only surviving parent, when the plaintiff was a child of nine years of age—and Davis, whereby the father contracted to surrender plaintiff's custody and control to Davis, and Davis—a single man who never married—agreed upon that consideration to rear the plaintiff, giving him the care and rights of a son, make him his heir and leave to him at his death all of his property.

The trial court found that the evidence established the making of the parol agreement; that Davis took charge of the plaintiff under the agreement when he was thus a child, and plaintiff's father never thereafter exercised any control over him; that the plaintiff lived with Davis thereafter, giving him the affection and obedience of a son, and performing chores and services around his home as needed, for which he received no wages or money consideration. Davis failed to bequeath any of his property to plaintiff, dying intestate, leaving an estate of both real and personal property. Before his death he had not placed the plaintiff in possession of any of it.

Judgment for the defendants was rendered in the trial court. On the appeal, this was reversed by the honorable Court of Civil Appeals for the First District and judgment rendered for the plaintiff.

As it affected the land belonging to Davis, the contract was plainly condemned by the statute of frauds. It was merely a parol agreement whereby in consideration of the father's surrender of the custody of the plaintiff and the latter's living with Davis as a son, Davis' lands owned at his death should become the plaintiff's property. It was in effect but a parol sale of Davis' lands to be performed by him in the future, and has no higher dignity than such a sale. The question presented by this feature of the case is whether the performance of the contract by the plaintiff relieves it from the operation of the statute of frauds, or, as more accurately stated, renders the contract enforceable in equity notwithstanding the statute.

The Court of Civil Appeals has held that it does, despite the fact that there was never any possession of the lands by the plaintiff in Davis' lifetime.

To sustain this holding, there must be created by judicial authority another exception to the operation of the statute of frauds, one unsanctioned by any previous decision of this court, and of larger consequence than any heretofore recognized by it. This is evident. For if it be the law that a contract of this kind may, under the circumstances here present, be enforced against a decedent's estate, the entire inheritances of families are, for the benefit of strangers to the blood, put at the mercy of parol evidence.

From an early time it has been the rule of this court, steadily adhered to, that to relieve a parol sale of land from the operation of the statute of frauds, three things were necessary: 1. Payment of the consideration, whether it be in money or services. 2. Possession by the vendee. And 3. The making by the vendee of valuable and permanent improvements upon the land with the consent of the vendor; or, without such improvements, the presence of such facts as would make the transaction a fraud upon the purchaser if it were not enforced. Payment of the consideration, though it be a payment in full, is not sufficient. This has been the law since Garner v. Stubblefield, 5 Tex. 552. Nor is possession of the premises by the vendee. Ann Berta Lodge v. Leverton, 42 Tex. 18. Each of these three elements is indispensable, and they must all exist.

Regardless of the disposition of other courts to engraft other exceptions upon a plain and salutary statute which had its origin in the prolific frauds and perjuries with which parol contracts concerning lands abounded, this court has always refused to further relax the statute. We think the wisdom of its course has been justified.

Equity has no concern in such cases except to prevent the perpetration of a fraud. . . . The statute is valid; it is imperative; it is emphatic. Its simple requirement that contracts for the transfer of lands be in writing, imposes no hardship. The effect of its relaxation in what seemed to the courts hard cases has produced abuses almost as great as would have its rigorous enforcement, in the substitution of a doubtful state of the law for a rule that was plain and certain and easily capable of observance. . . .

By its requirement of payment of the consideration, adverse possession by the purchaser, and his making of valuable and permanent improvements in order for the contract to be exempt from the statute, it insures the application of the exemption only for the avoidance of actual fraud, and secures, as it should, the full operation of the statute in all other cases. Its purpose is both to prevent the perpetration of fraud and to safeguard the titles of lands. It is a rule founded in sound reason and common experience, and is fair and just.

There is no fraud in refusing to enforce the contract where only the consideration is paid.

[I]n Bradley v. Owsley, 74 Tex. 69, 11 S. W. 1052, it is announced: "The rule in this state is well established that verbal contracts for the sale of land will not be enforced without proof of possession and valuable improvements permanent in character or of other facts making the transaction a fraud on the purchaser if not enforced." See also Altgelt v. Escalera, 51 Tex. Civ. App. 108, 110 S. W. 989, and Terry v. Craft, 87 S. W. 844.

With this the established, and in our opinion the sound, rule of decision in this State, there can be no occasion for enlarging it. . . .

The parol contract here has no basis for its enforcement, other than the plaintiff's performance by his assuming with Davis the relation and rendering him the service of a son. That was the consideration for Davis' agreement to make him the owner of his estate. The case, therefore, is simply one where the consideration for a parol agreement to transfer the title to land has been paid, with no possession of the land surrendered and no valuable and permanent improvements made by the purchaser on the faith of the agreement. In no other character of case resting only upon the payment of the consideration could such a contract be enforced in this State.

Aside from the invalidity of the contract as to the land of the estate under the statute of frauds[,] . . . it is a character of contract which should be held void as a matter of public policy. A parent has no property interest in his child and should not be permitted to deal with his child as property. . . .

The judgment of the honorable Court of Civil Appeals is reversed and the judgment of the District Court is affirmed.

NOTES & QUESTIONS:

1. Don and Jan (sellers) put up a "For Sale by Owner" sign to sell their residence without the help of a realtor. An their very first open house Mr. Smith tells Don and Jan he likes the house, wants to buy it, and will pay their asking price. Nothing is in writing; they shake on it. They wait several weeks and call Mr. Smith to find out when they will conclude the sale. Mr. Smith tells them his wife did not like the house and they won't be completing any purchase. Can Don and Jan seek specific performance?

2. What if, instead, Don and Jan have the conversation with Mr. Smith about the purchase and before he leaves that day Mr. Smith gives them $5,000 cash as a deposit. Mr. Smith tells them that he loves the house and wants to complete the transaction quickly because he is selling his current home and will need a place to live soon. They continue to show the property

and a couple of days later another couple offers $10,000 more than Mr. Smith. Don and Jan enter into a written agreement with the new buyers. They tell Mr. Smith they are very sorry but received a better offer. Can Mr. Smith seek specific performance?

3. Would it make any difference in your answer to Question 2 if Mr. Smith only gave the $5,000 in cash and never said anything about selling his current home?

4. Would it make any difference in your answer to Question 2 if Mr. Smith gave the $5,000 and was allowed to move into the house before the agreed-upon closing date?

2. Marketable Title and Equitable Conversion

At the time of signing a valid contract for sale under the statute of frauds something happens to the title. There is a split of the legal and equitable title, a concept referred to as equitable conversion. What legal impact does the split of legal and equitable title have on the parties to the contract? What happens if problems arise during the executory period when the title is "split"?

In addition, every contract for the sale of real property impliedly includes a covenant that marketable title will be delivered by the seller at the time of closing unless there is specific language to the contrary. What does marketable title mean? What can cause title to be considered unmarketable?

These are the concepts we will now explore.

Texas Title Examination Standards

Chapter II
Marketable Title

Standard 2.10 Marketable Title Defined

All title examinations should be based on marketability of title. A marketable title is a record title that is free from reasonable doubt such that a prudent person, with knowledge of all salient facts and circumstances and their legal significance, would be willing to accept it. To be marketable, a title need not be absolutely free from every possible suspicion. There mere possibility of a defect that has no probably basis does not show an unmarketable title.

Comment:

Except as otherwise provided in these standards, if a title examination reveals the need to rely on facts outside the record the title is unmarketable. An example would be facts that must be proven by parol evidence or by presumptions of fact that would probably, in the event of suit, become genuine issues of fact. Whether the potential lawsuit would likely be won by the party with the apparent record title is immaterial, because threat or probable likelihood of litigation renders the title unmarketable. On the other hand, a title need not be perfect to be marketable. A doubt about title must be a reasonable doubt and be serious enough to affect its value.

Caution:

Matters that may make a title unmarketable include:

(1) Land acquired by limitation title.
(2) Title that is subject to an outstanding oil and gas lease.
(3) Title that is subject to an outstanding covenant.
(4) Title that is subject to an outstanding easement.
(5) Title that is subject to a mortgage, judgment lien or tax lien.

Unmarketable Issues

While the above definition is from the Texas Title Examination Standards, the definition of marketable (or merchantable) title is a common definition to all jurisdictions. With that definition in mind, read the following case involving difficulties during the executory period.

Lohmeyer v. Bower
Supreme Court of Kansas, 1951
227 P.2d 102

PARKER, J.

This action originated in the district court of Lyon county when plaintiff filed a petition seeking to rescind a contract in which he had agreed to purchase certain real estate on the ground title tendered by the defendants was unmerchantable. The defendants Bower and Bower, husband and wife, answered contesting plaintiff's right to rescind and by cross-petition asked specific performance of the contract. The case was tried upon the pleadings and stipulated facts by the trial court which rendered judgment for the defendants generally and decreed specific performance of the contract. The plaintiff appeals from that judgment.

Pertinent provisions of the contract, entered into between the parties, essential to disposition of the issues raised by the pleadings, read:

> Witnesseth, That in consideration of the stipulations herein contained, and the payments to be made by the second party as hereinafter specified, the first party hereby agrees to sell unto the second party for following described real estate, situated in the County of Lyon, State of Kansas, to-wit:

Lot numbered Thirty-seven (37) on Berkley Road in Berkley Hills Addition to the City of Emporia, according to the recorded plat thereof.

and to convey the above described real estate to the second party by Warranty Deed with an abstract of title, certified to date showing good merchantable title or an Owners Policy of Title Insurance in the amount of the sale price, guaranteeing said title to party of the second part, free and clear of all encumbrances except special taxes subject, however, to all restrictions and easements of record applying to this property, it being understood that the first party shall have sufficient time to bring said abstract to date or obtain Report for Title Insurance and to correct any imperfections in the title if there be such imperfections.

***

That the first party cannot deliver title as agreed, the earnest money paid by the second party shall be returned to said second party and this contract cancelled.

1· STORY Cov.

Zoning Ordinance

[The abstract of title showed that the original subdivider of the Berkley Hills Addition had, in 1926, imposed a restrictive covenant on lot 37 requiring any house erected on lot 37 to be two stories in height. Lot 37 had a one-story house on it that the Bowers had placed there. Additionally, there was a zoning ordinance providing that "[i]n no case shall a frame building be erected within three feet of the side or rear lot line, nor within six feet of another building, unless the space between the studs on such side be filled solidly with not less than 2 ½ inches of brickwork or other equivalent incombustable material." The frame house on lot 37 was located within 18 inches of the north line of the lot in violation of the ordinance. Dr. Lohmeyer brought the zoning ordinance to the attention of the Bowers, and they offered to purchase and convey to Lohmeyer two feet along the entire north side of lot 37. Dr. Lohmeyer refused their offer.]

[S]ince resort to the contract makes it clear appellees agreed to convey the involved property with an abstract of title showing good merchantable title, free and clear of all encumbrances, it becomes apparent the all decisive issue presented by the pleadings and the stipulation is whether such property is subject to encumbrances or other burdens making the title unmerchantable and if so whether they are such as are excepted by the provision of the contract which reads "subject however, to all restrictions and easements of record applying to this property."

Decision of the foregoing issue can be simplified by directing attention early to the appellant's position. Conceding he purchased the property, subject to all restrictions of record he makes no complaint of the restrictions contained in the declaration forming a part of the dedication of Berkley Hills Addition nor of the ordinance restricting the building location on the lot but bases his right to rescission of the contract solely upon presently existing violations thereof. This, we may add, limited to restrictions imposed by terms of the ordinance, relating to the use of land or the location and character of buildings that may be located thereon, even in the absence of provisions in the contract excepting them, must necessarily be his position for we are convinced, although it must be conceded there are some decisions to the contrary, the rule supported by the better reasoned decisions, indeed if not by the great weight of authority, is that municipal restrictions of such character, existing at the time of the execution of a contract for the sale of real estate, are not such encumbrances or burdens on title as may be availed of by a vendee to avoid his agreement to purchase on the ground they render his title unmerchantable.

On the other hand there can be no question the rule respecting restrictions upon the use of land or the location and type of buildings that may be erected thereon fixed by covenants or other private restrictive agreements, including those contained in the declaration forming a part of the dedication of Berkley Hills Addition, is directly contrary to the one to which we have just referred. Such restrictions, under all the authorities, constitute encumbrances rendering the title to land unmerchantable.

There can be no doubt regarding what constitutes a marketable or merchantable title in this jurisdiction. This court has been called on to pass upon that question on numerous occasions[:]

> "A marketable title to real estate is one which is free from reasonable doubt, and a title is doubtful and unmarketable if it exposes the party holding it to the hazard of litigation.
>
> To render the title to real estate unmarketable, the defect of which the purchaser complains must be of a substantial character and one from which he may suffer injury. Mere immaterial defects which do not diminish in quantity, quality or value the property contracted for, constitute no ground upon which the purchaser may reject the title. Facts must be known at the time which fairly raise a reasonable doubt as to the title; a mere possibility or conjecture that such a state of facts may be developed at some future time is not sufficient."

Under the rule just stated, and in the face of facts such as are here involved, we have little difficulty in concluding that the violation of section 5-224 of the ordinances of the city of Emporia as well as the violation of the restrictions imposed by the dedication declaration so encumber the title to Lot 37 as to expose the party holding it to the hazard of litigation and make such title doubtful and unmarketable. It follows, since, as we have indicated, the appellees had contracted to convey such real estate to appellant by warranty deed with an abstract of title showing good merchantable title, free and clear of all encumbrances, that they cannot convey the title contracted for and that the trial court should have rendered judgment rescinding the contract. This, we may add is so, notwithstanding the contract provides the conveyance was to be made subject to all restrictions and easements of record, for, as we have seen, it is the violation of the restrictions imposed by both the ordinance and the dedication declaration, not the existence of those restrictions, that renders the title unmarketable. The decision just announced is not without precedent or unsupported by sound authority.

Finally appellees point to the contract which, it must be conceded, provides they shall have time to correct imperfections in the title and contend that even if it be held the restrictions and the ordinance have been violated they are entitled to time in which to correct those imperfections. Assuming, without deciding, they might remedy the violation of the ordinance by buying additional ground the short and simple answer to their contention with respect to the violation of the restrictions imposed by the dedication declaration is that any changes in the house would compel the purchaser to take something that he did not contract to buy.

Conclusions heretofore announced require reversal of the judgment with directions to the trial court to cancel and set aside the contract and render such judgment as may be equitable and proper under the issues raised by the pleadings.

It is so ordered.

NOTES & QUESTIONS:

1. In the contract signed by Dr. Lohmeyer, he agreed to take subject to all of the restrictions and easements on record. Why would he sign such a contract?

2. Dr. Lohmeyer also agreed that the sellers must provide him "with an abstract of title, certified to date showing good merchantable title or an Owners Policy of Title Insurance." What is the difference between the two? Does that change the implied covenant of marketable title? If so, how?

   In Creative Living, Inc. v. Steinhauser, 335 N.Y.S.2d 897 (App. Div. 1974), aff'd without opinion, 365 N.Y.S.2d 987 (App. Div. 1975) the contract provided that the seller would have a title such as a title insurer would insure. The court stated that "[t]his provision in the contract made the title company the final judge of title and when the title company was prepared to insure title in accordance with the contract no further requirement had to be met."

3. The court took the position here, as do the majority of courts, that public land use restrictions such as zoning or wetlands designations do not make title unmarketable. It is only the violations of these regulations that make title unmarketable . However, the presence of a covenant does make title unmarketable. Look back to the definition of marketable title. Can you explain what the difference is? *See* Decatur v. Barnett, 398 S.E.2d 706 (Ga. Ct. App. 1990), *rev'd on other grounds*, 403 S.E.2d 46 (Ga. 1991).

4. Suppose there is unimproved land that is in an area with a zoning ordinance that prohibits the operation of any liquor stores or nightclubs on the property. The buyer is looking to purchase this property to build a new liquor store. The buyer enters into the contract and then finds out about the zoning ordinance. Can the buyer rescind the contract based on the covenant of marketable title? If not, what could the buyer have done to protect himself?

5. Several other issues have differing impacts on the concept of marketable title. For example, building codes and even building code violations do not impact marketability. The rationale is that the building code and any violation relates to the physical condition of the property and not the title to it. The covenant of marketable title is about title. However, what if a purchaser discovers that there is no access to land during the executory period? In Sinks v. Karleskint, 474 N.E.2d 767 (Ill. App. 1985), the purchasers of a 40-acre tract alleged that title was not marketable because the tract had no legal access, which the purchasers knew. The court held the title was marketable. The court reasoned that lack of access affects market value, not marketability of title. A title is marketable, said the court, if the seller has a fee simple, the title is free from any encumbrances, and the buyer is entitled to possession. *See also* Campbell v. Summit Plaza Associates, 192 P.3d 465 (Colo. App. 2008). Not all courts would agree with *Sinks* or *Campbell*. *See* Janian v. Barnes, 742 N.Y.S.2d 445 (App. Div. 2002) (lack of legal access renders title unmarketable).

NOTES ON EQUITABLE CONVERSION:

1. Both purchasers and sellers of real property are normally entitled to specific performance as a remedy for the other's breach of contract. As outlined in the introductory note, the buyer is viewed in equity as the owner from the date of the contract (thus having the "equitable title"); the seller has a claim for money secured by a vendor's lien on the land. The seller is also said to hold the legal title as trustee for the buyer. Because of this split in the title, the doctrine of equitable conversion impacts several legal issues in the executory period.

2. *Risk of Loss.* Based on this explanation of equitable conversion, consider what happens in the following situation. The parties enter into a valid sales contract with a closing date set for July 10, 2015. On July 4, some rowdy neighbors pop fireworks, one lands on the roof of the house under contract and it burns to the ground. Closing is only six days away. Is the seller entitled to specific performance under the contract if the buyer refuses to complete the purchase? The answer is, it depends. Using the doctrine of equitable conversion it has been held under the traditional rule that the buyer bears the risk of loss. *See* Powell on Real Property § 81.03[2] (Michael Allan Wolf ed. 2000). This would require the buyer to complete the purchase on July 10 with the house gone and still pay the purchase price under the contract. However, that is not the answer that most people expect. The seller is in possession and has the best chance of protecting the property from harm, the seller should still have property hazard insurance that would pay for the damage, and the buyer does not normally have insurance covering the property until the day legal title transfers.

Because the traditional rule does not comport with the normal expectations, some states have adopted the Uniform Vendor and Purchaser Act (1935). Texas adopted the act and it is found in the Texas Property Code.

Tex. Prop. Code § 5.007 Vendor & Purchaser Risk Act

(a) Any contract made in this state for the purchase and sale of real property shall be interpreted as including an agreement that the parties have the rights and duties prescribed by this section, unless the contract expressly provides otherwise.

(b) If, when neither the legal title nor the possession of the subject matter of the contract has been transferred, all or a material part of the property is destroyed without fault of the purchaser or is taken by eminent domain, the vendor may not enforce the contract, and the purchaser is entitled to recover any portion of the contract price paid.

(c) If, when either the legal title or possession of the subject matter of the contract has been transferred, all or a material part of the property is destroyed without the fault of the vendor or is taken by eminent domain, the purchase is not relieved from the duty to pay the contract price, nor is the purchaser entitled to recover any portion of the price already paid.

(d) This section shall be interpreted and construed to accomplish its general purpose to make uniform the law of those states that enact the Uniform Vendor and Purchaser Risk Act.

In looking at the Texas statute, if the fireworks example occurred in Texas, under subsection (b) the buyer would not have to go through with the purchase and would not be at risk of losing any earnest money *unless* the sales contract contained some provision to the contrary. This is more in line with normal expectations.

If the purchaser has the risk of loss, and the seller has insurance, in most states the seller holds the insurance proceeds as trustee for the buyer. *See* William B. Stoebuck & Dale A. Whitman, The Law of Property § 10.13, at 792-797 (3d ed. 2000). The parties should include a provision regarding risk of loss in the contract of sale and buy insurance accordingly.

3. *Death During the Executory Period.* Although not as frequent an occurrence as damage to the property, one of the parties could die during the executory period. What does that mean for the transaction? This is another area where the doctrine of equitable conversion is applied to provide an answer. Once there is the split in legal and equitable title, the seller's interest is classified as personal property (right to the sales proceeds), and the buyer's interest is classified as real property (right to obtain legal title).

There is a valid contract between Oliver and Ann. Oliver is selling Blackacre to Ann for $50,000. Before closing, Oliver dies with a will leaving all of his personal property to Charles and all of his real property to Diane. Ann goes to closing with Oliver's estate. Who will receive the sales proceeds?

What if instead of Oliver dying before closing, Ann dies? Ann left a will leaving all of her real property to Emma and all of her personal property to Frank. When Oliver goes to closing with Ann's estate, who will take title to Blackacre?

3. Seller's Disclosure/Duty to Disclose Defects

The purchase of real property is typically the largest purchase any individual will make during the course of his or her lifetime. In addition to the buyer's concerns about the quality of the title to the land, there are also concerns about the physical condition of the land. What exactly is the buyer getting for his money? The person in the position of the most knowledge about the physical condition of the property is the seller, but for many years the seller of real property was not required to provide any information to the buyer regarding the physical condition of that property. The purchaser of real property bought under the doctrine of "caveat emptor" (let the buyer beware).

Over time the concern grew about the ability of the seller to possibly unload horrible problems onto an unwary buyer. Therefore, the courts first became involved in addressing the duty to disclose on the part of the seller and eventually state legislatures stepped in to provide statutory guidance regarding the duty to disclose. Texas is one of those states that have provided such statutory guidance. We will first examine the common law concept and then evaluate the Texas Property Code requirements for a seller of real property.

Johnson v. Davis
Supreme Court of Florida, 1985
480 So. 2d 625

ADKINS, J.

We have before us a petition to review the decision in Johnson v. Davis, 449 So. 2d 344 (Fla. 3d DCA 1984), which expressly and directly conflicts with Banks v. Salina, 413 So. 2d 851 (Fla. 4th DCA 1982), and Ramel v. Chasebrook Construction Co., 135 So. 2d 876 (Fla. 2d DCA 1961). We have jurisdiction and approve the decision of the district court.

In May of 1982, the Davises entered into a contract to buy for $310,000 the Johnsons' home, which at the time was three years old. The contract required a $5,000 deposit payment, an additional $26,000 deposit payment within five days and a closing by June 21, 1982. The crucial provision of the contract, for the purposes of the case at bar, is Paragraph F which provided:

F. Roof Inspection: Prior to closing at Buyer's expense, Buyer shall have the right to obtain a written report from a licensed roofer stating that the roof is in a watertight condition. In the event repairs are required either to correct leaks or to replace

damage to facia or soffit, seller shall pay for said repairs which
shall be performed by a licensed roofing contractor.

The contract further provided for payment to the "prevailing party" of all costs and reasonable fees in any contract litigation.

Before the Davises made the additional $26,000 deposit payment, Mrs. Davis noticed some buckling and peeling plaster around the corner of a window frame in the family room and stains on the ceilings in the family room and kitchen of the home. Upon inquiring, Mrs. Davis was told by Mr. Johnson that the window had had a minor problem that had long since been corrected and that the stains were wallpaper glue and the result of ceiling beams being moved. There is disagreement among the parties as to whether Mr. Johnson also told Mrs. Davis at this time that there had never been any problems with the roof or ceilings. The Davises thereafter paid the remainder of their deposit and the Johnsons vacated the home. Several days later, following a heavy rain, Mrs. Davis entered the home and discovered water "gushing" in from around the window frame, the ceiling of the family room, the light fixtures, the glass doors, and the stove in the kitchen.

Two roofers hired by the Johnsons' broker concluded that for under $1,000 they could "fix" certain leaks in the roof and by doing so make the roof "watertight." Three roofers hired by the Davises found that the roof was inherently defective, that any repairs would be temporary because the roof was "slipping," and that only a new $15,000 roof could be "watertight."

The Davises filed a complaint alleging breach of contract, fraud and misrepresentation, and sought rescission of the contract and return of their deposit. The Johnsons counterclaimed seeking the deposit as liquidated damages.

The trial court entered its final judgment on May 27, 1983. The court made no findings of fact, but awarded the Davises $26,000 plus interest and awarded the Johnsons $5,000 plus interest. Each party was to bear their own attorneys' fees.

The Johnsons appealed and the Davises cross-appealed from the final judgment. The Third District found for the Davises affirming the trial court's return of the majority of the deposit to the Davises ($26,000), and reversing the award of $5,000 to the Johnsons as well as the court's failure to award the Davises costs and fees. Accordingly, the court remanded with directions to return to the Davises the balance of their deposit and to award them costs and fees.

The trial court included no findings of fact in its order. However, the district court inferred from the record that the trial court refused to accept the Davises' characterization of the roof inspection provision of the contract. The district court noted that if there was a breach, the trial court would have ordered the return of the Davises' entire deposit because there is no way to distinguish the two deposit payments under a breach of contract theory. We agree with this interpretation and further find no error by the trial court in this respect.

The contract contemplated the possibility that the roof may not be watertight at the time of inspection and provided a remedy if it was not in such a condition. The roof inspection provision of the contract did not impose any obligation beyond the seller correcting the leaks and replacing damage to the facia or soffit. The record is devoid of any evidence that the seller refused to make needed repairs to the roof. In fact, the record reflects that the Davises' never even demanded that the areas of leakage be repaired either by way of repair or replacement. Yet the Davises insist that the Johnsons breached the contract justifying rescission. We find this contention to be without merit.

We also agree with the district court's conclusions under a theory of fraud and find that the Johnsons' statements to the Davises regarding the condition of the roof constituted a fraudulent misrepresentation entitling respondents to the return of their $26,000 deposit payment. In the state of Florida, relief for a fraudulent misrepresentation may be granted only when the following elements are present: (1) a false statement concerning a material fact; (2) the representor's knowledge that the representation is false; (3) an intention that the representation induce another to act on it; and, (4) consequent injury by the party acting in reliance on the representation.

The evidence adduced at trial shows that after the buyer and the seller signed the purchase and sales agreement and after receiving the $5,000 initial deposit payment the Johnsons affirmatively repeated to the Davises that there were no problems with the roof. The Johnsons subsequently received the additional $26,000 deposit payment from the Davises. The record reflects that the statement made by the Johnsons was a false representation of material fact, made with knowledge of its falsity, upon which the Davises relied to their detriment as evidenced by the $26,000 paid to the Johnsons.

The doctrine of caveat emptor does not exempt a seller from responsibility for the statements and representations which he makes to induce the buyer to act, when under the circumstances these amount to fraud in the legal sense. To be grounds for relief, the false representations need not have been made at the time of the signing of the purchase and sales agreement in order for the element of reliance to be present. The fact that the false statements as to the quality of the roof were made after the signing of the purchase and sales agreement does not excuse the seller from liability when the misrepresentations were made prior to the execution of the contract by conveyance of the property. It would be contrary to all notions of fairness and justice for this Court to place its stamp of approval on an affirmative misrepresentation by a wrongdoer just because it was made after the signing of the executory contract when all of the necessary elements for actionable fraud are present. Furthermore, the Davises' reliance on the truth of the Johnsons' representation was justified and is supported by this Court's decision in Besett v. Basnett, 389 So. 2d 995 (1980), where we held "that a recipient may rely on the truth of a representation, even though its falsity could have been ascertained had he made an investigation, unless he knows the representation to be false or its falsity is obvious to him." Id. at 998.

In determining whether a seller of a home has a duty to disclose latent material defects to a buyer, the established tort law distinction between misfeasance and nonfeasance, action and inaction must carefully be analyzed. The highly individualistic philosophy of the earlier common law consistently imposed liability upon the commission of affirmative acts of harm, but shrank from converting the courts into an institution for forcing men to help one another. This distinction is deeply rooted in our case law. Liability for nonfeasance has therefore been slow to receive recognition in the evolution of tort law.

In theory, the difference between misfeasance and nonfeasance, action and inaction is quite simple and obvious; however, in practice it is not always easy to draw the line and determine whether conduct is active or passive. That is, where failure to disclose a material fact is calculated to induce a false belief, the distinction between concealment and affirmative representations is tenuous. Both proceed from the same motives and are attended with the same consequences; both are violative of the principles of fair dealing and good faith; both are calculated to produce the same result; and, in fact, both essentially have the same effect.

Still there exists in much of our case law the old tort notion that there can be no liability for nonfeasance. The courts in some jurisdictions, including Florida, hold that where the parties are dealing at arm's length and the facts lie equally open to both parties, with equal opportunity of examination, mere nondisclosure does not constitute a fraudulent concealment. The Fourth District affirmed that rule of law in Banks v. Salina, 413 So.2d 851 (Fla. 4th DCA 1982), and found that although the sellers had sold a home without disclosing the presence of a defective roof and swimming pool of which the sellers had knowledge, "[i]n Florida, there is no duty to disclose when parties are dealing at arms length." Id. at 852.

These unappetizing cases are not in tune with the times and do not conform with current notions of justice, equity and fair dealing. One should not be able to stand behind the impervious shield of caveat emptor and take advantage of another's ignorance. Our courts have taken great strides since the days when the judicial emphasis was on rigid rules and ancient precedents. Modern concepts of justice and fair dealing have given our courts the opportunity and latitude to change legal precepts in order to conform to society's needs. Thus, the tendency of the more recent cases has been to restrict rather than extend the doctrine of caveat emptor. The law appears to be working toward the ultimate conclusion that full disclosure of all material facts must be made whenever elementary fair conduct demands it.

The harness placed on the doctrine of caveat emptor in a number of other jurisdictions has resulted in the seller of a home being liable for failing to disclose material defects of which he is aware. This philosophy was succinctly expressed in Lingsch v. Savage, 213 Cal. App. 2d 729, 29 Cal. Rptr. 201 (1963):

It is now settled in California that where the seller knows of facts materially affecting the value or desirability of the property which are known or accessible only to him and also knows that such facts are not known to or within the reach of the diligent attention and observation of the buyer, the seller is under a duty to disclose them to the buyer.

In Posner v. Davis, 76 Ill.App.3d 638, buyers brought an action alleging that the sellers of a home fraudulently concealed certain defects in the home which included a leaking roof and basement flooding. Relying on *Lingsch*, the court concluded that the sellers knew of and failed to disclose latent material defects and thus were liable for fraudulent concealment. Numerous other jurisdictions have followed this view in formulating law involving the sale of homes.

We are of the opinion, in view of the reasoning and results in *Lingsch*, *Posner* and the aforementioned cases decided in other jurisdictions, that the same philosophy regarding the sale of homes should also be the law in the state of Florida. Accordingly, we hold that where the seller of a home knows of facts materially affecting the value of the property which are not readily observable and are not known to the buyer, the seller is under a duty to disclose them to the buyer. This duty is equally applicable to all forms of real property, new and used.

In the case at bar, the evidence shows that the Johnsons knew of and failed to disclose that there had been problems with the roof of the house. Mr. Johnson admitted during his testimony that the Johnsons were aware of roof problems prior to entering into the contract of sale and receiving the $5,000 deposit payment. Thus, we agree with the district court and find that the Johnsons' fraudulent concealment also entitles the Davises to the return of the $5,000 deposit payment plus interest. We further find that the Davises should be awarded costs and fees.

The decision of the Third District Court of Appeal is hereby approved.

It is so ordered.

NOTES & QUESTIONS:

1. Did the court in *Johnson* need to impose an affirmative duty to disclose to provide relief to the buyers? Why or why not?

2. At what point in time does the defect get discovered in *Johnson*? Consider how that is different from the cases below. Should that make a difference in the available relief to the buyer?

3. Does imposing a duty to disclose impose an obligation on the seller to conduct a home inspection before putting a home up for sale? Why or why not?

4. Should there be a similar duty to disclose in commercial transactions? Why or why not?

Texas has adopted a statutory disclosure form. The duty is for the seller to complete the form accurately and honestly and provide it to the buyer before entering into the sales contract. This is the minimum requirement. If a buyer asks additional questions about the condition of the property the common law rules of no fraudulent misrepresentation and no fraudulent concealment still apply. This form applies to most resale transactions but does not apply to the sale of a new construction home. The material will cover issues related to new homes and physical defects later in this chapter.

Tex. Prop. Code § 5.008 Duty to Disclose

a) A seller of residential real property comprising not more than one dwelling unit located in this state shall give to the purchaser of the property a written notice as prescribed by this section or a written notice substantially similar to the notice prescribed by this section which contains, at a minimum, all of the items in the notice prescribed by this section.

(b) The notice must be executed and must, at a minimum, read substantially similar to the following:

SELLER'S DISCLOSURE NOTICE

CONCERNING THE PROPERTY AT _____

(Street Address and City)

THIS NOTICE IS A DISCLOSURE OF SELLER'S KNOWLEDGE OF THE CONDITION OF THE PROPERTY AS OF THE DATE SIGNED BY SELLER AND IS NOT A SUBSTITUTE FOR ANY INSPECTIONS OR WARRANTIES THE PURCHASER MAY WISH TO OBTAIN. IT IS NOT A WARRANTY OF ANY KIND BY SELLER OR SELLER'S AGENTS.

Seller ____ is ____ is not occupying the Property.

If unoccupied, how long since Seller has occupied the Property?

1. The Property has the items checked below:

Write Yes (Y), No (N), or Unknown (U).

Range

Oven

Microwave

Dishwasher

Trash Compactor

Disposal

Washer/Dryer Hookups

Fire Detection Equipment

Intercom System

Smoke Detector— Hearing Impaired

Carbon Monoxide Alarm

Emergency Escape Ladder

Attic Fan(s)

Exhaust Fan(s)

Central A/C

Central Heating

Wall/Window Air Conditioning

Plumbing System

Septic System

Window Screens

Rain Gutters

Security System

Fences

Pool

Sauna

Spa

Hot Tub

Pool Equipment

Pool Heater

Automatic Lawn Sprinkler System

TV Antenna

Cable TV Wiring

Satellite Dish

Ceiling Fan(s)

Fireplace(s) & Chimney (wood burning)

Fireplace(s) & Chimney (Mock)

Natural Gas Lines

Gas Fixtures

Liquid Propane Gas:

LP Community

LP on Property (Captive)

Public Sewer System

Patio/Decking

Outdoor Gril

Garage: Attached Not Attached

Carport

Garage Door Opener(s): Electronic Control(s)

Water Heater: Gas Electric

Water Supply: City Well MUD Co-op

Roof Type:

Age: __ (approx)

Are you (Seller) aware of any of the above items that are not in working condition, that have known defects, or that are in need of repair?
___ Yes ___ No ___ Unknown.

If yes, then describe. (Attach additional sheets if necessary):

2. Does the property have working smoke detectors installed in accordance with the smoke detector requirements of Chapter 766, Health and Safety Code?*
___ Yes ___ No ___ Unknown.

If the answer to the question above is no or unknown, explain. (Attach additional sheets if necessary): _____

*Chapter 766 of the Health and Safety Code requires one-family or two-family dwellings to have working smoke detectors installed in accordance with the requirements of the building code in effect in the area in which the dwelling is located, including performance, location, and power source requirements. If you do not know the building code requirements in effect in your area, you may check unknown above or contact your local building official for more information. A buyer may require a seller to install smoke detectors for the hearing impaired if: (1) the buyer or a member of the buyer's family who will reside in the dwelling is hearing impaired; (2) the buyer gives the seller written evidence of the hearing impairment from a licensed physician; and (3) within 10 days after the effective date, the buyer makes a written request for the seller to install smoke detectors for the hearing impaired and specifies the locations for installation. The parties may agree who will bear the cost of installing the smoke detectors and which brand of smoke detectors to install.

3. Are you (Seller) aware of any known defects/malfunctions in any of the following?

Write Yes (Y) if you are aware, write No (N) if you are not aware.

Interior Walls	Roof	Plumbing/Sewers/Electrical
Ceilings	Foundation/Slab(s)	
Floors	Basement	Lighting
Exterior Walls	Walls/Fences	Septic Systems
Doors	Driveways	Fixtures
Windows	Sidewalks	

Other Structural Components (Describe):_____

If the answer to any of the above is yes, explain. (Attach additional sheets if necessary):_____

4. Are you (Seller) aware of any of the following conditions? Write Yes (Y) if you are aware, write No (N) if you are not aware.

Active Termites (includes wood-destroying insects)

Previous Structural or Roof Repair

Urea formaldehyde Insulation

Previous Flooding

Radon Gas

Previous Fires

Present Flood Insurance Coverage

Unplatted Easements

Termite or Wood Rot Damage Needing Repair

Hazardous or Toxic Waste

Previous Termite Damage

Asbestos Components

Previous Termite Treatment

Improper Drainage

Lead Based Paint

Water Penetration

Aluminum Wiring

Located in 100-Year Floodplain

Landfill, Settling, Soil Movement, Fault Lines

Subsurface Structure or Pits

Single Blockable Main Drain in Pool/Hot Tub/Spa*

Previous Use of Premises for Manufacture of Methamphetamine

If the answer to any of the above is yes, explain. (Attach additional sheets if necessary):_____

*A single blockable main drain may cause a suction entrapment hazard for an individual.

5. Are you (Seller) aware of any item, equipment, or system in or on the property that is in need of repair? ___ Yes (if you are aware) ___ No (if you are not aware). If yes, explain (attach additional sheets as necessary).

_____

6. Are you (Seller) aware of any of the following?

Write Yes (Y) if you are aware, write No (N) if you are not aware.

Room additions, structural modifications, or other alterations or repairs made without necessary permits or not in compliance with building codes in effect at that time.

Homeowners' Association or maintenance fees or assessments.

Any "common area" (facilities such as pools, tennis courts, walkways, or other areas) co-owned in undivided interest with others.

Any notices of violations of deed restrictions or governmental ordinances affecting the condition or use of the Property.

Any lawsuits directly or indirectly affecting the Property.

Any condition on the Property which materially affects the physical health or safety of an individual.

Any rainwater harvesting system located on the property that is larger than 500 gallons and that uses a public water supply as an auxiliary water source.

Any portion of the property that is located in a groundwater conservation district or a subsidence district.

If the answer to any of the above is yes, explain. (Attach additional sheets if necessary): _____

7. If the property is located in a coastal area that is seaward of the Gulf Intracoastal Waterway or within 1,000 feet of the mean high tide bordering the Gulf of Mexico, the property may be subject to the Open Beaches Act or the Dune Protection Act (Chapter 61 or 63, Natural Resources Code, respectively) and a beachfront construction certificate or dune protection permit may be required for repairs or improvements. Contact the local government with ordinance authority over construction adjacent to public beaches for more information.

8. This property may be located near a military installation and may be affected by high noise or air installation compatible use zones or other operations. Information relating to high noise and compatible use zones is available in the most recent Air Installation Compatible Use Zone Study or Joint Land Use Study

prepared for a military installation and may be accessed on the Internet website of the military installation and of the county and any municipality in which the military installation is located.

Date _____

Signature of Seller _____

The undersigned purchaser hereby acknowledges receipt of the foregoing notice.

Date _____

Signature of Purchaser _____

(c) A seller or seller's agent shall have no duty to make a disclosure or release information related to whether a death by natural causes, suicide, or accident unrelated to the condition of the property occurred on the property or whether a previous occupant had, may have had, has, or may have AIDS, HIV related illnesses, or HIV infection.

(d) The notice shall be completed to the best of seller's belief and knowledge as of the date the notice is completed and signed by the seller. If the information required by the notice is unknown to the seller, the seller shall indicate that fact on the notice, and by that act is in compliance with this section.

(e) This section does not apply to a transfer:

(1) pursuant to a court order or foreclosure sale;

(2) by a trustee in bankruptcy;

(3) to a mortgagee by a mortgagor or successor in interest, or to a beneficiary of a deed of trust by a trustor or successor in interest;

(4) by a mortgagee or a beneficiary under a deed of trust who has acquired the real property at a sale conducted pursuant to a power of sale under a deed of trust or a sale pursuant to a court ordered foreclosure or has acquired the real property by a deed in lieu of foreclosure;

(5) by a fiduciary in the course of the administration of a decedent's estate, guardianship, conservatorship, or trust;

(6) from one co-owner to one or more other co-owners;

(7) made to a spouse or to a person or persons in the lineal line of consanguinity of one or more of the transferors;

(8) between spouses resulting from a decree of dissolution of marriage or a decree of legal separation or from a property settlement agreement incidental to such a decree;

(9) to or from any governmental entity;

(10) of a new residence of not more than one dwelling unit which has not previously been occupied for residential purposes; or

(11) of real property where the value of any dwelling does not exceed five percent of the value of the property.

(f) The notice shall be delivered by the seller to the purchaser on or before the effective date of an executory contract binding the purchaser to purchase the property. If a contract is entered without the seller providing the notice required by this section, the purchaser may terminate the contract for any reason within seven days after receiving the notice.

(g) In this section:

(1) "Blockable main drain" means a main drain of any size and shape that a human body can sufficiently block to create a suction entrapment hazard.

(2) "Main drain" means a submerged suction outlet typically located at the bottom of a swimming pool or spa to conduct water to a recirculating pump.

Robbins v. Capozzi
Court of Appeals of Texas, Tyler, 2002
100 S.W.3d 18

Appellant Susan Robbins ("Robbins") appeals the trial court's grant of summary judgment in favor of Appellees, LaDonna Capozzi ("Capozzi"), Adleta & Poston ("A & P") and Susan Bratton ("Bratton"). Robbins raises three issues on appeal. We affirm.

Background
In 1999, Capozzi purchased Unit C at the 3537 Normandy condominium project ("Unit C") in Highland Park from Mockingbird Corporation as a place for her daughter, Meghan Capozzi ("Meghan"), to live while attending SMU. Unit C is part of a five-unit condominium complex with enough garage space to house two cars for each unit.

In order to enter the Unit C garages, a 90-degree turn must be made from a driveway that runs along the side of the garages. Before any of the condominiums were sold, the developers, Wallace Swanson ("Swanson") and Allie Beth Allman ("Allman"), satisfied themselves that the garages would accommodate different types of cars. Swanson successfully parked a large Jaguar sedan in one of the Unit C garages and both Swanson and Allman parked Allman's Mercedes SUV in one of the garages.

Shortly after her mother bought Unit C, Meghan discovered that SMU did not allow freshmen to live off campus and had to give up the idea of living in the condominium during her freshman year. Although Meghan did not live at Unit C, she went there on occasion and stored some of her belongings there. Whenever she did so, she parked her Audi A4 sedan in one of the Unit C garages. Meghan successfully negotiated the 90-degree turn from the driveway into the garage by backing up and maneuvering her vehicle into the garage. One of Meghan's friends also successfully maneuvered his car, a Mazda MX-3, into one of the garages.

Meghan decided that it would be more convenient for her to park her car in the driveway next to her front door instead of in the Unit C garages. She believed the third space would not only eliminate the need to line up her car to park in the Unit C garages but would also allow her to access her own unit more easily. She also planned to have two roommates living with her the following year, giving rise to the need for a total of three parking spaces for the property. Meghan's father, John Capozzi, discussed the idea with Allman and in February of 2000, Mockingbird Corporation executed and recorded a "Common Element Designation for 3537 Normandy, a Condominium" (the "Driveway Designation"), designating an additional parking space in the driveway of the complex (the "driveway space") to be used by the owner of Unit C. Once the Driveway Designation was recorded, Meghan parked her car in the driveway space whenever she visited the condo.

---

[1] Google Earth V 6.2.2.6613. (December 10, 2009). Highland Park, Texas. 32° 50′ 18.92″N, 96° 47′ 30.16″W, Eye alt 1028 feet. 2010 Europa Technologies. http://www.earth.google.com [December 10, 2009].

[2] Google Earth V 6.2.2.6613. (December 10, 2009). Highland Park, Texas. 32° 50′ 18.92″N, 96° 47′ 30.16″W, Eye alt 558 feet. 2010 Google. http://www.earth.google.com [December 10, 2009].

Meghan later decided that she would leave SMU and transfer to another university in the Northeast. Capozzi decided to sell Unit C and hired A & P as the broker. In March of 2000, Capozzi, as Seller, and Robbins, as buyer, entered into a "Residential Condominium Contract (Resale)-All Cash, Assumption Third Party Conventional or Seller Financing" (the "Condo Contract") for the sale of the property. In the Seller's Disclosure Notice (the "notice") tendered to Robbins pursuant to the Condo Contract, Capozzi checked boxes indicating that the garage was in "Working Condition" and had "no known defects." Robbins also received a copy of the Driveway Designation as part of a "Condominium Information Statement" that included copies of all recorded documents affecting the complex. Robbins, who drove a Toyota 4-Runner SUV at the time, visited the property four times before she bought it but never tried to park her SUV in any of the Unit C garages. The parties closed on the Condo Contract, and Robbins received her deed to the property in April.

Shortly before Robbins moved into Unit C in late April, she discovered that she could not maneuver her vehicle into either of Unit C's garages. Robbins and her father then attempted to park other different-sized vehicles in the garages and could not get them into the garages. One of Robbins's co-workers parked a two-door Acura coupe in one of the garages after he pulled up to the entrance and drove his car forward and backward, turning each time to line his car up in order to have an unimpeded entry into the garage. It took the co-worker about ten minutes to complete this process. Later that month, Robbins learned that Meghan had experienced difficulties maneuvering her car into the parking spaces and that Capozzi and her husband had negotiated the Driveway Designation.

In September, Robbins filed suit against Capozzi, A & P, and A & P's agent, Susan Bratton, asserting claims for common law fraud, a violation of sections 17.46(b)(5) and (23) of the Deceptive Trade Practices Act ("DTPA"), and fraud in a real estate transaction in violation of section 27.01 of the Texas Business and Commerce Code. Robbins alleged that the fraud arose out of all three defendants' failure to disclose the difficulties Meghan encountered when parking her car in the Unit C garages. Robbins sought rescission of the transaction, return of the purchase price paid for the property, exemplary damages, costs and attorney's fees.

Capozzi, A & P, and Bratton answered, claiming that none of them knew of anyone who claimed to be unable to park any particular vehicle in either of the Unit C garages.

The trial court granted summary judgment to Capozzi, A & P and Bratton on all of Robbins's claims. In a bench trial on September 18, the trial court ruled that Capozzi was entitled to recover her attorney's fees under the Condo Contract.

Robbins filed a motion for new trial on October 19, which was overruled by operation of law. Robbins then filed her notice of appeal on December 19.

Statutory and Common Law Fraud Claims

In her first and second issues, Robbins argues that the trial court erred in granting summary judgment on the statutory and common law fraud claims she asserted against each defendant.

Robbins contends that Capozzi's representation on the seller's disclosure that the Unit C parking garage was in "working condition" and had "no known defects" was false because Robbins could not maneuver her Toyota 4-Runner into the garage. Robbins further contends that this representation was material because Robbins's deposition testimony, attached to her response to Capozzi's motion for summary judgment, revealed that she would not have bought Unit C if she had been told about the parking difficulties. Robbins also argues that a genuine issue of material fact exists as to whether or not Capozzi had a duty to disclose to Robbins (1) the difficulties Meghan had when parking her vehicle in the garage and (2) the reason the Driveway Designation had been amended to provide a third parking space for Unit C outside of the enclosed parking structure.

It is undisputed that Capozzi represented that the garage was in "working condition" and had "no known defects"; however, Robbins has not presented any evidence to raise a fact issue on the falsity of this representation. She has not directed us to anything in the record demonstrating that the garage was not in working condition or was defective in any way.

She only complains that she could not drive her vehicle into the garage because the width of the driveway that ran along the side of the garage was not large enough to compensate for the width of the turning radius of her vehicle. Thus, Robbins's complaint is, in substance, that the driveway is defective. We first note that Capozzi's representations relate only to the garage and not to the driveway. However, even if the term "garage" includes the driveway, the record does not support Robbins's contention that the driveway is defective.

Capozzi testified that five different vehicles (an Audi A4, a Mazda MX-3, a full-size Jaguar, a Mercedes C280, and a Mercedes SUV) have been parked in the Unit C garages. In April of 2001, A & P conducted an inspection of the garages. A & P's employee, Duke Jimerson, drove a 1997 Mercedes C280 sedan into one of the Unit C garages three times with no difficulty. Robbins even testified in her deposition that her co-worker parked a car in the garage, albeit after ten minutes of maneuvering his vehicle. Therefore, Robbins has not shown that the driveway is defective, but merely that the driveway does not accommodate the turning radius of her particular vehicle and possibly that of her co-worker's vehicle. Although this situation may be an inconvenience, it is not a defect. Consequently, Robbins has not shown that Capozzi's representations were false. Robbins also argues that Capozzi's failure to disclose the difficulties Meghan encountered while parking her car constituted fraud. As a general rule, a failure to disclose information does not constitute fraud unless there is a duty to disclose the information. Bradford v. Vento, 48 S.W.3d 749, 755 (Tex.2001). Thus, silence may be equivalent to a false representation only when the particular circumstances impose a duty on the party to speak and he deliberately remains silent. Id. Whether such a duty exists is a question of law. Id. A seller of real estate is under a duty to disclose those material facts which would not be discoverable by the buyer in the exercise of ordinary care and due diligence. Pairett v. Gutierrez, 969 S.W.2d 512, 515 (Tex. App. Austin 1998, pet. denied). "Material" means a reasonable person would attach importance to and would be induced to act on the information in determining his choice of actions in the transaction in question. American Medical Int'l, Inc. v. Giurintano, 821 S.W.2d 331, 338 (Tex. App. Houston [14th Dist.] 1991, no writ). Likewise, a seller of real estate has no duty to disclose material facts which would be discoverable by the buyer in the exercise of ordinary care and due diligence.

The record demonstrates that Robbins visited the property four times before the closing date but never tried to park her vehicle in the Unit C garages because when she looked at the garages, she thought she would have no problem driving into them. The record also supports Robbins's assertion that the parking at Unit C was material because Robbins testified at her deposition that she would not have bought the property if she had known about Meghan's parking difficulties.

However, it is also undisputed that Robbins was provided a copy of the Driveway Designation before the closing date and had the opportunity to inquire about the reasons the Driveway Designation was obtained but chose not to.[3] Robbins also knew the size and turning capabilities of her own vehicle; therefore, she was in a much better position than Capozzi to discover whether or not her vehicle would be able to turn into the Unit C garages. Had Robbins exercised ordinary care and due diligence by attempting to park her vehicle in either of the garages before the closing date, she would have discovered that she could not turn her vehicle into the garages. Therefore, we hold that Capozzi did not have a duty to disclose any problems Meghan encountered when attempting to park her car in any of the Unit C garages. Robbins's common law fraud issue, as it relates to Capozzi, is overruled.

Susan Bratton and A & P

Robbins argues that Bratton and A & P are liable for common law fraud because (1) Bratton acted in concert with Capozzi in preparing the Seller's Disclosure Notice and (2) a two-page sales flyer Bratton prepared for the marketing of Unit C failed to disclose the third parking space created by the Driveway Designation even though Bratton was aware of the difficulties Meghan encountered when parking her car in Unit C's garages. Robbins contends that A

---

[3] Capozzi testified that she obtained the Driveway Designation because it was "more convenient" for her daughter to "pull up" and park at the door of the condominium than to take the "extra time" to "line up" her car in order to park in the garage.

& P is liable for the actions of Bratton, its agent, under a theory of respondent superior.[4]

In order to defeat Bratton's and A & P's motion for summary judgment, Robbins had to raise a genuine issue of material fact on each element of common law fraud. As is the case with Capozzi, Robbins has failed to show that any of the representations Bratton made were false. The evidence is undisputed that Robbins was made aware of the Driveway Designation before the closing date, yet failed to inquire about the reasons behind the designation and also failed to determine, after four visits to Unit C, whether her vehicle would be able to turn into the Unit C garages. Whether Robbins's vehicle would be capable of turning into one of the Unit C garages is the type of information that a buyer would be expected to discover by ordinary inquiry. See *Bradford*, 48 S.W.3d at 756. Robbins's common law fraud issue, as it relates to Bratton and A & P, is overruled.

Conclusion

The trial court did not err in granting summary judgment in favor of Capozzi because Robbins failed to raise a genuine issue of material fact on her statutory fraud, common law fraud, and DTPA claims. The trial court also committed no error in awarding Capozzi her attorney's fees pursuant to the provision in the Condo Contract.

Therefore, the trial court's judgment is affirmed.

Cole v. Johnson
Court of Appeals of Texas, Fort Worth, 2005
157 S.W.3d 856

Introduction

This case involves the nondisclosure of certain information regarding the foundation of a home purchased by Lucas Cole and allegedly also by his wife, Alberta Cole (collectively, "the Coles"), from Larry C. Johnson and Rhea F. Johnson (collectively, "the Johnsons"). In four points, the Coles assert error on the part of the trial court in granting summary judgment on behalf of, and awarding attorney's fees to, the Johnsons, resulting in the dismissal of the Coles' suit.

Factual Background

This is a case of a faulty foundation's failure. On October 15, 2000, Lucas Cole entered into a contract with the Johnsons to purchase their home at 3302 Tranquility Drive, Arlington, Tarrant County, Texas. On November 17, 2000, the

---

[4] Robbins's attempt to hold A & P liable for Bratton's actions under a theory of respondeat superior was not challenged by A & P.

INDICATES COLES HAVE MADE ASSESSMENT OF PROPERTY

sale of the house was completed. Among the closing papers was a two-page notarized document signed by Lucas Cole on November 17, 2000, which indicated that the sale price was being lowered two thousand dollars in lieu of foundation repairs, that the Johnsons would be held harmless for any present or future repairs, and that the property was being purchased in an "as-is" condition. For reasons that are not indicated in the record, Alberta Cole, the wife of Lucas Cole, was not named as a party and did not sign the Residential Sales Contract, the Acknowledgment of Receipt of the Sellers' Disclosure Notice, or the November 17, 2000 notarized document, although she was named as a "buyer" in the notarized document.

In connection with the purchase of the home, numerous other documents were executed or provided by the Johnsons, including (1) a fifteen-page concrete and soils testing report dated May 11, 1993 from the Hooper Group, Inc. to Koos and Associates, Inc., (2) a ten-page foundation investigation dated May 28, 1993 submitted to United States Automobile Association Insurance ("USAA") by Koos Engineering and Associates ("Koos"), (3) a four-page report from McHale Consulting Engineering ("McHale") to Ram Jack Foundation Repair ("Ram Jack") dated March 1, 1995, (4) core drilling and testing reports from Don Illingworth to Terracon Consultants, Inc. ("Terracon") dated February 22, 1996, (5) a ten-page report with attachments from to Don Illingworth and Associates, Inc. dated March 1, 1996 concerning sub-surface exploration and laboratory testing, (6) several pages of bid estimates and a contract for work between Extra Mile Construction Company and the Johnsons dated June 17, 1996, (7) other documents relating to bid estimates and pier placements by Ram Jack, (8) a foundation report summary running from 1993 to 2000, and (9) other miscellaneous documents related to the foundation and work thereon, all totaling fifty-five pages.

FOUNDATION REPAIRS ON RECORD

These documents revealed that USSA and Koos prepared a foundation and soil study concerning the property in 1993 and, as a result, Ram Jack installed twelve piers to repair the foundation. In 1995, McHale Engineering did another foundation and soils study for Ram Jack resulting in the application of mudjacking to the center of the home. In 1996, Terracon prepared a soils study for the homeowner to ascertain the type of foundation that would be needed if an additional room were added to the home. Also in 1996, work was performed on the drainage along the west and the south sides of the house by Extra Mile Construction. In 2000, two additional piers were installed, the Ram Jack piers were adjusted, and brick masonry was repaired by Extra Mile Construction.

The disclosure statement, to which the fifty-five pages of documentation was attached, indicated that the foundation and drainage had been inspected four times by Koos, Ram Jack, McHale, and Terracon; that the foundation had been repaired with the explanation of "see report"; that there had been house settling and soil movement with the explanation of "see reports" for the house settling; that repairs had been made to the foundation of the property since its original construction; that the seller had obtained a written report on the condition of the foundation, which was attached to the disclosure statement; that the seller had obtained a written report about drainage; that repairs had been made to the drainage of the property since its original construction; that the owner was not aware of any undisclosed defective condition; that the owner was unaware of any current defective condition to the drainage; and that there was no builder's warranty or other non-manufacturer's warranty on the property.

After the closing on the home, during a telephone conversation between Rhea Johnson and Alberta Cole, Rhea mentioned to Alberta that the Ram Jack foundation work had failed, that Ram Jack had refunded their fee to the Johnsons, and that the Ram Jack warranty had been released in connection with the refund.

Procedural Background

Subsequent to the conversation between Alberta and Rhea, the Coles filed suit against the Johnsons and others alleging breach of contract, violation of the DTPA, negligent misrepresentation, common law fraud, statutory fraud in a real estate transaction, and negligence, all based on the Rhea/Alberta telephone conversation. They specifically alleged that the Johnsons withheld substantial information concerning recommendations for repairs that they had elected not to undertake and the resulting concealed, unrepaired foundation defect. They prayed for economic damages, mental anguish, "additional damages," prejudgment interest, attorney's fees, and costs of suit. The Johnsons answered with a general denial, asserted affirmative defenses, and requested attorney's fees.

On March 19, 2004, a hearing was heard on a "traditional" summary judgment motion filed by the Johnsons and Ebby Halliday Real Estate Inc., d/b/a Ebby Halliday. As a result of the hearing, certain objections to the Coles' summary judgment response and evidence were denied in part and granted in part, summary judgment was granted to the Johnsons, and attorney's fees and costs were awarded to the Johnsons. The summary judgment signed by the trial court concludes with, "This judgment finally disposes of all claims and all parties and is appealable." Therefore, it is a final judgment subject to appeal. See Lehmann v. Har-Con Co., 39 S.W.3d 191, 206 (Tex. 2001). The trial court did not specify the reasons for its grant of summary judgment. This appeal followed.

Points on Appeal

In their first point, the Coles assert that the trial court erred if it granted summary judgment to the Johnsons based on the finding that the Johnsons were absolved of any further duty to disclose additional information regarding the Ram Jack repair work above and beyond what had been disclosed prior to the sale of the property. As previously stated, all the Coles' causes of action are based on the

Rhea/Alberta telephone conversation and the alleged omission of information provided to the Coles regarding the failure of the Ram Jack pier work.

Specifically, they complain that "the 1995 foundation repair by of [sic] Ram Jack's 1993 foundation work had failed and resulted in a refund to them [the Johnsons] of the money paid to Ram Jack for the 1993 job and cancellation of a warranty it had extended to the Johnsons for that work," which was not disclosed to them. The Coles, citing SmithKline Beecham Corporation v. Doe, 903 S.W.2d 347, 353 (Tex.1995), Hoggett v. Brown, 971 S.W.2d 472, 487 (Tex. App.—Houston [14th Dist.] 1997, pet. denied), and Ralston Purina Company v. McKendrick, 850 S.W.2d 629, 636 (Tex. App.—San Antonio 1993, writ denied), assert that the Johnsons breached "a general duty to disclose information in a transaction [that] is not absolved when a party makes a partial disclosure that, although true, conveys a false impression."

The Coles assert that this omission denied them the opportunity to evaluate the information which should have been disclosed to them. However, the Coles ignore the final four words of their own argument, that is, that a partial disclosure may not absolve the disclosing party if the partially disclosed information conveys a false impression. Moreover, a seller of a house is charged only with disclosing such material facts as to put a buyer exercising reasonable diligence on notice of the condition of the house. Pfeiffer v. Ebby Halliday Real Estate, Inc., 747 S.W.2d 887, 890 (Tex. App.—Dallas 1988, no writ). The Coles were aware there was no foundation warranty for the premises. They were aware that the property had an extensive history of foundation problems and foundation work. They were aware that foundation and drainage repairs had been made following the Ram Jack foundation work. They were aware that the Ram Jack foundation work had not cured the foundation problems because the foundation had continued to move and had to be repaired following that work. Specifically, the McHale Engineering report, which was prepared after Ram Jack installed twelve piers in 1993 and after further attempted repairs in 1995, indicated that some of the pier tops were exposed and the piers appeared to be loose. This is a condition that occurs when the foundation heaves or rises. . . . The residence appears to be experiencing foundation movement around the perimeter of the residence. . . . [This] consists primarily of cracked masonry, out of plumb windows and deflection of the frieze board at the top of the wall.

The report further finds evidence of sheetrock cracking throughout the residence in the walls and in the ceilings and slab cracks in the entry tile and throughout the garage. The report opines that

> [the] residence is experiencing [heaving]. . . . This foundation heave appears to have occurred since the residence was underpinned. . . . The elevation differentials in this residence are significant. . . . The excess moisture below this residence may

have created considerable instability in the subgrade soil. As the subgrade soils dry over the next few years, mud jacking of the interior slab may have to be repeated.

It is obvious, even to a layman, that the foundation work performed by Ram Jack had not corrected all the problems with the property's foundation; that these problems were ongoing at the time of the McHale report; and that further problems might occur in the future.

HOLDING

The disclosures by the Johnsons did not convey a false impression and assuredly would have put a buyer using reasonable diligence on notice as to the residence's condition. This point is overruled.

Conclusion

Having overruled all the Coles' points, the judgment of the trial court is affirmed.

NOTES & QUESTIONS:

1. In looking at the statutory disclosure form, it appears that just about everything imaginable is covered. But what happens if after the disclosure form is completed and before closing occurs, something changes? The seller discovers that there is some defect that exists that is questioned in the form. Does the seller have an obligation to provide this new information? According to the Houston Court of Appeals in Bynum v. Prudential, there is no duty to provide any ongoing updates. Although the seller discovered the presence of asbestos during the executory period, the court stated that in looking at (d) of § 5.008, the language states that "the notice shall be completed to the best of seller's belief and knowledge as of the date the notice is completed and signed by the seller." There is nothing in the statute to indicate there is a duty to supplement. Bynum v. Prudential, 129 S.W.3d 781, 795 (Tex. App.–Houston [1st Dist.] 2004, pet. denied). While legally this may be true, as illustrated by Cole v. Johnson, that may not be the most prudent position to take.

2. Other issues often arise that are even more difficult to answer. For example, does a seller have an obligation to reveal a noisy or difficult neighbor? What about the presence of a nearby toxic waste dump? What about a death on the property? The answers to these questions vary greatly. It will depend on the state. Look at the Texas statute to answer these questions.

4. Other Disclosure Topics

In addition to concerns about the physical condition, a buyer will also be concerned with whether any restrictions and obligations come along with ownership of the property. On the § 5.008 Seller's Disclosure Form there is a question asking if the property is subject to membership in a mandatory owners' association. As you learned in the chapter on covenants, living in a residential subdivision can come with many strings attached. Because of this, there is an additional section of the Texas Property Code, provided below, that requires an additional notice to be provided in those circumstances.

Tex. Prop. Code § 5.012 Notice of Mandatory Owners' Association

(a) A seller of residential real property that is subject to membership in a property owners' association and that comprises not more than one dwelling unit located in this state shall give to the purchaser of the property a written notice that reads substantially similar to the following:

NOTICE OF MEMBERSHIP IN PROPERTY OWNERS' ASSOCIATION CONCERNING THE PROPERTY AT (street address) (name of residential community)

As a purchaser of property in the residential community in which this property is located, you are obligated to be a member of a property owners' association. Restrictive covenants governing the use and occupancy of the property and all dedicatory instruments governing the establishment, maintenance, or operation of this residential community have been or will be recorded in the Real Property Records of the county in which the property is located. Copies of the restrictive covenants and dedicatory instruments may be obtained from the county clerk.

You are obligated to pay assessments to the property owners' association. The amount of the assessments is subject to change. Your failure to pay the assessments could result in enforcement of the association's lien on and the foreclosure of your property.

Section 207.003, Property Code, entitles an owner to receive copies of any document that governs the establishment, maintenance, or operation of a subdivision, including, but not limited to, restrictions, bylaws, rules and regulations, and a resale certificate from a property owners' association. A resale certificate contains information including, but not limited to, statements specifying the amount and frequency of regular assessments and the style and cause number of lawsuits to which the property owners' association is a party, other than lawsuits relating to unpaid ad valorem taxes of an individual member of the association. These documents must be made available to you by the property owners' association or the association's agent on your request.

Date: _____   _____
                                        Signature of Purchaser

(a-1) The second paragraph of the notice prescribed by Subsection (a) must be in bold print and underlined.

(b) The seller shall deliver the notice to the purchaser before the date the executory contract binds the purchaser to purchase the property. The notice may be given separately, as part of the contract during negotiations, or as part of any other notice the seller delivers to the purchaser. If the notice is included as part of the executory contract or another notice, the title of the notice prescribed by this section, the references to the street address and date in the notice, and the purchaser's signature on the notice may be omitted.

(c) This section does not apply to a transfer:
   (1) under a court order or foreclosure sale;
   (2) by a trustee in bankruptcy;
   (3) to a mortgagee by a mortgagor or successor in interest or to a beneficiary of a deed of trust by a trustor or successor in interest;
   (4) by a mortgagee or a beneficiary under a deed of trust who has acquired the land at a sale conducted under a power of sale under a deed of trust or a sale under a court-ordered foreclosure or has acquired the land by a deed in lieu of foreclosure;
   (5) by a fiduciary in the course of the administration of a decedent's estate, guardianship, conservatorship, or trust;
   (6) from one co-owner to another co-owner of an undivided interest in the real property;
   (7) to a spouse or a person in the lineal line of consanguinity of the seller;
   (8) to or from a governmental entity;
   (9) of only a mineral interest, leasehold interest, or security interest; or
   (10) of a real property interest in a condominium.

(d) If an executory contract is entered into without the seller providing the notice required by this section, the purchaser may terminate the contract for any reason within the earlier of:
   (1) seven days after the date the purchaser receives the notice; or
   (2) the date the transfer occurs as provided by the executory contract.

(e) The purchaser's right to terminate the executory contract under Subsection (d) is the purchaser's exclusive remedy for the seller's failure to provide the notice required by this section.

NOTES:

1. You may notice that the types of transactions that do not require a § 5.008 disclosure form are also excluded here under (c), except for the new home purchase. The builder/vendor who sells a new construction home has the same obligation as any other seller with respect to disclosing the mandatory membership in a property owners association.

   While this disclosure is helpful, it has a weakness that is usually exploited. Under (b) the statute states that "[i]f the notice is included as part of the executory contract or another notice, the title of the notice prescribed by this section, the references to the street address and date in the notice, and the purchaser's signature on the notice may be omitted." This allows the notice to be buried within the standard sales contract and that is typically what occurs. The notice is there, but might not be very noticeable.

5. New Home Warranties

The area of new home construction has been a source of controversy and a tortured area of the law in Texas and in many states across the country. When purchasing an existing home, there is a requirement to provide a seller's disclosure, but the transaction does not come with any warranties from the seller regarding habitability or workmanship or any promises related to the physical condition of the property unless the seller affirmatively makes such warranties. When purchasing a new construction home, whether custom built or a spec home, there is no statutory requirement to complete a seller's disclosure form. The common law obligations not to fraudulently conceal, not to fraudulently misrepresent, and to disclose material latent defects known to the builder/vendor still exist. Because the home is new, the buyer normally expects the seller (builder) to provide warranties about the condition of the home being purchased. The courts and legislature in Texas have tried different approaches to dealing with these issues; however, none have been particularly successful in adequately protecting the consumer.

The law in Texas began with the common law imposition of the implied warranties of habitability and good workmanship. Several Texas Supreme Court cases evaluated these warranties over the years to determine if such warranties were waivable, and if so, how that could be accomplished. The legislature stepped in with the Residential Construction Liability Act (RCLA) to try to put in place a system that would require notice to the builder with an opportunity to cure any defects before litigation. After a few years of the RCLA, the Texas legislature enacted the Texas Residential Construction Commission Act, creating the Texas Residential Construction Commission (TRCC). The legislation included a sunset provision which had it set to end in 2009 unless that legislature decided to revive it. After examination, discussion, and great dissatisfaction from consumers, the Act was allowed to sunset and the TRCC no longer exists.

Today we are back to using the common law warranties and obligations that existed prior to the TRCC. The RCLA does remain in place as a gatekeeper to construction litigation.

Humber v. Morton
Supreme Court of Texas, 1968
426 S.W.2d 554

NORVELL, Justice.

The widow Humber brought suit against Claude Morton, alleging that Morton was in the business of building and selling new houses; that she purchased a house from him which was not suitable for human habitation in that the fireplace and chimney were not properly constructed and because of such defect, the house caught fire and partially burned the first time a fire was lighted in the fireplace. Morton defended upon two grounds: that an independent contractor, Johnny F. Mays, had constructed the fireplace and he, Morton, was not liable for the work done by Mays, and that the doctrine of "caveat emptor" applied to all sales of real estate. Upon the first trial of the case (which was to a jury), Mrs. Humber recovered a judgment which was reversed by the Eastland Court of Civil Appeals and the cause remanded for another trial because of an improper submission of the damage issue.

Upon the second trial, defendant Morton filed a motion for summary judgment supported by affidavits, one of which referred to and incorporated therein the statement of the evidence adduced upon the first trial. Plaintiff likewise made a motion for summary judgment. Defendant's motion was granted and that of the plaintiff overruled. Such judgment was affirmed by the Court of Civil Appeals upon the holdings that Mays was an independent contractor and that the doctrine of implied warranty was not applicable to the case. Mrs. Humber, as petitioner, brought the case here, but we shall refer to the parties by their trial court designations.

It conclusively appears that defendant Morton was a "builder-vendor." The summary judgment proofs disclose that he was in the business of building or assembling houses designed for dwelling purposes upon land owned by him. He would then sell the completed houses together with the tracts of land upon which they were situated to members of the house-buying public. There is conflict in the summary judgment proofs as to whether the house sold to Mrs. Humber had been constructed with a dangerously defective fireplace chimney. Construction engineers, who testified under oath for Mrs. Humber, as disclosed by the statement of facts upon the first trial which was made a part of the summary judgment record here, stated that the chimney was defective. Mr. Mays, who built the chimney, denied that his work was substandard or deficient in any way.

While there may be other grounds for holding that Mrs. Humber made a case to go to the jury, such as negligence attributable to Morton, failure to inspect and the like, we need not discuss these theories because we are of the opinion that the courts below erred in holding as a matter of law that Morton was not liable to Mrs. Humber because the doctrine of caveat emptor applied to the sale of a new house by a "builder-vendor" and consequently no implied warranty that the house was fit for human habitation arose from the sale. Accordingly, we reverse the judgments of the courts below and remand the cause to the district court for a conventional trial upon the merits.

Mrs. Humber entered into a contract when she bought the house from Morton in May of 1964 and such house, together with the lot upon which it was situated, was conveyed to her. According to Morton, the only warranty contained in the deed was the warranty of title, *i.e.*, "to warrant and forever defend, all and singular, the said premises unto the said Ernestine Humber, her heirs and assigns, . . ." and that he made no other warranty, written or oral, in connection with the sale. While it is unusual for one to sell a house without saying something good about it, and the statement that no warranty was made smacks of a conclusion, we shall assume that such conversation as may have taken place did not involve anything more than mere sales talk or puffing, and that no express warranties, either oral or written, were involved. However, it is undisputed that Morton built the house and then sold it as a new house. Did he thereby impliedly warrant that such house was constructed in a good workmanlike manner and was suitable for human habitation? We hold that he did. Under such circumstances, the law raises an implied warranty.

Preliminary to our discussion of the controlling issue in the case, the applicability of the caveat emptor doctrine, we should notice the reference of the Court of Civil Appeals to Article 1297, Vernon's Ann. Tex. Stats., which incidentally is not set out in the opinion, but is referred to by a quotation from Westwood Development Company v. Esponge, 342 S.W.2d 623 (Tex. Civ. App.1961, writ ref'd, n.r.e.). The statute is not deemed applicable here for a number of reasons. Article 1297 does not say that warranties as to fitness and suitability of structures upon land cannot arise unless expressed in the deed of conveyance. The article relates to covenants which may or may not arise from the use of certain specific words in a conveyance, namely, "grant" or "convey."

This article is part of Title 31, Revised Statutes, relating to conveyances. It relates to covenants of title which arise out of conveyances and not to collateral covenants such as the suitability of a house for human habitation. The presence of a collateral covenant of this type in a deed would be strange indeed. "It is not the office of a deed to express the terms of the contract of sale, but to pass the title pursuant to the contract." 26 C.J.S. Deeds s 1, p. 582. The article simply prescribes what covenants may be implied by the use of two designated words, "grant" or "convey." The implied warranty of fitness arises from the sale and does not spring from the conveyance.

It may be that the lower courts were striking at the nonstatutory doctrine of merger under which all prior negotiations with reference to a sale of land are said to be merged in the final transaction between the parties. The doctrine of merger, however, is a matter generally controlled by the intention of the parties. 26 C.J.S. Deeds s 91, p. 841. For example: A owns Blackacre and agrees with B to construct a house thereon and then conveys the house and lot to B after the house has been completed. There are numerous cases that an implied covenant or warranty to build in a workmanlike manner is not destroyed by the deed. See, e.g., Perry v. Sharon Development Co. (1937) 4 All E.R. 390 (CA); Jones v. Gatewood, 381 P.2d 158 (Okl.1963).

If the passage of a deed does not operate to extinguish a warranty, either expressed or implied, in the case of an uncompleted house, it is difficult to understand how the deed could operate to merge and thus destroy an implied warranty raised by law in the case of a sale of a completed new house. It would be a strange doctrine indeed for the law to raise an implied warranty from a sale and then recognize that such warranty could be defeated by the passage of title to the subject matter of the sale. The issue here is not whether the implied warranty was extinguished by a conveyance, but whether such warranty ever came into existence in the first place.

The cases which give some weight to the doctrine of merger in the implied warranty situation hold that the doctrine of caveat emptor applies to sales of real property, thus reducing the "merger" theory to the status of a "unicorn hunting bow." The merger doctrine implies that there is something to merge.

We return to the crucial issue in the case—Does the doctrine of caveat emptor apply to the sale of a new house by a builder-vendor?

Originally, the two great systems of jurisprudence applied different doctrines to sales of both real and personal property. The rule of the common law—caveat emptor—was fundamentally based upon the premise that the buyer and seller dealt at arm's length, and that the purchaser had means and opportunity to gain information concerning the subject matter of the sale which were equal to those of the seller. On the other hand, the civil law doctrine—

caveat venditor—was based upon the premise that a sound price calls for a sound article; that when one sells an article, he implies that it has value. 77 C.J.S. 1159, Sales s 315, Sales 275, Sales, 46 Am. Jur. 275, Sales s 87.

Today, the doctrine of caveat emptor as related to sales of personal property has a severely limited application. O. M. Franklin Serum Co. v. C. A. Hoover & Sons, 418 S.W.2d 482 (Tex.Sup.1967).

In 1884, the Supreme Court of the United States applied the doctrine of implied warranty, the antithesis of caveat emptor, to a real property situation involving false work and pilings driven into the bed of the Maumee River. The case of Kellogg Bridge Company v. Hamilton, 110 U.S. 108, 3 S. Ct. 537, 28 L. Ed. 86, arose in connection with the construction of a bridge. The Supreme Court, (the elder Mr. Justice Harlan writing), said:

"Although the plaintiff in error (Kellogg Bridge Company, defendant in the trial court) is not a manufacturer, in the common acceptation of that word, it made or constructed the false work which it sold to Hamilton. The transaction, if not technically a sale, created between the parties the relation of vendor and vendee. The business of the company was the construction of bridges. By its occupation, apart from its contract with the railroad company, it held itself out as reasonably competent to do work of that character. Having partially executed its contract with the railroad company, it made an arrangement with Hamilton whereby the latter undertook, among other things, to prepare all necessary false work, and, by a day named, and in the best manner, to erect the bridge then being constructed by the bridge company—Hamilton to assume and pay for such work and materials as that company had up to that time done and furnished. Manifestly, it was contemplated by the parties that Hamilton should commence where the company left off. It certainly was not expected that he should incur the expense of removing the false work put up by the company and commence anew. On the contrary, he agreed to assume and pay for, and therefore it was expected by the company that he should use, such false work as it had previously prepared. It is unreasonable to suppose that he would buy that which he did not intend to use, or that the company would require him to assume and pay for that which it did not expect him to use, or which was unfit for use. . . . In the cases of sales by manufacturers of their own articles for particular purposes, communicated to them at the time, the argument was uniformly pressed that, as the buyer could have required an express warranty, none should be implied. But, plainly, such an argument impeaches the whole doctrine of implied warranty, for there can be no case of a sale of personal property in which the buyer may not, if he chooses, insist on an express warranty against latent defects.

"All the facts are present which, upon any view of the adjudged cases, must be held essential in an implied warranty. The transaction was, in effect, a sale of this false work, constructed by a company whose business it was to do such work; to be used in the same way the maker intended to use it, and the latent defects in which, as the maker knew, the buyer could not, by any inspection or examination, at the time discover; the buyer did not, because in the nature of things he could not, rely on his own judgment; and, in view of the circumstances of the case, and the relations of the parties, he must be deemed to have relied on the judgment of the company, which alone of the parties to the contract had or could have knowledge of the manner in which the work had been done. The law, therefore, implies a warranty that this false work was reasonably suitable for such use as was contemplated by both parties. . . ."

In Texas, the doctrine of caveat emptor began its fade-out at an early date. In Wintz v. Morrison, 17 Tex. 369 (1856), involving a sale of personal property, the Texas Supreme Court quoted with approval the following from Story on Sales as to the trend of 19th century decisions:

"(T)he tendency of all the modern cases of warranty is to enlarge the responsibility of the seller, to construe every affirmation by him to be a warranty, and frequently to imply a warranty on his part, from acts and circumstances, wherever they were relied upon by the buyer. The maxim of Caveat emptor seems gradually to be restricted in its operation and limited in its dominion, and beset with the circumvallations of the modern doctrine of implied warranty, until it can no longer claim the empire over the law of sales, and is but a shadow of itself. . . ."

As to the present personal property rule of implied warranties or strict liability in tort, see, Decker, Putman, McKisson and Franklin, cited above.

While in numerous common law jurisdictions, the caveat emptor doctrine as applied to the vendor builder-new house situation has overstayed its time, it was said by way of dicta in a Texas Court of Civil Appeals case in 1944 that:

"By offering the (new) house for sale as a new and complete structure appellant impliedly warranted that it was properly constructed and of good material and specifically that it had a good foundation, ..." Loma Vista Development Co. v. Johnson, Tex. Civ. App., 177 S.W.2d 225, l.c. 227, rev. on other grounds, 142 Tex. 686, 180 S.W.2d 922.

This decision has been described as "a preview of things to come."

The rapid sickening of the caveat emptor doctrine as applied to sales of new houses was exposed by the *Miller-Perry-Howe-Weck-Jones-Glisan-Carpenter* syndrome. The history of this development is briefly set out in Carpenter v. Donohoe, 154 Colo. 78, 388 P.2d 399 (1964), and in more detail by Professor E. F. Roberts in "The Case of the Unwary Home Buyer: The Housing Merchant Did It," 52 Cornell Law Quarterly 835 (1967). See also, Williston on Contracts (3rd Ed. Jaeger) s 926A, wherein it is said: "It would be much better if this enlightened approach (implied warranty, Jones v. Gatewood, 381 P.2d 158 (Okl.)) were generally adopted with respect to the sale of new houses for it would tend to discourage much of the sloppy work and jerry-building that has become perceptible over the years." (citations omitted).

The *Glisan* case (Glisan v. Smolenske), 153 Colo. 274, 387 P.2d 260 (1963), was factually similar to the hypothetical example heretofore set out in this opinion. Smolenske had agreed to purchase a house from Gilsan while it was under construction. The court propounded and answered the implied warranty question, thusly:

"Was there an implied warranty that the house, when completed, would be fit for habitation? There is a growing body of law on this question, which, if followed, requires an answer in the affirmative.

"It is the rule that there is an implied warranty where the contract relates to a house which is still in the process of construction, where the vendor's workmen are still on the job, and particularly where completion is not accomplished until the house has arrived at the contemplated condition-namely, finished and fit for habitation." (citations omitted)

In the next year, 1964, the Colorado Supreme Court in Carpenter v. Donohoe, 154 Colo. 78, 388 P.2d 399, extended the implied warranty rule announced by it in *Glisan* to cover sales of a new house by a builder-vendor. The court said:

"That a different rule should apply to the purchaser of a house which is near completion than would apply to one who purchases a new house seems incongruous. To say that the former may rely on an implied warranty and the latter cannot is recognizing a distinction without a reasonable basis for it. This is pointedly argued in an excellent article, 'Caveat Emptor in Sales of Realty-Recent Assaults upon the Rule,' by Bearman, 14 Vanderbilt Law Rev. 541 (1960-61).

"We hold that the implied warranty doctrine is extended to include agreements between builder-vendors and purchasers for the sale of newly constructed buildings, completed at the time of contracting. There is an implied warranty that builder-vendors have complied with the building code of the area in which the structure is located. Where, as here, a home is the subject of sale, there are implied warranties that the home was built in workmanlike manner and is suitable for habitation."

While it is not necessary for us to pass upon a situation in which the vendor-purchaser relationship is absent, the case of Schipper v. Levitt & Sons, 44 N.J. 70, 207 A.2d 314 (1965), is important as much of the reasoning set forth in the opinion is applicable here. The Supreme Court of New Jersey recognized 'the need for imposing on builder-vendors an implied obligation of reasonable workmanship and habitability which survives delivery of the deed.' This was a case in which a person other than a purchaser had been injured by a defective water heater which had been installed in a new house by Levitt, the builder-vendor. The opinion cited and quotes from Carpenter v. Donohoe but proceeded upon the theory of strict liability in tort. The court placed emphasis upon the close analogy between a defect in a new house and a manufactured chattel. The opinion states:

"The law should be based on current concepts of what is right and just and the judiciary should be alert to the never-ending need for keeping its common law principles abreast of the times. Ancient distinctions which make no sense in today's society and tend to discredit the law should be readily rejected as they were step by step in *Henningsen* (Henningsen v. Bloomfield Motors, 32 N.J. 358, 161 A.2d 69, 75 AL.L.R.2d 1 (1960)) and *Santor* (Santor v. A and M Karagheusian, 44 N.J. 52, 207 A.2d 305, 16 A.L.R.3d 670 (1965)). . . .

"When a vendee buys a development house from an advertised model, as in a Levitt or in a comparable project, he clearly relies on the skill of the developer and on its implied representation that the house will be erected in reasonably workmanlike manner and will be reasonably fit for habitation. He has no architect or other professional adviser of his own, he has no real competency to inspect on his own, his actual examination is, in the nature of things, largely superficial, and his opportunity for obtaining meaningful protective changes in the conveyancing documents prepared by the builder vendor is negligible. If there is improper construction such as a defective heating system or a defective ceiling, stairway and the like, the well-being of the vendee and others is seriously endangered and serious injury is foreseeable. The public interest dictates that if such injury does result from the defective construction, its cost should be borne by the responsible developer who created the danger and who is in the better economic position to bear the loss rather than by the injured party who justifiably relied on the developer's skill and implied representation."

In Bethlahmy v. Bechtel, 415 P.2d 698 (Idaho 1966), it appeared that the trial court had rendered judgment in accordance with the 1959 holding of the Supreme Court of Oregon in Steiber v. Palumbo, a much cited case which is relied upon by the defendant here. The specific finding of the trial court was:

"There are no implied warranties in the sale of real property. The sale of this home carried with it, absent an express warranty, no promise that the floor would not leak."

The Idaho court was then called upon to deal with the Oregon decision and the later decisions of the Colorado Supreme Court in Carpenter and that of the New Jersey Supreme Court in *Schipper*. After a careful review of many decisions, including the Oregon, Colorado and New Jersey cases mentioned, the court said:

"The *Schipper* decision is important here because: (1) it illustrates the recent change in the attitude of the courts toward the application of the doctrine of caveat emptor in actions between the builder-vendor and purchaser of newly constructed dwellings; (2) it draws analogy between the present case and the long-accepted application of implied warranty of fitness in sales of personal property; and (3) the opinion had the unanimous approval of the participating justices. . . ."

"The foregoing decisions all (except the *Hoye* case) rendered subsequent to the 1959 Oregon decision, relied upon by the trial court, show the trend of judicial opinion is to invoke the doctrine of implied warranty of fitness in cases involving sales of new houses by the builder. The old rule of caveat emptor does not satisfy the demands of justice in such cases. The purchase of a home is not an everyday transaction for the average family, and in many instances is the most important transaction of a lifetime. To apply the rule of caveat emptor to an inexperienced buyer, and in favor of a builder who is daily engaged in the business of building and selling houses, is manifestly a denial of justice."

In September of 1967, the Houston Court of Civil Appeals handed down its opinion in Moore v. Werner, 418 S.W.2d 918 (no writ), in which, after citing a number of authorities, the court said:

"Many of the authorities cited involve personalty, but we see no reason for any distinction between the sale of a new house and the sale of personalty, especially in a suit between the original parties to the contract, one of whom constructed the house in question. It was the seller's duty to perform the work in a good and workmanlike manner and to furnish adequate materials, and failing to do so, we believe the rule of implied warranty of fitness applies.

If at one time in Texas the rule of caveat emptor had application to the sale of a new house by a vendor-builder, that time is now past. The decisions and legal writings herein referred to afford numerous examples and situations illustrating the harshness and injustice of the rule when applied to the sale of new houses by a builder-vendor, and we need not repeat them here. Obviously, the ordinary purchaser is not in a position to ascertain when there is a defect in a chimney flue, or vent of a heating apparatus, or whether the plumbing work covered by a concrete slab foundation is faulty. It is also highly irrational to make a distinction between the liability of a vendor-builder who employs servants and one who uses independent contractors. Compare, Conner v. Conejo Valley Development Co., 61 Cal. Rptr. 333 (1967). The common law is not afflicted with the rigidity of the law of the Medes and the Persians 'which altereth not,' and as stated in Cardozo in 'The Nature of the Judicial Process,' pp. 150-151 (quoted in 415 P.2d 698):

"That court best serves the law which recognizes that the rules of law which grew up in a remote generation may, in the fullness of experience, be found to serve another generation badly, and which discards the old rule when it finds that another rule of law represents what should be according to the established and settled judgment of society, and no considerable property rights have become vested in reliance upon the old rule. . . ."

The caveat emptor rule as applied to new houses is an anachronism patently out of harmony with modern home buying practices. It does a disservice not only to the ordinary prudent purchaser but to the industry itself by lending encouragement to the unscrupulous, fly-by-night operator and purveyor of shoddy work.

The judgments of the courts below are reversed and the cause remanded for trial in accordance with this opinion.

Centex Homes v. Buecher
Supreme Court of Texas, 2002
95 S.W.3d 266

The issue in this case is whether a homebuilder may disclaim the implied warranties of habitability and good and workmanlike construction that accompany a new home sale. The sales contract here provided that the builder's express limited warranty replaced all other warranties, including these two implied warranties. Holding that the implied warranties of habitability and good and workmanlike construction could not be waived, the court of appeals reversed the trial court's judgment and remanded the homeowners' claims for further proceedings. 18 S.W.3d 807.

We agree with the court of appeals that the implied warranty of habitability cannot be waived except under limited circumstances not implicated here. We disagree, however, that the implied warranty of good and workmanlike construction cannot be disclaimed. When the parties' agreement sufficiently describes the manner, performance or quality of construction, the express agreement may supersede the implied warranty of good workmanship. Although we do not agree in all respects with the court of appeals' reasoning, we affirm its judgment remanding this cause to the trial court.

Michael Buecher and other homeowners purchased new homes built by Centex Homes or Centex Real Estate Corporation doing business as Centex Homes. Each homeowner signed a standard form sales agreement prepared by Centex. The homeowners allege that the agreement contained a one-year limited express warranty in lieu of and waiving the implied warranties of habitability and good and workmanlike construction. Specifically, the disclaimer provision provided:

> At closing Seller will deliver to Purchaser, Seller's standard form of homeowner's Limited Home Warranty against defects in workmanship and materials, a copy of which is available to Purchaser. PURCHASER AGREES TO ACCEPT SAID HOMEOWNER'S WARRANTY AT CLOSING IN LIEU OF ALL OTHER WARRANTIES, WHATSOEVER, WHETHER EXPRESSED OR IMPLIED BY LAW, AND INCLUDING BUT NOT LIMITED TO THE IMPLIED WARRANTIES OF GOOD WORKMANLIKE CONSTRUCTION AND HABITABILITY. PURCHASER ACKNOWLEDGES AND AGREES THAT SELLER IS RELYING ON THIS WAIVER AND WOULD NOT SELL THE PROPERTY TO PURCHASER WITHOUT THIS WAIVER. Purchaser's initials in the margin indicate their approval of this section 8. (Emphasis in original.)

After Buecher and the other plaintiffs purchased their homes, they sued Centex alleging fraud, misrepresentation, negligence, and violation of the Texas Deceptive Trade Practices-Consumer Protection Act ("DTPA") in connection with the construction and sale of their new homes. The homeowners also sought (1) an injunction to prevent Centex from asserting that the implied warranties of habitability and good and workmanlike construction had been waived by the provisions in its sales contracts; (2) an injunction prohibiting Centex from asserting to any homeowner or subsequent purchaser that it had no liability for construction defects beyond the period set forth in the express warranty it gave in lieu of implied warranties;(3) a declaration that the disclaimer provision is unenforceable as a matter of law; and (4) notification to all purchasers and subsequent purchasers that Centex's waiver of implied warranties is void and unenforceable. . . .

A divided court of appeals, sitting en banc, reversed the trial court's judgment and remanded the cause for further proceedings. 18 S.W.3d 807, 811. The court of appeals held that a homebuilder may not disclaim or cause a homeowner to waive the implied warranties of habitability and good and workmanlike construction. *Id.* at 808.

In Humber v. Morton, 426 S.W.2d 554, 555 (Tex. 1968), this Court recognized that a builder of a new home impliedly warrants that the residence is constructed in a good and workmanlike manner and is suitable for human habitation. In replacing caveat emptor with these two implied warranties, we noted the significance of a new home purchase for most buyers and the difficulty of discovering or guarding against latent defects in construction:

> The old rule of caveat emptor does not satisfy the demands of justice in [the sale of new homes]. The purchase of a home is not an everyday transaction for the average family, and in many instances is the most important transaction of a lifetime. To apply the rule of caveat emptor to an inexperienced buyer, and in favor of a builder who is daily engaged in the business of building and selling houses, is manifestly a denial of justice. *Humber,* 426 S.W.2d at 561 (quoting Bethlahmy v. Bechtel, 91 Idaho 55, 415 P.2d 698 (1966)). . . .

Centex argues that we should adhere to [this court's prior decision in] Robichaux because it is consistent with decisions from other states allowing parties to expressly disclaim the implied warranties that ordinarily arise with new home sales. *See, e.g.,* Greeves v. Rosenbaum, 965 P.2d 669, 673 (Wyo. 1998); O'Mara v. Dykema, 328 Ark. 310, 942 S.W.2d 854, 859 (1997); Frickel v. Sunnyside Enters., Inc., 106 Wash. 2d 714, 725 P.2d 422, 426 (1986) (en banc); Dixon v. Mountain City Constr. Co., 632 S.W.2d 538, 542 (Tenn.1982); Petersen v.

Hubschman Constr. Co., 76 Ill.2d 31, 27 Ill. Dec. 746, 389 N.E.2d 1154, 1159 (1979); Griffin v. Wheeler-Leonard & Co., 290 N.C. 185, 225 S.E.2d 557, 567 (1976); Casavant v. Campopiano, 114 R.I. 24, 327 A.2d 831, 833 (1974). These cases, however, generally fail to differentiate between the implied warranty of good workmanship and the implied warranty of habitability.

All of these cases either ignore the implied warranty of habitability or treat it as part of the implied warranty of good workmanship. In Texas, however, the two warranties provide separate and distinct protection for the new home buyer. See Evans v. J. Stiles, Inc., 689 S.W.2d 399, 400 (Tex. 1985) (possible to breach warranty of good workmanship without breaching warranty of habitability); *accord* Chandler v. Madsen, 197 Mont. 234, 642 P.2d 1028, 1031 (1982) (distinguishing between the two implied warranties). Unfortunately, as in *Robichaux*, we have not always been careful to distinguish between the two. *See Robichaux*, 643 S.W.2d at 393. But because they are distinct and different warranties, it is important to consider the particular purpose of each when considering issues of waiver or disclaimer.

The implied warranty of good workmanship focuses on the builder's conduct, while the implied warranty of habitability focuses on the state of the completed structure. Through the implied warranty of good workmanship, the common law recognizes that a new home builder should perform with at least a minimal standard of care. (Citations omitted). This implied warranty requires the builder to construct the home in the same manner as would a generally proficient builder engaged in similar work and performing under similar circumstances. *See* Melody Home Mfg. Co. v. Barnes, 741 S.W.2d 349, 354-55 (Tex. 1987). The implied warranty of good workmanship serves as a "gap-filler" or "default warranty"; it applies unless and until the parties express a contrary intention. (Citations omitted). Thus, the implied warranty of good workmanship attaches to a new home sale if the parties' agreement does not provide how the builder or the structure is to perform.

The implied warranty of habitability, on the other hand, looks only to the finished product:

> [T]he implied warranty of habitability is a result oriented concept based upon specific public policy considerations. These include the propriety of shifting the costs of defective construction from consumers to builders who are presumed better able to absorb such costs; the nature of the transaction which involves the purchase of a manufactured product, a house; the buyer's inferior bargaining position; the foreseeable risk of harm resulting from defects to consumers; consumer difficulty in ascertaining defective conditions; and justifiable reliance by consumers on a builder's expertise and implied representations.

Davis, 72 Neb. L. Rev. at 1019 (footnotes omitted).

This implied warranty is more limited in scope, protecting the purchaser only from those defects that undermine the very basis of the bargain. Id. at 1015. It requires the builder to provide a house that is safe, sanitary, and otherwise fit for human habitation. *Kamarath,* 568 S.W.2d at 660. In other words, this implied warranty only protects new home buyers from conditions that are so defective that the property is unsuitable for its intended use as a home. As compared to the warranty of good workmanship, "the warranty of habitability represents a form of strict liability since the adequacy of the completed structure and not the manner of performance by the builder governs liability." Davis, 72 Neb. L. Rev. at 1015 (1993) (footnotes omitted).

These two implied warranties parallel one another, and they may overlap. For example, a builder's inferior workmanship could compromise the structure and cause the home to be unsafe. But a builder's failure to perform good workmanship is actionable even when the outcome does not impair habitability. *Evans,* 689 S.W.2d at 400. Similarly, a home could be well constructed and yet unfit for human habitation if, for example, a builder constructed a home with good workmanship but on a toxic waste site. Unfortunately, many courts, including this one, have not consistently recognized these distinctions.

We created the *Humber* implied warranties to protect the average home buyer who lacks the ability and expertise to discover defects in a new house. *Humber,* 426 S.W.2d at 561. Such buyer generally expects to receive a house that is structurally sound, habitable and free of hidden defects, and these implied warranties serve to protect the buyer's reasonable expectations. While the parties are free to define for themselves the quality of workmanship, there is generally no substitute for habitability. The implied warranty of habitability is thus an essential part of a new home sale.

The Supreme Court of Missouri has stated that while it does not "reject outright the possibility of a valid disclaimer or modification [of the implied warranty of habitability] under any set of facts," a valid waiver requires more than clear and unambiguous language. Crowder v. Vandendeale, 564 S.W.2d 879, 881 (Mo. 1978) (en banc). Under *Crowder,* the builder is required to prove that the buyer actually understood what he or she was waiving. *Id.* at 881 n. 4. We agree with the Missouri Supreme Court that the warranty of habitability can be waived only to the extent that defects are adequately disclosed. Thus only in unique circumstances, such as when a purchaser buys a problem house with express and full knowledge of the defects that affect its habitability, should a waiver of this warranty be recognized.

The implied warranty of good workmanship, however, defines the level of performance expected when the parties fail to make express provision in their contract. It functions as a gap-filler whose purpose is to supply terms that are omitted from but necessary to the contract's performance. See Restatement (Second) Contracts §§ 204 (1981) (Supplying an Omitted Essential Term). As a gap-filler, the parties' agreement may supersede the implied standard for workmanship, but the agreement cannot simply disclaim it. See generally Lenape Res. Corp. v. Tenn. Gas Pipeline Co., 925 S.W.2d 565, 570 (Tex. 1996) (interpreting UCC gap-filler).

In conclusion, we hold that the implied warranty of good workmanship may be disclaimed by the parties when their agreement provides for the manner, performance or quality of the desired construction. We further hold that the warranty of habitability may not be disclaimed generally. This latter implied warranty, however, only extends to defects that render the property so defective that it is unsuitable for its intended use as a home. Further, the implied warranty of habitability extends only to latent defects. It does not include defects, even substantial ones that are known by or expressly disclosed to the buyer.

In the trial court, the homeowners, who had purchased homes from Centex under standardized contracts disclaiming the implied warranty of habitability and the implied warranty of good and workmanlike construction, sought a judicial declaration as a class that the disclaimer was unenforceable. The trial court concluded that the disclaimer provision validly waived both implied warranties and dismissed the class claims. Without deciding whether a class action is appropriate in this case, we remand the class claims for consideration in light of our clarification of the purpose and protection afforded by these implied warranties.

The court of appeals' judgment is affirmed.

NOTES & QUESTIONS:

1. These cases help explain the warranties that exist and the potential for waiver. Keep in mind that these cases are dealing with the sale of new construction homes. Therefore, these doctrines apply in the residential context only. The concept of the warranty of habitability for new home construction is well established and accepted in most, if not all, states.[5] Additionally, almost all modern courts have imposed an implied warranty of workmanlike quality.[6]

2. Keep in mind that the view is very different with respect to commercial properties. In Texas, there is an implied warranty of suitability for newly constructed commercial properties. However, in commercial cases it can be freely waived by the agreement of the parties. This is another example where the commercial buyer is on different footing.

---

[5] See Joseph William Singer, Introduction to Property § 11.3.3.2 (2d ed. 2005).
[6] Id.

6. Remedies for Breach of the Sales Contract

Hopefully, the process goes smoothly and the parties reach closing. In the event that the contract for sale is breached, three remedies are available to the nondefaulting party, whether the buyer or the seller: (1) damages, (2) retention of the deposit (sellers) or restitution of the deposit (buyers), or (3) specific performance of the contract. Generally, the winner may elect which remedy he or she prefers.

<u>Jones v. Lee</u>
Court of Appeals of New Mexico, 1998
971 P.2d 858

DONNELLY, J.

Ihn P. Lee and Philomena Lee (Buyers) appeal from judgments determining that they breached a contract to purchase an Albuquerque, New Mexico, residence and awarding compensatory and punitive damages to Sam P. Jones and Sharon A. Jones (Sellers), and compensatory damages to Sonja Waldin and The Vaughn Company, Inc. (Broker-Agents). Buyers raise four issues on appeal: (1) whether the trial court erred in determining the applicability and measure of damages to be awarded to Sellers for breach of a real estate contract; (2) whether the trial court's award of consequential and special damages was proper and supported by substantial evidence; (3) whether the trial court erred in awarding punitive damages; and (4) whether the trial court erred in finding that Buyers were required to pay a broker's commission to Broker-Agents. Affirmed in part and reversed in part.

Facts and Procedural Background

Following negotiations between the parties, on June 25, 1994, Buyers entered into a written real estate contract wherein they agreed to purchase Sellers' residence for $610,000. Sellers had listed the property for sale with Metro 100 Realtors. The purchase agreement entered into between Buyers and Sellers also listed Broker-Agents as Sellers' agents. Several weeks after signing the purchase agreement and tendering $6,000 in earnest money, Buyers informed Sellers they were unable to consummate the agreement because of financial reasons. Buyers submitted a proposed termination agreement, dated August 23, 1994, to Sellers, whereby Buyers offered to void the contract in return for forfeiting their $6,000 earnest money deposit.

Sellers rejected the proposed termination agreement and when it became clear that Buyers were not going to honor the purchase agreement, Sellers relisted the property for sale. Sellers ultimately sold the property in November 1994 to another purchaser for $540,000, $70,000 below the contract price originally agreed upon by the defaulting Buyers.

On April 12, 1995, Sellers filed suit against Buyers, seeking damages for breach of the real estate purchase agreement.

The trial court adopted findings of fact and conclusions of law and entered a judgment in favor of Sellers, awarding them $70,000 in damages for the loss resulting from the resale of the realty at a lower price; $300 for a heating warranty required to be furnished the new buyers; $1,433 for a solar inspection required by the new buyers; $126 for a consultation on the solar system required by the new buyers; $2,250 for interest payments on the first and second mortgages until resale; $17,156, plus gross receipts tax, for a broker's commission; $11,000 for architect and contractor fees incurred on a home Sellers had planned to build following the sale of their home; and $10,172 for interest claimed to have been lost by Sellers on the net proceeds of the contract sale price. The compensatory and special damages awarded by the trial court totaled $112,748.94. In addition to the compensatory and special damages listed above, the trial court also awarded $33,000 in punitive damages, together with costs and prejudgment interest. The total damages awarded to Sellers amounted to $157,118.94, plus court costs.

Discussion
I. Applicability and Measure of Damages

Buyers argue that the trial court erred in awarding compensatory and special damages to Sellers and that it utilized an incorrect measure in calculating the amount of damages to be awarded. On appeal, a reviewing court will not overturn the trial court's findings of fact or award of damages if there is substantial and competent evidence to support such determination, or unless it is clearly demonstrated that the trial court employed an incorrect measure of damages.

If a purchaser defaults on a contract to purchase realty, as a general rule, the seller has three alternative remedies. The sellers may (1) seek relief in equity for rescission, (2) offer to perform and bring an action for specific performance, or (3) elect to retain the realty and file suit seeking an award of damages. Here, Sellers elected to sue for damages. Where a party elects to sue for damages resulting from a breach of land sale contract, the burden is on that party to present competent evidence to support such claim for damages. The rationale underlying the award of damages in a breach of contract case is to compensate the non-defaulting party with just compensation commensurate with his or her loss.

Buyers accurately note that New Mexico follows the "loss of the bargain" rule in determining damages resulting from a purchaser's breach of a contract to buy realty. The "loss of the bargain" rule has been reaffirmed by our Supreme

Court in Hickey v. Griggs, 106 N.M. 27, 30, 738 P.2d 899, 902 (1987). In *Hickey* the Court stated that when a purchaser breaches an executory real estate contract, the "vendor's measure of damages is the difference between the purchase price and the market value of the property at the time of the breach." *Hickey*, 106 N.M. at 30, 738 P.2d at 902.

Loss of The Bargain

Buyers argue that the trial court erred in calculating compensatory damages of $70,000 solely by determining the difference between the contract price agreed upon by the parties and the subsequent resale price of the property, without determining the fair market value of the property at the time of the breach. The parties stipulated that the fair market value on August 23, 1994, was $610,000; thus, Buyers argue that Sellers did not sustain any compensatory damages because "at the time of the breach . . . they held property worth exactly the same amount as the contract price[.]"

Buyers are correct that in order to apply the loss of the bargain rule, the trial court must determine the value of the property at the time of the breach and compare that amount with the contract price. See Aboud v. Adams, 507 P.2d 430, 436 (N.M. 1973); see also Arthur L. Corbin, Corbin on Contracts § 1098A, at 535 (1964) (where purchaser defaults on purchase of realty, "the vendor's damages are the full contract price minus the market value of the land at date of breach and also minus any payment received").

In *Aboud* our Supreme Court addressed an analogous situation to that presented here, observing:

> [T]he loss of the bargain rule was not properly applied as there was no finding made of the market value of the land in question at the time of the breach. The trial court simply took the difference between "what the Adams had agreed to pay and what he later sold [the property] for[.]"

The *Aboud* Court, quoting from 55 Am. Jur. Vendor and Purchaser § 526, at 920, further observed:

> [I]n this country in the case of a private sale of land, the right of the vendor to resell on account of the [purchaser's default] and recover any deficiency arising on the resale is generally denied.

Due to the trial court's failure to determine the market value of the property at the time of the breach, the Court in *Aboud* remanded the case to the trial court to expressly determine the market value, noting:

While a subsequent sale is evidence of the market value at the time of breach, it is not conclusive and the court must properly establish the market value at such time. Thus, evidence of the resale price is properly admitted as one of the factors in determining market value.

Where the market value at the time of the breach is the same as the contract price, the sellers are generally limited to the recovery of only nominal damages or forfeiture of any earnest money, unless the sellers have established that they have also incurred special damages resulting from such breach.

In the instant case, like *Aboud*, there was no finding determining the date of breach or the market value of the property at the time of the breach. These determinations are essential factors in applying the loss of the bargain rule and in calculating the amount of general damages resulting from a purchaser's breach of a real estate contract. Thus, we conclude that the cause must be remanded for adoption of express findings of fact in accordance with the rule.

We noted above that the parties stipulated to the fair market value of the property on August 23, 1994. Also, while the date agreed upon for closing is generally the time for measuring the property's value at the time of the breach, Sellers stated that the breach occurred on August 23, 1994, when Buyers tendered a proposed termination agreement.

The general rule is that stipulations are ordinarily binding on the parties absent fraud, mistake, improvidence, material change in circumstances, or unless equitable considerations require otherwise.

As indicated in *Aboud*, a subsequent sale of land may be considered evidence of the market value at the time of breach and should be considered with other evidence bearing on the issue. It is unclear from the appellate record, including our questioning and the attorneys' answers at oral argument, for what purpose and to what effect the parties agreed to the stipulation before the trial court concerning market value. It shall be for the trial court on remand to determine what effect to give the stipulation and to otherwise determine the market value at the time of breach, to compare that to the contract sale price, and to calculate general damages, if any.

II. Award of Special Damages

Buyers also challenge the trial court's award of special damages. Special damages may be awarded by the fact finder in a breach of contract case if the damages are shown to have resulted as the natural and probable consequence of the breach and, at the time of the formation of the contract, the breaching party reasonably knew or should have anticipated from the facts and circumstances that the damages would probably be incurred.

1. Solar System and Heating Warranty

Buyers challenge the trial court's special damages award of $1,433 for an inspection of the solar system, $126 for a consultation on the solar system, and $300 for a heating warranty incident to the resale of the residence. The trial court found that these damages were reasonably foreseeable by a person in Buyers' situation when the contract was formed. We agree. Whether a situation is reasonably foreseeable is generally a question of fact to be determined by the fact finder from the evidence and circumstances. As observed in *Camino Real Mobile Home Park Partnership*, 119 N.M. at 446, 891 P.2d at 1200, the foreseeability of damages rule "anticipates an explicit or tacit agreement by the defendant 'to respond in damages for the particular damages understood to be likely in the event of a breach[.]'" Here, although the purchase agreement between Buyers and Sellers did not specifically require an inspection of the solar system or consultation regarding its effectiveness, nevertheless, Paragraph 15 of the residential purchase agreement indicated that Sellers, at closing, would see to it that the heating and solar system would be "in the same condition as of the date of acceptance, normal wear and tear excepted and subject to the provisions of Paragraphs 10 and 12" of the agreement. Since the contract contemplated that an inspection would be made of the solar and heating systems, and these are major components of the residence, there was evidence in the record from which the trial court could reasonably determine that inspection of these systems and consultation with a specialist concerning such systems would be a reasonably foreseeable requirement imposed by a future purchaser. Similarly, our review of Paragraph 10 of the real estate sales agreement indicates the existence of evidence from which the trial court could find that Sellers may be required to pay for a heating warranty from a future purchaser.

Paragraph 10 is a paragraph in the form contract indicating a list of warranties, the costs of which are sometimes borne by the sellers. The existence of this list in the contract is evidence upon which the trial court could find that the cost of the warranty was reasonably foreseeable.

2. Interest

After Buyers' default, Sellers relisted the property for sale and continued making payments on the first and second mortgages on the property until the subsequent sale. Sellers presented evidence that the interest payments on the mortgages totaled $4,500. The trial court found that the mortgage interest that Sellers continued to pay on their residence following the breach by Buyers was foreseeable. However, the trial court acknowledged that Sellers enjoyed the benefit of the continued occupancy of the residence and therefore reduced this award of interest by one-half.

The trial court correctly determined that Sellers may be entitled to damages resulting from the payment of mortgage interest due to Buyers' breach of contract to purchase realty because such damages were reasonably foreseeable. Where a buyer defaults on a residential purchase agreement, thus forcing the seller to replace the property on the market for sale, the lapse of time between the original closing date and a subsequent sale may give rise to the incurring of special damages by the seller.

3. Fees Incident to Separate Lot

The trial court also awarded $11,000 special damages for architect's and contractor's fees incurred by Sellers in planning to build a new home on a lot acquired by Sellers in 1992.

Sellers' response to Buyers' request for admissions conceded that prior to 1995, Sellers did not notify Buyers of the existence of the lot purchased by them in December 1992. Sellers admitted at trial that they did not know whether Buyers were aware of Sellers' strained financial status or the fact that they had previously purchased a lot on which they contemplated constructing a new house. In preparation for the construction of a new house, Sellers hired an architect and consulted with a contractor, thereby incurring expenses for $9,000 and $2,000 respectively. Sellers admitted that they had originally paid $150,000 for the lot and subsequently sold it for $194,000. We agree with Buyers that there is insufficient evidence in the record to establish that the architect's and the contractor's expenses incurred by them prior to the execution of the 1995 purchase agreement were reasonably foreseeable to Buyers when the parties executed the agreement. See *Wall*, 104 N.M. at 2, 715 P.2d at 450 (special damage arising from breach of contract must be expenses which are not expected to occur regularly to other plaintiffs and which are shown to have been within the contemplation of the parties at the time of the formation of the contract). As such, Sellers are not entitled to recover their claim for these fees.

III. Award of Punitive Damages

The trial court awarded punitive damages against Buyers for their conduct in attempting to persuade Sellers to agree to terminate the contract. The trial court found, among other things:

> [Buyers] and their family members engaged in acts of extremely poor judgment toward [Sellers] in their efforts to persuade [Sellers] to agree to a termination of the contract. One of these acts, [Buyers'] and their son's attempting to contact Mrs. Jones at her house, reasonably frightened Mrs. Jones but did not intimidate [Sellers] into agreeing to termination of the contract.

> [Buyers] made misrepresentations of fact regarding their financial situation in their efforts to persuade [Sellers] to agree to a termination of the contract.

At the time of their breach of the contract, [Buyers] had approximately $577,000 in a checking account, and earned income of more than $16,000.00 per month, plus bonuses.

[Buyers'] failure to consummate the contract to purchase was wanton, utterly reckless and in utter disregard of their contractual obligations, and was sufficient to warrant the imposition of punitive damages. [Buyers'] conduct evidenced such a cavalier attitude toward their own obligations and the harm inflicted on [Sellers] as to establish their intent to harm [Sellers].

An equitable and reasonable award of punitive damages is $33,000.00.

Buyers argue that the punitive damage award is unsupported by substantial evidence and is incorrect as a matter of law because it was linked to an incorrect computation of compensatory damages. Absent proof that the conduct of a party resulting in a breach of contract was malicious, fraudulent, oppressive, or recklessly committed, with a wanton disregard of the other party's rights, an award of punitive damages is improper. Because the purpose of punitive damages is to punish and deter improper conduct, there must be some evidence of a culpable mental state on the part of the party who has caused the breach. Thus, absent a showing that the breaching party intended to inflict harm on the non-breaching party or conduct which violates community standards of decency, the actions of the breaching party will not serve as a basis for an award of punitive damages.

In explaining the punitive damages award, the trial court stated that the award was "approximately a third of the compensatory damages." The trial court found that Buyers "made intentional misrepresentations of fact to Norwest Mortgage regarding [Buyers'] financial ability to close the transaction in order to be relieved of their obligation under the contract" and that "[a]t the time of their intentional breach, [Buyers] had sufficient capital and income to finance the purchase of the property."

Our review of the record indicates a factual basis from which the trial court could properly assess punitive damages against Buyers. The trial court found that the conduct of Buyers included acts intended to persuade Sellers to agree to terminate the agreement. Additionally, despite Sellers' request that Buyers communicate with them through their attorneys or Broker-Agents, Buyers attempted to contact them directly and, on one occasion, severely frightened Mrs. Jones by pounding on the front door of the residence so forcibly that the lock on the door to the residence had to be replaced.

Because the trial court, in assessing the award of punitive damages against Buyers, stated that it based the award of punitive damages, in part, on its computation of compensatory damages, and we have determined that the award of compensatory damages was not calculated on the "loss of the bargain rule," we remand the issue of the award of punitive damages to the trial court for the adoption of additional findings of fact and conclusions of law concerning the amount, if any, of punitive damages, after the trial court calculates its award of damages, if any, based on loss of the bargain.

Conclusion

For the reasons discussed herein, the cause is remanded for redetermination of the amount of compensatory and special damages, and/or the award of punitive damages, consistent with the matters discussed herein.

It is so ordered.

NOTES & QUESTIONS:

1. Remember that while both buyers and sellers have the same legally available remedies, from a practical standpoint the buyer or seller may choose different options depending on the circumstances. For example, there may be very little in the way of actual damages and the buyer is unable to complete the purchase due to finances. In that case the seller would choose to keep the earnest money as liquidated damages. If the seller breaches, again there may be very little in the way of actual damages. Getting earnest money refunded does not really help. This may be a situation where the buyer demands specific performance.

Chapter 7
Acquiring Property by Purchase: The Real Estate Closing and Post-Closing Title Issues

If the executory period comes to an end as planned, that means that there has now been a closing of the transaction. This marks a new period of time with respect to questions and problems related to title. During the executory period, there was an implied or express promise to provide marketable or merchantable title at the time of closing. The contract will no longer be the operative document guiding title questions moving forward. That is because once all of the promises have been performed and the parties are ready for closing, the next document required is the deed.

A. Deeds: The Instrument of Conveyance

The deed is the instrument that actually serves as the mechanism to convey legal title to the property to the new owner. The transfer for legal title must be in writing. Deeds are subject to the statute of frauds as well as the statute of conveyances. Just as we looked at the statute of frauds in the context of the contract for the sale of real estate, there are very basic requirements for a valid deed. To meet the requirements a deed must be (1) in writing, (2) identify the grantor and grantee, (3) include conveyancing language, (4) contain a valid property description, and (5) be signed by the grantor.

You will notice a few differences between the requirements for a deed and a contract and that is due to the purpose of the two documents. The contract is to obtain a promise that the transfer of legal title will occur and to address the rights and obligations leading up to that point. It is the blueprint for the sales transaction. The deed is used to transfer legal title to real property and is used whether a purchase or a gift. While both documents must be in writing, identify the parties and the property, the contract uses language of promises to buy and sell while the deed is a conveyance or transfer from grantor to grantee. That also is the reason why there is only a signature of the grantor. In the contract, both parties are making promises that the other will want enforced. In the deed, only the seller/grantor is conveying and promising. There is no reason for the grantee to sign. Finally, in the contract there must be a price or means to determine the price. There is no requirement that any consideration be included in a deed. Again, a deed may be conveying title as a gift and there is no consideration. That cannot be a requirement or there could never be a valid gift!

Deeds will have different content in order to achieve certain results regarding promises that have been made by the parties but there are some common elements required for any deed to be a valid conveyance. These are elements we will examine in order to determine a deed is "valid on its face." The requirements of the statute of conveyances are that there is a valid execution, delivery, and acceptance. If any of these components are missing then the transfer is *void ab initio,* meaning void from its inception.

Tex. Prop. Code § 5.021 Instrument of Conveyance
A conveyance of an estate of inheritance, a freehold, or an estate for more than one year, in land and tenements, must be in writing and must be subscribed and delivered by the conveyor or by the conveyor's agent authorized in writing.

1. Types of Deeds: Covenants of Title

Think back to the doctrine of merger. The doctrine of merger dictates that all issues relating to title in the sales contract will merge into the deed at the time of closing. This approach makes sense because the only purpose of the deed is to convey legal title to the property. It should be and will be the operative document after closing. This means that it is of utmost importance to a grantee to ensure that the proper language is included in a deed. Not only does the grantee want to be sure that the deed contains the requirements to meet the statute of frauds and statute of conveyances, the grantee will want to be sure to obtain some promises regarding the quality of the title being received. Once the grantee has the deed, there is no valid argument regarding marketability of title any longer. Thus, we must turn our attention to the possible covenants of title that may be contained in a deed.

Additional language can be included in a deed to provide promises regarding the quality of title being received. These covenants of title are not required for the deed to be a valid instrument of conveyance but are desired by the buyer. If the buyer is using an institutional lender to finance the purchase, that lender is also going to require covenants of title to be included in the deed. There are three different types of deeds commonly used in transactions: quitclaim, special warranty, and general warranty. We will consider each type of deed and the contents. We will also define each standard covenant of title that may be included in a deed.

a. The Quitclaim Deed—You Get Whatever I May Have

As this sample Quitclaim Deed illustrates, the quitclaim deed is an effective instrument to convey title to real property. However, a quitclaim deed is very different from the other two types we will consider. The quitclaim deed makes no promises whatsoever about the title being conveyed. This is not the type of deed that should be used in a purchase transaction. It can be a useful tool to release uncertain claims and to clear up any gaps or defects in the chain of title. Basically the grantor is saying that whatever it is I have, I am quitclaiming to you, the grantee.

Remember that during the material covering the executory period, the discussion of marketable title involved several issues that could cause problems with delivering marketable title by the time of closing. A quitclaim deed is an instrument that could be used to clear up some of those title issues. For example, if a title is only a limitations title then it is not marketable. If the seller who is claiming a limitations title wants to provide a marketable title, that seller could approach the record title holder and seek a quitclaim deed from that individual. The idea is that the record title holder really no longer owns anything because someone has acquired it through adverse possession, but the record does not reflect that. By obtaining a quitclaim deed to record in the public records, all of the links will be in place and marketable title can be delivered. The record title holder would not want to make any promises regarding the quality of title being transferred but would prefer to quitclaim any right, title, or interest they may have. Thus, the quitclaim deed under these circumstances would not be suspect. It would be serving a useful function.

Quitclaim

Date:

Grantor:

Grantor's Mailing Address: [include county]

Grantee:

Grantee's Mailing Address: [include county]

Consideration:

Property (including any improvements):

For the Consideration, Grantor quitclaims to Grantee all of Grantor's right, title, and interest in and to the Property, to have and to hold it to Grantee and Grantee's heirs, successors, and assigns forever. Neither Grantor nor Grantor's heirs, successors, or assigns will have, claim, or demand any right or title to the Property or any part of it.
When the context requires, singular nouns and pronouns include the plural.

_____

[Name of grantor]

_____

[Name of grantee]

---

b. Warranty Deeds and Covenants of Title

While the quitclaim deed can serve some legitimate purposes, the general warranty and special warranty deeds are the most common. There are six typical covenants of title that can be included in a deed. Rarely are all six used in one deed, although it is completely possible to do so.

Under common law, any covenants of title must be expressly stated in the deed. There are six standard covenants of title that are used. Each is a different contractual promise regarding the quality of the title to the land and is promising protection against title defects. Let's consider the different available covenants.

Covenant of seisin is a promise that the grantor owns and is in possession of what he purports to convey.

Covenant of right to convey is a promise that the grantor has the right to transfer the title to the property.

Covenant against encumbrances is a promise that the land is not subject to any encumbrances, such as easements, covenants, mortgages, deeds of trust, leases, or other liens other than those taken subject to in the deed.

Covenant of warranty is a promise to warrant and defend against any lawful claims of superior title. There is a covenant of general warranty that makes the grantor liable for any defects that exist in the title even if not caused by the grantor. The covenant of special warranty makes the grantor liable only for those defects caused by the grantor but not others.

Covenant of quiet enjoyment is a promise that the grantee's possession will not be disturbed and that if disturbed the grantee will be compensated for damages.

Covenant of further assurances is a promise that the grantor will execute any documents needed to clear the grantee's title. Unlike the other covenants, this one may be enforced by damages or specific performance.

The first three covenants are labeled as "present covenants." This means that in a majority of states these promises do not run with the land and can only be enforced by the immediate grantor and grantee. Additionally, by being labeled as a present covenant, the breach occurs at the time of delivery of the deed with a defect in existence. The statute of limitations to bring an action for recovery will begin to run at that time.

The last three covenants are labeled as "future covenants." This means that in all states these promises run with the land and a remote grantee can sue upon the covenant. These also require a breach to occur. Simply delivering the deed with a defect in existence does not trigger a breach and the running of the statute of limitations. There must be a breach that will be caused by an actual or constructive eviction and the statute of limitations will begin to run at that time.

If a deed is to contain all of these standard covenants of title it would need to expressly include all of the promises. The only way that a covenant of title will be implied is if a state's statute creates such implied covenants. The Texas Property Code does create some implied covenants of title under certain circumstances. The statute is as follows:

Tex. Prop. Code § 5.023 Implied Warranties[1]

    (a) Unless the conveyance expressly provides otherwise, the use of "grant" or "convey" in a conveyance of an estate of inheritance or fee simple implies only that the grantor and the grantor's heirs covenant to the grantee and the grantee's heirs or assigns:

        (1) that prior to the execution of the conveyance the grantor has not conveyed the estate or any interest in the estate to a person other than the grantee; and

        (2) that at the time of the execution of the conveyance the estate is free from encumbrances.[2]

    (b) An implied covenant under this section may be the basis for a lawsuit as if it had been expressed in the conveyance.

The statute tells us that in Texas, if the words "grants" or "conveys" are used, then implied covenants of title exist. Many other states have similar statutes that imply covenants. It is possible to use the words "grants" or "conveys" for standard conveyancing language and to also include an express disclaimer of all express and implied covenants of title so that there are no promises in the deed. This type of deed would not really be a quitclaim deed but it also would not be a warranty deed. It would simply be a deed to the property.

In order to be considered either a general warranty deed or a special warranty deed the deed must at least contain the covenant of general warranty or covenant of special warranty respectively. The following are samples of both general warranty deeds and special warranty deeds. Examine the language closely to determine what the difference is to provide the limitation on liability.

Tex. Prop. Code § 5.022 General Warranty Deed

    (a) The following form or a form that is the same in substance conveys a fee simple estate in real property with a covenant of general warranty:

---

[1] Covenants of title and warranties of title are the same thing. The names are used interchangeably.

[2] Texas Property Code § 5.024 defines an encumbrance to include a tax, an assessment, and a lien on real property.

The State of Texas

County of _____

Know all men by these presents, That I, _____, of the
_____ (give name of city, town, or county), in the state
aforesaid, for and in consideration of _____ dollars, to me in
hand paid by _____, have granted, sold, and conveyed, and by
these presents do grant, sell, and convey unto the said _____,
of the _____ (give name of city, town, or county), in the state
of _____, all that certain _____ (describe the
premises). To have and to hold the above described premises, together with
all and singular the rights and appurtenances thereto in any wise belonging,
unto the said _____, his heirs or assigns forever. And I do
hereby bind myself, my heirs, executors, and administrators to warrant and
forever defend all and singular the said premises unto the said
_____, his heirs, and assigns, against every person
whomsoever, lawfully claiming or to claim the same, or any part thereof.

Witness my hand, this _____ day of
_____, A.D. 19___.

Signed and delivered in the presence of _____

(b) A covenant of warranty is not required in a conveyance.

(c) The parties to a conveyance may insert any clause or use any form not in contravention of law.

NOTES & QUESTIONS

1. This form deed provided in the Texas Property Code creates a deed that contains three covenants. What are the three covenants? Where do you find them?

2. What should a grantor do if the buyer contracted to receive a general warranty deed at closing but had also agreed in the contract to take subject to neighborhood restrictions, utility easements, and other easements of record?

Below is a sample special warranty deed. Where is the language different from the general warranty deed above?

The State of Texas

County of _____

Know all men by these presents, That I, _____, of the _____ (give name of city, town, or county), in the state aforesaid, for and in consideration of _____ dollars, to me in hand paid by _____, have granted, sold, and conveyed, and by these presents do grant, sell, and convey unto the said _____, of the _____ (give name of city, town, or county), in the state of _____, all that certain _____ (describe the premises). To have and to hold the above described premises, together with all and singular the rights and appurtenances thereto in any wise belonging, unto the said _____, his heirs or assigns forever. And I do hereby bind myself, my heirs, executors, and administrators to warrant and forever defend all and singular the said premises unto the said _____, his heirs, and assigns, against every person whomsoever, lawfully claiming or to claim the same, or any part thereof, then the claim is by, through, or under Grantor but not otherwise.

Witness my hand, this _____ day of _____, A.D. 19___.

Signed and delivered in the presence of _____.

---

2. Coverage Provided by Covenants of Title

The promises contained in a deed are contractual in nature. Therefore, covenants provide relief only if the specific promise matches up to a defect it is intended to cover. The statute of limitations will also be a possible bar to recovery as well as not being able to sue a certain grantor. Consider these issues while reading the following cases. Even though a deed may contain several promises, there still may not be any available relief under the covenants of title.

Brown v. Lober
Supreme Court of Illinois, 1979
389 N.E.2d 1188

UNDERWOOD, J.

Plaintiffs instituted this action in the Montgomery County circuit court based on an alleged breach of the covenant of seisin in their warranty deed. The trial court held that although there had been a breach of the covenant of seisin, the suit was barred by the 10-year statute of limitations in section 16 of the Limitations Act. Plaintiffs' post-trial motion, which was based on an alleged breach of the covenant of quiet enjoyment, was also denied. A divided Fifth District Appellate Court reversed and remanded. We allowed the defendant's petition for leave to appeal.

The parties submitted an agreed statement of facts which sets forth the relevant history of this controversy. Plaintiffs purchased 80 acres of Montgomery County real estate from William and Faith Bost and received a statutory warranty deed, containing no exceptions, dated December 21, 1957. Subsequently, plaintiffs took possession of the land and recorded their deed.

On May 8, 1974, plaintiffs granted a coal option to Consolidated Coal Company (Consolidated) for the coal rights on the 80-acre tract for the sum of $6,000. Approximately two years later, however, plaintiffs "discovered" that they, in fact, owned only a one-third interest in the subsurface coal rights. It is a matter of public record that, in 1947, a prior grantor had reserved a two-thirds interest in the mineral rights on the property. Although plaintiffs had their abstract of title examined in 1958 and 1968 for loan purposes, they contend that until May 4, 1976, they believed that they were the sole owners of the surface and subsurface rights on the 80-acre tract. Upon discovering that a prior grantor had reserved a two-thirds interest in the coal rights, plaintiffs and Consolidated renegotiated their agreement to provide for payment of $2,000 in exchange for a one-third interest in the subsurface coal rights. On May 25, 1976, plaintiffs filed this action against the executor of the estate of Faith Bost, seeking damages in the amount of $4,000.

The deed which plaintiffs received from the Bosts was a general statutory form warranty deed meeting the requirements of section 9 of "An Act concerning conveyances". That section provides:

"Every deed in substance in the above form, when otherwise duly executed, shall be deemed and held a conveyance in fee simple, to the grantee, his heirs or assigns, with covenants on the part of the grantor, (1) that at the time of the making and delivery of such deed he was lawfully seized of an indefeasible estate in fee simple, in and to the premises therein described, and had good right and full power to convey the same; (2) that the same were then free from all encumbrances; and (3) that he warrants to the grantee, his heirs and assigns, the quiet and peaceable possession of such premises, and will defend the title thereto against all persons who may lawfully claim the same. And such covenants shall be obligatory upon any grantor, his heirs and personal representatives, as fully and with like effect as if written at length in such deed."

The effect of this provision is that certain covenants of title are implied in every statutory form warranty deed. Subsection 1 contains the covenant of seisin and the covenant of good right to convey. These covenants, which are considered synonymous, assure the grantee that the grantor is, at the time of the conveyance, lawfully seized and has the power to convey an estate of the quality and quantity which he professes to convey.

Subsection 2 represents the covenant against encumbrances. An encumbrance is any right to, or interest in, land which may subsist in a third party to the diminution of the value of the estate, but consistent with the passing of the fee by conveyance.

Subsection 3 sets forth the covenant of quiet enjoyment, which is synonymous with the covenant of warranty in Illinois. By this covenant, "the grantor warrants to the grantee, his heirs and assigns, the possession of the premises and that he will defend the title granted by the terms of the deed against persons who may lawfully claim the same, and that such covenant shall be obligatory upon the grantor, his heirs, personal representatives, and assigns." Biwer v. Martin (1920), 294 Ill. 488, 497, 128 N.E. 518, 522.

Plaintiffs' complaint is premised upon the fact that "William Roy Bost and Faith Bost covenanted that they were the owners in fee simple of the above described property at the time of the conveyance to the plaintiffs." While the complaint could be more explicit, it appears that plaintiffs were alleging a cause of action for breach of the covenant of seisin. This court has stated repeatedly that the covenant of seisin is a covenant in praesenti and, therefore, if broken at all, is broken at the time of delivery of the deed.

Since the deed was delivered to the plaintiffs on December 21, 1957, any cause of action for breach of the covenant of seisin would have accrued on that date. The trial court held that this cause of action was barred by the statute of limitations. No question is raised as to the applicability of the 10-year statute of limitations. We conclude, therefore, that the cause of action for breach of the covenant of seisin was properly determined by the trial court to be barred by the statute of limitations since plaintiffs did not file their complaint until May 25, 1976, nearly 20 years after their alleged cause of action accrued.

In their post-trial motion, plaintiffs set forth as an additional theory of recovery an alleged breach of the covenant of quiet enjoyment. The trial court, without explanation, denied the motion. The appellate court reversed, holding that the cause of action on the covenant of quiet enjoyment was not barred by the statute of limitations. The appellate court theorized that plaintiffs' cause of action did not accrue until 1976, when plaintiffs discovered that they only had a one-third interest in the subsurface coal rights and renegotiated their contract with the coal company for one-third of the previous contract price. The primary issue before us, therefore, is when, if at all, the plaintiffs' cause of action for breach of the covenant of quiet enjoyment is deemed to have accrued.

This court has stated on numerous occasions that, in contrast to the covenant of seisin, the covenant of warranty or quiet enjoyment is prospective in nature and is breached only when there is an actual or constructive eviction of the covenantee by the paramount titleholder.

The cases are also replete with statements to the effect that the mere existence of paramount title in one other than the covenantee is not sufficient to constitute a breach of the covenant of warranty or quiet enjoyment: "(T) here must be a union of acts of disturbance and lawful title, to constitute a breach of the covenant for quiet enjoyment, or warranty." (Barry v. Guild (1888), 126 Ill. 439, 446, 18 N.E. 759, 761.) "(T)here is a general concurrence that something more than the mere existence of a paramount title is necessary to constitute a breach of the covenant of warranty." (Scott v. Kirkendall (1878), 88 Ill. 465, 467.) "A mere want of title is no breach of this covenant. There must not only be a want of title, but there must be an ouster under a paramount title." Moore v. Vail (1855), 17 Ill. 185, 189.

The question is whether plaintiffs have alleged facts sufficient to constitute a constructive eviction. They argue that if a covenantee fails in his effort to sell an interest in land because he discovers that he does not own what his warranty deed purported to convey, he has suffered a constructive eviction and is thereby entitled to bring an action against his grantor for breach of the covenant of quiet enjoyment. We think that the decision of this court in Scott v. Kirkendall (1878), 88 Ill. 465, is controlling on this issue and compels us to reject plaintiffs' argument.

In *Scott*, an action was brought for breach of the covenant of warranty by a grantee who discovered that other parties had paramount title to the land in question. The land was vacant and unoccupied at all relevant times. This court, in rejecting the grantee's claim that there was a breach of the covenant of quiet enjoyment, quoted the earlier decision in Moore v. Vail (1855), 17 Ill. 185, 191:

" 'Until that time, (the taking possession by the owner of the paramount title,) he might peaceably have entered upon and enjoyed the premises, without resistance or molestation, which was all his grantors covenanted he should do. They did not guarantee to him a perfect title, but the possession and enjoyment of the premises.' "

Relying on this language in *Moore*, the *Scott* court concluded:

> We do not see but what this fully decides the present case against the appellant. It holds that the mere existence of a paramount title does not constitute a breach of the covenant. That is all there is here. There has been no assertion of the

adverse title. The land has always been vacant. Appellant could at any time have taken peaceable possession of it. He has in no way been prevented or hindered from the enjoyment of the possession by any one having a better right. It was but the possession and enjoyment of the premises which was assured to him, and there has been no disturbance or interference in that respect. True, there is a superior title in another, but appellant has never felt "its pressure upon him."

Admittedly, *Scott* dealt with surface rights while the case before us concerns subsurface mineral rights. We are, nevertheless, convinced that the reasoning employed in *Scott* is applicable to the present case. While plaintiffs went into possession of the surface area, they cannot be said to have possessed the subsurface minerals. "Possession of the surface does not carry possession of the minerals. To possess the mineral estate, one must undertake the actual removal thereof from the ground or do such other act as will apprise the community that such interest is in the exclusive use and enjoyment of the claiming party."

Since no one has, as yet, undertaken to remove the coal or otherwise manifested a clear intent to exclusively "possess" the mineral estate, it must be concluded that the subsurface estate is "vacant." As in *Scott*, plaintiffs "could at any time have taken peaceable possession of it. (They have) in no way been prevented or hindered from the enjoyment of the possession by anyone having a better right." Accordingly, until such time as one holding paramount title interferes with plaintiffs' right of possession (*E.g.*, by beginning to mine the coal), there can be no constructive eviction and, therefore, no breach of the covenant of quiet enjoyment.

What plaintiffs are apparently attempting to do on this appeal is to extend the protection afforded by the covenant of quiet enjoyment. However, we decline to expand the historical scope of this covenant to provide a remedy where another of the covenants of title is so clearly applicable. As this court stated in Scott v. Kirkendall (1878):

> To sustain the present action would be to confound all distinction between the covenant of warranty and that of seizin, or of right to convey. They are not equivalent covenants. An action will lie upon the latter, though there be no disturbance of possession. A defect of title will suffice. Not so with the covenant of warranty, or for quiet enjoyment, as has always been held by the prevailing authority.

The covenant of seisin, unquestionably, was breached when the Bosts delivered the deed to plaintiffs, and plaintiffs then had a cause of action. However, despite the fact that it was a matter of public record that there was a reservation of a two-thirds interest in the mineral rights in the earlier deed, plaintiffs failed to bring an action for breach of the covenant of seisin within the 10-year period following delivery of the deed. The likely explanation is that plaintiffs had not secured a title opinion at the time they purchased the property, and the subsequent examiners for the lenders were not concerned with the mineral rights. Plaintiffs' oversight, however, does not justify us in overruling earlier decisions in order to recognize an otherwise premature cause of action. The mere fact that plaintiffs' original contract with Consolidated had to be modified due to their discovery that paramount title to two-thirds of the subsurface minerals belonged to another is not sufficient to constitute the constructive eviction necessary to a breach of the covenant of quiet enjoyment.

Accordingly, the judgment of the appellate court is reversed, and the judgment of the circuit court of Montgomery County is affirmed.

Appellate court reversed; circuit court affirmed.

QUESTIONS:

1. What was the defect complained of by the Browns?

2. What covenants of title did they have in their deed? Are they present or future covenants?

3. Why didn't the covenants of title provide them relief?

4. Is there anything the Browns can do at this time to be able to utilize a covenant of title? What if they find the person who owns the other two-thirds of the minerals and pay them for the minerals. Can they then bring suit on the covenant of title?

Frimberger v. Anzellotti
Appellate Court of Connecticut, 1991
594 A.2d 1029

LAVERY, J.

The defendant appeals from the judgment of the trial court awarding the plaintiff damages for breach of the warranty against encumbrances and innocent misrepresentation of real property that the defendant conveyed to the plaintiff by warranty deed.

The defendant claims that the court was incorrect in finding that she breached the warranty deed covenant against encumbrances, and in awarding damages for diminution of value to the property caused by a wetlands violation as well as damages for costs of correcting that violation. We agree with the defendant and reverse the decision of the trial court.

The record and memorandum of decision disclose the following facts. In 1978, the defendant's brother and predecessor in title, Paul DiLoreto, subdivided a parcel of land located in Old Saybrook for the purpose of constructing residences on each of the two resulting parcels. The property abuts a tidal marshland and is, therefore, subject to the provisions of General Statutes § 22a-28 et seq.

DiLoreto built a bulkhead and filled that portion of the subject parcel immediately adjacent to the wetlands area, and then proceeded with the construction of a dwelling on the property. On February 21, 1984, DiLoreto transferred the subject property to the defendant by quit claim deed. On December 31, 1985, the defendant conveyed the property to the plaintiff by warranty deed, free and clear of all encumbrances but subject to all building, building line and zoning restrictions as well as easements and restrictions of record.

During the summer of 1986, the plaintiff decided to perform repairs on the bulkhead and the filled area of the property. The plaintiff engaged an engineering firm which wrote to the state department of environmental protection (DEP) requesting a survey of the tidal wetlands on the property. On March 14, 1986, working with the plaintiff's engineers, the DEP placed stakes on the wetlands boundary and noted that there was a tidal wetlands violation on the property. In a letter to the plaintiff dated April 10, 1986, the DEP confirmed its findings and indicated that in order to establish the tidal wetlands boundary, as staked for regulatory purposes, the plaintiff must provide DEP with an A-2 survey of the property. At some point after April, 1986, and before March, 1988, the plaintiff engaged a second group of engineers who met with DEP officials and completed an A-2 survey.

On March 28, 1988, members of the DEP water resources unit met with the plaintiff's new engineers to stake out the wetlands boundary again. On April 13, 1988, as confirmation of that meeting, Denis Cunningham, the assistant director of the DEP water resources unit, wrote to the plaintiff to advise him that the filled and bulkheaded portion of the property, and possibly the northwest corner of the house were encroaching on the tidal wetlands boundary, thereby creating a violation of General Statutes § 22a-30. This letter suggested that to correct the violation, the plaintiff would have to submit an application to DEP demonstrating the necessity of maintaining the bulkhead and fill within the tidal wetlands. Instead of filing the application, the plaintiff filed the underlying lawsuit against the defendant, claiming damages for breach of the warranty against encumbrances and innocent misrepresentation.

The trial court determined that the area had been filled without obtaining the necessary permits required under General Statutes § 22a-32. The court found that the defendant had breached the warranty against encumbrances and had innocently misrepresented the condition of the property by allowing the plaintiff to purchase the property in reliance on the defendant's warranty against encumbrances. The court awarded the plaintiff damages and costs in the amount of $47,792.60, a figure that included the costs to correct the wetlands violation as well as the diminution of value of the property caused by the wetlands violation. The defendant brought the present appeal.

This appeal turns on a determination of whether an alleged latent violation of a land use statute or regulation, existing on the land at the time title is conveyed, constitutes an encumbrance such that the conveyance breaches the grantor's covenant against encumbrances. An encumbrance is defined as "every right to or interest in the land which may subsist in third persons, to the diminution of the value of the land, but consistent with the passing of the fee by the conveyance." H. Tiffany, Real Property (1975) § 1002). All encumbrances may be classed as either (1) a pecuniary charge against the premises, such as mortgages, judgment liens, tax liens, or assessments, or (2) estates or interests in the property less than the fee, like leases, life estates or dower rights, or (3) easements or servitudes on the land, such as rights of way, restrictive covenants and profits. It is important to note that the covenant against encumbrances operates in praesenti and cannot be breached unless the encumbrance existed at the time of the conveyance. Id.

The issue of whether a latent violation of a restrictive land use statute or ordinance, that exists at the time the fee is conveyed, constitutes a breach of the warranty deed covenant against encumbrances has not been decided in Connecticut. There is, however, persuasive and authoritative weight in the legal literature and the case law of other jurisdictions to support the proposition that such an exercise of police power by the state does not affect the marketability of title and should not rise to the level of an encumbrance. *See, e.g.,* Domer v. Sleeper, 533 P.2d 9 (Alaska 1975) (latent building code violation not an encumbrance); McCrae v. Giteles, 253 So. 2d 260, 261 (Fla. App. 1971) (violation of housing code noticed and known by vendor not an encumbrance); Monti v. Tangora, 99 Ill. App. 3d 575, 54 Ill. Dec. 732, 425 N.E.2d 597 (1981) (noticed building code violations not an encumbrance); Silverblatt v. Livadas, 340 Mass. 474, 164 N.E.2d 875 (1960) (contingent or inchoate lien which might result from building code violation not an encumbrance); Fahmie v. Wulster, 81 N.J. 391, 408 A.2d 789 (1979) (discussed infra); Woodenbury v. Spier, 122 App. Div. 396, 106 N.Y.S. 817 (1907) (a lis pendens filed to enforce housing code violations after conveyance not an encumbrance); Stone v. Sexsmith, 28 Wash. 2d 947, 184 P.2d 567 (1947).

Of the cases cited from other jurisdictions, Fahmie v. Wulster, *supra*, provides the closest factual analogue to the case before us. In *Fahmie*, a closely held corporation that originally owned certain property requested permission from the New Jersey bureau of water to place a nine foot diameter culvert on the property to enclose a stream. The bureau required instead that a sixteen and one-half foot diameter culvert should be installed. The corporation went ahead with its plan and installed the nine foot culvert.

The property was later conveyed to Wulster, the titular president of the corporation, who had no knowledge of the installation of the nine foot culvert. Nine years after the installation of the culvert, Wulster conveyed the property, by warranty deed, to Fahmie.

In anticipation of the subsequent resale of the property, Fahmie made application to the New Jersey economic development commission, division of water policy and supply, to make additional improvements to the stream and its banks. It was then that the inadequate nine foot culvert was discovered, and the plaintiff was required to replace it with a sixteen and one-half foot diameter pipe. Fahmie sued Wulster for the cost to correct the violation claiming a breach of the deed warranty against encumbrances.

The New Jersey Supreme Court concluded that it was generally the law throughout the country that a claim for breach of a covenant against encumbrances cannot be predicated on the necessity to repair or alter the property to conform with land use regulations. By so doing, the *Fahmie* court refused to expand the concept of an encumbrance to include structural conditions existing on the property that constitute violations of statute or governmental regulation. The court concluded that such a conceptual enlargement of the covenant against encumbrances would create uncertainty and confusion in the law of conveyancing and title insurance because neither a title search nor a physical examination of the premises would disclose the violation. The New Jersey court went on to state that "[t]he better way to deal with violations of governmental regulations, their nature and scope being as pervasive as they are, is by contract provisions which can give the purchaser full protection [in such situations]." *Id.*, 81 N.J. at 397, 408 A.2d 789.

The case before us raises the same issues as those raised in *Fahmie*. Here, the court found that in 1978 the wetlands area was filled without a permit and in violation of state statute. The alleged violation was unknown to the defendant, was not on the land records and was discovered only after the plaintiff attempted to get permission to perform additional improvements to the wetlands area.

Although the DEP first advised the plaintiff of the alleged violation in 1986, it did not bring any action to compel compliance with the statute. Rather, it suggested that the violation may be corrected by submitting an application to DEP. As of the date of trial, the plaintiff had not made such an application, there had been no further action taken by the DEP to compel compliance, and no administrative order was ever entered from which the plaintiff could appeal. Thus, the plaintiff was never required by DEP to abate the violation or restore the wetlands.

Our Supreme Court has stated that for a deed to be free of all encumbrances there must be marketable title that can be sold "at a fair price to a reasonable purchaser or mortgaged to a person of reasonable prudence as a security for the loan of money." Perkins v. August, 109 Conn. 452, 456, 146 A. 831 (1929). To render a title unmarketable, the defect must present a real and substantial probability of litigation or loss at the time of the conveyance. Latent violations of state or municipal land use regulations that do not appear on the land records, that are unknown to the seller of the property, as to which the agency charged with enforcement has taken no official action to compel compliance at the time the deed was executed, and that have not ripened into an interest that can be recorded on the land records do not constitute an encumbrance for the purpose of the deed warranty. Monti v. Tangora, 99 Ill. App. 3d 575, 581-82, 54 Ill. Dec. 732, 425 N.E.2d 597 (1981). Although, under the statute, DEP could impose fines or restrict the use of the property until it is brought into compliance, such a restriction is not an encumbrance.

Because the plaintiff never actually filed the application, any damages that he may have suffered were speculative. The court based its assessment of damages on a proposed application and the anticipated costs of complying with that proposed application. The fact that the alleged violation was first noted by DEP only after the plaintiff made requests to rework the bulkhead and filled area, leads us to the conclusion that no litigation or loss was imminent. This position is confirmed by the fact that, as of the date of trial, no order was entered by DEP to compel the plaintiff to rectify the violative condition and no application was made by the plaintiff to gain approval of existing conditions.

We adopt the reasoning of Fahmie v. Wulster, and hold that the concept of encumbrances cannot be expanded to include latent conditions on property that are in violation of statutes or government regulations. To do so would create uncertainty in the law of conveyances, title searches and title insurance. The parties to a conveyance of real property can adequately protect themselves from such conditions by including protective language in the contract and by insisting on appropriate provisions in the deed. As the Illinois Appellate Court held in Monti v. Tangora, "[t]he problem created by the existence of code violations is not one to be resolved by the courts, but is one that can be handled quite easily by the draftsmen of contracts for sale and of deeds. All that is required of the law on this point is that it be certain. Once certainty is achieved, parties and their draftsmen may place rights and obligations where they will. It is the stability in real estate transactions that is of paramount importance here." Monti v. Tangora, *supra*, at 582, 54 Ill. Dec. 732, 425 N.E.2d 597.

The plaintiff in this case is an attorney and land developer who had developed waterfront property and was aware of the wetlands requirement. He could have protected himself from any liability for wetlands violation either by requiring an A-2 survey prior to closing or by inserting provisions in the contract and deed to indemnify himself against potential tidal wetlands violations or violations of other environmental statutes.

The judgment is reversed as to the award of damages for breach of the warranty against encumbrances and for innocent misrepresentation of real property, and the case is remanded with direction to render judgment in favor of the defendant on those issues.

NOTES & QUESTIONS:

1. What promises did the plaintiff receive in his deed?

2. What is the defect complained of?

3. Does the covenant against encumbrances provide any relief?

4. Is the covenant against encumbrances the same as the covenant of marketable title during the executory period?

5. If plaintiff had discovered the wetlands violation during the executory period, what could he have done?

6. A buyer is free to take property subject to an existing lien and agree to pay that lien. However, absent such an agreement, the presence of a lien is an encumbrance that makes title unmarketable.

7. If there was an agreement that the grantee would pay unpaid taxes owed on the property, what could the grantor do in drafting the deed to avoid a claim against him for the unpaid taxes?

Smith v. Armes
Court of Civil Appeals of Texas, Fort Worth, 1948
208 S.W.2d 409

[Ed. Note: Plaintiff J. C. Armes purchased a lot from defendants A. J. Smith and his wife Ethel P. Smith for $600. The lot was described by metes and bounds and was purported to be 80 feet wide. Plaintiff discovered that the property was only 70 feet wide, relied on the general warranty deed to sue defendants, and was awarded damages of $125 for the 10-foot deficiency in quantity. The warranty reads: "And we do hereby bind ourselves, our heirs, executors and administrators to Warrant and Forever Defend all and singular the said premises unto the said J. C. Armes, his heirs and assigns, against every person whomsoever lawfully claiming or to claim the same or any part thereof." Defendants' complaint on appeal was based on the fact that there was no special warranty and no covenant of quantity being made and, therefore, the quantity of the lot was not covered by the general warranty deed.

It is our view that the general warranty contained in the deed from defendants to plaintiff cannot be construed as a covenant of quantity in the lot but was only a warranty of the title thereto and recovery could not be had upon that warranty unless and until the title failed. In 12 Tex. Jur. 27, sec. 18, it is said: "As regards covenants of warranty, it is a general rule that a deficit in the quantity of the land conveyed does not result in a cause of action on such a covenant; it is breached only by a failure of title."

In Brown v. Yoakum, Tex. Civ. App., 170 S.W. 803, writ refused, it was held that the general covenant of warranty does not include a warranty of the quantity of land conveyed unless the property is sold by the acre and the quantity warranted, and it was further held that in the absence of warranty of quantity there can be no reduction of the purchase price for a deficiency in the quantity unless there is proof of fraud or mistake.

In Nicholson v. Slaughter Co., Tex. Civ. App., 217 S.W. 716, writ refused, it was held that where land is sold in bulk for a lump sum and not by the acre with the quantity warranted, the general warranty of title does not include a warranty of the quantity of land conveyed.

In Barnes v. Lightfoot, 26 Tex. Civ. App. 113, 62 S.W. 564, writ dismissed, it was held that where land was not sold by the acre, though the deed called for a certain number of acres, and upon measurement it was found to be short of the number of acres the tract was said to contain, the purchaser could not recover against the seller under the general warranty of the title, absent a warranty of the quantity contained in the tract, especially where there were no allegations made or proof shown of fraud or mistake. There can be no doubt that a grantor could obligate himself to warrant the quantity represented in his conveyance, but to do so such intention to warrant the quantity must be made in the instrument of conveyance.

In 12 Tex. Jur., p. 20, sec. 13, it is said: "A grantor may covenant that the land measures up to the quantity specified. When such is the case, the grantee may sue for the appropriate relief in the event of a breach. This covenant may be created only by proper words showing the intention to covenant as to quantity. Words of mere description in a deed constitute neither an express nor implied covenant for quantity." The authorities cited in the footnote abundantly support the text.

Substantially the same rule as that above quoted may be found in 12 Tex. Jur., p. 70, sec. 46.

As pointed out above, plaintiff's suit is based solely upon the warranty of title and proof that the lot conveyed was short in foot frontage. There were no allegations nor proof that a fraud was perpetrated by defendants, nor that the deficit was the result of a mistake. The deed of conveyance is set out in full in the statement of facts and there is no warranty of quantity to be found in the instrument, nor does plaintiff claim that there was such a warranty, other than from the fact he thought he was buying a lot 80 ft. wide and that defendants thought they owned 80 ft. in the lot.

For the reasons herein stated, the judgment of the trial court cannot stand and it is therefore reversed and judgment is entered for defendants.

NOTES & QUESTIONS:

1. If a grantee is concerned about the quantity of land being purchased, what can he do to protect himself in the deed?

2. What if instead of the land not being as much as he thought it was, the grantee discovered after the closing that the grantor owned only a 1/3 fractional share in the property and that the other 2/3 share was owned by two additional cotenants? What can the grantee do? Would any covenants of title in a General Warranty Deed or Special Warranty Deed provide relief?

3. What if the deed contains the correct property description for land that Grantor has good title to and can convey, but in looking at the property the grantor pointed out other land and represented to the grantee that the other land, which is rich in timber, was what was actually being conveyed? So the deed is for Blackacre, which Grantor owns, but Grantor had represented to Grantee that he was getting Whiteacre. Is there any protection in the General Warranty Deed from Grantor to Grantee? How may Grantee recover? Can he?

3. Establishing a Breach

As previously stated, present covenants are breached at the time of delivery of the deed. However, future covenants are promising the grantor will do something in the future if a problem occurs. We saw in *Brown v. Lober* that even though there was a problem and promise that matched, there was not yet a breach of the future covenant of quiet enjoyment, thus no recovery. We will now turn our attention to what is required to establish that breach.

<u>**Cross v. Thomas**</u>
Court of Civil Appeals of Texas, Fort Worth, 1953
264 S.W.2d 539

On March 11, 1947, appellees, D. W. Thomas and wife, executed a general warranty deed to appellant Floyd M. Cross to Lots 1, 2, 3, 4, 5, 6, 7, 8 and 9, in Block 9, Interurban Addition, Third Filing, to the City of Fort Worth, and also a strip of land adjoining and lying east of Lots 5 and 6.

[Ed. Note: The plaintiff Cross made claims that Thomas made misrepresentations and was fraudulent in representing the state of the title to Cross. The jury found that D. W. Thomas represented to appellant that he had good and marketable title to all the property described in his deed; that appellant relied upon such statements, but to the issue as to whether such representation was false and fraudulent, the jury answered "No." The court stated that "Mere expression of opinion as to the sufficiency of the title, when the means of information are equally accessible to both parties, and when no confidential relations exist between them, do not constitute fraud on the part of the vendor. A purchaser has no right to rely on the statement of the vendor that his title is good, where all the facts are laid before him, for this is no more than the statement of an opinion. To constitute fraud the vendor must falsely state, or fraudulently conceal, some fact material to the title." Maupin, Marketable Title to Real Estate, p. 264, § 106.]

Since the delivery of appellees' deed to appellant, appellant acquired deeds from other claimants of the property the title to which was in dispute, and paid therefore $2,550.

On Motion for Rehearing

Appellant asks that we consider point two in his brief, which is that he was entitled to recover for a breach of warranty, if not damages for misrepresentation of title. We did consider the point, but did not write on it further. . . . No issue was submitted or requested on that ground of recovery.

We do not think that appellant could recover for breach of warranty in the absence of evidence and findings that he was ejected from the premises, actually or constructively, by a holder of a title superior to his own. Rancho Bonito Land & Live-Stock Co. v. North, 92 Tex. 72, 45 S.W. 994; Schneider v. Lipscomb County Nat. Farm Loan Ass'n, 146 Tex. 66, 202 S.W.2d 832, 172 A.L.R. 1. A reputable lawyer testified that his examination of an abstract of title to the property in dispute disclosed that the record title was in the parties from whom appellant later acquired deeds. There was no other evidence as to their title. We believe that whether an abstract shows title in a particular person is a question of law and not of fact. Brackenridge v. Claridge, 91 Tex. 527, 44 S.W. 819, 43 L.R.A. 593; Moser v. Tucker, Tex. Civ. App., 195 S.W. 259; Bourland v. Huffhines, Tex. Civ.

App., 269 S.W. 184; Wakeland v. Robertson, Tex. Civ. App., 219 S.W. 842; Crenshaw v. True, Tex. Civ. App., 295 S.W. 632. Furthermore, we find in the record no evidence that anybody ever asserted superior title to the property in such manner as would constitute a constructive eviction of appellant. All that is shown is that when appellant was convinced that others held superior title, he offered to and did pay them for deeds conveying their supposed title to himself. This has been held not to amount to constructive disseisin. 12 Tex. Jur., p. 43, sec. 27, and cases there cited. Had he waited for an assertion of adverse title, his own title might have been perfected by limitation. There is nothing in the record to indicate that he would have lost anything by waiting. If the lapse of time would have secured him against loss, the vendor is entitled to the benefit of that contingency, as well after as before the conveyance. Rancho Bonito Land & Live Stock Co. v. North, *supra*. The mere existence of a superior title in another is not a breach of warranty because that does not work an eviction of a buyer who has entered upon the land. Jones' Heirs v. Paul's Heirs, 59 Tex. 41.

Since it does not conclusively appear that there was superior title in those from whom appellant later acquired deeds, nor that there was either actual or constructive eviction, and since no such issues were submitted or requested, if it cannot be said that appellant waived the ground of recovery based upon his allegations of breach of warranty, it must be said that such issues, if raised, were found by the Court in such manner as will support the judgment. Rule 279, T.R.C.P.

The motion for rehearing is overruled.

NOTES & QUESTIONS:

1. The court in *Brown* and the court in *Cross* both stated that mere knowledge of a defect without more is not sufficient to trigger a breach of the covenant of quiet enjoyment or general warranty. The court in *Cross* says that there must be an assertion of superior title and a yielding thereto. Each part of that statement must be defined and applied. What will serve as an assertion? What is superior title? What is a yielding to the superior title?

2. A voluntary yielding to someone with superior title that is unasserted is also not a constructive eviction and triggers no breach of the covenant of warranty. *See* Patton v. McFarlane, 3 Pen. & W. 419 (Pa. 1832); Felts v. Whitaker, 129 S.W.2d 682 (Tex.Civ.App.—Fort Worth 1939), *aff'd*, 155 S.W.2d 604 (Tex.1941).

3. It is, in general, not necessary that the grantee should await his actual dispossession by the holder of the paramount title. The holder of superior title has the right summarily to obtain possession under it and if that right is asserted and the covenantee may anticipate its actual exercise and

surrenders possession as a result, then such *ouster in pais* amounts to a constructive eviction supporting a covenant action. Schneider v. Lipscomb County, 202 S.W.2d 832 (Tex. 1947); Drew v. Towle, 27 N.H. 412 (N.H. 1853).

4. Even if there is an assertion of superior title, there is neither actual nor constructive eviction while the covenantee remains in possession. Without an eviction, there can be no recovery on a covenant of warranty. Mead v. Stackpole, 40 Hun. 473 (N.Y. Gen. Term 1886).

5. A final judicial determination of the title adverse to the grantee has been held to constitute a constructive eviction. Once judgment is entered regarding the trespass to try title action, the breach of the covenant of warranty has occurred and statute of limitations starts to run. Schneider v. Lipscomb Co., 202 S.W.2d 832 (Tex. 1947); Beach v. Nordman, 117 SW 785 (Ark. 1909).

6. A purchase by a covenantee of an outstanding paramount title, when that title is actually and hostilely asserted, will constitute such a constructive eviction as will entitle him to damages upon his covenant of warranty. Davenport v. Bartlett, 9 Ala. 179 (Ala. 1846); Eversole v. Early, 44 NW 897 (Iowa 1890); Cross v. Thomas, 264 S.W.2d 539 (Tex. Civ. App.—Ft. Worth 1953).

7. Where at the time of conveyance the grantee finds the premises in possession of one claiming under paramount title, the covenant for quiet enjoyment or warranty is held to be broken, without any other act on the part of either the grantee or the one in possession claiming paramount title. Felts v. Whitaker, 129 S.W.2d 682 (Tex. Civ. App.—Ft. Worth 1939); Shankle v. Ingram, 45 S.E. 578 (NC 1903).

8. The foreclosure of a mortgage or other lien is a sufficient constructive eviction to entitle the covenantee to sue for breach of the covenant of warranty. Collier v. Cowger, 12 SW 702 (Ark. 1889); Sherman v. Piner, 91 S.W.2d 1185 (Tex. Civ. App.—Eastland 1936).

TITLE COVENANT PROBLEMS:

All of these questions are being posed as of the date the issue is discovered. Do not assume any facts in giving your answers. If you need additional facts, indicate what facts and why.

1. Barney owns a life estate in Blackacre, which is real property located in Dallas, Texas. Barney executes a general warranty deed using the form that is provided in the Texas Property Code conveying Blackacre in fee simple absolute to Marshall. The deed meets all of the requirements of a valid deed and legal title is transferred to Marshall on February 25, 2006. On September 1, 2010, Marshall finds out that Barney had only a life estate in Blackacre.
   a. What covenants of title does Marshall have available to him?
   b. Can he bring an action against Barney based on any of these covenants? Why or why not?
   c. How long does Marshall have to bring these action(s)?

2. Barney owns Blackacre, a 40-acre forest tract in east Texas, in fee simple absolute. He conveys the tract to Marshall on February 25, 2006, by a valid Texas form general warranty deed. Marshall records his deed that day. He does nothing with the property and leaves it as forest land. On February 7, 2007, Barney conveys Blackacre to Ted under a Texas form general warranty deed. Ted did not conduct a title search and does not know about Marshall. Ted takes possession of Blackacre and builds a house. Ted learns of Marshall's deed on September 1, 2010. (Note: All states will recognize Marshall as the true owner of Blackacre under these facts, unless Ted has managed to acquire title by adverse possession.)
   a. What covenants of title does Ted have available to him?
   b. Can he bring an action against Barney based on any of these covenants? Why or why not?
   c. Would your answer to the above question change if Ted abandoned Blackacre once he found out about Marshall? Why or why not?
   d. What if, when Ted finds out about Marshall, he contacts him and offers to pay Marshall for his interest in Blackacre?
   e. Would it affect your answer if Marshall sends a letter to Ted stating that Marshall is the true owner of Blackacre and he is going to sue Ted, so Ted leaves?
   f. What if Marshall files suit and in response Ted leaves Blackacre?
   g. What if Marshall sued to have title quieted in him and Ted says, "fine, sue me, but I'm not leaving"?
   h. What if Marshall sues and is successful in his lawsuit, receiving a judgment indicating he is indeed the superior title holder?

3. Barney owns Blackacre in fee simple absolute. He has a mortgage on the property in favor of First City Bank, which is properly recorded. Marshall does not conduct a title search and has no knowledge of the existing lien.

Barney executes and delivers a valid general warranty deed using the form provided in the Texas Property Code. Marshall accepts the deed and legal title passes on February 25, 2006.

On March 1, 2010, Marshall discovers the loan is in default and the bank intends to foreclose on the property at a foreclosure sale on the first Tuesday in April. What can Marshall do? Does he have any available covenants of title?

4. Damages for Breach of Title Covenants

Once a defect and promise match up and a breach occurs, when relief is sought by the grantee, what will be the recoverable damages? It will depend somewhat on the nature of the covenant. Is the grantee obligated to do anything to mitigate the possible damages that may occur?

<u>**Ledbetter et ux. v. Howard et ux.**</u>
Court of Civil Appeals of Texas, Waco, 1965
395 S.W.2d 951

McDONALD, Chief Justice.
This is an appeal by the seller, from a judgment for the buyer, in a suit for damages for breach of the warranty in a deed.

Plaintiffs, Howard and wife, sued defendants Ledbetter and wife for breach of the warranty of title in a deed. Plaintiffs on May 6, 1960 bought a house and lot in Waco, Texas from defendants, paying $1,000 in cash and assuming $5,771.84 unpaid balance on a note owed Bankers Life Company. Plaintiffs lived in the house from May 1960 to November 1961, after which date they rented the house for $55 per month. On November 23, 1964 the Treasury Department seized the house for taxes owed by defendants' predecessor in title.

Plaintiffs sued for $3,752.19 (which represented the $1,000 paid in cash; $1161.12 paid to Bankers Life on the principal of the note; $943.74 paid Bankers Life as interest on deferred balance; and $647.33 paid Bankers Life as escrow funds for payment of taxes and insurance).

Defendants answered by general denial, and filed cross action for $680 (plus attorneys' fees), allegedly due defendants from plaintiffs on a note.

Trial was before the court without a jury, which found plaintiffs entitled to the $3,752.19 sued for; and defendants entitled to $748 on their cross action against plaintiffs; and rendered judgment for plaintiffs for $3,004.19.

Defendants appeal, contending the trial court erred:

Issues

1) In rendering judgment for plaintiffs when plaintiffs did not allege and prove they were unable to pay off the tax lien prior to foreclosure by the U.S. Government.

2) In rendering judgment for plaintiffs when defendants tendered a title to the property clear of the U.S. Treasury lien.

3) In rendering judgment for the $943.74 interest, and $647.33 escrow funds paid by plaintiffs to Bankers Life, since plaintiffs did not allege and prove such interest and escrow funds were in excess of the reasonable rental value of the property.

① We revert to defendants' 1st contention. Defendants sold the property to plaintiffs and warranted the title. Such titled failed because the U.S. Treasury asserted a tax lien against the property, and subsequently foreclosed it. The plaintiffs had no duty to diminish the damages accruing from breach of a covenant of general warranty by purchasing or extinguishing the title asserted against them. Schneider v. Lipscomb Co. Nat. Farm Loan Ass'n., 146 Tex. 66, 202 S.W.2d 832.

② Defendants' 2nd contention is that plaintiffs were not entitled to judgment because defendants tendered them a title to the property free of the U. S. tax lien. Plaintiffs were dispossessed of the house and lot on November 23, 1964 by the U.S. tax authorities. Thereafter, the tax authorities held a tax sale and the defendants bought the property in for some $1,500; and in their answer tendered a deed to the property free and clear of the tax lien. The tender came too late. Plaintiffs had already been dispossessed of their property, and had instituted their suit on the defendants' warranty of title, prior to the tender.

③ Defendants' 3rd contention complains that the trial court erred in rendering judgment for plaintiffs for the $943.74 interest defendant paid Bankers Life on the deferred balance of the note; and the $647.33 plaintiffs paid Bankers Life as escrow funds with which to pay taxes and insurance on the property.

The measure of damages for breach of warranty is the value of the property at the time the warranty was made; generally shown by the amount of the consideration paid. 20 Am. Jur.2d p. 691. The plaintiff may further recover for interest and taxes paid if he was never in possession or if his occupancy was not beneficial. Where the buyer has been in beneficial possession up to the time of eviction, he can recover only for the interest and taxes which are in excess of the reasonable rental value of the premises.

Plaintiffs alleged the reasonable rental value of the property to be $60 per month; and the proof showed plaintiffs lived on the property from May 1960 to November 1961; and rented the property for $55 per month from November 1961 until November 1964. The rental value of the property was thus $3,470; and in excess of the $1,591.07 interest and escrow payments contended for. Therefore, plaintiffs were not entitled to recover for the interest and escrow moneys. 20 Am. Jur. 2d p. 708, 716; Huff v. Reilly, CCA (n. w. h.), 26 Tex. Civ. App. 101, 64 S.W. 387; Brown v. Hearon, 66 Tex. 63, 17 S.W. 395.

The trial court erred in rendering judgment for the $943.74 interest and $647.33 escrow funds paid by plaintiffs, and the judgment is excessive in such amount.

Plaintiff, by cross point, contends the trial court erred in holding defendants entitled to recover $748 against them. Defendants alleged that plaintiff executed a note payable to defendants for $1,000, upon which was unpaid $680. Plaintiff plead limitation as to the note; and the trial court sustained plaintiffs' objection to the introduction of the note in evidence. Nevertheless the trial court entered judgment for defendant against plaintiff for the $680 (plus $68 attorneys' fees as provided in the note). The note was not overdue before May 1, 1961; the 4 year Statute of Limitations is applicable to such note; and the note was not barred by limitations since defendants' cross action was filed on April 15, 1965. As noted, trial was before the Court without a jury. While the basis for the trial court's action in rendering judgment for the $748 does not appear with certainty, the note was admissible in evidence, and the action of the trial court in rendering judgment for defendant thereon is correct.

The judgment is reformed, deleting the $1,591.07 excessive amount; and affirmed for the balance of $1,413.12, on which plaintiffs are entitled to interest at 6% from the date of eviction, November 23, 1964. The judgment is further reformed to provide for such interest. Costs are divided 1/2 against each party. As reformed, the judgment is affirmed.

Reformed and affirmed.

NOTES & QUESTIONS:

1. *Ledbetter* makes clear that the grantee has no duty to mitigate damages in order to be able to recover. The grantees had no obligation to pay off the tax lien in order to avoid losing possession of the land and having a complete failure of title.

2. What is the appropriate measure of damages for recovery? For the covenants of seisin, right to convey, quiet enjoyment, and warranty, the grantee will be complaining of either a complete or partial failure of title. This means that the grantee will be seeking recovery of damages to represent the value of what was lost. What is used to measure the value? There are different approaches to the measure of actual damages that can be recovered with the future covenants. For present covenants, the suit in most places is only between the immediate grantor and grantee, the purchase price is clear, and the grantee can recover full or partial amount of the purchase price that represents the failure of title.

However, with the future covenants the question becomes a little more difficult. Because the future covenants run with the land, a remote grantor may be sued, or even if the immediate grantor is sued, the value of the land may have changed drastically. The majority approach to actual damages is that the grantee may recover the purchase price and if recovering against a remote grantor, that amount will be capped at the amount the grantor received when making the promise. This means that a grantee may not receive full recovery if forced to sue a remote grantor and the property appreciated in value as it typically does.

What would happen if the grantee sued a remote grantor and the property had actually depreciated in value? The grantee paid less than the remote grantor received? Is the grantee limited in recovery to what she paid, or can she recover the full amount that the grantor received? Look to Hollingsworth v. Mexia to answer that question.

Hollingsworth v. Mexia
Court of Civil Appeals of Texas, 1896
37 S.W. 455

WILLIAMS, J.

Facts

S. R. and E. A. Mexia are suing J. C. Burnet in a trespass to try title action. The basis of that cause of action is that both parties are claiming a possessory interest in the land, basically both are claiming FSA ownership. There were multiple parcels of land involved but the dispute surrounds only two parcels. For those two parcels Burnet is not claiming title because of legal record title but based on adverse possession. Burnet is in possession and Mexia wants possession.

Burnet then brings Hollingsworth into the suit claiming that if he loses in the trespass to try title suit that Hollingsworth will have to pay him damages for a breach of the covenant of general warranty.

Hollingsworth is a common grantor for both chains of title. Hollingsworth had conveyed to Aguilera who then conveyed to Mexia, the plaintiff in this case. After conveying to Aguilera, Hollingsworth made a second conveyance to Carroll. On March 10, 1879 Hollingsworth gave Carroll a General Warranty Deed and was paid $5,200. Carroll then conveyed part of that land, including the tracts at issue in this case, to Burnet on April 13, 1887 also with a General Warranty Deed. Burnet paid $1,000 to Carroll.

In the suit, Hollingsworth is making the same claim as Burnet, that Burnet has title to the land based on adverse possession. Hollingsworth needs Burnet to win the underlying trespass to try title suit with Mexia so that no damages will be owed under the covenant of general warranty. If Burnet loses title to the land, Hollingsworth has to pay damages.

Burnet loses the underlying trespass to try title suit and the issue on appeal involves how much the damages are that are owed to Burnet by Hollingsworth who is a remote grantee.

The chain of title to the land in dispute is as follows:

	Hollingsworth	
Aguilera	|	Carroll (GWD) ($5200)
	|	
Mexia	|	Burnet (GWD) ($1,000)

From this judgment Hollingsworth prosecutes this writ of error.

The pleading of the defendant showed on its face that he had paid for the land, to his immediate vendor, Carroll, a less sum than the latter had paid to plaintiff in error; and it is contended that under these facts the defendant could not recover of the plaintiff in error more than he had paid to Carroll. Upon the question of law thus presented as to the right of a plaintiff, who has been evicted from land, to recover of a remote warrantor of the title the sum received by such warrantor from his immediate grantee as the price of the land, though the plaintiff himself paid to his immediate grantor a less sum, there is an irreconcilable conflict among the decision in other states. The following decisions hold that the recovery can be had of the full amount received by the original warrantor regardless of what plaintiff himself had paid for the land: Brooks v. Black (Miss.) 8 Sount. 332; Lowrance v. Robertson, 10 S. C. 8; Mischke v. Baughn, 52 Iowa, 528, 3 N.W. 543; Dougherty v. Duvall, 9 B. Mon. 57. See, also Hunt v. Orwig, 17 C. Mon. 73, and Cock v. Curtis (Mich.) 36 N. W. 692. Other cases cited below, hold to the contrary view, that the recovery restricted to the amount paid by the plaintiff for the land which he has lost on the ground that this is his damage. Williams v. Beeman, 2 Dev. 483; Mette v. Dow, 9 Lea. 93; Whitzman v. Hirsh, 87 Tenn. 513, 11 S.W 421; Moore v. Frankenfleld 25 Minn. 540; Crisfield v. Storr, 36 Md. 129; Taylor v. Wallace (Colo. Sup.) 37 Pac. 963.

Treating the question, then, as open in this state, we are of the opinion that the judgment rendered in this case is correct. The subject has been very fully discussed in the cases cited above, and perhaps it is unnecessary to do more than refer to them. But it seems to us that what we consider the error in the views of those courts holding that the plaintiff in such cases is limited in his recovery to the amount paid by him for the land arises from an inattention to the true meaning of the rule which makes the purchase money and interest the measure of damages for breach of warranty, and to the course of reasoning through which it was established. At an early day the question as to the measure of damages as between a covenantor and his immediate covenantee for breach of warranty arose, and received great attention. The cases of Staats v. Ten Eyck, 3 Caines, 112, and Pitcher v. Livingston, 4 Johns. 1, are the leading ones on the subject, in which the rule and the reasons upon which it is founded were carefully considered and stated, and have been adopted and followed in most of the states, including our own. Garrett v. Gaines, 6 Tex. 443; Turner v. Miller, 42 Tex. 420. The rule was mainly deduced from the history of the covenant, which was substituted for the ancient common-law warranty, the obligation under which was to restore to the party evicted other land, worth as much as that which he had lost had been worth at the time of the warranty; and instead of the land it was held that, under the covenant of warranty, the warrantor should pay back its value at the time of the warranty as fixed by the price agreed upon between the parties at that time. The rule was fortified by the argument that it enabled both parties, at the time of their contract, to know the extent of the liability which might arise upon the covenant, and did not leave the vendor of land subject to unforeseen damages which might result from the rapid appreciation of property, or from costly and luxurious improvements which might be made by subsequent possessors. It is, confessedly, not based entirely upon the idea of compensation for the loss sustained by the person evicted, for it excluded a recovery for the value of the land at the time of eviction further than that may be compensated by restoration of the price received by the vendor. 3 Sedg. Dam. §§ 951, 957, 964. Going behind the mere formula by which the rule is usually expressed, and looking at the reasoning upon which it was based, we find that it was adopted in order to fix and limit the liability incurred by the covenantor at the time of the conveyance, rather than to ascertain the extent of loss sustained by any covenantee at the time of eviction. That liability cannot be increased or diminished by any subsequent enhancement or depreciation in value of the land. Nor can it be increased by the contracts made between subsequent vendors and their vendees.

The covenantor in a warranty receives the price for which he has sold the land, and the true meaning of his covenant, as fixed by those decisions, which have established the general rule of damages, is that he will, in case the land is entirely lost, restore that price to the person who has lost the land. This rule, it is true, applies perfectly in only those cases where there is total eviction, and in cases of partial loss it has been modified so as to allow a recovery of only such proportion of the consideration as the amount of the loss bears to the whole of it. Again, the doctrines regulating the rights of principal and surety and the subject of subrogation have no application. The right of the person evicted to sue upon remote covenants is not derived from a subrogation to the rights of his vendor, nor is there anything like the relation of principal and surety. The covenant of warranty, until it has been broken, passes, as a strictly legal right, with the land, when that is conveyed. Rawle, Cov. pp. 334-336, 359. An intermediate owner of the land has no right of action upon the covenants under which he held until he has been made to respond to the claims of his covenants. But the party evicted has the original right of action against all. Eustis v. Fosdick, 88 Tex. 615, 32 S.W. 872.

All of the cases which have adopted the rule given in Mette v. Dow are based, it seems to us, upon the same assumption pointed out in that decision. In some of the cases which maintain the position of plaintiff in error it is objected that the other rule would give a different measure of damages to the person evicted against each of the warrantors in his chain of title, as he could recover from any one of them what that one had received as the price of the land. But this arises only from the difference in their contracts and is precisely what the general rule intends. The warrantor fixes by his contract the limit of his own liability, and that cannot be changed by the contracts of others. The person evicted can have but one satisfaction. The judgment of the district court is not erroneous, and it is affirmed.

NOTES & QUESTIONS:

1. The decision reached by the court in *Hollingsworth* is not one that would be reached by courts in all states. There is a concern that the grantee recovering more than her purchase price is receiving a windfall. However, the rationale in *Hollingsworth* is that of a contractual approach. If the grantor, who made this promise with a defect in existence, is not going to be harmed by the appreciation of land value, he will not be benefitted by the depreciation of it either.

2. This only accounts for the actual damages that can be recovered for a breach of a future covenant. There are other recoverable damages. The grantee can also recover any mortgage interest and property taxes paid to date. There is a difference of opinion as to whether the grantee's possession should impact the recovery. Some states, Texas included, do consider possession. The rule is that the grantee can only recover the amount of interest and taxes in excess of fair rental value during time of possession. However, if the grantee has not been in possession he can recover the full amount paid. Other states allow for full recovery regardless of any possession by the grantee.

    If the grantee has to defend the title in a lawsuit and loses out to the person with a superior title to the property, the grantee can recover those court costs and attorneys fees when suing under the breach of title covenant.

Finally, if the grantee has made improvements to the property since taking title, if he can qualify as a good faith improver, then the value of the improvement can be recovered not under the warranty from the grantor but from the person with superior title who will take possession of those improvements. This allows for full recovery by the grantee and allocates the expense of damages onto the parties that should be responsible.

3. The measure of damages when recovering on a covenant against encumbrances is different. An action on this covenant is not complaining about a complete or partial failure of title. This is seeking to remove the encumbrance from the land. The recoverable damages are either (1) the amount required to remove the encumbrance from the property, up to its FMV or (2) the diminished FMV due to the presence of the encumbrance. For example, if the encumbrance is a lien, the exact amount to remove the encumbrance is known and that will be the desired outcome. However, if the encumbrance is an easement with a pipeline company, that is not going to be removed. In that case the landowner could recover the diminished FMV for the property because he is now stuck with land burdened by the encumbrance.

5. Execution, Delivery, and Acceptance

Now that you have an understanding of what is contained in the deed and the benefits of having those contents, we will finish up our coverage of the deed with the concepts of execution, delivery, and acceptance. These are the requirements from the statute of conveyances that must be valid in order for title to transfer. No matter how well the document satisfies the statute of frauds to be valid on its face, if execution, delivery, or acceptance is invalid there is no transfer of title and the deed is void ab initio. These concepts cause particular difficulty because these elements cannot be seen by looking at the document. Now we must peer behind the paper to make sure the process was proper to validly convey title.

Valid execution requires a valid signature of the grantor or a signature by the grantee or a third party with the grantor's permission. Issues with forgery and fraud could prevent a valid execution. In most instances a fraudulently obtained signature will not result in the deed being void, however, a forgery does render the deed void. Even a person who would otherwise qualify as a bona fide purchaser cannot prevail over a forgery.

Acceptance is the grantee's acceptance of the legal title. Acceptance is rarely an issue. As long as the deed is not rejected there is a presumption that there was an acceptance. Evidence can be used to establish the deed was not accepted. If no acceptance, the deed is void.

Delivery is the most frequently contested issue. Valid delivery requires that the grantor must by words or actions manifest intent that the deed be immediately effective to transfer an interest in the land to the grantee. The grantor does not have to physically hand over the document for there to be a valid delivery. However, if the deed is in the grantee's possession, the grantee begins with a rebuttable presumption of valid delivery. If the grantor dies with the deed still in his possession, then the grantee starts with a rebuttable presumption against him that there was no valid delivery. Although recording is not required for a valid transfer of title, if the deed is recorded, the grantee also gets a rebuttable presumption of valid delivery.

Most Issues Arise w/ Delivery!

While issues do arise over the question of who has physical possession of the document, an issue that frequently occurs is that of an attempted conditional delivery of the deed.

Sweeney v. Sweeney
Supreme Court of Errors of Connecticut, 1940
11 A.2d 806

JENNINGS, J.

Maurice Sweeney, plaintiff's intestate, hereinafter called Maurice, deeded his farm to his brother John M. Sweeney, hereinafter called John, and the deed was recorded. John deeded the property back to Maurice. This deed is unrecorded and was accidentally burned. The question to be decided is whether the second deed was delivered and if so, whether or not a condition claimed to be attached to the delivery is operative. This must be determined on the finding. The following statement includes such changes therein as are required by the evidence:

The plaintiff is the widow and administratrix of Maurice but had not lived with him for the twenty years preceding his death in September, 1938, at the age of seventy-three years. Maurice lived on a tract of land of some hundred and thirty-five acres which he owned in East Hampton, where he ran a tavern. John assisted him in running the tavern to some extent. On February 2, 1937, Maurice and John went to the town clerk's office in East Hampton pursuant to an appointment made the preceding day. Maurice requested the town clerk to draw a deed of his East Hampton property to John and this was done. At the same time he requested that a deed be prepared from John to himself so that he, Maurice, would be protected if John predeceased him. Both deeds were duly executed. The first was left for recording and the second was taken away by Maurice and never recorded. A week or two later Maurice took to John the recorded deed and a week or two after that took the unrecorded deed to John's house. John kept both deeds and gave the second deed to his attorney after the institution of this action. It was destroyed when the latter's office was burned. After the execution of the deeds, Maurice continued to occupy the property, paid the fixed charges, received the rents and exercised full dominion over it until his death. In April, 1937, Maurice made a written lease to Ernest Myers of a portion of the premises and on June 18, 1938, a written lease to Frank and Esther Fricke for twenty years. The first lease is lost but the second was recorded. The defendant never collected any money from tenants or paid any fixed charges or repairs prior to the death of Maurice. On these facts the trial court concluded that there was no intention to make present delivery of John's deed to Maurice, that there was no delivery or acceptance thereof, that it was not intended to operate until John's death and rendered judgment for the defendant.

This deed was, in effect, manually delivered. Maurice continued to occupy the property and exercised full dominion over it without interference by John. It follows that all the essentials of a good delivery were present unless there is something in the contentions of John which defeats this result. He claims that there was no intention on his part to make present delivery.

It is, of course, true that physical possession of a duly executed deed is not conclusive proof that it was legally delivered. This is so under some circumstances even where there has been a manual delivery. Delivery must be made with the intent to pass title if it is to be effective.

The deed having been in effect actually delivered to Maurice, the execution of the attestation clause was prima facie proof that the deed was delivered. There is a rebuttable presumption that the grantee assented since the deed was beneficial to him. No fact is found which militates against this presumption. Where deeds are formally executed and delivered, these presumptions can be overcome only by evidence that no delivery was in fact intended. The only purpose in making the deed expressed by either party was the statement by Maurice that it was to protect him in case John predeceased him. Since this purpose would have been defeated had there been no delivery with intent to pass title, this conclusively establishes the fact that there was a legal delivery.

The defendant next claims that if there was a delivery, it was on condition and that the condition (the death of John before that of Maurice) was not and cannot be fulfilled. This claim is not good because the delivery was to the grantee. A conditional delivery is and can only be made by placing the deed in the hands of a third person to be kept by him until the happening of the event upon the happening of which the deed is to be delivered over by the third person to the grantee. Conditional delivery to a grantee vests absolute title in the latter. This is one of the instances where a positive rule of law may defeat the actual intention of the parties. The safety of real estate titles is considered more important than the unfortunate results which may follow the application of the rule in a few individual instances. To relax it would open the door wide to fraud and the fabrication of evidence. Although the doctrine has been criticized no material change has been noted in the attitude of the courts in this country.

The finding does not support the conclusion. The finding shows a delivery and, even if a conditional delivery is assumed, the condition is not good for the reasons stated. Since a new trial is necessary, the one ruling on evidence made a ground of appeal is noticed. The town clerk was permitted to testify to certain statements made by Maurice when the deed was drafted. Parol evidence is not admissible to vary the terms of the deed but may be received to show the use that was to be made of it. The ruling was correct as showing the circumstances surrounding delivery. There is error and a new trial is ordered.

NOTES & QUESTIONS:

1. What do you think the brothers were trying to accomplish with the two deeds? Think of what you have already learned in this course and consider what you would recommend to John and Maurice to accomplish their goals.

2. The laws in the state of Connecticut at that time provided that if a decedent died intestate, his surviving spouse would receive one-third of his property if there were surviving issue or a surviving parent of the deceased. However, if the facts were as we can gather from the case and he only had the surviving spouse and brother, under the statutes at the time his surviving spouse would receive 100 percent of his property. *See* Conn. Gen. Stat. § 5156 (1930).

3. The rule used by the court in *Sweeney* reflects the majority view on conditional delivery in a grantee. It is the view that is followed in Texas. However, there is a minority view on conditional delivery in the grantee. A few courts have held that if there is an attempted conditional delivery to the grantee then there is no delivery at all.

4. Is the concept of a conditional delivery any different if a third party is involved? Consider the scenario where John Sweeney drafts the exact same deed as he did in the case above, but instead of giving it to his brother and telling him that it will be effective upon his death if Maurice survives him, he gives the same instruction to his lawyer. Will this conditional delivery be effective?

Rosengrant v. Rosengrant
Court of Appeals of Oklahoma, 1981
629 P.2d 800

BOYDSTON, J.

This is an appeal by J. W. (Jay) Rosengrant from the trial court's decision to cancel and set aside a warranty deed which attempted to vest title in him to certain property owned by his aunt and uncle, Mildred and Harold Rosengrant. The trial court held the deed was invalid for want of legal delivery. We affirm that decision.

Harold and Mildred were a retired couple living on a farm southeast of Tecumseh, Oklahoma. They had no children of their own but had six nieces and nephews through Harold's deceased brother. One of these nephews was Jay Rosengrant. He and his wife lived a short distance from Harold and Mildred and helped the elderly couple from time to time with their chores.

In 1971, it was discovered that Mildred had cancer. In July, 1972 Mildred and Harold went to Mexico to obtain laetrile treatments accompanied by Jay's wife. Jay remained behind to care for the farm.

Shortly before this trip, on June 23, 1972, Mildred had called Jay and asked him to meet her and Harold at Farmers and Merchants Bank in Tecumseh. Upon arriving at the bank, Harold introduced Jay to his banker J. E. Vanlandengham who presented Harold and Mildred with a deed to their farm which he had prepared according to their instructions. Both Harold and Mildred signed the deed and informed Jay that they were going to give him "the place," but that they wanted Jay to leave the deed at the bank with Mr. Vanlandengham and when "something happened" to them, he was to take it to Shawnee and record it and "it" would be theirs. Harold personally handed the deed to Jay to "make this legal." Jay accepted the deed and then handed it back to the banker who told him he would put it in an envelope and keep it in the vault until he called for it.

In July, 1974, when Mildred's death was imminent, Jay and Harold conferred with an attorney concerning the legality of the transaction. The attorney advised them it should be sufficient but if Harold anticipated problems he should draw up a will.

In 1976, Harold discovered he had lung cancer. In August and December 1977, Harold put $10,000 into two certificates of deposit in joint tenancy with Jay.

Harold died January 28, 1978. On February 2, Jay and his wife went to the bank to inventory the contents of the safety deposit box. They also requested the envelope containing the deed which was retrieved from the collection file of the bank.

Jay went to Shawnee the next day and recorded the deed.

The petition to cancel and set aside the deed was filed February 22, 1978, alleging that the deed was void in that it was never legally delivered and alternatively that since it was to be operative only upon recordation after the death of the grantors it was a testamentary instrument and was void for failure to comply with the Statute of Wills.

The trial court found the deed was null and void for failure of legal delivery. The dispositive issue raised on appeal is whether the trial court erred in so ruling. We hold it did not and affirm the judgment.

The facts surrounding the transaction which took place at the bank were uncontroverted. It is the interpretation of the meaning and legal result of the transaction which is the issue to be determined by this court on appeal.

In cases involving attempted transfers such as this, it is the grantor's intent at the time the deed is delivered which is of primary and controlling importance. It is the function of this court to weigh the evidence presented at trial as to grantor's intent and unless the trial court's decision is clearly against the weight of the evidence, to uphold that finding.

The grantor and banker were both dead at the time of trial. Consequently, the only testimony regarding the transaction was supplied by the grantee, Jay. The pertinent part of his testimony is as follows:

A. (A)nd was going to hand it back to Mr. Vanlandingham (sic), and he wouldn't take it.

Q. What did Mr. Vanlandingham say?

A. Well, he laughed then and said that "We got to make this legal," or something like that. And said, "You'll have to give it to Jay and let Jay give it back to me."

Q. And what did Harold do with the document?

A. He gave it to me.

Q. Did you hold it?

A. Yes.

Q. Then what did you do with it?

A. Mr. Vanlandingham, I believe, told me I ought to look at it.

Q. And you looked at it?

A. Yes.

Q. And then what did you do with it?

A. I handed it to Mr. Vanlandingham.

Q. And what did he do with the document?

A. He had it in his hand, I believe, when we left.

Q. Do you recall seeing the envelope at any time during this transaction?

A. I never saw the envelope. But Mr. Vanlandingham told me when I handed it to him, said, "Jay, I'll put this in an envelope and keep it in a vault for you until you call for it."

A. Well, Harold told me while Mildred was signing the deed that they were going to deed me the farm, but they wanted me to leave the deed at the bank with Van, and that when something happened to them that I would go to the bank and pick it up and take it to Shawnee to the court house and record it, and it would be mine.

When the deed was retrieved, it was contained in an envelope on which was typed: "J. W. Rosengrant- or Harold H. Rosengrant."

The import of the writing on the envelope is clear. It creates an inescapable conclusion that the deed was, in fact, retrievable at any time by Harold before his death. The bank teller's testimony as to the custom and usage of the bank leaves no other conclusion but that at any time Harold was free to retrieve the deed. There was, if not an expressed, an implied agreement between the banker and Harold that the grant was not to take effect until two conditions occurred the death of both grantors and the recordation of the deed.

In support of this conclusion conduct relative to the property is significant and was correctly considered by the court. Evidence was presented to show that after the deed was filed Harold continued to farm, use and control the property. Further, he continued to pay taxes on it until his death and claimed it as his homestead.

Grantee confuses the issues involved herein by relying upon grantors' goodwill toward him and his wife as if it were a controlling factor. From a fair review of the record it is apparent Jay and his wife were very attentive, kind and helpful to this elderly couple. The donative intent on the part of grantors is undeniable. We believe they fully intended to reward Jay and his wife for their kindness. Nevertheless, where a grantor delivers a deed under which he reserves a right of retrieval and attaches to that delivery the condition that the deed is to become operative only after the death of grantors and further continues to use the property as if no transfer had occurred grantor's actions are nothing more than an attempt to employ the deed as if it were a will. Under Oklahoma law this cannot be done. The ritualistic "delivery of the deed" to the grantee and his redelivery of it to the third party for safe keeping created under these circumstances only a symbolic delivery. It amounted to a pro forma attempt to comply with the legal aspects of delivery. Based on all the facts and circumstances the true intent of the parties is expressed by the notation on the envelope and by the later conduct of the parties in relation to the land. Legal delivery is not just a symbolic gesture. It necessarily carries all the force and consequence of absolute, outright ownership at the time of delivery or it is no delivery at all.

The trial court interpreted the envelope literally. The clear implication is that grantor intended to continue to exercise control and that the grant was not to take effect until such time as both he and his wife had died and the deed had been recorded. From a complete review of the record and weighing of the evidence we find the trial court's judgment is not clearly against the weight of the evidence. Costs of appeal are taxed to appellant.

BRIGHTMIRE, Judge, concurring specially.

In a dispute of this kind dealing with the issue of whether an unrecorded deed placed in the custody of a third party is a valid conveyance to the named grantee at that time or is deposited for some other reason, such as in trust or for a testamentary purpose, the fact finder often has a particularly tough job trying to determine what the true facts are.

The law, on the other hand, is relatively clear. A valid in praesenti conveyance requires two things: (1) actual or constructive delivery of the deed to the grantee or to a third party; and (2) an intention by the grantor to divest himself of the conveyed interest. Here the trial judge found there was no delivery despite the testimony of Jay Rosengrant to the contrary that one of the grantors handed the deed to him at the suggestion of banker J. E. Vanlandengham.

So the question is, was the trial court bound to find the fact to be as Rosengrant stated? In my opinion he was not for several reasons. Of the four persons present at the bank meeting in question only Rosengrant survives which, when coupled with the self-serving nature of the nephew's statements, served to cast a suspicious cloud over his testimony. And this, when considered along with other circumstances detailed in the majority opinion, would have justified the fact finder in disbelieving it. I personally have trouble with the delivery testimony in spite of the apparent "corroboration" of the lawyer, Jeff Diamond. The only reason I can see for Vanlandengham suggesting such a physical delivery would be to assure the accomplishment of a valid conveyance of the property at that time. But if the grantors intended that then why did they simply give it to the named grantee and tell him to record it? Why did they go through the delivery motion in the presence of Vanlandengham and then give the deed to the banker? Why did the banker write on the envelope containing the deed that it was to be given to either the grantee "or" a grantor? The fact that the grantors continued to occupy the land, paid taxes on it, offered to sell it once and otherwise treated it as their own justifies an inference that they did not make an actual delivery of the deed to the named grantee. Or, if they did, they directed that it be left in the custody of the banker with the intent of reserving a de facto life estate or of retaining a power of revocation by instructing the banker to return it to them if they requested it during their lifetimes or to give it to the named grantee upon their deaths. In either case, the deed failed as a valid conveyance.

I therefore join in affirming the trial court's judgment.

NOTES & QUESTIONS:

1. What was the intent of Uncle Harold? Was he trying to part with a future interest right away? Or was he intending for nothing to happen until his death and then at that time a fee simple absolute would transfer?

2. Should it matter what the bank's customs and practices are in determining Harold's intent?

3. Would the outcome be any different if Harold had given the deed directly to Jay without involving the bank?

4. What would happen if the condition were not about death but about payment of the purchase price? Seller drafts a deed conveying fee simple absolute ownership of Blackacre to Buyer. Seller gives deed to a third party escrow agent with verbal instructions to hold the deed until the sales proceeds are paid and then at that time the deed could be given to the buyer for recording. Is this oral condition with a third party valid? Yes, it is. A verbal condition in the grantee is not valid in most places and allows delivery of FSA. However, a verbal condition to a third party would be upheld. Buyer would have to pay the purchase price.

   What if the facts change and the seller gives the deed to Blackacre to buyer with the verbal condition that the sales price must be paid in one week? Buyer takes the deed and refuses to pay the purchase price when due. Do we apply the majority rule that there is a valid delivery of FSA in the buyer and we ignore the verbal condition? Not in this instance. Because this involves the purchase price being paid to the seller, the court will find an implied equitable vendor's lien in the delivery and the buyer will still be legally obligated to pay the purchase money to the seller. It is always best to have an express vendor's lien, but equity will help the seller this this situation.

5. During the 2015 legislative session, a new concept was added to the Texas Estates Code. Chapter 114 of the Estate Code now allows for a Transfer on Death Deed.[3] Section 114.051 provides that "an individual may transfer the individual's interest in real property to one or more beneficiaries effective at the transferor's death by a transfer on death deed." Additionally, unlike other deeds, § 114.052 states that a transfer on death deed is revocable and under § 114.053 is a nontestamentary instrument. In order to be effective, § 114.055 provides specific requirememnts. The deed must contain the essential elements and

---

[3] Tex. Estates Code §§ 114.001-114.152. Enacted by S.B. 462, § 1, 84th Leg., eff. Sept. 1, 2015. The statutes are taken from the Uniform Real Property Transfer on Death Act. Thirteen states have adopted the act. The states include: Missouri (1989), Kansas (1997), Ohio (2000), New Mexico (2001), Arizona (2002), Nevada (2003), Colorado (2004), Arkansas (2005), Wisconsin (2006), Montana (2007), Oklahoma (2008), Minnesota (2008), and Indiana (2009).

formalities of a recordable deed, it must state that the transfer to the beneficiary is to occur at the transferor's death, and it must be recorded before the transferor's death in the deed records of the county in which the real property is located. Additionally, under § 114.056, the deed is effective without notice or delivery to the beneficiary during the transferor's life or consideration.

Would this instrument have been helpful to the parties in *Rosengrant* or *Sweeney*?

B. Basic Real Estate Finance

1. Introduction to Real Estate Finance

In the typical real estate transaction, the buyer is not likely to pay in cash. This is where real estate finance comes into the equation. As we saw with the real estate contract, most buyers negotiate for a Third Party Finance Addendum, which gives the buyer a set amount of time to get financing in order to make sure that he will be approved for the amount agreed upon to purchase the property. The buyer will be looking for affordable repayment terms including a low interest rate and possibly a lengthy repayment period. The available financing arrangements have changed drastically since the 1980s.

Historically, if a buyer was looking to purchase a home, he would go to his local bank or savings and loan to seek approval for fixed-rate 20-year loan. The lender would go through all of the buyer's financial information with a fine-tooth comb. The buyer would have to provide bank statements, pay stubs, tax returns, and likely go through an in-person interview. After the lender's due diligence, the buyer would find out if he had approval for a loan that would require the buyer to put 20 percent of the purchase price down in cash. If everything went through, the buyer would receive the funds and enter into two different instruments with the lender. One document, the promissory note, established the personal obligation to pay the debt. The second document, the mortgage or deed of trust, established the security interest in the real property.

Once buyers had other options than locally owned banks and savings and loans, the process became a little different. No longer did a buyer enter into an agreement with a local lender that would manage the loan for its entirety. With federally backed mortgages made possible through Fannie Mae and Freddie Mac, a secondary market for mortgages was created. Even if a loan originated with a local bank, it could be sold on the market to another investor who would actually then own the note and take the security interest in the property. With the growth and success of this secondary market, different types of lenders came onto the scene. Buyers had to go through less process to obtain approval for a loan. Often there were no documentation, stated income loans being made. Repayments were extended from 20 and 30 years to 40 years. Then the negative amortization loan was born where a borrower would make payments at less than the amount of the interest accruing, which meant that the additional unpaid interest was being added to the principal balance. The balance of the loan actually increased over time rather than decreased. Adjustable Rate Mortgages (ARMs) also became popular and more risk occurred. Borrowers could get a lower interest rate initially, knowing that the rate would increase significantly. However, these loans were encouraged because the idea was that the borrower would refinance before the rate adjusted and it would all work out.

The problem is that it didn't all work out. It all fell apart. We went through the mortgage and housing crisis beginning in 2007 and are still feeling the effects today. Credit is tighter, federal regulations are more expansive, and foreclosures have soared. Thus, it is important to understand some basic components of real estate finance and the foreclosure process.

Real estate finance is a complex area that is also addressed in its own upper-level elective course. What we will focus on are the very basic issues involved in real estate finance that will guide us through the rest of our discussions such as foreclosure and the priority system. Keep in mind that what the lending institution is getting in exchange for the money loaned to the buyer is a nonpossessory interest in the property in the form of a lien. (This topic ties into the discussion in the concurrent ownership chapter regarding the mortgage as lien v. mortgage as title theories.) The property that is being purchased is the collateral or security for the loan. Failure to pay back the loan according to all of the terms of the financing documents can cause the buyer to lose the property through a foreclosure proceeding.

There are different foreclosure proceedings but there is overlap in the rules that apply. Our coverage will differentiate between the judicial and nonjudicial foreclosure proceedings, discuss the role of the trustee at a nonjudicial foreclosure, and how the lender must go through certain steps in compliance with the Texas Property Code, as well as the financing documents in the transaction, to ensure the validity of the sale.

Real estate foreclosures have been at a heightened level for years and so are mistakes by lenders in the haste to process so many foreclosures. It is imperative that a real estate attorney working in this area have a command of the applicable provisions to provide for an efficient and valid sale for the lender and a fair and valid sale for the debtor.

a. Financing Real Estate Transactions: Two Documents, Two Roles

The required financing documents include a promissory note for the personal promise to pay the loan. This document sets out the terms of the financing and conditions of default. It also dictates the time to cure any default that might occur and the consequences. The second document is the security instrument to be used to secure the particular piece of real property as collateral for the debt. The security instrument could be a mortgage or deed of trust. Both documents are used across the country. In Texas, the preferred document is the deed of trust. The deed of trust confers the private power of sale allowing for a nonjudicial foreclosure process. The deed of trust also sets forth the duties of the trustee in the event of a foreclosure and the resulting status of the borrowers following a foreclosure. A mortgage is the document typically used when there will be a judicial foreclosure. The mortgage still secures the property as collateral but any foreclosure will occur through a judicial process that will be administered by the sheriff or constable.

While the lending documents are contractual in nature, there is a large body of federal law that imposes requirements for the initial financing requirements. Additionally, even though the deed of trust, mortgage and note contain provisions regarding default, cure time, and other foreclosure issues, these documents cannot change the minimum requirements in the Texas Property Code provisions that govern the foreclosure process. However, it is possible for the Promissory Note and Deed of Trust to provide for more protection which they actually do quite often with respect to the time allowed to cure the default.

Samples of both the Promissory Note (taken from the Texas Real Estate Forms Manual) and Deed of Trust (standard Fannie Mae/Freddie Mac form) are set forth below. The Texas Property Code sections will follow with the statutory requirements of foreclosure.

Promissory Note

Date:

Borrower:

Borrower's Mailing Address: [include county]

Lender:

Place for Payment: [include county]

Principal Amount:

Annual Interest Rate:

Maturity Date:

Annual Interest Rate on Matured, Unpaid Amounts:

Terms of Payment (principal and interest):

Security for Payment:

Other Security for Payment:

Borrower promises to pay to the order of Lender the Principal Amount plus interest at the Annual Interest Rate. This note is payable at the Place for Payment and according to the Terms of Payment. All unpaid amounts are due by the Maturity Date. After maturity, Borrower promises to pay any unpaid principal balance plus interest at the Annual Interest Rate on Matured, Unpaid Amounts.

Notwithstanding any other provision of this note, in the event of a default, before exercising any of Lender's remedies under this note or any [deed of trust/security agreement/instrument] securing [include if applicable: or collateral to] it, Lender will first give Borrower written notice of default and Borrower will have thirty days after notice is given in which to cure the default. If the default is not cured thirty days after notice, Borrower and each surety, endorser, and guarantor waive all demand for payment, presentation for payment, notice of intention to accelerate maturity, notice of acceleration of maturity, protest, and notice of protest, to the extent permitted by law.

If Borrower defaults in the payment of this note or in the performance of any obligation in any instrument securing or collateral to this note, Lender may declare the unpaid principal balance, earned interest, and any other amounts owed on the note immediately due. Borrower and each surety, endorser, and guarantor waive all demand for payment, presentation for payment, notice of intention to accelerate maturity, notice of acceleration of maturity, protest, and notice of protest, to the extent permitted by law.

Borrower also promises to pay reasonable attorney's fees and court and other costs if this note is placed in the hands of an attorney to collect or enforce the note. These expenses will bear interest from the date of advance at the Annual Interest Rate on Matured, Unpaid Amounts. Borrower will pay Lender these expenses and interest on demand at the Place for Payment. These expenses and interest will become part of the debt evidenced by the note and will be secured by any security for payment.

Borrower may prepay this note in any amount at any time before the Maturity Date without penalty or premium.

OR

Borrower may not make any prepayments without the prior written consent of Lender.

If any installment becomes overdue for more than [number] days, at Lender's option a late payment charge of $[amount] may be charged in order to defray the expense of handling the delinquent payment.

Interest on the debt evidenced by this note will not exceed the maximum rate or amount of nonusurious interest that may be contracted for, taken, reserved, charged, or received under law. Any interest in excess of that maximum amount will be credited on the Principal Amount or, if the Principal Amount has been paid, refunded. On any acceleration or required or permitted prepayment, any excess interest will be canceled automatically as of the acceleration or prepayment or, if the excess interest has already been paid, credited on the Principal Amount or, if the Principal Amount has been paid, refunded. This provision overrides any conflicting provisions in this note and all other instruments concerning the debt.

Each Borrower is responsible for all obligations represented by this note.

When the context requires, singular nouns and pronouns include the plural.

[Name of borrower]

RESIDENTIAL DEED OF TRUST[4]

Notice of confidentiality rights: If you are a natural person, you may remove or strike any or all of the following information from any instrument that transfers an interest in real property before it is filed for record in the public records: your Social Security number or your driver's license number.

Date:

Grantor:
Grantor's Mailing Address (including county):

Trustee:

---

[4] Prepared by the State Bar of Texas for use by lawyers only. 1999, 2000, 2002, 2004, 2006, 2009 by the State Bar of Texas. Revised 06/09.

Trustee's Mailing Address (including county):

Lender:
Lender's Mailing Address (including county):

Obligation
Note(s)
Date:
Original principal amount:
Borrower:
Lender:
Maturity date:

Other Debt:

Property (including any improvements):

Prior Lien(s) (including recording information):

Other Exceptions to Conveyance and Warranty:
For value received and to secure payment of the Obligation, Grantor conveys the Property to Trustee in trust. Grantor warrants and agrees to defend the title to the Property, subject to the Other Exceptions to Conveyance and
Warranty. On payment of the Obligation and all other amounts secured by this deed of trust, this deed of trust will have no further effect, and Lender will release it at Grantor's expense.

Clauses and Covenants

A. Grantor's Obligations

Grantor agrees to—
1. keep the Property in good repair and condition;
2. pay all taxes and assessments on the Property before delinquency;
3. defend title to the Property subject to the Other Exceptions to Conveyance and Warranty and preserve the lien's priority as it is established in this deed of trust;
4. maintain all insurance coverages with respect to the Property, revenues generated by the Property, and operations on theProperty that Lender reasonably requires ("Required InsuranceCoverages"), issued by insurers and written on policy forms acceptable to Lender, and deliver evidence of the

Required Insurance Coverages in a form acceptable to Lender at least ten days before the expiration of the Required Insurance Coverages;

    5. obey all laws, ordinances, and restrictive covenants applicable to the Property;

    6. keep any buildings occupied as required by the Required Insurance Coverages;

    7. if the lien of this deed of trust is not a first lien, pay or cause to be paid all prior lien notes and abide by or cause to be abided by all prior lien instruments; and

    8. notify Lender of any change of address.

B. Lender's Rights

    1. Lender or Lender's mortgage servicer may appoint in writing a substitute trustee, succeeding to all rights and responsibilities of Trustee.

    2. If the proceeds of the Obligation are used to pay any debt secured by prior liens, Lender is subrogated to all the rights and liens of the holders of any debt so paid.

    3. Lender may apply any proceeds received under the property insurance policies covering the Property either to reduce the Obligation or to repair or replace damaged or destroyed improvements covered by the policy. If the Property is Grantor's primary residence and Lender reasonably determines that repairs to the improvements are economically feasible, Lender will make the insurance proceeds available to Grantor for repairs.

    4. Notwithstanding the terms of the Note to the contrary, and unless applicable law prohibits, all payments received by Lender from Grantor with respect to the Obligation or this deed of trust may, at Lender'sdiscretion, be applied first to amounts payable under this deed of trust and then to amounts due and payable to Lender with respect to the Obligation, to be applied to late charges, principal, or interest in the order Lender in its discretion determines.

    5. If Grantor fails to perform any of Grantor's obligations, Lender may perform those obligations and be reimbursed by Grantor on demand for any amounts so paid, including attorney's fees, plus interest on those amounts from the dates of payment at the rate stated in the Note for matured, unpaid amounts. The amount to be reimbursed will be secured by this deed of trust.

    6. If there is a default on the Obligation or if Grantor fails to perform any of Grantor's obligations and the default continues after any required notice of the default and the time allowed to cure, Lender may—

        a. declare the unpaid principal balance and earned interest on the Obligation immediately due;

        b. direct Trustee to foreclose this lien, in which case Lender or Lender's agent will cause notice of the foreclosure sale to be given as provided by the Texas Property Code as then in effect; and

c. purchase the Property at any foreclosure sale by offering the highest bid and then have the bid credited on the Obligation.

7. Lender may remedy any default without waiving it and may waive any default without waiving any prior or subsequent default.

C. Trustee's Rights and Duties

If directed by Lender to foreclose this lien, Trustee will—

1. either personally or by agent give notice of the foreclosure sale as required by the Texas Property Code as then in effect;

2. sell and convey all or part of the Property "AS IS" to the highest bidder for cash with a general warranty binding Grantor, subject to the Prior Lien and to the Other Exceptions to Conveyance and Warranty and without representation or warranty, express or implied, by Trustee;

3. from the proceeds of the sale, pay, in this order—

    a. expenses of foreclosure, including a reasonable commission to Trustee;

    b. to Lender, the full amount of principal, interest, attorney's fees, and other charges due and unpaid;

    c. any amounts required by law to be paid before payment to Grantor; and

    d. to Grantor, any balance; and

4. be indemnified, held harmless, and defended by Lender against all costs, expenses, and liabilities incurred by Trustee for acting in the execution or enforcement of the trust created by this deed of trust, which includes all court and other costs, including attorney's fees, incurred by Trustee in defense of any action or proceeding taken against Trustee in that capacity.

D. General Provisions

1. If any of the Property is sold under this deed of trust, Grantor must immediately surrender possession to the purchaser. If Grantor fails to do so, Grantor will become a tenant at sufferance of the purchaser, subject to an action for forcible detainer.

2. Recitals in any trustee's deed conveying the Property will be presumed to be true.

3. Proceeding under this deed of trust, filing suit for foreclosure, or pursuing any other remedy will not constitute an election of remedies.

4. This lien will remain superior to liens later created even if the time of payment of all or part of the Obligation is extended or part of the Property is released.

5. If any portion of the Obligation cannot be lawfully secured by this deed of trust, payments will be applied first to discharge that portion.

6. Grantor assigns to Lender all amounts payable to or received by Grantor from condemnation of all or part of the Property, from private sale in lieu of condemnation, and from damages caused by public works or construction on or near the Property. After deducting any expenses incurred, including attorney's fees and court and other costs, Lender will either release any remaining amounts to Grantor or apply such amounts to reduce the Obligation. Lender will not be liable for failure to collect or to exercise diligence in collecting any such amounts. Grantor will immediately give Lender notice of any actual or threatened proceedings for condemnation of all or part of the Property.

7. Grantor assigns to Lender absolutely, not only as collateral, all present and future rent and other income and receipts from the Property. Grantor warrants the validity and enforceability of the assignment. Grantor may as Lender's licensee collect rent and other income and receipts as long as Grantor is not in default with respect to the Obligation or this deed of trust. Grantor will apply all rent and other income and receipts to payment of the Obligation and performance of this deed of trust, but if the rent and other income and receipts exceed the amount due with respect to the Obligation and deed of trust, Grantor may retain the excess. If Grantor defaults in payment of the Obligation or performance of this deed of trust, Lender may terminate Grantor's license to collect rent and other income and then as Grantor's agent may rent the Property and collect all rent and other income and receipts. Lender neither has nor assumes any obligations as lessor or landlord with respect to any occupant of the Property. Lender may exercise Lender's rights and remedies under this paragraph without taking possession of the Property. Lender will apply all rent and other income and receipts collected under this paragraph first to expenses incurred in exercising Lender's rights and remedies and then to Grantor's obligations with respect to the Obligation and this deed of trust in the order determined by Lender. Lender is not required to act under this paragraph, and acting under this paragraph does not waive any of Lender's other rights or remedies. If Grantor becomes a voluntary or involuntary debtor in bankruptcy, Lender's filing a proof of claim in bankruptcy will be deemed equivalent to the appointment of a receiver under Texas law.

8. Interest on the debt secured by this deed of trust will not exceed the maximum amount of nonusurious interest that may be contracted for, taken, reserved, charged, or received under law. Any interest in excess of that maximum amount will be credited on the principal of the debt or, if that has been paid, refunded. On any acceleration or required or permitted prepayment, any such excess will be canceled automatically as of the acceleration or prepayment or, if already paid, credited on the principal of the debt or, if the principal of the debt has been paid, refunded. This provision overrides any conflicting provisions in this and all other instruments concerning the debt.

9. In no event may this deed of trust secure payment of any debt that may not lawfully be secured by a lien on real estate or create a lien otherwise prohibited by law.

10. If Grantor transfers any part of the Property without Lender's prior written consent, Lender may declare the Obligation immediately payable and invoke any remedies provided in this deed of trust for default. If the Property is residential real property containing fewer than five dwelling units or a residential manufactured home, this provision does not apply to

a. a subordinate lien or encumbrance that does not transfer rights of occupancy of the Property;

b. creation of a purchase-money security interest for household appliances;

c. transfer by devise, descent, or operation of law on the death of a co-Grantor;

d. grant of a leasehold interest of three years or less without an option to purchase;

e. transfer to a spouse or children of Grantor or between co-Grantors;

f. transfer to a relative of Grantor on Grantor's death;

g. a transfer resulting from a decree of a dissolution of marriage, a legal separation agreement, or an incidental property settlement agreement by which the spouse of Grantor becomes an owner of the Property; or

h. transfer to an inter vivos trust in which Grantor is and remains a beneficiary and occupant of the Property.

11. When the context requires, singular nouns and pronouns include the plural.

12. The term Note includes all extensions, modifications, and renewals of the Note and all amounts secured by this deed of trust.

13. This deed of trust binds, benefits, and may be enforced by the successors in interest of all parties.

14. If Grantor and Borrower are not the same person, the term Grantor includes Borrower.

15. Grantor and each surety, endorser, and guarantor of the Obligation waive all demand for payment, presentation for payment, notice of intention to accelerate maturity, notice of acceleration of maturity, protest, and notice of protest, to the extent permitted by law.

16. Grantor agrees to pay reasonable attorney's fees, trustee's fees, and court and other costs of enforcing Lender's rights under this deed of trust if this deed of trust is placed in the hands of an attorney for enforcement.

17. If any provision of this deed of trust is determined to be invalid or unenforceable, the validity or enforceability of any other provision will not be affected.

18. The term "Lender" includes any mortgage servicer for Lender.

19. Grantor represents that this deed of trust and the Note are given for the following purposes:

_____

Signature of Grantors

(Acknowledgment by Notary Public)

AFTER RECORDING RETURN TO: _____

PREPARED IN THE LAW OFFICE OF: _____

The note and deed of trust are going to be essential components to the discussion of foreclosure. If things don't go as planned, the lender will want to take the land in satisfaction of the debt. Essentially what will occur is a forced conveyance of the land from the owner/debtor to the lender or some third party.

b. Foreclosure Process

Once the borrower is in default (which can include more than just nonpayment of the debt), the foreclosure process begins. The rationale for foreclosure comes from historical roots once again. The mortgage began as a transfer of title from the debtor to the lender with a condition subsequent for the debtor to get the land back after the debt was repaid. [5] The lender (mortgagee) would take possession of the property and the mortgage was paid from proceeds obtained from the land. Eventually around the 16th century the relationship changed so that the mortgage was viewed as simply a security for the debt rather than a transfer of any title to the land. However, some harsh consequences came about. For example, if the borrower was supposed to repay the debt by a certain date and that did not happen, the borrower lost the property forever.[6]

The chancellors in the courts of equity began extending the time, essentially rewriting terms of the contract. The additional time helped the borrower to not lose land that likely had equity, but it also left the lender without much recourse if the debt was not being paid. The courts of equity started imposing a time limit within which the borrower could redeem the property through its equity of redemption. This was an equitable concept to help prevent a foreclosure. If the foreclosure were allowed to proceed, that process would then cut off the equity

---

[5] *See* Joseph William Singer, Introduction to Property § 11.5 (2d ed. 2005).
[6] *Id.*

of redemption.[7] This was a strict foreclosure that would allow the debtor to automatically lose the property on a certain date. This eventually changed to require a foreclosure sale due to unfairness in the process.

Every state currently allows the judicial foreclosure sale process and that is the only process allowed in approximately half of the states.[8] The other states, Texas included, allow for both judicial and nonjudicial foreclosure sale proceedings. After a valid sale, whether judicial or nonjudicial, there are some postsale considerations as well. If the property sold for less than the debt owed, some states allow the lender to pursue a deficiency judgment.[9] Additionally, some states also provide a statutory right of redemption after the sale occurs. This means that in some states, even if the sale was conducted properly and is completely valid, by statute the debtor is given a set time period within which he can repurchase the property. Be sure to keep the concepts of equity of redemption and statutory right of redemption separate. The equity of redemption allows the debtor to prevent the foreclosure, while the statutory right of redemption allows the debtor to regain the property after foreclosure.[10]

i. Notice of Default with Time to Cure

Regardless of the process used, judicial or nonjudicial, the first step will be providing notice of default with time to cure. Under Texas Property Code § 51.001(d),

> Notwithstanding any agreement to the contrary, the mortgage servicer of the debt shall serve a debtor in default under a deed of trust or other contract lien on real property used as the debtor's residence with written notice by certified mail stating that the debtor is in default under the deed of trust or other contract lien and giving the debtor at least 20 days to cure the default before notice of sale can be given under Subsection (b). The entire calendar day on which the notice required by this subsection is given, regardless of the time of day at which the notice is given, is included in computing the 20-day notice period required by this subsection, and the entire calendar day on which

---

[7] Thompson on Real Property, Thomas Edition § 101.01(a) (David A. Thomas ed. 1994).

[8] *Id*. at § 101.01(b).

[9] Texas has deficiency judgment states in the Texas Property Code. We will address this basic concept in a little more detail after covering the sales process.

[10] Texas does not recognize the statutory right of redemption in the context of a foreclosure for a deed of trust or mortgage. There are limited situations involving property taxes and HOA liens that allow a statutory right of redemption.

notice of sale is given under Subsection (b) is excluded in computing the 20-day notice period.

No actual notice of default is required. Once the notice is placed in the mail to the debtor at his last address on file with the lender, the lender is deemed to have complied with this requirement.

If the default is not cured within the time allowed, then the lender will decide whether to proceed with a judicial or nonjudicial foreclosure. If there will be a judicial foreclosure a lawsuit will be filed to collect on the debt and the relief requested with be a judgment on the debt as well as an order of foreclosure. If there will be a nonjudicial foreclosure, then the lender simply sends a second notice.

ii. Notice of Sale

If the debtor does not cure during the time allowed, the lender must send a second notice. This is the notice of sale. It will inform the debtor that the entire debt has been accelerated and a sale of the property will take place. This notice of sale has particular content and distribution requirements. Under § 51.002 (a), (b), and (c),[11]

The contents of the notice must inform the debtor of the date of the sale which must be at least 21 days after the date of the notice, the earliest time that the sale will begin (and it must not begin later than three hours after the earliest time), and the location of the sale if no area is designated by the commissioners court. The notice would need to designate the area where the sale covered by that notice is to take place, and the sale must occur in that area.

The notice of sale must be:
(1) posted at the courthouse door of each county in which the property is located a written notice designating the county in which the property will be sold;
(2) filed in the office of the county clerk of each county in which the property is located a copy of the notice posted under Subdivision (1) and also making the notice available on the county clerk's website if one is

---

[11] Tex. Prop. Code § 51.002. Sale of Real Property Under Contract Lien

maintained and available for free access to the public; and

(3) served by certified mail on each debtor who, according to the records of the mortgage servicer of the debt, is obligated to pay the debt.

Service of a notice under this section by certified mail is complete when the notice is deposited in the United States mail, postage prepaid and addressed to the debtor at the debtor's last known address.

As of September 1, 2015, the Texas legislature also added some additional requirements regarding recordation of documents in the foreclosure process. In addition to providing notice to parties in a certain manner, newly enacted section 12.0012 now requires the county clerk to record certain instruments related to the foreclosure process.[12] An instrument that appoints or authorizes a trustee or substitute trustee to exercise the power of sale, a notice of sale for a n on-judicial foreclosure, a notice of default on which the sale occurred and a trustee's deed was issued, a document from the US Department of Defense indicating the debtor was not on active duty military service on the date of the sale, a statement of facts regarding a foreclosure sale or proof of service of the mailing of any foreclosure notice. In order to properly record these documents they must be attached as an exhibit to (1) a trusee or substitute trustee's deed, or (2) and affidavit of a trustee or substitute trustee related to the foreclosure sale.

iii.   Proper Date, Time, and Location of Sale

Under § 51.002(a), sale of real property under a power of sale conferred by a deed of trust or other contract lien must be a public sale at auction held between 10 a.m. and 4 p.m. of the first Tuesday of a month. As amended in 2017, if the first Tuesday of the month is January 1 or July 4, the public sale auction will be held between 10 a.m. and 4 p.m. on the first Wedenesday of the month. Except as provided by Subsection (h), the sale must take place at the county courthouse in the county in which the land is located, or if the property is located in more than one county, the sale may be made at the courthouse in any county in which the property is located. The commissioners court shall designate the area at the courthouse where the sales are to take place and shall record the designation in the real property records of the county. The sale must occur in the designated area. If no area is designated by the commissioners court, the notice

---

[12] Tex. Prop. Code § 12.0012. Instruments Concerning Real Property Subject to a Foreclosure Sale. Enacted by H.B. 2063, § 1, 84th Leg., eff. Sept. 1, 2015.

of sale must designate the area where the sale covered by that notice is to take place, and the sale must occur in that area.

The case below involves a nonjudicial foreclosure process in New Hampshire. As you read the *Murphy* case, consider what is different in this case from what is required under Texas law.

Murphy v. Fin. Dev. Corp.
Supreme Court of New Hampshire, 1985
495 A.2d 1245

DOUGLAS, J.

The plaintiffs brought this action seeking to set aside the foreclosure sale of their home, or, in the alternative, money damages. The Superior Court entered a judgment for the plaintiffs in the amount of $27,000 against two of the defendants, Financial Development Corporation and Colonial Deposit Company (the lenders).

The plaintiffs purchased a house in Nashua in 1966, financing it by means of a mortgage loan. They refinanced the loan in March of 1980, executing a new promissory note and a power of sale mortgage, with Financial Development Corporation as mortgagee. The note and mortgage were later assigned to Colonial Deposit Company.

In February of 1981, the plaintiff Richard Murphy became unemployed. By September of 1981, the plaintiffs were seven months in arrears on their mortgage payments, and had also failed to pay substantial amounts in utility assessments and real estate taxes. After discussing unsuccessfully with the plaintiffs proposals for revising the payment schedule, rewriting the note, and arranging alternative financing, the lenders gave notice on October 6, 1981, of their intent to foreclose.

During the following weeks, the plaintiffs made a concerted effort to avoid foreclosure. They paid the seven months' mortgage arrearage, but failed to pay some $643.18 in costs and legal fees associated with the foreclosure proceedings. The lenders scheduled the foreclosure sale for November 10, 1981, at the site of the subject property. They complied with all of the statutory requirements for notice.

At the plaintiffs' request, the lenders agreed to postpone the sale until December 15, 1981. They advised the plaintiffs that this would entail an additional cost of $100, and that the sale would proceed unless the lenders received payment of $743.18, as well as all mortgage payments then due, by December 15. Notice of the postponement was posted on the subject property on November 10 at the originally scheduled time of the sale, and was also posted at the Nashua City Hall and Post Office. No prospective bidders were present for the scheduled sale.

In late November, the plaintiffs paid the mortgage payment which had been due in October, but made no further payments to the lenders. An attempt by the lenders to arrange new financing for the plaintiffs through a third party failed when the plaintiffs refused to agree to pay for a new appraisal of the property. Early on the morning of December 15, 1981, the plaintiffs tried to obtain a further postponement, but were advised by the lenders' attorney that it was impossible unless the costs and legal fees were paid.

At the plaintiffs' request, the attorney called the president of Financial Development Corporation, who also refused to postpone the sale. Further calls by the plaintiffs to the lenders' offices were equally unavailing.

The sale proceeded as scheduled at 10:00 a.m. on December 15, at the site of the property. Although it had snowed the previous night, the weather was clear and warm at the time of the sale, and the roads were clear. The only parties present were the plaintiffs, a representative of the lenders, and an attorney, Morgan Hollis, who had been engaged to conduct the sale because the lenders' attorney, who lived in Dover, had been apprehensive about the weather the night before. The lenders' representative made the only bid at the sale. That bid of $27,000, roughly the amount owed on the mortgage, plus costs and fees, was accepted and the sale concluded.

Later that same day, Attorney Hollis encountered one of his clients, William Dube, a representative of the defendant Southern New Hampshire Home Traders, Inc. (Southern). On being informed of the sale, Mr. Dube contacted the lenders and offered to buy the property for $27,000. The lenders rejected the offer and made a counter offer of $40,000. Within two days a purchase price of $38,000 was agreed upon by Mr. Dube and the lenders and the sale was subsequently completed.

The plaintiffs commenced this action on February 5, 1982. The lenders moved to dismiss, arguing that any action was barred because the plaintiffs had failed to petition for an injunction prior to the sale. The master denied the motion. After hearing the evidence, he ruled for the plaintiffs, finding that the lenders had "failed to exercise good faith and due diligence in obtaining a fair price for the subject property at the foreclosure sale. . . ."

The master also ruled that Southern was a bona fide purchaser for value, and thus had acquired legal title to the house. That ruling is not at issue here. He assessed monetary damages against the lenders equal to "the difference between the fair market value of the subject property on the date of the foreclosure and the price obtained at said sale."

Having found the fair market value to be $54,000, he assessed damages accordingly at $27,000. He further ruled that "[t]he bad faith of the 'Lenders' warrants an award of legal fees." The lenders appealed.

The issue before us is whether the master erred in concluding that the lenders had failed to comply with the often-repeated rule that a mortgagee executing a power of sale is bound both by the statutory procedural requirements and by a duty to protect the interests of the mortgagor through the exercise of good faith and due diligence. We will not overturn a master's findings and rulings "unless they are unsupported by the evidence or are erroneous as a matter of law." Summit Electric, Inc. v. Pepin Brothers Const., Inc., 121 N.H. 203, 206, 427 A.2d 505, 507 (1981).

The master found that the lenders, throughout the time prior to the sale, "did not mislead or deal unfairly with the plaintiffs." They engaged in serious efforts to avoid foreclosure through new financing, and agreed to one postponement of the sale. The basis for the master's decision was his conclusion that the lenders had failed to exercise good faith and due diligence in obtaining a fair price for the property.

The court's past decisions have not dealt consistently with the question whether the mortgagee's duty amounts to that of a fiduciary or trustee. This may be an inevitable result of the mortgagee's dual role as seller and potential buyer at the foreclosure sale, and of the conflicting interests involved.

We need not label a duty, however, in order to define it. In his role as a seller, the mortgagee's duty of good faith and due diligence is essentially that of a fiduciary.

A mortgagee, therefore, must exert every reasonable effort to obtain "a fair and reasonable price under the circumstances," even to the extent, if necessary, of adjourning the sale or of establishing "an upset price below which he will not accept any offer." Lakes Region Fin. Corp. v. Goodhue Boat Yard, Inc., 118 N.H. at 107, 382 A.2d at 1111.

What constitutes a fair price, or whether the mortgagee must establish an upset price, adjourn the sale, or make other reasonable efforts to assure a fair price, depends on the circumstances of each case. Inadequacy of price alone is not sufficient to demonstrate bad faith unless the price is so low as to shock the judicial conscience.

We must decide, in the present case, whether the evidence supports the finding of the master that the lenders failed to exercise good faith and due diligence in obtaining a fair price for the plaintiffs' property.

We first note that "[t]he duties of good faith and due diligence are distinct. . . . One may be observed and not the other, and any inquiry as to their breach calls for a separate consideration of each." Wheeler v. Slocinski, 82 N.H. at 213, 131 A. at 600. In order "to constitute bad faith there must be an intentional disregard of duty or a purpose to injure." *Id.* at 214, 131 A. at 600–01.

There is insufficient evidence in the record to support the master's finding that the lenders acted in bad faith in failing to obtain a fair price for the plaintiffs' property. The lenders complied with the statutory requirements of notice and otherwise conducted the sale in compliance with statutory provisions. The lenders postponed the sale one time and did not bid with knowledge of any immediately available subsequent purchaser. Further, there is no evidence indicating an intent on the part of the lenders to injure the mortgagor by, for example, discouraging other buyers.

There is ample evidence in the record, however, to support the master's finding that the lenders failed to exercise due diligence in obtaining a fair price. "The issue of the lack of due diligence is whether a reasonable man in the [lenders'] place would have adjourned the sale," *id.* at 215, 131 A. at 601, or taken other measures to receive a fair price.

In early 1980, the plaintiffs' home was appraised at $46,000. At the time of the foreclosure sale on December 15, 1981, the lenders had not had the house reappraised to take into account improvements and appreciation. The master found that a reasonable person in the place of the lenders would have realized that the plaintiffs' equity in the property was at least $19,000, the difference between the 1980 appraised value of $46,000 and the amount owed on the mortgage totaling approximately $27,000.

At the foreclosure sale, the lenders were the only bidders. The master found that their bid of $27,000 "was sufficient to cover all monies due and did not create a deficiency balance" but "did not provide for a return of any of the plaintiffs' equity."

Further, the master found that the lenders "had reason to know" that "they stood to make a substantial profit on a quick turnaround sale." On the day of the sale, the lenders offered to sell the foreclosed property to William Dube for $40,000. Within two days after the foreclosure sale, they did in fact agree to sell it to Dube for $38,000. It was not necessary for the master to find that the lenders knew of a specific potential buyer before the sale in order to show lack of good faith or due diligence as the lenders contend. The fact that the lenders offered the property for sale at a price sizably above that for which they had purchased it, only a few hours before, supports the master's finding that the lenders had reason to know, at the time of the foreclosure sale, that they could make a substantial profit on a quick turnaround sale. For this reason, they should have taken more measures to ensure receiving a higher price at the sale.

While a mortgagee may not always be required to secure a portion of the mortgagor's equity, such an obligation did exist in this case. The substantial amount of equity which the plaintiffs had in their property, the knowledge of the lenders as to the appraised value of the property, and the plaintiffs' efforts to forestall foreclosure by paying the mortgage arrearage within weeks of the sale, all support the master's conclusion that the lenders had a fiduciary duty to take more reasonable steps than they did to protect the plaintiffs' equity by attempting to obtain a fair price for the property. They could have established an appropriate upset price to assure a minimum bid. They also could have postponed the auction and advertised commercially by display advertising in order to assure that bidders other than themselves would be present.

Instead, as Theodore DiStefano, an officer of both lending institutions testified, the lenders made no attempt to obtain fair market value for the property but were concerned only with making themselves "whole." On the facts of this case, such disregard for the interests of the mortgagors was a breach of duty by the mortgagees.

Although the lenders did comply with the statutory requirements of notice of the foreclosure sale, these efforts were not sufficient in this case to demonstrate due diligence. At the time of the initially scheduled sale, the extent of the lenders' efforts to publicize the sale of the property was publication of a legal notice of the mortgagees' sale at public auction on November 10, published once a week for three weeks in the *Nashua Telegraph*, plus postings in public places. The lenders did not advertise, publish, or otherwise give notice to the general public of postponement of the sale to December 15, 1981, other than by posting notices at the plaintiffs' house, at the post office, and at city hall. That these efforts to advertise were ineffective is evidenced by the fact that no one, other than the lenders, appeared at the sale to bid on the property. This fact allowed the lenders to purchase the property at a minimal price and then to profit substantially in a quick turnaround sale.

We recognize a need to give guidance to a trial court which must determine whether a mortgagee who has complied with the strict letter of the statutory law has nevertheless violated his additional duties of good faith and due diligence. A finding that the mortgagee had, or should have had, knowledge of his ability to get a higher price at an adjourned sale is the most conclusive evidence of such a violation.

More generally, we are in agreement with the official Commissioners' Comment to section 3–508 of the Uniform Land Transactions Act:

> The requirement that the sale be conducted in a reasonable manner, including the advertising aspects, requires that the person conducting the sale use the ordinary methods of making buyers aware that are used when an owner is voluntarily selling his land. Thus an advertisement in the portion of a daily newspaper where these ads are placed or, in appropriate cases such as the sale of an industrial plant, a display advertisement in the financial sections of the daily newspaper may be the most reasonable method. In other cases employment of a professional real estate agent may be the more reasonable method. It is unlikely that an advertisement in a legal publication among other legal notices would qualify as a commercially reasonable method of sale advertising. [13 Uniform Laws Annotated 704 (West 1980).]

As discussed above, the lenders met neither of these guidelines.

While agreeing with the master that the lenders failed to exercise due diligence in this case, we find that he erred as a matter of law in awarding damages equal to "the difference between the fair market value of the subject property . . . and the price obtained at [the] sale."

Such a formula may well be the appropriate measure where bad faith is found. In such a case, a mortgagee's conduct amounts to more than mere negligence. Damages based upon the fair market value, a figure in excess of a fair price, will more readily induce mortgagees to perform their duties properly. A "fair" price may or may not yield a figure close to fair market value; however, it will be that price arrived at as a result of due diligence by the mortgagee.

Where, as here, however, a mortgagee fails to exercise due diligence, the proper assessment of damages is the difference between a fair price for the property and the price obtained at the foreclosure sale. We have held, where lack of due diligence has been found, that "the test is not 'fair market value' as in eminent domain cases nor is the mortgagee bound to give credit for the highest possible amount which might be obtained under different circumstances, as at an owner's sale." Silver v. First National Bank, 108 N.H. 390, 392, 236 A.2d 493, 495 (1967) (citation omitted). Accordingly, we remand to the trial court for a reassessment of damages consistent with this opinion.

Because we concluded above that there was no "bad faith or obstinate, unjust, vexatious, wanton, or oppressive conduct," on the part of the lenders, we see no reason to stray from our general rule that the prevailing litigant is not entitled to collect attorney's fees from the loser. Harkeem v. Adams, 117 N.H. 687, 688, 377 A.2d 617, 617 (1977).

Therefore, we reverse this part of the master's decision.

Reversed in part; affirmed in part; remanded.

First State Bank v. Keilman
Court of Appeals of Texas, Austin, 1993
851 S.W.2d 914

JONES, Justice.

The opinion and judgment issued herein by this Court on December 23, 1992, are withdrawn, and this opinion is filed in lieu of the earlier one.

Background

On November 1, 1985, the Keilmans executed a promissory note payable to Frontier National Bank ("Frontier") in the principal amount of $157,000. The note obligated the Keilmans to pay interest at a rate equal to the lesser of the maximum lawful rate or Frontier's prime rate plus two percent per annum. The note was secured by a deed-of-trust lien on 563 acres of land located in Terrell County, Texas (the "property"), which had been purchased by the Keilmans in 1983. As additional security, the Keilmans pledged a $150,000 note receivable dated October 1, 1985. The Keilmans renewed and extended this loan several times. In the final renewal note, executed on August 11, 1986, the Keilmans promised to pay $152,000 plus interest.

In October 1988 the FDIC closed Frontier, and FSB purchased the Keilmans' renewal note from the receivership estate.

By March 1989 the Keilmans were in default. On April 25, 1989, FSB's attorney, Janice McKennon, formally notified the Keilmans by letter that they were in default and demanded payment of all past due sums. On May 15, 1989, McKennon informed the Keilmans by letter that FSB had accelerated their indebtedness and scheduled a trustee's sale of the property securing the loan for June 6, 1989, at the Terrell County courthouse.

On behalf of FSB, McKennon hired Terrell County Attorney Marsha Monroe to conduct the foreclosure sale and to bid on the property on behalf of FSB. FSB appointed Monroe as the substitute trustee under the deed of trust. Monroe filed the appointment of substitute trustee and the notice of sale with the Terrell County Clerk and posted the notice of sale on the courthouse bulletin board. Before the proposed foreclosure date, FSB obtained an appraisal that placed the value of the property at $16,462.20. Based on this appraisal, FSB calculated a bid price, and McKennon conveyed the proposed bid to Monroe.

A few days before the scheduled sale, Mr. Keilman spoke with Roy Touchstone, a loan officer at FSB, who said the foreclosure sale would proceed as planned. Touchstone also told Keilman of the appraisal received by FSB. Keilman strongly disagreed with the appraised value and began efforts to borrow money in order to bid against FSB at the foreclosure sale.

On June 6, 1989, Mr. Keilman and a companion, Carl Bierman, drove to Terrell County to attend the foreclosure sale, which was to occur on the courthouse steps between 10:00 a.m. and 1:00 p.m. Shortly before 10:30 a.m., Keilman decided to go to the local newspaper office to see if the sale had been advertised in the newspaper. Before leaving the courthouse, Keilman authorized Bierman to bid up to $16,000 for the property. Shortly after Keilman left, Monroe appeared on the courthouse steps to begin the sale. Bierman asked Monroe to wait until Keilman returned; however, Monroe refused and began the sale in Keilman's absence. Apparently having misunderstood Keilman's instructions, Bierman believed he was authorized to bid only up to $13,000. As a result, he stopped bidding when the price reached $13,000. Monroe sold the property to FSB for $13,200.

FSB credited the entire $13,200 toward the Keilmans' indebtedness on the renewal note. Touchstone then contacted the Keilmans by letter requesting a meeting in order to discuss a payment plan for the deficiency remaining on the note. After receiving no response, FSB filed suit to collect on the deficiency. The Keilmans counterclaimed, alleging that FSB materially altered the promissory note, wrongfully foreclosed on the property, and committed usury.

The jury found that FSB altered the note without the Keilmans' consent, wrongfully foreclosed on the property, committed usury, and engaged in a conspiracy with the substitute trustee to injure the Keilmans. The jury also found that the unpaid principal balance on the note was $40,000 and the accrued but unpaid interest was $18,000. Based on these findings, the trial court awarded the Keilmans $293,000 in statutory usury penalties, $18,200 in actual damages, $97,000 in exemplary damages, and $68,500 in attorney's fees; the trial court also rendered judgment that the note was void and that FSB take nothing on its deficiency claim.

On appeal, FSB asserts fifteen points of error. We will group the points of error and address each in the order of the following categories: (1) Material Alteration; (2) Wrongful Foreclosure; (3) Usury; (4) Attorney's Fees; and (5) FSB's Deficiency Claim.

Wrongful Foreclosure

In points of error eight through thirteen, FSB complains that the trial court erred in rendering judgment and awarding damages based on the jury's findings that FSB wrongfully foreclosed on the property. The Keilmans' wrongful foreclosure claim was based on three theories: (1) common-law wrongful foreclosure, (2) conspiracy, and (3) violation of the unconscionability provisions of the Deceptive Trade Practices Act (DTPA), Tex. Bus. & Com. Code Ann. § 17.45(5) (West 1987). We will discuss each theory separately. (NOTE: This edited version only discusses the common law wrongful foreclosure claim.)

1. Common Law Wrongful Foreclosure

In point of error eight, FSB complains that the evidence is legally and factually insufficient to support any finding that FSB wrongfully foreclosed on the property. We agree. The Keilmans asserted at trial that FSB "chilled the bidding," *i.e.*, took affirmative steps to adversely affect the sale price, at the foreclosure. Under Texas law, if a "defect" or "irregularity" occurs in the foreclosure process which deters third parties from bidding, then a debtor has a claim against the mortgagee for damages resulting from the "unfair" sale. Pentad Joint Venture v. First Nat'l Bank, 797 S.W.2d 92, 96 (Tex. App.—Austin 1990, writ denied). Mere inadequacy of consideration alone, however, does not render a foreclosure sale void if the sale was otherwise conducted legally and fairly. Tarrant Sav. Ass'n v. Lucky Homes, Inc., 390 S.W.2d 473, 475 (Tex. 1965).

A mortgagee's duty is to avoid affirmatively deterring prospective bidders by acts or statements made before or during a foreclosure sale. Pentad Joint Venture, 797 S.W.2d at 96. However, "a mortgagee is under *no duty* to take affirmative action, beyond that required by statute or the deed of trust, to ensure a 'fair' sale." *Id.* (emphasis added). In other words, a debtor may recover damages for common-law wrongful foreclosure only if the mortgagee either (1) fails to comply with statutory or contractual terms, or (2) complies with such terms, yet takes affirmative action that detrimentally affects the fairness of the foreclosure process.

The Keilmans assert four alleged irregularities as support for the jury's finding of wrongful foreclosure: (1) FSB failed to advertise the foreclosure sale in the manner required by the deed of trust; (2) FSB failed to sufficiently inform prospective bidders regarding the foreclosure sale; (3) the trustee failed to delay the sale until Mr. Keilman was present; and (4) FSB included statements in the notice of sale that conflicted with the terms of the deed of trust and misled prospective bidders.

a. Failure to Advertise

The deed of trust contained the following clause:

> [A]fter advertising the time, place and terms of the sale of the above described and conveyed property, then subject to the lien hereof, and mailing and filing notices as required by section 51.002, Texas Property Code, as then amended (successor to article 3810, Texas Revised Civil Statutes), and otherwise complying with that statute, the Trustee shall sell the above described property. (Emphasis added.)

The Keilmans do not contend that FSB failed to comply with the provisions of section 51.002; rather, they assert that FSB's posting of the notice at the county courthouse announcing the time, place, and terms of the upcoming public auction of the mortgaged property was insufficient to satisfy the requirement in the deed of trust that the sale be "advertised." The Keilmans argue that the foregoing deed of trust provision specifically required FSB to advertise the sale by means other than posting, such as advertising in a local newspaper. We disagree.

If the language of a contract is unambiguous, then a court will construe the contractual language as a matter of law. Coker v. Coker, 650 S.W.2d 391, 393 (Tex. 1983). Whether the language of a contract is ambiguous is itself a question of law for the court to decide by looking at the contract as a whole in light of the circumstances present when the contract was made. *Id.* at 394.

The Texas Supreme Court has adopted the following broad definition of "advertise" from Black's Law Dictionary (5th ed. 1979):

> To advise, announce, apprise, command, give notice of, inform, make known, publish. On [sic] call to the public attention

by any means whatsoever. Any oral, written, or graphic statement made by the seller in any manner in connection with the solicitation of business and includes, without limitation because of enumeration, statements and representations made in a newspaper or other publication or on radio or television or contained in any notice, handbill, sign catalog, or letter. . . . Smith v. Baldwin, 611 S.W.2d 611, 614-15 (Tex. 1980).

Even though the term "advertise" is very broad, we are not convinced that it is ambiguous in the present case. While the *manner* of advertising is not prescribed in the Keilmans' deed of trust, there is no indication in the record that the parties intended the term to be read in a narrow sense. Specifically, there is no evidence that FSB obligated itself to engage in one type of advertising over another. Therefore, the record does not support the Keilmans' bare assertion that a newspaper ad or similar advertisement was required. The intent of the parties must be taken from the agreement itself, not from the parties' present interpretation. First City Nat'l Bank v. Concord Oil Co., 808 S.W.2d 133, 137 (Tex. App.—El Paso 1991, no writ).

We conclude that, as used in the present circumstances, the term "advertise" is unambiguous and must be construed broadly. Under such construction, the term clearly includes the posting of notices in public places. Thus, by posting a notice of the upcoming sale at the Terrell County courthouse, FSB complied with the "advertising" requirement of the deed of trust. Because a mortgagee is under no duty to take affirmative action beyond that required by statute or deed of trust to ensure a "fair" sale, we conclude as a matter of law that FSB's advertisement of the foreclosure sale by posting a public notice at the courthouse instead of by other means, such as placing an ad in a local newspaper does not constitute a defect or irregularity that would give rise to a claim for damages.

b. Failure to Sufficiently Inform Prospective Bidders

FSB provided information regarding the foreclosure sale to prospective bidders by posting the notice of sale at the courthouse. The Keilmans do not contend that information provided in the notice of sale failed to comply with statutory requirements or the terms of the deed of trust; rather, they assert that the information provided failed to sufficiently inform prospective bidders and, therefore, unfairly "chilled the bidding."

The Keilmans claimed that the notice provided only a legal description rather than a street address; that neither the notice nor any other foreclosure document indicated that FSB was the proper seller; and that the notice obscured sources of possible information because it did not disclose the address or phone number of FSB or the trustee. Despite the truth of these claims, the notice was sufficient under Texas law. *See* Hutson v. Sadler, 501 S.W.2d 728, 731-32 (Tex. Civ. App.—

Tyler 1973, no writ) (notice was sufficient even though posted notice erroneously identified owner and holder of the note); FDIC v. Myers, 955 F.2d 348, 350 (5th Cir. 1992) (under Texas law, posted notice sufficient despite its failure to advertise specific time of sale, the nature of the property being sold, the identity of the lender, the address and telephone number of the trustee, and other potential information which would have enabled potential buyers to learn about the property); *see also* Stone v. Watt, 81 S.W.2d 552, 555 (Tex. Civ. App.—Eastland 1935, writ ref'd); Mortimer v. Williams, 262 S.W. 123, 125 (Tex. Civ. App.—Dallas 1924, no writ).

The Keilmans also presented evidence at trial that the notice of sale was tacked on a cluttered bulletin board, ending up underneath other papers. Although such is the state of many county courthouse bulletin boards, "[i]f the notices are actually posted the required number of days prior to the sale, it is not essential that they remain intact and visible during every one of the intervening days." Chambers v. Lee, 566 S.W.2d 69, 73 (Tex. Civ. App.—Texarkana 1978, no writ).

The notice of sale was sufficient under Texas law and the deed of trust imposed no additional requirements on the mortgagee. Because a mortgagee is under no duty to take affirmative action beyond that required by statute or deed of trust to ensure a fair sale, we conclude as a matter of law that the failure to place additional information in the notice does not constitute a defect or irregularity that would give rise to a claim for damages.

c. Foreclosure Sale in Debtor's Absence

Mr. Keilman testified that, after waiting for Monroe to appear and begin the foreclosure sale, he went to the local newspaper office to determine if the sale had been advertised there; that he authorized his companion, Carl Bierman, to bid up to $16,000; that Monroe came to the courthouse steps to begin the sale while Keilman was absent; that Bierman asked Monroe to wait until Keilman returned; that Monroe proceeded with the sale in Keilman's absence; and that Bierman bid up to $13,000 for the property. The Keilmans argue that Monroe's failure to delay the sale until Mr. Keilman returned constituted an irregularity that destroyed the legality and fairness of the sale. We disagree.

No provision of the deed of trust gave Mr. Keilman the right to be present at the sale or required Monroe to postpone the sale until he arrived. Under Texas law, the trustee has no legal duty to wait. *See* Bering v. Republic Bank of San Antonio, 581 S.W.2d 806, 808 (Tex. Civ. App.—Corpus Christi 1979, writ ref'd n.r.e.). Moreover, Keilman's agent, Bierman, was present to bid for him and did bid for him. The fact that Bierman misconstrued his instructions and did not bid up to $16,000 does not corrupt FSB's actions; the mistake, if any, was chargeable to the Keilmans.

Because a mortgagee is under no duty to take affirmative action beyond that required by statute or deed of trust to ensure a fair sale, we conclude as a matter of law that the substitute trustee's action in proceeding with the foreclosure sale in Mr. Keilman's absence does not constitute a defect or irregularity that would give rise to a claim for damages.

d. Statements in the Notice of Sale

The notice placed by Monroe in the Terrell County courthouse included the following language: "NO WARRANTIES, EITHER EXPRESSED OR IMPLIED, ARE OR SHALL BE MADE AS TO MERCHANTABILITY, FITNESS FOR PURPOSE, WORKMANSHIP OR QUALITY. No policy of title insurance will be furnished to the purchaser." The Keilmans argue that this statement disclaiming Uniform Commercial Code ("UCC") warranties regarding merchantability, fitness for purpose, workmanship, and quality, as well as the statement indicating that no title policy would be issued, conflicted with the terms of the deed of trust and could have misled prospective bidders. Therefore, they argue, FSB's inclusion of the disclaimers constituted an irregularity invalidating the foreclosure sale. We disagree.

The deed of trust provides that if the trustee sells the property, the trustee shall "make due conveyance to the Purchaser or Purchasers, with general warranty binding Grantors, their heirs and assigns." The UCC warranties referenced in the notice could apply only to the improvements on the land. No provision in the notice of sale stated or suggested that the general warranty of title was being disclaimed, and no provision in the deed of trust requires the trustee to make, as part of the conveyance, any UCC warranties. Because only the UCC warranties were disclaimed, the statement in the notice of sale did not conflict with the terms of the deed of trust. Further, no provision in the deed of trust required the trustee to provide the purchaser with a title policy. Because the deed of trust does not require a title policy, the statement in the notice of sale that none would be provided did not conflict with the terms of the deed of trust.

Further, including the disclaimers did not constitute an affirmative act that "chilled the bidding." Under Texas law, "[o]ne who bids upon property at a foreclosure sale does so at his peril." Henke v. First S. Properties, Inc., 586 S.W.2d 617, 620 (Tex. Civ. App.—Waco 1979, writ ref'd n.r.e.). Statements that UCC warranties are disclaimed as to any improvements on the property, and that no title policy will be provided, are fully consistent with a prospective bidder's realistic expectations. We conclude as a matter of law that placing such statements in the public notice of the foreclosure sale does not constitute a defect or irregularity that would give rise to a claim for damages.

e. Conclusion

Of the four "irregularities" identified by the Keilmans, the first three were actually complaints that FSB did not take *additional steps* to encourage third party participation in the foreclosure sale. As stated above, however, the mortgagee is under no duty to take affirmative action, beyond that required by statute or deed of trust, to ensure such participation. Accordingly, the first three alleged irregularities do not give rise to a claim for damages. The fourth "irregularity" identified by the Keilmans complains of FSB's affirmative act in placing disclaimers In the notice of sale. We concluded above that such disclaimers neither conflicted with the terms of the deed of trust nor misled prospective bidders. Accordingly, the fourth alleged irregularity does not give rise to a claim for damages. In the present case, there is no evidence that the actions of FSB on which the Keilmans base their common-law wrongful-foreclosure claim were improper. Accordingly, we conclude the record here contains no evidence that the foreclosure sale was conducted illegally or unfairly.

Based on the foregoing analysis, we sustain this portion of FSB's eighth point of error. Because we have concluded that there is no evidence that FSB "chilled the bidding" in the present case, the Keilmans are not entitled to recover any damages. Accordingly, we need not reach point of error nine, which raises the issue of whether the debtor has the burden of proving a *gross* inadequacy of price in order to recover damages in a "chilled bidding" case. *Compare* University Sav. Assn. v. Springwoods Shopping Ctr., 644 S.W.2d 705 (Tex. 1982) (citing the test established in American Sav. & Loan Assoc. v. Musick, 531 S.W.2d 581 (Tex. 1975), for a suit seeking damages for wrongful foreclosure), and Charter Nat'l Bank-Houston v. Stevens, 781 S.W.2d 368 (Tex. App.—Houston [14th Dist.] 1989, writ denied).

Duty of Trustee

Under Texas law, the trustee's duty is to act with "absolute impartiality and fairness" to all concerned, including the mortgagor. Hammonds v. Holmes, 559 S.W.2d 345, 347 (Tex. 1977). However, a trustee does not owe a *fiduciary duty* to the mortgagor. *See* FDIC v. Myers, 955 F.2d 348, 350 (5th Cir. 1992). The Keilmans cite American Savings & Loan Association v. Musick, 517 S.W.2d 627 (Tex. Civ. App.—Houston [14th Dist.] 1974), *rev'd on other grounds,* 531 S.W.2d 581 (Tex. 1975), for the proposition that a deed of trust creates a fiduciary relationship between the trustee and mortgagor. While the court in that case did use the phrase "fiduciary relationship," the opinion clearly indicates that the duty owed is simply a duty to strictly comply with the terms of the deed of trust. 517 S.W.2d at 631; *see also University Sav. Ass'n,* 644 S.W.2d at 706. In other words, a trustee fulfills his duty to act with impartiality and fairness by strictly complying with the terms of the deed of trust.

Conclusion

The mere fact that Monroe accepted a bid below the loan amount and that FSB acquired the property for less than the loan amount is not evidence of conspiracy. Neither Monroe, as trustee, nor FSB, as mortgagee, engaged in any action that breached any duty owed to the Keilmans. The evidence demonstrates that Monroe strictly complied with the terms of the deed of trust in acting as trustee at the foreclosure sale. In short, all actions taken by Monroe and FSB were lawful acts. Further, their purpose was not shown to be unlawful. There is no evidence that FSB's purpose was anything other than to foreclose its lien on a property securing a loan that was in default. Nor is there any evidence that Monroe's purpose was anything other than to comply with the terms of the deed of trust in acting as trustee and conducting the foreclosure. We conclude that the record contains no evidence of an unlawful conspiracy between Monroe and FSB. Accordingly, we sustain this portion of FSB's eighth point of error.

NOTES & QUESTIONS:

1. Consider the differences in the two cases. Which is the better approach?

2. How would you determine a fair price using the holding of the *Murphy* court? How would you determine what constitutes "chilled bidding" under the holding of the *FSB v. Keilman* case?

2. Mortgage Substitutes: The Installment Land Contract

There are other options for financing that do not follow the traditional route of an institutional lender with notes and deeds of trust executed along with a deed to transfer title to the property. Often there are individuals with less than perfect credit, or no credit, or low income who want to purchase a home but will not have the traditional options available. This opens the door for opportunities for seller financing.

In some instances, if a seller has already paid for the property in full, the seller might be willing to act as the lender, collecting principal and interest payments over time. In this transaction the seller would deliver the deed just as in a regular closing. However, instead of receiving the sales proceeds in one lump sum from the buyer or his lender, the seller also takes a note and deed of trust or mortgage to ensure he will receive the payments in regular installments until paid in full. In this situation, if the buyer defaults, the seller/lender will have to go through the same foreclosure procedures as any institutional lender.

There is another means of financing that is much different. It is referred to as the installment land contract or, in Texas, as the contract for deed. There is no closing initially. The buyer and seller enter into a long-term executory contract.

This contract will contain many different terms that you have seen thus far. It will include payment terms, interest rates, payoff dates, and additional requirements on the buyer like paying property taxes and carrying property hazard insurance. In this case the seller will transfer possession to the buyer, the buyer will make installment payments at agreed-upon intervals until the debt is paid in full. Only then will a deed be executed and delivered for the buyer to accept. This could be 5, 10, 20 years in the future. It is a very extended executory period. While the objective is the same, the legal relationship is much different. This has led to confusion and sometimes deception.

Bean v. Walker
New York Supreme Court, Appellate Division
Fourth Department, 1983
464 N.Y.S.2d 895

DOERR, J.

Presented for our resolution is the question of the relative rights between a vendor and a defaulting vendee under a land purchase contract. Special Term, in granting summary judgment in favor of plaintiffs, effectively held that the defaulting vendee has no rights. We cannot agree.

The facts may be briefly stated. In January 1973 plaintiffs agreed to sell and defendants agreed to buy a single-family home in Syracuse for the sum of $15,000.[13] The contract provided that this sum would be paid over a 15-year period at 5% interest, in monthly installments of $118.62. The sellers retained legal title to the property which they agreed to convey upon payment in full according to the terms of the contract. The purchasers were entitled to possession of the property, and all taxes, assessments and water rates, and insurance became the obligation of the purchasers. The contract also provided that in the event purchasers defaulted in making payment and failed to cure the default within 30 days, the sellers could elect to call the remaining balance immediately due or elect to declare the contract terminated and repossess the premises. If the latter alternative was chosen, then a forfeiture clause came into play whereby the seller could retain all the money paid under the contract as "liquidated" damages and "the same shall be in no event considered a penalty but rather the payment of rent."

Defendants went into possession of the premises in January 1973 and in the ensuing years claim to have made substantial improvements on the property. They made the required payments under the contract until August 1981 when they defaulted following an injury sustained by defendant Carl Walker. During the

---

[13] The house now has an alleged market value of $44,000.

years while they occupied the premises as contract purchasers defendants paid to plaintiff $12,099.24, of which $7,114.75 was applied to principal. Thus, at the time of their default, defendants had paid almost one-half of the purchase price called for under the agreement. After the required 30-day period to cure the default, plaintiffs commenced this action sounding in ejectment seeking a judgment "that they be adjudged the owner in fee" of the property and granting them possession thereof. The court granted summary judgment to plaintiffs.

If the only substantive law to be applied to this case was that of contracts, the result reached would be correct. However, under the facts presented herein the law with regard to the transfer of real property must also be considered. The reconciliation of what might appear to be conflicting concepts is not insurmountable.

While there are few New York cases which directly address the circumstances herein presented, certain general principles may be observed. It is well settled that the owner of the real estate from the time of the execution of a valid contract for its sale is to be treated as the owner of the purchase money and the purchaser of the land is to be treated as the equitable owner thereof. The purchase money becomes personal property. Thus, notwithstanding the words of the contract and implications which may arise therefrom, the law of property declares that, upon the execution of a contract for sale of land, the vendee acquires equitable title. The vendor holds the legal title in trust for the vendee and has an equitable lien for the payment of the purchase price. The vendee in possession, for all practical purposes, is the owner of the property with all the rights of an owner subject only to the terms of the contract. The vendor may enforce his lien by foreclosure or an action at law for the purchase price of the property—the remedies are concurrent. The conclusion to be reached, of course, is that upon the execution of a contract an interest in real property comes into existence by operation of law, superseding the terms of the contract.

Cases from other jurisdictions are more instructive. In Skendzel v. Marshall, 301 N.E.2d 641, [(Ind. 1973)] the court observed that while legal title does not vest in the vendee until the contract terms are satisfied, he does acquire a vested equitable title at the time the contract is consummated. When the parties enter into the contract all incidents of ownership accrue to the vendee who assumes the risk of loss and is the recipient of all appreciation of value. The status of the parties becomes like that of mortgagor-mortgagee. Viewed otherwise would be to elevate form over substance. The doctrine that equity deems as done that which ought to be done is an appropriate concept which we should apply to the present case.

Where sale of real property is evidenced by contract only and the purchase price has not been paid and is not to be paid until some future date in accordance with the terms of the agreement, the parties occupy substantially the position of mortgagor and mortgagee at common law. In New York a mortgage merely creates a lien rather than conveying title, but this was not always so. At common law the mortgage conveyed title, and it was to protect the buyer from summary ejectment that Courts of Equity evolved the concept of "equitable" title as distinct from "legal" title. The doctrine of equitable conversion had important consequences. The equitable owner suffered the risk of loss as does a contract vendee in possession today, but concomitantly, the equitable owner was also entitled to any increase in value; "since a purchaser under a binding contract of sale is in equity regarded as the owner of the property, he is entitled to any benefit or increase in value that may accrue to it" (6 Warren's Weed, New York Real Property, Vendee and Vendor, § 6.01). Similarly, upon the parties' death, the vendor's interest is regarded as personal property (i.e., the right to receive money), while the vendee's interest is treated as real property.

Because the common-law mortgagor possessed equitable title, the legal owner (the mortgagee) could not recover the premises summarily, but had to first extinguish the equitable owner's equity of redemption. Thus evolved the equitable remedy of mortgage foreclosure, which is now governed by statute. In our view, the vendees herein occupy the same position as the mortgagor at common law; both have an equitable title only, while another person has legal title. We perceive no reason why the instant vendees should be treated any differently than the mortgagor at common law.

Thus the contract vendors may not summarily dispossess the vendees of their equitable ownership without first bringing an action to foreclose the vendees' equity of redemption. This view reflects the modern trend in other jurisdictions.

The key to the resolution of the rights of the parties lies in whether the vendee under a land sale contract has acquired an interest in the property of such a nature that it must be extinguished before the vendor may resume possession. We hold that such an interest exists since the vendee acquires equitable title and the vendor merely holds the legal title in trust for the vendee, subject to the vendor's equitable lien for the payment of the purchase price in accordance with the terms of the contract. The vendor may not enforce his rights by the simple expedient of an action in ejectment but must instead proceed to foreclose the vendee's equitable title or bring an action at law for the purchase price, neither of which remedies plaintiffs have sought.

The effect of the judgment granted below is that plaintiffs will have their property with improvements made over the years by defendants, along with over $7,000 in principal payments on a purchase price of $15,000, and over $4,000 in interest. The basic inequity of such a result requires no further comment. If a forfeiture would result in the inequitable disposition of property and an exorbitant monetary loss, equity can and should intervene.

The interest of the parties here can only be determined by a sale of the property after foreclosure proceedings with provisions for disposing of the surplus or for a deficiency judgment.

By our holding today we do not suggest that forfeiture would be an inappropriate result in all instances involving a breach of a land contract. If the vendee abandons the property and absconds, logic compels that the forfeiture provisions of the contract may be enforced. Similarly, where the vendee has paid a minimal sum on the contract and upon default seeks to retain possession of the property while the vendor is paying taxes, insurance and other upkeep to preserve the property, equity will not intervene to help the vendee. Such is not the case before us.

Accordingly, the judgment should be reversed, the motion should be denied and the matter remitted to Supreme Court for further proceedings in accordance with this Opinion.

3. Mortgage Substitutes: The Texas Contract for Deed

According to at least one Texas Court of Appeal, "it is a matter of common knowledge, of which we can take judicial notice, that many poor people are unable to obtain conventional financing when they wish to purchase residential property. Frequently it is necessary for them to pay out the entire purchase price of the land prior to procuring title and prior to securing a mortgage on the property with a lending agency in order to finance any improvements."[14] The Texas Legislature originally enacted the provisions in the Texas Property Code governing contracts for deed because the Legislature found the following:

1. the proliferation of colonies and substandard housing developments that lack adequate infrastructure creates serious and unacceptable health risks for the residents in these areas;
2. many residents building homes in these areas do not have access to traditional financing and the assistance of a professional builder, which promotes expansion of substandard housing;
3. the contract-for-deed arrangement allows low-income persons to purchase property and build homes on the property;
4. statutory law in this state does not ensure [an adequate flow of information and protection for the purchaser]; and
5. a purchaser under a contract-for-deed arrangement is faced with significant problems requiring statutory protection because of:

---

[14] Sanchez v. Brandt, 567 S.W.2d 254, 258 (Tex. Civ. App.—Corpus Christi 1978, writ ref'd n.r.e.).

A. the inadequacy of infrastructure in the areas where this arrangement is commonly used; and

B. the unregulated status of the contract-for-deed arrangement.[15]

One commentator described the problem leading to the enactment of the legislation as follows:

> Las Lomas is one of more than 1,000 colonias located along the Texas-Mexico border. Many of these communities were established decades ago by developers who bought undesirable land, divided it into subdivisions and sold the lots to low-income families. Over the years, developers invested little or no money in infrastructure such as sewage, water, and roads, leaving thousands of families living without such basic necessities as running water or paved roads.
>
> Rather than selling the lots through banks or other traditional financial institutions, the developers issued contracts for deed, high interest notes that are often virtually impossible to pay off. Families would pay for years only to find that they had been paying only interest and had made no headway on the principal of the loan. Because contracts for deed are set up as a kind of rent-to-own arrangement, a family that missed one payment could lose the property, including any improvements that had been made.[16]

Taking the intended purpose for the legislation into consideration, the Legislature initially limited the applicability of the statute to counties determined to be within 200 miles of an international border and to have a per capita income that averaged 25 percent below the state average.[17] The provision limiting the statute's applicability to specific counties was removed in 2001 when the Legislature adopted several amendments to the statutory provisions relating to executory contracts for deed.[18]

---

[15] Act of May 27, 1995, 74th Leg., R.S., ch. 994, § 1, 1995 Tex. Gen. Laws 4982.

[16] Pamela Brown, Lawyers Team Up to Help in Colonia, 63 Tex. B.J. 462, 462 (2000); *see also* Flores v. Millennium Interests, Ltd., 185 S.W.3d 427, 434- 35, No. 04-1002, 2005 WL 2397521, at * 6-7 (Tex. Sept. 30, 2005) (Wainwright, J., concurring) (describing problem leading to legislation).

[17] Act of May 27, 1995, 74th Leg., R.S., ch. 994, § 3, 1995 Tex. Gen. Laws 4983-84; Flores, at 429, 2005 WL 2397521, at * 2 n. 1.

[18] See Act of May 18, 2001, 77th Leg., R.S., ch. 693, § 1, 2001 Tex. Gen. Laws 1319.

Tex. Prop. Code § 5.062 Applicability

(a) This subchapter applies only to a transaction involving an executory contract for conveyance of real property used or to be used as the purchaser's residence or as the residence of a person related to the purchaser within the second degree by consanguinity or affinity, as determined under Chapter 573, Government Code. For purposes of this subchapter, and only for the purposes of this subchapter:

   (1) a lot measuring one acre or less is presumed to be residential property; and

   (2) an option to purchase real property that includes or is combined or executed concurrently with a residential lease agreement, together with the lease, is considered an executory contract for conveyance of real property.

(b) This subchapter does not apply to the following transactions under an executory contract:

   (1) the sale of state land; or

   (2) a sale of land by:

      (A) the Veterans' Land Board;

      (B) this state or a political subdivision of this state; or

      (C) an instrumentality, public corporation, or other entity created to act on behalf of this state or a political subdivision of this state, including an entity created under Chapter 303, 392, or 394, Local Government Code.

(c) This subchapter does not apply to an executory contract that provides for the delivery of a deed from the seller to the purchaser within 180 days of the date of the final execution of the executory contract.

(d) Section 5.066 and Sections 5.068-5.080 do not apply to a transaction involving an executory contract for conveyance if the purchaser of the property:

   (1) is related to the seller of the property within the second degree by consanguinity or affinity, as determined under Chapter 573, Government Code; and

   (2) has waived the applicability of those sections in a written agreement.

(e) Sections 5.066, 5.067, 5.071, 5.075, 5.079, 5.081, and 5.082 do not apply to an executory contract described by Subsection (a)(2).

§ 5.063 Notice

(a) Notice under Section 5.064 must be in writing and must be delivered by registered or certified mail, return receipt requested. The notice must be conspicuous and printed in 14-point boldface type or 14-point uppercase typewritten letters, and must include on a separate page the statement:

NOTICE

YOU ARE NOT COMPLYING WITH THE TERMS OF THE CONTRACT TO BUY YOUR PROPERTY. UNLESS YOU TAKE THE ACTION SPECIFIED IN THIS NOTICE BY (date) THE SELLER HAS THE RIGHT TO TAKE POSSESSION OF YOUR PROPERTY.

(b) The notice must also:
    (1) identify and explain the remedy the seller intends to enforce;
    (2) if the purchaser has failed to make a timely payment, specify:
        (A) the delinquent amount, itemized into principal and interest;
        (B) any additional charges claimed, such as late charges or attorney's fees; and
        (C) the period to which the delinquency and additional charges relate; and
    (3) if the purchaser has failed to comply with a term of the contract, identify the term violated and the action required to cure the violation.
(c) Notice by mail is given when it is mailed to the purchaser's residence or place of business. The affidavit of a person knowledgeable of the facts to the effect that notice was given is prima facie evidence of notice in an action involving a subsequent bona fide purchaser for value if the purchaser is not in possession of the real property and if the stated time to avoid the forfeiture has expired. A bona fide subsequent purchaser for value who relies upon the affidavit under this subsection shall take title free and clear of the contract.

§ 5.604 Seller's Remedies on Default

A seller may enforce the remedy of rescission or of forfeiture and acceleration against a purchaser in default under an executory contract for conveyance of real property only if:
    (1) the seller notifies the purchaser of:
        (A) the seller's intent to enforce a remedy under this section; and
        (B) the purchaser's right to cure the default within the 30-day period described by Section 5.065;
    (2) the purchaser fails to cure the default within the 30-day period described by Section 5.065;
    (3) Section 5.066 does not apply; and

(4) The contract has not been recorded in the county in which the property is located.[19]

§ 5.065 Right to Cure Default

Notwithstanding an agreement to the contrary, a purchaser in default under an executory contract for the conveyance of real property may avoid the enforcement of a remedy described by Section 5.064 by complying with the terms of the contract on or before the 30th day after the date notice is given under that section.

§ 5.066 Equity Protection; Sale of Property[20]

(a) If a purchaser defaults after the purchaser has paid 40 percent or more of the amount due or the equivalent of 48 monthly payments under the executory contract or, regardless of the amount the purchaser has paid, the executory contract has been recorded, the seller is granted the power to sell, through a trustee designated by the seller, the purchaser's interest in the property as provided by this section. The seller may not enforce the remedy of rescission or of forfeiture and acceleration after the contract has been recorded.

(b) The seller shall notify a purchaser of a default under the contract and allow the purchaser at least 60 days after the date notice is given to cure the default. The notice must be provided as prescribed by Section 5.063 except that the notice must substitute the following statement:

NOTICE

YOU ARE NOT COMPLYING WITH THE TERMS OF THE CONTRACT TO BUY YOUR PROPERTY. UNLESS YOU TAKE THE ACTION SPECIFIED IN THIS NOTICE BY (date) A TRUSTEE DESIGNATED BY THE SELLER HAS THE RIGHT TO SELL YOUR PROPERTY AT A PUBLIC AUCTION.

(c) The trustee or a substitute trustee designated by the seller must post, file, and serve a notice of sale and the county clerk shall record and maintain the notice of sale as prescribed by Section 51.002. A notice of sale is not valid unless it is given after the period to cure has expired.

(d) The trustee or a substitute trustee designated by the seller must conduct the sale as prescribed by Section 51.002. The seller must:

(1) convey to a purchaser at a sale conducted under this section fee simple title to the real property; and

---

[19] The 84th legislature added (4) and it takes effect September 1, 2015.

[20] Subsection (a) was amended by the 84th legislature and is effective September 1, 2015.

(2) warrant that the property is free from any encumbrance.

(e) The remaining balance of the amount due under the executory contract is the debt for purposes of a sale under this section. If the proceeds of the sale exceed the debt amount, the seller shall disburse the excess funds to the purchaser under the executory contract. If the proceeds of the sale are insufficient to extinguish the debt amount, the seller's right to recover the resulting deficiency is subject to Sections 51.003, 51.004, and 51.005 unless a provision of the executory contract releases the purchaser under the contract from liability.

(f) The affidavit of a person knowledgeable of the facts that states that the notice was given and the sale was conducted as provided by this section is prima facie evidence of those facts. A purchaser for value who relies on an affidavit under this subsection acquires title to the property free and clear of the executory contract.

(g) If a purchaser defaults before the purchaser has paid 40 percent of the amount due or the equivalent of 48 monthly payments under the executory contract, the seller may enforce the remedy of rescission or of forfeiture and acceleration of the indebtedness if the seller complies with the notice requirements of Sections 5.063 and 5.064.

§ 5.079 Title Transfer[21]

(a) A recorded executory contract shall be the same as a deed with a vendor's lien. The vendor's lien is for the amount of the unpaid contract price, less any lawful deductions, and may be enforced by foreclosure sale under Section 5.066 or by judicial foreclosure. A general warranty is implied unless otherwise limited by the recorded executory contract. If an executory contract has not been recorded or converted under Section 5.081, the seller shall transfer recorded, legal title of the property covered by the executory contract to the purchaser not later than the 30th day after the date the seller receives the purchaser's final payment due under the contract.

NOTES & QUESTIONS:

Consider the differences in the Texas statutes and the approach taken in *Bean v. Walker*. Which system works better to protect potential equity of the buyer?

---

[21] The language of § 5.079(a) was changed significantly by the legislature. This new language is effective September 1, 2015. The other subsections of this statute are omitted.

Chapter 8
Providing Title Assurance: Priorities and the Recording System

A. Introduction

We have already covered the marketable title covenant a in the executory period and the covenants of title in a deed. These are both components of the title assurance system. However, there are other components in the system essential to help prevent the types of disputes you have already seen. Remember that in Brown v. Lober, the Browns did not receive title to all of the minerals. Had they conducted a title search during the executory period that might have been discovered. Had they purchased a title insurance policy, that might have been discovered and if not, would have been insured against. In Ledbetter v. Howard, the parties took title that was subject to an outstanding tax lien. Had they conducted a title search during the executory period that might have been discovered.

The goal of the system of title assurance is that buyers will end up owning exactly what they thought they would own. No surprises! If parties will avail themselves of all parts of the system, this goal can be achieved. In this section we will examine:

(1) The chain of title and title search;
(2) Priority rules for competing interests in the same property (this is the underlying decision before we have a breach of warranty claim to be brought);
(3) The bona fide purchaser and good faith creditor; and
(4) The role of title insurance.

B. The Recording System

The public records office is central to the recording system. This is the place in each county where all of the recorded property records are organized and indexed to be searchable by the public. The public has access to these documents free of charge. These documents are in the vast majority of counties indexed based on names. Title companies can be hired to perform title searches. Title companies used to have their own "title plants" where hard copies of the records from the county office were stored and indexed according to property description. Now title companies use a computerized system but still index and search based on property description. This fundamental difference will lead to some interesting discussions in material to come.

Title insurance companies serve as a backup to the recording system. Title insurance is sold and can be purchased for extra assurance that you have superior title and funds available to pay in case that is actually incorrect. Sometimes attorneys will be consulted because of questions that arise in title searches but attorneys typically do not conduct title searches today. The process of using a title company is less expensive and comes with an insurance policy. Also, lawyers are not in the insurance business and would prefer to avoid potential professional malpractice liability for something missed in a search.

Before we learn the process of searching the public records system, let us first consider why it is important to have a recording system. There are many reasons that this system is important. First, we have seen time and time again that when dealing with land we need clear rules to promote alienability and economic efficiency. If documents are recorded and accessible, landowners should feel comfortable with the transactions they are engaging in and feel certain and secure about the title to the land. Second, another common theme is the avoidance of self-help. If we have an organized system that promotes certainty and free alienability, we will lessen the chances of having a disgruntled landowner who feels compelled to use violence and brute force to prevail. Third, having the recording system allows for ownership and possession to be independent. In the very beginning of this course we saw heated disputes occur over a fox and a baseball. Those were items of personal property that did not have title instruments that could be recorded for orderly determination of ownership. In fact, with those items of personal property, physical possession of the object was determinative of ownership. With a system of public records, a landowner does not have to feel compelled to be on Blackacre at every moment to protect his title. Fourth, having the recording system provides a repository for documents that might otherwise be lost. Again, thinking about ownership through possession, you don't want to have to walk around holding the deed to your property to protect your ownership. Also, you don't want to have to worry about having the only copy that might be destroyed by fire or flood. These important documents essentially have a back-up at the public records building.

There are many rules and concepts to come that build on the foundation of understanding the recording system, the indexes, and the rules that govern disputes over land. Consider the situation where Barney owned Blackacre in fee simple absolute and conveyed the land to Marshall. Marshall takes his deed and records it in the public records. He has no present plans to use or occupy the land but wants to build a vacation home there in the future. In the meantime, Barney decides to sell the land a second time to make some quick cash. Barney conveys the land to Ted one year later. Ted does not conduct a title search and has no actual knowledge of the conveyance to Marshall. Ted later sells the land to Lily, who then sells to Robin. Robin goes into possession, builds a house, and begins occupying it. Marshall discovers Robin on his land one day and wants her out! Situations just like this occur. Does this mean that our system has failed Robin? No. This means that Robin, and Lily, and Ted were not reasonably prudent purchasers. Based on these facts, Marshall acted completely responsibly and recorded his deed. His interest is first in time, first in right, and that deed is recorded for all the world to see. Had Ted bothered to go and look at the records, he would find Marshall's deed. Had Lily bothered to go and look, she would have found Marshall's deed. Had Robin bothered to go and look at the records she would have found Marshall's deed.

However, change the facts so that although Marshall is still first in time but does not record his deed right away. Barney sells to Ted as a second conveyance, but this time Marshall is not in possession of the land and his deed is not yet recorded in the public records. Ted had no actual knowledge of the prior conveyance to Marshall and had no way of knowing about it. The system could not do what it was designed to do because Marshall did not utilize it properly. This is why there are additional rules that we will consider about priority disputes and exceptions to the first-in-time rule.

But before we can do all of that, let's take a look at the system and the indexes to understand how to find the information.

1. The Indexes

There are volumes upon volumes of documents recorded at any county's public records office. In order for the public to be able to find anything, there must be an orderly, user-friendly, indexing system. Most counties use a grantor/grantee name index system. Very few places have a tract index that indexes by property description. As mentioned above, title companies have such indexes but not most counties.

So, if we think about Robin and her unfortunate circumstances, how could she have prevented that from happening? By conducting a search of the public records! She is trying to find out: (1) the history of all of the past owners of the land back to a certain point in time; (2) all conveyances entered into by the various owners; and (3) whether any other interests exist in this land. Ultimately, (1) *who* is the current owner and (2) *what* does he own?

What do you search to answer those questions? First, search the deed indexes looking for deeds with the same property description. Second, search for deeds of trust, mechanics liens, easements, covenants, and any adverse conveyances. Third, you may need to search other records as well: probate court filings, judgments in district and county courts, family court records. The purchaser wants a complete picture of what could be impacting the title. This is not a situation where ignorance is bliss. When it comes to land, ignorance can lead to a majorly expensive headache.

You will be looking at the indexes to begin the process of putting together the information. In McLennan County, after April 1996, records are all on the computer. However, all records before that date are in the bound volumes linked to the indexes. Counties differ as to dates that electronic recording began and whether the county has gone back to put older records on the computerized system. This is something that a lawyer would need to consider because every county has a different approach.

Photograph of the McLennan County Public Records Office

Start in the Grantee indexes for Deeds. The first step is to find the current grantor's name in the grantee index. You need to find when he took title to the property and from whom. This will help with the next step.

The front cover of the index, like the one in the photo, will tell you:

1. What type of instruments are indexed;
2. What letters of the alphabet it covers; and
3. For what time period.

There are many different indexes in the Records Office such as indexes for deeds, deeds of trust and mechanic liens, marriage and death records, and even cattle brands.

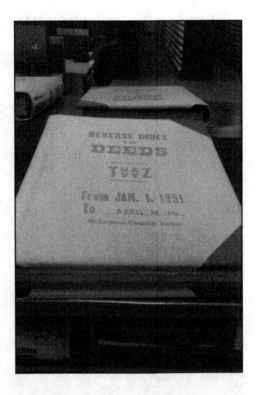

As the purchaser, begin by searching the grantee index starting with your grantor/seller in the current transaction. You need to find the deed that your seller received when he took title to the property. When you find that entry in the index, it will also tell you the name of the grantor in that transaction

You will need to then take the name of the grantor in that transaction and look in the grantee index to find when that person received title to the land. You will continue this process until you have searched back in time for a sufficient number of years.

Page from the Grantee Index in the McLennan County Public Records Office

In gathering the information in the index, you need to get the page and volume number, and confirm the correct property description and the names of all grantors. Gathering this information will allow you to locate the actual documents involved in the prior transactions. In order to do this, you need to pull the actual document listed in the index. From that you will obtain the name of the grantor in that deed and also find the date of the instrument *and* the date it was recorded (it will not always be the same date!). What is the relevance of the two dates? Date of the instrument = date the interest was acquired for priority purposes. Date the instrument was recorded = date for constructive notice purposes.

- Use the information from the index to pull the recorded documents

- Why can't you rely solely on the index?

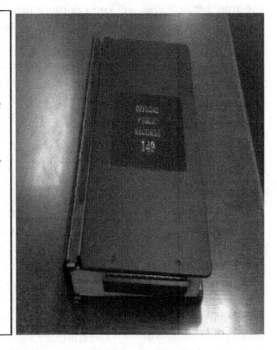

After going back far enough, the buyer will then begin searching from that point forward in the grantor indexes looking for any adverse conveyances by each grantor and making sure each part of the chain of title links up. The search is conducted using each grantor's name from the date the grantor is shown to have received the interest (date of the instrument) until the date the next person recorded (not necessarily the date of the instrument). You will follow this process through the present date with present grantor's name.

There is more information in the document that is recorded than what the index reveals. You have an obligation to look at the actual recorded document. You want to acquire as much actual knowledge about a piece of land as possible to avoid problematic transactions. If you find adverse conveyances by the grantor, the process will also need to include searching for documentation indicating whether the adverse conveyance has terminated (if possible) or still remains on the title. If you found a deed of trust for the purchase money, can you locate a release of lien for that debt? If an easement was granted, can you locate a release of that easement or possible transactions merging the dominant and servient estate ownership as to effectively terminate the easement? If there were restrictive covenants recorded, has there been anything recorded indicating termination of the covenants or did the covenant document itself indicate an ending date?

You need to determine what is the adverse conveyance and what should we be concerned with as a result? Remember, at this stage we are concerned with marketability of title, can the problem be fixed or do we need to walk away from the transaction? You will keep coming forward in time for each person's name you have obtained and searching for all adverse conveyances.

By the time this process is concluded, the current purchaser should have a wealth of information before ever completing the transaction. The purchaser should (1) feel assured that the seller has good title; (2) know of issues to be resolved; or (3) know to walk away.

The problem that we will look at next is that sometimes the documents are not recorded properly or are not recorded at all. What impact should that have on this process?

2. Types of Recording Acts

Now that we have covered the indexes and means of conducting a title search, we will turn to examples that illustrate that sometimes there are competing interests in the same piece of real property. The court has to determine which interest would prevail. The general common law rule is that of "first in time, first in right." That concept has been involved in these materials since the beginning of the course. Who was first in time to acquire the fox? Who was a prior possessor with the chimney sweep and jeweler? Who had possession of the baseball? This rule of first in time is a core principle to property law as that meets societal expectations and helps promote certainty and order.

Originally at common law, we adhered to the basic principle of first in time, first in right. However, an equitable concept evolved to protect one who was considered to be a bona fide purchaser.[1] Equitable exceptions to the rule developed that allowed an equitable interest first in time to lose out to a subsequent bona fide purchaser. Additionally, a first-in-time interest could be estopped from asserting that first-in-time right if by words or actions an otherwise bona fide purchaser was led to believe the state of the title was different from what it actually is. The case of Johnson v. Darr in the next section provides an example of how the equitable exceptions could work if the party

---

[1] The concept of the bona fide purchaser will be developed after looking at the statutory exception. The bona fide purchaser is a limited class of people who can take advantage of any of the exceptions whether common law or statutory.

asserting them were a bona fide purchaser. That case will ultimately rest on the recording statute and its application.

Outside of these equitable concepts, we also turn our attention back to the public records system. The public records provide a place where documents are recorded so that it is easy to determine which interest is first in time. We want the public records system to be as complete and accurate as possible so that we limit the number of disputes related to land to as small a number as possible. In order to promote recording of instruments, every state has a recording statute. The statutes take different forms but the basic idea behind all of them is that certain documents are required to be recorded and if they are not, the first in time interest may feel the penalty effect of losing out to an interest that came later in time.[2]

The logic behind this is that if there are two people with competing interests in the real property, the person who ultimately loses should be the one who could have prevented or avoided the problem. Had the first in time interest been properly recorded, no one could come along and claim any exception to the general rule of first in time, first in right.

First, we will examine each type of recording statute. Then we will work on applying the different statutes and comparing the outcomes in each situation.

a. The Race Recording Statute

Louisiana and North Carolina are the only two states that still use a race recording statute. With a race recording statute the person who wins the race to the courthouse to record his document will prevail. There is no inquiry into good faith or acting without notice. With this type of statute the bad guy who actually knows of an earlier conveyance can still win by simply recording his document first. Because this statute rewards the wrongdoer, almost every state has abandoned this approach. This statute does lend itself simplicity and certainty. The only inquiry is who recorded first? This eliminates the need for evidence outside of the record regarding intent and notice of a second-in-time interest.

Here is the North Carolina statute, which provides an example of a race statute:

> No (i) conveyance of land, or (ii) contract to convey, or (iii) option to convey, or (iv) lease of land for more than three years shall be valid to pass any property interest as against lien creditors or purchasers for valuable consideration from the donor, bargain, or lessor *but from the time of registration thereof*

---

[2] Originally at common law there were no exceptions to the rule. However, with the statutory recording acts there was now a method for someone to cut in line. You will understand as this material progresses that only very narrowly defined circumstances allow this second-in-time interest to prevail.

in the county where the land lies, or if the land is located in more than one county, then in each county where any portion of the land lies to be effective as to land in that county.[3]

b. The Race-Notice Recording Statute

The race-notice recording statute is used in about half of the states. This statute retains the first recording aspect of the race statute but now does not allow the bad guy to win. This statute adds in a requirement that the second-in-time person trying to gain priority must be acting in good faith and not have any form of notice of the first-in-time interest. This type of statute provides an incentive to record, so as not to feel the penalty effect, and it also prevents the bad guy from winning.

The following language is from the Washington statute:

> A conveyance of real property, when acknowledged by the person executing the same (the acknowledgment being certified as required by law), may be recorded in the office of the recording officer of the county where the property is situated. Every such conveyance not so recorded is void as against any subsequent purchaser or mortgagee in good faith and for a valuable consideration from the same vendor, his heirs, or devisees, of the same real property or any portion thereof *whose conveyance is first duly recorded*.[4]

c. The Notice Recording Statute

The notice recording statute is used in the other half of the states. This statute does not include a requirement that the second-in-time interest record first. It requires the second-in-time person be in good faith and take without notice. This means that if the first-in-time interest fails to record, that interest will feel the penalty effect if there is a subsequent good faith purchaser for value or bona fide purchaser. There is still an incentive to record because without being recorded this opens the door for the subsequent good faith purchaser for value or bona fide purchaser to exist.

Texas is one of the states that has a notice recording statute. The Texas Statute provides:[5]

---

[3] N.C. Gen. Stat. § 47-18(a).
[4] Wash. Rev. Code § 65.08.070.
[5] Tex. Prop. Code § 13.001(a).

A conveyance of real property or an interest in real property or a mortgage or deed of trust is void as to a creditor or to a subsequent purchaser for a valuable consideration without notice unless the instrument has been acknowledged, sworn to, or proved and filed for record as required by law.

RECORDING STATUTE PROBLEMS

Often it is difficult to understand the differences between these statutes without actually working with them. The recording first without consideration for any type of notice versus having no notice and recording first versus having no notice but with no requirement to record first to prevail create big differences in the outcome of a particular dispute. The following problems are designed to help understand the differences.

For each of the following problems, determine who has priority under each of the three recording statutes (race, race/notice, and notice). Assume that (1) each grantee has given value for his conveyance, (2) the search is to be conducted using a name index, and (3) A's interest is first in time and subject to the recording statute. In each diagram "ur" stands for unrecorded and "r" is for recorded.

1. *O* conveys Blackacre to *A* who does not record her deed. Then *O* conveys Blackacre a second time to *B* who has actual knowledge of the prior conveyance to *A*. *B* records his deed. *A* then records her deed.
   In a dispute between *A* and *B*, who wins?
   Race statute?
   Race/notice statute?
   Notice statute?

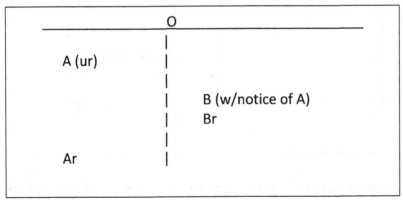

2. *O* conveys Blackacre to *A*, who does not record her deed. *O* then conveys Blackacre a second time to *B* who does not have any form of notice of *A*. *B* records his deed. *A* then records her deed.
   In a dispute between *A* and *B*, who wins?

Race statute?
Race/notice statute?
Notice statute?

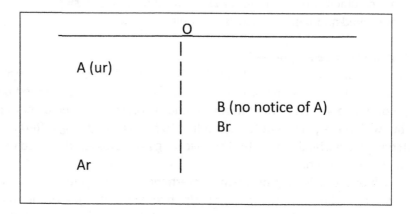

3. *O* conveys Blackacre to *A*, who does not record her deed. *O* then conveys Blackacre a second time to *B* who does not have any form of notice of *A*. *A* records her deed. *B* then records his deed.
In a dispute between *A* and *B*, who wins?
Race statute?
Race/notice statute?
Notice statute?

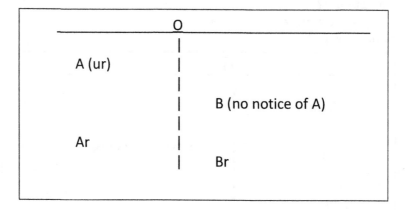

In comparing the statutes using these examples, do you understand the difference in the first-in-time person recording to not feel the penalty effect versus a requirement that the second-in-time interest record first to take priority? That is a key difference to understand with these statutes.

3. Applying the Acts to Resolve the Dispute

In addition to understanding the mechanics and order of recording, there are many components to the recording statutes. In order to use the exception, the first-in-time interest must be one that falls within the recording statute. In the examples that you just completed, the instructions told you to assume the first-in-time interest came within the act. In practice, an attorney must look to the particular act to know what documents must be recorded.

Each of the example statutes above indicate what type of documents must be recorded in order to avoid the penalty effect. The North Carolina statute specifies a (i) conveyance of land, or (ii) contract to convey, or (iii) option to convey, or (iv) lease of land for more than three years. The Washington statute requires "a conveyance of real property" to be recorded. The Texas statute requires "a conveyance of real property or an interest in real property or a mortgage or deed of trust."

Therefore, to even consider the recording statute as an available exception to the general rule, there must be the right interest involved. Keep that in mind as you read the following case.

Johnson et al. v. Darr et al.
Texas Supreme Court, 1925
272 S.W. 1098

WARD, Special Chief Justice.[6]

This is an action instituted by J. M. Darr and others as trustees for the fraternal beneficiary organization known as Woodmen of the World (Respondents) against W. T. Johnson and others (Petitioner) to establish a trust, remove cloud, and enjoin sale under attachment lien and judgment of foreclosure involving two tracts of land in the city of El Paso. The cause was tried upon an agreed statement of facts, and judgment was entered in the trial court in favor of Respondent for one of the tracts involved, and for the Petitioner for the other. On appeal the honorable Court of Civil Appeals at El Paso reversed the case and rendered judgment for Woodmen of the World, for both tracts; Justice Higgins dissenting.

---

[6] This case has an interesting role in Texas history. Justice Ward who authored this opinion is a woman. The other two justices who heard this case and wrote concurring opinions were also women. This was the first all-female supreme court in the United States. And it happened in Texas in 1925.

The agreed statement of facts is fully set out in the opinion of that court. 257 S.W. 682. The facts in substance are that the trustees of the Woodmen of the World, for a nominal consideration, on August 24, 1921, conveyed the title to the two tracts of land involved in the suit to F. P. Jones. On the same date Jones executed an agreement to hold it in trust for them and to re-convey when called upon to do so. The agreement to hold in trust and re-convey was evidenced in writing, as follows:

> "The State of Texas, County of El Paso.
> "Whereas, Tornillo Camp, No. 42, Woodmen of the World . . . in regular session ordered the managers as auditors and trustees . . . to sell, transfer and convey to the undersigned, the following real estate (then follows description); and, whereas, said officers have executed and delivered said deed, thereby transferring and conveying said property to the undersigned; this is to acknowledge that I have received said conveyance in trust and agree to re-convey the same to such person as said officers shall direct, at any time they may request said conveyance. Dated, signed and acknowledged August 24th, 1921. Filed for record October 24th, 1922."

The deed to Jones was recorded, but the agreement of Jones was not recorded until October, 1922. Meanwhile, creditors of Jones levied an attachment upon the property in June, 1922, and in December, 1922, obtained judgment for their debt and foreclosure of attachment lien. Shortly after the levy of attachment lien this suit was filed by Darr et al., trustees for Woodmen of the World.

Petitioners contend that the declaration of trust executed by Jones is such an instrument as must be recorded to protect the equitable title of defendants in error against attaching creditors. Article 6824 is as follows:

6824

> ". . . All bargains, sales and other conveyances whatever, of any land, tenements and hereditaments, whether they may be made for passing any estate of freehold of inheritance, or for a term of years; . . . shall be void as to all creditors and subsequent purchasers for valuable consideration without notice, unless they shall be acknowledged or proved and filed with the clerk, to be recorded as required by law."

Respondents insist that said instrument, though entitled to record under article 6823, is not within the scope of article 6824, and therefore their equitable title was superior to the attachment lien.

If Respondents are correct in their contention, no necessity exists to consider any other questions raised by the assignments. Thus the first question presented is whether or not the instrument above set out falls within the purview of article 6824, requiring certain instruments to be recorded.

When a right is solely and exclusively of legislative creation, and does not derive existence from the common law or principles of equity, and creates a new right by statute, the courts will not extend the application of the statute, but will limit its application to the exact words of the act. "He who would avail himself of such a summary remedy must bring himself within both the letter and spirit of the law." Sutherland on Statutory Construction (2d Ed.) § 572.

The terms of article 6824 should doubtless be construed for the suppression of the mischief it was designed to prevent, and all conveyances within its spirit and scope should be brought under its operation. To go further would be for the courts to assume legislative functions and transcend the authority of a judicial tribunal. The instrument under consideration created a trust in lands, and under no rational rule of construction can it be regarded as a conveyance or passing of an estate in land. It is merely the written acknowledgment of a trust created by the agreement of the parties when the deed was executed, placing the naked legal title in Jones and retaining the equitable title in the trustees of the Woodmen of the World. The deed being absolute on its face but in fact passing only the naked legal title to Jones, are the lands so conveyed subject to the creditors' attachment lien?

It will not be questioned that, had the trustees been less diligent in attempting to protect the interest of their organization and left the proof of the trust to parol evidence, no interest in the land would have been acquired by the attachment lien, as against the equitable title remaining in the Woodmen of the World, and, if proof of the trust had been left to parol, the attaching creditors would have acquired no more interest in the land than Jones had. Grace v. Wade, 45 Tex. 522; Parker v. Coop, 60 Tex. 111; McKamey et al. v. Thorp et al., 61 Tex. 648; Blankenship v. Douglas, 26 Tex. 227, 82 Am. Dec. 608; Oberthier v. Stroud, 33 Tex. 522; Senter & Co. v. Lambeth, 59 Tex. 259; Henderson v. Rushing, 47 Tex. Civ. App. 485, 105 S. W. 840; First State Bank of Amarillo v. Jones, 107 Tex. 623, 183 S. W. 874.

It is the settled law in this state that attachment lien creditors acquire no greater interest in the land than that owned by the debtor, at the date of the levy, except where such common-law rule has been abrogated by the registration laws expressly defining the effect of unrecorded conveyances and mortgages against purchasers and creditors without notice.

But Petitioners contend that, because the instrument was entitled to record, it must be recorded to protect the equitable title remaining in defendants in error. That instruments permitted to be recorded are not required to be recorded in order to protect the equitable title against attaching creditors is held in Adams v. Williams, 112 Tex. 469, 477, 248 S. W. 676, the opinion by the Commission of Appeals saying:

"There having been, under the facts certified, a valid assignment of the two vendor's lien notes in controversy to Mrs. Cooper, the lien securing the same and the right to enforce such lien by foreclosure upon the land, and the sale thereof, if necessary, passed to her with the debt evidenced by said notes. * * * Article 6824 of our registration statutes (Vernon's Sayles' Ann. Civ. St. 1914) has no application to the assignment of promissory notes as such."

The equitable title of the Respondents was the superior title. It existed independent of the written instrument executed by Jones, and could have been enforced in a court of equity, had the instrument never been executed. That being true, regardless of the registration statute, the title of the Respondents was superior to the lien of the attaching creditors, and was not within or affected by article 6824. Henderson v. Rushing et al., 47 Tex. Civ. App. 485, 105 S.W. 840; Hawkins v. Willard (Tex. Civ. App.) 38 S.W. 365; Cetti v. Wilson et al. (Tex. Civ. App.) 168 S.W. 996; Long v. Field et al., 31 Tex. Civ. App. 241, 71 S.W. 774; Uhl v. Weiden et al., 122 Mich. 638, 81 N.W. 571.

In Hawkins v. Willard, *supra*, Josephine Hawkins acquired 160 acres of land from Walker by deed dated February 1, 1886, recorded December, 1889. In order to obtain money to pay Walker the balance of purchase price, and for no other purpose, she deeded the land to her son December, 1889, so that he might mortgage it for that purpose. Failing to raise the money by this means, she obtained it elsewhere, paid off the balance to Walker, and recorded his release 1890. Her son B. O. Hawkins re-conveyed to her in November, 1891, but this deed, though made before, was not recorded until after the land had been levied upon as the property of B. O. Hawkins by his creditors. The sole consideration for the deed back to his mother by B. O. Hawkins was to reinvest her with the legal title. The creditors sought to apply article 6824, and asserted that failure to record the deed from Hawkins to his mother subordinated her equitable title to their liens. The court held:

"It may be conceded, no actual notice being charged against the plaintiff in execution, that the levy would prevail over the unrecorded deed from B. O. Hawkins to appellant. But this is because of our registration statute, which declares such unrecorded conveyances to be void as to creditors. McKamey v. Thorp, 61 Tex. 648, and cases there cited. The deed from B. O. Hawkins being thus null, did appellant show an equitable right superior to that acquired by execution levy without notice thereof? Undoubtedly, the conveyance to B. O. Hawkins, though absolute in form, was in reality in trust; and, while it placed the legal title in him, he held it, particularly after the purpose of the conveyance had otherwise been accomplished, in trust solely for his mother. Such a trust, whether it be regarded as a resulting or an express trust, may be established by parol in this state. Black v. Caviness, 2 Tex. Civ. App. 118, 21 S.W. 635; Clark v. Haney, 62 Tex. 511; Hudson v. Wilkinson, 45 Tex. 444; Bailey v. Harris, 19 Tex. 109. It was not, therefore, within either our statute of frauds (which requires certain rights to be evidenced by writing) or our registration statute (which requires certain written instruments to be recorded). Briscoe v. Bronaugh, 1 Tex. 326; Orme v. Roberts, 33 Tex. 768, and numerous other cases. For a review of the leading and earlier cases, see Parker v. Coop, 60 Tex. 111. This equitable right of appellant was not lost by her failure to have the re-conveyance of the bare legal title placed on record, as was expressly held in Blankenship v. Douglas, supra.

The decisions of this state uniformly hold that the registration statutes do not apply to equitable titles. That bona fide purchasers for value are protected against the assertion of such title is because of the doctrine of estoppel, and not the registration statutes.

We are of the opinion that the instrument evidencing the trust was not required by the statute to be recorded, and that the title of defendants in error was not affected by the attachment lien. We therefore affirm the judgment of the Court of Civil Appeals reversing and rendering the decision of the trial court.

NOTES & QUESTIONS:

1. What was the problem that prevented the creditors from being successful? The first-in-time document was not recorded for quite some time. Would a different exception have worked? Why or why not?

2. An interesting piece of Texas history accompanies this case. One of the parties—Woodmen of the World—began as a fraternal organization that most professional men belonged to at the time. In fact, all of the justices sitting on the Texas Supreme Court at the time were members of Woodmen of the World. They recused themselves from this case, as it had to do with title to property owned by their organization. The governor then had to appoint three justices to sit in their place. The problem was that most of the male attorneys in the state who were qualified to sit on the supreme court were also members of Woodmen of the World.

   The governor had to look to female attorneys in the state who were qualified to sit as the court. The governor at the time was none other than Governor Pat Neff. Pat Neff was born near McGregor, Texas. He graduated from McGregor High School and then went on to graduate from Baylor University in 1894 and the University of Texas Law School in 1897. Pat Neff began practicing law at Waco in 1897. He won two gubernatorial elections in 1920 and 1922. When he completed his service as governor, he resumed his law practice in Waco. He became president of Baylor University, serving from 1932 to 1947.[7]

Hortense Ward was the first woman to become a lawyer in Texas. She studied law through correspondence courses while working as a court stenographer. She passed the Texas bar exam in 1910, at the age of 35. She became a partner with her husband in the Houston law firm of Ward & Ward. Hortense Ward had an active and productive career. She led a successful effort to persuade the Texas legislature to grant property rights to married women, co-authored the constitutional amendment providing for Prohibition in Texas, supported women's suffrage, and became the first woman to vote in Harris County.

On the day of oral arguments, the courtroom was filled with lawyers and women when the special judges took their seats upon the bench. They first conferred with Governor Pat Neff in his office where they received their commissions. The current Chief Justice administered the oath, which included having the women' swear that they had never fought in a duel. None of the three women raised their right hands. (The same oath was later taken by Miriam Ferguson as Governor of Texas.) The other two specially appointed female justices were Ruth Virginia Brazzil and Hattie L. Henenberg. All three wrote opinions: Justice Ward wrote the opinion for the court, and the others wrote concurrences.[8]

3. Even if we can make a determination that the first-in-time interest does fall within the recording statute, there are many other issues that arise in applying these statutes. There are often situations where a document is recorded but not properly so. Additionally, the second-in-time person wanting to cut in line must be able to qualify for the exception. We will now turn our attention to problems with recording of the first-in-time document that may allow someone to come in and cut in line. We will then follow with a discussion of who the right person is to use the statute.

---

[7] Historical data on Pat Neff obtained from Texas Archival Resources Online, http://www.lib.utexas.edu/taro/tslac/40030/tsl-40030.html.

[8] The information on the interesting history of this case was provided by research conducted by Professor Patricia Wilson, Baylor Law School.

4. Problems with Recording and the Impact on Priority

There are many times when a document that is required to be recorded by the statute is in the public records, but will still trigger the penalty effect of the statute. How can that be? Many problems can occur with the recording of instruments that make the recording essentially ineffective.

Looking back to the example recording statutes above, each of the statutes includes some language regarding how the instrument must be recorded. The North Carolina statute requires that there must be "registration thereof in the county where the land lies, or if the land is located in more than one county, then in each county where any portion of the land lies to be effective as to land in that county." It is important to record the instrument in the correct county records or it is pointless. A person is not going to do a title search in a different county than where the land is located. It would not make sense to require a search of all counties to find information about land in a particular county or counties.

In addition to being recorded in the right location, the statutes also address what is required to record the document. The Washington statute states, that "[a] conveyance of real property, when acknowledged by the person executing the same (the acknowledgment being certified as required by law), may be recorded in the office of the recording officer of the county where the property is situated." This statute tells us that the document must be acknowledged and recorded in the right location. Without a proper acknowledgment, although the deed itself is valid and transferred title from grantor to grantee, it will not be properly recorded in the public records to provide notice to subsequent purchasers. The grantee should require the grantor to provide a proper acknowledgment at the time of taking the deed in order to properly record. If the grantee does not take this step to protect himself, he could potentially lose out to a subsequent purchaser.

The acknowledgment is simply the part that is added to a deed to sign before a notary public. This requirement is to help prevent forged or fraudulent documents from becoming a part of the public record. In some states witnesses can be used, but most recording statutes require an acknowledgement. This is a sample acknowledgment that is seen on most deeds.

State of _____
County of _____

    I hereby certify that on this day before me, a notary public, personally appeared the above named ___[Grantor]_____, who acknowledged that he voluntarily signed the foregoing instrument on the day and year therein mentioned.

    In testimony whereof, I hereunto subscribe my name and affix my official seal on this _____ day of _____, 20___.

Signature of Notary Public

Notary   Public   in   and for_____ County,

State of _____

My Commission Expires

_____

> Notary Seal is placed on the document

The Texas statute states that the document must be "acknowledged, sworn to, or proved and filed for record as required by law." There are additional property code provisions that help with the "required by law" component of the statute. Texas Property Code § 11.001 gives the place of recording. Comparable to the statutes from North Carolina and Washington, to be effectively recorded "an instrument relating to real property must be eligible for recording and must be recorded in the county in which a part of the real property is located."[9] Then Texas Property Code § 12.001 defines what is required to be eligible for recording.

Tex. Prop. Code
§ 12.001 Instruments Concerning Property

    (a) An instrument concerning real or personal property may be recorded if it has been acknowledged, sworn to with a proper jurat, or proved according to law.

    (b) An instrument conveying real property may not be recorded unless it is signed and acknowledged or sworn to by the grantor in the presence of two or more credible subscribing witnesses or acknowledged or sworn to

---

[9] Tex. Prop. Code § 11.001(a).

before and certified by an officer authorized to take acknowledgements or oaths, as applicable.

The benefit of properly recording is also reflected in § 13.002. It states that "[a]n instrument that is properly recorded in the proper county is: (1) notice to all persons of the existence of the instrument; and (2) subject to inspection by the public."[10]

However, even if the content of the deed is proper, it is acknowledged, and it is placed in the public records of the proper county, there can still be a problem with the recording. In order to be properly recorded the instrument must also be within the chain of title to the property. The chain of title refers to the recorded transactions in sequence from the sovereign of the soil to the present owner. Think back to the indexes and title searching. In conducting a standard title search using grantor and grantee indexes, the searcher is looking for specific names during a defined period of time. This means that if the instrument is recorded too early or recorded too late, it will be outside of the chain of title. This deed will be unconnected to the chain of title and will be lost. It is described as a wild deed.

While these issues impact the proper recording of the first-in-time interest to be protected from a subsequent purchaser, that ties directly to the concept of the bona fide purchaser who is trying to use the statute. If the first-in-time person *properly* records, there will never be a subsequent bona fide purchaser. As seen in the Texas Property Code § 13.002, the impact of proper recording is notice to all. This is a form of notice known as constructive record notice. We will tie all of these pieces together in the coming sections, but they are related and dependent concepts. While the focus is on proper recording providing notice, that is really also getting to the fact that a person will not be a bona fide purchaser to use the recording statute or even one of the common law equitable exceptions.

Consider that while reading the following cases that involve timing issues and notice of a prior interest.

Moore v. Curry
Supreme Court of Texas, 1872
236 Tex. 668

WALKER, J.

The patent to the land in controversy was issued to Leroy H. Smith, and the title in him is not disputed. He sold the land first to Whitesides in 1845. Whitesides neglected to record his deed until after Smith resold the land to Henry Bowman. Bowman sold to Jones, and Jones to the appellant, Moore.

---

[10] Tex. Prop. Code § 13.002.

Curry, the appellee, claims the land through mesne conveyances from Whitesides. The contest is between a senior unrecorded and a junior recorded deed from Smith, the patentee.

The doctrine which gives a junior title precedence when recorded, over a senior unrecorded title, as laid down by all writers on equity, is that the vendee in the second deed must be a bona fide purchaser without notice and for a valuable consideration.

This doctrine is recognized and very clearly stated, both in the case of Watkins v. Edwards, 23 Texas 443, and in Beatty et al. v. Whitaker, 23 Texas 526, that to postpone a prior unregistered conveyance in favor of a subsequent vendee, it must appear that he had bona fide paid the purchase money, and had neither actual nor constructive notice of the title of the prior vendee.

And a party who has not paid the purchase money cannot claim priority over one who has an older unrecorded deed. The appellant in this case fails to prove the payment of the purchase money from Bowman to Smith. This is the first link in his title from the patentee. His counsel very ably argue, that though they have not proven the consideration for this deed, that Moore had, nevertheless, obtained a good title and that those who purchased from Bowman are not chargeable with any defect in his title; upon the doctrine that a purchaser without notice takes a good title though his vendor be chargeable with notice. The deed through Bowman to Jones was recorded before Whitesides recorded his deed, and the plaintiff has proven the payment of the consideration for this deed. Jones, then, is a bona fide purchaser, without notice and for valuable consideration, and his title must prevail.

In our former opinion delivered in this case we were led to adopt an error in supposing that Whitesides had recorded his title before the deed from Bowman to Jones was recorded, having corrected this error, it becomes our duty to reverse the judgment of the District Court, and render a judgment for appellant, which is accordingly done.

NOTES & QUESTIONS:

1. The deed from Smith to Whitesides is the first-in-time deed and it is recorded. What was the problem with the recording?

2. Even though Whitesides did not record his deed immediately, could he at some point have recorded his deed and prevented the problem that occurred? If so, when?

3. After reading this case, consider these two examples. Again, you will be determining who has priority under each of the three types of recording statutes. Assume that (1) each grantee has given value for his conveyance,

(2) the search is to be conducted using a name index; and (3) *A's* interest is one that is subject to the recording statute.

4. *O* conveys Blackacre to *A* and she does not record. *O* then conveys to *X* who has actual knowledge of the earlier conveyance to *A*. *X* records his deed. *A* records her deed. Then *X* conveys to *Z* who has no actual knowledge of *A*.

   In a dispute between *A* and *Z*, who wins?
   Race statute?
   Race/notice statute?
   Notice statute?

```
                            O
        _____
                            |
        A(ur)               |
                            |
                            |
                            |   X (w/actual notice of A)
                            |   Xr
                            |
        Ar                  |
                            |
                            |   Z (no notice of A)
```

   In this example, would it make a difference if the parties searched with a tract index at a title company rather than a grantor/grantee name index? Why or why not?

5. *O* conveys Blackacre to *A* who does not record her deed. *O* then conveys to *X* who has knowledge of the *O* to *A* conveyance. *A* records her deed. Then *X* records his deed. *X* conveys to *Z*.

   In a dispute between *A* and *Z*, who wins?
   Race statute?
   Race/notice statute?
   Notice Statute?

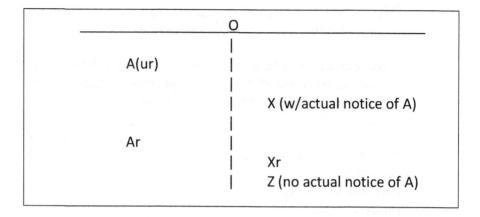

In this example, would it make a difference if the parties searched with a tract index at a title company rather than a grantor/grantee name index? Why or why not?

6. The Moore v. Curry case provided one example of how recording at the wrong time can allow the first-in-time interest to lose out. Now we will turn to another example of how recording issues can cause problems for a first-in-time interest. This case also illustrates the importance of properly determining what is indeed first in time.

Board of Education of Minneapolis v. Hughes
Supreme Court of Minnesota, 1912
136 N.W. 1095

BUNN, J.

Action to determine adverse claims to a lot in Minneapolis. The complaint alleged that plaintiff owned the lot, and the answer denied this, and alleged title in defendant L. A. Hughes. The trial resulted in a decision in favor of plaintiff, and defendants appealed from an order denying a new trial.

The facts are not in controversy and are as follows: On May 16, 1906, Carrie B. Hoerger, a resident of Faribault, owned the lot in question, which was vacant and subject to unpaid delinquent taxes. Defendant L. A. Hughes offered to pay $25 for this lot. His offer was accepted, and he sent his check for the purchase price of this and two other lots bought at the same time to Ed. Hoerger, husband of the owner, together with a deed to be executed and returned. The name of the grantee in the deed was not inserted; the space for the same being left blank. It was executed and acknowledged by Carrie B. Hoerger and her husband on May

17, 1906, and delivered to defendant Hughes by mail. The check was retained and cashed. Hughes filled in the name of the grantee, but not until shortly prior to the date when the deed was recorded, which was December 16, 1910. On April 27, 1909, Duryea & Wilson, real estate dealers, paid Mrs. Hoerger $25 for a quitclaim deed to the lot, which was executed and delivered to them, but which was not recorded until December 21, 1910. On November 19, 1909, Duryea & Wilson executed and delivered to plaintiff a warranty deed to the lot, which deed was filed for record January 27, 1910. It thus appears that the deed to Hughes was recorded before the deed to Duryea & Wilson, though the deed from them to plaintiff was recorded before the deed to defendant.

The questions for our consideration may be thus stated: (1) Did the deed from Hoerger to Hughes ever become operative? (2) If so, is he a subsequent purchaser whose deed was first duly recorded, within the language of the recording act?

1. The decision of the first question involves a consideration of the effect of the delivery of a deed by the grantor to the grantee with the name of the latter omitted from the space provided for it, without express authority to the grantee to insert his own or another name in the blank space. It is settled that a deed that does not name a grantee is a nullity, and wholly inoperative as a conveyance, until the name of the grantee is legally inserted. It is clear, therefore, and this is conceded, that the deed to defendant Hughes was not operative as a conveyance until his name was inserted as grantee.

Defendant, however, contends that Hughes had implied authority from the grantor to fill the blank with his own name as grantee, and that when he did so the deed became operative. This contention must, we think, be sustained. Whatever the rule may have been in the past, or may be now in some jurisdictions, we are satisfied that at the present day, and in this state, a deed which is a nullity when delivered because the name of the grantee is omitted becomes operative without a new execution or acknowledgment if the grantee, with either express or implied authority from the grantor, inserts his name in the blank space left for the name of the grantee. In State v. Young, 23 Minn. 551, . . . the language of Judge Mitchell is pertinent here in answer to more than one of plaintiff's contentions: "We therefore hold that parol authority is sufficient to authorize the filling of a blank in a sealed instrument, and that such authority may be given in any way by which it might be given in case of an unsealed instrument."

As in the case at bar, there was no claim that any express authority was given. It was held that this was unnecessary-that authority could be implied from circumstances, when the facts proved, all taken together and fairly considered, justify the inference. In Casserly v. Morrow, 101 Minn. 16, 111 N. W. 654, the name of an assignee in an assignment of a mortgage was absent when the instrument was delivered. The Chief Justice said: "If, however, Morrow's name was inserted as assignee in the instrument by the authority of the mortgagee, express or implied from circumstances, and then recorded, he was the legal owner of record of the mortgage and entitled to foreclose."

Unquestionably the authorities are in conflict; but this court is committed to the rule that in case of the execution and delivery of a sealed instrument, complete in all respects save that the blank for the name of the grantee is not filled, the grantee may insert his name in the blank space, provided he has authority from the grantor to do so, and, further, that this authority may be in parol, and may be implied from circumstances. We consider this the better rule, and also that it should be and is the law that when the grantor receives and retains the consideration, and delivers the deed in the condition described to the purchaser, authority to insert his name as grantee is presumed. Any other rule would be contrary to good sense and to equity. The same result could perhaps be reached by applying the doctrine of estoppel; but we prefer to base our decision on the ground of implied authority. Clearly the facts in the case at bar bring it within the principle announced, and we hold that Hughes, when he received the deed from Mrs. Hoerger, had implied authority to insert his name as grantee, in the absence of evidence showing the want of such authority. The delay in filling up the blank has no bearing on the question of the validity of the instrument when the blank was filled.

It is argued that holding that parol authority to fill the blank is sufficient violates the statute of frauds. This theory is the basis of many of the decisions that conflict with the views above expressed; but we do not think it sound. The cases in this state, and the Wisconsin, Iowa, and other decisions referred to, are abundant authority to the proposition that the authority of the grantee need not be in writing. Our conclusion is, therefore, that the deed to Hughes became operative as a conveyance when he inserted his name as grantee.

2. When the Hughes deed was recorded, there was of record a deed to the lot from Duryea & Wilson to plaintiff, but no record showing that Duryea & Wilson had any title to convey. The deed to them from the common grantor had not been recorded. We hold that this record of a deed from an apparent stranger to the title was not notice to Hughes of the prior unrecorded conveyance by his grantor. He was a subsequent purchaser in good faith for a valuable consideration, whose conveyance was first duly recorded; that is, Hughes' conveyance dates from the time when he filled the blank space, which was after the deed from his grantor to Duryea & Wilson. He was, therefore, a 'subsequent purchaser,' and is protected by the recording of his deed before the prior deed was recorded. The statute cannot be construed so as to give priority to a deed recorded before, which shows no conveyance from a record owner. It was necessary, not only that the deed to plaintiff should be recorded before the deed to Hughes, but also that the deed to plaintiff's grantor should be first recorded.

Our conclusion is that the learned trial court should have held on the evidence that defendant L. A. Hughes was the owner of the lot.

Order reversed, and new trial granted.

NOTES & QUESTIONS:

1. Which interest is actually first in time, first in right? Why?

2. Would the outcome be any different if the deed to Hughes had actually taken effect on May 17, 1906?

3. What is the problem with recording in this case?

4. Now consider the following example in light of the Bd. Of Educ. v. Hughes case. Again, you will be determining who has priority under each of the three types of recording statutes. Assume that (1) each grantee has given value for his conveyance, (2) the search is to be conducted using a name index; and (3) A's interest is one that is subject to the recording statute.

   In 2000, O conveys Blackacre to A, who does not record her deed. In 2001, A then conveys to B. B records her deed (A to B). Then in 2003, O conveys Blackacre to Z who has no notice of the earlier conveyances. Z records his deed. Finally, in 2004 B records the deed A received from O.

   In a dispute between B and Z, who wins?
   Race statute?
   Race/notice Statute?
   Notice statute?

O
A(ur)
B
Br
Z (no notice of A)
Zr
B rec O to A
Deed

In this example, would it make a difference if the parties searched with a tract index at a title company rather than a grantor/grantee name index? Why or why not?

Now that we have considered a variety of situations where recording happened too late, let us consider one example where recording actually occurs too early. You have probably already been amazed at the fact that people actually forge documents, convey the same land twice, and act carelessly with important documents like deeds. There are, in fact, situations where a person is not only conveying land that he does not currently own, but actually is conveying land that he has not *ever* owned. When this occurs, it is often because the person is negotiating the purchase of the land and expects to get it in the near future. However, the party conveying does not actually own anything at this point. What is to stop the person from conveying land he does not own to A, and then after legally acquiring title through a deed, to deny the fact that A received anything at all?

There is an equitable doctrine that operates to keep A from being harmed by O's actions. This is the doctrine of estoppel by deed or the doctrine of after acquired title. Both are labels for the same concept. The doctrine of estoppel by deed protects the buyer, A, by preventing the grantor, O, from taking back title to the property that O had already conveyed.[11] That doctrine only protects A from O. It does not operate to protect A if O engages in a subsequent conveyance.

Consider the following situation. Oliver wants to give Blackacre to his daughter Ann for her birthday, but he has not yet sealed the deal with the current owner, Xavier. Not wanting to have his plans thwarted, Oliver gives Ann a deed on her birthday in 2012 and she records it. In 2013, Oliver gets a deed from Xavier for the property. Oliver records it. Later, in 2014, when Oliver is having financial problems, he sells Blackacre to Beth who pays valuable consideration and has no actual knowledge of the earlier conveyance to Ann. Beth records her deed that day. In a dispute between Ann and Beth, who wins in each jurisdiction?

```
                              X
           _____O_____(2013)_____

                              |
           2012   A(r)         |
                              |
                              |
                              |   B (no notice of A)  (2014)
                              |   B(r)
                              |
```

---

[11] James William Singer, Introduction to Property § 11.4 (2d ed. 2005).

5. Bona Fide Purchasers and Good Faith Creditors: Questions of Notice and Consideration

Always falling back on the concept of first in time, first in right, it should be difficult for someone to be able to find an exception to the rule. We have been considering the exceptions that exist, with a focus on the recording statutes. It is important to keep in mind that not only must there be an interest that falls under the statute (or an equitable exception) but the person trying to use the statute must be the right person—a bona fide purchaser or possibly a good faith creditor.

To establish status as a bona fide purchaser (BFP), the person must be acting in good faith, without any form of notice of the prior interest, and must have paid good and valuable consideration. There are three prongs to this definition that must be satisfied. If any one of them fails, the party is not a BFP and cannot use the statute or the common law exceptions. So, for example, if *A* has a deed that is supposed to be recorded and it isn't, *A* will not lose to *B* if *B* is not a BFP. *B* could fail as a BFP for any of the reasons, it does not matter. *B* must jump through all of the hoops successfully to cut in line.

A good faith creditor (GFC), is similar to the BFP in all respects except for consideration. A good faith creditor must also be acting in good faith without any form of notice of the prior interest. However, the GFC has not given good and valuable consideration. The GFC will have a value component, but it will be different. We will further define this difference later in this section.

The prior section focused on applying the recording statute and examining issues when even a recorded document would not provide notice. As stated in that section, the proper recording of the first-in-time interest has a direct impact on the ability of someone second in time to qualify as a bona fide purchaser. Thus, we were really already considering the lack of notice requirement of a bona fide purchaser from the constructive record notice viewpoint. Now, we will turn our attention to the other forms of notice, actual and inquiry. Additionally, to complete the definition of the bona fide purchaser we will examine issues impacting good faith and also determine what is consideration or value. Finally, we will compare the bona fide purchaser, who can use any of the priority exceptions, to a good faith creditor, who may only use a recording statute if the language of the statute allows.

a. Other Notice Issues Impacting the BFP or GFC

In order to be a BFP or GFC, a party cannot have any form of notice. There are three types of notice: actual, constructive record notice, and inquiry notice. Actual notice is not usually the issue. Actual notice would mean that the person has an actual subjective awareness of the prior interest. The second-in-time person is not usually acting with actual knowledge of the fact that there was already a prior interest granted in the property. Thus, we turn to the other two forms of notice, which are usually at issue.

Constructive record notice is notice that is imputed on all subsequent parties when instruments are properly recorded in the public records. Once an instrument is properly recorded, it provides notice to everyone, even if no one ever looks at the records. This is a benefit given to an instrument that is properly recorded. It provides a protective shield that prevents someone from claiming they did not know and had no way to know about the prior interest.

There is also inquiry notice. Inquiry notice occurs when there are certain facts or circumstances that should trigger a reasonable investigation. If the person does not investigate, he will be charged with notice of whatever a reasonable investigation would have revealed. The most common situations that trigger a duty to inquire arise from statements in a recorded document in the chain of title or possession by someone other than the grantor.

The following cases provide examples of both a duty to inquire based on references in a recorded document (*Harper*) and based on possession by someone other than the grantor (*Madison*).

Harper v. Paradise
Supreme Court of Georgia, 1974
210 S.E.2d 710

INGRAM, J.

This appeal involves title to land. It is from a judgment and directed verdict granted to the appellees and denied to the appellants in the Superior Court of Oglethorpe County.

Appellants claim title as remaindermen under a deed to a life tenant with the remainder interest to the named children of the life tenant. This deed was delivered to the life tenant but was lost or misplaced for a number of years and was not recorded until 35 years later.

Appellees claim title as uninterrupted successors in title to an intervening mortgagee who purchased the property at a sheriff's sale following the foreclosure of a security deed given by the life tenant to secure a loan which became in default. Prior to the execution of the security deed by the life tenant, she obtained a quitclaim deed from all but one of the then living heirs of the original grantor who died earlier. Appellees also claim prescriptive title as a result of the peaceful, continuous, open and adverse possession of the property by them and their record predecessors in title for more than 21 years.

The life tenant died in 1972 and her children and representatives of deceased children, who were named as the remaindermen, then brought the present action to recover the land. The trial court determined that appellees held superior title to the land and it is this judgment, adverse to the remaindermen, that produced the present appeal to this court.

The above condensation of the title contentions of the parties can be understood best by reciting in detail the sequential occurrence of the facts which produced these conflicting claims of title.

On February 1, 1922, Mrs. Susan Harper conveyed by warranty deed a 106.65-acre farm in Oglethorpe County to her daughter-in-law, Maude Harper, for life with remainder in fee simple to Maude Harper's named children. The deed, which recited that it was given for Five Dollars and "natural love and affection," was lost, or misplaced, until 1957 when it was found by Clyde Harper, one of the named remaindermen, in an old trunk belonging to Maude Harper. The deed was recorded in July, 1957.

Susan Harper died sometime during the period 1925-1927 and was survived by her legal heirs, Price Harper, Prudie Harper Jackson, Mildred Chambers and John W. Harper, Maude Harper's husband. In 1928, all of Susan Harper's then living heirs, except John W. Harper, joined in executing an instrument to Maude Harper, recorded March 19, 1928 which contained the following language: "Deed, Heirs of Mrs. Susan Harper, to Mrs. Maude Harper. Whereas Mrs. Susan Harper did on or about the . . . day of March, 1927, make and deliver a deed of gift to the land hereinafter more fully described to Mrs. Maude Harper the wife of John W. Harper, which said deed was delivered to the said Mrs. Maude Harper and was not recorded; and Whereas said deed has been lost or destroyed and cannot be found; and Whereas the said Mrs. Susan Harper has since died and leaves as her heirs at law the grantors herein; Now therefore for and in consideration of the sum of $1.00, in hand paid, the receipt of which is hereby acknowledged, the undersigned Mrs. Prudence Harper Jackson, Price Harper and Ben Grant as guardian of Mildred Chambers, do hereby remise, release and forever quit claim to the said Mrs. Maude Harper, her heirs and assigns, all of their right, title, interest, claim or demand that they and each of them have or may have had in and to the (described property). To have and to hold the said property to the said Mrs. Maude Harper, her heirs and assigns, so that neither the said grantors nor their heirs nor any person or persons claiming under them shall at any time hereafter by any way or means, have, claim or demand any right, title or interest in and to the aforesaid property or its appurtenances or any part thereof. This deed is made and delivered to the said Mrs. Maude Harper to take the place of the deed made and executed and delivered by Mrs. Susan Harper during her lifetime as each of the parties hereto know that the said property was conveyed to the said Mrs. Maude Harper by the said Mrs. Susan Harper during her lifetime and that the said Mrs. Maude Harper was on said property and in possession thereof."

On February 27, 1933, Maude Harper executed a security deed, recorded the same day, which purported to convey the entire fee simple to Ella Thornton to secure a fifty dollar loan. The loan being in default, Ella Thornton foreclosed on the property, receiving a sheriff's deed executed and recorded in 1936. There is an unbroken chain of record title out of Ella Thornton to the appellees, Lincoln and William Paradise, who claim the property as grantees under a warranty deed executed and recorded in 1955. The appellees also assert title by way of peaceful, continuous, open and adverse possession by them and their predecessors in title beginning in 1940.

The appellees trace their title back through Susan Harper, but they do not rely on the 1922 deed from Susan Harper to Maude Harper as a link in their record chain of title. If appellees relied on the 1922 deed, then clearly the only interest they would have obtained would have been Maude Harper's life estate which terminated upon her death in 1972. No forfeiture shall result from a tenant for life selling the entire estate in lands; the purchaser shall acquire only his interest.

Appellees contend that the 1928 instrument executed by three of Susan Harper's then living heirs must be treated under Code s 67-2502 as having been executed by the heirs as agents or representatives of Susan Harper, thereby making both the 1922 and 1928 deeds derivative of the same source. That Code section provides: "All innocent persons, firms or corporations acting in good faith and without actual notice, who purchase for value, or obtain contractual liens, from distributees, devisees, legatees, or heirs at law, holding or apparently holding land or personal property by will or inheritance from a deceased person, shall be protected in the purchase of said property or in acquiring such a lien thereon as against unrecorded liens or conveyances created or executed by said deceased person upon or to said property in like manner and to the same extent as if the property had been purchased of or the lien acquired from the deceased person."

Appellees argue that since both deeds must be treated as having emanated from the same source, the 1928 deed has priority under Code s 29-401 because it was recorded first. Code s 29-401 provides: "Every deed conveying lands shall be recorded in the office of the clerk of the superior court of the county where the land lies. The record may be made at any time, but such deed loses its priority over a subsequent recorded deed from the same vendor, taken without notice of the existence of the first."

In opposition to the appellees' reliance on Code s 67-2502, the appellants cite the case of Mathis v. Solomon. In that case, the grantor by deed of 1923 conveyed to his wife for life, then to his heirs in remainder. This deed was not recorded until 1928. In 1926, the life tenant and one of the remaindermen conveyed the fee simple by warranty deed, recorded in 1927, to B. L. Fetner. Fetner conveyed by quitclaim deed to the defendants in 1930, and that deed was recorded in 1937. The remaindermen who had not joined in the 1926 deed to Fetner sued the defendants to recover the property. This court held in favor of the remaindermen, saying that Code s 67-2502 "enacted in favor of bona fide purchasers from 'distributees, devisees, legatees, or heirs at law, holding or apparently holding land or personal property by will or inheritance from a deceased person,' cannot be extended beyond its terms so as to aid a bona fide purchaser from a life tenant as against a remainderman who does not join in the conveyance." The court further said that Code s 96-205 (relating to voluntary conveyances and re-enacted, in substantially the same form as Code Ann. s 29-401.1), "while including bona fide purchasers from administrators, executors, and others who in effect sell land as agent of the grantor making the voluntary conveyance, does not include purchasers acquiring title from other sources."

In *Mathis*, the deed to the life tenant conveyed the remainder interest to the grantor's heirs. Thus, a subsequent purchaser from the life tenant and only one of those heirs could not rely on Code s 67-2502 since the remaining heirs of the original grantor did not join in the deed. As these heirs of the original grantor were remaindermen, their interests could not be defeated by the later deed which was recorded first.

In the present case, the remaindermen in the deed to the life tenant were not the heirs of the grantor. They were named children of the life tenant grantee. Therefore, after the death of the original grantor, Susan Harper, her heirs could have joined in a deed to an innocent person acting in good faith and without actual notice of the earlier deed. If such a deed had been made, conveying a fee simple interest without making any reference to a prior unrecorded lost or misplaced deed, Code s 67-2502 might well apply to place that deed from the heirs within the protection of Code s 29-401.

However, the 1928 deed relied upon by appellees was to the same person, Maude Harper, who was the life tenant in the 1922 deed. The 1928 deed recited that it was given in lieu of the earlier lost or misplaced deed from Susan Harper to Maude Harper and that Maude Harper was in possession of the property. Thus Maude Harper is bound to have taken the 1928 deed with knowledge of the 1922 deed. The recitals of the 1928 deed negate any contention that the grantors in that deed were holding or apparently holding the property by will or inheritance from Susan Harper. Indeed, the recitals of the 1928 deed actually serve as a disclaimer by the heirs that they were so holding or apparently holding the land.

Therefore, Code s 67-2502 is not applicable under the facts of this case and cannot be used to give the 1928 deed priority over the 1922 deed under the provisions of Code s 29-401. The recitals contained in the 1928 deed clearly put any subsequent purchaser on notice of the existence of the earlier misplaced or lost deed, and, in terms of Code s 29-401, the 1928 deed, though recorded first, would not be entitled to priority.

We conclude that it was incumbent upon the appellees to ascertain through diligent inquiry the contents of the earlier deed and the interests conveyed therein. See Henson v. Bridges, 218 Ga. 6(2) holding that "a deed in the chain of title, discovered by the investigator, is constructive notice of all other deeds which were referred to in the deed discovered," including an unrecorded plat included in the deed discovered. Although the appellees at trial denied having received any information as to the existence of the interests claimed by the appellants, the transcript fails to indicate any effort on the part of the appellees to inquire as to the interests conveyed by the lost or misplaced deed when they purchased the property in 1955. A thorough review of the record evinces no inquiry whatsoever by the defendants, or attempt to explain why such inquiry would have been futile. Thus it will be presumed that due inquiry would have disclosed the existent facts.

The appellees also contend that they have established prescriptive title by way of peaceful, continuous, open and adverse possession by them and their predecessors in title beginning in 1940. However, the remaindermen named in the 1922 deed had no right of possession until the life's tenant's death in 1972. "Prescription does not begin to run in favor of a grantee under a deed from a life tenant, against a remainderman who does not join in the deed, until the falling in of the life-estate by the death of the life tenant." Mathis v. Solomon, supra, p. 312, of 188 Ga., p. 25 of 4 S.E.2d.

A remaining enumeration of error asserted by appellants which deals with the admissibility into evidence of a title examiner's certificate of title is unnecessary to decide in view of the conclusions reached above. The trial court erred in granting appellees' motion for directed verdict and in overruling the appellants' motion for directed verdict. Therefore, the judgment of the trial court is reversed with direction that judgment be entered in favor of the appellants.

NOTES & QUESTIONS:

1. What did the court find triggered the duty to inquire?

2. What would a reasonable investigation be under the circumstances? What information would that investigation reveal? What should Paradise have done to be able to qualify as a BFP?

Madison v. Gordon
Supreme Court of Texas, 2001
39 S.W.3d 604

PER CURIAM.

This case involves a title dispute and the characteristics of possession necessary to give a subsequent purchaser constructive notice of a possessor's claim. The court of appeals held that possession alone gives a purchaser constructive notice. 9 S.W.3d 476, 479. We disagree. Under Texas law, possession giving rise to constructive notice must be visible, open, exclusive, and unequivocal.

The purchaser in this case proved as a matter of law that the claimant's possession was not exclusive or unequivocal. Accordingly, we reverse the court of appeals' judgment and render judgment for the purchaser.

Ronald Gordon owned a four-plex in LaMarque. He lived in one unit and rented out the others. Gordon has resided on this property since 1988. However, a number of title transfers have occurred, beginning in 1991. This dispute arises between Gordon and the fourth subsequent transferee, Anna Marie Madison, who is claiming bona fide purchaser status.

The first transfer occurred in 1991 when Gordon, while in jail, hired an attorney, Alton Williams, to defend him. Gordon signed a warranty deed conveying his property to a bondsman. The deed was properly recorded. Gordon also signed a note payable to the bondsman and secured by the property. The deed does not reflect this note. A year later, the bondsman conveyed the property to Williams, who properly recorded the deed. Williams then borrowed money and secured the loan with the property the following year. This deed of trust was also properly recorded.

In late 1993, Williams, in need of cash and unable to secure a loan, asked Madison, his fiancé, to purchase the LaMarque property. Madison agreed to do so and applied for a loan. The bank approved her application, and, in February 1994, Madison signed a note and deed of trust, payable to the bank. The bank recorded both documents. Williams then conveyed the property to Madison by warranty deed reflecting the vendor's lien recognized in Madison's note. Williams used the proceeds to pay his prior loan and taxes on the property.

In 1995, Gordon sued Madison, Williams, the bondsman, and the bank to recover title to the property. He also sued each defendant for fraud, civil conspiracy, and Deceptive Trade Practices Act violations. Madison counterclaimed against Gordon to quiet title and for attorney fees and costs as sanctions for a frivolous DTPA suit. Madison also filed a cross-claim against Williams for misrepresentation.

Gordon and Madison both filed summary judgment motions. Gordon's summary judgment motion claimed that the initial transfer to the bondsman was intended as a mortgage and that the bondsman's subsequent transfer to Williams was thus fraudulent. He also claimed that Madison could not assert bona fide purchaser as an affirmative defense because she had actual or, alternatively, constructive notice of his claims.

Madison's summary judgment motion invoked her status as bona fide purchaser. She claimed she was a bona fide purchaser because she acquired the property in good faith, for value, and without notice, actual or constructive, of any third-party claim or interest. She claimed that Williams told her nothing about Gordon and that she did not otherwise have actual notice. She also claimed she had no constructive notice through the county's deed records because those records showed only Williams as the property's owner. She further contended that Gordon was on notice that the deed records showed Williams as the owner since sometime in 1992, yet he did nothing about it. Additionally, she claimed that, although Gordon has continued living on the property since 1988, he last claimed the property as his homestead and last paid property taxes in 1991—the year he transferred the property to the bondsman.

The trial court concluded that Madison was a bona fide purchaser, granted Madison's motion, and denied Gordon's motion. The trial court granted Gordon's motion to sever, and he appealed. The court of appeals reversed the trial court's judgment and rendered judgment for Gordon on Madison's affirmative defense. 9 S.W.3d at 480. It held that, as a matter of law, Madison was not a bona fide purchaser because Gordon's possession gave her constructive notice of his claim. 9 S.W.3d at 480. The court of appeals also remanded to the trial court the issue of whether Williams' transfer to Madison was illegal. 9 S.W.3d at 480. But the court of appeals affirmed the trial court's summary judgment for Madison on Gordon's fraud, civil conspiracy, and DTPA claims and on her counterclaim for attorney's fees. 9 S.W.3d at 480. Only Madison filed a petition for review in this Court. The sole issue in her petition is whether Gordon's possession gave Madison constructive notice of his claims. Gordon did not file a response to Madison's petition.

Status as a bona fide purchaser is an affirmative defense to a title dispute. *See* Cooksey v. Sinder, 682 S.W.2d 252, 253 (Tex. 1984) (per curiam). A bona fide purchaser is not subject to certain claims or defenses. *See* Carter v. Converse, 550 S.W.2d 322, 329 (Tex. Civ. App.—Tyler 1977, writ ref'd n.r.e.). To receive this special protection, one must acquire property in good faith, for value, and without notice of any third-party claim or interest. Houston Oil Co. v. Hayden, 104 Tex. 175, 135 S.W. 1149, 1152 (1911); *Carter*, 550 S.W.2d at 329. Notice may be constructive or actual. Flack v. First Nat'l Bank, 226 S.W.2d 628, 631 (Tex. 1950); American Surety Co. v. Bache, 82 S.W.2d 181, 183 (Tex. Civ. App.—Fort Worth 1935, writ ref'd). Actual notice rests on personal information or knowledge. Flack, 226 S.W.2d at 631. Constructive notice is notice the law imputes to a person not having personal information or knowledge. *Flack*, 226 S.W.2d at 632.

One purchasing land may be charged with constructive notice of an occupant's claims. This implied-notice doctrine applies if a court determines that the purchaser has a duty to ascertain the rights of a third-party possessor. *See* Collum v. Sanger Bros., 98 Tex. 162, 82 S.W. 459, 460 (1904); American Surety Co., 82 S.W.2d at 183. When this duty arises, the purchaser is charged with notice of all the occupant's claims the purchaser might have reasonably discovered on proper inquiry. Dixon v. Cargill, 104 S.W.2d 101, 102 (Tex. Civ. App.—Eastland 1937, writ ref'd); *see also* Flack, 226 S.W.2d at 632. The duty arises, however, only if the possession is visible, open, exclusive, and unequivocal. *See* Strong v. Strong, 128 Tex. 470, 98 S.W.2d 346, 350 (1936) (holding claimant residing as "a member of [the record title-owner's] family" was not open or exclusive); *see also* Shaver

v. National Title & Abstract Co., 361 S.W.2d 867, 869 (Tex. 1962) (holding buried pipeline not "visible"); Paris Grocer Co. v. Burks, 101 Tex. 106, 105 S.W. 174, 176 (1907) (holding severed portion of a tract of land, though fenced off, was "too uncertain and equivocal" to give purchaser notice); Boyd v. Orr, 170 S.W.2d 829, 834 (Tex. Civ. App.—Texarkana 1943, writ ref'd) (holding minor children's occupancy in mother's homestead was "not the character of possession as would constitute constructive notice"); DeGuerin v. Jackson, 50 S.W.2d 443, 448 (Tex. Civ. App.—Texarkana 1932) (holding there was no "visible" circumstance pointing to claimant as possessor of field and noting that "all authorities agree" that the possession must be "open, visible, and unequivocal" to impute notice to a potential purchaser), aff'd, 124 Tex. 424, 77 S.W.2d 1041 (1935).

In *Strong*, we described the kind of possession sufficient to give constructive notice as "consist[ing] of open, visible, and unequivocal acts of occupancy in their nature referable to exclusive dominion over the property, sufficient upon observation to put an intending purchaser on inquiry as to the rights of such possessor." *Strong*, 98 S.W.2d at 350. Possession that meets these requirements—visible, open, exclusive, and unequivocal possession—affords notice of title equivalent to the constructive notice deed registration affords. *Strong*, 98 S.W.2d at 348. However, we also held that "ambiguous or equivocal possession which may appear subservient or attributable to the possession of the holder of the legal title is not sufficiently indicative of ownership to impute notice as a matter of law of the unrecorded rights of such possessor." *Strong*, 98 S.W.2d at 350.

Gordon's possession as a tenant in a multi-unit structure did not satisfy the criteria necessary to give Madison constructive notice. His possession was neither exclusive nor unequivocal. As rental property, one would expect occupants on the property. Indeed, Gordon was one of four tenants living on the property, and there was nothing to indicate he would later claim title. Gordon's occupancy simply does not meet the exclusive requirement necessary to impute notice of his claims to Madison.

Nor does Gordon's possession meet *Strong*'s requirement that possession be unequivocal. When an occupant's possession is compatible with another's ownership assertion, the occupant's possession cannot be said to be unequivocal. See *Strong*, 98 S.W.2d at 350. Here, Gordon's occupancy was compatible with Williams' assurances of ownership. Thus his possession was "ambiguous or equivocal possession which may [have] appear[ed] subservient or attributable to" Williams. See *Strong*, 98 S.W.2d at 350. Accordingly, his possession was not unequivocal.

There are cases that seemingly support Gordon's position that possession alone gives rise to constructive notice. See, e.g., Moore v. Chamberlain, 109 Tex. 64, 195 S.W. 1135 (1917); *Collum*, 82 S.W. at 459; Aldridge v. North E. Indep. Sch. Dist., 428 S.W.2d 447 (Tex. App.—San Antonio 1968, writ ref'd); Bell v. Smith, 532

S.W.2d 680 (Tex. Civ. App.—Fort Worth 1976, no writ). Though these cases correctly concluded that the third-party's possession gave rise to constructive notice, they do not mention *Strong*'s requirements that the possession be visible, open, exclusive, and unequivocal. But in each of these cases, the occupant lived in a single-unit dwelling. Arguably, this sole possession of property implicates visibility, openness, exclusivity, and unequivocality. Consequently, while it would have been better to assess the *Strong* requirements, we do not question the ultimate outcome in these cases.

Texas law requires visible, open, exclusive, and unequivocal possession to put a purchaser on notice of a possessor's claims. Gordon's possession does not satisfy these requirements. Therefore, Madison is a bona fide purchaser, not subject to Gordon's claims. Accordingly, without hearing oral argument, we reverse the court of appeals' judgment and render judgment for Madison.

NOTES & QUESTIONS:

1. What is required to qualify as possession to trigger a duty to inquire? Does it depend on the type of property involved?

2. Most courts use a standard similar to that of adverse possession. When we cover adverse possession in the next chapter, you will see that in considering the element of actual possession, often the nature of the property involved does inform the requirement of the nature of possession to qualify as actual possession. This same type of approach is used for a duty to inquire based on possession. The subsequent purchaser must investigate activity that appears to be possession that is not subservient to the grantor.

b. Consideration Issues for Bona Fide Purchaser and Good Faith Creditor Status

What is consideration? This is the distinguishing factor between a BFP and a GFC. In a recording statute like the one in Texas, there is protection for both bona fide purchasers and good faith creditors. However, most states do not protect creditors under the statute and the common law exceptions only protect purchasers, not creditors. The difference really comes down to timing of when the value was given in relation to obtaining an interest in the land. A bank that lends the purchase money for real property is actually a purchaser. A bank that lends money in exchange for a deed of trust is actually a purchaser. A person or company who lends funds or advances credit, later obtains a judgment, and then takes a lien against "any and all real property *O* owns in *X* county" is not a purchaser. What is the difference? The timing. The bank that gives the purchase money or some other loan and gets a deed of trust or mortgage on the property is giving the value in exchange for a security interest in the real property at that time. The bank is only advancing the value because it is receiving collateral in exchange. It is essentially purchasing its interest in the land.

However, the creditor who advances funds or credit without seeking anything in return is not a purchaser. Even if a lien is ultimately obtained, that is just for an antecedent debt, not new consideration. That creditor did not purchase an interest in *O*'s real property. Thus, if there is an interest earlier in time than the creditor, the creditor is in no worse position that it was before. However, if the bank or another person acts as a purchaser and there is a prior interest, that purchaser is in a worse position. The purchaser only advanced the value in exchange for that interest.

Keep that distinction in mind while reading the next case.

McKamey v. Thorp
Supreme Court of Texas, 1884
61 Tex. 648

WILLIE C. J.

[Ed. Note: The facts were that Mrs. McKamey inherited property from her father, which would have been considered her separate property. She sold this property, and the proceeds from that sale would have similarly been considered her separate property. She turned this money over to her husband to invest for her benefit, which he did, including purchasing the property at issue in the case. Although this new property, too, would have been Mrs. McKamey's separate property, title was placed in both her name and her husband's name, thus giving the appearance that it was community property owned by both Mr. and Mrs. McKamey. The property was subsequently sold to pay Mr. McKamey's debt to a man by the name of Thompson. Thompson purchased the property at the sheriff's sale by "bidding his debt," that is, offering to buy the property for the amount of money Mr. McKamey owed Thompson. Thompson subsequently sold the property to Thorpe and the other defendants.

Thorpe and the other defendants were aware of Mrs. McKamey's interest, and thus, if he was to prevail against her claim to superior title, Thorpe needed show that Thompson had superior title because of either the recording statute or one of the other exceptions.

The court determined that a resulting trust existed in Mrs. McKamey's favor, meaning that she had an equitable interest in the property. Because her resulting trust was not subject to the recording statute, Thompson did not have priority based on Mrs. McKamey's failure to record her interest.

The court next turned to the issue of whether Thompson was a bona fide purchaser, such that he might have priority based on one of the other exceptions.]

[The title of Thompson] must depend upon whether or not he had notice at the time of sale, and if not, then whether or not he was a purchaser for valuable consideration.

As Thompson bought the property in controversy without notice of Mrs. McKamey's title, the only question for our decision is: Was he a purchaser for valuable consideration, having paid the amount of his bid by crediting it upon his judgment against the defendant in execution?

A review of our decisions will show that in a few cases intimations have been made to the effect that one buying under such circumstances is to be treated as a bona fide purchaser, and that in other cases the rule has been distinctly laid down to the contrary.

In Blankenship v. Douglas, 26 Tex. 225, an intimation was thrown out to the effect that a creditor thus buying was a bona fide purchaser, but it was added that it was not intended to express any authoritative opinion upon the point.

In Wallace v. Campbell, 54 Tex. 90, 91, it was said that such a purchase might be bona fide when a previous judgment or execution lien had been secured upon the property sold. The creditor would then hold through his previous lien and not merely through his purchase at the judicial sale.

It may be also remarked that in such case a purchaser surrenders an existing security, viz., the previous lien of his judgment or execution, and this is held equivalent to the payment of a valuable consideration. Love v. Taylor, 26 Miss. 574; Padgett v. Lawrence, 10 Paige ch., 179. It is obvious from this that where there is no such prior lien acquired, as in case of a resulting trust, the foundation of the creditor's title through the purchase at sheriff's sale is removed and the title itself must fall. These decisions are, therefore, not authority for holding that a judgment creditor, purchasing at his own sale, without any previous lien acquired upon the property, is a purchaser for valuable consideration.

On the contrary, in Ayers v. Duprey, 27 Tex. 594, it was held that "it will not constitute a bona fide purchase that the creditor bids off the premises and applies the bid on his own judgment. That is a precedent debt, and the consideration is not advanced upon the faith of the "judgment." Whilst this point was not necessary to a decision of the cause, it was raised by the record and passed upon by the court. In the subsequent case of Delespine v. Campbell, 52 Tex.,12, the doctrine on this subject as stated in Ayers v. Duprey, is approved and followed.

The decided tendency of our decisions seems therefore, to be in favor of the doctrine that a creditor buying at his own sale and crediting his bid upon the judgment is not a purchaser for value. And this view seems to be supported by very high authority. 1 Story's Eq., sec. 420, note 3 and authorities cited.

Our Revised Statutes, under which this case must be decided, provide that "a purchaser under execution shall be deemed to be an innocent purchaser without notice in all cases where he would be deemed to be such had the sale been made voluntarily by the defendant in person." Art. 2318.

We have therefore, only to inquire in what cases a purchase from a defendant, in execution at private sale, is deemed a bona fide purchaser, in order to determine when he will be considered when buying at sheriff s sale.

It seems to be held by the great weight of American authors that a creditor who buys from his debtor, and pays the consideration money by merely crediting the amount upon a pre-existing debt, is not a bona fide purchaser for value. This doctrine proceeds upon the principle that the creditor receiving the conveyance divests himself of no right, and place himself in no worse situation than he would have been if he had received notice of the prior title existing in the property in favor of a third party. He is treated as advancing nothing on the faith of his purchase, and is losing nothing if the apparent title of his vendor should prove worthless. Dickerson v. Tillinghast, *supra*; Wright v. Douglass, 10 Barb., 107.

As a natural result of this principle, if a valid security such as a mortgage of judgment lien, is surrendered, or in addition to the precedent debt a new consideration is advanced, or new liabilities are incurred, the purchase will become bona fide. Love v. Taylor, *supra*; Padgett v. Larence, *supra*. And in most of the American courts the purchaser of negotiable paper is held not to be within the rule, but this arises from consideration pertaining to mercantile law alone and the necessities of commerce, which require that such paper should pass from hand to hand more freely than any other species of property. Swife v. Tyson, 16 Pet , 1; Brush v. Scribner, 11 Conn. 388.

None of these exceptions are of course applicable to a purchase, like the present, of land by a creditor who has advanced no new consideration, surrendered no security, but merely credited the consideration money upon a larger indebtedness held by him against his debtor.

From the decisions made by this court previously to the Revised Statutes, the principle upon which they rest, and the authorities cited to sustain them, it would seem that the article of our statute cited above is but declaratory of the law as it already existed.

In any event it cannot be said that in placing execution sales upon the same plane with the private conveyances made by the debtor, the statute has given the creditor purchasing any better position than he before possessed. For it is sometimes held that an execution creditor purchasing at his own sale, and crediting his bid on the judgment, may be a bona fide purchaser, when, if he had received a conveyance voluntarily from the debtor from the same consideration, he would not have occupied that position. Compare Dickerson v. Tillinghast, *supra*, with Wood v. Chapin, 3 Kern., 509.

Indeed there may be some reason for the difference, as the purchaser at sheriff's sale must needs [sic] pay a portion of his bid in settlement of the expenses of the cause, which the private purchaser does not and in addition it is the policy of the law to encourage the judgment creditor to bid at his own sales and thus create competition, and cause the property to bring a larger price for the benefit of the debtor. But be this as it may, the statute places both classes of purchasers upon the same footing, and a purchaser at sheriff's sale cannot be protected unless the law would also shield him had he bought privately from his debtor, the defendant in execution.

Thompson was not, therefore, a bona fide purchaser of the property in controversy, and his vendees, the defendants, having bought with notice of Mrs. McKamey's claim, judgment should have been rendered for the plaintiffs below. The judgment is therefore reversed, and will be rendered here in favor of the appellants that they recover the land sued for, and their costs, and have their writ of possession against the appellees.

REVERSED AND RENDERED.

NOTES & QUESTIONS:

1.   Even if there is consideration from a legal standpoint, what is good and valuable? How much is enough. There is no real bright line when dealing with the amount, which leaves this as a fact question. All courts agree that the consideration does not have to be full fair market value. Additionally, all courts agree that the amount must be more than nominal because then it is more like a gift than a purchase. However, what if the amount is somewhere in the middle? That is where the specific facts and circumstances often dictate the outcome.

c.   The BFP and GFC: In Good Faith

The last component of BFP and GFC status is that the person is acting in good faith. Facts and circumstances surrounding the transaction may make it appear to not be In good faith, even if there is no notice and good and valuable consideration was advanced.

Imagine O approaches B on a Friday afternoon about selling him a property that B could use as another rental property in his business. O tells B he is having cash flow problems and offers to sell the property to B for $25,000 (FMV is $35,000) if he can pay in cash before 8:00 a.m. on Monday. B has no idea that O has just sold the property earlier in the morning to A. The deed from O to A is not yet recorded in the public records. B is not in possession of the property. The price is close to FMV and would be good and valuable consideration. If B purchases the property and records his deed and then has a dispute with A, who wins? It depends. Is B acting in good faith? There is a document that is not yet recorded to provide constructive notice. There is no actual or inquiry notice. The amount of consideration is good and valuable. It will come down to whether B is acting in good faith. In order to allow the first in time, first in right to prevail, the courts may find that B did not act in good faith due to the circumstances surrounding the sale (need cash in hand by 8:00 a.m. Monday when approached late in the day on Friday?).

Another issue that can impact good faith is the presence of a quitclaim deed in the chain of title. There are three different approaches taken to quitclaim deeds:

(1) As a matter of law, a person accepting a quitclaim deed does not take in good faith. Additionally, the holder of a title in which there appears, however remote, a quitclaim deed may not assert the claim of innocent purchaser as against an outstanding title or secret trust or equity that was existing when the quitclaim was executed. (Texas)

(2) A quitclaim deed in the chain of title puts the purchaser on inquiry notice and must conduct a reasonable investigation; the purchaser could possibly qualify as a BFP if the reasonable investigation would not have revealed any prior interest.

(3) A quitclaim deed in and of itself has no impact on BFP status; treated the same as a warranty deed.

The final issue that impacts good faith is a forgery. If a deed is a forgery, it is void and passes nothing, not even to one who would otherwise qualify as a BFP. Additionally, if there is a forgery in the chain of title, per se no one in that chain of title can be in good faith, even if the later purchaser is completely unaware). This may seem harsh to the otherwise innocent BFP, but it is more important to keep forgeries from having an impact on land titles.

6. The Shelter Rule as an Exception to BFP/GFC Status

There are circumstances where a person who is a party to a priority dispute will prevail, even though he is not actually a BFP or GFC. This happens because of the shelter rule. The shelter rule provides that one who is not a bona fide purchaser (BFP), but who takes an interest in property from a BFP, may be sheltered in the latter's protective status. The BFP who records first obtains full rights in the property over the earlier buyer who did not record.[12] Why have such a rule? It is not to protect the subsequent party who does not qualify as a BFP or GFC, but it is to protect the person who did qualify for a priority exception. If that person cannot provide shelter to someone who takes from him, then the priority will be useless. The shelter allows him to convey the property to another even if

---

[12] Am. Jur. Vendor § 419. Strekal v. Espe, 114 P.3d 67 (Colo. Ct. App. 2004); Richart v. Jackson, 758 A.2d 319 (Vt. 2000). The Shelter Rule also provides shelter for a GFC if that person is allowed priority under the state's recording statute. So, a BFP can shelter anyone, a GFC can provide shelter if using a recording statute that allows the GFC to take priority.

the underlying facts and circumstances are now known. This allows for good economic use and marketability of the land.

Consider this example:

O conveys Blackacre to *A* and she does not record her deed. *O* then conveys to *X* who has no notice of the prior conveyance to *A*. *X* records his deed. Then *A* records her deed. *X* then conveys to *C* who has actual notice of the earlier *O* to *A* conveyance.

In a dispute between *A* and *C*, who wins?

Race statute?

Race/notice statute?

Notice statute?

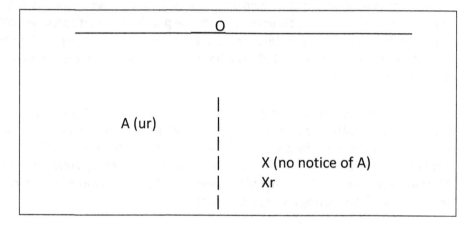

Is the result any different if instead of *C* having notice of *A*, C received the property through gift or inheritance and provided no consideration?

REVIEW PROBLEMS: APPLYING THE TEXAS RECORDING STATUTE AND BFP/GFC RULES

The correct answer for each problem is given, using Texas law. State the reason for the conclusions reached. *Unless otherwise noted*, all purported transfers are of legal title subject to the recording statute.

1. *O* conveys Blackacre to *A* and the deed is unrecorded. *O* then conveys Blackacre to *B*, who satisfies the requirements of a bona fide

purchaser. *B* does not record. *B* then conveys to *C* who has notice of the earlier *O* to *A* conveyance. *C* takes good title against *A*. Why?

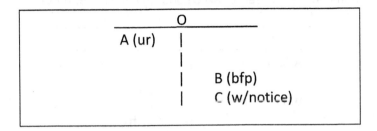

2. *O* conveys Blackacre to *A* and *A* does not record the deed. *O* then conveys Blackacre to *B*, who has actual knowledge of *A*'s interest. *B* does not record. *B* then conveys to *C*, who qualifies as a bona fide purchaser. *C* takes good title against *A*. Why?

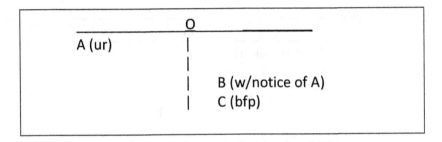

3. *O* conveys Blackacre to *A*, who records the deed. *A* then conveys to *B*, who does not record. *O* then conveys to *C*. *C* does not record. *B*'s title is good against *C*, regardless of *C*'s good faith and payment of value. Why?

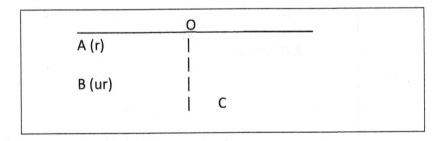

4. *O* conveys Blackacre to *A* who does not record. *A* then conveys to *B*, who records the *A* to *B* deed. *O* then conveys to *C*, who qualifies as a bona fide purchaser. *C* takes good title against *B*. Why?

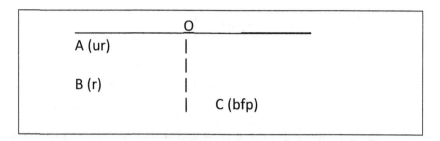

5. *O* enters into a contract of sale for Blackacre with *A*. *A* records the contract. *O* then conveys Blackacre by deed to *B*. *A*'s contract of sale has priority over *B*'s interest. Why?

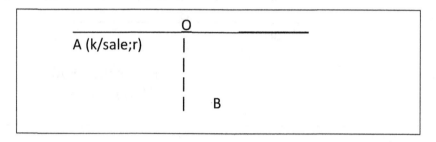

6. *O* enters into a contract of sale for Blackacre with *A*. *A* does not record the contract. *O* then conveys Blackacre by deed to *B*. *B* qualifies as a BFP. *B* does not record. *B* takes legal title free from *A*'s contract of sale. Why?

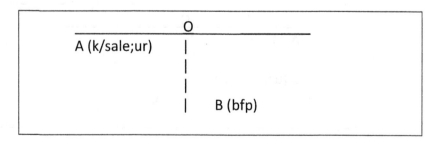

7. *O* conveys Blackacre to *A*. *A* does not record her deed. *O* then conveys Blackacre to *B*, who has notice of *A*. *B*'s deed is unrecorded. Then *A*

records her deed. *B* then conveys to *C*. *A* prevails over *C* regardless of *C*'s actual good faith and value. Why?

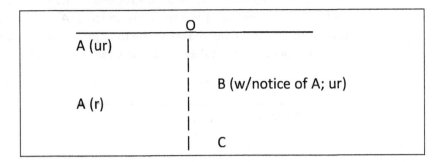

8. *O* conveys Blackacre to *A*. *A* does not record her deed. *O* has outstanding debts and *O*'s creditor *B* gets a judgment against him and obtains a lien against "any and all property *O* owns in McLennan County." Under the Texas recording statute, *B*'s lien is good against *A*. Why?

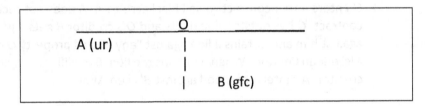

9. *O* conveys Blackacre to *A*. *A* does not record her deed. *O* has outstanding debts and *O*'s creditor *B* gets a judgment against him and obtains a lien against "any and all property *O* owns in McLennan County." *B* has a foreclosure sale and *C* purchases at the foreclosure sale with notice of *A*'s interest. Under the Texas recording statute, *C* takes good title against *A*. Why? → GFC GETS PRIORITY UNDER RECORDING STAT.

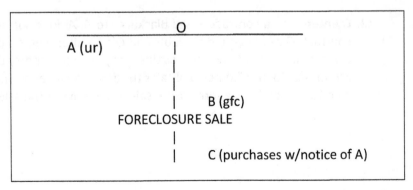

10. *O* conveys Blackacre to *A*. *A* does not record her deed. *O* has outstanding debts and *O*'s creditor *B* gets a judgment against him and obtains a lien against "any and all property *O* owns in McLennan County." When *B* obtains the lien, *B* has notice of *A*'s interest. *B* has a foreclosure sale and *C* purchases at the foreclosure sale. *C* qualifies as a bona fide purchaser. *C* takes good title against *A*. Why?

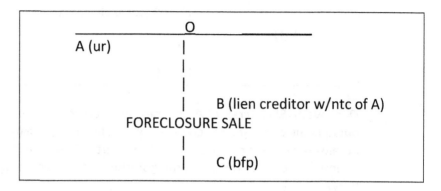

11. *O* enters into a contract to sell Blackacre to *A*. *A* does not record the contract. *O* has outstanding debts and *O*'s creditor *B* gets a judgment against him and obtains a lien against "any and all property *O* owns in McLennan County." When *B* obtains the lien, *B* qualifies as a good faith creditor. *A*'s interest is good against *B*'s lien. Why?

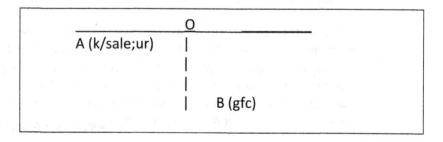

12. *O* enters into a contract to sell Blackacre to *A*. *A* does not record the contract. *O* has outstanding debts and *O*'s creditor *B* gets a judgment against him and obtains a lien against "any and all property *O* owns in McLennan County." When *B* obtains the lien, *B* qualifies as a good faith creditor. *B* conducts a foreclosure sale and *C* buys at the sale without

any notice of *A*. *C* takes legal title free of *A*'s interest. Why?

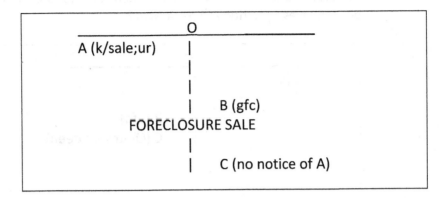

13. *O* conveys Blackacre to *A*. *A* does not record her deed. *O* then conveys to *B* by quitclaim deed. *B* then conveys to *C*, who gives value and has no notice of *A*'s interest. In Texas, neither *B* nor *C* can take title better than *A*'s. Why?

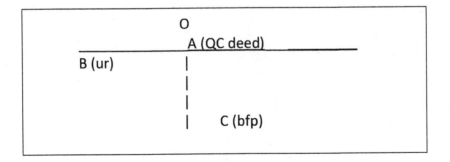

14. *O* conveys to *A* via quitclaim deed. *A* conveys to *B*. *B* does not record her deed. *A* then conveys to *C* who qualifies as a BFP. *C* takes good title against *B*. Why?

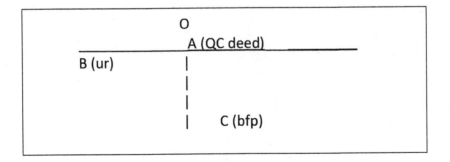

15. *O* conveys Blackacre to *A*. *A* does not record. *O* then conveys to *B* who qualifies as a bona fide purchaser. *B* then conveys to *C* via quitclaim deed. *C* takes good title against *A*. Why?

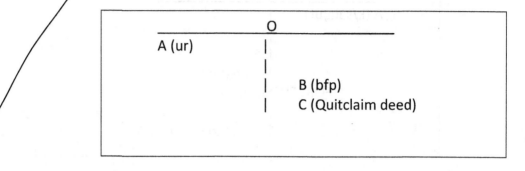

```
                              O
  _____|_____
  A (ur)                     |
                             |
                             |        B (bfp)
                             |        C (Quitclaim deed)
                             |
```

B ESTABLISHES PRIORITY + SHELTERS C

Chapter 9
Acquiring Property by Adverse Possession

Adverse possession is a means of acquiring title to property without a conveyance, without a deed. There are a variety of public policy reasons behind adverse possession that we will discuss. Adverse possession is also referred to as "title by limitation" because it is a variation on the statute of limitation. It is not a statute of limitation but in some instances has the same effect. If a plaintiff brings a trespass to try title suit in Texas, the defendant claiming adverse possession may assert it as an affirmative defense. The defense is basically that although the plaintiff may have had record title to the property through a deed or other instrument, the defendant has acquired title through adverse possession. It is as if the record title holder conveyed the property to the adverse possessor without any actual conveyance.

We have just spent weeks dealing with all of the aspects of conveying real property through the real estate transaction. We picked apart the contract, the deed, the process, the recording system, and attempts to obtain good title. We even analyzed what happens if you don't have good title or lose out to the priority of another interest, and what remedies you may have. What we are about to cover is a completely different manner of obtaining legal title to real property—no contract, no deed, no consideration, no title searches, but a challenge nonetheless.

Why is this doctrine even necessary?

Let's think about the priority exceptions we just discussed and the first in time first in right rule. We have O who owns Blackacre and he's a real scoundrel. He sold Blackacre to his friend A on October 1, 2000. He conveys the property with a general warranty deed that was recorded the same day.

O is in law school racking up a bunch of debt and is in need of some cash, so he sells Blackacre again to his law school classmate B. B didn't do so well with the title search problem in his property class and decides not to worry about it. Surely O is a trustworthy guy. So B buys the property from O. Blackacre has a FMV of $100,000 and B pays $45,000. The deed from O to B is a quitclaim deed. This transaction is completed on August 1, 2007.

B is second in time and he cannot be a BFP because he had constructive record notice of the person first in time.[1] In a dispute between the A and B, B is

---

[1] In Texas the quitclaim deed would also prevent B from being in good faith.

going to lose because he cannot be a BFP to take advantage of any of the exceptions. However, if *B* takes possession of the property and establishes all of the required elements for the right period of time, *B* can take legal title to the property away from *A* who is otherwise first in time, first in right.

Under circumstances like this example, most people can accept and understand the role of adverse possession. However, adverse possession has been in the news more recently for bizarre actions by individuals that have the public wondering why this legal doctrine even exists.

In December 2007, the *Los Angeles Times* reported a story about a Colorado couple who successfully adversely possessed one-third of the lot located next to them, which was valued at $1 million.[2] The story reported that for more than 20 years, a retired judge and his lawyer wife trespassed on their neighbor's land. The court ultimately awarded title to the couple, stating the couple had demonstrated that their attachment to the land was "stronger than the true owners' attachment." Others in the community were outraged. A sign was placed facing their home that read "You will never enjoy a stolen view."

In July 2011, the acts of Kenneth Robinson started a swarm of attempted adverse possessions in Texas.[3] Mr. Robinson moved into a $300,000 home in Flower Mound, Texas, claiming it as his own. He claimed that a little known law called adverse possession allowed him to claim the home. The owners had vacated the property and it was in the process of foreclosure. Mr. Robinson saw an opportunity and moved in, but his attempt proved unsuccessful when Bank of America had him evicted after eight months of occupancy.[4]

There are occasions, usually rare occasions, where adverse possession occurs because the person knows he doesn't own the property and uses it anyway. There are also occasions when someone is on land that they think is their own but can acquire it through adverse possession. Neighbors often end up adversely possessing part of another's driveway or yard due to fencing and survey issues.

---

[2] Correll, Dee Dee. This Land Is Not Their Land—Now, Los Angeles Times (Dec. 3, 2007).

[3] Sanburn, Josh. Man Gets $300,000 Home for $16, Time Moneyland (July 18, 2011). Following this story about Mr. Robinson there were cases coming up all over the state. On October 26, 2011, abclocal.go.com reported that a woman was charged with burglary for squatting in a Fort Bend County home. The woman told the investigator that she learned about taking possession of distressed properties after attending a seminar in Houston. In November 2011, WFAA.com reported that constables continued to evict adverse possessors in Tarrant County.

[4] Dorning, Anne-Marie. Texas Squatter with $16 McMansion Kicked Out After 8 Months, Good Morning America Yahoo News, http://gma.yahoo.com/teas-squatter-16-mcmansion-kicked-8-months-173113977--abc-news.html (Feb. 7, 2012).

No matter how it happens or why it happens, it is a transfer of legal title without a document and without any money changing hands. This is why it is often referred to as "title by theft."

During the 19th century, American courts modified English adverse possession law to suit the unique American conditions. States have individual statutes to dictate the time length required. Sometimes the statutes make additional requirements aside from the standard elements. We will cover the standard elements of adverse possession to understand their meaning and application. Then we will turn to the variety of Texas statutes and their particular application.

A. Introduction and History of Adverse Possession

While referred to as "title by theft, " adverse possession actually has some beneficial uses in property law. While it seems contrary to common sense at first glance, there are explanations for the valid use of this legal doctrine.

As early as 2000 BC, as written in the Code of Hammurabi, a person who spent three years using a house, garden, or field owned by a soldier absent on military duty acquired title to the property even if the soldier later returned. Why would that happen to a member of the military? The practical reality of the time was that the landowner would most likely die in battle and would not return to the land. By allowing this early form of adverse possession, the land was kept in productive use, which was essential at the time.

Adverse possession became part of the English legal system in 1275 with the Statute of Westminster, which limited actions for recovery of land by precluding a suitor from alleging dated claims. By 1639, there was a statute of limitations that required suits to recover possession of land to be brought within 20 years. The prudent landowner would inspect his property regularly and eject any trespassers. If the owner did not bother to do that during a 20-year period, then it could be reasonably interpreted as the owner's acceptance of the possessor's title.

During the settling of America and westward expansion, the doctrine of adverse possession became even more crucial. Think about the movie *Far and Away*. In the newly independent United States, adverse possession flourished. There were vast undeveloped wilderness lands that the American government wanted occupied and colonized. There were many disputes because many times the land was not surveyed or, even if it was, the boundary lines were not clearly marked. Often the land title was held by absentee speculators. The pioneer settlers without any title claims often appropriated vacant land, cleared timber, and started farms. There was massive title confusion. Adverse possession helped to clear that confusion.

B. Policy Rationale and Function of Adverse Possession

Adverse possession statutes are often referred to as specialized statutes of limitations, but that is misleading. The ordinary statute of limitations simply acts as an affirmative defense if suit is brought. If adverse possession were purely a statute of limitations, the claimant would have to wait to be sued and then assert the claim to the land. However, that is not the case. The adverse possession statutes also provide affirmative rights to the claimant.

Example: *A* takes possession of Blackacre, a farm owned by *O*, and eventually satisfies all of the requirements of adverse possession. *A* now holds title to Blackacre. If *O* now sues to eject *A* from possession, *A* will assert his title to the property as a defense to the action. Here, adverse possession works like an ordinary statute of limitations.

However, what if *O* never files suit? As a successful adverse possessor, *A* now owns Blackacre but *A* doesn't have a deed or any instrument recording his title in the public records. *A* has a practical problem of how he will use or convey the land as he wishes. In order to correct the title, *A* will need to record a judgment or deed confirming his ownership. *A* is entitled to file a quiet title action against *O* or demand a quitclaim deed from *O* in *A*'s favor. A regular statute of limitations doesn't confer any such rights on the holder of that defense.

There are a variety of policy rationales for adverse possession. If you keep these rationales in mind when reading the cases, it might help you to understand why the court is reaching a certain result. You may not agree with the result, but you may at least appreciate the application.

1. <u>Limitations Model</u>: This model views adverse possession as a specialized statute of limitations, the level of possession required for adverse possession is said to give notice to the supposed owner of the occupant's apparent claim to title and the owner then has the opportunity to bring suit to eject the occupant.

2. <u>Administrative Model</u>: This model views adverse possession as a useful method for curing minor title defects, thereby protecting title of the possessor.

3. <u>Development Model</u>: This model proposes that the law of adverse possession of wild, undeveloped lands is best explained as a tool to facilitate economic development. By vesting title in the industrious settler, rather than absentee landowner, adverse possession prompted rapid development of the nation's wilderness lands. This theory allows for the reallocation of land to productive users.

4. <u>Efficiency/Personhood Model</u>: This model blends diverse approaches that focus on avoiding injury to the adverse possessor. Over time, the adverse possessor becomes more attached to the land that he has enjoyed and used and it cannot be torn away without his resenting the act. The adverse possessor places a high personal value on the land while the absentee landowner has virtually abandoned it.

Adverse possession is a creature of statute and will vary from place to place. We will discuss the elements needed for adverse possession as well as specific adverse possession requirements in Texas.

C. Elements of Adverse Possession

Possession must be:
(1) actual;
(2) exclusive;
(3) open and notorious;
(4) adverse or hostile under a claim of right; *and*
(5) continuous;
(6) for the statutory period

1. Actual Possession

The adverse possessor must take actual possession of the land and more than mere entry onto the land is needed. There must be sufficient acts to establish possession rather than use. Recall from Chapter 4 that use can result in a prescriptive easement. We need possession to acquire title.

As seen with most of the elements, there are differing views of how the elements work. You will see variation among the states. The majority view for actual possession is that the claimant must physically use the particular parcel of land in the same manner that a reasonable owner would. The acts necessary to meet this requirement vary from parcel to parcel depending on the nature, character, and location of the land and the use to which it may be devoted.

Depending on the parcel of land, this requirement could be satisfied by residence, cultivation, improvement, grazing, pasturing, hunting, fishing, timber harvesting, mining, or other economically productive activities.

For example, adverse possessor *A1* can obtain actual possession of a house by residing there because this is how an ordinary owner would use a residence. If *A2* attempts to adversely possess a 100-acre tract of farm land, he must cultivate the land as an average owner would do. *A3* seeking to obtain title to a 1,000-acre parcel of wild, undeveloped land, need only perform the activities that are suited to the land in its natural condition such as timber harvesting, mining, grazing, etc.

The minority view of actual possession is held by only ten states, including California, Florida, and New York. Those states specify by statute the particular conduct that constitutes actual possession. For example, Florida's statute requires the possessor to "cultivate, improve or enclose the property." The case of Van Valkenburgh v. Lutz below provides the New York statutes that dictate what actual possession means in that state

<u>**Van Valkenburgh v. Lutz**</u>
Court of Appeals of New York, 1952
106 N.E2d 28

DYE, J.

These consolidated actions were brought to compel the removal of certain encroachments upon plaintiffs' lands, for delivery of possession and incidental relief. The subject property consists of four unimproved building lots designated as 19, 20, 21 and 22 in block 54 on the official tax map of the city of Yonkers, N.Y. These lots together form a parcel somewhat triangular in shape with dimensions of approximately 150 by 126 by 170 feet fronting on Gibson Place, a street to be laid out within the subdivision running in a northeasterly direction from Leroy Avenue and now surfaced for automobile travel as far as lots 26, 27 and 28. The subject premises were purchased by the plaintiffs from the city of Yonkers by deed dated April 14, 1947. At that time the defendants were, and had been since 1912, owners of premises designated as lots 14 and 15 in block 54, as shown on the same map. The defendants' lots front on Leroy Avenue and adjoin lot 19 owned by the plaintiffs at the rear boundary line. All of these lots, though differently numbered, appear on a map of the subdivision of the Murray Estate opened prior to 1912 and numbering 479 lots. At that time that part of the Murray subdivision was covered with a natural wild growth of brush and small trees. (Diagram and notation is added to Google Earth photo).[5]

---

[5] Google Earth V 6.2.2.6613. (March 24, 2009). Yonkers, New York. 40° 54' 39.03"N, 73° 53' 16.67"W, Eye alt 233 m. Europe Technologies 2007. http://www.earth.google.com [March 24, 2009].

The defendants interposed an answer denying generally the allegations of the complaint and alleging as an affirmative defense, and as a counterclaim, that William Lutz had acquired title to the subject premises by virtue of having held and possessed the same adversely to plaintiffs and predecessors for upwards of thirty years.

The issue thus joined was tried before Hon. Frederick P. Close, Official Referee, who found that title to said lots "was perfected in William Lutz by virtue of adverse possession by the year 1935" and not thereafter disseized. The judgment entered thereon in favor of the defendants was affirmed in the Appellate Division, Second Department, without opinion, one Justice dissenting on the ground that the evidence was insufficient to establish title by adverse possession.

To acquire title to real property by adverse possession not founded upon a written instrument, it must be shown by clear and convincing proof that for at least fifteen years (formerly twenty years) there was an "actual" occupation under a claim of title, for it is only the premises so actually occupied "and no others"' that are deemed to have been held adversely. The essential elements of proof being either that the premises (1) are protected by a substantial inclosure, or are (2) usually cultivated or improved.[6]

---

[6] The applicable New York adverse possession statutes at the time were sections 34, 38, 39, and 40 of the New York Civil Practice Act. The provisions are set forth below.

Concededly, there is no proof here that the subject premises were "protected by a substantial inclosure" which leaves for consideration only whether there is evidence showing that the premises were cultivated or improved sufficiently to satisfy the statute.

We think not. The proof concededly fails to show that the cultivation incident to the garden utilized the whole of the premises claimed. Such lack may not be supplied by inference on the showing that the cultivation of a smaller area, whose boundaries are neither defined nor its location fixed with certainty, "must have been substantial" as several neighbors were "supplied with vegetables." This introduces an element of speculation and surmise which may not be considered since the statute clearly limits the premises adversely held to those "actually" occupied "and no others," which we have recently interpreted as requiring definition by clear and positive proof.

Furthermore, on this record, the proof fails to show that the premises were improved. According to the proof the small shed or shack (about 5 by 10 1/2 feet) which, as shown by survey map, was located on the subject premises about 14 feet from the Lutz boundary line. This was built in about the year 1923 and, as Lutz himself testified, he knew at the time it was not on his land and, his wife, a defendant here, also testified to the same effect.

---

§ 34. An action to recover real property or the possession thereof cannot be maintained by a party other than the people, unless the plaintiff, his ancestor, predecessor, or grantor, was seized or possessed of the premises in question within fifteen years before the commencement of the action. . . .

§ 38. For the purpose of constituting an adverse possession, by a person claiming a title founded upon a written instrument, or judgment, or decree, land is deemed to have been possessed and occupied in either of the following cases:

1. Where it has been usually cultivated or improved.

2. Where it has been protected by a substantial inclosure.

3. Where, although not inclosed, it has been used for the supply of fuel or of fencing timber, either for the purposes of husbandry or for the ordinary use of the occupant.

Where a known farm or single lot has been partly improved, the portion of the farm or lot that has been left not cleared or not inclosed, according to the usual course and custom of the adjoining county, is deemed to have been occupied for the same length of time as the part improved and cultivated.

§ 39. Where there has been an actual continued occupation of premises under a claim of title, exclusive of any other right, but not founded upon a written instrument or a judgment or decree, the premises so actually occupied, and no others, are deemed to have been held adversely.

§ 40. For the purpose of constituting an adverse possession by a person claiming title not founded upon a written instrument or a judgment or decree, land is deemed to have been possessed and occupied in either of the following cases, and no others:

1. Where it has been protected by a substantial inclosure.

2. Where it has been usually cultivated or improved.

The statute requires as an essential element of proof, recognized as fundamental on the concept of adversity since ancient times, that the occupation of premises be 'under a claim of title', in other words, hostile, and when lacking will not operate to bar the legal title, no matter how long the occupation may have continued.

Similarly, the garage encroachment, extending a few inches over the boundary line, fails to supply proof of occupation by improvement. Lutz himself testified that when he built the garage he had no survey and thought he was getting it on his own property, which certainly falls short of establishing that he did it under a claim of title hostile to the true owner. The other acts committed by Lutz over the years, such as placing a portable chicken coop on the premises which he moved about, the cutting of brush and some of the trees, and the littering of the property with odds and ends of salvaged building materials, cast-off items of house furnishings and parts of automobiles which the defendants and their witnesses described as "personal belongings", "junk", "rubbish" and "debris", were acts which under no stretch of the imagination could be deemed an occupation by improvement within the meaning of the statute, and which, of course, are of no avail in establishing adverse possession.

We are also persuaded that the defendant's subsequent words and conduct confirms the view that his occupation was not "under a claim of title". When the defendant had the opportunity to declare his hostility and assert his rights against the true owner, he voluntarily chose to concede that the plaintiffs' legal title conferred actual ownership entitling them to the possession of these and other premises in order to provide a basis for establishing defendant's right to an easement by adverse possession the use of a well-defined "traveled way" that crossed the said premises. In that action, William Lutz, a defendant here (now deceased), chose to litigate the issue of title and possession and, having succeeded in establishing his claim of easement by adverse possession, he may not now disavow the effect of his favorable judgment, or prevent its use as evidence to show his prior intent. Declarations against interest made by a prescriptive tenant are always available on the issue of his intent.

On this record we do not reach the question of disseisin by oral disclaimer, since the proof fails to establish actual occupation for such time or in such manner as to establish title. What we are saying is that the proof fails to establish actual occupation for such a time or in such a manner as to establish title by adverse possession.

The judgments should be reversed, the counterclaim dismissed and judgment directed to be entered in favor of plaintiff Joseph D. Van Valkenburgh for the relief prayed for in the complaint subject to the existing easement with costs in all courts.

FULD, J (dissenting).

In my judgment, the weight of evidence lies with the determination made by the court at Special Term and affirmed by the Appellate Division. But whether that is so or not, there can be no doubt whatsoever that the record contains some evidence that the premises here involved were occupied by William Lutz, defendant's late husband, for fifteen years under a claim of title and that, of course, should compel an affirmance.

The four lots in suit, located in the city of Yonkers, comprise a fairly level parcel of land, triangular in shape, with approximate dimensions of 150 by 126 by 170 feet. It is bounded on the north by a 'traveled way', on the west and south by Gibson Place, an unopened street, and on the southeast by a vacant lot. Immediately to the east of the parcel, the land descends sharply to Leroy Avenue, forming a steep hill; on the hill are situated two lots, purchased by Lutz in 1912, upon which his family's home has stood for over thirty years.

Wild and overgrown when the Lutzes first moved into the neighborhood, the property was cleared by defendant's husband and had been, by 1916, the referee found, developed into a truck farm "of substantial size." Lutz, together with his children, worked the farm continuously until his death in 1948; indeed, after 1928, he had no other employment. Each year, a new crop was planted and the harvest of vegetables was sold to neighbors. Lutz also raised chickens on the premises, and constructed coops or sheds for them. Fruit trees were planted, and timber was cut from that portion of the property not used for the farm. On one of the lots, Lutz in 1920 built a one-room dwelling, in which his brother Charles has lived ever since.

Although disputing the referee's finding that the dimensions of Lutz's farm were substantial, the court's opinion fails to remark the plentiful evidence in support thereof. For instance, there is credible testimony in the record that "nearly all" of the property comprised by the four lots was cultivated during the period to which the referee's finding relates. A survey introduced in evidence indicates the very considerable extent to which the property was cultivated in 1950, and many witnesses testified that the farm was no larger at that time than it had ever been. There is evidence, moreover, that the cultivated area extended from the "traveled way" on one side of the property to a row of logs and brush placed by Lutz for the express purpose of marking the farm's boundary at the opposite end of the premises.

According to defendant's testimony, she and her husband, knowing that they did not have record title to the premises, intended from the first nevertheless to occupy the property as their own. Bearing this out is the fact that Lutz put down the row of logs and brush, which was over 100 feet in length, to mark the southwestern boundary of his farm; this marker, only roughly approximating the lot lines, extended beyond them into the bed of Gibson Place. The property was, moreover, known in the neighborhood as "Mr. Lutz's gardens," and the one-room dwelling on it as "Charlie's house"; the evidence clearly indicates that people living in the vicinity believed the property to be owned by Lutz. And it is undisputed that for upwards of thirty-five years until 1947, when plaintiffs became the record owners no other person ever asserted title to the parcel.

With evidence such as that in the record, I am at a loss to understand how this court can say that support is lacking for the finding that the premises had been occupied by Lutz under a claim of title. The referee was fully justified in concluding that the character of Lutz's possession was akin to that of a true owner and indicated, more dramatically and effectively than could words, an intent to claim the property as his own. Recognizing that "A claim of title may be made by acts alone quite as effectively as by the most emphatic assertions," Barnes v. Light, 116 N.Y. 34, 39, we have often sustained findings based on evidence of actual occupation and improvement of the property in the manner that "owners are accustomed to possess and improve their estates". La Frombois v. Jackson, 8 Cow. 589, 603.

That Lutz knew that he did not have the record title to the property a circumstance relied upon by the court is of no consequence, so long as he intended, notwithstanding that fact, to acquire and use the property as his own. As we stated in Ramapo Mfg. Co. v. Mapes, 216 N.Y. 362, 370-371, the bona fides of the claim of the occupant is not essential, and it will not excuse the negligence of the owner in forbearing to bring his action until after the time in the statute of limitations shall have run against him to show that the defendant knew all along that he was in the wrong.

Quite obviously, the fact that Lutz alleged in the 1947 easement action twelve years after title had, according to the referee, vested in him through adverse possession that one of the plaintiffs was the owner of three of the lots, simply constituted evidence pointing the other way, to be weighed with the other proof by the courts below. While it is true that a disclaimer of title by the occupant of property, made before the statutory period has run, indelibly stamps his possession as nonadverse and prevents title from vesting in him, a disclaimer made after the statute has run carries with it totally different legal consequences. Once title has vested by virtue of adverse possession, it is elementary that it may be divested, not by an oral disclaimer, but only by a transfer complying with the formalities prescribed by law. Hence, an oral acknowledgment of title in another, made after the statutory period is alleged to have run, "is only evidence tending to show the character of the previous possession." Smith v. Vermont Marble Co., 99 Vt. 384, 294. Here, Official Referee Close, of the opinion that the 1947 admission was made by Lutz under the erroneous advice of his attorney, chose to rest his decision rather on evidence of Lutz's numerous and continual acts of dominion over the property proof of a most persuasive character. Even if we were to feel that the referee was mistaken in so weighing the evidence, we would be powerless, to change the determination, where, as we have seen, there is some evidence in the record to support his conclusion.

In view of the extensive cultivation of the parcel in suit, there is no substance to the argument that the requirements of sections 39 and 40 of the Civil Practice Act were not met. Under those provisions, only the premises "actually occupied" in the manner prescribed that is, "protected by a substantial inclosure" or "usually cultivated or improved" are deemed to have been held adversely. The object of the statute, we have recognized, "is that the real owner may, by unequivocal acts of the usurper, have notice of the hostile claim, and be thereby called upon to assert his legal title." Monot v. Murphy, 207 N.Y. 240, 245. Since the character of the acts sufficient to afford such notice "depends upon the nature and situation of the property and the uses to which it can be applied", it is settled that the provisions of sections 39 and 40 are to be construed, not in a narrow or technical sense, but with reference to the nature, character, condition, and location of the property under consideration.

Judge Dye considers it significant that the proof "fails to show that the cultivation incident to the garden utilized the whole of the premises claimed." There surely is no requirement in either statute or decision that proof of adverse possession depends upon cultivation of "the whole" plot or of every foot of the property in question. And, indeed, the statute which, as noted, reads "usually cultivated or improved" has been construed to mean only that the claimant's occupation must "consist of acts such as are usual in the ordinary cultivation and improvement of similar lands by thrifty owners." The evidence demonstrates that by far the greater part of the four lots was regularly and continuously used for farming, and, that being so, the fact that a portion of the property was not cleared should not affect the claimant's ability to acquire title by adverse possession: any frugal person, owning and occupying lands similar to those here involved, would have permitted, as Lutz did, some of the trees to stand while clearing the bulk of the property in order to provide a source of lumber and other tree products for his usual needs. The portion of the property held subservient to the part actively cultivated is as much "occupied" as the portion actually tilled. The nature of the cultivation engaged in by Lutz was more than adequate, as his neighbors' testimony establishes, to give the owner notice of an adverse claim and to delimit the property to which the claim related. The limits of the parcel in suit were indicated in a general way by boundaries natural as well as man-made: the declivity to Leroy Avenue, the "traveled way," and Gibson Place. Apart from that, however, the evidence discloses that the bulk of each of the four lots was cultivated, and even putting to one side the fact that the cottage, called "Charlie's house," had been actually occupied and lived in for upwards of thirty years such substantial use was enough to put the owner on notice that his whole lot was claimed.

In short, there is ample evidence to sustain the finding that William Lutz actually occupied the property in suit for over fifteen years under a claim of title. Since, then, title vested in Lutz by 1935, the judgment must be affirmed. To rule otherwise, on the ground that the weight of evidence is against that finding a view which I do not, in any event, hold is to ignore the constitutional provision that limits our jurisdiction to the review of questions of law.

I would affirm the judgment reached by both of the courts below.

NOTES & QUESTIONS:

1. Which of the statutes defining actual possession applied to the *Lutz* case? Why?

2. The other sections of the statutes bring in the concept of possession under "color of title." When an adverse possessor enters onto land with an instrument of title, although defective in some respect, the possessor gets the benefit of constructive possession. Therefore, in the case of Mr. Lutz, if the garden and chicken coops and house for Charlie did not cover the entirety of tracts 19-22, he could have acquired title by adverse possession to the land he actually possessed. However, had Mr. Lutz entered the land with some defective instrument of title and still only actually possessed part of the triangular tract, he would have been given constructive possession of the remainder of the land described in the deed. This "color of title" and constructive possession rule is one that clearly shows how a blatant trespasser is treated differently from one who may be acting with some degree of good faith.

3. In addition to actual possession, the state of mind seemed to be at issue. When discussing "Charlie's house" the court stated that the building of the structure did not count for adverse possession purposes because Lutz knew that it was not on his land. Additionally, when addressing the garage encroachment, the court stated that the encroachment did not count for adverse possession purposes because Lutz mistakenly believed it was on his land. What does that mean is required for the adverse and hostile element in New York? More on that concept in a minute.

2. Adverse or Hostile Possession Under a Claim of Title or Claim of Right

This is the most confusing element. This element involves the adverse possessor's state of mind. There is little judicial agreement on how to label this element. Most courts agree that the terms "adverse" and "hostile" mean the same thing. Some courts use this "claim of title" or "claim of right" language as well but that is also just a part of this adverse/hostile possession element. The most common phrasing is adverse possession under a claim of right.

There are different tests to determine if the element is met.

1. <u>Objective Test</u>: The adverse possessor's subjective state of mind is irrelevant as long as he possesses the land of another without permission. This is the majority view today.

A enters into possession of Blackacre, a 100-acre farm, fully aware that it is actually owned by *O*. Without *O*'s permission, *A* resides in the farm house, cultivates the land, and takes related steps over a ten-year period that meets the other adverse possession criteria. Under the objective test, *A*'s possession is deemed adverse and hostile under a claim of right simply because she used the land without *O*'s consent. The same result would have occurred under the objective test if she believed in good faith that she owned Blackacre or if she had no belief at all about who owned the land.

2. <u>Good Faith Test</u>: The adverse possessor must believe in good faith that he owns title to the land. He innocently but mistakenly thinks he is the true owner. This is a minority view used in some states. It is difficult to be able to ascertain this subjective intent, especially in cases where tacking is involved, thus the move to the objective standard. While this is the minority view, commentators suggest that even if not an express requirement most courts impliedly require this good faith belief of ownership because the adverse possessors who ultimately prevail are only good faith occupants.

Under the good faith test, if we go back to the example of *A* occupying the farm house and cultivating the land, *A* would not prevail when she entered the land knowing she wasn't the owner. She also would not have prevailed if she entered the land and did not have any particular belief about the ownership. *A* would only prevail if she had the good faith belief of ownership.

3. <u>Intentional Trespass Test</u>: The adverse possessor must know that he does not own the land and subjectively intend to take title from the true owner. In looking back at the farm example, under this test, *A* would only prevail if she had the requisite knowledge that she did not own the property and she can also establish that she intended to take title from *O* by possessing the property. This test is rarely used. The reason for that is because with this test we allow the intentional wrongdoer to win out over people who were acting in good faith or without any bad intent. However, the objective standard would also allow that person to prevail.

4. <u>Claim of Right Test</u>: As explained by Joseph William Singer, the requirement of an adverse possessor being under a claim of right requires a slightly different mental inquiry. With the claim of right standard, if the adverse

possessor never intended to claim the land as her own, then there will not be the requisite mental state for adverse and hostile possession.[7]

With the adverse and hostile standard, one commonality in any jurisdiction is that the land cannot be possessed with the permission of the owner. If that is the case, none of the time of permissive use counts towards the statutory period.

Consider these different standards for adverse and hostile as you read the next two cases from the Texas Supreme Court.

Billy Ellis et al. v. Jansing et ux.
Supreme Court of Texas, 1981
620 S.W.2d 569

WALLACE, Justice.

This is an appeal from a summary judgment in a trespass to try title case. The trial court rendered judgment for Billy Ellis and Charles M. McDonald, plaintiffs. The court of civil appeals reversed the judgment of the trial court and remanded for trial. 610 S.W.2d 812. We reverse the judgment of the court of civil appeals and affirm the judgment of the trial court.

The Petitioners, Ellis and McDonald, own Lot 4 and the Respondents, the Jansings, own the adjoining Lot 3 of Castle Heights Addition to the City of Waco. The common source of title was A. B. Shoemake. In 1937 Shoemake entered into an agreement with the City of Waco whereby he dedicated "for the use and accommodation of the City of Waco, the owners of contiguous lots and the general public," a 15 foot easement which extended across the westernmost part of Lot 4 owned by Ellis and McDonald and adjoined the easternmost boundary of the Jansings' Lot 3. Mr. Shoemake erected a concrete retaining wall 8 to 10 feet high, topped by a 4 foot chain link fence, located approximately 3 1/2 feet east of the 15 foot easement and, for the purposes of our discussion, ran the length of the easement. This retaining wall extends some 2 to 3 feet above the surface of the 15 foot easement and the Jansings' property. Ellis and McDonald's property is 8 to 10 feet lower than the easement and the Jansings' property.

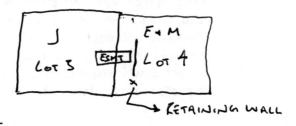

---

[7] Joseph William Singer, Property § 4.2.5 Adverse and Hostile (4th ed. 2014).

The City of Waco built an underground concrete pipe storm sewer beneath the entire length of the 15 foot easement. The storm sewer is still in use and is still checked periodically by City employees.

The issues before us are: (1) whether Tex. Rev. Civ. Stat. Ann. art. 5517 (1958) is applicable to this fact situation, and (2) whether Respondents produced summary judgment evidence sufficient to raise a fact issue on title by adverse possession under the ten year statute of limitation, Tex. Rev. Civ. Stat. Ann. art. 5510 (1958).

Article 5517 states:

> The right of the State, all counties, incorporated cities and all school districts shall not be barred by any of the provisions of this Title, nor shall any person ever acquire, by occupancy or adverse possession, any right or title to any part or portion of any road, street, alley, sidewalk, or grounds which belong to any town, city, or county, or which have been donated or dedicated for public use to any such town, city, or county by the owner thereof, or which have been laid out or dedicated in any manner to public use in any town, city, or county in this State.

The instrument by which the 15 foot easement in question was dedicated states, in pertinent part:

> . . . the strips of ground hereinafter described shall at all times hereafter be and remain open as for an alley and passageway for the use and accommodation of the City of Waco, *A* the owners of contiguous lots and the general public, which said property, to be so used as such alley and passageway is described as follows: (There follows a metes and bounds description of the 15 foot easement in question.)

The court of civil appeals, in reversing the judgment of the trial court, held that Article 5517 was not applicable because this is a dispute between two individuals over the ownership of the fee to the property subject to the easement. The court of civil appeals attempted to distinguish this fact situation from those cases where individuals were attempting to perfect title by adverse possession against public bodies. The court of civil appeals erred in its interpretation of Article 5517. Although the court correctly interpreted the first part of the statute, which states that the right of the State, counties, incorporated cities and all school districts shall not be barred by any provisions of the statutes setting out the statute of limitations as it applies to actions for the title of real estate, the court ignored the following language:

> . . . nor shall any person ever acquire, by occupancy or adverse possession, any right or title to any part or portion of any road, street, alley, sidewalk, or grounds which belong to any town, city, or county, or which have been donated or dedicated for public use to any such town, city, or county by the owner thereof, or which have been laid out or dedicated in any manner to public use in any town, city, or county in this State.

We hold that it was the intention of the Legislature in enacting Article 5517 to protect the rights of those persons to whom the property was dedicated from any person claiming by adverse possession. A dedication for use by the general public, as in this case, protects the right of use by the public generally, not just the city, county or other public body.

The document whereby this 15 foot easement was dedicated clearly shows an intention to dedicate it to the city of Waco, to adjacent property owners, and to the general public as an alley and passageway. We hold that Article 5517 is applicable to this case and prohibits a claim of adverse possession by the Respondents with respect to the 15 foot easement in question. Spencer v. Levy, 173 S.W. 550 (Tex. Civ. App. Austin 1915, writ ref'd).

The cement retaining wall is 3.85 feet east of the easement property at the north end and 3.35 feet east of the easement at the south end. The Jansings contend that even if they are prohibited by Article 5517 from claiming adverse possession to the 15 foot easement strip, they perfected title by adverse possession to the strip between the easement and the concrete retaining wall. The Jansings further contend that the summary judgment evidence raises a fact issue as to whether such limitation title was perfected by them and their predecessor in title, Newman E. Copeland, et ux.

The Jansings took title to their property on May 22, 1970, and the present action was filed on August 8, 1979. To have matured limitation title under the ten year statute, Article 5510, they must tack their adverse possession, if any, to that of Newman E. Copeland and wife.

By deposition, Mr. Copeland testified that when he and his wife took possession of the property they assumed that their boundary line was the concrete retaining wall. Mr. Copeland stated there was a flower bed along the retaining wall, he dug up the flowers, and thereafter grass grew over the entire 15 foot easement and the strip between the easement and the retaining wall. The Copeland's yard was never fenced, and entrance onto the easement and adjoining strip between the easement and retaining wall was not obstructed. He further testified that he did not represent to the Jansings that their property line extended to the retaining wall or that he owned the property all the way to the retaining wall. Mr. Copeland also testified he had never represented to anybody that he owned or claimed the 15 foot easement or the adjoining 3 feet between the easement and the retaining wall. In his affidavit attached to Defendant's Answer to Plaintiff's Motion for Summary Judgment, Mr. Copeland stated that when he purchased the property the concrete wall and chain link fence on top thereof was in place, it was his understanding that the fence was the eastern boundary line of the property, and it was his belief that his property extended to the retaining wall and fence. He stated that he used that property as part of his yard, and during the time of his occupancy he maintained it as part of his yard, keeping the grass mowed, trimming and removing trees and other growth the same as the other parts of the yard. He then stated:

> My use and claim to the property, including that up to the fence, was at all times uninterrupted by the adverse claim of any person, my use was open and notorious and adverse, exclusive, and continuous for all of the period of the time that I owned it from the date of my deed to the date of acquiring until the time we conveyed it to Mr. and Mrs. Jansing. No one has ever disputed my right to the use and enjoyment of said property or my claim to the title thereof.

Not Fact Issue To Survive Summary Jgmt

This portion of the affidavit in which Mr. Copeland states he held open, notorious, exclusive, continuous and adverse possession to the property in question, represents legal conclusions and is ineffective to raise a fact issue in a summary judgment hearing. Life Insurance Company of Virginia v. Gar-Dal, Inc., 570 S.W.2d 378 (Tex. 1978). "In ruling on a motion for summary judgment, only admissible testimony having probative force is to be considered." Crain v. Davis, 417 S.W.2d 53 (Tex. 1967); Box v. Bates, 162 Tex. 184, 346 S.W.2d 317 (1961).

This leaves us with the question of whether the testimony of Mr. Copeland that he bought the property thinking that the boundary was the concrete retaining wall and maintained it as part of his yard was sufficient to raise a fact issue of adverse possession. Mr. Copeland testified he never claimed or intended to claim any property other than that described in his deed, or what he thought was contained in his deed, and he never intended to claim any property owned by the abutting property owners.

SUBJECTIVE?

We hold these facts are legally insufficient to sustain a claim of adverse possession. Miller v. Fitzpatrick, 418 S.W.2d 884 (Tex. Civ. App. Corpus Christi 1967, writ ref'd n.r e.). "Mere occupancy of land without any intention to appropriate it will not support the statute of limitations." Wright v. Vernon Compress Company, 156 Tex. 474, 296 S.W.2d 517 (1956). "No matter how exclusive and hostile to the true owner the possession may be in appearance, it cannot be adverse unless accompanied by the intent on the part of the occupant to make it so. The naked possession unaccompanied with any claim of right will never constitute a bar." Orsborn v. Deep Rock Oil Corp., 153 Tex. 281, 267 S.W.2d 781 (1954), quoting Houston Oil Company v. Stepney, 187 S.W. 1078 (Tex. Civ. App. Beaumont 1916, writ ref'd).

MUST HAVE INTENT

The Copelands did not commence adverse possession; therefore there was nothing to which the Jansings could tack their claim of adverse possession.

We reverse the judgment of the court of civil appeals and affirm the judgment of the trial court which con-firmed title in Ellis and McDonald to all of Lot 4 subject to the 15 foot easement.

NOTE: ADVERSE POSSESSION AGAINST THE GOVERNMENT:

According to common law, a person cannot adversely possess against the government. This is still the majority rule today. While some states have chosen to change this by statute, they are relatively few. The Texas Civil Practice and Remedies code has actually codified the common law rule of no adverse possession against a governmental entity.

Texas Civil Practice & Remedies Code § 16.061. Rights Not Barred

(a) A right of action of this state or a political subdivision of the state, including a county, an incorporated city or town, a navigation district, a municipal utility district, a port authority, an entity acting under Chapter

54, Transportation Code, a school district, or an entity created under Section 52, Article III, or Section 59, Article XVI, Texas Constitution, is not barred by any of the following sections: 16.001-16.004, 16.006, 16.007, 16.021-16.028, 16.030-16.032, 16.035-16.037, 16.051, 16.062, 16.063, 16.065-16.067, 16.070, 16.071, 31.006, or 71.021.

Tran v. Macha
Supreme Court of Texas, 2006
213 S.W.3d 913

PER CURIAM.

Neighboring relatives shared the use of a driveway for many years, thinking it belonged to one of them when in fact it belonged to the other. The court of appeals held this mutual mistake and mutual use transferred title by adverse possession. We disagree, and thus reverse.

In the 1920s, land on what is now Case Street in the City of West University Place in Harris County was subdivided into lots 55 feet wide. But during construction in the 1930s and '40s, several houses were built on the mistaken assumption that the lots were only 50 feet wide. As a result, each house was increasingly shifted to the east side of its lot, until the house on Lot 5 was built next to that lot's eastern boundary with Lot 6. This case concerns a driveway built on a 20-foot strip of land just east of that boundary-a strip everyone assumed was on Lot 5, but was actually on Lot 6.

When Lillian Haliburton bought Lot 5 in 1970, Lot 6 was owned by her brother's family, the Buddes. For many years, both families used the driveway on the disputed strip. The driveway led to a garage built on both lots, which Haliburton used for parking and storage. Although Haliburton was no longer living at the time of trial, there was testimony that family members all presumed mistakenly that the driveway and garage belonged to her Lot 5.

In 1995, the Buddes sold Lot 6 to the defendants, Minh Thu Tran and Norman L. Roser. In 2001, Haliburton sold Lot 5 to the plaintiffs, William and Nita Macha, who already owned Lot 4 to the west. During the latter transaction, a survey revealed that the driveway was not a part of Lot 5, so the Machas secured a quitclaim deed conveying any interest Haliburton might have acquired in the strip by adverse possession. When Tran and Roser learned of the survey, they obtained a permit and erected a fence around the strip. This suit ensued.

A jury found the strip had passed by adverse possession to Haliburton, and thence to the Machas. The First Court of Appeals affirmed, holding in a divided opinion that Haliburton's use of the strip and everyone's mistaken belief that she owned it were legally sufficient evidence of adverse possession. See 176 S.W.3d 128 (Tex. App.—Houston [1st Dist.] 2004). We disagree.

Under Texas law, adverse possession requires "an actual and visible appropriation of real property, commenced and continued under a claim of right that is inconsistent with and is hostile to the claim of another person." Tex. Civ. Prac. & Rem. Code § 16.021(1). The statute requires visible appropriation; mistaken beliefs about ownership do not transfer title until someone acts on them. *See, e.g.*, Bywaters v. Gannon, 686 S.W.2d 593, 595 (Tex. 1985). Thus, there must be adverse possession, not just adverse beliefs.

The statute requires that such possession be "inconsistent with" and "hostile to" the claims of all others. Joint use is not enough, because "possession must be of such character as to indicate unmistakably an assertion of a claim of exclusive ownership in the occupant." Rhodes v. Cahill, 802 S.W.2d 643, 645 (Tex. 1990) (quoting Rick v. Grubbs, 147 Tex. 267, 214 S.W.2d 925, 927 (1948)); McDonnold v. Weinacht, 465 S.W.2d 136, 141 (Tex. 1971). Here, Haliburton shared use of the strip with the Buddes, so her use was not inconsistent with or hostile to their ownership. *See, e.g.*, Brooks v. Jones, 578 S.W.2d 669, 673 (Tex. 1979) ("It has long been the law in Texas that when a landowner and the claimant of an easement both use the same way, the use by the claimant is not exclusive of the owner's use and therefore will not be considered adverse.").

The court of appeals held that Haliburton adversely possessed the strip by building a driveway and garage on it. 176 S.W.3d at 132. But nothing in the record shows she did either. To the contrary, both were in place before she bought Lot 5, and nothing shows who built them or when. We agree that building a structure on property may be sufficient evidence of adverse possession. *See* City of El Paso v. Fort Dearborn Nat'l Bank, 96 Tex. 496, 74 S.W. 21, 23 (1903); McDow v. Rabb, 56 Tex. 154, 161 (1882). But the record here shows only that Haliburton used the driveway and garage, not that she built them.

The court of appeals also held that "adverse possession need not be intentional, so long as it is visible, open, and notorious." 176 S.W.3d at 133. It is true that "hostile" use does not require an intention to dispossess the rightful owner, or even know that there is one. *See* Calfee v. Duke, 544 S.W.2d 640, 642 (Tex. 1976). But there must be an intention to claim property as one's own to the exclusion of all others; "[m]ere occupancy of land without any intention to appropriate it will not support the statute of limitations." Ellis v. Jansing, 620 S.W.2d 569, 571 (Tex. 1981) (quoting Wright v. Vernon Compress Co., 156 Tex. 474, 296 S.W.2d 517, 522 (1956)); Nona Mills Co. v. Wright, 101 Tex. 14, 102 S.W. 1118, 1120 (1907). Here, there is no evidence Haliburton ever intended to exclude the Buddes, or that they used the driveway only with her express permission.

It may seem harsh that adverse possession rewards only those who believe "good fences make good neighbors," and not those who are happy to share. But the doctrine itself is a harsh one, taking real estate from a record owner without express consent or compensation. Before taking such a severe step, the law reasonably requires that the parties' intentions be very clear.

Accordingly, without hearing oral argument, we reverse the court of appeals' judgment and render judgment for the defendant.

NOTES ON "ADVERSE AND HOSTILE":

1. Where does the Texas standard for "adverse and hostile" fall? Is it the majority objective test, the minority good faith test, or the rare intentional trespass test? Does it fit in any of these?

2. Absent unusual circumstances, a tenant's possession is not deemed adverse or hostile toward the landlord. By definition, a landlord expressly consents to the tenant's occupancy. The statutory period for adverse possession will begin running if the tenant unequivocally repudiates his status as a tenant and claims title to the land. Similarly, possession by the owner's agent or a member of the owner's family is normally permissive and not adverse or hostile.

3. Additionally, possession by one cotenant is normally not considered adverse or hostile because each cotenant is entitled to 100 percent possession of the property. In order to begin adverse possession, the cotenant in possession must unequivocally claim sole ownership of the land by either (1) physically ousting the cotenants, or (2) taking other steps that clearly notify the cotenants of the claim. Absent physical ouster, many jurisdictions insist on actual notice to cotenants while others simply require open and notorious actions that demonstrate hostility.

3. Exclusive Possession

In order to satisfy this element, possession must not be shared with either the true owner or the general public. However, absolute exclusivity is not a requirement. The claimant's possession must be as exclusive as would characterize an owner's normal use for such land. Isolated visits by third parties do not destroy exclusivity. An occasional hiker or hunter who crosses through the uninhabited tract of land would not interrupt *A*'s possession. The adverse possessor must only exclude third parties to the extent that a reasonable owner would do so.

An interesting question arises when two adverse possessors both occupy the same property. Suppose *A1* and *A2* both occupy Blackacre, a farm owned by *O*. Arguably neither has exclusive possession. Does the presence of *A1* interrupt *A2*'s exclusive possession and vice versa? In this situation, courts normally rule that the two adverse possessors who hold joint possession will acquire title as tenants in common.

4. Open and Notorious Possession

The acts of the possessor must be so visible and obvious that a reasonable owner who inspects the land will receive notice of an adverse title claim. It is not necessary to show the owner obtained actual knowledge of the claim or that the owner conducted an inspection. The owner is charged with knowledge that a diligent inspection would reveal. Secret or hidden activities do not satisfy this requirement.

Suppose O owns title to Blackacre, a 40-acre parcel of unimproved farm land. Adverse possessor A grows corn on the land for 15 years. A plows the land, plants seeds, sprays pesticides, nurtures the crops, and finally harvests the corn. On these facts, A's possession is open and notorious. If O inspected Blackacre, O would see clear evidence of A's activity on the land and learn about A's title claim.

Now suppose that A never cultivated the land. Instead, A visits at night once a month to observe the stars. A is careful to show no light during these visits and his activities leave behind no visible trace that O might discover aside from a few footprints. A has not met the requirement of open and notorious possession.

What acts establish open and notorious possession? Actions such as residing on the land, building fences or other improvements, or cultivating crops are almost always sufficient.

The "open and notorious" provision is almost always troublesome in the case of wild, unimproved land such as forests, prairies, wetlands, or deserts. The acts that constitute possession of such lands are often minor and infrequent and most courts seem to accept a lower degree of openness and notoriety. Depending on the circumstances, activities such as grazing livestock, cutting wild hay, harvesting timber, gathering firewood, clearing brush, fishing, hunting, posting "no trespassing" signs, or a combination of these activities may satisfy the requirement.

A court in Alaska held that building an outhouse and other improvements, tree planting, camping, and related acts were open and notorious. A court in Michigan held that building a hunting cabin, visiting the cabin six times each year, selling pulpwood, and related activities was held to be open and notorious possession.

So, in the example involving the undeveloped farm land, if A went out there only at night to observe the stars but left behind "No trespassing" signs and also built a small observatory for his telescope then that could be sufficient for open and notorious possession. If the owner made an inspection of the premises it would be apparent that someone may be claiming title to the property.

5. Continuous Possession

The continuous possession element is concerned with the frequency of the possession. There must be possession that is continuous enough during the statutory period. This element does not mandate that the claimant physically occupy the land every minute. The required continuity is measured by the location, nature, and character of the land. The possession need only be as continuous or sporadic as those of a reasonable land owner. Depending on the nature of the land, possession may be deemed continuous even if long periods of time go by without use of the land.

For wild, unimproved land activities as rare as gathering firewood a few times a year or using the land for grazing for a few weeks may be sufficient if a reasonable owner would do the same. For example, thinking back to the couple in Colorado who adversely possessed 1/3 of the neighboring lot, they cut the grass, stacked firewood, and held parties on the land. They were not physically on the land every day. However, for an unimproved piece of real property, the degree of activity was sufficient to meet the element.

For someone like Mr. Robinson occupying a residence in a suburb, the claimant must presumably live in the house. However, even in this situation the reasonable homeowner leaves for work, runs errands, visits friends, takes vacations, etc., and the adverse possessor must do the same.

In addition to the frequency of the possession, another issue arises in this context and that is of tacking. Sometimes in the cases one person cannot make out the entire statutory period on his own. Tacking is permissible only if the successive claimants are in privity with each other. Privity arises when one claimant transfers possessory rights to another, most commonly through a deed, but sometimes through a devise or intestate succession. There is no privity between successive trespassers.[8]

As seen in both the *Ellis* and *Tran* cases, people often need to count the time of a prior possessor along with their own. In both *Ellis* and *Tran*, the possessors were claiming additional land adjacent to the land that they held under a deed. The land that they were claiming was not land described in the deeds. However, the tacking question was not even raised in those cases because that type of tacking was always permitted because they also were not viewed in the same light as successive trespassers. There was a connection or relationship between the consecutive trespassers. In the Howard v. Kunto case below, in addition to

---

[8] Texas Civil Practice & Remedies Code § 16.023. Tacking of Successive Interests:

> To satisfy a limitations period, peaceable and adverse possession does not need to continue in the same person, but there must be privity of estate between each holder and his successor.

the frequency of use, there is an issue of tacking. See if you understand how the court was deciding something new on that issue.

Howard v. Kunto
Court of Appeals of Washington, 1970
477 P.2d 210

PEARSON, J.

Land surveying is an ancient art but not one free of the errors that often creep into the affairs of men. In this case, we are presented with the question of what happens when the descriptions in deeds do not fit the land the deed holders are occupying. Defendants appeal from a decree quieting title in the plaintiffs of a tract of land on the shore of Hood Canal in Mason County.

At least as long ago as 1932 the record tells us that one McCall resided in the house now occupied by the appellant-defendants, Kunto. McCall had a deed that described a 50-foot-wide parcel on the shore of Hood Canal. The error that brings this case before us is that 50 feet described in the deed is not the same 50 feet upon which McCall's house stood. Rather, the described land is an adjacent 50-foot lot directly west of that upon which the house stood. In other words, McCall's house stood on one lot and his deed described the adjacent lot. Several property owners to the west of defendants, not parties to this action, are similarly situated.

Over the years since 1946, several conveyances occurred, using the same legal description and accompanied by a transfer of possession to the succeeding occupants. The Kuntos' immediate predecessors in interest, Millers, desired to build a dock. To this end, they had a survey performed which indicated that the deed description and the physical occupation were in conformity. Several boundary stakes were placed as a result of this survey and the dock was constructed, as well as other improvements. The house as well as the others in the area continued to be used as summer recreational retreats.

The Kuntos then took possession of the disputed property under a deed from the Millers in 1959. In 1960 the respondent-plaintiffs, Howard, who held land east of that of the Kuntos, determined to convey an undivided one-half interest in their land to the Yearlys. To this end, they undertook to have a survey of the entire area made. After expending considerable effort, the surveyor retained by the Howards discovered that according to the government survey, the deed descriptions and the land occupancy of the parties did not coincide. Between the Howards and the Kuntos lay the Moyers' property. When the Howards' survey was completed, they discovered that they were the record owners of the land occupied by the Moyers and that the Moyers held record title to the land occupied by the Kuntos. Howard approached Moyer and in return for a conveyance of the land upon which the Moyers' house stood, Moyer conveyed

[handwritten margin note: Bunch of Bad Surveys]

to the Howards record title to the land upon which the Kunto house stood. Until plaintiffs Howard obtained the conveyance from Moyer in April, 1960, neither Moyer nor any of his predecessors ever asserted any right to ownership of the property actually being possessed by Kunto and his predecessors. This action was then instituted to quiet title in the Howards and Yearlys. The Kuntos appeal from a trial court decision granting this remedy.

At the time this action was commenced on August 19, 1960, defendants had been in occupance of the disputed property less than a year. The trial court's reason for denying their claim of adverse possession is succinctly stated in its memorandum opinion: "In this instance, defendants have failed to prove, by a preponderance of the evidence, a continuity of possession or estate to permit tacking of the adverse possession of defendants to the possession of their predecessors."

Finding of fact 6, which is challenged by defendants, incorporates the above concept and additionally finds defendant's possession not to have been "continuous" because it involved only "summer occupancy."

Two issues are presented by this appeal:

(1) Is a claim of adverse possession defeated because the physical use of the premises is restricted to summer occupancy?

(2) May a person who receives record title to tract A under the mistaken belief that the has title to tract B (immediately contiguous to tract A) and who subsequently occupies tract B, for the purpose of establishing title to tract B by adverse possession, use the periods of possession of tract B by his immediate predecessors who also had record title to tract A?

In approaching both of these questions, we point out that the evidence, largely undisputed in any material sense, established that defendant or his immediate predecessors did occupy the premises, which we have called tract B, as though it was their own for far more than the 10 years as prescribed in RCW 4.16.020.5.

We also point out that findings of fact is not challenged for its factual determinations but for the conclusions contained therein to the effect that the continuity of possession may not be established by summer occupancy, and that a predecessor's possession may not be tacked because a legal "claim of right" did not exist under the circumstances.

We start with the oft-quoted rule that: (T)o constitute adverse possession, there must be actual possession which is Uninterrupted, open and notorious, hostile and exclusive, and under a Claim of right made in good faith for the statutory period.

We reject the conclusion that summer occupancy only of a summer beach home destroys the continuity of possession required by the statute. It has become firmly established that the requisite possession requires such possession and dominion "as ordinarily marks the conduct of owners in general in holding, managing, and caring for property of like nature and condition."

We hold that occupancy of tract *B* during the summer months for more than the 10-year period by defendant and his predecessors, together with the continued existence of the improvements on the land and beach area, constituted "uninterrupted" possession within this rule. To hold otherwise is to completely ignore the nature and condition of the property.

We find such rule fully consonant with the legal writers on the subject. In F. Clark, Law of Surveying and Boundaries, s 561 (3d ed. 1959) at 565: "Continuity of possession may be established although the land is used regularly for only a certain period each year."

Further, at 566:

> This rule [which permits tacking] is one of substance and not of absolute mathematical continuity, provided there is no break so as to sever two possessions. It is not necessary that the occupant should be actually upon the premises continually. If the land is occupied during the period of time during the year it is capable of use, there is sufficient continuity.

We now reach the question of tacking. The precise issue before us is novel in that none of the property occupied by defendant or his predecessors coincided with the property described in their deeds, but was contiguous.

In the typical case, which has been subject to much litigation, the party seeking to establish title by adverse possession claims more land than that described in the deed.

In such cases it is clear that tacking is permitted.

In Buchanan v. Cassell, the Supreme Court stated: "This state follows the rule that a purchaser may tack the adverse use of its predecessor in interest to that of his own where the land was intended to be included in the deed between them, but was mistakenly omitted from the description."

The general statement which appears in many of the cases is that tacking of adverse possession is permitted if the successive occupants are in 'privity.' The deed running between the parties purporting to transfer the land possessed traditionally furnishes the privity of estate which connects the possession of the successive occupants. Plaintiff contends, and the trial court ruled, that where the deed does not describe any of the land which was occupied, the actual transfer of possession is insufficient to establish privity.

To assess the cogency of this argument and ruling, we must turn to the historical reasons for requiring privity as a necessary prerequisite to tacking the possession of several occupants.

The requirement of privity had its roots in the notion that a succession of trespasses, even though there was no appreciable interval between them, should not, in equity, be allowed to defeat the record title. The "claim of right," "color of title" requirement of the statutes and cases was probably derived from the early American belief that the squatter should not be able to profit by his trespass.

However, it appears to this court that there is a substantial difference between the squatter or trespasser and the property purchaser, who along with several of his neighbors, as a result of an inaccurate survey or subdivision, occupies and improves property exactly 50 feet to the east of that which a survey some 30 years later demonstrates that they in fact own. It seems to us that there is also a strong public policy favoring early certainty as to the location of land ownership which enters into a proper interpretation of privity.

On the irregular perimeters of Puget Sound exact determination of land locations and boundaries is difficult and expensive. This difficulty is convincingly demonstrated in this case by the problems plaintiff's engineer encountered in attempting to locate the corners. It cannot be expected that every purchaser will or should engage a surveyor to ascertain that the beach home he is purchasing lies within the boundaries described in his deed. Such a practice is neither reasonable nor customary. Of course, 50-foot errors in descriptions are devastating where a group of adjacent owners each hold 50 feet of waterfront property.

The technical requirement of "privity" should not, we think, be used to upset the long periods of occupancy of those who in good faith received an erroneous deed description. Their "claim of right" is no less persuasive than the purchaser who believes he is purchasing more land than his deed described.

In the final analysis, however, we believe the requirement of "privity" is no more than judicial recognition of the need for some reasonable connection between successive occupants of real property so as to raise their claim of right above the status of the wrongdoer or the trespasser. We think such reasonable connection exists in this case.

Where, as here, several successive purchasers received record title to tract A under the mistaken belief that they were acquiring tract B, immediately contiguous thereto, and where possession of tract B is transferred and occupied in a continuous manner for more than 10 years by successive occupants, we hold there is sufficient privity of estate to permit tacking and thus establish adverse possession as a matter of law.

We see no reason in law or in equity for differentiating this case from Faubion v. Elder, where the appellants were claiming more land than their deed described and where successive periods of occupation were allowed to be united to each other to make up the time of adverse holding. This application of the privity requirement should particularly pertain where the holder of record title to tract B acquired the same with knowledge of the discrepancy.

Judgment is reversed with directions to dismiss plaintiffs' action and to enter a decree quieting defendants' title to the disputed tract of land in accordance with the prayer of their cross-complaint.

NOTES AND QUESTIONS:

1. There are other issues that arise with continuous possession when future interests are involved. A future interest is immune from adverse possession until the interest holder is entitled to immediate possession of the land. Until that point, the interest holder has no right of action against the adverse claimant.

2. *L* holds a life estate in Blackacre, followed by an indefeasibly vested remainder in *R*. Adverse possessor *A* occupies Blackacre in 2000 and remains in possession through 2010. Assuming that the jurisdiction uses a ten-year period and *A* meets the other standards, *A* acquires only *L*'s life estate in Blackacre in 2010. *A* technically holds a life estate *pur autre vie* because it is still measured by *L*'s life. The statutory period against *R*'s remainder interest does not begin to run until *R* is entitled to possession, that is when *L* dies. Suppose *L* dies in 2011 and the life estate ends. *R* now holds fee simple absolute in Blackacre. If *A* still holds possession then the period for adverse possession against *R*'s title begins to run.

   What if the facts change so that when *A* begins the period of adverse possession in 2000, *O* owns the property in fee simple absolute. After adverse possession begins, *O* conveys a life estate to *L* and a vested remainder in fee simple to *R*. When *A* remains in possession meeting all of the requirements for adverse possession until 2010, what estate does *A* own? Why?

3. The defeasible fee estates also raise interesting distinctions with adverse possession. Remember both the fee simple determinable and the fee simple subject to executory interest end automatically if a condition occurs. That means that once the condition occurs, if the owner of the present possessory estate remains, the period of adverse possession begins at that time. However, if the estate is a fee simple subject to condition subsequent, the future interest must take steps to re-enter the land. Until then, the present possessory estate just continues. In that case the adverse possession will not begin until the future interest attempts to take steps and the present possessory estate holder remains in possession.

D. Texas Adverse Possession Statutes

Texas has a variety of statutes ranging from 3 years to 25 years. The shorter the time period, the more onerous the requirements become to satisfy the statute. For every statute, all of the standard adverse possession elements must be met. However, for some of the statutes there are extra requirements added on to the standard ones. Because of that, the ten-year statute is the one most often used in Texas as it is the "bare possession statute." That means it requires only the basic adverse possession elements. The 25-year statute will be used only if the owner is under a legal disability. The three- and five-year statutes are more rarely used and will only work in very specific circumstances.

Tex. Civ. Prac. & Rem. Code
§ 16.024 "Three Year Color of Title"
A person must bring suit to recover real property held by another in peaceable and adverse possession under title or color of title not later than three years after the day the cause of action accrues.

§ 16.025 "Five Year Duly Registered Deed"
    (a) A person must bring suit not later than five years after the day the cause of action accrues to recover real property held in peaceable and adverse possession by another who:
        (1) cultivates, uses, or enjoys the property;
        (2) pays applicable taxes on the property; and
        (3) claims the property under a duly registered deed.
    (b) This section does not apply to a claim based on a forged deed or a deed executed under a forged power of attorney.

Phelps v. Pecos Valley Southern Ry. Co.
Court of Civil Appeals of Texas, El Paso, 1916.
182 S.W. 1156

HIGGINS, J.
This is an action of trespass to try title, brought by Phelps against the appellee. J. W. Parker is the common source of title. On January 4, 1909, he conveyed the premises in controversy to M. L. Swinehart. This deed was not recorded. By deed dated May 6, 1910, recorded February 14, 1911, Swinehart conveyed the same to appellee. Appellee went into possession on or about March 1, 1910, and remained in continuous, peaceable, and adverse possession until the filing of this suit on May 21, 1914. By deed dated November 10, 1909, recorded November 10, 1909, Parker, for a valuable consideration, conveyed the premises

to the Jesse French Piano & Organ Company, who, in turn, conveyed same to Phelps by deed dated October 30, 1914, recorded November 4, 1914. This deed was executed in ratification of a prior ineffective deed of said company to Phelps, dated December 29, 1909, which was filed for record January 5, 1910. On November 10, 1909, and December 2, 1909, the Jesse French Piano & Organ Company and Phelps had no notice, actual or constructive, of the deed from Parker to Swinehart, and the entry upon the land by the appellee on March 1, 1910, was the first notice Phelps had of its claim to the land. The only question presented is whether appellee acquired title under the three-year statute of limitation.

Article 6824, R. S., provides that all conveyances of land shall be void as to subsequent purchasers for a valuable consideration without notice unless they shall be acknowledged and filed for record as required by law; but the same, as between the parties and their heirs, and as to subsequent purchasers with notice thereof, or without valuable consideration, shall nevertheless be valid and binding. By article 5672 R. S., it is provided that every suit to recover real estate, as against one in peaceable and adverse possession thereof under title or color of title, must be brought within three years next after the cause of action shall have accrued. The point at issue between the parties resolves itself into this: Does an unrecorded deed constitute color of title within the meaning of articles 5672 and 5673, R. S.? If so, judgment was properly rendered for appellee.

Appellant calls to our attention the cases of Cox v. Bray, 28 Tex. 247, Wall v. Lubbock, 52 Tex. Civ. App. 405, 118 S. W. 886, Watson v. Watson, 55 S. W. 183, and Lynn v. Burnett, 34 Tex. Civ. App. 335, 79 S. W. 64, where it was held that void deeds were insufficient to support the three-year statute; also to Latimer v. Logwood, 27 S. W. 960, where a like holding was made with respect to a void judgment. Upon the authority of these cases, it is insisted appellee could not acquire a prescriptive right under the statute because the unrecorded deed from Parker to Swinehart was void as to him; he having purchased the premises for value and without notice thereof. The cases cited are distinguishable. In each of them the instrument relied upon as the basis of the prescriptive right was void ab initio and a complete nullity. Such is not the case here. The deed from Parker to Swinehart was valid and binding between the parties, as well as to subsequent purchasers with notice or without a valuable consideration. The word "void" means that which has no force or effect. It is often used as in effect meaning voidable only; and it is seldom, except in a very clear case, to be regarded as implying a complete nullity, but, in a legal sense, is to be taken subject to a large qualification in view of all the circumstances calling for its application and the rights and interests to be affected in a given case. The term "void" can only accurately be applied to those contracts that have no effect whatever; which are mere nullities and incapable of confirmation or ratification. It is rarely that things are wholly void and without force and effect as to all persons and for all purposes and incapable of being made otherwise. Things are voidable which are valid and effectual until they are avoided by some act. The distinction between void and voidable transactions is a fundamental one, though it is often obscured by carelessness of language. As applied to contracts, the distinction between the terms is often one of great practical importance, and, whenever accurately used, the term "void" can only properly be applied to such contracts as are mere nullities and incapable of confirmation or ratification. These rules to which we have just adverted are well settled, and it is apparent that an unrecorded deed is not to be considered a void instrument as against a subsequent purchaser in the sense that it has no force or effect, or as a mere nullity, which is incapable of ratification or confirmation. Upon the contrary, it is plain that the term "void" in article 6824 is used in the sense of "voidable." It is undoubtedly true that a void deed is lacking in that intrinsic fairness and honesty demanded by article 5673 in order to constitute color of title. The cited cases are referable to this principle. It is equally true, however, that an instrument valid between the parties thereto is intrinsically fair and honest, although it may be voidable at the suit of a third party for proper cause. Hence the soundness of appellant's contention may be admitted—that a void deed is so lacking in intrinsic fairness and honesty that it does not constitute color of title—but this is beside the question when we consider that the deed from Parker to Swinehart was not void, but voidable merely at the instance of the subsequent vendee of Parker, the Jesse French Piano & Organ Company, and its vendee, Phelps.

In order to determine whether appellee's unrecorded deed constitutes color of title, it is only necessary to inquire whether it is intrinsically fair and honest. The deed is clearly valid as between Parker and Swinehart, and therefore neither void in the correct sense of the term, nor lacking in intrinsic fairness and honesty. The fact that it was unrecorded is what constitutes it color of title. Had the instrument been duly recorded, appellee would have had title to the premises notwithstanding appellant's subsequently acquired and subsequently recorded deed. It is apparent that Swinehart's failure to record his deed did not operate to make it void as between him and his grantor, nor did such failure affect the fairness and honesty of the transaction between them. While he undoubtedly would be estopped to assert title as against one holding under a subsequently acquired deed for value without notice, this does not render his deed "void" in the technical sense of that term nor make it lacking in intrinsic fairness and honesty. Article 5673, R. S., not only defines "color of title," but aptly illustrates it as follows:

> And by "color of title" is meant a consecutive chain of such transfer down to such person in possession, without being regular, as if one or more of the memorials or muniments be not registered, or not duly registered, or be only in writing, or such

like defect as may not extend to or include the want of intrinsic fairness and honesty.

Chief Justice Stayton, speaking for our Supreme Court in Grigsby et al. v. May et al., 84 Tex. 240, 19 S.W. 343, and discussing the definition of "color of title" as given in article 5673, says:

> This definition doubtless was intended to give instances in which the chain of transfer would not be regular, within the meaning of the statute; but want of registration or of due registration in the chain giving color of title could have no operation in the matter of notice, and evidently was not intended to affect the right of a person holding under color of title; for, notwithstanding such irregularities may exist, the same protection is given as would be were the party holding under "title."

Continuing, and still discussing the definition as illustrated by the words of the statute, Judge Stayton says:

> The other illustration is where one or more of the muniments of title "be only in writing," which evidently was intended to cover cases in which the evidence of right, though in writing, was not executed in the manner prescribed by law; and, under the statute, these are not defects which make the muniments wanting in "intrinsic fairness and honesty." The statute, however, in effect, does declare that like defects in regularity will cause the claim to be only 'color of title,' and does not deprive those of this effect unless they be wanting in intrinsic fairness and honesty."

In the same case, the court refers to the case of Pearson v. Burditt, 26 Tex. 173, 80 Am. Dec. 649, and quotes and adopts the explanation there given of the words "intrinsic fairness and honesty," embraced in the definition of "color of title" in the statute, in the following language:

> All the examples of irregularity given have relation to the muniment of right, and for this reason it was decided in Pearson v. Burditt that "the term, 'intrinsic fairness and honesty,' embraced in the definition of color of title in our statute, relates to the means of proving the right of property in the land, so as to make the title equitably equal to a regular chain." By "equitably

equal to a regular chain" we understand to have been meant simply that, if the muniments in the chain of transfer were in fact freely executed by the persons whose acts they appear to be, then they are sufficient if, upon their faces, they show such right to land as a court of equity would enforce as between the parties to the instrument; and that this is what was intended is evident from the facts of the case then under consideration by this court.

As between Parker and Swinehart, the deed of January 4, 1909, was in all respects regular and binding upon both, and as a result possessed the intrinsic fairness and honesty which is demanded by the statute of all the links in a regular chain of transfer from and under the sovereignty. This deed, therefore, although unrecorded, is not in any sense void, as contended for by appellant, and proof of its execution, together with proof of three years' peaceable and adverse possession, was a complete bar to plaintiff's action. As is indicated above, an examination of the adversely cited authorities will show that in every instance, the instrument attacked was void in the strictest sense as between the parties thereto, and therefore lacking in intrinsic fairness and honesty. It has never been held, so far as we are advised, that a deed which is valid and binding between the parties is, because unrecorded, void in the strict sense of that term, or that it is so lacking in intrinsic fairness and honesty that it does not constitute color of title. Indeed, such a holding would be manifestly incongruous, in view of article 5673, which expressly defines color of title as a consecutive chain of transfer, down to the person in possession, without being regular, and instances such an irregularity as failure to register, or duly register, one or more of the muniments.

Affirmed.

QUESTIONS:

How should this case be diagrammed reflecting the competing claims in the chain of title? Do title warranties help any of the parties to this dispute?

Foster v. Roberts
Court of Appeals of Texas, Texarkana, 2002
2002 WL 31426432

Opinion by Justice GRANT.

Murrell and Carolyn Foster appeal from a summary judgment rendered against them in their lawsuit against Butler and Linda Roberts. The Fosters sued the Robertses in an attempt to recover real property, which they contend was at one time their homestead.

On July 3, 2001, the Fosters filed an action in trespass to try title against the Robertses challenging their title to the property. The Robertses filed a Motion for Summary Judgment based on the defensive theory of adverse possession relying on the three-year and five-year statutes. The trial court granted the motion.

On appeal, the Fosters contend generally that the deed by which the Roberts obtained title to the property was void and therefore without any effect because it was based on an unlawful and unconstitutional foreclosure of a vendor's lien on a Texas rural homestead. Their argument is based on their position that the deed is void on its face and that the adverse possession statutes do not apply. They also argue that because their lawsuit sought to recover the land and not to cancel the deed, then the defenses provided by adverse possession do not apply.

The summary judgment proof shows a lending institution foreclosed on the property on January 1, 1991, and in 1993 the institution sold the property to the Robertses. The deed was filed of record on September 22, 1993.

In support of their arguments, the Fosters direct this court to cases typified by Harris v. Bryson & Hartgrove, 34 Tex. Civ. App. 532, 80 S.W. 105 (1904, writ ref'd), and Dowdell v. McCardell, 193 S.W. 182 (Tex. Civ. App.—Beaumont 1917, no writ). Those cases provide no support for the Fosters' position, however, because they hold that the deed requirement set out in the five-year limitations provision is met where the deed is not void on its face.

The Fosters do not contend that this deed is void on its face, and the deed itself does not appear to be deficient. Rather, they argue that the deed should be held to be void because title to the property never transferred to the lending institution. Therefore, they argue, any deed the lending institution produced could not convey title and was necessarily void. In support of this position, they direct this court to Slaughter v. Qualls, 139 Tex. 340, 162 S.W.2d 671 (1942). In that case, the Texas Supreme Court found that a trustee's deed was absolutely void, although it appeared on its face to be valid, because a homestead was sold in a foreclosure sale when the mortgagor was not in default.

However, in *Slaughter*, the limitations statute that was applied was a general four-year limitations provision, and the question raised was the ability of the party to sustain his direct suit to cancel the deed. Adverse possession was not at issue. Slaughter is therefore not directly applicable to this case.

The Fosters contend that under the adverse possession provision, the possessor attempting to use that limitations provision must show that he or she has a right under title or color of title. As defined by Section 16.021, title means a regular chain of transfers of the property, while color of title is defined as a chain of title that is not regular, but only for reasons specified by statute. If the Fosters could show the deed was void, then the Robertses could not conclusively negate their cause of action, because a void deed is neither title, nor color of title. Field Measurement Serv., Inc. v. Ives, 609 S.W.2d 615, 620 (Tex. Civ. App.—Corpus Christi 1980, writ ref'd n.r.e.).

However, we need not address this issue under the three-year adverse possession statute if the five-year limitations theory will support the granting of the summary judgment, because when a trial court's order granting summary judgment does not specify the ground on which it relied for its ruling, we affirm the summary judgment if any of the theories advanced are meritorious. Star-Telegram, Inc. v. Doe, 915 S.W.2d 471, 473 (Tex.1995).

The five-year provision differs substantially from the three-year provision. It does not require a good title, but only that the possessor "claims the property under a duly registered deed." This distinction has long explicitly been set out in case law, as early as Neal v. Pickett, 280 S.W. 748 (Tex. Comm'n App. 1926, holding approved). The court recognized that in the five-year limitations statute, the function of a "deed" was merely to give notice of the adverse claim and that a void deed is as competent to provide notice as a valid one. The court also recognized that an exception exists if the deed is void on its face, because it is then "not a deed at all within the meaning of the law ." *Id.* at 752; Taylor v. Phillips Petroleum Co., 295 S.W.2d 738, 744 (Tex. Civ. App.—Galveston 1956, writ ref'd n.r.e.).

The deed is part of the record, and as noted above, is regular on its face. Further, there is no allegation or proof that would bring this case within the exception to the five-year statute as either a forgery or as a deed executed under a forged power of attorney.

The undisputed evidence shows the deed was duly recorded, that the Robertses used and cultivated the property, and that they had timely paid all applicable taxes. The undisputed evidence shows that nearly eight years elapsed from the date of the recordation of the deed before the Fosters filed suit.

We conclude the trial court properly rendered summary judgment in favor of the Robertses. We affirm the judgment of the trial court.

Tex. Civ. Prac. & Rem. Code § 16.026 "Ten Year Bare Possession Statute"

(a) A person must bring suit not later than 10 years after the day the cause of action accrues to recover real property held in peaceable and adverse possession by another who cultivates, uses, or enjoys the property.

(b) Without a title instrument, peaceable and adverse possession is limited in this section to 160 acres, including improvements, unless the number of acres actually enclosed exceeds 160. If the number of enclosed acres exceeds 160 acres, peaceable and adverse possession extends to the real property actually enclosed.

(c) Peaceable possession of real property held under a duly registered deed or other memorandum of title that fixes the boundaries of the possessor's claim extends to the boundaries specified in the instrument.

When is the Ten Year Bare Possession Statute used? It is used any time there is an adverse possessor who does not enter the land with any title instrument or if the adverse possessor has a title instrument that does not satisfy the requirements of the more stringent Three Year and Five Year statutes. As seen in (c), having an instrument of title is still helpful in determining the quantity of land that can be acquired. The adverse possession will extend to the boundaries in the instrument. This would allow the adverse possessor to acquire title to more than 160 acres and to land that is not actually enclosed.

With all of these statutes, the legislature still saw fit to add one more in 2017. The Fifteen Year Adverse Possession statute was created to address the very limited and specific problem of cotenant adverse possession when that cotenancy arose by intestate succession. Consider the following very common scenario to understand the need for this new statute.

Mom owns Blackacre 100 percent in fee simple absolute. She dies intestate with four surviving children. Based on the laws of intestate succession, each child now inherits a 25 percent undivided share as a tenant in common in Blackacre. The oldest child moves onto the property and is paying the taxes and trying to maintain the premises. The property is not insured and there is a major hail storm. The roof needs to be replaced and oldest child does not have the money. A contractor will replace the roof and allow for payments to made over time if the contractor can obtain a mechanic's lien on the property. However, the oldest child has inherited a fractional share of ownership, but nothing in the deed records reflects her as an owner of anything, not even the 25 percent share. No lien, repairs can be made. She wants to claim a homestead exemption for property taxes, but again, the property is not in her name. She has been living on the property for 20 years and her siblings have never made any demand to enter and have never contributed to any expenses. What can she do about the title?

Texas Civil Practice & Remedies Code § 16.0265. Adverse Possession by Cotenant Heir: 15-Year Combined Limitations Period

(a) In this section, "cotenant heir" means one of two or more persons who simultaneously acquire identical, undivided ownership interests in, and rights to possession of, the same real property by operation of the applicable intestate succession laws of this state or a successor in interest of one of those persons.

(b) One or more cotenant heirs of real property may acquire the interests of other cotenant heirs in the property by adverse possession under this section if, for a continuous, uninterrupted 10-year period immediately preceding the filing of the affidavits required by Subsection (c):

(1) the possessing cotenant heir or heirs:

(A) hold the property in peaceable and exclusive possession;

(B) cultivate, use, or enjoy the property; and

(C) pay all property taxes on the property not later than two years after the date the taxes become due; and

(2) no other cotenant heir has:

(A) contributed to the property's taxes or maintenance;

(B) challenged a possessing cotenant heir's exclusive possession of the property;

(C) asserted any other claim against a possessing cotenant heir in connection with the property, such as the right to rental payments from a possessing cotenant heir;

(D) acted to preserve the cotenant heir's interest in the property by filing notice of the cotenant heir's claimed interest in the deed records of the county in which the property is located; or

(E) entered into a written agreement with the possessing cotenant heir under which the possessing cotenant heir is allowed to possess the property but the other cotenant heir does not forfeit that heir's ownership interest.

(c) To make a claim of adverse possession against a cotenant heir under this section, the cotenant heir or heirs claiming adverse possession must:

(1) file in the deed records of the county in which the real property is located an affidavit of heirship in the form prescribed by Section 203.002, Estates Code, and an affidavit of adverse possession that complies with the requirements of Subsection (d);

(2) publish notice of the claim in a newspaper of general circulation in the county in which the property is located for the four consecutive weeks immediately following the date the affidavits required by Subdivision (1) are filed; and

(3) provide written notice of the claim to the last known addresses of all other cotenant heirs by certified mail, return receipt requested.

(d) The affidavits required by Subsection (c) may be filed separately or combined into a single instrument. The affidavit of adverse possession must include: [specific requirements are listed]

(e) A cotenant heir must file a controverting affidavit or bring suit to recover the cotenant heir's interest in real property adversely possessed by another cotenant heir under this section not later than the fifth anniversary of the date a right of adverse possession is asserted by the filing of the affidavits required by Subsection (c).

(f) If a controverting affidavit or judgment is not filed before the fifth anniversary of the date the affidavits required by Subsection (c) are filed and no notice described by Subsection (b)(2)(D) was filed in the 10-year period preceding the filing of the affidavits under Subsection (c), title vests in the adversely possessing cotenant heir or heirs in the manner provided by Section 16.030, precluding all claims by other cotenant heirs.

(h) Without a title instrument, peaceable and adverse possession is limited in this section to 160 acres, including improvements, unless the number of acres actually enclosed exceeds 160 acres. If the number of enclosed acres exceeds 160 acres, peaceable and adverse possession extends to the real property actually enclosed.

1. DISABILITY TOLLING:

Like other types of statutes of limitation, there is a provision that provides limited tolling for certain legal disabilities. However, the 25-year statute works along with the disability tolling to basically provide that in Texas after 25 years, the adverse possession will be complete even if the true owner has been under a legal disability for his whole life.

Disability tolling statutes vary from state to state and the application can be complicated. We will consider a few basic points with respect to disability tolling.

Tex. Civ. Prac. & Rem. Code
§ 16.022 Effect of Disability
(a) For the purposes of this subchapter, a person is under a legal disability if the person is:

(1) younger than 18 years of age, regardless of whether the person is married;

(2) of unsound mind; or

(3) serving in the United States Armed Forces during time of war.

(b) If a person entitled to sue for the recovery of real property or entitled to make a defense based on the title to real property is under a legal disability at the time title to the property vests or adverse possession commences, the time of the disability is not included in a limitations period.

(c) Except as provided by Sections 16.027 and 16.028, after the termination of the legal disability, a person has the same time to present a claim that is allowed to others under this chapter.

§ 16.027 "Notwithstanding Disability"

A person, regardless of whether the person is or has been under a legal disability, must bring suit not later than 25 years after the day the cause of action accrues to recover real property held in peaceable and adverse possession by another who cultivates, uses, or enjoys the property.

The only disability that will count for tolling purposes is a legal disability that exists at the time the adverse possession begins. If a disability arises after adverse possession begins, there will be no tolling.

For example, on January 1, *A* entered onto an unoccupied farm and began a period of adverse possession. On January 4, three days later, the owner of the farm was adjudicated insane and remained insane for 23 years, then recovered and sued to regain possession of the farm from *A*. The time period for adverse possession is ten years.

Who wins? *A* wins. A established adverse possession after ten years because there is no disability tolling in this instance. The disability did not arise until after adverse possession began and it does not count.

But what if the owner was insane before *A*'s adverse possession began? Once *A* satisfies the elements for 25 years, even if the owner is still insane, the time will run and *A* will take title to the property.

Chapter 10
Acquiring Property by Gift

A. Introduction to Gifts

We have covered the purchase of real property, adverse possession, the rule of finders, and the rule of capture. We now turn our attention to the gift, which is our last topic regarding acquiring property. You have actually already taken a small peek at the concept of a gift of real property in Chapter 7 when discussing delivery of deeds and the conditional delivery. In those cases there were gifts of real property involved. We will now incorporate personal property again to consider the legal requirements of a valid gift.

Let's start with a definition. A gift is a voluntary, immediate transfer of property without consideration from one person (donor) to another (donee). It is a noncontractual, gratuitous transfer of property made without legal consideration. Along with legal definitions, there are legal elements or requirements of a valid gift. Let us consider these requirements.

B. Inter Vivos Gifts

Inter vivos gifts are gifts that are completed during the donor's lifetime. When we studied the *Rosengrant* and *Sweeney* cases, we saw examples of attempted inter vivos gifts of real property. In both cases the court had to make a determination of valid delivery. In making the decision of a valid delivery, the court focused on the donative intent. When examining gifts of real property, there is a deed and the language of the deed will be examined to try to glean the grantor's intent for the gift. However, with personal property, there are no deeds.

The nature of a gift of personal property raises red flags. The law is skeptical of situations where someone would part with something of value without compensation. This area of the law lends itself to deceit and fraud. Therefore, the courts are usually very strict in examining evidence of a potential gift. In order to have a valid gift there must be evidence of donative intent, delivery, and acceptance. We will examine each requirement separately.

1. Donative Intent

Donative intent is an important requirement with personal property as well as real property. There are reasons why real or personal property may change hands without transferring title and ownership of the property. With real property you have learned how the landlord-tenant relationship works. A person could be in possession as a tenant without the owner having any intent to make a gift of the land.

For personal property, the idea of transferring possession without ownership is even more common. Every time you take your clothes to the dry cleaner or leave your car with a valet you are transferring possession without title. These are called bailment relationships. The court must be sure that the transfer is not something less than a transfer of ownership.

2. Delivery → 3 TYPES

Delivery is an element that often causes difficulty. As we saw with delivery of deeds, delivery requires an intent of the donor to make an immediate transfer of ownership to the donee. Without a valid delivery, there is no gift. Statements and actions by the donor serve as the best evidence of the donor's intent. Oral or written statements may serve as evidence of donative intent. The court will be looking at what was said in these statements very closely to make the distinction: Is there an intent to make a transfer of ownership now, later, or not at all?

There are different forms of delivery. However, not all forms of delivery are suitable for every item. Delivery is the actual, physical delivery of the object. This is commonly referred to as "manual delivery." Historically, manual delivery has been required in all cases except when the manual delivery is impractical or impossible. The general rule has been, however, if it can be physically handed over, it must be handed over.

The next type of delivery is constructive delivery. This occurs when the donor physically transfers to the donee the means of obtaining access to and control of the property, most commonly by handing over a key. The third type of delivery is symbolic delivery. Symbolic delivery occurs when an object that represents or symbolizes the gift is physically handed to the donee, usually a writing.

The conflict in modern cases is how strictly to adhere to the manual delivery requirement. There are modern cases where courts have found a valid constructive delivery even if manual delivery was possible. The rationale was that when the evidence of donative intent is concrete and undisputed, there is every indication the donor intended to make a present transfer and when the steps taken by the donor must have been deemed by the donor as sufficient to pass the donor's interest. The Restatement (Third) of Donative Transfers proposes that if a donee can provide clear and convincing evidence of donative intent, then no delivery is required.[1] However, that is still just a proposal. The state that has come closest to adopting such a standard is California. California adopted a statute that allows a symbolic delivery by a writing under any circumstance.[2]

Having donative intent and making a delivery normally occur simultaneously. However, with the inter vivos gift that is not a requirement. You will see when discussing the gift causa mortis that the requirement is different. This means that in a situation where possession transfers and then intent follows, the gift is completed as soon as the elements are both satisfied (along with acceptance which is presumed). Additionally, if there is the intent expressed and then the transfer of possession follows, the gift is completed as soon as both elements are satisfied (along with acceptance which is presumed).

3. Acceptance → PRESUMED!

As with acceptance with deeds, acceptance of a gift is presumed. The donee may reject or disclaim a gift and if that occurs, the gift will not be valid. However, this is not a usual source of dispute with gifts. There are occasions where someone may not want to accept a gift—tax consequences, expensive upkeep, or the presence of hazardous substances on land. However, in the vast majority of cases the gift is accepted and valid.

While all elements of a gift are not usually at issue in a dispute, in the following case they are. How does the donee manage to deal with attacks on all fronts?

Gruen v. Gruen
Court of Appeals of New York, 1986
496 N.E.2d 869

SIMONS, J.

Plaintiff commenced this action seeking a declaration that he is the rightful owner of a painting which he alleges his father, now deceased, gave to him. He concedes that he has never had possession of the painting but asserts that his father made a valid gift of the title in 1963 reserving a life estate for himself. His father retained possession of the painting until he died in 1980. Defendant, plaintiff's stepmother, has the painting now and has refused plaintiff's requests that she turn it over to him. She contends that the purported gift was testamentary in nature and invalid insofar as the formalities of a will were not

---

[1] Restatement (Third) of Property, Wills and Other Donative Transfers § 6.2, Illustration 22 (2003).

[2] Cal. Civ. Code § 1147 (West 2007).

met or, alternatively, that a donor may not make a valid inter vivos gift of a chattel and retain a life estate with a complete right of possession. Following a seven-day nonjury trial, Special Term found that plaintiff had failed to establish any of the elements of an inter vivos gift and that in any event an attempt by a donor to retain a present possessory life estate in a chattel invalidated a purported gift of it. The Appellate Division held that a valid gift may be made reserving a life estate and, finding the elements of a gift established in this case, it reversed and remitted the matter for a determination of value. That determination has now been made and defendant appeals directly to this court from the subsequent final judgment entered in Supreme Court awarding plaintiff $2,500,000 in damages representing the value of the painting, plus interest. We now affirm.

The subject of the dispute is a work entitled "Schloss Kammer am Attersee II" painted by a noted Austrian modernist, Gustav Klimt. It was purchased by plaintiff's father, Victor Gruen, in 1959 for $8,000. On April 1, 1963, the elder Gruen, a successful architect with offices and residences in both New York City and Los Angeles during most of the time involved in this action, wrote a letter to plaintiff, then an undergraduate student at Harvard, stating that he was giving him the Klimt painting for his birthday but that he wished to retain the possession of it for his lifetime. This letter is not in evidence, apparently because plaintiff destroyed it on instructions from his father. Two other letters were received, however, one dated May 22, 1963, and the other April 1, 1963. Both had been dictated by Victor Gruen and sent together to plaintiff on or about May 22, 1963. The letter dated May 22, 1963 reads as follows:

ORIGINAL LETTER DESTROYED [handwritten annotation in left margin]

> Dear Michael:
>
> I wrote you at the time of your birthday about the gift of the painting by Klimt.
>
> Now my lawyer tells me that because of the existing tax laws, it was wrong to mention in that letter that I want to use the painting as long as I live. Though I still want to use it, this should not appear in the letter. I am enclosing, therefore, a new letter and I ask you to send the old one back to me so that it can be destroyed
>
> I know this is all very silly, but the lawyer and our accountant insist that they must have in their possession copies of a letter which will serve the purpose of making it possible for you, once I die, to get this picture without having to pay inheritance taxes on it.
>
> Love,
>
> s/Victor.

Enclosed with this letter was a substitute gift letter, dated April 1, 1963, which stated:

> Dear Michael:
>
> The 21st birthday, being an important event in life, should be celebrated accordingly. I therefore wish to give you as a present the oil painting by Gustav Klimt of Schloss Kammer which now hangs in the New York living room. You know that Lazette and I bought it some 5 or 6 years ago, and you always told us how much you liked it.
>
> Happy birthday again.
>
> Love,
>
> s/Victor.

Plaintiff never took possession of the painting nor did he seek to do so. Except for a brief period between 1964 and 1965 when it was on loan to art exhibits and when restoration work was performed on it, the painting remained in his father's possession, moving with him from New York City to Beverly Hills and finally to Vienna, Austria, where Victor Gruen died on February 14, 1980. Following Victor's death plaintiff requested possession of the Klimt painting and when defendant refused, he commenced this action.

The issues framed for appeal are whether a valid inter vivos gift of a chattel may be made where the donor has reserved a life estate in the chattel and the donee never has had physical possession of it before the donor's death and, if it may, which factual findings on the elements of a valid inter vivos gift more nearly comport with the weight of the evidence in this case, those of Special Term or those of the Appellate Division. The latter issue requires application of two general rules. First, to make a valid inter vivos gift there must exist the intent on the part of the donor to make a present transfer; delivery of the gift, either actual or constructive to the donee; and acceptance by the donee. Second, the proponent of a gift has the burden of proving each of these elements by clear and convincing evidence.

Donative Intent

There is an important distinction between the intent with which an inter vivos gift is made and the intent to make a gift by will. An inter vivos gift requires that the donor intend to make an irrevocable present transfer of ownership; if the intention is to make a testamentary disposition effective only after death, the gift is invalid unless made by will.

Defendant contends that the trial court was correct in finding that Victor did not intend to transfer any present interest in the painting to plaintiff in 1963 but only expressed an intention that plaintiff was to get the painting upon his death. The evidence is all but conclusive, however, that Victor intended to transfer ownership of the painting to plaintiff in 1963 but to retain a life estate in it and that he did, therefore, effectively transfer a remainder interest in the painting to plaintiff at that time. Although the original letter was not in evidence, testimony of its contents was received along with the substitute gift letter and its covering letter dated May 22, 1963. The three letters should be considered together as a single instrument and when they are they unambiguously establish that Victor Gruen intended to make a present gift of title to the painting at that time. But there was other evidence for after 1963 Victor made several statements orally and in writing indicating that he had previously given plaintiff the painting and that plaintiff owned it. Victor Gruen retained possession of the property, insured it, allowed others to exhibit it and made necessary repairs to it but those acts are not inconsistent with his retention of a life estate. Furthermore, whatever probative value could be attached to his statement that he had bequeathed the painting to his heirs, made 16 years later when he prepared an export license application so that he could take the painting out of Austria, is negated by the overwhelming evidence that he intended a present transfer of title in 1963. Victor's failure to file a gift tax return on the transaction was partially explained by allegedly erroneous legal advice he received, and while that omission sometimes may indicate that the donor had no intention of making a present gift, it does not necessarily do so and it is not dispositive in this case.

Defendant contends that even if a present gift was intended, Victor's reservation of a lifetime interest in the painting defeated it. She relies on a statement from Young v. Young, that " '[a]ny gift of chattels which expressly reserves the use of the property to the donor for a certain period, or as long as the donor shall live, is ineffectual.'" The statement was dictum, however, and the holding of the court was limited to a determination that an attempted gift of bonds in which the donor reserved the interest for life failed because there had been no delivery of the gift, either actual or constructive. The court expressly left undecided the question "whether a remainder in a chattel may be created and given by a donor by carving out a life estate for himself and transferring the remainder." We answered part of that question in Matter of Brandreth, 62 N.E. 563, when we held that "[in] this state a life estate and remainder can be created in a chattel or a fund the same as in real property". The case did not require us to decide whether there could be a valid gift of the remainder.

Defendant recognizes that a valid inter vivos gift of a remainder interest can be made not only of real property but also of such intangibles as stocks and bonds.

Indeed, several of the cases she cites so hold. That being so, it is difficult to perceive any legal basis for the distinction she urges which would permit gifts of remainder interests in those properties but not of remainder interests in chattels such as the Klimt painting here. The only reason suggested is that the gift of a chattel must include a present right to possession. The application of Brandreth to permit a gift of the remainder in this case, however, is consistent with the distinction, well recognized in the law of gifts as well as in real property law, between ownership and possession or enjoyment. Insofar as some of our cases purport to require that the donor intend to transfer both title and possession immediately to have a valid inter vivos gift, they state the rule too broadly and confuse the effectiveness of a gift with the transfer of the possession of the subject of that gift. The correct test is " 'whether the maker intended the [gift] to have no effect until after the maker's death, or whether he intended it to transfer some present interest.' " (McCarthy v. Peret, 281 N.Y. 407, 24 N.E.2d 102). "As long as the evidence establishes an intent to make a present and irrevocable transfer of title or the right of ownership, there is a present transfer of some interest and the gift is effective immediately. Thus, in Speelman v. Pascal, [222 N.Y.S.2d 324], we held valid a gift of a percentage of the future royalties to the play "My Fair Lady" before the play even existed. There, as in this case, the donee received title or the right of ownership to some property immediately upon the making of the gift but possession or enjoyment of the subject of the gift was postponed to some future time.

Defendant suggests that allowing a donor to make a present gift of a remainder with the reservation of a life estate will lead courts to effectuate otherwise invalid testamentary dispositions of property. The two have entirely different characteristics, however, which make them distinguishable. Once the gift is made it is irrevocable and the donor is limited to the rights of a life tenant not an owner. Moreover, with the gift of a remainder title vests immediately in the donee and any possession is postponed until the donor's death whereas under a will neither title nor possession vests immediately. Finally, the postponement of enjoyment of the gift is produced by the express terms of the gift not by the nature of the instrument as it is with a will.

Delivery

In order to have a valid inter vivos gift, there must be a delivery of the gift, either by a physical delivery of the subject of the gift or a constructive or symbolic delivery such as by an instrument of gift, sufficient to divest the donor of dominion and control over the property. As the statement of the rule suggests, the requirement of delivery is not rigid or inflexible, but is to be applied in light of its purpose to avoid mistakes by donors and fraudulent claims by donees. Accordingly, what is sufficient to constitute delivery "must be tailored to suit the circumstances of the case." The rule requires that " '[t]he delivery necessary to consummate a gift must be as perfect as the nature of the property and the circumstances and surroundings of the parties will reasonably permit.' "

Defendant contends that when a tangible piece of personal property such as a painting is the subject of a gift, physical delivery of the painting itself is the best form of delivery and should be required. Here, of course, we have only delivery of Victor Gruen's letters which serve as instruments of gift. Defendant's statement of the rule as applied may be generally true, but it ignores the fact that what Victor Gruen gave plaintiff was not all rights to the Klimt painting, but only title to it with no right of possession until his death. Under these circumstances, it would be illogical for the law to require the donor to part with possession of the painting when that is exactly what he intends to retain.

Nor is there any reason to require a donor making a gift of a remainder interest in a chattel to physically deliver the chattel into the donee's hands only to have the donee redeliver it to the donor. As the facts of this case demonstrate, such a requirement could impose practical burdens on the parties to the gift while serving the delivery requirement poorly. Thus, in order to accomplish this type of delivery the parties would have been required to travel to New York for the symbolic transfer and redelivery of the Klimt painting which was hanging on the wall of Victor Gruen's Manhattan apartment. Defendant suggests that such a requirement would be stronger evidence of a completed gift, but in the absence of witnesses to the event or any written confirmation of the gift it would provide less protection against fraudulent claims than have the written instruments of gift delivered in this case.

[handwritten margin note: PHYSICAL DELIVERY WOULD BE IMPRACTICAL]

Acceptance

Acceptance by the donee is essential to the validity of an inter vivos gift, but when a gift is of value to the donee, as it is here, the law will presume an acceptance on his part. Plaintiff did not rely on this presumption alone but also presented clear and convincing proof of his acceptance of a remainder interest in the Klimt painting by evidence that he had made several contemporaneous statements acknowledging the gift to his friends and associates, even showing some of them his father's gift letter, and that he had retained both letters for over 17 years to verify the gift after his father died. Defendant relied exclusively on affidavits filed by plaintiff in a matrimonial action with his former wife, in which plaintiff failed to list his interest in the painting as an asset. These affidavits were made over 10 years after acceptance was complete and they do not even approach the evidence in Matter of Kelly where the donee, immediately upon delivery of a diamond ring, rejected it as "too flashy." We agree with the Appellate Division that interpretation of the affidavit was too speculative to support a finding of rejection and overcome the substantial showing of acceptance by plaintiff.

Accordingly, the judgment appealed from and the order of the Appellate Division brought up for review should be affirmed, with costs.

NOTES, QUESTIONS, AND PROBLEMS:

1. In examining the issue of intent, was the intent of the donor to part with a future interest now, to part will the full ownership now, or to part with something only at death? How can you determine that?

2. What role do the various letters from the donor play in the court's rationale? What would have been the outcome had the donee destroyed or lost all of the letters?

3. Carol owns a piano that she wishes to give to her daughter Marcia as a birthday present. Carol and Marcia live 300 miles apart. On Marcia's birthday, Carol sends a card with a handwritten note Marcia that reads, "Today I give you the Steinway piano in my living room. You learned to play the piano on it and I know it means so much to you. Have a wonderful birthday! Love, Mom." Has Carol made a valid inter vivos gift of the piano to Marcia? Why or why not? If Carol dies suddenly two days later and the other beneficiaries under her will claim the piano, will Marcia prevail?

4. Carol owns an heirloom diamond necklace that all women in the family have worn on their wedding days. Carol wants the necklace to pass to her oldest daughter, Marcia. Carol gives Marcia a key to the safe deposit box at the bank where she keeps the necklace and says to Marcia, "The necklace is yours. I want you to have it as my oldest daughter. Take this key to the safe deposit box so you can go and pick it up whenever you want." Has Carol made a valid inter vivos gift to Marcia?

C. Gift Causa Mortis

The gift causa mortis is an interesting creature. It is essentially an emergency substitute for a will. The gift causa mortis allows a donor to make a deathbed transfer of property without following the formalities of a will. However, this can only be used for personal property, not real property. The gift causa mortis requires donative intent, delivery, and acceptance. However, due to its unique nature there are additional requirements and a more strict delivery requirement than with an inter vivos gift.

The gift causa mortis requires that the donor be confronting the substantial certainty of death in the near future from a particular illness or affliction. If the donor dies from the anticipated peril then the gift is complete. However, if the donor survives, in some states the gift if automatically revoked. In other states the gift is revoked if the donor asks for the property, but otherwise will be a completed valid gift. The natural apprehension of death does not allow for a gift causa mortis. If the death is not truly imminent, there is time to obtain a valid will and thus the gift causa mortis will not be applicable.

Consider the situation where Carol is about to undergo a quadruple bypass surgery and the doctors have not given her a good chance of survival. At the hospital, Carol removes her favorite sapphire ring and hands it to Alice saying, "since I am about to die, I want you to have this." Carol dies on the operating table. Is there a valid gift causa mortis to Alice? What if Carol recovers? What would happen if the ring were at home in Carol's dresser? Carol told Alice that the sapphire ring in her dresser at home was hers since she was about to die. If Carol dies on the operating table, is this a valid gift causa mortis? If Carol recovers, what happens?

Chapter 11
Protecting Property: Texas Homestead Laws

A. Introduction to Texas Homestead Laws

You probably have all heard the old saying that a person's home is his or her castle. Well, that becomes quite clear when looking at the protections afforded by Texas Homestead laws. The protection is afforded by the Texas Constitution and is further defined in the Texas Property Code, Texas Probate Code, and Texas Family Code.

The protection afforded by the Homestead laws protects the right to possession of property for a surviving spouse or minor child in the situation of the death of the title holder and also protects possession by preventing creditors from seizing homestead property except under very specific and limited circumstances.

The coverage of the homestead material will focus on defining what exactly the homestead is and what type of property may be protected by homestead laws. We will look at the rules for establishing the homestead and the different types of homesteads that can be created. After establishing the homestead, what legal rights and responsibilities does that include? We will look at laws regarding the homestead with respect to taxes on homestead property, selling homestead property, liens that may and may not attach to homestead property, and creating the legal life estate and what that entails.

Finally, as with all other interests in property, we will discuss how this protection may end. What constitutes abandonment of the homestead and what effect does the abandonment have on the property?

1. History of Texas Homestead Laws

In May 1837, New York banks ceased payments to investors, leading other banks across the nation to do the same. In a short period of time, currency lost its value and many companies crashed with fortunes being lost. Unemployment skyrocketed—especially in the West and South with a loss of agricultural exports and crop failures. Public calls for banking reform increased anxiety and a six-year depression followed.

While this may sound like an article ripped from recent headlines, this was the status of the economic situation in 1837 with Texas being hit hard. As a result, Texas Homestead laws were born.

Prior to 1840, Texas was under the rule of France, Spain, and Mexico. Spanish civil law provided a statutory protection against execution on certain items of personal property, tools of trade, and the dwelling houses of knights and noblemen, but the protection was not absolute. Spanish law also provided that a certain amount of a husband's estate would go to the wife if she had no property of her own to support herself. There was an exemption for antecedent debts against the property of colonists and impresarios under the laws of the Republic of Texas.

The first statutory provision for homestead protection was enacted in 1839. The provision exempted 50 acres of land or one town lot and improvements not to exceed $500 in value. This provision was briefly repealed in 1840 but re-enacted in 1843. Since 1843, Texas has continually had homestead protections in place. In 1843, Congress also extended homestead protection into the probate process.

Texas adopted a new constitution when it joined the United States in 1845. The new constitution included a homestead provision that increased the amount protected to 200 acres; the value of land of an urban homestead, however, could not exceed $2,000. The joinder requirement was also created at this time. The wife had to consent to the sale of the homestead property in an effort to provide the wife with some protection from her husband's actions. Homestead protection applied only to families and not to single individuals. The constitutions of 1861 and 1855 contained the same provisions.

The constitution of 1876 introduced the business homestead. An urban homestead may be used for the purpose of a home "or as a place to exercise the calling or business of the head of a family." This constitution also provided survivorship rights to surviving spouses. In 1897, an amendment added the provision that protected proceeds of a voluntary sale of a homestead for six months after such sale.

In 1970, the value of the urban homestead that could be protected was increased to $10,000. In 1973, the scope of the homestead protected was finally expanded to single adults. In 1983, the homestead protection was limited based on acreage for the first time, rather than value. The urban homestead was limited to one acre. In 1989, the definition of rural homestead was added.

Some of the most significant changes in homestead protections occurred during the 1990s. In 1995, Texas voters amended the Texas Constitution, which triggered amendments to the Property Code expanding the list of exceptions to homestead protection; owelty of partition judgments and a refinance of a lien on a homestead were added to the list of liens permissible to attach to homestead property.

In 1997, the voters amended the constitution to expand exemptions more. The 1997 amendments allowed for the home equity loan and reverse mortgage to be available to Texas property owners. It also allowed different requirements to validly attach a home improvement lien by imposing different requirements. The last amendments with respect to the content or extent of homestead law occurred in 1999, when the constitution was amended to increase the size of the urban homestead and made other changes to the urban homestead. Despite some discussions in the legislature in recent years the only changes made have been fine-tuning the provisions already in place and nothing has been expanded since 1999.

B. Establishing the Homestead: What Is Homestead Property?

Texas Homestead laws are not intended to be used as a means to shield all assets from creditors or to allow a person to pick and choose what is entitled to protection. While Texas Homestead laws do provide a great degree of protection, there are limits. The Texas Constitution and Property Code both lay out the requirements of what exactly can fall within the reach of the laws and also how much can actually be protected. For the average person, the question of what is homestead is rather straightforward. Think of the typical family or individual living in a house in a residential neighborhood. This is the only property the person owns. It is where he lives. That is the homestead. However, when people own multiple pieces of property or large parcels of land consisting of hundreds or thousands of acres, what is homestead can become a much more difficult question.

When a person does own multiple parcels or hundreds or thousands of acres, the classification of urban or rural is incredibly important. Fortunately there is now a provision in the Texas Property Code to assist with making the distinction between a rural and an urban homestead. If the characteristics of the property do not fit the definition of urban provided in the statute, the property is rural.

But, what if we are dealing with someone who does not own the typical home in a residential neighborhood but instead has a residence that is a little different? Think about the show *Treehouse Masters*,[1] or the person who lives in a mobile home in a trailer park, or the person who lives on a boat. Would these homes qualify as a homestead?

---

[1] *Treehouse Masters*, Animal Planet, first aired May 31, 2013.

Texas Const. art. XVI, § 51 Amount of Homestead; Uses

The homestead, not in a town or city, shall consist of not more than two hundred acres of land, which may be in one or more parcels, with the improvements thereon; the homestead in a city, town or village, shall consist of lot or contiguous lots amounting to not more than 10 acres of land, together with any improvements on the land; provided, that the homestead in a city, town or village shall be used for the purposes of a home, or as both an urban home and a place to exercise a calling or business, of the homestead claimant, whether a single adult person, or the head of a family; provided also, that any temporary renting of the homestead shall not change the character of the same, when no other homestead has been acquired; provided further that a release or refinance of an existing lien against a homestead as to a part of the homestead does not create an additional burden on the part of the homestead property that is unreleased or subject to the refinance, and a new lien is not invalid only for that reason.

Tex. Prop. Code § 41.002. Definition of Homestead

(a) If used for the purposes of an urban home or as both an urban home and a place to exercise a calling or business, the homestead of a family or a single, adult person, not otherwise entitled to a homestead, shall consist of not more than 10 acres of land which may be in one or more contiguous lots, together with any improvements thereon.

(b) If used for the purposes of a rural home, the homestead shall consist of:

    (1) for a family, not more than 200 acres, which may be in one or more parcels, with the improvements thereon; or

    (2) for a single, adult person, not otherwise entitled to a homestead, not more than 100 acres, which may be in one or more parcels, with the improvements thereon.

(c) A homestead is considered to be urban if, at the time the designation is made, the property is:

    (1) located within the limits of a municipality or its extraterritorial jurisdiction or a platted subdivision; and

    (2) served by police protection, paid or volunteer fire protection, and at least three of the following services provided by a municipality or under contract to a municipality:

        (A) electric;

        (B) natural gas;

        (C) sewer;

        (D) storm sewer; and

        (E) water.

(d) The definition of a homestead as provided in this section applies to all homesteads in this state whenever created.

Norris v. Thomas
Supreme Court of Texas, 2007
215 S.W.3d 851

Justice WILLETT delivered the opinion of the Court, joined by Chief Justice JEFFERSON, Justice HECHT, Justice GREEN, and Justice JOHNSON.

We confront today a question of first impression: whether a boat qualifies as a homestead under article XVI, sections 50 and 51 of the Texas Constitution. Since 1845, our state constitution has protected a homestead from forced sale to satisfy the claims of creditors. Thomas Norris claimed his 68-foot yacht as a homestead to shield it from bankruptcy creditors, prompting the United States Court of Appeals for the Fifth Circuit to certify this question to us: "Does a motorized waterborne vessel, used as a primary residence and otherwise fulfilling all of the requirements of a homestead except attachment to land, qualify for the homestead exemption under Article 16, §§ 50 and 51 of the Texas Constitution?" Under the facts presented in this case, and given the Constitution's explicit realty-based language, we answer the question, "No."

I. Background

In September 2003, Norris filed a voluntary bankruptcy petition under Chapter 7 of the United States Bankruptcy Code Under the Code a debtor may claim a homestead exemption as allowed by state law. Norris claimed his 68-foot yacht as exempt property under the Texas homestead exemption. The boat, which Norris valued at $399,000 in his bankruptcy schedules, has four bedrooms, three bathrooms, a galley, and an upper and lower salon. Although his petition indicated that his street address was 13909 Nacogdoches Road, San Antonio, Texas, Norris testified at a January 2004 bankruptcy court hearing that the address is a business postal center where the Norrises receive mail. Norris further stated that he took up permanent residence on the boat after the Norrises sold their previous home in Lake McQueeny, Texas, in 2000, and that the boat is his only home. Norris's attorney stated at the hearing that "primarily, [Norris] lives on that boat while it's dry-docked" at Corpus Christi, and that the boat received water, phone service, and electricity through connections to a dock. Norris also testified at the hearing that since purchasing the boat in 1997 he had cruised extensively to places such as New Orleans, Florida, and Alabama. At the time the bankruptcy petition was filed in September 2003, the boat was docked in Port Aransas, Texas. Norris testified at the January 2004 hearing that he had moved the boat to a marina in Corpus Christi, Texas, where he had a month-to-month lease. Although the boat is described in the record as "dry-docked," there is no indication that Norris ever permanently affixed the boat to real estate or intended to do so.

The bankruptcy court held that the Texas homestead exemption, even broadly construed, does not include boats. The federal district court agreed, concluding that the boat was a movable chattel "by virtue of its self-powered mobility" and not entitled to homestead protection. Norris appealed to the Fifth Circuit, which certified the question to this Court.

II. Discussion

We construe homestead laws generously; however, courts cannot unduly stretch the homestead laws beyond their constitutional and statutory moorings and protect that which is not a homestead.

A. Texas Constitutional and Statutory Provisions

Neither the Texas Constitution nor the Property Code defines "homestead" with specificity. Section 50 of article XVI shields homesteads from forced sale, providing generally that "[t]he homestead of a family, or of a single adult person, shall be, and is hereby protected from forced sale, for the payment of all debts. . . ." Section 51, in turn, restricts the maximum size of a protected homestead, limiting rural and urban homesteads by acres of land and including any land-based improvements. The Texas Property Code resembles section 51 and likewise describes a homestead as a home or a home and business with certain acreage limitations with any "improvements thereon." Though neither of these provisions expressly exclude boats from homestead protection, they both discuss homesteads in terms of land and any improvements that sit atop the land. More specifically, when describing the scope of the protection, section 51 and the Property Code state the acreage limitation and then variably say, when describing any attached structures, "with the improvements thereon" or "with any improvements on the land" or "with any improvements thereon."

B. Precedent

Texas's strong pro-homestead tradition pre-dates statehood, and the Republic of Texas was determined to protect homesteads from creditors. In 1886, roughly a half-century after Texas homestead laws originated, we opined on their reach and limits. In Cullers v. James, we held that a house may be a homestead even if the owner has no proprietary interest in the land on which the house stands. The James family leased a three-or four-acre tract of land from Robert Walker (though the property was actually Walker's wife's separate property). The land contained improvements such as a house, a gin-house, gin machinery, and a mill that were "so fixed as to make [them] part of the land." But since James had no interest in the land, the Court viewed the improvements as personal property instead of realty. Nonetheless, the Court held that the house and gin-house qualified as a homestead.

Cullers established that a house can be a homestead even if the owner has no ownership interest in the land. It also made clear that the term "improvements" as protected by article XVI, section 51 includes the residence itself. In the 121 years since *Cullers*, we have defined improvements to real property with greater precision, distinguishing them from mere personalty, and holding that "personalty does not constitute an improvement until it is annexed to realty." This Court put it plainly in Sonnier v. Chisholm-Ryder Co.: "There can be no improvement without annexation to realty, and until personalty is annexed to realty, it by definition cannot be an improvement." Not only that, but the annexed object cannot be deemed an improvement to land unless it is intended to be "a permanent addition to the realty."

Since *Cullers*, the courts of appeals have issued several homestead-related opinions that bear more directly on today's issue, and they share a common thread: homestead protection turns not on who owns the underlying land, but on the degree to which the residence "thereon" or "on the land" is attached to it. This Court reviewed four of these pertinent cases, refusing the writ in the first and finding no reversible error in the others. We continue to believe that their attachment-based analysis is correct.

In Clark v. Vitz, Vitz built a "house-trailer" that his family used as its primary residence for two years. He later purchased a lot with a brick house, placed the house trailer twenty-five feet from the house, and set the trailer on four wooden blocks. Vitz ran electrical service to the house trailer from the residence and planned to connect the trailer to the residence's plumbing. The court held that Vitz's attachment of the house-trailer to his residence made the trailer part of the homestead.

In Gann v. Montgomery, the Ganns owned a "house trailer, mounted on wheels, of the type usually pulled behind an automobile." After a few years, the Ganns moved the trailer to Mr. Gann's parents' backyard. Gann executed a promissory note secured by a chattel mortgage on the trailer. Gann then entered the United States Army and was stationed at the Fort Worth Army Airfield. His family still lived in the trailer, now parked at the airfield and still on wheels. The mortgage holder brought suit to foreclose on the chattel mortgage lien. The court, citing *Cullers*, noted the distinction between a chattel that is attached to realty and a chattel that is not. After quoting from *Cullers*, the court said:

> Taken alone, this language might indicate a belief by the Supreme Court that the homestead exemption could attach to any chattel, such as a covered wagon, or a houseboat, or any other type of movable vehicle or conveyance, which for the time being might be occupied by the claimant and his family as living quarters. But when we examine the opinion in the light of the

facts of the case, and consider the disposition made of the entire case, we come to a different conclusion.

The court then noted the distinction between personal property—such as the gin machinery in *Cullers*—and a permanent fixture attached to realty that is personal property only because the owner of the fixture does not own the land. The court cited *Clark* as consistent with this dichotomy in that the house trailer was only a homestead because it had been attached to the realty and set alongside the house, essentially becoming an extra room. The court held that house trailers without the characteristics of permanent fixtures attached to realty are not protected homesteads.

In Capitol Aggregates, Inc. v. Walker, the Walkers owned a "mobile trailer home" connected to the gas, water, and sewage systems of a trailer park. They removed the wheels and set the house on cement blocks. The court found it persuasive that the house was "as physically attached to the land as frame houses" and held that the trailer house was a homestead.

Finally, in Minnehoma Financial Co. v. Ditto, Ditto purchased a "mobile home." He attached the mobile home to his property by removing the wheels, placing it on concrete blocks secured by eight-foot buried anchors, and connecting it to electricity and water. The court held that the mobile home was a homestead:

> We agree with Ditto that a mobile home may be deemed an improvement to the realty when attached to the realty in a manner indicating an intention that it be a permanent part of the real estate. The nature of a mobile home does not preclude its being given homestead protection. If a mobile home is attached in such a manner to a homestead, it is entitled to homestead protection.

Nonetheless, the court held that the trailer home was not protected because a lien attached before the mobile home became part of Ditto's homestead.

C. Application

Applying these precedents to the instant facts, we agree that the proper test for whether a residence attains homestead status is whether the attachment to land is sufficient to make the personal property a permanent part of the realty. Significantly, both the Constitution and the Property Code use the word "thereon" when describing any protected homestead improvements; the Constitution also stipulates "on the land," which is plainly not the same as "in the water."

As we said in *Cullers*, "The greater part of [the personal property] was . . . so fixed as to make it part of the land. . . ." Ninety-two years later, the *Ditto* court held "a mobile home may be deemed an improvement to the realty when attached to the realty in a manner indicating an intention that it be a permanent part of the real estate." The *Gann* court similarly reasoned "the homestead right may attach to a chattel if it has been annexed to the freehold so as to have become a fixture and to have acquired the character of realty." Movable chattels do not possess the characteristics of a fixture attached to real property and do not acquire the character of realty. As the *Walker* court put it, "[i]t is their attachment to realty which gives them homestead character."

In *Clark*, setting a trailer home on four wooden blocks and connecting it to electrical service was sufficient to attach the trailer to real property. In *Gann*, where the house trailer remained on wheels, merely parking the movable trailer on real property was insufficient to attach the trailer to the property. In *Walker*, removing the wheels of a mobile trailer home, setting it on cement blocks, and connecting it to water, sewer, and gas service was sufficient to attach the mobile trailer to real property. And in *Ditto*, removing the wheels of a mobile home, setting it on concrete blocks with eight-foot buried anchors, and connecting it to electrical and plumbing service was sufficient to give it homestead protection.

In the pending case, although Norris's dock-based connections to utilities and plumbing are like the land-based utility connections in *Clark, Walker,* and *Ditto*, a boat is sufficiently distinct from a mobile home or house trailer to justify a different outcome, particularly given the Constitution's unequivocal requirement that protected improvements be on the land. Norris's boat, unlike a dwelling that is permanently affixed to land, retains its independent, mobile character even when attached to dock-based amenities because it has self-contained utility and plumbing systems and also boasts its own propulsion. Norris, in fact, admits to traveling in the boat extensively throughout the Gulf of Mexico prior to filing for bankruptcy, and he moved the boat from Port Aransas to Corpus Christi after the bankruptcy filing. *Gann* was the only case where parties moved their home and still sought homestead protection, which the court denied. Though Norris took steps to tether the boat to realty, these steps do not sufficiently alter the boat's mobile character or, apparently, prevent Norris from cruising. We hold that Norris's boat remains a movable chattel; it does not rest "thereon" or "on the land" as Texas homestead law clearly requires; it has not become a permanent part of the real estate; and it has not sufficiently attached to real property to merit homestead protection. In our view, the homestead exemption from creditors found in the Constitution and the Property Code contemplates a requisite degree of physical permanency and attachment to fixed realty—"thereon" and "on the land" constitute the operative language—that is not present in the pending case.

The dissent bemoans the Court's "cramped interpretation" and urges a more "family-supportive 'homestead' concept" that the Legislature and at least one executive agency have embraced in other areas of Texas law. The Tax Code, for example, specifically includes mobile homes in its definition of "residence homestead" and more generally employs a looser definition that essentially focuses on whether the structure is owned and occupied as a principal residence. In addition, state regulations that determine eligibility for certain welfare-related programs define "homestead" expansively to include "[a]ny structure, including a houseboat or motor-home that the household uses as its residence. . . ." The dissent, while conceding that these context-specific provisions do not govern the instant dispute, argues these more protective provisions counsel a more "functional approach."

We believe these provisions cut the other way, demonstrating if anything that policymakers are adept at adopting different definitions for different purposes. The Legislature is certainly free to put a proposed amendment before Texas voters to delete "thereon" and "on the land" and expand our Constitution's current land-based homestead exemption to cover boats explicitly. Indeed, amending the Texas Constitution is no Sisyphean task, having been done 439 times since its adoption in 1876, making our Constitution one of the nation's longest. But the authority to overhaul Texas homestead law and shield boats from bankruptcy creditors is not ours. This is a quintessential policy judgment, and our confined role is determining what Texas law is, not what it should be. If houseboat-homesteads are in Texas's future, it should be because Texas voters have amended our laws to say so, not this Court.

III. Conclusion

Unless and until Texas law changes, a boat can be a home, but it cannot be a homestead. Our realty-focused constitution and laws frame a homestead in terms of tracts, parcels, acres, and lots together with any land-based improvements.

In order to qualify as a homestead, a residence must rest on the land and have a requisite degree of physical permanency, immobility, and attachment to fixed realty. A dock-based umbilical cord providing water, electricity, and phone service may help make a boat habitable, but the attachment to land is too slight to warrant homestead protection.

Accordingly, Norris's yacht does not qualify as an exempt homestead under article XVI, sections 50 and 51 of the Texas Constitution, and we answer the certified question, "No."

Justice O'NEILL delivered a dissenting opinion, joined by Justice WAINWRIGHT, Justice BRISTER, and Justice MEDINA.

The Court's cramped interpretation of homestead is inconsistent with this Court's precedents and the policies underlying the constitutional exemption. Accordingly, I respectfully dissent.

C. Occupancy and Use of the Property as a Homestead

Not only does there have to be land with improvements thereon, not just any land and improvements can be considered homestead. If we go back to consider the public policy behind homestead laws, there is a central theme of trying to keep people in their homes so that even in times of great distress, like the death of a spouse or financial difficulties, a person or a family has the opportunity to still remain in a home. However, not every person acquires a homestead in the same manner. Next we will consider how to handle a variety of common situations like acquiring undeveloped land and building improvements on it or moving from one home to another. In these situations, where is the homestead? When can we first impress homestead character upon the property?

1. Undeveloped Land

Gilmore v. Dennison
Commission of Appeals of Texas, Section A, 1938
115 S.W.2d 902

HICKMAN, Commissioner.

Plaintiff in error, Gilmore, the owner of a money judgment against defendant in error, Dennison, caused an execution to be issued thereon and levied upon 164 1/2 acres of land in Jefferson county as the property of Dennison to satisfy the judgment. Upon the petition of Dennison the district court permanently enjoined the sale of the land under execution upon the ground that same constituted the homestead of Dennison and his family. The Court of Civil Appeals affirmed the trial court's judgment. 91 S.W.2d 371.

The sole question presented is whether the evidence raised an issue of fact on the homestead question. The opinion of the Court of Civil Appeals sets out the testimony in narrative form, the substance of which is as follows:

Dennison, in his own behalf, testified that he was married and had eight children; that he was a farmer; that he lived in Nome so that he could send his children to school; that he owned the 164 1/2 -acre tract of land and it was the only real estate he owned; that the land was located about five miles from Nome; that he acquired it in 1919; that he had never lived on the land or spent a night there; that it had no improvements on it; that he intended to live on the land when he got able to build a house on it; that he had done nothing toward building a house on the land and had not put any lumber on it for the purpose of building a house; that he had worked the land himself part of the time and leased it part of the time; and that he used all of the rents and revenues from the land to buy groceries for his family. Further evidence was that in 1926 Dennison designated this property as his homestead.

The question presented is not an open one in this jurisdiction. By a long line of decisions, some of which are cited below, the rule has been established that in order to impress upon property a homestead character, in the absence of actual occupancy thereof, there must be an intention by the head of the family to reside upon it with his family as a home, coupled with some overt act of preparation evidencing that intention. Mere intention alone is not sufficient. The effect of Dennison's own testimony is that he intends at some indefinite time in the future to reside upon this property as a home, provided he becomes able to erect improvements thereon. No overt act evidencing that intention was testified to. Such testimony falls short of presenting a fact issue on the homestead question. Lasseter v. Blackwell, Tex. Com. App., 227 S.W. 944; Silvers v. Welch, 127 Tex. 58, 91 S.W.2d 686; L. E. Whitham & Co. v. Briggs' Estate, Tex. Com. App., 58 S.W.2d 49; Franklin v. Coffee, 18 Tex. 413, 70 Am. Dec. 292; Hinton v. Uvalde Paving Co., Tex. Civ. App., 77 S.W.2d 733, *error refused*; Guajardo v. Emery, Tex. Civ. App., 73 S.W.2d 615, *error refused*; Brooks v. Chatham, 57 Tex. 31; Nunn on Exemptions, p. 99.

No reason is perceived for remanding the cause for another trial. This opinion is based upon the testimony of defendant in error himself and he has stated fully the facts upon which he bases his claim.

It is accordingly our order that the judgments of both the district court and Court of Civil Appeals be reversed and that judgment be here rendered dissolving the injunction.

Opinion adopted by the Supreme Court.

Harkrider-Keith-Cooke Co. v. Smith
Court of Civil Appeals of Texas, 1926
284 S.W. 612

McCLENDON, C.J.

Suit by Claude W. Smith, appellee, against Harkrider-Keith-Cooke Company, appellant to restrain sale of S.E. 1/4 of block 19, Claws addition to town of Coleman, under execution upon a judgment against Carl Cheaney, and to remove cloud from title. Trial to the court. Judgment for plaintiff for relief sought. Defendant appeals.

The following facts are undisputed: On May 13, 1921, appellant recovered in the justice court of precinct No. 1, Coleman county, a judgment against Cheaney and another for $42 besides interest and costs. An abstract of this judgment was, on January 7, 1922, recorded and indexed in Coleman county, so as to fix a lien on real estate in the country then or thereafter owned by Cheaney. This judgment was kept alive by executions as the law requires.

The property in suit was conveyed to Cheaney by a Mrs. Nowlin by deed of May 8, 1923, for the recited cash consideration of $250. On June 7, 1923, Cheaney gave a deed of trust on the property in favor of Temple Trust Company "to secure the payment of the note therein described, same being a loan made on said date by Temple Trust Company to Carl Cheaney for the purpose of improving the property in question." On December 26, 1923, Cheaney and wife conveyed the property to J. W. Waites, and on December 30, 1923, Waites conveyed it to appellee, Smith. Each of these instruments was recorded on the day of its execution. On April 29, 1925, appellant caused an execution issued under his judgment against Cheaney to be levied upon the property, and the property was advertised to be sold under this levy on the first Tuesday in June, 1925. Appellee brought this suit to enjoin the sale and remove cloud from his title by virtue of the apparent abstract of judgment lien, alleging that the property was the homestead of Cheaney and wife from the time Cheaney acquired it until he conveyed it to Waites.

Appellant's brief contains nine assignments of error. The first three question the sufficiency of the evidence to support the claim of homestead. . . .

At the time the property was purchased by Cheaney it was vacant and unimproved, and appellant's contentions, as set forth in its first two propositions, are that the burden of proof was on appellee to show the homestead character of the property at that time in order to defeat the judgment lien, and that this burden was not met since the evidence showed only a subsequent improvement and occupancy of the property by Cheaney. The evidence upon the homestead issue is confined to the testimony of Waites alone. Cheaney was not called as a witness, and the record discloses no reason why he was not called.

We quote the following from Waites' testimony underscoring the portions to which objections were preserved in bill of exceptions 1, 2, and 3:

> "I was acquainted with that property on May 8, 1923, the date of the deed from Mrs. Nowlin to Carl Cheaney. There were no improvements whatever, of any kind, on that property at that time—it was just a vacant town lot. I paid the cash consideration for that deed; I paid for all papers; I paid for all of the transactions of the papers and also for the lot, and for the $250 consideration in the deed. I paid that $250 cash consideration to Mrs. Nowlin. It was Carl Cheaney's intention, in buying that property to buy it for a home. He didn't own any other property in Coleman at that time if he did anywhere I don't know it. He was living in the house with me here in Coleman. At that time Mr. Cheaney had a wife and one baby.

"As to what I did, if anything, immediately after that deed was executed to Carl Cheaney: Well I had a lot of material left from the Allen and Scarbrough job, and moved that on the job there and put Carl to work. I moved a house over on that lot just after Carl Cheaney got that deed. I built a five-room building there, and as soon as I got it completed Carl Cheaney and his wife and baby moved into it. Carl Cheaney continued to reside on that property and used it for a home up until the time he sold it back to me, which was on December 26, 1923, as shown by the deed. He was still living in it when I got the deed. He had no other home that I knew anything about and was using that as his home. After I got the house completed—somewhere about that time, don't know the date—Carl Cheaney executed a deed of trust to the Temple Trust Company on that property. The deed of trust shows June 7, 1923; I guess that is about right, along there somewhere. The Temple Trust Company didn't advance any money until I actually got the property completed, and after I got it completed the Temple Trust Company took up the deed of trust—in this deed of trust. That was on June 27, 1923, not quite a month after the deed from Mrs. Nowlin. Carl Cheaney was living in the house at the time he sold it to me; he was living in the house at the time the deed was delivered to me.

"I bought the land from Mrs. Nowlin. Carl Cheaney was living in the house with me then. He knew that I was buying it for them for a home. Mr. Cheaney and me talked the matter over. He just made the remark, him and his wife both, that they would love to have a home, and I bought it for that purpose for them. I told them if they would go on and work for me and save and do their part I would help them to build a home. So this money I paid out on the lot was my own individual money. I let him work that out, and then I let him work out something like $250 more—in fact I borrowed him some. He commenced trying to save up to get a home, so then we borrowed some from the Temple Trust Company. At the very time he took the deed from Mrs. Nowlin to that property I bought it intending to make him a deed to it, and improvement were put on it for him a home at that particular time."

Under the decisions of this state, where a family has no homestead, the acquisition of unimproved property with the intention of its becoming homestead, followed in a reasonable time by acts evidencing that intention and the subsequent actual use and occupancy of the property as a homestead, impresses the homestead character upon the property from the moment of its acquisition, and precludes the attaching of a lien by reason of a previously abstracted judgment. Cameron v. Gebhard, 85 Tex. 610, 22 S.W. 1033, 34 Am. St. Rep. 832; Freiberg v. Walzem, 85 Tex. 264, 20 S.W. 60, 34 Am. St. Rep. 808; Gallagher v. Keller, 87 Tex. 472, 29 S.W. 647; Dobkins v. Kuykendall, 81 Tex. 180, 16 S.W. 743; Macmanus v. Campbell, 37 Tex. 267; King v. Wright (Tex. Civ. App.) 38 S.W. 530; Wallis v. Wendler, 27 Tex. Civ. App. 235, 65 S.W. 43; Jones v. Lanning (Tex. Civ. App.) 201 S.W. 443.

After a very careful review of the decisions upon this subject, the Supreme Court, speaking through Mr. Associate Justice Brown in the first cited case, say:

> "From these decisions it is apparent that intention is almost the only thing that may not be dispensed with in some state of case; and it follows that this intention in good faith to occupy is the prime factor in securing the benefits of the exemption. Preparation—that is, such acts as manifest this intention—is but the corroborating witness to the declaration of intention, the safeguard against fraud, and an assurance of the bona fides of the declared intention of the party.
>
> "If a homestead cannot be acquired until it is occupied, then no one can acquire a homestead exempted from forced sale unless he buys an improved place; and then he must have a race with the sheriff for possession. The unimproved lands of the country and the vacant lots of our cities cannot be acquired for the purpose of making a home by the man who is indebted, except at the risk of turning it over to a creditor. If a man owes nothing, or is able to pay all that he owes, he does not need the exemption; it he has other property, he can protect his home by pointing out that other property for sale; but if he has nothing but the homestead, he comes within the necessity of the constitutional provision, and to him is the chief value of exemption."

The evidence above quoted is clearly sufficient to support the trial court's judgment, if in fact it does not conclusively show that the property was purchased for homestead purposes. Preparations were at once begun to place a dwelling house on the property, and this object was consummated before the deed of trust was executed to the Temple Trust Company, at which time only a month had elapsed since Cheaney acquired the property. The conclusion that the evidence supports the finding that the homestead character attached to the property at the very moment of Cheaney's purchase is to obvious to require discussion. . . .

Finding no reversible error in the trial court's judgment, it is affirmed.

2. Homestead Intent

In both the *Gilmore* and *Harkrider* cases above, there was no homestead in existence when the family acquired the land upon which they would build their home. In those cases the critical inquiry was the use and occupancy needed to impress homestead character upon the land. The next case focuses on the situation of owning one home and then purchasing another. It is often said that the purchase of a new home does not necessarily mean there is a new homestead. In order to establish homestead status we look at the use, occupancy, and itent. Consider these elements when reading the cases below.

Caulley v. Caulley
Supreme Court of Texas, 1991
806 S.W.2d 795

MAUZY, Justice.

Robert and Ruth Caulley were divorced in Ohio in 1981. In 1987, Ruth filed suit in Harris County seeking to enforce an Ohio divorce judgment that ordered Robert to pay Ruth alimony. She obtained a money judgment for $34,625 against Robert from the 269th District Court of Harris County. On September 10, 1987, the Harris County District Clerk issued a writ of execution on the judgment and forwarded the writ to the Sheriff of Houston County, where Robert owned property. The writ was returned "Nulla Bona" because a homestead exemption was on file in the Houston County Clerk's office. Ruth then filed an Application for Turnover Order in the 269th District Court. She disputed the homestead exemption and asked the court to order the district clerk to reissue a writ of execution on the property, and to order that each of Robert's paychecks be turned over to her until her judgment against him was satisfied. On February 2, 1988, the trial court again ordered the district clerk to issue a writ of execution upon the Houston County property. The trial court also appointed a receiver and ordered Robert to turn over $2500 of his $2700 net monthly wages to the receiver in order to satisfy the money judgment against him.

Robert appealed and contended in the court of appeals that the homestead designation is determined by the claimant's state of mind. He also contended that the turnover statute (Tex. Civ. Prac. & Rem. Code § 31.002) is unconstitutional under Art. XVI, § 28 (prohibition against garnishment) when used to order a judgment debtor to turn over his wages to a creditor. The court of appeals rejected Robert's arguments and affirmed the judgment of the trial court. 777

S.W.2d 147. We affirm the lower courts' judgment regarding the homestead designation, but we reverse the trial court's order that Robert must turn over 90% of his net wages in order to satisfy the judgment against him.

I. Homestead Exemption

One month after the September, 1981 divorce from Ruth, Robert married Christine in Texas. Before the marriage, Christine had an urban home in Harris County upon which she had established a homestead exemption. After the marriage, the couple made this home their residence. In 1983, Robert and Christine jointly purchased a 150-acre farm in Houston County. This was the property upon which the trial court ordered execution.

Along with the original issuance of a writ of execution, an abstract of judgment was recorded in the Houston County Clerk's office on September 23, 1987. On October 16, 1987, Robert filed a declaration that the Houston County property was his rural homestead. On October 19, 1987, Christine sought to "undesignate" the couple's Harris County residence as an urban homestead. Once homestead rights are shown to exist in property, they are presumed to continue, and anyone asserting abandonment has the burden of proving it by competent evidence. Sullivan v. Barnett, 471 S.W.2d 39 (Tex.1971). The trial court entered Findings of Fact and Conclusions of Law in which it found that the urban home in Harris County was the homestead of Robert and Christine. Robert contended on appeal that there was no evidence to support this finding by the trial court.

The court of appeals reasoned that testimony at trial revealed that Robert and Christine "spent at least 60% of the nights of the year" at their Harris County home. 777 S.W.2d at 150. Additionally, the court of appeals held that Robert tried to designate the Houston County property as homestead only after Ruth sought to enforce her judgment against that property. Id. Thus, the court of appeals correctly held that some evidence supported the trial court's finding that the urban home in Harris County was the homestead of Robert and Christine. Robert argued in both the court of appeals and in this Court that the Houston County property would become the couple's permanent home in a few years and that this indicates an intention on their part to make this their homestead property. While occupying a piece of property as homestead, a person cannot establish a homestead right in another place by "attempting to live there in the future". O'Brien v. Woeltz, 94 Tex. 148, 58 S.W. 943, 945, modified on rehearing, 94 Tex. 154, 59 S.W. 535 (1900); Johnston v. Martin, 81 Tex. 18, 16 S.W. 550, 550-551 (1891). Therefore, Robert's argument is without merit. We hold that the trial court and the court of appeals correctly decided that the Houston County property was not Robert's and Christine's homestead, and we affirm that portion of the judgment.

The following cases raises several issues about the homestead. As we have seen, there is a need to characterize a family or individual status when dealing with rural land. While urban land receives a flat ten-acre limit regardless of status, there is still a significant distinction between single and family status when dealing with rural land. How do we determine what a family is? Not all families look the same. The *Carpenter* case assists with a definition to use in determining family status.

Additionally, an individual or family may own multiple tracts of land. Some of the land is occupied as a home and some could be used for the family business or the individual's business. Would it be possible to have the land used for business purposes and also receive homestead protection if within the allowed acreage?

NCNB Texas National Bank v. Carpenter
Court of Appeals of Texas, Fort Worth, 1993
849 S.W.2d 875

DAY, Justice.

NCNB Texas National Bank and Greg Stephenson, Substitute Trustee (NCNB), appeal from the trial court's order granting summary judgment, declaratory judgment, and attorney's fees in favor of Brooks and Pearl Carpenter (the Carpenters).

We reverse and remand for trial on the merits.

The undisputed facts in this case are as follows: By warranty deed dated January 31, 1976, the Carpenters acquired a 187.93-acre tract of land in Erath County, Texas. The Carpenters assumed and agreed to pay to Stephenville Bank & Trust Company a promissory note in the original amount of $50,000, dated October 2, 1972 (the $50,000 first lien note). From 1976 until the present, the land has been used for agricultural purposes, including grazing cattle and livestock and raising hay. A barn, but no residence, is located on the property. The Carpenters' residence is located on a separate 27-acre tract of land in Erath County near the City of Stephenville, Texas.

On December 1, 1983, Interfirst Bank Stephenville, N.A. (Interfirst), NCNB's predecessor-in-interest, made a loan consolidating all the previously existing loans that Randall Carpenter had with Interfirst (the 1983 loan). As consideration for the loan, Brooks and Pearl Carpenter gave a deed of trust for the 187.93 acres to Karen Domel, Trustee, for the benefit of Interfirst (the 1983 deed of trust). Brooks Carpenter orally represented to Interfirst's loan officer, Monty Bedwell, that the 187.93-acre tract was not the Carpenters' homestead. The 1983 deed of trust also makes the following representation:

Grantors [Brooks and Pearl Carpenter] expressly represent the property hereinabove mentioned and conveyed to the Trustee forms no part of any property owned, used, or claimed by the Grantors as exempted from forced sale under the laws of the State of Texas, and Grantors renounce all and every claim thereto under any such law or laws.

Not Homestead

The Carpenters and Interfirst agreed at the time the 1983 loan was made that it was inferior to the $50,000 first lien note.

At the closing of the 1983 loan, Brooks and Pearl Carpenter, Randall Carpenter, and Randall's wife, Isla, executed a written commercial loan purpose statement that contained an exempt property disclaimer virtually identical to the one in the 1983 deed of trust.

In 1986 the 1983 loan was renewed and extended (the 1986 loan). By deed of trust dated February 27, 1986, Brooks and Pearl Carpenter again represented that the 187.93-acre tract was not their homestead. The 1986 deed of trust contained the following representation:

> 28. Designation of Homestead. Grantors [Brooks and Pearl Carpenter] expressly represent that the property hereinabove mentioned and conveyed to the Trustee forms no part of any property owned, used or claimed by Grantors as exempted from forced sale under the laws of the State of Texas, and Grantors renounce all and every claim thereto under any such law or laws and hereby expressly designate as their homestead and as constituting all the property owned, used or claimed by them as exempt under such laws other property owned by them. [Emphasis supplied.]

Before making the 1983 loan, and at least semi-annually thereafter, Bedwell visited the 187.93-acre tract and observed that it was used to graze cattle and for a haying operation in conjunction with a dairy business. Bedwell was also aware that the Carpenters owned more than 400 rural acres in Erath County, in addition to the 187.93 acres in question.

Sometime after 1986, the Carpenters defaulted on the 1986 loan. Accordingly, by letter dated March 30, 1990, NCNB demanded that the Carpenters pay the 1986 note in full within ten days. In response, the Carpenters, through their attorney, notified NCNB that they claimed the 187.93-acre tract as part of their homestead. NCNB then advised the Carpenters, by letter dated May 14, 1990, and an accompanying notice of substitute trustee's sale, that NCNB intended to foreclose its lien on the 187.93-acre tract on June 5, 1990.

Claiming Homestead

On April 23, 1990, Brooks Carpenter filed an application for a 1-d-1 agricultural appraisal of the 187.93 acres. On or about May 16, 1990, Brooks Carpenter obtained a survey deleting 15 acres from the 187.93-acre tract. The

Carpenters assert that the remaining 172.93 acres, along with the 27-acre tract upon which they reside, constitute their rural homestead.

On May 30, 1990, the Carpenters petitioned in Erath County District Court for a temporary restraining order and a temporary injunction prohibiting NCNB from foreclosing on the lien against the 172.93 acres. The trial court granted the Carpenters' requests. The suit was subsequently transferred to Tarrant County by court order entered upon the parties' joint motion for change of venue.

The Carpenters then filed a motion for summary judgment in Tarrant County. By their motion, the Carpenters sought a declaration (1) that NCNB's lien against the 172.93 acres is void, thus prohibiting foreclosure, (2) that the 172.93-acre tract and the 27 acres upon which the Carpenters reside is their rural homestead, and (3) attorney's fees. The trial court granted the Carpenters' motion, and NCNB appeals from that order.

NCNB raises the following grounds on appeal: (1) summary judgment is improper in this case because distinct factual disputes exist as to whether the Carpenters: (a) used and occupied the 172.93 acres as their homestead, (b) established their homestead claim as a matter of law, (c) are estopped from claiming the property as their homestead, and (d) had abandoned their homestead claim to the property; (2) the trial court improperly held that NCNB must establish estoppel as a matter of law; and (3) the declaratory judgment and award of attorney's fees are also improper since the Carpenters failed to establish their homestead claim as a matter of law.

In its first point of error, NCNB complains the trial court improperly declared the 172.93 acres part of the Carpenters' homestead. In its second point of error, NCNB challenges the propriety of summary judgment in favor of the Carpenters, contending that fact issues exist concerning whether the Carpenters: (1) used and occupied the property in question as their homestead; (2) are estopped to claim the property is their rural homestead; and (3) abandoned their homestead claim to the property. We agree with NCNB that there are factual disputes concerning at least the Carpenters' homestead claim and NCNB's estoppel claim.

In their motion for summary judgment, the Carpenters asserted that they have been in actual possession of the property from the time they acquired it in 1976 to the present and have continually used it "for agricultural purposes, including the grazing of cattle and livestock and the raising of agricultural products such as hay" to support their family. The Carpenters also asserted that Bedwell knew the Carpenters were using the property for these purposes, as well as for a dairy land operation, prior to the time the Carpenters executed the 1986 note and deed of trust. The Carpenters made similar assertions regarding their possession and use of the property, and Bedwell's knowledge of it, in their affidavits in support of their motion for summary judgment.

In its response to the Carpenters' motion for summary judgment, NCNB contended that the property in dispute was not occupied or used as a home by the Carpenters. In his affidavit in support of NCNB's response, Bedwell stated that, based on his personal visits to and observation of the property, the land was being used for a hay field operation in conjunction with a dairy business. Bedwell also stated, however, that at the time of the 1983 and 1986 loans, he had personal knowledge of the fact that Randall and Jerry Carpenter, the Carpenters' sons, were working the hay operation and grazing cattle on the property in conjunction with their (i.e., Randall and Jerry's) dairy operation. Finally, Bedwell stated that he also had personal knowledge that Brooks Carpenter's business was a trucking operation operated from another location in Erath County.

The Texas Constitution makes the following provisions regarding homesteads:

> The homestead of a family . . . shall be, and is hereby protected from forced sale, for the payment of all debts except for the purchase money thereof, or a part of such purchase money, the taxes due thereon, or for work and material used in constructing improvements thereon. . . . No mortgage, trust deed, or other lien on the homestead shall ever be valid, except for the purchase money therefor, or improvements made thereon. . . .

Tex. Const. art. XVI, § 50.

> The homestead, not in a town or city, shall consist of not more than two hundred acres of land, which may be in one or more parcels, with the improvements thereon . . . provided, that the same shall be used for the purposes of a home, or as a place to exercise the calling or business of the homestead claimant, whether a single adult person, or the head of a family. . . .

≤ 200 ACRE

Tex. Const. art. XVI, § 51. See also Tex. Prop. Code Ann. § 41.002(b)(1) (Vernon Supp. 1993).

The party claiming the homestead exemption—in this case, the Carpenters—has the burden of establishing the homestead character of the property. First Interstate Bank v. Bland, 810 S.W.2d 277, 286 (Tex. App.—Fort Worth 1991, no writ). To establish a homestead claim in rural property, the claimant must: (1) reside on part of the property; and (2) use the property for purposes of a home. Fajkus v. First Nat'l Bank, 735 S.W.2d 882, 884 (Tex. App.— Austin 1987, writ denied); Tex. Const. art. XVI, § 51. Although actual residence on part of the rural property is required, one need not reside on all the parcels so long as the other tracts are used for the support of the family. Fajkus, 735 S.W.2d at 884.

In the instant case, the parties agree that the Carpenters reside on part of the property they are claiming as their rural homestead. The dispute between NCNB and the Carpenters centers solely around whether the Carpenters used the 172.93 acres as a home. The Carpenters claim they have continually used this tract of land for agricultural purposes and to support their family, and that NCNB had knowledge of this use through Bedwell, NCNB's senior loan officer. Conversely, NCNB asserts the Carpenters' sons, and not the Carpenters, were in actual use of the property when the loans were made.

In order for either a family business or residence homestead to exist, a family must exist. The requirement of family is met whenever there is a group of people who have a social status as a family—that is, a group living together subject to one domestic government. There must be a legal or moral responsibility on the head of the family for the rest of the members of the family, and a corresponding dependence of the others upon the head of the family. Henry S. Miller Co. v. Shoaf, 434 S.W.2d 243, 244 (Tex. Civ. App.—Eastland 1968, writ ref'd n.r.e.). *See also* Roco v. Green, 50 Tex. 483, 490 (1878); Central Life Assur. Soc. v. Gray, 32 S.W.2d 259, 260 (Tex. Civ. App.—Waco 1930, writ ref'd). A moral obligation for support and care exists where there is a necessity for such care and support, although that necessity need not be absolute. *Shoaf*, 434 S.W.2d at 245.

In addition to the situation involving a husband, wife, and minor children, Texas courts have found that a family exists for homestead exemption purposes in the following circumstances: (1) a divorcee and her mother constitute a family if the divorcee has a moral obligation to support and care for her mother, *Shoaf*, 434 S.W.2d at 243, 246; (2) brother and sister constitute a family when the brother has a moral obligation to support and care for his sister, *Gray*, 32 S.W.2d at 260-61; (3) a father and minor son constitute a family—whether or not the father has custody of the child—because the father has a legal and moral obligation to support the child, White v. Edzards, 399 S.W.2d 935, 937 (Tex. Civ. App.—Texarkana 1966, writ ref'd n.r.e.). In each of these instances, the court allowed the head of the family to claim a homestead exemption under article 16, section 50 of the Texas Constitution.

In contrast, the court in L. E. Witham & Co. v. Briggs' Estate, 58 S.W.2d 49 (Tex. Comm'n App. 1933, holding approved), held that a mother and adult son, who lived together and shared expenses, did not constitute a "family" within the meaning of article 16, section 50. Id. at 49-50. The court stated it would be:

> unreasonable to hold that a mother is under any legal or moral obligation to support her adult son, who is able-bodied and capable of supporting himself. Nor can it reasonably be said that the mother, who is capable of supporting herself and does support herself, is dependent on her son for support. *Id.*

Consequently, the court held that the mother could not claim a homestead exemption to avoid foreclosure of a paving lien on the property in question. *Id.* at 50.

By their summary judgment evidence, the Carpenters failed to conclusively establish two facts essential to their family homestead claim: (1) that they, personally, used the 172.93 acres as a home (2) to support their family. The Carpenters claimed they personally possessed and used the property for agricultural purposes from 1976 to the present. Bedwell's affidavit controverts this claim, however. Bedwell stated the land was actually used by the Carpenters' sons, Randall and Jerry, at the time the 1983 and 1986 loans were made.

The Carpenters also claimed they used the property to support their family. The Carpenters put on no evidence, however, that they, together with Randall and Jerry, constitute a single "family" as that term is defined in the case law for homestead exemption purposes. The record does not contain Randall's and Jerry's ages, but it does show that Randall was married at the time the 1983 loan was made. Absent a showing by the Carpenters that they were under a legal or moral obligation to support and care for Randall and/or Jerry and that a necessity for such support and care existed at the time the 1983 and 1986 loans were made, the Carpenters cannot claim the 172.93 acres as their homestead if, in fact, Randall and Jerry occupied and used the property instead of their parents.

The disagreement over who was in actual possession and use of the 172.93 acres also bears directly on NCNB's estoppel claim.

No estoppel can arise in favor of a lender or encumbrancer who has attempted to secure a lien on homestead property that is in actual use and possession of the homestead claimant, based solely upon declarations, whether written or oral, which state to the contrary. Lincoln v. Bennett, 138 Tex. 56, 156 S.W.2d 504, 506 (1941); *First Interstate Bank*, 810 S.W.2d at 287. Moreover, when a homestead claimant is in actual occupancy of his homestead, it will be deemed that a lender or encumbrancer acted with knowledge of the occupant's right to invoke the rule of homestead. *First Interstate Bank*, 810 S.W.2d at 285; *see also* Englander Co. v. Kennedy, 424 S.W.2d 305, 308- 09 (Tex. Civ. App.—Dallas), writ ref'd n.r.e. per curiam, 428 S.W.2d 806 (Tex. 1968). Possession and use of land by one who owns it and who resides upon it makes it the homestead in law and in fact. *First Interstate*, 810 S.W.2d at 286; *Lifemark Corp. v. Merritt,* 655 S.W.2d 310, 314 (Tex. App.—Houston [14th Dist.] 1983, writ ref'd n.r.e.).

NCNB relied upon the defense of estoppel at the summary judgment hearing. NCNB contended that estoppel was founded on the Carpenters' declarations in the 1983 and 1986 deeds of trust and the commercial loan purpose statement. The 1983 deed of trust and the commercial purpose statement contain clauses disclaiming any homestead interest in the 172.93 acres. The 1986 deed of trust contains a designation of homestead paragraph in which the Carpenters, as grantors, state that they expressly designate as their homestead other property owned by them. No homestead property is specifically described, however.

Additionally, NCNB contended that the use of the property in question was not inconsistent with Brooks Carpenter's oral representations and the representations made in the deeds of trust that the 172.93 acres did not constitute the Carpenters' homestead.

In his affidavit, Bedwell stated twice that he made the 1983 and 1986 loans "solely in reliance upon both the oral and written representations of Brooks Carpenter" and other members of the Carpenter family that the property in question was not their homestead. Nonetheless, Bedwell also alleged other facts in his affidavit to show that the use of the property was not inconsistent with Brooks Carpenter's representations that the property was not his homestead, such as actual use by Randall and Jerry Carpenter in conjunction with their dairy business. Bedwell also stated that he knew personally that the Carpenters owned over 400 acres in rural Erath County, in addition to the 172.93 acres, that they could have claimed as their homestead.

A homestead claimant may be estopped to claim the homestead exemption where physical facts open to observation lead to a conclusion that the property in question is not the homestead, the use of the property is not inconsistent with the claimant's representations that the property is disclaimed as the homestead, and the representations were intended to be and were actually relied upon by the lender. *First Interstate Bank*, 810 S.W.2d at 285-86.

If Randall and Jerry Carpenter, rather than Brooks and Pearl Carpenter, were occupying and using the 172.93 acres when the 1983 and 1986 loans were made, this fact could have caused Bedwell to conclude, based on the Carpenters' oral and written representations, that the property in question was not Brooks and Pearl Carpenter's homestead. The Carpenters do not dispute that they intended for NCNB to rely on their representations that the property was not their homestead. Moreover, Bedwell contends that he did, indeed, rely upon those representations, as borne out by his personal observations, when making the loans.

Accordingly, because material fact issues exist regarding who actually possessed and used the 172.93 acres and whether Randall and Jerry Carpenter were part of Brooks and Pearl Carpenter's "family," we find that the trial court improperly: (1) declared the property in question part of Brooks and Pearl Carpenter's rural homestead; (2) declared NCNB's lien on 172.93 of the 187.93 acres void ab initio; and (3) granted summary judgment for the Carpenters. We sustain NCNB's first and second points of error. In light of our holding regarding these points of error, we deem it unnecessary to consider NCNB's points of error three through five.

We reverse the trial court's judgment and remand this case for trial on the merits.

NOTES & QUESTIONS:

It is important to remember that at the time of the *Carpenter* case, the only debts that could attach to a homestead were the purchase money lien, mechanics lien, and tax lien. What the Carpenters were attempting to do was use the equity in the land to refinance existing debts. If the land was all homestead, the lien would not be constitutionally permissible and therefore, void. Today, the home equity lien validly attaches to the homestead as long as certain conditions are met. We will consider that in more detail later In this chapter.

However, in this case the Carpenters affirmatively stated and signed documents indicating the land was not their homestead. The bank's secondary argument was that even if the land were actually homestead, the Carpenters should be estopped from asserting the homestead protection as a result of their words and actions regarding the homestead status. What type of argument is the bank making?

3. Homestead for Future Interests

If the homestead status is essentially meant to protect the primary residence, then should a future interest in a piece of real property have homestead protection? The answer to that question seems pretty straightforward—no. We have already looked a multiple scenarios where just intending for land or a house to be homestead isn't enough. What if the house was the person's homestead until divorce and then the facts change?

The following cases both involve divorce proceedings with a homestead involved. In the *Laster* case, the house was the community property of the spouses and the judge allowed the wife to remain in sole possession of the home with the minor children. The husband's right to possession was delayed until a future date. In the *Lawrence* case, the house was separate property but become the couple's homestead. Upon divorce, the court awarded the wife sole possession for the remainder of her lifetime and the husband's possession was delayed until the time of her death. What impact, if any, does this change in the right to possession have on homestead?

Laster v. First Huntsville Properties Company
Supreme Court of Texas, 1991
826 S.W.2d 125

COOK, Justice.

This case presents the question whether one ex-spouse who, pursuant to a consent decree of divorce, holds a future interest in property subject to the homestead right of the other ex-spouse, can mortgage that interest. We hold that such an interest can be validly mortgaged. For the following reasons, the judgment of the court of appeals is affirmed and this cause is remanded to the trial court for a determination of the rights of the parties.

I

When Melissa and Richard Laster divorced in 1976, they entered into an agreed judgment which, among other things, divided the couple's property. Under the decree, Melissa was given a 73.83 percent interest in the community property residence and Richard was given the remaining undivided 26.17 percent interest. Melissa and the children were also given the right to the use and occupancy of the residence until the younger of the two children reached eighteen years of age or was no longer in school.

This right in the residence was further made subject to Melissa making the monthly payments on the residence, maintaining the premises, and ensuring that any absence from the residence did not exceed three years. The judgment provided that at the occurrence of one or more of these conditions, Melissa's right of use and occupancy of the residence would terminate and the rights of the parties in the property would be determined in accordance with their interests as set out in the judgment. Melissa currently remains in sole possession of the residence.

In 1979, Richard executed a deed of trust conveying his interest in the residence to secure payment on a promissory note, upon which he later defaulted. Richard's interest was sold by substitute trustee's deed in 1981 to the First National Bank of Huntsville, which later sold the property to First Huntsville Realty Corporation in 1983. First Huntsville Properties purchased the property from First Huntsville Realty in 1985. The couple's youngest child turned eighteen in 1988, and First Huntsville Properties filed suit seeking to partition the residence in 1989. In Melissa's answer, she alleges the entire property was, both at the time the deed of trust was executed and at the time suit was filed, subject to her homestead interest in the entire residence. Thus, she claims, the residence is protected from forced sale.

A bench trial was had and the trial court rendered judgment holding that: the residence was protected from forced sale by Melissa's continuing homestead right in the entire residence; the continuing homestead right was paramount to First Huntsville's interest in the property; and the writ of partition was thereby denied as "premature." The court further stated that in light of its holding, it was unnecessary to determine the question of the parties' respective interests in the residence. In the findings of fact and conclusions of law filed later, however, the court stated that First Huntsville Properties had acquired title to Richard's 26.17 percent interest in the residence "subject to the right of occupancy of Melissa L. Laster."

First Huntsville Properties appealed, claiming that Melissa no longer had a homestead right which extended to its undivided interest in the property at the time the partition action was filed and, therefore, partition should be granted. The court of appeals reversed the trial court's judgment, holding that the trial court erred in not partitioning the residence because First Huntsville's interest in the property which was held in cotenancy with Melissa, was paramount to her homestead right. Melissa appeals from that judgment.

II

Melissa argues the court of appeals erred both when it held that a cotenant's right to seek partition was paramount to another cotenant's homestead rights, and when it did not find that the mortgage executed by Richard was void because it was levied against homestead property to secure general indebtedness. We turn first to the issue of what relation the parties bear to one another in regards to the residence.

A

The court of appeals found that Melissa and Richard held their respective interests in the residence as "joint owners," with Melissa retaining a homestead interest in the whole until the younger of the two children reached eighteen. The court also determined that, by way of Richard's mortgage, Melissa and First Huntsville now hold the residence as tenants in common. The court of appeals did not discuss whether the mortgage was void under Texas homestead laws. Although we agree that First Huntsville and Melissa are now cotenants in the residence, we disagree with the court's reasoning in reaching this result.

The term "joint owner" is utilized in the statute which authorizes partition of jointly held property. See Tex. Prop. Code § 23.001. This term, however, is imprecise because its use does not signify any one type of ownership. The term has, in the past, been used to refer both to property held in joint tenancy and property held in cotenancy. In the context that the term is used by the court of appeals in the instant case, it appears the court considered Melissa and Richard to be tenants in common in the residence. This classification is incorrect.

A cotenancy is formed when two or more persons share the unity of exclusive use and possession in property held in common. 4A R. Powell & P.

Rohan, Real Property, 601[1] (1991); 2 H. Tiffany, Real Property, § 319 (3rd ed. 1939). The present right to possession of the property is essential because one who is never entitled to possession of property held in common is not a cotenant. Reed v. Turner, 489 S.W.2d 373, 381 (Tex. Civ. App.—Tyler 1972, writ ref'd n.r.e.); LeBus v. LeBus, 269 S.W.2d 506, 510 (Tex. Civ. App.—Fort Worth 1954, writ ref'd n.r.e.). Therefore, Melissa and Richard did not hold the residence as tenants in common because the divorce decree gave Melissa the right to the use and possession of the residence to the exclusion of Richard.

In Texas, the homestead right constitutes an estate in land. Woods v. Alvarado State Bank, 118 Tex. 586, 593–94, 19 S.W.2d 35, 37–38 (1929). This estate is analogous to a life tenancy, with the holder of the homestead right possessing the rights similar to those of a life tenant for so long as the property retains its homestead character. Fiew v. Qualtrough, 624 S.W.2d 335, 337 (Tex. App.—Corpus Christi 1981, writ ref'd n.r.e.); Sparks v. Robertson, 203 S.W.2d 622, 623 (Tex. Civ. App.—Austin 1947, writ ref'd). Although the homestead estate is not identical to a life estate because one's homestead rights can be lost through abandonment, "it may be said that the homestead laws have the effect of reducing the underlying ownership rights in a homestead property to something akin to remainder interests and vesting in each spouse an interest akin to an undivided life estate in the property." United States v. Rodgers, 461 U.S. 677, 686, 103 S. Ct. 2132, 2138, 76 L. Ed.2d 236 (1983).

Therefore, the divorce decree created in Melissa rights in the residence analogous to those of a life tenant, and created in Richard a future interest in the residence similar to that held by a vested remainderman.[2] See generally Guilliams v. Koonsman, 154 Tex. 401, 406, 279 S.W.2d 579, 582 (1955) (setting out the rule used to determine whether a remainder interest has vested); Medlin v. Medlin, 203 S.W.2d 635, 641 (Tex. Civ. App.—Amarillo 1947, writ ref'd) (a remainderman's interest in property is usually vested). It is undisputed that at the time Richard mortgaged his interest in the residence, the property as a whole was designated as Melissa's homestead. The question arises, then, whether the mortgage executed by Richard against his interest in the residence is void under the Texas homestead laws.

B

The homestead of a single adult or family is protected from forced sale for the payment of a debt unless the debt is for purchase money on the homestead,

---

[2] [Ed. Note: The court's classification of Melissa's interest as that of a life estate is incorrect. In the next case, the divorce decree actually does award exclusive possession of the home to the wife until her death or her abandonment of the homestead. However, in this divorce decree Melissa is awarded sole occupancy of the home until the minor children reach age 18 or are no longer in school. This is not in any way granting Melissa the right to sole occupancy until her death. Thus, the classification is inaccurate.]

for work and materials used to construct improvements on the homestead property, or for unpaid taxes. Tex. Const. art. XVI, § 50; Tex. Prop. Code § 41.002. Any attempt to mortgage homestead property, except as approved by the Texas Constitution, is void. A mortgage or lien that is void because it was illegally levied against homestead property can never have any effect, even after the property is no longer impressed with the homestead character.

This homestead protection, however, can arise only in the person or family who has a present possessory interest in the subject property. Accordingly, one who holds only a future interest in property with no present right to possession is not entitled to homestead protection in that property.

Applying this rule to the present situation, no homestead right arose in Richard's interest in the residence because he held only a future right to possession in the property subject to Melissa's homestead rights. It has long been the rule that the holder of a vested future interest in property can mortgage or alienate that interest. Since Richard held no protective homestead right which would prevent the mortgage of his interest, we now turn to the issue of whether Melissa's homestead right in the entire property served to invalidate the mortgage. The case of Johnson v. Prosper State Bank, 125 S.W.2d 707, 709–11 (Tex. Civ. App.—Dallas 1939), aff'd, 134 Tex. 677, 138 S.W.2d 1117 (1940), is instructive on this point.

In Johnson, a bank properly abstracted a judgment rendered for the non-payment of a note for general indebtedness against the real property interests the debtor owned or would obtain in the future. The abstract was perfected in 1934. In 1929, the debtor's mother had died intestate, causing certain real estate to pass to the debtor subject to his father's continued homestead interest in the property. The debtor's father died in 1935, and the property passed to the debtor under his father's will.

In 1936, the bank sought a writ of partition against the debtor's inherited land for the payment of the abstracted judgment. The debtor argued that the bank had no interest in the inherited property because the lien had been placed on homestead property. The court held that a homestead right could not exist on his interest in the property at the time the lien attached, because a future estate "whether vested or contingent, will not support a claim of homestead, irrespective of intention and preparation of one out of possession to occupy the land when and if the right of possession and occupancy become a reality." As his homestead right did not arise until after the death of his parents, the court found that the bank's preexisting lien was valid and enforceable against the debtor's ownership interest in the property.

Thus, in accordance with the general rule that one's homestead rights will not protect property in which no possessory interest is held, a non-possessory, future interest in property is not protected by the homestead right of the person with the present right to occupy the property. In the instant case, the deed of trust executed by Richard did not create a lien against the homestead itself but instead created a lien against his non-possessory interest in the property which was not impressed with any homestead interest.

As the mortgage attached only to Richard's interest and did not affect any property interest protected by Melissa's homestead right, the mortgage was not invalidated by that protection. Therefore, Richard executed a valid lien against his interest. When the youngest child reached eighteen years of age, Melissa's court-awarded homestead estate in the entire residence ended, entitling Richard, or his successor in interest, to fee simple ownership of the undivided 26.17 percent interest. Thus, Richard's interest in the property is now owned in fee simple by First Huntsville Properties and held in cotenancy with Melissa's remaining 73.83 percent interest.

C

The last question to be resolved is whether Melissa's remaining homestead rights in the property prevent the forced sale and partition of the residence. On divorce, a trial court has broad power to order the "just and right" division of the divorcing couple's estate, including the ability to award the use of the homestead to one spouse, even if title to the homestead property is held by the other spouse. The power to order a "just and right" division also includes the power to order the sale of the homestead and the partition of the proceeds.

In the instant case, Melissa and Richard agreed, with the trial court's approval, to simply postpone the partition of the homestead until both children either obtained the age of eighteen or no longer attended school. Pursuant to the divorce decree in this case, the division of the homestead can now take place just as if the court had ordered the division at the time of divorce. Furthermore, it would be manifestly unjust to allow Richard's rights in the estate to be prejudiced simply because the division of the homestead property took place after the younger of the two children turned eighteen rather than at the time of divorce.

After the partition sale, Melissa's homestead right carries over to her portion of the proceeds of sale. Melissa may seek continued homestead protection for the proceeds of the partition sale as she could for the proceeds of any other type of sale of her homestead interest. Melissa has not been divested of her homestead rights.

III

For the foregoing reasons, we hold that the mortgage and transfer of Richard's interest in the residence was permissible under the constitution and laws of Texas. We further hold that, under the divorce decree in this case, the residence is now subject to division just as if it had been apportioned at the time of divorce. We affirm the judgment of the court of appeals and remand this cause to the trial court for a disposition of the rights of the parties consistent with this opinion.

DOGGETT, J., joins in the court's judgment but not its opinion.
GAMMAGE, J., dissents, joined by MAUZY, J.

<u>**Lawrence v. Lawrence**</u>
Court of Appeals of Texas, Texarkana, 1995
911 S.W.2 450

CORNELIUS, Chief Justice.

[Ed. Note: This suit arose following a divorce between John Thomas Lawrence, Sr. and Irene Lawrence. The divorce court, in dividing the property, awarded Irene $50,000, to be paid by Lawrence, Sr. Additionally, because of Lawrence, Sr.'s wrongful acts that substantially contributed to the divorce (infidelity? abuse?), the divorce court awarded Irene the "exclusive use, benefit, enjoyment, and right of occupancy" of ten acres that were Lawrence, Sr.'s separate property. Essentially, Irene had a life estate while Lawrence, Sr., had a reversion.

After the entry of the divorce decree, Lawrence, Sr., purported to convey the 10 acres to his son, John Thomas Lawrence, Jr. This lawsuit arose when Irene sought a declaratory judgment that her $50,000.00 judgment lien arising from the divorce action attached to the ten-acre tract (specifically to the reversionary interest). Lawrence, Jr., as the owner of the reversionary interest, asserted his father's homestead right to claim that Irene's lien did not attach to the ten acres. Lawrence, Jr., supported his claim with Lawrence, Sr.'s affidavit, in which Lawrence, Sr., said he lived on the ten acres, claimed it as his homestead before the divorce, and claimed no other property as his homestead. The court granted a summary judgment in favor of Irene, holding that her judgment lien did attach. Lawrence, Jr., appealed the summary judgment.]

A single adult's homestead is protected from forced sale for the payment of a debt unless the debt is for homestead purchase money, for work and materials used to build improvements on homestead property, or for unpaid taxes. Tex. Const. art. XVI, § 50; Tex. Prop. Code Ann. § 41.002 (Vernon Supp.1995); Laster v. First Huntsville Properties Co., 826 S.W.2d 125, 130 (Tex. 1991). The homestead protection can arise only in one who has a present possessory interest in the subject property. Laster v. First Huntsville Properties Co., *supra*. One who holds only a future interest with no present right to possession is not entitled to homestead protection in that property. Id.

Lawrence Jr. claims his homestead interest as successor in interest from his father. As a subsequent purchaser of homestead property, Lawrence Jr. may assert his father's homestead protection against a prior lien holder so long as there is no gap between the time of homestead alienation and Lawrence Jr.'s recordation of his title. Intertex, Inc. v. Kneisley, 837 S.W.2d 136, 138 (Tex. App.—Houston [14th Dist.] 1992, writ denied) (citing Posey v. Commercial Nat'l Bank, 55 S.W.2d 515, 517 (Tex. Comm'n App. 1932, judgm't adopted)).

Lawrence Jr. argues primarily that property may lose its homestead character only through death, abandonment, or alienation, Posey v. Commercial Nat'l Bank, *supra*, and that none of those applies here. He also contends, citing Speer & Goodnight v. Sykes, 102 Tex. 451, 119 S.W. 86, 88 (1909), and Posey v. Commercial Nat'l Bank, *supra*, that although the court awarded a life estate in the ten-acre tract to Irene Lawrence, the life estate did not divest Lawrence Sr. of his homestead right because the termination of his possessory right in the homestead was by court order, not voluntary abandonment. He points out that in both the cited cases the nonpossessory party retained a homestead interest even without a right of possession.

In Speer & Goodnight v. Sykes, *supra*, Mrs. Sykes was granted a divorce, custody of the children, one-half the homestead where the children were then living, and the use and control of the other half during the children's lifetime. Mr. Sykes settled a short distance away with the children and continued to support the children. Mrs. Sykes never claimed custody of the children. The court subsequently awarded the whole tract to Mrs. Sykes, apparently as part of a settlement for an assault she suffered during the marriage. She soon sold it. Mr. Sykes then returned to the tract with his children, claiming half of it as homestead. The court ruled Mr. Sykes's removal by legal process did not divest him of his homestead rights, but only suspended his right of possession during the time Mrs. Sykes might have used it to support the minor children. He had a right to reoccupy the tract as a homestead when the ex-wife sold her interest.

In Posey v. Commercial Nat'l Bank, *supra*, another case involving minor children, Mr. Posey granted a life estate in their home to Mrs. Posey in anticipation of divorce. The court held that the deed was coerced in anticipation of court action, and thus was not voluntary abandonment of the homestead, so Mr. Posey's remainder could not be subject to his debts.

Not only Speer & Goodnight v. Sykes, *supra*, and Posey v. Commercial Nat'l Bank, *supra*, but also the cases of Rimmer v. McKinney, 649 S.W.2d 365 (Tex. App.—Fort Worth 1983, no writ), and Sakowitz Bros. v. McCord, 162 S.W.2d 437 (Tex. Civ. App.—Galveston 1942, no writ), expressly hold that a party's dispossession from his homestead by judicial act or threat of judicial action does not defeat his homestead right. These cases were decided before Laster v. First Huntsville Properties Co., *supra,* so we can only assume that the Supreme Court intended to change the law by its decision in *Laster*. Yet, the *Laster* opinions, both majority and dissenting, do not even cite any of the earlier cases, either to overrule them or to attempt to distinguish them. We can discern no fact that distinguishes *Laster* from *Posey* and *Speer*, except possibly the fact that in *Laster* the court decree ousting the homestead claimant was a consent decree. Nevertheless, because of the explicit and unambiguous language of the majority opinion in *Laster*, we conclude that one who holds only a future interest in property with no present right of possession cannot claim a homestead right in the property, regardless of how he was dispossessed.

Lawrence Jr. also argues that Irene Lawrence's judgment lien is not the type of lien a judgment creditor can execute against a homestead. Exocet Inc. v. Cordes, 815 S.W.2d 350, 352 (Tex. App.—Austin 1991, no writ). If, however, the ten acre tract was not Lawrence Sr.'s homestead after the divorce, the property is nonexempt, and Irene Lawrence's judgment lien can be executed.

Lawrence Jr. also argues that Thompson v. Thompson, 149 Tex. 632, 236 S.W.2d 779, 785-86 (1951), demonstrates that the law does not always require a party claiming a homestead right to have right of immediate possession. The opinion in *Thompson* states that, while the law generally requires a present possessory interest for a homestead claim, it does not always require it. That case involved a widow's right to renounce her claims under her husband's will and claim oil royalties under the open mines doctrine. The court held that when the couple granted a lease for the minerals under the couple's homestead, the couple did not sever the minerals from the surface estate and thereby deprive the widow of sufficient possessory interest to stand on her statutory rights to royalties from producing wells. The question involved present possession of the mineral estate. The widow had present possessory right to the surface, which neither Lawrence Sr. or the ex-husband in Laster v. First Huntsville Properties Co., *supra,* had at the pertinent time.

The apparent anomaly in Laster v. First Huntsville Properties Co., *supra,* might be explained by the 1973 amendment to the Texas Constitution, Tex. Const. art. XVI, § 50 (1876, amended 1973), which allowed a single person to claim homestead protection. Before the enactment of that amendment and the state equal rights amendment, Tex. Const. art. I, § 3a, a single person with no dependent presumably could not establish a homestead. See Lane v. Phillips, 69 Tex. 240, 6 S.W. 610 (1887); Steves v. Smith, 107 S.W. 141, 49 Tex. Civ. App. 126 (1908, writ ref'd). Also, absent fraud, the husband rather than the wife generally determined the family homestead's location. Arlin Properties, Inc. v. Utz, 465 S.W.2d 231, 233 (Tex. Civ. App.—Fort Worth 1971, no writ). The courts in Speer & Goodnight v. Sykes, *supra,* and Posey v. Commercial Nat'l Bank, *supra,* recognized that under existing law a father who continued to support his minor children after divorce had the right to designate a homestead for the children's protection.

Irene Lawrence suggests that the difference in holdings may be understood by comparing Schulz v. L.E. Whitham & Co., 119 Tex. 211, 27 S.W.2d 1093, 1095 (1930), which cited Speer & Goodnight v. Sykes, *supra,* to Laster v. First Huntsville

Properties Co., *supra*. The *Schulz* court held the ex-husband had the right to claim homestead protection for his family even though he no longer lived with the family on the property. Under the law at the time, the husband had the right to designate the homestead, and the property maintained that character so long as he discharged his moral and legal obligations to support his family.

Irene Lawrence also argues that Lawrence Sr., in his affidavit, does not even contend that he claimed the property as his homestead until he sold it to Lawrence Jr., but only claimed it up to the date of the divorce decree. On this basis, she posits that the summary judgment evidence does not show that Lawrence Sr. claimed the property as his homestead at the time of sale and so Lawrence Jr. would not be successor in interest to his homestead right. We will not construe the summary judgment affidavit that narrowly. Instead, we construe it as saying Lawrence Sr. claimed the land as his homestead until he could no longer legally claim it as such, i.e., at the date he was legally ousted from possession. Speer & Goodnight v. Sykes, *supra,* and Posey v. Commercial Nat'l Bank, *supra.*

Lawrence Sr. as of the date of the divorce had no present possessory interest in the tract, only a future interest. Laster v. First Huntsville Properties Co., *supra,* which apparently reflects the current law, requires a present possessory interest for a party to claim a homestead right. As a holder of a future interest only, Lawrence Sr. is not entitled to a homestead exemption on the property. Id. The trial court deprived Lawrence Sr. of any present possessory interest by granting a life estate in his separate property to Irene Lawrence. Without a present possessory interest, as a matter of law he could not assert a homestead claim, and Lawrence Jr. could not be successor to that claim. Lawrence Jr. fails to raise a genuine issue of material fact as to his affirmative defense of homestead. The court properly granted summary judgment. It is affirmed.

4. Change in Designation

The homestead status arises due to the use, occupancy, and intent components. The landowner is not required to file any documents to designate property as homestead; however, in the event that there is more land owned than can be homestead protected or just multiple properties, a voluntary designation can be filed in the property records. It serves as some objective evidence of the subjective intent of the owners. Once "officially" designated, can that designation be changed? What if a formal designation has never been made but must be determined in the instance of a surviving spouse choosing to remain in the homestead?

Tex. Prop. Code § 41.005. Voluntary Designation of Homestead

(a) If a rural homestead of a family is part of one or more parcels containing a total of more than 200 acres, the head of the family and, if married, that person's spouse may voluntarily designate not more than 200 acres of the property as the homestead. If a rural homestead of a single adult person, not otherwise entitled to a homestead, is part of one or more parcels containing a total of more than 100 acres, the person may voluntarily designate not more than 100 acres of the property as the homestead.

(b) If an urban homestead of a family, or an urban homestead of a single adult person not otherwise entitled to a homestead, is part of one or more contiguous lots containing a total of more than 10 acres, the head of the family and, if married, that person's spouse or the single adult person, as applicable, may voluntarily designate not more than 10 acres of the property as the homestead.

(c) Except as provided by Subsection (e) or Subchapter B, to designate property as a homestead, a person or persons, as applicable, must make the designation in an instrument that is signed and acknowledged or proved in the manner required for the recording of other instruments. The person or persons must file the designation with the county clerk of the county in which all or part of the property is located. The clerk shall record the designation in the county deed records. The designation must contain:

    (1) a description sufficient to identify the property designated;

    (2) a statement by the person or persons who executed the instrument that the property is designated as the homestead of the person's family or as the homestead of a single adult person not otherwise entitled to a homestead;

    (3) the name of the current record title holder of the property; and

    (4) for a rural homestead, the number of acres designated and, if there is more than one survey, the number of acres in each.

(d) A person or persons, as applicable, may change the boundaries of a homestead designated under Subsection (c) by executing and recording an instrument in the manner required for a voluntary designation under that subsection. A change under this subsection does not impair rights acquired by a party before the change.

(e) omitted

(f) If a person or persons, as applicable, have not made a voluntary designation of a homestead under this section as of the time a writ of execution is issued against the person, any designation of the person's or persons' homestead must be made in accordance with Subchapter B.

(g) omitted

Riley v. Riley

Court of Appeals of Texas, Texarkana, 1998
972 S.W.2d 149

GRANT, Justice.

James William Riley, Bessie B. Goldschmidt and Marian R. Tepe, heirs of Elbert E. Riley, Jr., deceased, appeal from an order in probate court. Appellants are the surviving half-brother, sister, and half-sister of Elbert E. Riley, Jr., deceased. Appellee, Bobbie N. Riley, Administratrix of the Estate of Elbert E. Riley, Jr., is the surviving wife of Elbert E. Riley, Jr.

Appellants contend that Bobbie Riley's homestead interest in the mineral-producing property is limited and, therefore, the probate court should have provided for a credit against the reimbursement claim. [The reimbursement claim is edited out of the opinion for our purposes.]

This case was initiated in August 1994, when Bobbie Riley filed a claim agsinst the estate. On May 18, 1995, over Appellants' objection, the probate court entered an order in favor of Bobbie Riley. Appellants appealed the order, which was affirmed by the Second Court of Appeals.

Two pieces of property are at issue in this case. At the time the Rileys married, Elbert Riley owned land known as the Home Place (160 acres) and the River Place (74.7 acres). The Rileys lived on the Home Place throughout their marriage. Bobbie Riley has continued to live there since Elbert Riley's death. The Rileys farmed and ranched all of the property during their marriage for part of their support. The River Place, consisting of two tracts, 59.7 acres and 15 acres, was subject to an oil and gas lease when they married, and there has been production of oil and gas from the property.

Appellants argue that the probate court erred in its determination of the homestead property because Bobbie Riley has a homestead right in only 100 acres of the separate real property of her deceased husband's estate and, therefore, did not have homestead rights in the separate property oil and gas production of the estate.

By statute, a single person living alone is entitled to 100 acres as a rural homestead. Tex. Prop. Code Ann. § 41.002(b)(2) (Vernon Supp. 1998). Appellants argue that Bobbie Riley is only entitled to homestead rights in 100 acres, and because she lives in a home on the property in question, the homestead would logically be located where the home is located, the 160–acre Home Place tract. The River Place, which produces oil and gas royalties, would be excluded from Bobbie Riley's homestead, they argue. Further, Appellants contend they are entitled to one half of the approximately $36,000 in oil and gas royalties received by Bobbie Riley since Elbert Riley's death, pursuant to Section 38 of the Probate Code, which sets out the rules of descent and distribution in cases of intestacy.

Section 41.002(b)(2) of the Property Code deals with exemption from creditors and states that, for a single, adult person, for the purposes of a rural home, the homestead shall consist of not more than 100 acres, which may be in one or more parcels, with the improvements thereon, if that person is not otherwise entitled to a homestead. Tex. Prop. Code Ann. § 41.002(b)(2) (Vernon Supp. 1998). Bobbie Riley is "otherwise entitled to a homestead" under Sections 282 and 283 of the Probate Code and Article XVI, Section 52 of the Texas Constitution, which gives a deceased spouse's survivor and minor children the right to occupy the homestead for life.

The Texas Constitution sets out the definition and acreage limitations of homesteads as 200 acres. Section 271 of the Probate Code provides that in administering an estate, the court shall "set apart for the use and benefit of the surviving spouse and minor children and unmarried children remaining with the family of the deceased, all such property of the estate as is exempt from execution or forced sale by the constitution and laws of the state." Tex. Prob. Code Ann. § 271(a) (Vernon Supp. 1998) (emphasis added). Section 272 provides that "the homestead shall be delivered to the surviving spouse, if there be one, and if there be no surviving spouse, to the guardian of the minor children and unmarried children, if any, living with the family."

During their marriage, the Rileys were entitled to claim a rural homestead of 200 acres on Elbert Riley's separate property land. A surviving spouse has the same homestead rights in the property as both spouses had prior to the death of one spouse. The status of the homestead is immediately ascertainable upon the death of the decedent. Bobbie Riley is rightfully entitled to 200 acres as her homestead under the Texas Constitution.

We next address whether homestead acreage can be comprised of different parcels. If used for the purposes of a rural home, the homestead may be in one or more parcels. Tex. Prop. Code Ann. § 41.002(b)(1) (Vernon Supp.1998). To establish a homestead claim in rural property, the claimant must reside on part of the property and use the property for purposes of a home, although the claimant need not reside on all the parcels so long as the other tracts are used for the support of the family. NCNB Texas Nat'l Bank v. Carpenter, 849 S.W.2d 875, 879 (Tex. App.—Fort Worth 1993, no writ).

Bobbie Riley is entitled to 200 acres and to designate which 200 acres she wants to claim as her homestead as long as it is part of the property used by the family for homestead. She claims a homestead in 140 acres of the Home Place and 59.7 acres of the River Place, including the production of oil and gas.

The question, then, is whether a claimant may select only a portion of that land on which her home is located so that she may also select a portion of land elsewhere to make up her 200 acres of homestead. Specific to this case, may Bobbie Riley designate as her homestead a 140–acre portion of the 160 acres which is the site of her residence so that she can also designate 59.7 mineral-rich acres elsewhere?

A homestead claimant may exclude part of a tract actually occupied to obtain more acreage in another tract. However, such claimant must show that the second tract satisfies the requirement that the land is used for support of the family. Bobbie Riley testified that both parcels of property were farmed and ranched during the marriage for their support and that both parcels are presently used for running livestock. Testimony that cattle is grazed on the property shows use of the property in a manner which establishes homestead rights. Bobbie Riley also testified that the River Place has been oil- and gas-producing property since her marriage to Elbert Riley. The evidence supports the conclusion that the Rileys used the properties in such a manner as to establish homestead rights in the properties.

Bobbie Riley may properly designate as her homestead a 140–acre portion of the 160–acre Home Place, which is the site of her residence, and also designate 59.7 acres of the River Place.

Appellants argue that they are entitled to one half of the royalties received by Bobbie Riley since the date of Elbert Riley's death. Bobbie Riley argues that she is entitled to claim a homestead in the oil and gas royalties under the "open mine doctrine."

The open mine doctrine is an exception to the general rule that a life tenant is entitled to nothing but interest on mineral royalties and bonuses. Under the open mine doctrine, a homestead claimant is entitled to receive and expend all oil and gas royalties from the homestead, where the homestead property was producing oil or gas when the right in the property came into existence. Because the 59.7 acres Bobbie Riley has designated as her homestead were producing at the time her homestead rights in the property came into existence, she is entitled to the royalties from that designation.

However, Bobbie Riley's homestead designation did not include the 15–acre River Place tract. Therefore, the open mine doctrine does not apply to this tract. We have held that the probate court's order dated March 14, 1997, properly granted conveyance of all real property, including the 15–acre River Place tract, to Bobbie Riley.

In the interest of justice, we sever and remand for a new trial the portion of the case involving the royalties, if any, paid attributable to the 15–acre tract. The order of the probate court in all other respects is affirmed.

D. Homestead Problems

Using the cases above, answer the following problems.

Problem #1

Mr. Brady is the divorced father of three minor children. The children, Greg, Peter, and Bobby, reside primarily with their mother during the school year, visiting their father on alternating weekends and for four weeks during the summer. Mr. Brady lives on a parcel of land consisting of 130 acres, located in Texas, which he owns in fee simple absolute. The land would be categorized as rural under the Texas Property Code definition. How much land can Mr. Brady claim as homestead? Why?

Problem #2

Eventually Mr. Brady marries Carol who is the divorced mother of three minor children, Marsha, Jan, and Cindy. Mr. Brady moved into the house in which Carol and her three children were already residing before their marriage. The new Mr. and Mrs. Brady buy a house that they intend to move to and claim as their homestead in the next few years, likely after the youngest children finish school. When can the new property be their homestead and enjoy the protections afforded by the homestead laws? Why?

Problem #3

Ross and Emily are a recently divorced couple in Texas. Prior to their divorce, they made their residence on land owned by Ross as his separate property. As part of the divorce proceeding, the judge awarded Emily the exclusive right to possess. The court's decree specifically stated, "Emily shall have exclusive use, benefit, enjoyment and right of occupancy of the ten acre tract, during her life for the purpose of restoring Emily to her prior homestead, and as a result of Ross's wrongful acts which substantially contributed to the dissolution of the marriage." In addition, the court awarded Emily $50,000 and entered a judgment against Ross in that amount. The same day, Emily obtained a judgment lien against the ten acres. Subsequently Ross executed a deed transferring the ten acres to his best friend, Chandler.

Ross has not paid the $50,000 judgment and Emily now wishes to foreclose her judgment lien against the property. If successful, she will be able to sell the property, to which Chandler now claims title, to pay off the $50,000 judgment entered in her favor. Of course, she will bid her debt, and she will stand a good chance of ending up with title to the land herself. Chandler, however, claims that because the land was the homestead of Ross, Emily's judgment lien never attached, and thus she has no right to foreclose. Who is right, Emily or Chandler? Why?

Problem #4

     Mr. Brady is the owner, in fee simple absolute, of 300 noncontiguous acres located in Texas. The property would satisfy the Property Code's definition of rural property. This is Mr. Brady's separate property, acquired before his marriage to his current wife, Carol. The house in which Mr. & Mrs. Brady reside is located on one parcel of 50 acres. The other parcel of 250 acres, not too far away from the Bradys' home, is used for farming and ranching to support Mr. & Mrs. Brady.

     Recently Mr. Brady died. He was survived by only Mrs. Brady and Bobby, his son from a prior marriage. Mr. Brady devised all 300 acres to Bobby in his will. A dispute has arisen between Bobby and Mrs. Brady because Mrs. Brady has taken the position that she is entitled to a life estate giving her possession of 200 acres, and the 200 acres she has chosen consists of 150 acres of the property used for ranching and the 50 acres on which her house sits.

    a. How much land is Carol entitled to count as homestead? Why?

    b. Can she designate the land as her homestead in the way described above? Why or why not?

E. Legal Consequences of Establishing the Homestead

     Once a homestead is established and its character is determined, it is as if a magic force field surrounds the homestead and protects it from a multitude of debts during life and at death under certain circumstances. Additionally, as we saw in the Homestead Problems that we just answered, there are issues impacting possession of the homestead property during life in the event of divorce and also upon the death of the owner of the homestead. We will now turn our attention to these concepts to understand the variety of ways in which the homestead character changes the rules of the game that exist for other nonhomestead property.

1. Joinder of Spouses

     Because the homestead is to meant protect not only the record title holder but also the family, homestead status impacts the otherwise unrestricted management of separate property. Normally, if property is separate property, it remains as such even after marriage and the title holder's spouse has no interest in or control over the property. However, separate property that is homestead is different. As we have already seen in the Lawrence v. Lawrence and Riley v. Riley cases, there is an interest in the spouse. Thus, there are requirements that a spouse join in certain transactions involving the homestead.

Texas Family Code
§ 5.001. Sale, Conveyance, or Encumbrance of Homestead

Whether the homestead is the separate property of either spouse or community property, neither spouse may sell, convey, or encumber the homestead without the joinder of the other spouse except as provided in this chapter or by other rules of law.

§ 5.002. Sale of Separate Homestead After Spouse Judicially Declared Incapacitated

If the homestead is the separate property of a spouse and the other spouse has been judicially declared incapacitated by a court exercising original jurisdiction over guardianship and other matters under Chapter XIII, Texas Probate Code, the owner may sell, convey, or encumber the homestead without the joinder of the other spouse.

§ 5.003. Sale of Community Homestead After Spouse Judicially Declared Incapacitated

If the homestead is the community property of the spouses and one spouse has been judicially declared incapacitated by a court exercising original jurisdiction over guardianship and other matters under Chapter XIII, Texas Probate Code, the competent spouse may sell, convey, or encumber the homestead without the joinder of the other spouse.

§ 5.101. Sale of Separate Homestead Under Unusual Circumstances

If the homestead is the separate property of a spouse, that spouse may file a sworn petition that gives a description of the property, states the facts that make it desirable for the spouse to sell, convey, or encumber the homestead without the joinder of the other spouse, and alleges that the other spouse:
  (1) has disappeared and that the location of the spouse remains unknown to the petitioning spouse;
  (2) has permanently abandoned the homestead and the petitioning spouse;
  (3) has permanently abandoned the homestead and the spouses are permanently separated; or
  (4) has been reported by an executive department of the United States to be a prisoner of war or missing on public service of the United States.

§ 5.102. Sale of Community Homestead Under Unusual Circumstances

If the homestead is the community property of the spouses, one spouse may file a sworn petition that gives a description of the property, states the facts that make it desirable for the petitioning spouse to sell, convey, or encumber the homestead without the joinder of the other spouse, and alleges that the other spouse:

(1) has disappeared and that the location of the spouse remains unknown to the petitioning spouse;

(2) has permanently abandoned the homestead and the petitioning spouse;

(3) has permanently abandoned the homestead and the spouses are permanently separated; or

(4) has been reported by an executive department of the United States to be a prisoner of war or missing on public service of the United States.

As illustrated by these statutes, if there is a spouse, that spouse's interest must be protected and that requires the spouse's involvement except in some narrowly defined circumstances. So, think back to the real estate assignment and the question regarding the marital status of the seller. Do you now understand why that was a critical piece of information for the buyer to obtain before closing?

2. Debt Protection

Once the homestead status is in place, one of the most important functions of the laws is the protection from debt. As we saw with the public policy behind the creation of the Texas Homestead laws, protecting the family (and later the individual) from the impact of certain debts is an essential component of homestead. In *Gilmore, Harkrider, Caulley, Carpenter, Lawrence,* and *Laster,* homestead status was advanced to protect from debts attaching to the property. The Texas Constitution plays a significant role in protecting Texas landowners.

Policymakers in Texas have been very careful in making changes to the constitution to allow additional debts to attach to the homestead. Thus, there is a list in the constitution of liens that may permissibly attach to homestead. In a sense, these debts are powerful enough and connected enough to the land to allow them to penetrate the homestead forcefield that surrounds the property. The last change to the list was in 1997. Since that time the only changes have been in modifying some of the provisions for home equity loans and reverse mortgages. We will cover some of the most unique features of the debt protections provisions. Keep in mind that there are many more details than what we are able to cover.

Texas Const. art. XVI, § 50 Homestead; Protection from Forced Sale; Mortgages, Deeds of Trust and Liens[3]

(a) The homestead of a family, or of a single adult person, **shall be, and is hereby protected from forced sale, for the payment of all debts except for:**

---

[3] (Amended 2007.)

(1) the **purchase money** thereof, or a part of such purchase money;

(2) the **taxes** due thereon;

(3) an **owelty of partition** imposed against the entirety of the property by a court order or by a written agreement of the parties to the partition, including a debt of one spouse in favor of the other spouse resulting from a division or an award of a family homestead in a divorce proceeding;

(4) the **refinance of a lien against a homestead**, including a federal tax lien resulting from the tax debt of both spouses, if the homestead is a family homestead, or from the tax debt of the owner;

(5) **work and material used in constructing new improvements thereon,** if contracted for in writing, or **work and material used to repair or renovate existing improvements thereon if:** [Mechanic's Lien]

   (A) the work and material are contracted for in writing, with the consent of both spouses, in the case of a family homestead, given in the same manner as is required in making a sale and conveyance of the homestead;

   (B) the contract for the work and material is not executed by the owner or the owner's spouse before the fifth day after the owner makes written application for any extension of credit for the work and material, unless the work and material are necessary to complete immediate repairs to conditions on the homestead property that materially affect the health or safety of the owner or person residing in the homestead and the owner of the homestead acknowledges such in writing;

   (C) the contract for the work and material expressly provides that the owner may rescind the contract without penalty or charge within three days after the execution of the contract by all parties, unless the work and material are necessary to complete immediate repairs to conditions on the homestead property that materially affect the health or safety of the owner or person residing in the homestead and the owner of the homestead acknowledges such in writing; and

   (D) the contract for the work and material is executed by the owner and the owner's spouse only at the office of a third-party lender making an extension of credit for the work and material, an attorney at law, or a title company;

(6) an **extension of credit that:** [Home Equity Loan]

   (A) is secured by a voluntary lien on the homestead created under a written agreement with the consent of each owner and each owner's spouse;

    (B) is of a principal amount that when added to the aggregate total of the outstanding principal balances of all other indebtedness secured by valid encumbrances of record against the homestead does not exceed 80 percent of the fair market value of the homestead on the date the extension of credit is made;

    (C) is without recourse for personal liability against each owner and the spouse of each owner, unless the owner or spouse obtained the extension of credit by actual fraud;

    (D) is secured by a lien that may be foreclosed upon only by a court order;

    (E) Omitted

    (F) is not a form of open-end account that may be debited from time to time or under which credit may be extended from time to time unless the open-end account is a home equity line of credit;

    (G) - (M) omitted;

    (N) is closed only at the office of the lender, an attorney at law, or a title company;

    (O) -(Q) omitted.

  (7) a reverse mortgage; or

  (8) the conversion and refinance of a personal property lien secured by a manufactured home to a lien on real property, including the refinance of the purchase price of the manufactured home, the cost of installing the manufactured home on the real property, and the refinance of the purchase price of the real property.

(b) An owner or claimant of the property claimed as homestead may not sell or abandon the homestead without the consent of each owner and the spouse of each owner, given in such manner as may be prescribed by law.

(c) No mortgage, trust deed, or other lien on the homestead shall ever be valid unless it secures a debt described by this section, whether such mortgage, trust deed, or other lien, shall have been created by the owner alone, or together with his or her spouse, in case the owner is married.

(d) -(j) omitted

(k) "Reverse mortgage" means an extension of credit:

  (1) that is secured by a voluntary lien on homestead property created by a written agreement with the consent of each owner and each owner's spouse;

  (2) that is made to a person who is or whose spouse is 62 years or older;

  (3) that is made without recourse for personal liability against each owner and the spouse of each owner;

  (4) under which advances are provided to a borrower based on the equity in a borrower's homestead;

(5) that does not permit the lender to reduce the amount or number of advances because of an adjustment in the interest rate if periodic advances are to be made;

(6) that requires no payment of principal or interest until:

    (A) all borrowers have died;

    (B) the homestead property securing the loan is sold or otherwise transferred;

    (C) all borrowers cease occupying the homestead property for a period of longer than 12 consecutive months wlthoul prior written approval from the lender; or

    (D) the borrower:

        (i) defaults on an obligation specified in the loan documents to repair and maintain, pay taxes and assessments on, or insure the homestead property;

       (ii) commits actual fraud in connection with the loan; or

     (iii) fails to maintain the priority of the lender's lien on the homestead property, after the lender gives notice to the borrower, by promptly discharging any lien that has priority or may obtain priority over the lender's lien within 10 days after the date the borrower receives the notice, unless the borrower:

          (a) agrees in writing to the payment of the obligation secured by the lien in a manner acceptable to the lender;

          (b) contests in good faith the lien by, or defends against enforcement of the lien in, legal proceedings so as to prevent the enforcement of the lien or forfeiture of any part of the homestead property; or

          (c) secures from the holder of the lien an agreement satisfactory to the lender subordinating the lien to all amounts secured by the lender's lien on the homestead property;

(7) that provides that if the lender fails to make loan advances as required in the loan documents and if the lender fails to cure the default as required in the loan documents after notice from the borrower, the lender forfeits all principal and interest of the reverse mortgage, provided, however, that this subdivision does not apply when a governmental agency or instrumentality takes an assignment of the loan in order to cure the default;

(8) that is not made unless the owner of the homestead attests in writing that the owner received counseling regarding the advisability and availability of reverse mortgages and other financial alternatives;

(9) that requires the lender, at the time the loan is made, to disclose to the borrower by written notice the specific provisions contained in

Subdivision (6) of this subsection under which the borrower is required to repay the loan;

(10) that does not permit the lender to commence foreclosure until the lender gives notice to the borrower, in the manner provided for a notice by mail related to the foreclosure of liens under Subsection (a)(6) of this section, that a ground for foreclosure exists and gives the borrower at least 30 days, or at least 20 days in the event of a default under Subdivision (6)(D)(iii) of this subsection, to:

(A) remedy the condition creating the ground for foreclosure;

(B) pay the debt secured by the homestead property from proceeds of the sale of the homestead property by the borrower or from any other sources; or

(C) convey the homestead property to the lender by a deed in lieu of foreclosure; and

(11) that is secured by a lien that may be foreclosed upon only by a court order, if the foreclosure is for a ground other than a ground stated by Subdivision (6)(A) or (B) of this subsection.

[Remaining provisions omitted.]

Tex. Prop. Code § 41.001. Interests in Land Exempt from Seizure

(a) A homestead and one or more lots used for a place of burial of the dead are exempt from seizure for the claims of creditors except for encumbrances properly fixed on homestead property.

(b) Encumbrances may be properly fixed on homestead property for:

(1) purchase money;

(2) taxes on the property;

(3) work and material used in constructing improvements on the property if contracted for in writing as provided by Sections 53.254(a), (b), and (c);

(4) an owelty of partition imposed against the entirety of the property by a court order or by a written agreement of the parties to the partition, including a debt of one spouse in favor of the other spouse resulting from a division or an award of a family homestead in a divorce proceeding;

(5) the refinance of a lien against a homestead, including a federal tax lien resulting from the tax debt of both spouses, if the homestead is a family homestead, or from the tax debt of the owner;

(6) an extension of credit that meets the requirements of Section 50(a)(6), Article XVI, Texas Constitution; or

(7) a reverse mortgage that meets the requirements of Sections 50(k)-(p), Article XVI, Texas Constitution.

(c) The homestead claimant's proceeds of a sale of a homestead are not subject to seizure for a creditor's claim for six months after the date of sale.

3. Impact of Death on Surviving Spouse and/or Minor Children

In the event that the owner or an owner of the homestead property dies with a surviving spouse or minor children, there are certain provisions which keep the homestead status from being abandoned. Think back to the *Riley* case where Bobbie Riley lived in the homestead with her husband. Her husband was the sole owner of the separate property. Upon his death, if he does not leave the homestead to her in his will, she will not have 100 percent ownership of it and could lose her right to possess. However, if the property is homestead, the surviving spouse is give the right to remain in possession of the property and it cannot be partitioned during the spouse's lifetime. Because there is this right of occupancy, there is an accompanying debt protection even at death.

The Texas Constitution and statutory provisions set out the protections afforded at death. The following two cases illustrate questions that arise regarding the right of occupancy. This area has seen a change in the law in recent years to address the status of single adult children living at home. The statutes set forth below provide the current law regarding the right of occupancy and debt protection. However, in the case that follows, you will see that just a few years ago the state of the law was different.

Texas Const. art. XI, § 52. Descent and distribution of homestead; Restrictions on partition

On the death of the husband or wife, or both, the homestead shall descend and vest in like manner as other real property of the deceased, and shall be governed by the same laws of descent and distribution, but it shall not be partitioned among the heirs of the deceased during the lifetime of the surviving husband or wife, or so long as the survivor may elect to use or occupy the same as a homestead, or so long as the guardian of the minor children of the deceased may be permitted, under the order of the proper court having the jurisdiction, to use and occupy the same.

Texas Estates Code
Chapter 102. Probate Assets: Decedent's Homestead[4]

---

[4] Added by Acts 2009, 81st Leg., ch. 680, § 1, eff. Jan. 1, 2014.

§ 102.002. Homestead Rights Not Affected by Character of the Homestead
The homestead rights and the respective interests of the surviving spouse and children of a decedent are the same whether the homestead was the decedent's separate property or was community property between the surviving spouse and the decedent.

§ 102.003. Passage of Homestead
The homestead of a decedent who dies leaving a surviving spouse descends and vests on the decedent's death in the same manner as other real property of the decedent and is governed by the same laws of descent and distribution.

§ 102.004. Liability of Homestead for Debts[5]
If the decedent was survived by a spouse or minor child, the homestead is not liable for the payment of any of the debts of the estate, other than:
(1) purchase money for the homestead;
(2) taxes due on the homestead;
(3) work and material used in constructing improvements on the homestead if the requirements of Section 50(a)(5), Article XVI, Texas Constitution, are met;
(4) an owelty of partition imposed against the entirety of the property by a court order or written agreement of the parties to the partition, including a debt of one spouse in favor of the other spouse resulting from a division or an award of a family homestead in a divorce proceeding;
(5) the refinance of a lien against the homestead, including a federal tax lien resulting from the tax debt of both spouses, if the homestead is a family homestead, or from the tax debt of the decedent;
(6) an extension of credit on the homestead if the requirements of Section 50(a)(6), Article XVI, Texas Constitution, are met; or
(7) a reverse mortgage.

§ 102.005. Prohibitions on Partition of Homestead
The homestead may not be partitioned among the decedent's heirs:
(1) during the lifetime of the surviving spouse for as long as the surviving spouse elects to use or occupy the property as a homestead; or
(2) during the period the guardian of the decedent's minor children is permitted to use and occupy the homestead under a court order.

Chapter 353. Exempt Property and Family Allowance

---

[5] Amended by Acts 2013, 83rd Leg., ch. 1136 (H.B. 2912), § 8, eff. Jan. 1, 2014.

§ 353.051. Exempt Property to Be Set Aside[6]

(a) Unless an application and verified affidavit are filed as provided by Subsection (b), immediately after the inventory, appraisement, and list of claims of an estate are approved or after the affidavit in lieu of the inventory, appraisement, and list of claims is filed, the court by order shall set aside:

    (1) the homestead for the use and benefit of the decedent's surviving spouse and minor children; and

    (2) all other estate property that is exempt from execution or forced sale by the constitution and laws of this state for the use and benefit of the decedent's:

        (A) surviving spouse and minor children;

        (B) unmarried adult children remaining with the decedent's family; and

        (C) each other adult child who is incapacitated.

(b) Before the inventory, appraisement, and list of claims of an estate are approved or, if applicable, before the affidavit in lieu of the inventory, appraisement, and list of claims is filed:

    (1) the decedent's surviving spouse or any other person authorized to act on behalf of the decedent's minor children may apply to the court to have exempt property, including the homestead, set aside by filing an application and a verified affidavit listing all property that the applicant claims is exempt; and

    (2) any of the decedent's unmarried adult children remaining with the decedent's family, any other adult child of the decedent who is incapacitated, or a person who is authorized to act on behalf of the adult incapacitated child may apply to the court to have all exempt property, other than the homestead, set aside by filing an application and a verified affidavit listing all property, other than the homestead, that the applicant claims is exempt.

(c) At a hearing on an application filed under Subsection (b), the applicant has the burden of proof by a preponderance of the evidence. The court shall set aside property of the decedent's estate that the court finds is exempt.

---

[6] Amended by Acts 2011, 82nd Leg., ch. 810 (H.B. 2492), § 2.01, eff. Jan. 1, 2014; Acts 2011, 82nd Leg., ch. 1338 (S.B. 1198), § 2.46, eff. Jan. 1, 2014. Proposed Legislation: 2015 Texas Senate Bill No. 995, Texas Eighty-Fourth Legislature (June 18, 2015)

In the Estate of Farrell Jefferson Casida

Court of Appeals of Texas, Beaumont, 2000

13 S.W.3d 519

RONALD L. WALKER, Chief Justice.

This is an appeal from an order of the trial court containing various rulings connected with the administration of the estate of the deceased, Farrell Jefferson Casida. Casida's wife, Annie Laurie Casida, predeceased him. In his will, the deceased named his step-daughter, Carolyn DuBois, as independent executrix of said estate. Thereafter, the decedent's son, Roy Steven Casida, filed a variety of instruments, including application to set apart the decedent's homestead and exempt property; complaint demanding possession of estate property; and others. The trial court's final order from which this appeal originates approved denied Roy's application to set apart decedent's homestead and exempt property, and ordered Roy "and all other occupants" to vacate the house which was the subject of Roy's application for homestead status. On appeal, Roy raises seven points of error. With the exception of points 5 and 7, Roy's points of error complain in one way or another of the trial court's denial of his application to set apart the homestead, and his request for possession of said homestead so as to continue residing there.

The record before us reflects that the trial court heard evidence from only two witnesses, Carolyn and Roy. Roy testified that the home, located at 31927 Parkway Drive, Magnolia, Texas, was titled to the deceased and was the deceased's homestead, that Roy's mother predeceased his father, that he [Roy] lived at the house for the "last few years," and that under his father's will the only beneficiaries were himself and his half-sister, Carolyn. During her testimony, Carolyn admitted that at one time the decedent did indeed claim the Parkway Drive house as his homestead. However, the gist of Carolyn's testimony was an attempt to prove that the decedent had essentially abandoned the homestead for approximately the last ten years of his life.

It is well recognized that the party claiming a homestead exemption has the burden of establishing the homestead character of the property. *See* Sanchez v. Telles, 960 S.W.2d 762, 770 (Tex. App.—El Paso 1997, writ denied). The record reflects that the homestead status of the property was uncontested at least until the last ten years of the decedent's life. When homestead rights are once shown to exist in property, they are presumed to continue, and anyone asserting an abandonment has the burden of proving it by competent evidence. Sullivan v. Barnett, 471 S.W.2d 39, 43 (Tex. 1971). The party claiming abandonment must plead it and carry the burden of proving it. Id. Said burden is a heavy one, viz:

> This Court recently stated that ". . . beginning as early as 1857, in an opinion by Chief Justice Hemphill in Gouhenant v.

Cockrell, 20 Tex. 96 [(1857)], our courts have held that 'it must
be undeniably clear and beyond almost the shadow, at least (of)
all reasonable ground of dispute, that there has been a total
abandonment with an intention not to return and claim the
exemption.' " Burkhardt v. Lieberman, 138 Tex. 409, 159 S.W.2d
847, 852 [(1942)]; Rancho Oil Co. v. Powell, 142 Tex. 63, 175
S.W.2d 960, 963 (Tex. 1943). See also Womack v. Redden, 846
S.W.2d 5, 7 (Tex . App.—Texarkana 1992, writ denied).

While the evidence did establish the decedent lived at various locales in the
State of Arizona for about the last ten years of his life, the evidence also indicated
that the decedent traveled a great deal. Furthermore, the decedent did return
"home" anywhere from two to four times a year until his death. While testimony
indicated that decedent died in Arizona, there was no evidence that he had ever
bought any real property in Arizona nor any evidence that he had purchased a
house there. There was also no indication that the decedent had ever removed
any furnishings from the Parkway Drive house to Arizona. At any rate, the
independent executrix did not file any pleadings claiming abandonment.

This case was tried to the court. No findings of fact were filed, therefore the
judgment of the trial court implies all necessary findings of fact in support of it.
Pharo v. Chambers County, Tex., 922 S.W.2d 945, 948 (Tex. 1996). Nevertheless,
there must be some evidence in the record to support even implied findings that
there was a "total abandonment with an intention not to return and claim the
exemption" on the part of the decedent. See Womack v. Redden, 846 S.W.2d at
7. From the testimony before us we find that the trial court abused its discretion
in its implied finding that Carolyn met her burden of proving abandonment.
Carolyn's own testimony is not "clear, conclusive and undeniable" that the
decedent did indeed totally abandon the homestead with no intention of ever
returning. See Taylor v. Mosty Bros. Nursery, Inc., 777 S.W.2d 568, 569 (Tex.
App.—San Antonio 1989, no writ). "The acquiring of a new home is not always
the acquiring of a new homestead, and one does not necessarily abandon a
homestead by merely moving his home." Rancho Oil Co., 175 S.W.2d at 963.

We now turn to the propriety of recognizing the Parkway Drive property as
an exempt homestead of the decedent and not merely a general asset of the
estate, and the propriety of Roy's continued occupancy of the homestead. The
mere existence of an unmarried adult child remaining with the family is sufficient
to cause the homestead to descend free from the claims of creditors. National
Union Fire Ins. Co. of Pittsburgh, Pa. v. Olson, 920 S.W.2d 458, 461 (Tex. App.—
Austin 1996, no writ). We expand on this longstanding holding by providing the
following discussion taken from Milner v. McDaniel, 120 Tex. 160, 36 S.W.2d 992,
993-94 (1931).

It has often been determined by the Supreme Court of this state that, upon the death of an owner using and occupying property as a homestead, when there remains a constituent member of the family (wife, husband, minor child, or unmarried daughter), the title passes to all of the heirs and is subject only to the right of use by those entitled to occupy it as a homestead; the estate thus taken by the heirs to the property is unburdened by the claims of creditors of the community estate. Childers v. Henderson, 76 Tex. 664, 13 S.W. 481 [(1890)]; Cameron v. Morris, 83 Tex. 14, 18 S.W. 422 [(1892)]; Zwernemann v. Von Rosenburg, 76 Tex. 522, 13 S.W. 485 [(1890)]; Lacy v. Lockett, 82 Tex. 190, 17 S.W. 916, 918 [(1891)]; Roots v. Robertson, 93 Tex. 365, 55 S.W. 308 [(1900)].

. . . .

The foregoing authorities firmly establish the principle that a homestead cannot be subjected to the payment of community debts when there remains any constituent member of a family, as designated by the Constitution and statutes of this state, to take and occupy it as such. Under such circumstances it descends and vests in all the heirs free from community debts, even though some of the heirs may be adults and not entitled to any homestead interest in the property.

In the instant case, the right to have the property descend free and clear of the debts of the decedent because of its status as exempt homestead property only answers one prong of what Roy, and indeed all of the participants in this case, see as the interrelated issue of his "right" to continue to reside on the homestead property. As the Court in National Union Fire Ins. Co. pointed out, these are two distinct issues. *Id.* at 461. The most succinct explanation is to be found in the following taken from 18 m. K. Woodward & Ernest F. Smith, III, Texas Practice: Probate and Decedents' Estates § 868 (1971):

> That portion of Section 271 of the Probate Code which authorizes the setting apart of the homestead for an adult unmarried daughter[7] has been held unconstitutional to the extent that such setting apart would defeat the claims of the heirs. In so holding, the courts have relied upon the fact that the adult unmarried daughter is not one of the persons listed in Article 16, Section 52 of the Constitution as entitled to claim a homestead after the death of the owner. From this, the courts have reasoned that the legislature is as powerless to enlarge this category as it is to reduce it. Thus the existence of an adult unmarried daughter will not prevent a partition by the heirs or devisees and, indeed, she cannot continue occupying the homestead over their objection.

---

[7] A subsequent amendment to § 271 has extended the rights conferred upon the adult unmarried daughter to all adult children remaining with the family of the deceased.

Oddly enough, however, the existence of an adult unmarried daughter, as in the case of a surviving wife or minor child, will cause the land to descend free of debts. The result is ironical, not to say irrational. As one authority has pointed out:

> The sole purpose of the legislature was to shelter and protect this adult unmarried daughter in her parents' home, safe from dispossession by either creditor or heir. This legislative purpose proved abortive because it violated the constitution. . . . Yet these same statutes, though wholly thwarted of their purpose so far as concerns the adult unmarried daughter, are held still to endow her with such potency that her sole existence on the homestead is sufficient to cleave the homestead from her parents' creditors and deliver it free and clear to all of the heirs. The irony is that she cannot claim the right to remain on it even after she alone has thus ransomed it. Still more ironical, she has to be on the homestead in order to rout the creditors, and then she cannot stay on it.

[Footnotes to citations omitted.]

While the cases cited in the foregoing excerpt are quite old they have yet to be overruled or significantly modified on this issue. Applying the state of the law to the facts before us, while Roy's status as unmarried adult child living with the decedent on the homestead permits the homestead to descend to the devisees free and clear from debts of the decedent under the provisions of § 271 of the Probate Code, it does not provide Roy the right to reside on the homestead if Carolyn, in her capacity as devisee, objects and moves to partition the homestead in order to obtain her share per the terms of the decedent's will. *See* Thompson v. Kay, 124 Tex. 252, 77 S.W.2d 201, 214-15 (1934); National Union Fire Ins. Co., 920 S.W.2d at 461-62. We therefore sustain Roy's points of error three and four, only to the extent that they complain of trial court error in failing to recognize the homestead character of the property at 31927 Parkway Drive, Magnolia, Texas, and the fact that said property should be set aside as exempt in accordance with § 271 of the Probate Code. See Tex. Prob. Code Ann. § 271 (Vernon Supp.2000). We overrule points of error one, two, three, four, and six as far as Roy's occupancy of the homestead is concerned.

AFFIRMED IN PART; REVERSED IN PART AND REMANDED.

F. Abandonment of the Homestead

At some point either the landowner may want to claim that there is no longer homestead status with the property or a creditor may want homestead status to be terminated in order to be able to reach the asset. Once homestead status is established, it will remain until abandoned. As with other areas of property law where the concept of abandonment occurs, it is more than just a non-use. There is a need for non-use of the homestead property with an intent to no longer use. This issue came up in the *Casida* case in the prior section, the *Laster* case earlier in the chapter, and also in the *Harkrider* and *Caulley* cases at the beginning of the chapter. The burden is on the party claiming abandonment to establish that it has occurred. It is a very heavy burden.

Tex. Prop. Code
§ 41.003. Temporary Renting of a Homestead

Temporary renting of a homestead does not change its homestead character if the homestead claimant has not acquired another homestead.

§ 41.004. Abandonment of a Homestead

If a homestead claimant is married, a homestead cannot be abandoned without the consent of the claimant's spouse.

Churchill v. Mayo
Court of Appeals of Texas, Houston [1st Dist.], 2006
224 S.W.3d 340

ELSA ALCALA, Justice.

Appellant, Evelyn Churchill, appeals from a summary judgment rendered by the trial court in favor of appellee, Donna Mayo, as administratrix of the estate of the decedent, Kenneth David Churchill. The trial court's judgment found that Evelyn had abandoned her homestead rights in the property that is the subject of this dispute and ordered Mayo to sell the homestead property and partition the proceeds. Evelyn asserts that the trial court by rendering summary judgment against her, because her affidavit, raised a genuine issue of material fact on Mayo's claim that Evelyn was not entitled to and had abandoned the homestead. We reverse the judgment and remand the cause.

Background

Evelyn and Kenneth married in 1984. In 1989, Kenneth died intestate. The trial court appointed Mayo, one of Kenneth's nieces, to be the administratrix of Kenneth's estate. In 1990, the trial court ordered Mayo to set aside real property located in Fort Bend County for Evelyn's use as a homestead. See Tex. Prob. Code Ann. § 284 (Vernon 2003). Mayo immediately challenged the trial court's order declaring the property as Evelyn's homestead by filing an Application for Partition of Real Property by Sale and Partial Distribution. Evelyn responded by affidavit dated May 30, 1990 that stated that Evelyn was in France to care for her ill father, that she had traveled to the house four times in 1989, that she intended to return to the house, and that she had not abandoned it.

Fourteen years later, in 2004, Mayo and the other heirs filed a First Amended Application for Partition of Real Property by Sale and Partial Distribution. In that application, it was alleged that Evelyn had never attempted to occupy the property, that she had rented or leased the property to tenants, and that she had resided in France prior to and after Kenneth's death. The First Amended Application requested that the court (1) find that Evelyn had never occupied the property as her homestead, (2) find that Evelyn had abandoned the property, and (3) order the sale of the property and distribution of the proceeds. Mayo later filed a no-evidence motion for summary judgment asserting that there was no evidence that Evelyn had established homestead rights or, alternatively, that there was no evidence that Evelyn had not abandoned those rights.

Evelyn filed a response to Mayo's no-evidence motion, which response included copies of four tax statements as its evidence. Evelyn's response stated, "Not only has [Evelyn] returned to the property on many occasions, she has also maintained the tax payments on said property from 1989 until 2003. (See as an example attached Tax documents of year 2002)." The four tax statements are entitled "Tax Statement Fort Bend County L.I.D. # 2," "Fort Bend County 2002 Tax Statement," "2002 Fort Bend ISD Tax Statement," and "City of Sugar Land Tax Statement."

Evelyn also filed an affidavit that stated that she was entitled to the homestead and had not abandoned it. Although the affidavit was not attached to her response to the no-evidence motion for summary judgment, the affidavit was entitled "Affidavit in Support of Evelyn T. Churchill's Traverse, Response to Administratrix Donna Kathleen Mayo's 'No Evidence' Motion for Interlocutory Summary Judgment" and was thus clearly identified as part of Evelyn's summary judgment evidence. Her affidavit stated:

> Before me, the undersigned authority, personally appeared Evelyn T. Churchill, who, being by me duly sworn, deposed as follows:

> My name is Evelyn T. Churchill, I am of sound mind, capable of making this affidavit, and personally acquainted with the facts herein stated:

> . . .

> 5. I lived with [Kenneth] in the house that is contested in these probate proceedings. We lived together as man and wife.

> . . .

> 9. The contested property is my homestead, I consider it my homestead and I have not abandoned it nor have I any intend [sic] to abandon it.

10. I fully believe that I am entitled to homestead rights as I was the wife of the decedent and we lived as man and wife. Furthermore, I have never remarried after the death of [Kenneth] and I am leaving [sic] temporarily in my son's homestead.

11. I have supported and maintained the homestead by paying taxes on the property, paying for its upkeep, and maintaining insurance upon the property.

12. I never intended to prevent any heir of their inheritance. I rented the aforesaid property at the recommendations of my legal counsel Mr. G. Scott Fiddler. . . . Furthermore, the rental was intended to be temporary until the estate is closed.

The trial court found that Evelyn had established homestead rights, but that she had abandoned the property "at least as early as March 16, 1990, and that she has leased/rented the property to third parties possibly commencing as early as March 16, 1990." The court thus rendered summary judgment because Evelyn had failed to produce competent summary judgment evidence that she had not abandoned the property.

Abandonment of Homestead

Abandonment of a homestead occurs when the homestead claimant ceases to use the property and intends not to use it as a home again. Kendall Builders, Inc. v. Chesson, 149 S.W.3d 796, 808 (Tex. App.—Austin 2004, pet. denied). Merely changing residence is not, alone, an abandonment of the homestead. Id.; see Farrington v. First Nat'l Bank, 753 S.W.2d 248, 251 (Tex. App.—Houston [1st Dist.] 1988, writ denied) (noting that "mere fact of acquiring and moving" to new property does not show abandonment, absent intent not to return). Moving from homestead property due to health reasons is not sufficient to show abandonment. Morris v. Porter, 393 S.W.2d 385, 390 (Tex. Civ. App.—Houston 1965, writ ref'd n.r.e.). Nor does temporary renting of the homestead constitute abandonment of the homestead. Hollifield v. Hilton, 515 S.W.2d 717, 721 (Tex. Civ. App.—Fort Worth 1974, writ ref'd n.r.e.). Proof of intent not to use the property as a home again is required to show abandonment. Id.; Morris, 393 S.W.2d at 388. Intent is generally a fact question and may be shown by circumstantial evidence. City of Houston v. Jackson, 135 S.W.3d 891, 898 (Tex. App.—Houston [1st Dist.] 2004, no pet.).

"[A]nyone asserting abandonment [of a homestead] has the burden of proving it by competent evidence." Caulley v. Caulley, 806 S.W.2d 795, 797 (Tex. 1991) (citing Sullivan v. Barnett, 471 S.W.2d 39, 43 (Tex. 1971)). Moreover, "[o]nce homestead rights are shown to exist in property, they are presumed to continue." Id. The issue of abandonment of the homestead, therefore, is one upon which Mayo bore the burden of proof.

In her second issue, Evelyn asserts that she produced more than a scintilla of evidence that she has not abandoned the homestead, and thus, summary judgment was improper. Having held that the trial court erroneously struck Evelyn's affidavit, we further hold that the affidavit should have been considered as part of her summary judgment evidence, in addition to the four tax statements that she supplied. Evelyn's affidavit states that she had lived in the house with Kenneth when they were married, that the house is her homestead, that she did not abandon it, that she did not have any intent to abandon it, that she was living temporarily at in her son's homestead, and that she rented the property temporarily. Evelyn further asserts in the affidavit that she has supported and maintained the homestead by paying taxes on the property, paying for its "upkeep," and maintaining insurance on the property. Consistent with that last statement, Evelyn's summary judgment proof includes four tax statements for 2002, made billable to her. Given the tax statements and Evelyn's affidavit, we conclude that Evelyn presented more than a scintilla of evidence that she had not abandoned homestead rights in the property in response to Mayo's motion for summary judgment. *See Patriacca*, 98 S.W.3d at 306 (stating that reviewing court must view evidence in light most favorable to non-movant). Because Evelyn's proof raises a genuine issue of material fact, the trial court erred by rendering the summary judgment against her.

We sustain Evelyn's second issue.

Conclusion

Reversed the judgment of the trial court and remanded.

NOTES:

As Churchill v. Mayo illustrates, the abandonment question is a very fact-intensive inquiry. Many objective facts will be evaluated to determine if an abandonment has occurred. Once it does, then the property is just like any other and we are no longer concerned with issues of joinder, debt protection, or exclusive rights of occupancy. The forcefield is lifted and the property is vulnerable again.

TABLE OF CASES

695

INDEX